1001 VIDEO GAMES
YOU MUST PLAY BEFORE YOU DIE

1001 VIDEO GAMES
YOU MUST PLAY BEFORE YOU DIE

GENERAL EDITOR TONY MOTT

PREFACE BY PETER MOLYNEUX

UNIVERSE

A Quint**essence** Book

First published in the United States of America in 2010 by
UNIVERSE PUBLISHING
A Division of Rizzoli International Publications, Inc.
300 Park Avenue South
New York, NY 10010
www.rizzoliusa.com

Fourth printing, updated 2013
2013 2014 2015 / 10 9 8 7 6 5 4

ISBN: 978-0-7893-2090-2

Library of Congress Control Number: 2010923742

QSS.VIDG2

This book was designed and produced by
Quint**essence**
230 City Road
London EC1V 2TT
www.1001beforeyoudie.com

Update Editor	Helena Baser
Update Designer	Alison Hau
Editors	Frank Ritter, Simon Ward, Terry Burrows, Tamsin Oxford
Designer	Rod Teasdale
Production Manager	Anna Pauletti
Editorial Director	Jane Laing
Publisher	Mark Fletcher

Color reproduction by Chroma Graphics Pte Ltd., Singapore.
Printed in China by Midas Printing International Ltd.

CONTENTS

PREFACE

By Peter Molyneux, games developer

When I was invited to contribute the foreword to this book I didn't hesitate in saying yes, not only because it's the work of some of the brightest talents in the field of game writing, but because it's a celebration of what I believe is the world's most engaging form of entertainment. Video games have been my favorite way to pass time since I first saw a dedicated *Pong* console among the toasters and TVs in an electrical retailer way back in the 1970s. *Pong*, made by Atari, is a simple game involving batting a square-shaped ball back and forth to the accompaniment of bleepy sound effects, but I was bewitched immediately, and knew that I had to have one of my own. So I got the console home, plugged it into a portable black-and-white television... and within half an hour became consumed by boredom. Ten minutes later I took the machine apart in order to see how it worked. It never worked again, of course.

But I remained just as interested in playing games as I was in trying to decipher them. As the 1970s rolled around to the 1980s, video games had become a worldwide phenomenon. I began visiting pubs, not to drink beer but to play the arcade games you would always find there, nestled in corners. My visits to local cinemas were no longer about sitting down and watching the latest blockbuster movies but playing the arcade machines

Dune II, Command & Conquer, Super Mario 64, Tomb Raider, Ico, Eternal Darkness, Metal Gear Solid, Half-Life, The Legend Of Zelda: Ocarina Of Time, Halo and *Uncharted 2*. Age hasn't been kind to some of the older entries within these pages, but even the clunkiest-looking examples contain themes or ideas that have been important within the context of gaming's evolution, and to anyone with a serious interest in the medium, the list as a whole provides a fascinating illustration of the progress made since its formative years during the 1970s.

You can look at this book as a catalog of games you must play before you die, but you can also look at it as an illustration of social and cultural change in our world. There was a world before games, and a very different world afterward. In making unbelievably sophisticated technology understandable—and interactive—within seconds, the change they have brought about has been immense. Video games do a better job than any other electronic medium in making technology accessible (compare the user experience with grappling with a spreadsheet or word processor, for example), and their influence today can be found everywhere.

Video games will continue to change the world. Right now we're living in a particularly transformative age and undergoing more significant evolution than at any other time in gaming history. Consider the impact of social games via Facebook, the empowerment of players via user-generated content, the opportunities available to independent game-makers, and the incredible diversity of options providing for downloadable content (once upon a time, getting hold of new games involved long waits between releases and then a trip to the store; nowadays, you can get new content piped into your home every day). Nintendo did a great deal to broaden gaming's appeal with its DS and Wii consoles, and more recently Microsoft and Sony have moved further toward shaking things up, too. Microsoft's Natal, in particular, by removing the traditional controller from the equation, represents an enormous step forward for gaming. As a consequence, it makes us designers really sweat—but it's an immensely rewarding challenge.

The world has changed by a degree I couldn't have imagined when I first returned home with my *Pong* console, to the point that nowadays, no matter where you are in the world, no matter what your age or gender, you cannot say that video games aren't for you. There are certainly plenty of examples for everyone within the 1001 collected here. Hopefully you'll be as inspired by them as I have been throughout my gaming life.

Guildford, United Kingdom

INTRODUCTION

By Tony Mott

When I mentioned to a friend that I was working on this book, his immediate response was: "You really think there are 1001 video games worth playing?" I couldn't help but feel put out by his reaction. Of course there are 1001 video games worth playing. There are many more than that, in fact, but 2177 obviously doesn't have 1001's trim symmetry. (Also, 1001 is six fewer syllables to pronounce in a book store.) I don't imagine that the editors of *1001 Books* or *1001 Movies* faced such cynicism, but of course the sort of preconceptions that tend to linger around video games do not afflict most other forms of media. Compared to television, literature or music, the lowly video game isn't very widely understood.

Perhaps we shouldn't expect it to be. Though the earliest video games were conceived on devices such as laboratory oscilloscopes during the 1950s, the first commercial example did not appear until 1971. Books have been manufactured for many hundreds of years, while movies have their origins in the late 1800s. In comparative evolutionary terms, video games may have learned to walk, but they are still in the process of learning to feed themselves without smearing food into their hair. And, just as children are so often dismissed or chided by tutting adults, video games tend to be marginalized, often registering on the radars of social commentators only when it is time to serve up the latest round of condemnation. Over the years I have met many apparently otherwise sensible people who simply prefer not to engage with video games, preferring instead to believe that the world of gaming begins and ends with *Space Invaders*, a game that was released in 1978.

In reality, of course, over the past 40 years video games have evolved to the point that the key trait that defined them in the beginning— their interactivity—is about the only thing the early examples have in common with today's state of the art. *1001 Video Games You Must Play Before You Die* presents a vivid illustration of the progress made since the first *Computer Space* arcade cabinet was wheeled into an American bar in 1971, and I hope that in bringing together such a large number of video games this book proves to be an inspiration for all of us who make and play them. Nowadays there exist all sorts of books about video games, but to my knowledge there has never been one offering a critical collection as comprehensive as the one you're holding in your hands. Many lists detailing the "world's 100 best video games" have been published over the years—indeed, I've been responsible for a few

—but *1001 Video Games You Must Play Before You Die* is a more ambitious collection. Some of the most talented names working in video-game writing today have produced the content within these pages, drawing on many years of experience and, in every case, deep-rooted passion for the medium, and I'm confident that we have assembled an incisive, trustworthy companion for anyone with an interest in video games.

Why produce this book? On the one hand, it's a celebration of video gaming, and serves as a guide to 1001 examples whose delights deserve an audience, but it's also recognition of accomplishment. Not enough credit is given to the diversity that now exists within video games. They have evolved not only in predictable ways, exploring broader and more complex themes while their audio-visual fidelity has risen in line with the advance of technology, but in the way we interact with them, too. Now, via devices such as Microsoft's Kinect, they can be played by simply standing in front of the television and moving your body. They can be played with keyboards, joysticks, and mice, via PlayStation 3 and Xbox 360 joypad controllers, by prodding iPhone or Nintendo DS touch screens, or by waving a Nintendo Wii or PlayStation Move motion controller. You can even cut out any kind of physical exertion and wear a headset that facilitates control directly from your brain. The only common thread, in fact, is the one at the center of all this entertainment: interactivity.

A widening of perspective among those who make video games has brought about this variety. The true revolution within the medium didn't happen with the release of *Space Invaders*, or, later, as a consequence of technology being able to render realistic-looking 3D worlds on our screens. It happened when video game companies began to look beyond the young male demographic that, a long time ago, they identified as their key consumer, and whose focus-tested makeup they dedicated their energies to feeding. Research has shown that the average video game player today is in his or her mid-thirties—and it is very often a "her," with some studies suggesting that the gender split is in the region of 50:50. We have reached a point at which there are video games for everyone, regardless of age, sex, or strand of society.

Where once video games were informed by pen-and-paper, role-playing games like Dungeons & Dragons and sci-fi movie blockbusters like *Star Wars*, such staples no longer dominate the sales charts as they once did, and the form of the video game has evolved alongside the way we interact with it. In addition to embarking on monster slaying quests and martial arts tournaments, the players of today's video games can compete in cooking challenges, dance or sing along to their favorite tunes, get fit via exercise regimes, care for pets, manage farms, and explore the exotic world of hairdressing, to name but a few activities. Meanwhile the decision of game creators to put more power into consumers' hands is having a profound effect on the relationship we have with our entertainment, giving life to a new world of user generated content. And all of this is increasingly happening against an online backdrop — the act of playing shared with friends (and strangers). Which brings us back to video gaming's beginnings, when formative industry powerhouse Atari's first release, *Pong*, was released as a two player game predominantly because its designers believed that a game that encouraged social interaction would have a better chance of succeeding in bars across America. (They were correct: *Pong* was a minor phenomenon in the early '70s.)

Given that this book is dedicated to the history of video games, many of the entries within its pages fall into the category of "traditional" video game, but there are plenty more leftfield examples, too. In terms of organization, we have ordered them by year of release. Each entry details the game's format, original release date, developer, and genre. Many games have appeared on three or more platforms, in which case its format is referenced as "various," although in certain cases where a definitive version exists that should be played in preference to others, that is the only format noted.

How to go about playing all of these games? Unlike other media, such as books, video games don't tend to have long shelf lives. Instead, the traditional publishing model will see a game released with an attendant marketing push, at which point it has its opportunity to sink or swim. Sometimes a particularly profitable hit will be republished at a later date, but too few are given multiple bites of the cherry. More significantly, the devices on which we have played video games have been superseded by technologically superior hardware, and it's only in recent years that backward compatibility—allowing GameCube games to be played on the Wii console that succeeded it, for example—has become a popular feature on console platforms. Even on a platform as ostensibly static as the PC, the evolution of operating systems mean that it can be a trial getting even a five-year-old game running on a brand new computer. Fortunately, enthusiasts around the world have worked hard to preserve video game history, and emulators exist that can resurrect on your PC's desktop just about every home-gaming platform ever released—googling "emulators" will get you started. Elsewhere on the Internet, eBay represents a treasure trove of old games and gaming gear. For PC owners, Good Old Games (www.gog.com) republishes many classics for the platform, each one downloadable from the site for $10 or less. On consoles, creators of classic Japanese arcade games, including Capcom, Sega, and Namco, have released various collections that bring together notable arcade hits from the 1980s, including the likes of *Ghosts 'n Goblins*, *Space Harrier*, and *Pac-Man*, which run on many of today's platforms. Then there are initiatives on the part of console manufacturers Nintendo, Sony, and Microsoft; via their respective online gaming services users are able to purchase an extensive selection of legendary titles, including the standard-setting *Super Mario World*, the seminal *Final Fantasy VII*, and a galaxy of games that once lined the walls of video arcades the world over. With enough desire and persistence you should be able to track down even the strangest-looking curiosities featured within these pages.

As Peter Molyneux notes in his preface, some of the older examples in this book are a little ragged around the edges, but don't write off a game just because it looks like some kind of digital cave painting. The ships that sail the seas of 1982's *Utopia*, for example, are hardly works of art—how could they be, consisting of so few pixels?—but the game as a whole is a key entry in the strategy game genre and counts among its progeny such all-conquering series as *SimCity* and *Civilization*.

I would encourage open-mindedness throughout. After all, it's the willingness to look beyond convention and expectation that has so energized the world of video games down the years, and continues to push it forward today. It's not always easy. None of the industry's big publishers foresaw Facebook or Apple's iPhone as gaming platforms waiting to explode, but that is precisely what happened, shaking away dusty, old-fashioned paradigms in the process. The one constant in the world of video games is change, and the more prepared we are to embrace it, the better placed we'll be to benefit. At some point in the future hopefully we'll be able to document such change in a subsequent edition of this book.

Index of games

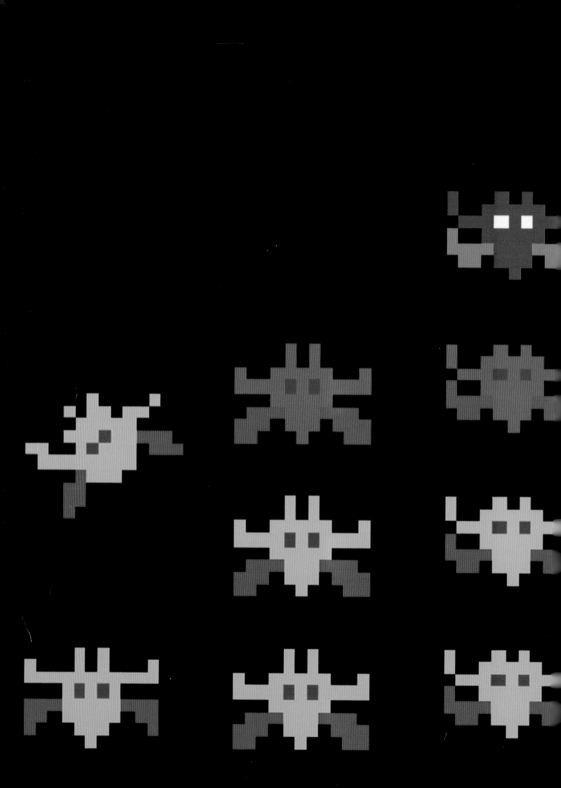

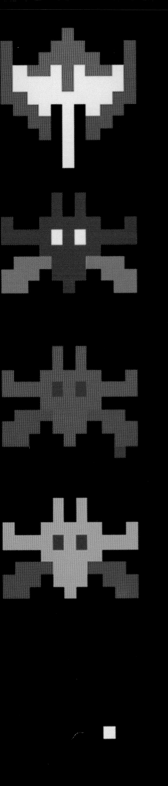

- The first home video game console—the **Magnavox Odyssey**—is launched in 1972; 100,000 units are sold in the first year

- In 1975 **Atari** releases the coin-op table tennis game *Pong* on a home console; it is called *Home Pong*

- *Pac-Man*, *Centipede*, and other video games are first made available on home PCs such as the **Tandy TRS-80**

- Games are sold to players on floppy disk or cassettes, wrapped in plastic bags

- *Space Invaders* and *Asteroids* are released in 1979, triggering the golden age of arcade games

1970s

```
HOW GOOD A SHOT ARE YOU WITH YOUR
RIFLE?

    1 - ACE MARKSMAN
    2 - GOOD SHOT
    3 - FAIRLY FAIR
    4 - NEED PRACTICE
    5 - SHAKY KNEES

ENTER ONE OF THE ABOVE -- THE BETTER YOU
CLAIM YOU ARE, THE FASTER YOU'LL HAVE TO
BE WITH YOUR GUN TO BE SUCCESSFUL.

PRESS 'RETURN' WHEN YOU ARE DONE.
```

The Oregon Trail

Original release date : 1971

Platform : Various

Developer : MECC

Genre : Edutainment

Millions of children grew up in the 1980s with *The Oregon Trail* installed on a classroom PC. Notionally presented as educational software, students learned almost nothing about the *actual* Oregon Trail—mostly that it was a place where you shot bears, forded rivers, and occasionally died of cholera. Yet for a generation, *The Oregon Trail* was a glorious Trojan horse that somehow made it okay to play computer games during school hours. It's a solid turn-based strategy game in its own right, too. So while it may have been a terrible history lesson, it did teach kids how to make a game plan and manage the balance of risk versus reward. Surely that was more important than some dusty old pioneers, anyway.

You begin in the city of Independence, where you choose your lot in life: farmer, carpenter, or banker. The cushier jobs may have more cash available to them, but even as a banker, the game is punishingly difficult. The pioneer life was no cakewalk, after all, so you have to manage resources carefully as your wagon lopes toward Oregon. Do you keep your family fat and healthy or starve them to stretch the food budget? Buy more bullets for hunting or grab a spare part in case of a breakdown? The long grind of the trail is broken up by landmarks, most memorably river crossings. It's here that many foolhardy players have met their demise by wading into eight-feet-deep waters just to save a buck on ferry fare.

The Oregon Trail has seen countless ports and remakes since its 1971 debut, but the canonical version is probably the 1985 version for Apple II computers. It's this edition, with color graphics that were remarkably detailed for the time, that most players remember as their first encounter with that strange beast known as "edutainment." **JT**

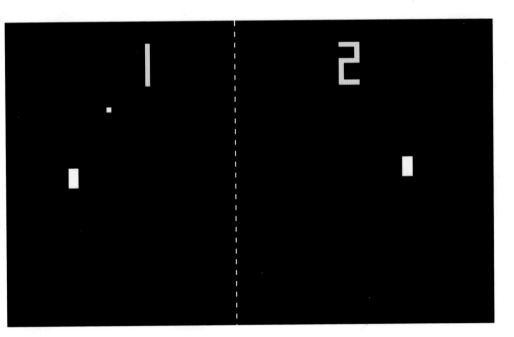

Pong

Original release date : 1972
Platform : Various
Developer : Atari
Genre : Sports

According to legend, shortly after the first *Pong* prototype was installed at Andy Capp's Tavern in Sunnyvale, California, Atari received a phone call from the bar's owner, who complained that the machine had broken. The engineer who'd built the game, Al Alcorn, drove to the pub to take a look. He found that the hardware was working just fine. The problem was an unexpected one: Patrons had fed so many quarters into the coin slot that the machine could take no more. An industry had been born.

Pong conquered bars and arcades, and, eventually, living rooms too, with a dedicated home version. A game whose instructions can be summed up in one sentence, "Avoid missing ball for high score," is easy for anybody to pick up and immediately understand. Players control one of two rectangular paddles along either side of the screen, trying to prevent the ball from escaping their side of the playing field, and sneak it past their opponent's paddle on the other. As an electronic version of table tennis, *Pong* is simple and intuitive. Its lineage as a pub game is obvious— the rules are hardly different from those of foosball.

Pong also demonstrates a subtle and important lesson of good game design, still applicable today, which is that the little things matter. Depending on where the ball strikes the paddle, players can give it "English," changing the angle of its trajectory to keep opponents off balance. *Pong*'s other unheralded accomplishment is its creation of credible artificial intelligence. Though playing against a human opponent is preferable, *Pong*'s computer-controlled second player is a worthy substitute. Good without being great, it's capable both of great saves and boneheaded mistakes. Though, unlike Andy Capp's customers, it's still on top of its game at last call. **MK**

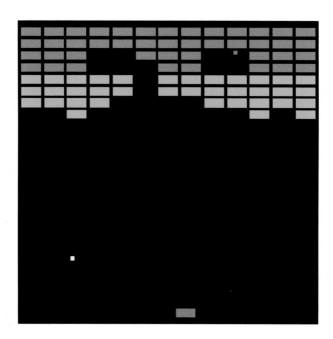

Breakout

Original release date : 1976
Platform : Various
Developer : Atari
Genre : Action

Nearly four decades on and video games still regularly draw inspiration from Atari's formative, blockbusting arcade game. In a very real way, *Breakout* defined the proto-vocabulary of its medium: taking the paddle and ball of *Pong*'s redacted approximation of table tennis and repurposing it into something unique, novel, and only possible in a video game.

Conceptualized by Atari founder, Nolan Bushnell, and one of the company's most influential engineers, Steve Bristow, the top third of *Breakout*'s screen is lined with bricks. You bounce a ball off these bricks to make them disappear, one by one, catching the ball on its rebound with a sliding paddle to prevent it from disappearing

off the bottom of the screen. The skill comes in directing your shots in such a way as to hit the remaining bricks at the top of the screen, scaling up from *Pong*'s need to simply hit the ball to take into greater account the angle at which you strike it. Walls too must be used to bounce the ball around the play area, introducing yet more scope for strategy and showboating.

Originally played on a black-and-white monitor in arcades, cabinet screens had strips of tinted acetate applied to give the impression of color. Increased difficulty was introduced to the game by having the paddle shrink to half its size once the ball has broken through the top row of bricks and hit the top of the play area.

The understated elegance of both the core idea and its execution ensures that *Breakout* remains a playable classic to this day. One of the cornerstones of the medium of sports games, its influence can be felt in countless contemporary titles from PopCap's pachinko hybrid *Peggle* to Q-Games' *Reflect Missile*. **SP**

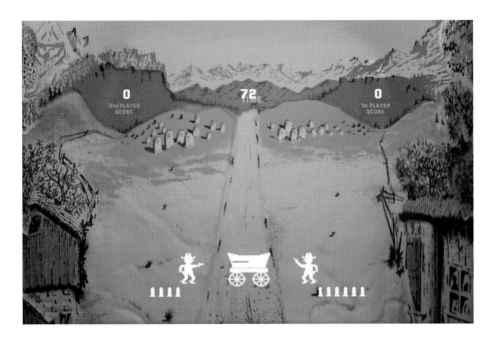

Boot Hill

Original release date : 1977
Platform : Arcade
Developer : Midway
Genre : Shoot 'Em Up

You could argue that *Boot Hill* is really just *Pong* redesigned by a John Wayne fan. Two players take on the role of cowboys on opposite sides of a Western backdrop lined with cacti and the odd wagon. Just as in Atari's landmark bat-and-ball game, you can ricochet your shots off the top and bottom of the screen. Yet unlike *Pong*, with its famously concise instructions to avoid missing the projectile at all costs, the aim is to *dodge* everything your opponent fires at you.

With only six shots in your revolver and a merciless time limit set on the action, the game is surprisingly realistic. Just as in a real-life gunfight, you're torn between coming out blasting (and unwisely emptying your clip in

a flash; there's no reload) or taking your time and trying to plug your CPU or human opponent with a single, well-aimed shot. Designed by Dave Nutting, as a jazzed-up semi-sequel to his earlier *Gun Fight* (1975), *Boot Hill* builds on *Pong*'s simple projectile physics and lets you fantasize about becoming a quick-draw shooter.

One of the problems of resurrecting retro coin-op games is that you can't always recreate the tactile realities of their cabinets—emulation on a modern PC only goes so far. Back in the day, a large part of *Boot Hill*'s attraction came from its cabinet's low-tech approach, which used mirrors to project its monochrome action onto a hand-drawn overlay of a frontier town. Playing without it isn't half as fun, especially since you don't get to see Boot Hill itself—a graveyard where dead players are transported and turned into headstones while a funeral march blasts from the speakers. The graveyard is a cheap trick, yet it does nod to the high-stakes at risk in every Old West gunfight: *bang*, *bang*, you're *really* dead. **JRu**

Combat

Original release date : 1977
Platform : VCS
Developer : Atari
Genre : Shoot 'Em Up

Anyone buying one of the seminal Atari VCS gaming consoles would find the *Combat* cartridge bundled as a part of the package. So from the five years following its launch in 1977, millions slammed the plastic wedge into their faux-wood-grained machines and thumbed away at rubberized joysticks, lobbing square electronic bullets at the person on the couch next to them. And yet the chunky tanks, jet fighters, and bombers eternally warring in *Combat* never quite managed to enter the public consciousness in the same way as Pac-Man, Space Invaders, or Mario. That's because the enemy in *Combat* was *us*. It's easy to forget that before games evolved into predominantly single-person experiences, they were more usually player-versus-player contests. *Combat* is an early, vital example of the multiplayer shooter.

Atari claimed that *Combat* was able to deliver twenty-seven different games, but back then the addition of a cloud, barrier, or different kind of bullet was considered dramatic enough to earn another tick on the back of the box. There are really only a couple different ways to play: with tanks or with planes. The most game-changing variation adds bullets that ricochet. The "tank pong" flavor transforms volleys into trigonometric contests, making a connected bank shot mandatory to score a hit. Game play itself is simple: Opponents tilt joysticks to jockey for position, aim, and fire. Hits score a point and put the enemy in a debilitating, momentary tailspin. The formula isn't all that different from the kill, spawn, and repeat of the contemporary first-person shooter.

The end result was the same in 1977 as it is today— when players are evenly matched and competition gets heated, the graphics and sounds fade into the background. It's just *you* against *them*. **GM**

Space Invaders

Original release date : 1978
Platform : Arcade
Developer : Taito
Genre : Shoot 'Em Up

Everybody knows *Space Invaders*. Almost everybody's played it too, struggling through wave after wave after deadening wave of planet Earth's least imaginative attackers; firing at endless wobbling drones, who track back and forth, getting ever closer until mankind is reduced to a single turret, scurrying around the bottom of the screen, taking its last few careful potshots from behind the slowly disintegrating shield.

If *Pac-Man* is about memory and *Donkey Kong* is all about story, then *Space Invaders* is fascinated with panic: the unshakable twitchiness that picks up as the last invaders evade your frantic shots; as the speed increases and the nasty little deep-space squids get lower and lower until you're within touching distance of their mandibles.

The game's controls are simple to the point of being invisible, and the objective so direct that *Space Invaders* couldn't help but be a classic. (It was so successful in Japan that the Ministry of Finance was forced to mint more of the 100-yen coins the arcade machine ate in such staggering quantities.) That said, *Space Invaders* does have a few subtleties in store—from the passing UFO that can give you a much-needed points boost (particularly if you're using one of a handful of well-used methods to predict its arrival), to the matter of locating the best places to aim and fire as you keep ahead of the descending horde.

Sparse and monochromatic, *Space Invaders* is one of those games whose appeal younger generations will struggle to understand. At the time of release, however, this was nothing less than a full-blown phenomenon. Clones, such as *Galaga*, would go on to break bold new ground of their own, but without Taito's humble mega-hit, video game history would most probably be unrecognizable territory. **CD**

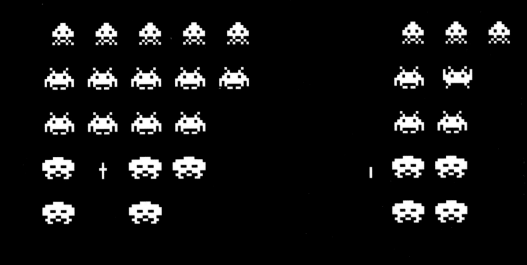

Adventure

Original release date : 1979
Platform : VCS
Developer : Atari
Genre : Adventure

All the early adventure games on home computers were purely text based. Players would type in commands, such as "go north," "drink potion," "throw rock," "kill snake," and subsequently be rewarded with a paragraph or two informing them of just how their plan had played out. You needed a keyboard to make them work properly. In other words—and unless you were a fan of computer fonts—there wasn't much in the way of spectacle along the way. Everything relied on imagination—a dangerous foundation on which to build a business.

In 1979, however, all that changed when Atari effectively ported Will Crowther's legendary text adventure, *Colossal Cave Adventure,* to its VCS home console. Somewhat basic graphics replaced the time-worn prose, the VCS's controller stood in for the keyboard, and a rather primitive—but wonderfully evocative—genre took its first baby steps toward the elaborate and florid fantasy worlds available to today's players.

A programming marvel at the time, the game fit into the space of just 4K (by way of comparison, the standard Google logo takes up 8K). *Adventure* also provided the gaming world with one of its first Easter eggs. Designer Warren Robinett, tiring of his years of anonymous toil spent at the coal-face of game production, hid his name within one of the game's rooms—a chamber that could only be opened by using a single-pixel key known as "The Dot." Stiff as the challenge was, and slight the reward, it wasn't long before someone had uncovered the secret and told everyone about it—proof that even in the early days of the genre, adventure games were already capable of generating real devotion in their audiences. Some things, then, never change. **CD**

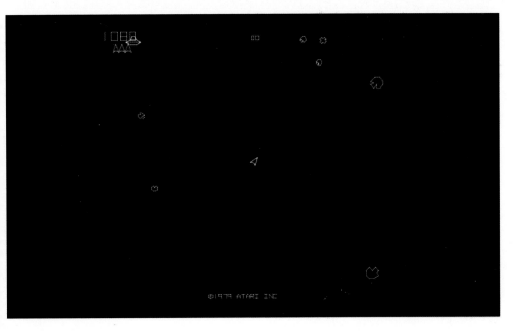

Asteroids

Original release date : 1979
Platform : Arcade
Developer : Atari
Genre : Shoot 'Em Up

Games these days tend to have complex stories; three-dimensional characters; and rousing, near-cinematic soundtracks. They start with a bang, pace themselves carefully for a big finale, and leave you wanting more— generally even teasing a sequel as the fireworks die down. They have epic drama, decent performances, and elaborately detailed worlds. *Asteroids* doesn't, and never did. *Asteroids* has boulders, unforgiving physics, and very little else. Oh, yes. You play as a triangle.

Despite such inauspicious details, Atari's coin-op champion remains more than just a dusty curio today. At the time of release, the sharp laser-etched vector visuals and frantic rock-blasting explosions made it quite the looker, and it's proved rather timeless in its simplicity, blinking out of the screen in the twenty-first century with a chic sense of stripped-back assurance a lot of modern games have tried, unsuccessfully, to emulate.

More important, though, is the quality of the game play itself. *Asteroids* is still good for a sweaty half hour as you blast chunks of space matter into shrapnel, dodge the oncoming debris by boosting cautiously around the screen, and lie in wait for the points-heavy flying saucer that twitters through the mayhem every so often, just itching to be blown to pieces.

A stark hi-scoring compulsion, *Asteroids* is a lot smarter than it looks. Veteran Atari developer Ed Logg was something of a perfectionist, paying attention to everything from the heft of the game's physics to the peculiarly memorable leaderboard font, and his craftsmanship shows in every facet of the game itself. These rocks may be made from nothing but light, but even now they remain entirely capable of bowling you over. **CD**

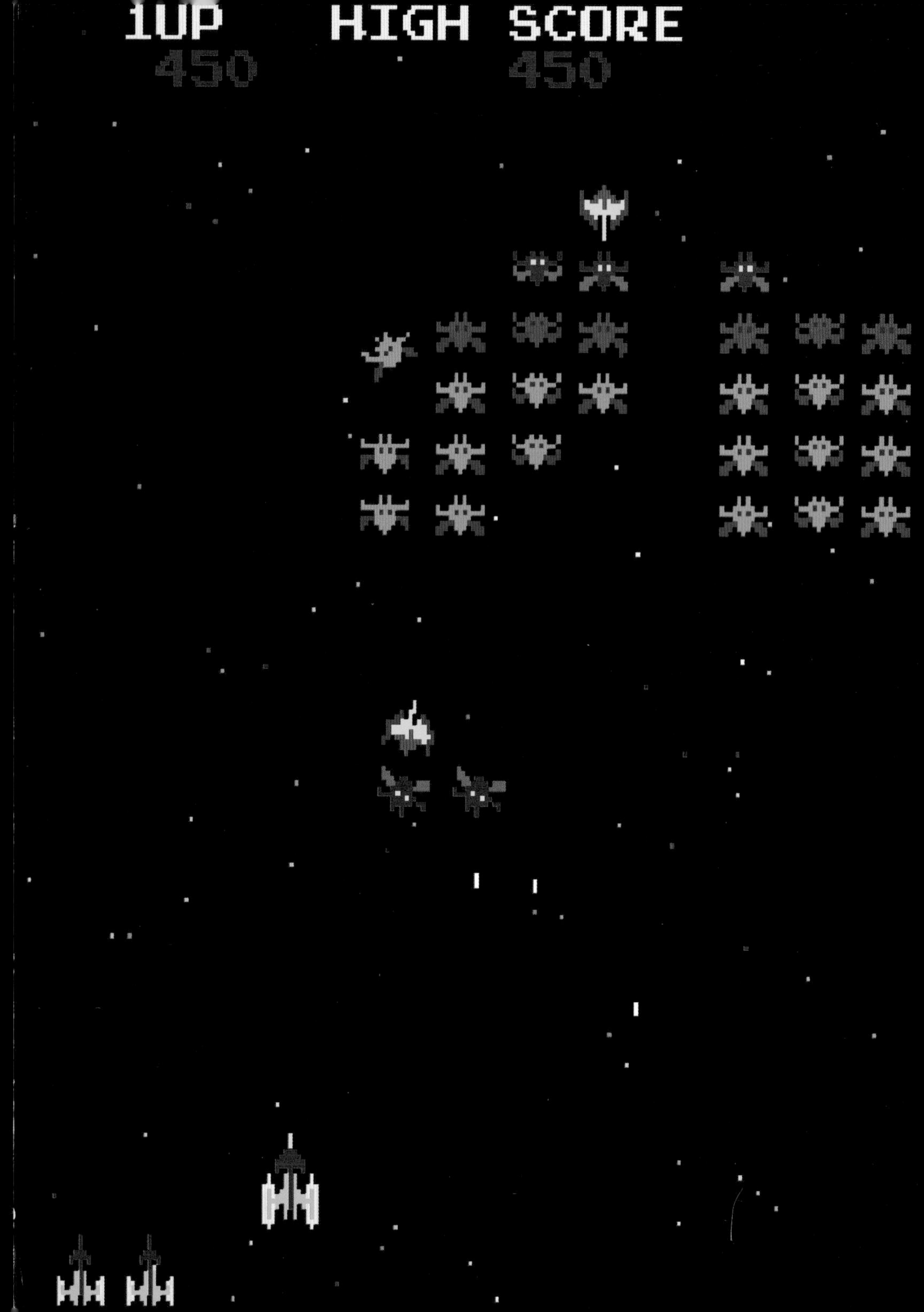
1UP
450
HIGH SCORE
450

Galaxian

Original release date : 1979
Platform : Arcade
Developer : Namco
Genre : Shoot 'Em Up

Galaxian was the first release by Namco, a former merry-go-round manufacturer whose later hits (perhaps you've heard of Pac-Man) would leave this debut in the dust. To the modern gamer, Galaxian looks like an evolutionary step that's best forgotten: the missing link between the groundbreaking but rigid Space Invaders and Galaxian's own successor, Galaga.

On release, Galaxian was revolutionary, boasting a full-color display and replacing the clumsy aliens of Space Invaders with sharp-winged, sinister, yet vividly colored, ships. (The flagship enemy type became a minor icon and a bonus item in both Pac-Man and Dig Dug.) Another significant advancement was in the movement of the enemy's attack, the robotic to-and-fro motion of Space Invaders enhanced by squadrons of fighters unexpectedly peeling out of formation to dive-bomb your positions. Namco's game even had a theme tune. Clearly it represented a step forward (something certain arcade operators recognized by making one game of Galaxian cost twice as much as what players expected to pay).

But it didn't step far enough. You're still limited to just one shot at a time—and with so much happening on the screen, that limit feels unnatural. You have to plan every shot and watch every attack, even as kamikaze line up for a crack at you. And even the dive-bombing mechanic feels limited next to the complex and graceful patterns that would emerge in Galaga, the sequel that endures as one of the most highly regarded classics of the golden age of video gaming. But Galaxian is still worth a credit or two, even if you're not a history buff. With its appealing visuals and well-balanced game play, Galaxian delivers a well-executed shooter game that, in truth, can only be faulted for what its maker hadn't yet invented. **CDa**

Lunar Lander

Original release date : 1979
Platform : Arcade
Developer : Atari
Genre : Flight Simulator

Cold and actually rather serious in tone, Lunar Lander may sound like a knockabout science-fiction romp, but this classic arcade game is tainted with a very slight whiff of education. In essence, Atari's offering is a bare-bones physics simulator in which you balance fuel consumption, thrust, gravity, and momentum to land the titular spacecraft on a brightly abstracted moon, frantically recalculating your strategy on the fly, to avoid blowing yourself into pieces in the process.

It may sound fairly dull, but—surprisingly—it isn't at all. In its peculiar mixture of abstraction and precision, Lunar Lander actually feels real in a way almost none of its competitors ever have. Other space games may offer flashy nebulae, swift pirouetting craft, and intergalactic adventure filled with alien encounters and laser battles, but Lunar Lander is the only one to allow you to briefly lose yourself in the fantasy, that you're genuinely onboard an Apollo mission, staring feverishly at the control panel, praying that you aren't about to get your away-team buddies comprehensively pulverized before they get to plant their flags.

And, in its own modest little way, Lunar Lander was forward thinking, too. Physics is now one of the great battlegrounds of modern gaming, a back-of-the-box bullet point in everything from shooters like Half-Life 2 to quirky puzzlers like Boom Blox. Lunar Lander got there first, when other games were still drawing childish mazes or trying to convince you that a large letter X was actually a racing car. Atari's classic might be light on genuine fun, then, and a title that appeals to the more bookish, solitary manner of children, but it's also an early indicator of the potential scope and quirks of games that the industry is only now reaching to embrace. **CD**

- *Pac-Man* is released in 1980, attracting players of both sexes to game arcades

- Released in 1982, the **Commodore 64** becomes the most popular US game platform

- The **Nintendo NES** first appears in 1983; its US launch in 1985 is accompanied by the release of eighteen titles, including *Super Mario Bros.*

- Home computer gaming overtakes the playing of games in arcades in 1984

- In the late 1980s dedicated sound cards improve the gaming experience

- **Nintendo** releases the *Game Boy* handheld video game device in 1989

1980s

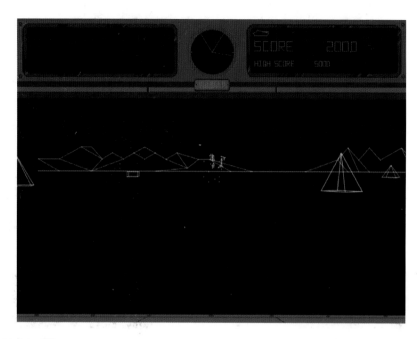

Battle Zone

Original release date : 1980
Platform : Arcade
Developer : Atari
Genre : Shoot 'Em Up

When it was first released back in the dark mists of time known as 1980, *Battle Zone*'s sharp three-dimensional graphics were so astonishing and unprecedented that people who played the game started going a little bit crazy. Some of them made up impossible stories about the things they'd achieved within the tank fighter's world, such as driving up the side of the erupting volcano that lurked, eternally, on the game's horizon, and dropping inside to explore the mysterious caldera.

Even if you weren't an out-and-out fantasist, designer Ed Rotberg's action game still had a lot of pleasures waiting in store for you. Its three-dimensional arena, filled with rampaging wire-frame tanks, was built from the smooth, unbroken lines of vector display units. That means that even today, the game has a clean, futuristic vibe that has barely aged, while the action itself, focusing on shooting at a variety of enemies and threats—ranging from speedy supertanks to nasty guided missiles to even the odd UFO—manages to be both twitchy and strategic in equal measure. Shooting things feels really good in such a stylish universe, and avoiding getting shot—moving out of harm's way at the last possible moment—remains one of the great pleasures of the golden age of arcades.

Such was the game's overwhelming success that Rotberg received unrequited attention from an unexpected source: the US military asked him to build a bespoke version of his classic game with more realistic physics as a tool for training army personnel. Despite such ambiguous offshoots, it's this entirely harmless original that earned the developer a place in the history books and gave gamers everywhere one of their first genuine jaw-dropping graphical experiences. **CD**

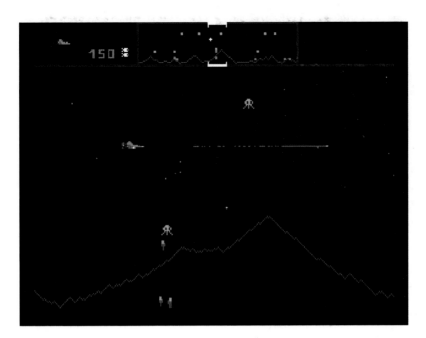

Defender

Original release date : 1980
Platform : Arcade
Developer : Williams
Genre : Shoot 'Em Up

Like *Donkey Kong*, another arcade game that would change the industry's formative landscape, initial reports on *Defender*, Eugene Jarvis's space side scroller, suggested it simply wouldn't catch on. With backward and forward movement, fire, smart bomb, and hyperspace, there were too many buttons, the enemies came at you in awkward strands of death, and the whole thing had no recognizable top or bottom. Play *Defender* like *Space Invaders*, as many arcade players initially would, and you'd be blown up from behind when an enemy you couldn't even see wobbled out from behind the screen.

Defender was, however, a marvel. Jarvis, who had grown up wanting to make pinball machines rather than arcade games, had understood that the player of tomorrow wanted something more than just predictable enemies to memorize and destroy by rote. They wanted ever-changing action, tricksy foes, and explosive options. They wanted something to protect—the tiny spacemen, in this case—as well as something to destroy. They wanted glowing spectacles as their enemies erupted into sprays of pixels. Most of all, they wanted the incredible levels of control that Jarvis's game would offer.

It came at a price, of course. *Defender* is hilariously difficult at first, with fledgling pilots careering into a mutated alien, hyperspacing into the path of a bullet, or surviving long enough to lose all their spacemen and end up sucked into the nebulous and terrifying void.

The result was a game that saw the future more clearly than most of its peers. Memory and repetition were never going to be enough to keep arcades busy for very long. Sooner or later, players would want something devious enough to really make them sweat. **CD**

Eamon

Original release date : 1980
Platform : Apple II
Developer : Donald Brown
Genre : Text Adventure

In the 1970s, the original adventure games passed freely from computer to computer, picking up contributions from geeks along the way. This early spirit of community paved the way to *Eamon*, Donald Brown's text-based adventure series that combined stats-driven combat and head-scratching interactive fiction. Brown started the franchise by creating the tutorial adventure and the main hall, which served as the character's home base. From there, players could swap floppies containing new adventures designed by Brown or by anyone else who cared to chip in.

The *Eamon* community wrote almost 250 adventures spanning every genre and idiom. The quality of these adventures varied, but fans published lengthy newsletters that ran reviews and kept one another apprised of what was out there, while in the dark age of dial-up modems, new adventures were shared on bulletin boards.

The game itself certainly feels quaintly from another era, but *Eamon*'s true legacy lies in the community that came together to build it. **CDa**

Missile Command

Original release date : 1980
Platform : Arcade
Developer : Atari
Genre : Shoot 'Em Up

The digital version of a game that schoolchildren play by scratching lines across the back of their notebooks, *Missile Command* demands spatial reasoning and ace timing. Nuclear missiles rain down on your cities. To stop them, you must counterstrike from one of your ground bases. Your defense missiles burst into a cloud, destroying anything caught in its radius. Fire blindly, though, and not only will you let a few warheads through, you'll also use up your stockpile, leaving you open to total annihilation.

As a piece of pop culture, *Missile Command* is perched between two eras. The premise can't help but evoke American fears of Russian nukes. After all, just three years later, *The Day After* would teach a television audience what radiation sickness looked like. But the game's giant trackball interface anticipates the dawn of mouse-driven computing: Modern players will feel right at home, rolling the cursor around the screen.

Today, the game is a trying proposition, but players with a sharp eye can feel nostalgic for a time when we knew where the missiles would come from. **CDa**

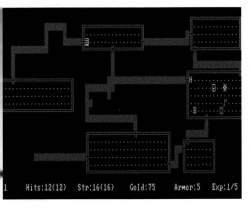

`1    Hits:12(12)    Str:16(16)    Gold:75    Armor:5    Exp:1/5`

`300    IOIOI EJD`

Rogue

Original release date : 1980
Platform : Various
Developer : Michael Toy, Glenn Wichman, Ken Arnold
Genre : Strategy / Role-Playing

Rogue first appeared on college Unix systems in 1980. It contains infinite variety via a series of randomly generated, ASCII-rendered dungeons that must be explored in a bid to retrieve the Amulet of Yendor from somewhere beyond the twenty-fifth level—an unlikely achievement given the imposing difficulty of even the earliest dungeon layers.

Practically no information is disclosed to the player, so every new game is a voyage of discovery, not just of the dungeon's layout, but also of the monsters and items within. Progression to the deeper parts of the dungeon is such a rarity that there are inevitably new monsters to meet. Quaffing potions and reading scrolls along the way is always a calculated risk; you might discover that you've just gulped down a potion of strength ("You feel stronger. What bulging muscles!"), but if you've guzzled a potion of blindness ("A cloak of darkness falls") you can kiss goodbye any chance of surviving to the later levels.

Other obstacles include simple hunger, which can wipe out even the bravest adventurer; dead ends; and a cruel variety of traps. **DM**

Tempest

Original release date : 1980
Platform : Arcade
Developer : Atari
Genre : Shoot 'Em Up

Tempest was born from an ideas book and a nightmare. Hot off the success of *Missile Command*, Dave Theurer was browsing Atari's book of game concepts and stumbled across the idea for a first-person version of *Space Invaders*. He sketched out the concept, marrying it to the new technology of color vector graphics. The clincher, though, was the nightmare in which Theurer dreamed he was watching hideous monsters clawing their way out of a hole in the ground.

The idea is simple: You are the pilot of the Claw, hanging at the top of a tunnel in space. Spinning around the edge, you fire at an array of fast-moving monsters coming at you from the hole at the center.

Unique to *Tempest* was the game's control system. You navigate by rotating the cabinet's "paddle"—a weighty, smooth-moving dial that is both quick and precise. The controller makes the game thrillingly fast and fluid, allowing the player to strafe half the board with a flick of the wrist and then spin back to mop up survivors with a fearless, steel-nerved aim. **CDa**

MUD

Original release date : 1980
Platform : Various
Developer : Roy Trubshaw, Richard Bartle
Genre : Adventure

1975's *Adventure* popularised text-based fantasy in video games, largely by incorporating Dungeons & Dragons into a virtual world. Three years later, Roy Trubshaw, a student at Essex University in the UK, took that formula and added multiple players. The result was *MUD* (Multi User Dungeon), the first virtual world.

There's plenty to say about *MUD*'s history, but the salient facts are that in late 1980 its development and maintenance was taken over by Richard Bartle, another Essex University student, who went on to create many of the features that define *MUD*'s reputation. It would run in various forms until the late '80s, its popularity greatly boosted when it became possible to 'dial in' from external networks. The seeds of World Of Warcraft were sown here.

MUD is a simple concept: your goal is to become a wizard (or witch). But the genius lies in its player-to-player interaction. For the first time, you could talk to other adventurers, squabble over loot, help each other out, and get into axe fights. To look at, the interface is almost identical to its precursor's, and the scoring system is simple: pick up items, perform tasks, or defeat competing players for various amounts of points. But killing other players is the most rewarding task, imbuing this virtual world with a little survival of the fittest—despite the social structures created by players, rogues prospered.

The world is more than just backdrop to the gameplay. By encouraging people to role-play their fantasy characters, the very bareness of the elements such as 'Large Mountains' and 'Thatched Cottages' became an advantage, an invitation to the imagination. And that is *MUD*'s legacy: the first game to realize not just how empowering a player's imagination is, but how powerful it can be when mixed with the imaginations of others. **RS**

Pac-Man

Original release date : 1980
Platform : Arcade
Developer : Namco
Genre : Maze

He's not the superstar he once was, but Pac-Man is probably still the most readily identifiable video game mascot—more universally recognizable than Mario, Sonic The Hedgehog, and Master Chief.

The inspiration for Pac-Man's simple yellow circle and its gaping mouth occurred—in the apocryphal yet charming story—when arcade developer Toru Iwatani took a slice out of a pizza and looked at the shape made by the remaining sections of pie.

The story may well have survived because the world of *Pac-Man* is all about eating: he races through mazes, gobbling pills—not forgetting the special power pills that will allow him to turn the tables on the ghosts pursuing him—with no thought in the world except what he can chow down on next. And for the best part of a decade, audiences around the world couldn't get enough of him. At the height of Pac-Mania, even his spooky enemies—Blinky, Pinky, Inky, and Clyde—were household names, and books that featured in bestseller lists taught players the most successful patterns for beating the game and earning the really big scores.

The patterns are important to mastering *Pac-Man*, in fact, and, arguably, one of the game's weaknesses. Lacking any particularly inspiring AI, Pac-Man's pursuers race around the maze, following predictable paths, meaning players can effectively beat the game through memory and timing rather than inventive reactions. It's an exploit, for sure, but it doesn't change the fact that Namco's game is at its best (and most enjoyable) when played fast and loose, with players taking the risks on stretching a power-pill streak as far as it will go, making mad dashes for the high-scoring fruit, and racing through those eerily familiar mazes like a Pac-Man possessed. **CD**

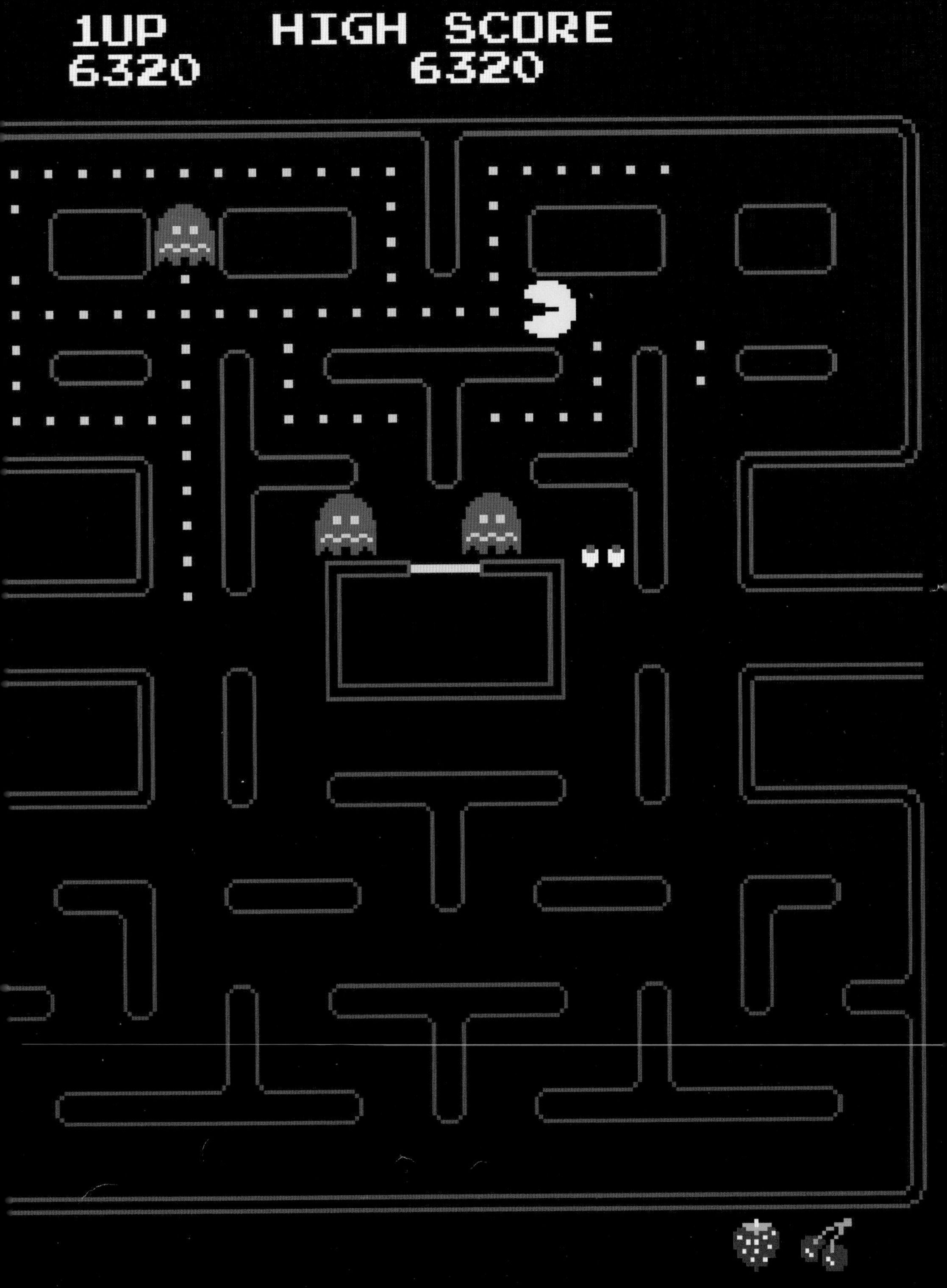
1UP
6320
HIGH SCORE
6320

Phoenix

Original release date : 1980
Platform : Arcade
Developer : Amstar Electronics
Genre : Shoot 'Em Up

Of all the space shooters to follow in the footsteps of Taito's legendary *Space Invaders*, *Phoenix* may be the creepiest. Whereas games like *Galaxian* rendered their foes as vaguely birdlike attackers, *Phoenix* took the next logical step: Your enemies can actually appear first as eggs, sidewinding down the screen and then hatching before your eyes into giant menaces that take multiple shots to bring down. Their eerie cries as they dive-bomb you from formation, and the shrieks as you pick off their wings, still cut right to the nerve. It is almost a letdown when, after four scenes of feathered hellbirds, you reach the boss—a giant battleship with an armored underside that must be progressively chipped away by your projectiles in order to get to the skinny little alien at its core.

Designed by the otherwise forgotten producer Amstar Electronics, the game consists of five scenes—two that pit you against a formation of birds, two against the hatching eggs, and, finally, the boss fight against the mothership. While *Phoenix*'s boss encounter isn't the most challenging, it can claim to have been the first.

The game's most interesting tactical innovation is a shield protecting against all forms of attack, but which takes several seconds to recharge between uses. A player can deal with the swooping birds by blasting away and then triggering the shield just in time for the enemy to crash into it. This makes the game more sophisticated than a simple nostalgia trip.

Mention should also be made of the clever audio design—one of the earliest examples of a disturbing atmosphere seeping into the bright, simple violence of a video arcade game. In 2005, *Phoenix* was reborn for younger generations on Xbox, PlayStation 2, PSP, and the PC as part of the *Taito Legends* series. **CDa**

Zork I

Original release date : 1980
Platform : Various
Developer : Infocom
Genre : Adventure

Of all the classics that Infocom produced in its early 1980s heyday, its first, *Zork I*, may be the worst possible place to start. A descendant of *Colossal Cave Adventure*, and originally bearing the drab name *Dungeon*, *Zork I* spent many years evolving on a mini-computer at the Massachusetts Institute of Technology.

Its commercial release is a hodgepodge of unrelated mythological references and fantasy signifiers, gated by puzzles both logical and loopy—finding your way through a maze by leaving a breadcrumb trail of objects? That's sensible. Scaring off a cyclops by yelling "Odysseus"? That's a little esoteric. Infocom's later text adventures prized carefully crafted stories, memorable characters, and puzzles that were at least a little more sensible than the ones that greeted explorers who broke into the white house to discover a vast world underneath.

At heart, *Zork I* is little more than a treasure hunt. But if anything saves it from feeling dated, it's the charm and the humor that shine through every inventory item and room description. The writers didn't just force you to bring a light into the caves, they invented a dark-dwelling monster—a Grue—to keep you in line. Grues would feature in many future Infocom games. Also noteworthy was the role of the Thief, gaming's first major nonplayer character. He is an autonomous antagonist who moves through the world but plays a crucial role in your beating the game.

Infocom remains synonymous with interactive fiction twenty years after the company closed its doors. The game reminds us that since the birth of computing, programmers have tried to bring adventure, fantasy, and the imagination of a Tolkien or a Gygax to the binary world. *Zork I* has the distinction of being one of the first milestones on that journey. **CDa**

Warlords

Original release date : 1980
Platform : Arcade, VCS
Developer : Atari
Genre : Shoot 'Em Up

Long before Nintendo marginalized the once-ubiquitous D-pad with its N64 controller, Atari was providing smooth analogue input in classic paddle-driven arcade games such as *Pong* and *Breakout*. Building on those games' defense and block-breaking mechanics, *Warlords*, despite not being a huge hit at the time, epitomizes the competitive party nature of the early 1980s arcade scene. Available in a four-player cocktail cabinet with color display, or a black-and-white two player upright unit, the game was ported to Atari's VCS the following year. Its vociferous fans covet the arcade version, however, due to its superior graphics and smoother movement.

That advantage soon becomes apparent once the dragon that flies around the screen during the attack sequence launches its first fireball. Each player must defend their corner of the screen, a task with which they are supported by a thick fort wall and moveable shield capable of catching the dragon's expulsion and redirecting it at opposing players. Every successful hit chips away at the wall, gradually exposing the eponymous warlords; a single direct hit, and it's game over for the unlucky defender. Additional fireballs are added to the chaos as players fall, requiring deft paddle work and a cool head to prevail. As if that wasn't enough, the velocity of the fireball can be altered by the speed and direction it ricochets from the shield, leading to bluffs and double-bluffs as players do their best to outsmart one another. When only one contestant remains, a point is scored before the next fast-paced round begins.

Warlords has been updated for today's generation of gamers via an Xbox Live Arcade version, but it's difficult not to lament the lack of paddle control and the pinpoint accuracy afforded by the original. **BM**

Centipede

Original release date : 1980
Platform : Arcade
Developer : Atari
Genre : Shoot 'Em Up

So much of the early history of gaming is focused on space and war, subjects guaranteed to appeal to the young male audience that filled the arcades of the early 1980s. *Centipede* is the game that bucked the trend. It's microcosmic rather than cosmic, it brings the conflict home, and it's notable for being perhaps the first game to attract female players to the arcades. How did it do that?

The obvious answer would be that it was designed by a woman. Dona Bailey was the only female programmer working at Atari at the time, and *Centipede* was her one and only game, created with Atari legend Ed Logg. But there has to be more to it than that. On the face of it, *Centipede* is a typical shooter, but with one key difference: Instead of a joystick, it's controlled by a trackball, offering a much more intuitive method of moving about. It's more direct, removing the layer of abstraction between the player and the action that the joystick puts in place, and allowing for precise movement in two dimensions rather than the one prevalent in other shooters of the time.

In addition, consider the setting. *Centipede* isn't about epic space battles, it's about pest control in the back garden. The action is as intense as the fiercest shooters of its era, but the setting can be identified with from real life rather than from the cinema screen. Testosterone-fueled it isn't. And it's a closed system with its own internal logic that's easy to grasp. It becomes about trying to create order from chaos, controlling the number of mushrooms, attempting to herd the centipede and preventing other garden invaders from doing too much damage. If you'd like, it's gaming at its most down-to-earth, and beyond its appeal to the fairer sex, it's also challenging enough to give the most hardened of players a tough time. A rare combination, indeed. **JM**

Galaga

Original release date : 1981
Platform : Arcade
Developer : Namco
Genre : Shoot 'Em Up

Although thought of as a classic of the early arcade era, *Galaga* is essentially little more than a *Space Invaders* clone. Ships attack in waves, while a lone fighter must see them off with nothing but twitchy reflexes and a single fire button. And yet a few simple hops in technology made for a dazzlingly refined experience. Compared to Taito's austere classic, *Galaga* is a deep-space fireworks display: Enemies whirl and jitter and course about the screen, as if attached to invisible Catherine wheels; lasers sear the air and stars slip past in a jaunty range of unlikely colors.

If *Space Invaders'* alien menace seems culled from the bottom of the sea, with their empty eyes and twitching tentacles, *Galaga's* are from the nasty little world of insects: buzzing wasps and dragonflies, larvae and butterflies. And while *Space Invaders'* meanies inch progressively lower in a slow back-and-forth descent that is easy to understand (even if it can be tricky to elude), *Galaga's* seem ever impatient to burst from their original formations, zooming down like kamikaze, disappearing off the bottom of the screen, only to warp right back to the top, looping in and out of view until the player is forced to give in to overstimulated panic.

It makes for a game with a lot more spectacle, but more options too: position yourself just right when a long line of baddies swoop in, and you can finish them all off without moving. But if you're more dangerous, so is the enemy, with its tractor beams and the ability to wriggle out of harm's way at the last second.

So while there's no doubt that *Galaga* remains heavily indebted to Taito's classic, and to *Galaxian*, its predecessor, it has always had just enough novelty of its own to keep things fresh. It may have been following templates, then, but it wasn't afraid to embellish their rules. **CD**

Donkey Kong

Original release date : 1981
Platform : Arcade
Developer : Nintendo
Genre : Platform

One of the more famous video game facts, *Donkey Kong's* awkward title came straight out of a Japanese-English dictionary: The game's soon-to-be-legendary designer, Shigeru Miyamoto, wanted stylish synonyms for the phrase "stubborn gorilla," and his choices would initially land Nintendo in hot water with movie studios over the rights to another famous gorilla. Its design, however, came straight from the future: a blast of elaborate cartoon japery that set ablaze an arcade scene filled, for the most part, with aliens and space rocks, and where the most charismatic figurehead yet created was a yellow circle who appeared to suffer a crippling drug addiction.

Miyamoto's game had jokes when most other games didn't even have characters. It had decent animation when other games had shimmering blips that just sort of wriggled around. And it introduced two characters who would dominate the gaming landscape for decades to come. In addition to Donkey Kong, we were introduced to a carpenter named Jumpman. Renamed Mario and given a career change—he becomes a plumber—he was already doing what would later make him so famous: leaping from platform to platform and dodging obstacles, in an endless quest to save Pauline, his kidnapped love interest.

At first viewing, Nintendo's American team were pretty much certain that the game would destroy their ailing division, but, inevitably, the truth was that *Donkey Kong* would launch the toy maker into the global stratosphere. It may not be as character filled as Miyamoto's later games— and Mario, at times, has a mean glint in his eyes as he races after his accomplice Yoshi—but the precision, the imagination, and the physics that would make the series great were all to be found here, for the first time, and it's still good, simple fun today. **CD**

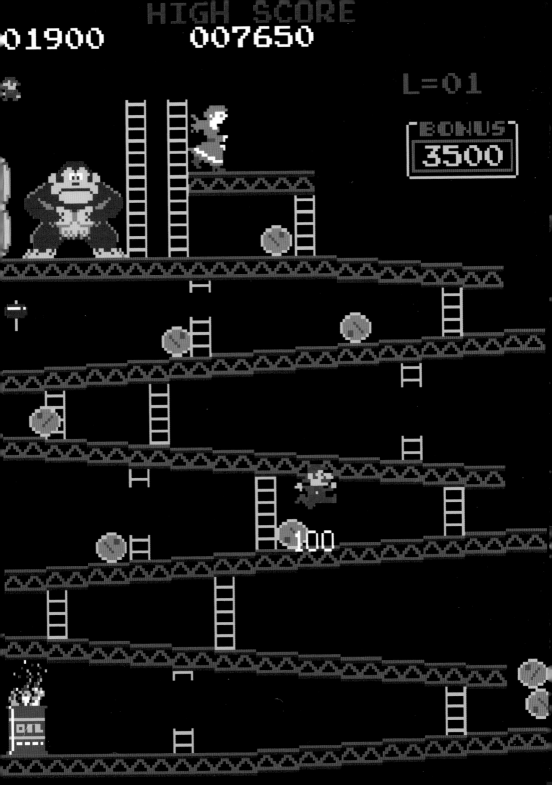

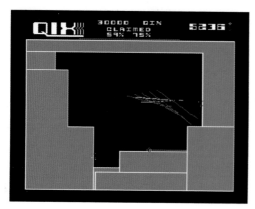

Qix

Original release date : 1981
Platform : Arcade
Developer : Randy Pfeiffer, Sandy Pfeiffer
Genre : Action

Scramble

Original release date : 1981
Platform : Arcade
Developer : Konami
Genre : Shoot 'Em Up

It makes sense that the writers of *Futurama* kept a *Qix* cabinet in their office. Taito's arcade puzzler is mathematically minded—the kind of game that a robot (although one more sober than *Futurama*'s cigar-smoking Bender) might cook up. Players race to divide space, drawing lines and capturing territory by moving a diamond-shaped marker horizontally and vertically through an empty playing field. Levels are cleared when a predetermined percentage of territory has been claimed. And there's a risk-versus-reward factor: slowly drawn lines are worth more points, but getting caught halfway through sketching a division means doom.

The game's titular enemy wreaks havoc with all sense of order. The Qix is a wavy, mercurial force that swoops and undulates like something (gasp) organic. Like an electronic specter, the Qix haunts the playing field, unconcerned with the player's movement. It's this force of nature that makes *Qix* interesting, transforming it from a contest between number crunchers into a struggle between the orderly and logical and the utterly unpredictable. **GM**

Often placed alongside other early side-scrolling shooters, *Scramble* isn't about shooting so much as ducking and weaving. The mission is to fly through hostile territory to bomb an enemy base. Five stages lie in your way, with surface-to-air rockets, zippy UFOs, and even a comet storm waiting to stop you. Tall mountains and skyscrapers impede your progress as the course grows trickier and narrower, until you're threading through tunnels on the way to your goal.

Your jet is armed with two weapons: a front-firing gun and a vertical bomb that lobs forward in an arc. The bomb is difficult to control and even experienced players find themselves missing narrow targets on the ground while struggling to dodge comets. And on top of all this, you also have to contend with the jet's limited fuel supply.

While slower and more convoluted than some of its peers, the varied courses and challenges made *Scramble* an enduring hit on home systems, which has stuck around to the latest generation—a visually reimagined version on Xbox 360 via Xbox Live Arcade. **CDa**

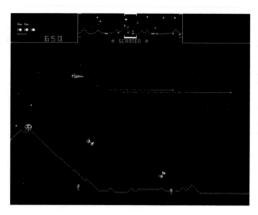

Stargate

Original release date : 1981
Platform : Arcade
Developer : Vid Kidz
Genre : Shoot 'Em Up

Stargate was designed by Eugene Jarvis and Larry DeMar as a sequel to the hugely popular *Defender*, which, within six months of its launch, was one of the biggest coin-op earners in arcade history. But the commercial requirement for a sequel posed a question: In a market where the customer was always ready to defect to the latest novel craze, how did you follow a game that players still found so challenging? The answer was to make it even tougher.

Although working with the *Defender* format, *Stargate* introduced fifteen different types of alien—some cruelly designed to unbalance techniques learned at length to master the original game. Also new, the central feature of the game field was the Stargate itself, which enabled the ship to warp from one side of the planet to the other, but behaved differently depending on the state of play.

Stargate was featured in an episode of the US sitcom *NewsRadio*, during which studio manager Dave revealed that he failed his high school SAT exams due to his addiction to the game. Playing *Stargate* for the first or the hundredth time, you can understand his plight. **MKu**

Venture

Original release date : 1981
Platform : Various
Developer : Exidy
Genre : Dungeon Crawler

Crude graphics were a fact of life in the earliest video games, but few games looked as primitive as *Venture*, which tried to conjure up a fantasy world with geometric visuals. Your dungeon is a rectangle, and it's filled with other boxy rooms where treasure and monsters lie. The hero, Winky—a smiling circle with a bow and arrow—races between rooms, grabs the goods, and dodges a series of archetypal foes, from skeletons and snakes to two-headed ettins, all of them rendered as stick figures.

The game looks so primitive that it lost almost nothing in the move from the arcade to home consoles. But for its limited technology, the game shows imagination: Each monster has a different gait, offers a new challenge, and, in a unique twist, the corpses themselves are toxic, spelling instant death you if you bump into them.

The constant peril and fast pace convey a thrill beyond the graphics: Winky's always on the move; linger, and the boss monsters will get him for sure. And while Winky never made it into the video game hero canon there is a charm and ambition about *Venture* that is timeless. **CDa**

Ms. Pac-Man

Original release date : 1981
Platform : Arcade
Developer : Midway
Genre : Maze

The original *Pac-Man* may be the choice of purists, but there are plenty of arcade aficionados prepared to argue that *Ms. Pac-Man* is the superior game—even though it wasn't even supposed to exist in the first place.

The game started out at General Computer Corporation, a small outfit that reverse engineered the *Pac-Man* code and created a hack called *Crazy Otto*, featuring new mazes and other enhancements. The Otto character was simply Pac-Man with a crude pair of legs tacked on. But when American *Pac-Man* distributor Midway saw *Crazy Otto*, its execs were impressed enough to purchase the rights, replace Otto's legs with a pretty red bow, and call it *Ms. Pac-Man*.

Most of the tweaks in this semi-illicit sequel, such as dancing bonus fruits, are mild, although the use of four different maze designs introduced a variety lacking in the original. But the game play update that had a more significant impact for coin-op jockeys was an element of randomness programmed into the ghosts' behavior. Rather than following predictable algorithms, as they do in *Pac-Man*, the multicolored ghouls in *Ms. Pac-Man* can surprise you. The upshot: players have to occasionally improvise instead of following a foolproof pattern.

The most groundbreaking aspect of this game, though, is Ms. Pac-Man's personality—in fact, she is one of the first video game characters to have one. Let's face it: Pac-Man is an icon, but he's got no charisma. The addition of that "Ms." prefix made all the difference. Portrayed as an alluring minx on the cabinet art and in the in-game cut-scenes, Ms. Pac-Man may still be a two-dimensional sprite on the screen, but she has a little depth. Little wonder that, despite her shady origins, she ended up being adopted as an indispensable part of *Pac-Man* lore. **JT**

Frogger

Original release date : 1981
Platform : Arcade
Developer : Konami
Genre : Action

In theory, you should never lose at *Frogger*. The gaming world's first frog superstar has a straightforward task: to get across a highway, and then a river—dodging vehicles in the first stretch, jumping across logs and turtles on the second. The surrounding world is oblivious to its struggle: The cars speed along on their own, and the alligators and poisonous frogs that patrol the river come and go regardless of where it hops. All you have to do is spot the path through the obstacles and complete it. If you find the right trail, you can make it in seconds. The whole thing should be a cinch, because only you can put yourself in trouble; the game hardly notices you're there.

That, however, is all easier said than done. Moving too quickly is one of the things that leads to mistakes. Panic is another. The obstacle course gets harder as cars speed up and sections of the river change their flow. You're tempted to make a jump onto a turtle when you know it's about to sink underwater—dragging you to your doom. And it's easy to get impatient around the slow-moving cars, even though the game will count you as dead for hitting either the front *or* the rear. You're led to make errors by fearing your own vulnerability, by your eagerness to grab that difficult far-left berth on the safe end of the board, or by the chance to grab a fly for extra points.

A monster hit of the coin-operated arcade era, *Frogger* anticipates the pleasure of platformers like *Super Mario Bros.*, and it appeals to players who would rather keep themselves alive than kill everything else around them. The frog's predicament draws the player into an environment that may be colorful and pleasing but is also full of threats. It's a place where shiny opportunities are put there to tempt you off the safe path, and where mastering the world breeds ridiculous joy. **CDa**

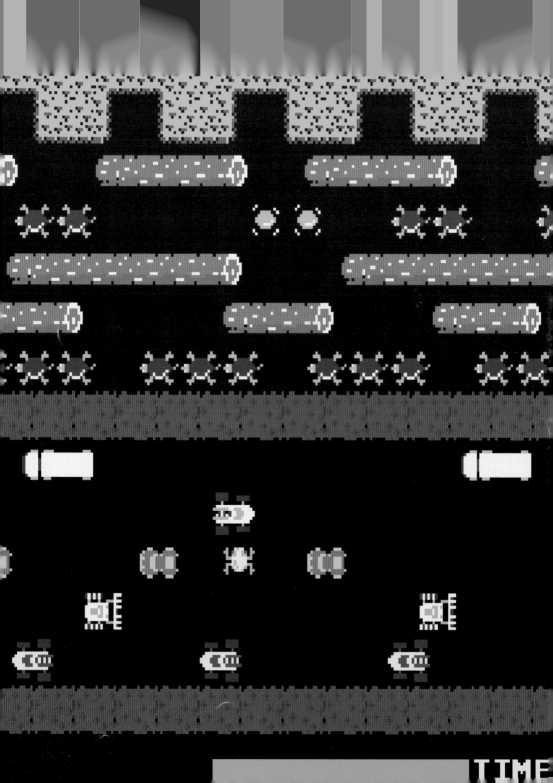

Gorf

Original release date : 1981
Platform : Arcade
Developer : Midway
Genre : Shoot 'Em Up

"Long live Gorf!" cries the Gorf arcade machine when you begin a game, thanks to its Votrax speech synthesizer chip. While the title's legacy lives on, however, Gorf is one of the most frequently overlooked *Space Invaders*–inspired titles from the arcade heyday of the early 1980s.

Gorf (which stands for "Galactic Orbiting Robot Force") is likely passed over because what makes it so groundbreaking—it was the first game to feature distinct levels—also unfortunately makes it a jack-of-all-trades and master of none. Within its five missions, Gorf apes its contemporaries, with the first being a battle against slowly approaching, crab-walking invaders, and the third bluntly called "Galaxians." The final mission distinguishes itself by featuring one of arcade gaming's earliest bosses (the Flag Ship) before looping back to the first mission with the difference of increased difficulty.

This multistage design at such an early point in gaming's history unfortunately means that each of Gorf's missions aren't as polished as the precise, singular design of a competing title, such as *Galaxian*, and several aspects, such as mundane graphics and slightly vague collision detection, make the whole package feel rather less evolved. One unique aspect in particular, the "quark laser" (which allows the player's spaceship to "cancel" its one shot allowed at any time and re-fire), feels like a quirk rather than a game-enhancing mechanic.

But it's all in the voice. Thanks to the flexibility of its speech synthesizer unit, Gorf's robotic master can taunt the player with twenty-five different phrases, often directly referencing your current rank (gained by repeatedly beating a set of missions). The game is flawed, but Gorf draws you back, because you can't let a machine insult you and then get away with it. Long live Gorf, indeed. **MKu**

Ultima I

Original release date : 1981
Platform : Various
Developer : Origin Systems
Genre : Role-playing

A milestone in computer role-playing game (CRPG) history, the early days of Richard Garriott's Ultima series were inauspicious. Originally designed for the Apple II computer, *Ultima I: The First Age of Darkness* was first self-published and sold in Ziploc bags. Popularity became such that by the time of the third installment, it had turned from a student hobby to a million-dollar industry.

Ultima I: The First Age of Darkness takes place in the medieval-styled land of Sosaria. The two main characters are the protagonist—a character who the player creates at the start of the game—and the evil wizard, Mondain, whose Gem of Immortality makes him seemingly invincible. The player's task is to overthrow Mondain. This is achieved by completing a series of quests—usually by venturing into a dungeon and killing monsters—which enables the player to acquire a time machine, go back into the past, and kill Mondain before he has discovered the powerful stone.

In spite of its importance in the story of the CRPG genre, *Ultima I* now seems an impossibly dated and awkward game, in everything from setting to design. But back in 1981, it seemed to offer a groundbreaking level of imagination, enabling the player to take on new roles and explore entire worlds with freedom. The game was also a technical marvel, its top-down tile-based graphics allowing for the creation of large, colorful environments, even on a system with limited storage space. These top-down, third-person views alternated with dungeons viewed in the first-person—*Ultima I* even included a space combat section.

There were other graphically-rich video games inspired by Dungeons & Dragons out there—Sir-Tech's *Wizardry*, to name one notable example—but few can argue with *Ultima I*'s impact on the international CRPG scene, both as a commercial and an artistic prospect. **MKu**

Gravitar

Original release date : 1982
Platform : Arcade
Developer : Atari
Genre : Shoot 'Em Up

The perfect game for anyone who thought that *Asteroids* needed more in the way of crash landings, *Gravitar* takes the same spin-and-thrust flight mechanic and expands it into an engrossing game of space exploration. Your ship begins in the middle of a cluster of planets, and sets out in search of fuel. As you get close to a planet, the perspective switches to the landscape and then zooms even closer as you get nearer to the ground, where your targets lie. And that's where the challenge kicks in, because, as the title suggests, the main characteristic of *Gravitar* is that it is a game centered on the effects of gravity.

Designed by Mike Hally (who later went on to design Atari's hit *Star Wars* arcade game), *Gravitar* was a complete dud in the arcades. Indeed, units were often converted to run the *Black Widow* game, which used the same hardware. It wasn't until the late 1980s that it was given a proper home release for the Atari 2600.

It's easy to see why *Gravitar* didn't thrive in the arcade: This is a complex game that takes practice and finesse, and even *Asteroids* doesn't prepare you for it. You can only move the ship by spinning and rocketing forward: to change direction, you have to spin, counterthrust, and then begin moving back the other way—which is far too many steps to deal with if you're falling straight at the ground. And if you do manage to persevere over all of that, in later levels you'll contend with *invisible* planets—so you can't even *see* what you're trying to avoid.

Above all, the tricky flight mechanic is the best reason to give *Gravitar* another look. It's fascinating as a larval space exploration game, as you learn how to switch perspectives from an open map, to an outer-space dogfight, to a raid on a planet. And even modern games rarely offer the chance to tackle thrust, fuel, *and* the inexorable pull of gravity. **CDa**

Joust

Original release date : 1982
Platform : Arcade
Developer : Williams
Genre : Action

Arcade games of old often tended to be a little arbitrary in their choice of themes—I'm a yellow ball with a drug habit.... I'm an Italian carpenter with a girlfriend who's been kidnapped by my pet gorilla.... You know the sort of thing. But *Joust* is spectacularly weird by any standard. It isn't about days of old when knights battled for maidens outside of tottering fairy tale castles. It's about days when they did all that riding on ostriches—and, in two-player games, on storks.

It's better than it sounds. Played on a series of platforms overlooking a pit of lava, *Joust* flings wave after wave of enemies (knights mounted on giant buzzards) at the player. The player's task is simple: to ride at them and gore them with a lance. With a joystick to move left and right, and a button to take you into the sky in flappy little bursts, the game is simple to play but tricky to master, particularly when the waves increase in ferocity, and enemies start dropping eggs that spawn more powerful enemies if they are not destroyed.

As surprising as it may seem, *Joust* was rather a popular game—so much so that a sequel, *Joust 2: Survival of the Fittest*, was released in 1986. But it's safe to say that the audience's expectations for digital entertainment have moved on a little since then, and—barring a global outbreak of brain herpes in the decision-making ranks of global entertainment corporations—this Williams classic is unlikely to get a further airing. Fans might, instead, want to track it down on both the Xbox 360 Live Arcade service and the PlayStation Network. Beyond that, this ostrich-battling sim is a poignant reminder of what we lost when the arcade dream faded: As games become more commercial and more mainstream, the scope for this kind of insanity is, inevitably, somewhat diminished. For shame. **CD**

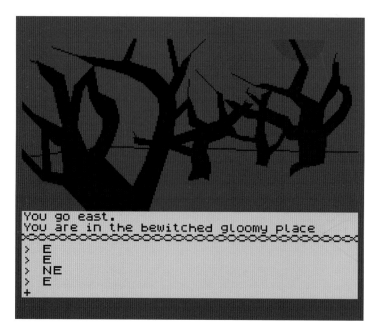

The Hobbit

Original release date : 1982

Platform : Various

Developer : Beam Software

Genre : Text Adventure

A familiar criticism of blockbuster novels is that they read like the recounting of a video game playthrough: someone travels to a location, solves a puzzle, or finds a clue that leads them to their next objective, and so on. For those authors or producers who adapt popular fiction into video games, however, the issue is more that the plots are somehow less engaging off the page—the developers and authors do not appear to know how to make their chosen medium as powerful as the original novel as a storytelling device. Not so in the case of JRR Tolkien's 1937 novel or the 1982 computer game adaptation *The Hobbit*.

A text adventure developed by the Melbourne-based Beam Software, every copy of *The Hobbit* was accompanied by the book, which, rather than serve as a "walkthrough" for the game, simply fired the player's imagination with its rich descriptions and adventurous story. Enlightened by Tolkien's vocabulary, gamers could play a text adventure that revolutionized the genre's traditionally simplistic parser interface. Previous games generally allowed only verb-noun input, but *The Hobbit* allowed players to input advanced sentences, with pronouns, adverbs, punctuation, and more, allowing them to ask an in-game character about an object while using another object to perform a task—all within the same sentence.

More than that, characters had their own AI and would act on their own accord (famously, dwarf Thorin would forever be sitting down to sing about gold), and while that meant occasionally they could end up getting themselves killed (rendering the game unfinishable), Middle-earth was as full of life as Tolkien's descriptions. *The Hobbit* was an open world of emergent game play before the concepts had even been imagined. **MKu**

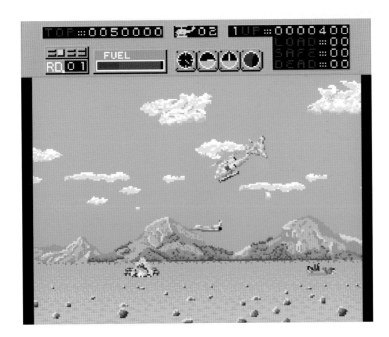

Choplifter

Original release date : 1982
Platform : Various
Developer : Brøderbund
Genre : Shoot 'Em Up

Innocent civilians are a real hassle. When you're not protecting them or shooting past them, you have to lead them by the hand to safety, all the time leaving yourself exposed to more danger—or at least more hassle. The "escort" mission is regularly one of the most aggravating parts of a game, but *Choplifter*, one of the first games to use the concept, actually makes it fun. In *Choplifter*, players fly a helicopter into enemy territory under heavy fire. Blowing up tanks, planes, and anti-aircraft artillery is easy; rescuing the civilians—who are huddled inside buildings in the middle of it all—is the hard part. Instead of mobbing you the second you land à la the fall of Saigon, they stroll up to the chopper like business travelers already on their second

dry martini. And if you get shot down while you're carting them back to base, they happily die by your side.

A realistic (for its day, anyway) war zone combines with a plausibly awkward control scheme. The chopper's front gun leans down, forcing you to pull back to aim at anything coming straight for you. And if you want to change direction or to switch to ground targets, you don't use the joystick: you actually have to press a separate button to switch your orientation.

Originally released for the Apple II computer, *Choplifter* was ported to most of the home systems of its day, and Sega brought it to the arcade in 1985—one of the few occasions that a game has moved from home system to coin-op. And though it's difficult to find nowadays, its legacy lives on—art-game designer Messhof's *The Thrill of Combat* (2009) reimagines it populated by maniacs who murder civilians instead of saving them, for example; mercifully for the hapless citizens on the ground, the chopper in that game is even *harder* to handle. **CDa**

Robotron 2084

Original release date : 1982
Platform : Arcade
Developer : Williams
Genre : Shoot 'Em Up

In the early days of the arcades, only two things really mattered to most developers: separating players from their money extremely quickly, and simultaneously making sure they'd still want to come back for more later that day. No designers were quite as effective at this tricky task as Williams's legendary Eugene Jarvis, whose first game, *Defender*, offered spectacle and swift deaths aplenty, along with some of the most forward-thinking game mechanics of the age. That said, he outdid himself with *Robotron 2084*, a pixelated bloodbath that killed off most new players in roughly fifteen seconds, leaving them stumbling back into daylight, pondering what had just happened and wondering where all their loose change had disappeared.

Even if it wasn't a compulsive masterpiece, *Robotron 2084* would go down in history as the first twin-stick shooter, in which the player moves with one joystick and fires, in any direction, with the other. It's simple in its premise, but tricky to master—and such a huge degree of control means that unscrupulous game designers can choose to fling enemies at you from all directions.

And that's precisely what *Robotron 2084* does, introducing an entire ecology of deadly robots, some that are invulnerable to attack, others that spawn terrible minions that will run you over or shoot at you, and yet more that merely follow you around, hoping to overwhelm you with sheer numbers. With a final wrinkle coming in the form of human family members who need to be collected for score boosts, *Robotron 2084* is the action game genre reduced to its brilliant bare minimum.

It may not look like much nowadays, but few modern games can match it for sheer class. If you're still on the fence, check out the fairly decent port available on Xbox Live Arcade. **CD**

Dig Dug

Original release date : 1982
Platform : Arcade
Developer : Namco
Genre : Maze

Video gaming's preeminent cross between mining and mazes, *Dig Dug* casts you as a little chap with a pump who can effortlessly burrow through the ground. Each level starts with Dig Dug at the top of a solid block of earth containing two types of beasties: bespectacled red types known as Pookas or cute dragons called Fygars. You are then charged with searching out the monsters before either forcing them so full of air that they burst (a rather sadistic exercise lent an element of compulsion by having to tap the button multiple times to operate your pump) or dropping rocks on their heads.

It's a slower-paced affair than you might expect from an early 1980s arcade game, and the fact you can see the enemy positions and plan your route of attack adds a tactical element to proceedings—the final monster on each screen will make a dash to the surface for freedom, so you always have to bear in mind the order in which you attack enemies. And to make things even trickier, the mazes you create in the ground can turn against you as earth weakens, monsters escape, and rocks begin falling toward you. It's frantic stuff.

Dig Dug's excellence shares more than a little common ground with *Pac-Man*: It's the quick switch between hunter and hunted. You start each level in total control and gradually relinquish a little of the initiative with each attack on the enemies before having to fight a frantic rearguard action. Finally, you have to close out each level by stopping the last monster from escaping—a moment that can crush even the most stouthearted of warriors.

Now available on most of the download services, *Dig Dug*'s simplicity means that it's lost little of its appeal. Fans may also want to check out the sequel, which adds tilted perspective to great success. **RS**

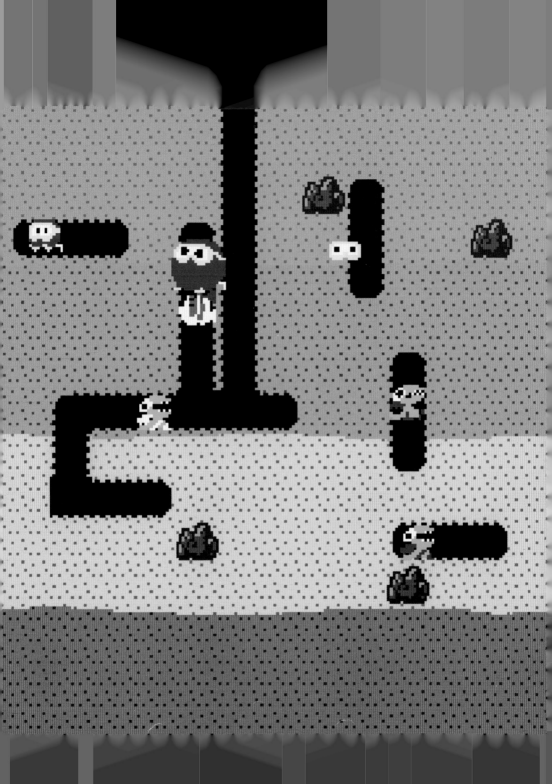

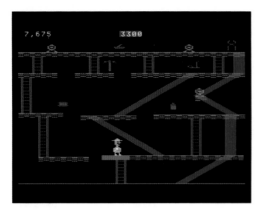

Miner 2049er

Moon Patrol

Original release date : 1982
Platform : Various
Publisher: Big Five Software
Genre : Platform

Original release date : 1982
Platform : Arcade
Publisher: Irem
Genre : Action

The most painful moment in *Miner 2049er* comes when you think you're almost finished—and then realize that you missed a spot. Programmed by Bill Hogue, *Miner 2049er* is a platformer set in a radioactive future, where Bounty Bob searches level after level of an underground mine and "scrubs" the floor with his feet while ducking or crushing the irradiated monsters that prowl the depths beside him. While a series of girders form most of each level, Bob must also deal with slides, matter transporters, and moving platforms. Most important of all, to get to the next level, every single pixel must be scrubbed.

As an early platformer, *Miner 2049er* had charm and clever level design. Across all ten or eleven maps (depending on your platform), no two were alike, and they combined the thrill of victory with the compulsive satisfaction of cleaning a map until it's spotless. Okay, it's practically *homo erectus* in a post–*Super Mario Bros.* world, but it was a milestone for its day. And after years in the wilderness, *Miner 2049er* has now returned to bedevil new generation on mobile devices. **CDa**

One of the most awkward vehicles in gaming history, your vehicle in *Moon Patrol* is neither fast nor deadly. Its big tires roll hypnotically over the uneven ground, speeding up or choking back, depending on the obstacles you spot ahead. Meanwhile, the aliens that taunt you from above can be pegged with a gun that resembles a peashooter.

Moon Patrol is the Thelonious Monk to the airborne shoot 'em up's Charlie Parker: eccentric and plodding, and all the more brilliant for it. While the skyline of a lunar civilization rolls by via parallax scrolling—the first time a game used the technique—you're focused on an obstacle course that challenges you on a gentle curve, gradually adding a greater number of threats. A more aggressive designer may have saddled the buggy with serious firepower, but get used to the controls, and you'll find that you have exactly what you need to keep the peace and clear your path as you travel.

The game ranks your times against the other ones posted at the arcade, bringing a sense of competition to one of the slowest driving games in history. **CDa**

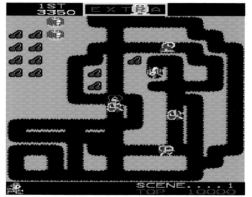

Mr. Do!

Q*Bert

Original release date : 1982
Platform : Arcade
Developer : Universal
Genre : Maze

Original release date : 1982
Platform : Arcade
Developer : Gottlieb
Genre : Puzzle

The conceptual disconnect of a killer clown with a lethal bouncy ball and who loves to eat his dessert is probably nothing new to fans of Japanese games.

At first blush, *Mr. Do* is a weirder, uglier cousin of the popular *Dig Dug*—lots of tunneling, taking out monsters, and, in this case, guarding pieces of food. But *Mr. Do* adds a few other wrinkles. In *Dig Dug*, the protagonist walks around with a bike pump and inflates his enemies to death; *Mr. Do* stars a clown who carries a large ball that he hurls down the tunnels at his enemies. This is tougher than it sounds, because the ball keeps bouncing until it kills something or comes back at you.

The game has two modes: gatherer or hunter. In both modes you advance either by grabbing the fruits strewn before you or by killing the monsters—either with the ball or by causing boulder-like apples to fall on their heads. The ultimate goal is the dessert at the center of the screen.

By the turn of the century, its status as a second-tier coin-op classic made it increasingly rare, and nowadays the arcade edition is hard to track down. **CDa**

*Q*Bert* works best if you don't ask too many questions. It's a game about a muppetlike thing with a tubelike nose who has to jump up and down a pyramid made up of colored cubes. The only thing we learn about his character is that he has a foul mouth: Every time he's caught or falls to his death, he shouts a gruff curse via a speech bubble. The world had seen nothing like it—and consequently it was a monster hit in the arcades.

*Q*Bert* appeals to the obsessive-compulsive gamer. The creature's job is to jump on to every space on the pyramid, flipping its color. Floating platforms take you safely back to the top so you can start down the other side, while enemies spring from the top of the pyramid to keep you on the move. That's about it, really.

*Q*Bert* married an addictive set of new mechanics and an MC Escher–esque board to a character who would hold his own against Donkey Kong and Pac-Man for the affection of millions, earning merchandise, sequels, and a spot on a Saturday morning cartoon. But what was he, exactly? Sometimes it's better not to ask. **CDa**

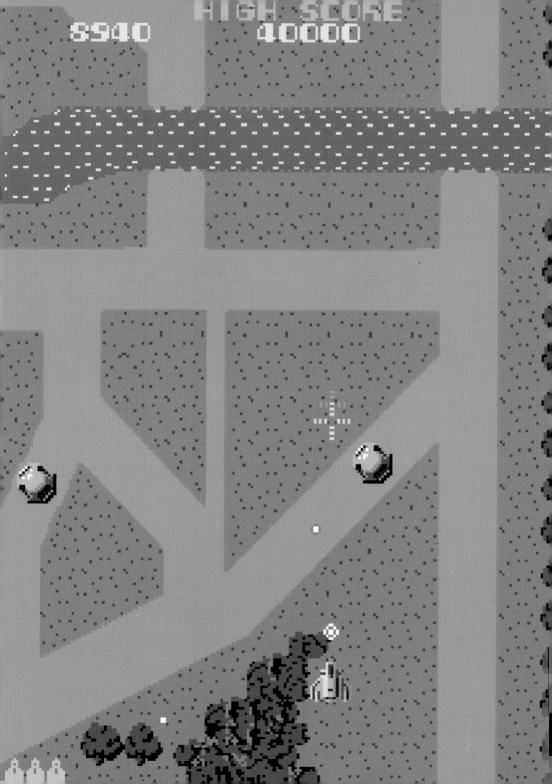

Xevious

Original release date : 1982
Platform : Arcade
Developer : Namco
Genre : Shoot 'Em Up

Brainchild of Masanobu "EVEZOO" Endoh—Easter egg hunters can be rewarded in *Xevious* by heading to the far right as the first level starts and shooting to reveal the hidden message "NAMCO ORIGINAL program by EVEZOO"—*Xevious* is a landmark in its genre.

It was the first shooter to feature a backdrop themed around something other than space. Instead, it plays out over detailed landscapes, and, as a result, has the unique feature that the player's craft—the iconically named Solvalou—has two modes of fire. Ordinary bullets are fired for flying enemies, but the unheralded threat of gun emplacements and tanks must be dealt with by the Solvalou's bombs, the aiming of which is aided by an on-screen crosshair.

Though seminal, and still enjoyable, *Xevious* only holds true legendary status within Japan, and, despite its regular inclusion on Namco's retro game collections, has never managed to capture the imagination of North American or European players. In retrospect, the game suffers from the lack of an ending and graphics that, while remarkable at the time, feature a dull palette and samey designs (nearly every enemy is a gray-colored geometric shape).

Flawed it may be, but the game is full of secrets, and challenges players with enemies who act unlike any that came before. Some of the enemies choose to shy away from your bullets rather than rush toward them, and others are impervious and require deft ship maneuvring. *Xevious* also features one of the earliest video game bosses: a massive flying saucer, the Andor Genesis, whose core must be destroyed in order to proceed.

Xevious might seem easy to overlook, then, but nevertheless it stands as a cornerstone in the evolution of the vertically scrolling shoot 'em up. **MKu**

Sokoban

Original release date : 1982
Platform : Various
Developer : Hiroyuki Imabayashi
Genre : Puzzle

Sokoban is a beautiful example of how a simple set of rules can result in something extraordinarily complex. It's a game that can be grasped in seconds: you're a warehouse keeper, you need to move a collection of crates to marked points in the warehouse, and you can only push (and not pull) them one at a time. Such elegance. The only fly in the ointment is the fact that the warehouse was designed by a madman, or perhaps a sadist. Or, more likely, a sadistic madman.

It's the level design that makes *Sokoban*. Its warehouses are cunning fabrications of open areas, corridors, and bottlenecks, built to trick you into maneuvering yourself into a dead end. As each new level appears you stare at it in horror, wondering how the hell you're supposed to get out of that one. An easy *Sokoban* level can be solved in a few minutes; the more complex ones can take hours or even days and require thousands of moves to complete. It's a game beloved of AI researchers because while simple levels can be solved by brute force, the harder ones are (so far, at least) beyond the capacity of the machines, requiring humans to put those crates in the right place.

Officially there are 306 *Sokoban* levels in existence, as made by the original publisher. Unofficially there are thousands; despite its global appeal, there have only been a handful of official releases outside of Japan. You're far more likely to come into contact with one of the many clones made available for practically every format than anything created by original designer Hiroyuki Imabayashi.

While attempts have been made to create clever variants, it's one of those games that got it right the first time. There may be improvements in the graphics, but the best knock offs of *Sokoban* are effectively identical to the versions released in the 1980s. **JM**

Tron

Original release date : 1982
Platform : Arcade
Developer : Bally Midway
Genre : Action

In the 1980s nerd flick *Tron*, Jeff Bridges plays Flynn, a video game designer turned video arcade owner, and in his first scene, we see him beating a (very dull) tank game while a crowd cheers on. A game for the film was inevitable, and while *Tron*'s two-dimensional top-down graphics don't match the movie's intensity, they nail its look and its most famous action sequences.

The game offers four distinct challenges, and at each level, they get harder: Instead of one tank that's three times stronger than you, you face nine, and so forth. You get to outmaneuver the tanks, throw your Frisbee-like disk at a viruslike infestation, and, best of all, race the light cycles, outrunning your opponents and penning them in with the trail you leave behind. The races are essentially like playing a competitive version of *Snake*, and the top-down perspective lacks the danger of the film's close-up shots. But no matter; the thrill of playing chicken and then breaking away at a perfect right-angle never gets old.

Tron is weakest when you're not in a vehicle. The disk-throwing activities feel bland, and breaking down the rotating, rainbow-colored barrier to the Master Control Program block by block is sheer hard labor. But the tank levels take fast moves and clever tactics to beat, and the racing remains nail-biting today. In some ways, the game predicts the future of movie tie-ins: a set of activities that copy, however awkwardly, exactly what you saw on the big screen. But at least the cabinet helps translate the look of the film to the arcade, with neon lines inscribed on its side panels and a translucent blue joystick to steer your way. The upcoming sequel to both the film and game promises remarkable effects and breathtaking visuals, but just how will *Tron Legacy* compare to the simple tension and compulsiveness of the original? **CDa**

Time Pilot

Original release date : 1982
Platform : Arcade
Developer : Konami
Genre : Shoot 'Em Up

For an uncompromising shooter, *Time Pilot*'s start screen had a way with words. "Play Time Pilot," it cajoled, adding "please deposit coin and try this game." It had no such manners once you did. One of the earliest games from Yoshiki Okamoto (responsible for many arcade classics, among them *Street Fighter II*), the most striking thing about the game is how effectively it manages to simulate dogfighting with the most basic of elements, as well as how unforgiving it remains to this day.

No matter how many coins you insert, there are no "continues" allowed here—though you can earn extra lives, which becomes essential in the quite bewildering later levels. Moving through five eras, the game ramps up from World War I biplanes that barely shoot to 1980s jet fighters, eventually taking in UFOs (in that far-flung year of 2001) that seem to be flown by hyperactive lunatics.

Apart from all the time travel, it's simple stuff. A two-dimensional shooter that lets you move in any direction, *Time Pilot* provides you with an infinite stream of bullets (there are no power-ups) with which to destroy a specific number of enemies before an airship appears; destroy that, and you warp to the next era.

Your craft always remains centered on the screen as you move. Neat little touches—like the number of frames of animation used as it turns, and the looping movements of enemy aircraft as they try to position themselves— make *Time Pilot* stand out among its jerkier contemporaries.

It may not be regarded quite as fondly today as Okamoto's *1942*, but *Time Pilot* is still an enjoyable blast, and arguably improves upon its obvious inspiration, *Asteroids*. And it really should have been responsible for an alternate timeline of its own, where all games say please when they want you to play. **RS**

Utopia

Original release date : 1982
Platform : Intellivision, Aquarius
Developer : Mattel Electronics
Genre : Strategy

Mattel's Intellivision console never achieved the popularity enjoyed by Atari's VCS (aka 2600) during the early 1980s, despite innovations such as controllers that have more in common with today's joypads than the often primitive joysticks of the era, and the Intellivoice Voice Synthesis Module, which connected to the base hardware to provide (limited) vocal accompaniment to certain games. And the console deserves kudos for some of its software, too, notably *Utopia*, which helped to define the evolution of the god and sim genres that would later prove sensational additions to gaming worldwide.

Utopia's success was more modest. It was, after all, a strategy game released at a point when the key goal for home consoles was to emulate the noisy, fast-paced action of the arcades. Further limiting the game's audience was its dependence on two players taking part, each one taking control of an island. The objective is to rule over your nation and ultimately accumulate more cash than your opponent. Farms can be purchased and put in place to provide revenues from crops, while trawling for fish delivers additional funds. The installation of factories, housing, hospitals, schools, and forts provides the deeper strategic content as you attempt to find that delicate balance between societal welfare and earnings potential.

Such considerations may make *Utopia* seem like a dull game, but the interactions between players provide plenty of spark, most notably when one sends out a PT boat in pursuit of the other's fishing vessel, or spends cash to create rebel uprisings within the opposing territory. The action, which plays out entirely in real time, transcends the limited presentation, and the intense competition it inspires is a hallmark that defines the best multiplayer games throughout history. **TB**

I, Robot

Original release date : 1983
Platform : Arcade
Developer : Atari
Genre : Shoot 'Em Up

Today, polygons serve as the fundamental building blocks for all but the most simplistic games, whether they're running on high-end PCs or modestly powered mobile phones. But in the early 1980s they were more exotic artifacts, and only rarely seen. The appearance of Atari's *I, Robot* in the arcades of 1983 was, therefore, something of an event. Originally titled *Ice Castles*, the game's brightly colored, filled three-dimensional objects and terrains were a quantum leap beyond the wire-frame spacecraft and landscapes of many traditional arcade machines. It presented solid-looking environments that felt like what they were supposed to be—visions of a far-off universe.

Game history is littered with technologically pioneering games that fail to supply substance to go with their innovations, but *I, Robot* delivers an engaging challenge within its revolutionary alien playscapes. Your task, as Unhappy Interface Robot #1984, is to change the color of the environment from red to blue by simply maneuvering over it, an idea lifted from *Q*Bert* but realized here with more variation and depth, thanks to increasingly complex level design. Birds and other hazards, such as bombs and flying sharks, impede your progress throughout, and particular care must be taken to avoid leaping across gaps in the environments while the menacing eye of Big Brother is open; failure to do so resulting in instant, laser-administered death.

I, Robot's distinctive styling is underlined by its inclusion of an alternate play mode entirely separate from the main game. Select "Doodle City" at the beginning of a session and you can cycle through three-dimensional objects and manipulate them around the screen to "paint" abstract art. It's not a concept other games rushed to follow, but then too few games are as boldly innovative as *I, Robot*. **TB**

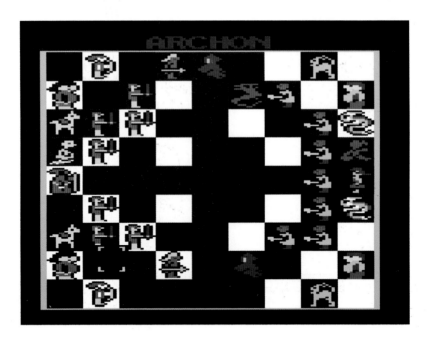

Archon

Original release date : 1983

Platform : Various

Developer : Free Fall Associates

Genre : Fighting / Strategy

German Grand Master Emanuel Lasker observed that "chess is, above all, a fight!" Free Fall Associates clearly took this literally when it created *Archon* (Greek for "ruler") by doing the unthinkable and building on chess's rather sturdy foundations. Superficially similar, *Archon* is actually a very different game, arming both sides with differing but well-balanced pieces and adding a real-time battle system that informed many subsequent strategy games.

After marching onto the board, each side's pieces are placed in turn according to their movement range. The opposing armies represent light and dark, and a light/dark cycle affects certain spaces on the board, providing stat boosts to the units occupying a like square. A spellcaster is

the king-equivalent and can use a variety of spells, such as healing, teleporting, or summoning monsters. And when two units occupy the same square, both are transported to a battle arena where they must exchange fire until one piece has lost all of its energy.

Obstacles phase in and out during the fracas, providing cover for the fleet of foot, and characters have varying speed, strength, and weapon attributes. A damaged unit remains damaged even in victory, so smart strategizing must be employed. Winning the game requires occupation of five power points (squares immune to magic, which also offer health boosts), the destruction of all opposing pieces, or the imprisonment of the last remaining piece (achieved by using a spell that stops the unit from moving until the light/dark cycle changes).

With *Archon*, two-player games can be fraught, fast, and highly enjoyable, thanks to the ability to turn the tides with the use of an underpowered piece. If chess is a fight, *Archon* is a bloody war. **BM**

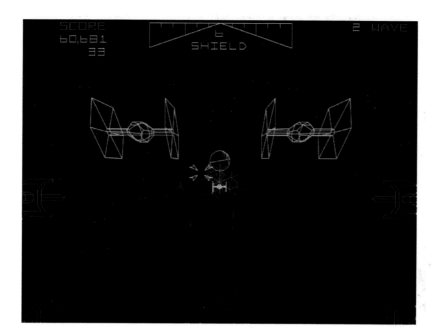

Star Wars

Original release date : 1983
Platform : Arcade
Developer : Atari
Genre : Shoot 'Em Up

One of the first in an endless series of tie-ins to the *Star Wars* franchise, this particular version focuses on the final spectacular sequence of the original movie (or *Star Wars: A New Hope*, if you're a more recent fan): the destruction of the Death Star. With vector graphics nailing the contours of the ships and landscapes, *Star Wars* leads you through three stages of the movie's final battle: shooting down TIE fighters on your approach; skimming along the surface of the Death Star, while turrets and more TIE fighters gun for you; and finally, racing down the trench to shoot a target about as big as a womp rat. Instead of ducking lasers, you dodge slow-moving fire bursts, and you can choose between fending off the missiles or going after their

source. And instead of lives, you get a shield that's worn down every time you're hit, which lets you keep flying to the bitter end, without interruption. And after you make your shot and blow up the Death Star, you get to do it again and again and again.

Though it was by no means the first *Star Wars* video game—that honor goes to the VCS/Intellivision title *Star Wars: The Empire Strikes Back*—it remains a fan favorite. The controller looks and feels like the one we saw in Luke Skywalker's cockpit, and the Death Star does explode vividly before our eyes. In fact, it was the perfect way to relive the film for a generation of kids who were as hooked on *Star Wars* as they were on, well, arcade games.

Nowadays, movie tie-in video games are more often than not a terrible dog's breakfast of scenes from the film and made-up activities, all shoehorned into a mediocre package. *Star Wars* chose the best piece of the movie and nailed it, and it delivers a finale that's as exciting now as it was for its time. **CDa**

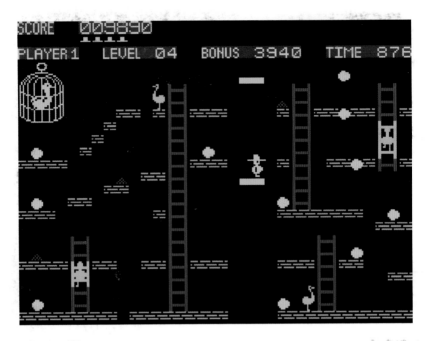

Chuckie Egg

Original release date : 1983
Platform : Various
Developer : Nigel Alderton
Genre : Platform

Manic Miner may get all the attention when gamers rake over the past, but the less-flashy *Chuckie Egg*, released the same year to a more muted response, is the better game.

Yes, *Manic Miner* is great, but it's also a game that insists you do things the right way, with little leeway for players who stray from the prescribed course. *Chuckie Egg*, despite its limited palette and cookie-cutter enemies, is a whole lot more free form and liberating; you don't feel that you're being pushed along a set path. Indeed, when you start the first level, there's no blindingly obvious direction in which to go, just a load of platforms and ladders, eggs that need to be grabbed and deadly hens that, instead of following simple back-and-forth paths, roam unpredictably.

Furthermore, your character moves with a speed and fluidity entirely unlike the leaden shuffling of just about all his platforming peers. Jumping is much more human in its execution: long, shallow leaps instead of miner Willy's lofty parabolas. It feels more *analogue*, more connected with the real world than other platform games, and your inability to simply jump over enemies gives you a real feeling of vulnerability that translates into a very human sense of only *just* having got away with it each time you successfully conclude a level.

To top it all, once you complete the game's eight levels, it loops back to the beginning and pulls the rug out from under you, releasing the caged duck that's been watching over the action, allowing it to fly freely around the level and home in on you constantly like a sniper's crosshair. The duck is an inspired touch that changes the game entirely and forces you to hone your skills even more keenly, and that's what sets *Chuckie Egg* apart from the platform crowd: It's about skill, not memorization. **JM**

Dragon's Lair

Original release date : 1983
Platform : Arcade
Developer : Cinematronics
Genre : Adventure / Interactive Fiction

At first glance, it seemed like the dawn of a new era: *Dragon's Lair* had done an end run around the chunky pixels and limited graphics processors of its day to deliver a genuine cinematic experience in the arcade. Using LaserDisc technology, the game delivered full-motion video sequences triggered by the player's performance. The adventure game had reached a milestone—at least that's the way it seemed.

The game action is controlled with a joystick and a single button, and at every decision point your inputs will either earn you another scene or a fully animated demise. Not only does it look amazing, but Don Bluth's animations put a screwball spin on the old story of a knight storming a castle to save a princess. Here, we have the exasperated Dirk the Daring putting up with trial after trial while the beautiful Princess Daphne—dizzy and flirty like a bubblier Marilyn Monroe—awaits his rescue.

Yet for all its glitz, *Dragon's Lair* is also a parlor trick. In truth, it's barely interactive—and often unfair. Some scenes are easy to figure out: If you're trying to catch the swinging rope, you wait until it's in reach before you make your move. But in others it's not clear what action you should take—or when you should take it. A split-second delay before you swing your sword or jump off a falling platform may make the difference between survival and death, and only through trial and error can you get the hang of it.

Still, the game does try to throw you a bone. If you flub one scene, it will move you on to another one, giving you a chance to see as much content as possible in a single play. And with enough practice, you can memorize all the steps to victory—a process that's more satisfying, and less expensive, with today's iPhone port of the game. **CDa**

Gyruss

Original release date : 1983
Platform : Arcade
Developer : Konami
Genre : Shoot 'Em Up

Gyruss is a rare example of a tube shooter—a game in which your ship moves in a circle around the screen, firing at enemies in the center. Atari's Tempest is the classic example of the genre, but Gyruss offers an interesting counterpoint. Where Tempest's aesthetic is sharp and eerie, Gyruss is elegant; the various-shaped aliens fly in from the sides in graceful formations, like mutant synchronized swimmers. No gridlines clutter the screen, and the flight patterns are mesmerizing—soothing, even—at least until the enemy gets serious about shooting back. And even the 8-bit version of Bach's Toccata and Fugue in D Minor—pumping out in unprecedented stereo sound—was vastly superior to the hackneyed soundtracks blaring beside Gyruss in early-1980s arcades.

Designed during his career at Konami by Yoshiki Okamoto, who had previously created Time Pilot and later worked on Street Fighter II at Capcom, the game is quite dizzying to play. The scrolling starfield of earlier space shooter games was rearranged for a three-dimensional perspective, so stars come into view at the center of the screen and fly outward, giving the impression of the player's ship moving through space at breathtaking speed.

With as slender a plot as any other golden-age arcade game, the simple aim of Gyruss is to shoot your way from the edge of the solar system back to Earth, defeating waves of attackers and other assorted objects that come your way between each planet. As slight as that may seem, it does give the gamer a sense of overall purpose.

Gyruss has seen many modern ports, such as in Konami Collector's Series: Arcade Advanced. It also received the slightly ignominious homage of appearing as a mini-game within Grand Theft Auto: San Andreas—where it was renamed They Crawled from Uranus! **CDa**

Mad Planets

Original release date : 1983
Platform : Arcade
Developer : Gottlieb
Genre : Shoot 'Em Up

Gottlieb was a pinball giant that tried its hand at arcade games with limited success, most notably the cartoony Q*bert. Less well known is 1983's Mad Planets, a particularly manic shooter that did itself no favors by being a bit too far out there for it to gain widespread appeal. Instead of the usual aliens, you're up against entire planets—planets that start small and weedy but quickly become massive, extremely dangerous, and follow crazy skewed orbits that would have had Newton scratching his head and going back to the drawing board.

Things are tough from the start. Nowhere on the screen is there a safe haven, so to even things up a little, you're given full freedom of movement—the whole screen is yours through which to maneuver, and a spinner enables you to turn and shoot in all directions. It may seem like a lot of freedom, but you need every degree of it because you are in almost permanent danger of a furious world slamming into you from any direction. The trick, learned early in the game, is to try to blast the planets when they're small. But they evolve so quickly that a level can turn from a duck shoot to utter chaos inside a second. Furthermore, you have to mind just how you shoot them: If you're not careful, you'll just pick off their moons—and a moonless planet becomes a mad planet, glowing red and slinging itself around ever faster.

It's fast and it's twitchy with a strange control scheme that makes it tricky to emulate and saw it almost untouched by home clones. Crazy Comets and Mega Apocalypse, both by Simon Nicol on the Commodore 64, were the only games to recreate the Mad Planets experience. Unique and rather special, if you can find the means to play Mad Planets properly, you'll discover a tough, daft, and rewarding space oddity. **JM**

M.U.L.E.

Original release date : 1983
Platform : Various
Developer : Ozark Softscape
Genre : Strategy

When Trip Hawkins first launched his fledgling Electronics Arts company, he approached publisher SSI with an offer for the rights to the business sim *Cartels & Cutthroats*. When he was turned down, Hawkins made a direct approach to Dan Bunten, the game's author, who promised to produce a far superior original instead. Nine months later *M.U.L.E.* shipped as EA's first product. A sophisticated multiplayer game, it not only launched what would soon become a multi-billion-dollar corporation, but is widely considered to be one of the most influential ever written. A detailed economic simulator with a focus on nonviolent competitive cooperation—a common theme for Bunten, who detested gaming's obsession with killing—*M.U.L.E.*'s pioneering steps laid foundations for countless other titles.

Up to four players are tasked with the management of a new colony on planet Irata in a scenario inspired by the Wild West. The simple purpose of the game is to amass the greatest wealth by balancing the supply and demand of four basic elements. This is achieved by configuring a Multiple Use Labor Element, which is programmed to harvest varying amounts of each element. Players buy whatever they need and sell what they don't need of their own harvest, and try to stay in profit.

The genius of *M.U.L.E.* is that, while victory is achieved through the accumulation of wealth, it is impossible for one player alone to harvest everything needed. The message is that collaboration and the well-being of the colony as a whole are a necessity or *all* players will fail.

SimCity, Command & Conquer, and *Viva Piñata* all owe a great debt to *M.U.L.E.*'s innovations. Indeed, Will Wright dedicated *The Sims* to Bunten, who died in 1998, and even included *M.U.L.E.*'s theme tune as a hidden extra in his 2008 game, *Spore*. **BM**

Planetfall

Original release date : 1983
Platform : Various
Developer : Infocom
Genre : Text Adventure

When *Planetfall* first shipped, sidekicks were rare. Floyd was a nonplayer character who tagged along with the player but took care of himself, proving amusing and also instrumental to the plot. Many gamers surprised themselves as they grew emotionally invested in an artificial life-form in an interactive fiction, who they only knew from text on a screen. When first-time author and soon-to-be legend Steve Meretzky mastered the delicate task of imbuing a functional resource with an endearing personality, he created a gaming milestone.

Of course, the rest of the game is good too; it's an Infocom text adventure coded at the height of the genre, by one if Infocom's greatest talents. A science-fiction story with a lively sense of humor, it acknowledges its debt to Douglas Adams—don't forget to grab your towel—but it also depicts in vivid detail a civilization on the brink of final destruction.

The player gets to play archaeologist, and ultimately savior, by wandering the buildings and laboratories and deducing the function of each artifact, as well as translating the comically pig-Latin-ish writing left behind by a lost race. And the game follows a timeline right from the opening scenes, when the player is given a limited number of moves to flee a doomed spaceship and crash-land on the planet. Take too long while you're down there, and you may fail in your quest.

The game had the advantage of being accessible to newcomers, with clear and logical problems that make for an easy introduction to text adventures. It's one of the company's best-loved games, instantly creating Meretzky's reputation as a funnyman and storyteller—but the person who really became famous was Floyd, one of the first characters in gaming who felt like more than a name. **CDa**

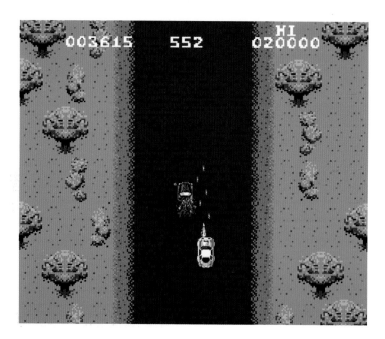

Spy Hunter

Original release date : 1983
Platform : Arcade
Developer : Midway
Genre : Action

With its smart weapons, cool cars, and the persistent buzz generated by the slinky rendition of the *Peter Gunn Theme* pumping from the speakers, *Spy Hunter* was viewed as a very stylish game back in the arcades of the early 1980s. It was a title that played into any boy's favorite fantasies—secret agents, nasty weaponry, and a driving license—and made the moment they started slotting in the coinage all but an inevitability. But make no mistake, it was the action as much at the perfectly poised presentation that kept those young punters coming back for more.

In *Spy Hunter*, you play as a secret agent with a car that shoots bullets from the front grill, and you're tasked with the admirably simple mission of tooling down an endless highway—conveniently, it's a highway entirely without corners of any kind—fighting off a range of vehicular enemies, from stretch cars with machine-guns projecting from the sides, to buses with spikes in the wheels, and even the occasional helicopter, while upgrading your ride with smoke screens and oil slicks every now and then as you drive into the back of passing power-up vans.

All of this was supercool, for sure, but *Spy Hunter*'s most magical moment comes when the game's incomplete bridges force you to take your dream machine off-road—and it suddenly transforms itself into a boat by passing through a convenient shack, taking the land-based battle directly to the waves.

Uniquely suited to the obsessions of the 1980s, with its slick mixture of espionage and cars, *Spy Hunter* is a delightful, if not expensive, memory, for everyone who played it. It is also the subject of a frankly ridiculous PS2 title built around a movie starring Dwayne Johnson, although that game, thankfully, sank without a trace. **CD**

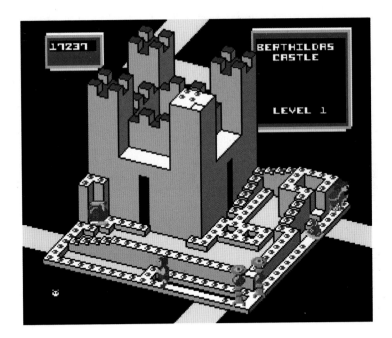

Crystal Castles

Original release date : 1983
Platform : Arcade
Developer : Atari
Genre : Action

For its day, *Crystal Castles* was awesomely ambitious: paths, bridges, ledges, and elevators decorate three-dimensional structures that are themselves laid out on an overworld map. The protagonist, Bentley Bear, conquers map after map by sweeping up gems as quickly as possible. Skeletons, witches, and animated trees plague Bentley's steps, and if he spends too long on a level, a swarm of bees will show up and chase him. Thanks to the game's trackball controller, it's possible to move very quickly indeed: One swipe sends you skimming across the screen, grabbing all the gems that lie in your path.

The design was certainly detailed: programmer Franz Lanzinger packed as much as he could into each screen—almost to a fault: Each of the thirty-seven maps feels crammed into view, and rendered in an unusual trimetric perspective that becomes quite disorienting in later levels. The controls are speedy but twitchy, especially when you try to take small steps or cover both sides of a broad path. The wide view also explains why none of the characters, who are actually quite cute, ever became arcade stars.

But *Crystal Castles* is charming and engrossing, flaws and all. The level design is ingenious, with semi-secret passages and sluggish elevators testing your reflexes, even as they tempt you to explore deeper.

Unusually, beating the game will actually end it, instead of taking you back to the beginning—an innovation for the time, and another reason why it feels more like the story-driven platformers that would later come to the home market than a typical repetitive coin-op.

It's been ported many times to home consoles and has even sprung up on Atari's official arcade web portal, where you can play a complete Flash version for free. **CDa**

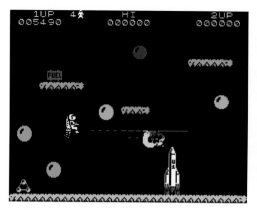

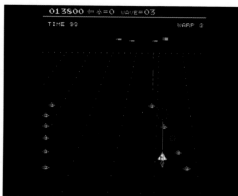

Jetpac

Original release date : 1983
Platform : Various
Developer : Ultimate Play the Game
Genre : Shoot 'Em Up

The game that launched the company that would one day become Rare—UK development powerhouse and creator of franchises like *Banjo-Kazooie* and the excellent *Viva Piñata*—*Jetpac* is a compact title that casts a very long shadow indeed. Part puzzle game and part twitchy platformer, the player is dropped into the role of a lone astronaut, Jetman, who must use his spacesuit's thrusters to blast himself around a series of simple planetary environments, collecting and reassembling the pieces of his ship, before loading it with fuel and subsequently roaring off into space. The real star of the game, though, is the simple yet extremely effective implementation of a physics model, tugging at you in a predictable and realistic manner as you race through the sky.

Jetpac provides plenty of entertainment for even modern-day space explorers, but just in case we'd forgotten its simple charms, Rare—now a part of the mighty Microsoft corporation—released an updated (if slightly overcomplicated) version, *Jetpac Refueled*, for the Xbox Live Arcade platform in 2007. **CD**

Juno First

Original release date : 1983
Platform : Arcade
Developer : Konami
Genre : Shoot 'Em Up

In the early 1980s it was uncommon for Japanese game designers to take inspiration from the West, so *Juno First* is something of an unusual specimen. The high-intensity horizontally scrolling shoot 'em up is flipped 90 degrees to become a high-intensity vertically scrolling one. But to sideline *Juno First* as a clone would be an injustice, because this is a supremely accomplished action game in its own right. Its pseudo–three-dimensional presentation, sending waves of enemies into the combat zone from a far-off horizon, makes the action much more dynamic than that of other similarly styled games of its era, which feel static in comparison. Since the game scrolls in both directions, retreat from the incoming enemies is an alternative option to the all-out attack style of play expected of the genre.

Juno First is a game in the classic high-score tradition, its intermittent bonus pods offering opportunities to crank up the points at an accelerated pace as your craft washes a spitting stream of laser fire across the screen. It will always live in the shadow of certain other examples, but to its modest fan base it remains a classic. **TB**

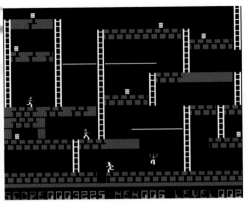

The Cold Room

AIR

High Score 000000   Score 002034

Lode Runner

Manic Miner

Original release date : 1983
Platform : Various
Developer : Douglas E. Smith
Genre : Platform

Original release date : 1983
Platform : Various
Developer : Matthew Smith
Genre : Platform

With its clever melding of puzzling and action, *Lode Runner* is an eminently playable platformer. It was, however, revolutionary for another reason, as one of the first games to offer a level editor. Giving players access to the building blocks of *Lode Runner*'s game world wasn't just a ploy to extend the game's lifespan and popularity—it gave the gaming community a then-rare opportunity to fully digest the concepts at work in every gold-scrounging level.

Lode Runner's scenario is almost primal. Set in a series of ornate caverns—multilayered mazes connected by ladders and bridges—the protagonist is a gold miner able to dig holes through soft rock. All around, guards try to prevent him from nabbing all the area's gold and escaping.

The original game shipped with 150 levels, but the modders crafted countless more. And the fact that the chase, dig, nab, and run of *Lode Runner* feels infinitely replayable is surely a testament to the rock-solid original design. But the game's longevity and timelessness also reflects well on us. Leave it to gamers to carry the torch, and they'll illuminate depths you never imagined. **GM**

Before *Jet Set Willy* and his frighteningly muddled mansion came *Manic Miner*, a far neater platformer, but with plenty of its own surreal touches and twists and an atmosphere every bit as thick with mysterious charm.

Trapped deep inside the tunnels and rocky chambers of a mine, players must help Willy get back to the surface, navigating an increasingly complex series of twenty different rooms, all of which require a key to be located before the exit can be unlocked. The range of different screens takes the miner on a genuinely bizarre journey at times, while the inclusion of a countdown clock based around Willy's ever-diminishing air supply only makes things more tense.

Paving the way for *Jet Set Willy*, one of 8-bit computing's most memorable games, *Manic Miner* remains a classic: taut, claustrophobic, and filled with designer Matthew Smith's strange humor. At the time, it was also the first ZX Spectrum game to feature extensive in-game music, plucked, rather stylishly, from the copyright-free back catalogues of maestros Grieg and Strauss. **CD**

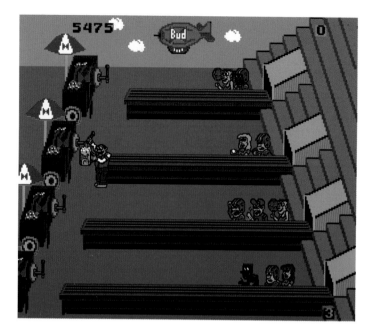

Tapper

Original release date : 1983
Platform : Arcade
Developer : Marvin Glass and Associates
Genre : Action

Tapper didn't simply live in the corner of your local watering hole. The arcade cabinet, outfitted with faux wood trim, a brass foot rest, and a joystick topped by a tap handle, feels like an extension of your local bar.

The game is a direct predecessor of *Diner Dash*. As the bartender, you pull drinks and slide them across the bar to your thirsty customers. Hurl one beer too many, and it'll crash on to the floor. Once they've quaffed their ale, drinkers send their empties right back at you. Those too will drop to the floor if not collected. More generous beer guzzlers will leave tips on the table. But it's risky to chase after this dough: Every moment you're away from the tap is a moment a stray mug could tumble to the sawdust.

The entire affair is colorful and slightly lurid. *Tapper* marked an early (and rare) instance where product placement was not just appropriate, but appealing. The Budweiser logo was prominent throughout. Maybe that's why a second version of the game—sans references to alcoholic beverages—was created when the machine staggered to arcades. Amiable cartoon customers, caricatures of cowboys, punks, basketball players, and aliens, helped make the notion of brew-swilling that much more attractive. And the nostalgic tinkle of a saloon piano and the satisfying crack of a frosty can of beer during the bonus round contributed additional auditory satisfaction.

The introduction of the white-washed *Root Beer Tapper* a year later wreaked havoc with character motivation (what customer would freak out over the slow pour of a noncaffeinated soft drink?). However, the move away from alcohol was a wise, early example of the self-regulation that would typify the gaming industry's approach to censorship. A case of better us than them. **GM**

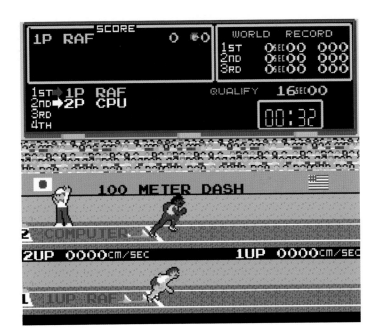

Track & Field

Original release date : 1984
Platform : Arcade
Developer : Konami
Genre : Sports

When the earliest game designers turned their attention to the Olympics, they captured humanity's greatest sporting event the only way they knew how: by making you mash buttons. *Track & Field* requires players to repeatedly tap buttons in order to make their athletes run, while another button unleashes an event-specific action—launching into the air for the long jump event, for example, or releasing a javelin. Button tapping is a crude way to enjoy activities that can sometimes look so graceful in real life, but it's obviously a very physical one, which heightens the game's appeal as a multiplayer attraction.

Track & Field can be played solo, but it comes into its own with up to three fellow athletes attempting to set the fastest times, springiest leaps, and longest throws. The six events (100-m dash, long jump, javelin, 110-m hurdles, hammer, high jump) allow players to compete head-to-head via two sets of controls. The solo events are the most technical, as you propel yourself right up to the line and then hold the button just long enough to find the perfect angle of launch (45 degrees being optimum, although some players swear by pitching it slightly higher or lower). The head-to-head running events, meanwhile, with two players battering buttons simultaneously, have been known to reduce overcompetitive types to exhausted wrecks—and arcade machines to disrepair.

Track & Field shipped in time to harvest interest in the 1984 Olympics in Los Angeles, and from that very first coin-op, Konami built a franchise that continues to this day with the likes of *New International Track & Field* for the Nintendo DS, while its simple but remarkably effective design has influenced countless imitators during the intervening years. **TB**

Ballblazer

Original release date : 1984
Platform : Various
Developer : Lucasfilm Games
Genre : Sports

Instead of trying to make a computer simulation of an existing sport with all the compromises that entails, with *Ballblazer* Lucasfilm Games invented a new sport altogether, one which played entirely to the strengths of home formats of the time.

It keeps things simple: It's a one-on-one game of football, only with hovercrafts, a floating ball, and moving goal posts. The controls are basic: The craft can be moved in four directions and can unleash a "force push" that can be used to launch the ball goalward, or to tackle and take the ball from the opposing player. Despite such limitations, however, *Ballblazer* works in three dimensions, thanks to a brilliant camera system: the hovercraft automatically faces whichever compass point is nearest the direction of the ball or, if you have control of the ball, the goal.

It's confusing at first, but once you adjust to the idea, it works amazingly well. The pitch may be huge and the graphics functional, but you always know which way to go, and this inspired piece of automation enables you to concentrate on getting to the ball, wrestling it off your opponent, and hopefully launching it between the posts. But that won't happen often. Indeed, your early games will be scrappy affairs until you get a feel for how *Ballblazer* works. Once you crack it, it's fluid and incredibly fast with an analogue feel and a physics model in which action has an equal and opposite reaction—as you'll note when you get kicked back after unleashing a shot.

It's minimalistic and expertly balanced, so much so that when LucasArts tried to sex it up for a 1990s sequel (*Masterblazer*), the result was a complete mess. Best of all, if *Ballblazer* were to become a real sport, your gaming skills would transfer across to it effortlessly—something that possibly makes it unique among sports games. **JM**

Bank Panic

Original release date : 1984
Platform : Arcade
Developer : Sanritsu Denki
Genre : Shoot 'Em Up

There aren't many video games about working in banks, probably because it's difficult to identify the fun potential in advising customers on mortgage rates. Wind the clock back to the days of the Wild West, however, and you have a setting more suited to entertainment, as illustrated by the fast-moving, bullet-riddled world of *Bank Panic*.

Panic is certainly the right word to describe what happens within the banks of Sanritsu Denki's game. You assume the role of a lawman, seeing off bandits with your pistol, forced to consistently make split-second decisions. You're faced with three doors at a time, and while you can see when one is about to open, you never know what's going to be on the other side. It might be a regular customer looking to make a deposit, in which case you let them go about their business; it might be a gun-toting robber, in which case it's time to unload; or, perhaps, it's a boy wearing a stack of hats, which can be shot away to reveal a bonus. As the game progresses, the action becomes more complicated. Normal citizens are sometimes pushed aside by robbers, for example, turning a moment of relief into a scrabble to reach for the fire button, while other criminals turn up with two revolvers (requiring two shots to kill), and occasionally bank doors will be rigged with bombs that must be shot before they detonate. All the action is played out to the background music's repeated cycle of "Dixie," the tempo of which speeds up frantically as the time runs down, adding yet another level of panic.

With three fire buttons (one for each door) and some dirty tricks under its belt (beware the townsfolk who turn up wearing the same clothes as the bad guys, for example, or robbers who duck away from the door), *Bank Panic* is one of the most complex arcade games of its era, requiring intense focus. It's also among the most enjoyable. **TB**

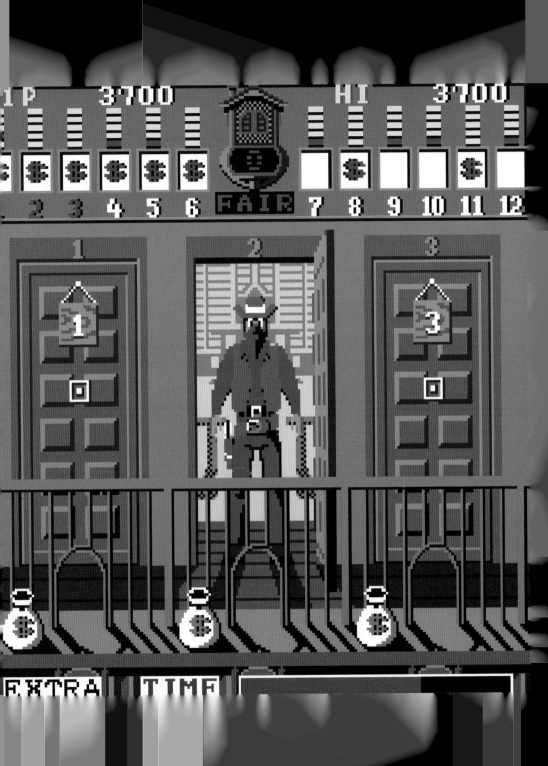

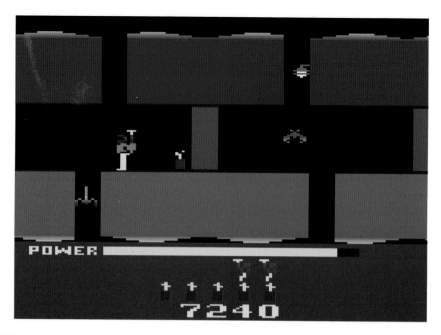

H.E.R.O.

Original release date : 1984
Platform : Various
Developer : John Van Ryzin
Genre : Platform

Take a look at an Xbox 360 controller. Two clickable analogue sticks, a D-pad, two analogue triggers, and nine buttons. Now consider the Atari VCS joystick. One digital stick and a fire button. Not much to work with, and as a result, the designers of yesteryear were often forced to be extremely imaginative with their control schemes.

If *H.E.R.O.*—a game in which you control a little man with a helicopter backpack, a laser gun, and a stash of explosives—were released today it would use a stick and three buttons, which would have been unheard-of extravagance back in 1984. Here we have left and right control movement, the up controls your helicopter backpack; down places explosives; the fire button activates

your laser. Not a control is wasted. It's an efficient and extremely elegant scheme befitting an ambitious game of underground rescue.

Your job is to descend into a series of mine shafts to find trapped workers, a task made more hazardous by deadly wildlife and blocked passageways that require blasting. Danger is everywhere; even blowing up a harmless wall requires you to make a swift getaway once you've dropped your dynamite. Ill-placed lanterns plunge rooms into darkness when you blunder into them, and life-terminating water lurks at the bottom of many caverns. And just to add to the fun you have a limited supply of dynamite—indeed, later levels do their utmost to get you to waste dynamite so that you run out just as the end of the level is in sight, thus forcing you to wait for the power to run out on your backpack, lose a life, and restart the level. Harsh, yes, but it means you just do it right the next time, and it's a small annoyance from a game that otherwise conjures an awful lot out of not very much at all. **JM**

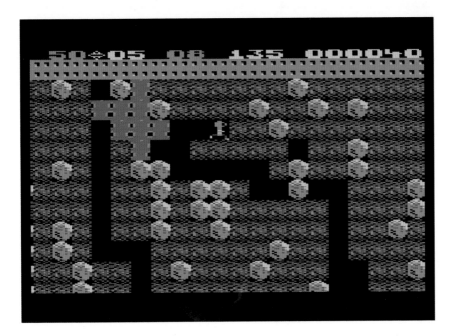

Boulder Dash

Original release date : 1984
Platform : Various
Developer : First Star Software
Genre : Maze

Boulder Dash took the design of arcade titles *Dig Dug* and *Mr. Do*—which feature two-dimensional maps and the player character tunneling through earth, avoiding enemies, and falling rocks (or, in *Mr. Do*'s case, apples)—and simplified it for home formats of the time. In doing so it created one of gaming's most enduring franchises.

Game play is simplicity itself. Taking the role of Rockford (a hero who, thanks to hardware limitations, looks more like a pixelated version of an anthropomorphic frog), the player tunnels around levels, collecting diamonds while avoiding tumbling boulders. Unlike *Dig Dug*'s Taizo Hori or *Mr. Do*, Rockford has no way to protect himself directly, so must use his wits to create a maze for his enemies,

carefully timing chases to make sure they end up on the business end of a falling rock.

Unusual in the video game industry as a title that has maintained the same rights holder since its inception—First Star Software still sells versions of the title to this day—*Boulder Dash* has received almost as many official sequels as it has clones, with often superb and usually wildly different ports to most home platforms, through Game Boy Advance to iPhone and iPod Touch.

Boulder Dash endures because unlike many of its contemporaries, it features no combat, and unlike other nonviolent titles, it allows players a variety of options to deal with threats: You create your own maze rather than simply navigate a predetermined one. It therefore requires a fine balance of on-the-fly puzzle solving and sharp reflexes, and ensures that any mistakes always feel like your own fault. As fresh and playable now as it was twenty years ago, *Boulder Dash* is a diamond well worth digging out. **MKu**

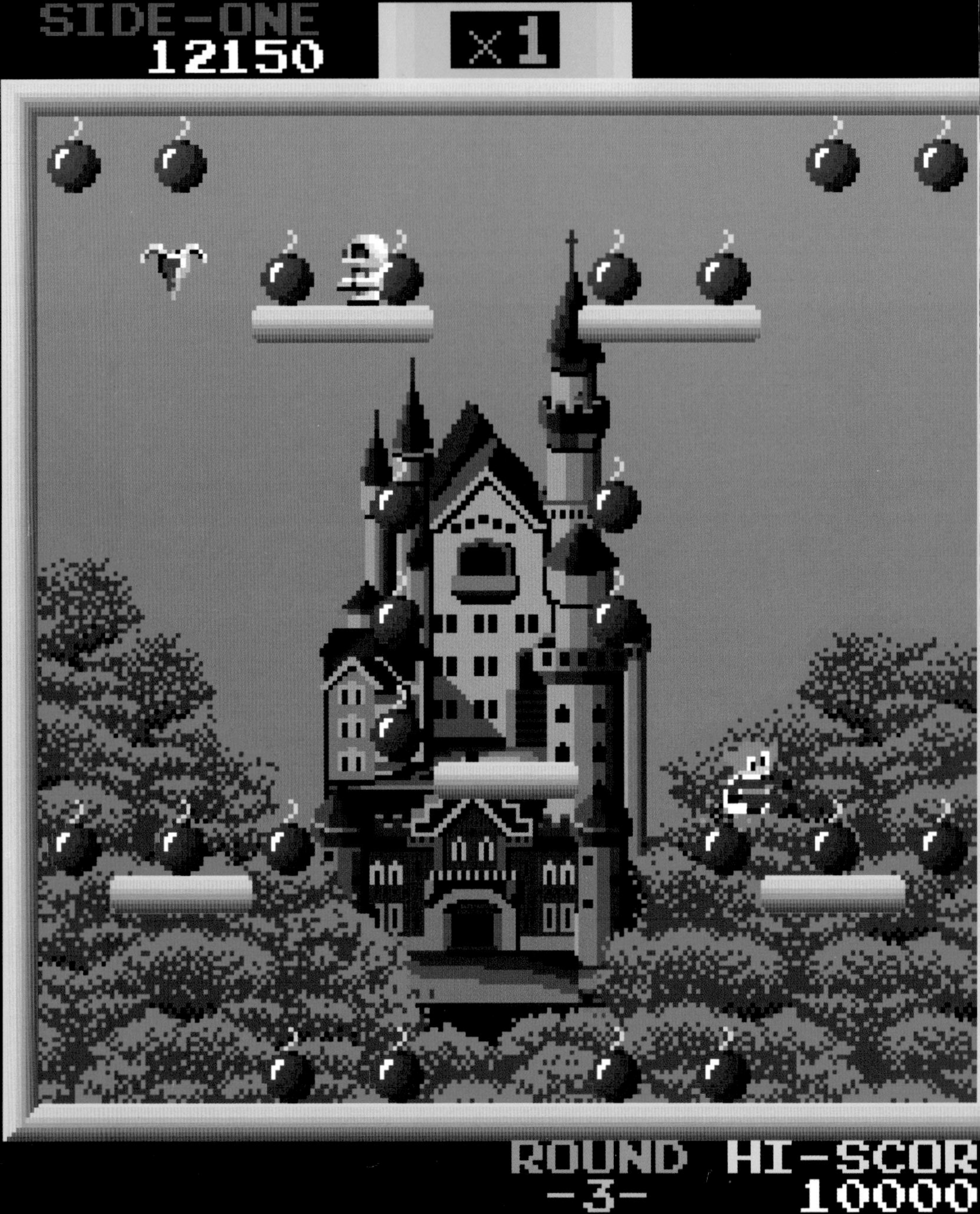
SIDE-ONE
12150
×1
ROUND
-3-
HI-SCOR
10000

Bomb Jack

Original release date : 1984
Platform : Various
Developer : Tehkan
Genre : Platform

The year 1984 was an explosive one. The IRA tried to blow up Margaret Thatcher in Brighton. Hezbollah targeted the US embassy in Beirut. Ronald Reagan made an off-color, on-microphone joke about bombing Russia. Meanwhile, in video arcades, a pudgy red-white-and-blue superhero called Jack jumped and glided to the rescue, defusing screen after screen of explosive devices planted in famous tourist destinations like the Sphinx, the Acropolis, and Castle Neuschwanstein. Were the artists of video gaming imitating life or was it just coincidence?

Nobody ever really knew what the true premise of *Bomb Jack* was supposed to be. But it's so fast and furious, it barely needs a plot. All you need to know is that the fuses are lit. What are you waiting for? Get moving! In fact, it's so manic that it's only after several (dozen) tries that you realize the bombs will never explode.

Instead, the burning fuses are part of the game's secondary challenge: defusing the bombs in order to gain bonus points. Sounds easy. But when you're besieged by mechanical birds, bouncing balls, and robots, dodging both enemies *and* the unexploded bombs, it's no mean feat. Especially since the deliberately unforgiving jumping physics means you'll have to work hard not to undershoot or overshoot your target.

Despite its international look, *Bomb Jack* is a thoroughly Japanese game. Its spring-heeled hero nods to Mario, as does its platforming. Its dodge-and-collect game play is straight out of *Pac-Man*, as is the siren triggered by its enemy-freezing power pills. Even its bombs are impossibly cute, more like ripe cherries than tools of asymmetric warfare. Maybe that explains its enduring appeal. There's been no shortage of bombs in the world since 1984. If only they were all as inexplosive as *Bomb Jack*'s. **JRu**

Elite

Original release date : 1984
Platform : Various
Developer : Ian Bell, David Braben
Genre : Strategy / Shoot 'Em Up

Few games have had the bravery to paint a portrait of such a vast, uncaring universe as is presented here in *Elite*. Created by Cambridge students Ian Bell and David Braben during the reign of Thatcher, this is a picture of merciless capitalism spread to the stars: a cruel galaxy cluster of market forces and sudden death, where squads of Vipers lurk in the next starfield, ready to gun you down; where running out of fuel light-years from a nearby planet spells certain death and where simply trying to dock your ship in an orbiting space station will probably kill you first, anyway.

Elite started life as an experiment in three-dimensional starfields, and quickly became a game of galactic dog fighting. Braben and Bell found the results a little boring, however, and instead came up with the idea of trading to make the universe feel a little more alive: everything from basic crops to gems, to—if you're willing to risk pursuit by the police—weapons and slaves (which fit into this entirely amoral economy). And finding the best exchange rate for the latest wares on which you took a high-priced gamble certainly adds an element of fiscal fear to the planets and nebulae through which you cruise.

Elite is big as well as clever, however, with eight massive galaxies to jump between, all spun out of a smart programming trick that uses the Fibonacci sequence to generate its stars and stats. You could think of *Elite* as an economics sim with a bit of shooting thrown in, which makes it sound cold and rather distant. But it's also epic, echoey, and filled with dazzling surprises and hidden adventures. No game before or since—except, perhaps, CCP's luminous *Eve Online*—has dared to treat science fiction with such seriousness. No game has been quite so immersive in its handling of lasers, intergalactic rockets, and attack ships. **CD**

Kung-Fu Master

Original release date : 1984
Platform : Arcade
Developer: Irem
Genre : Fighting

Ostensibly based on the Jackie Chan movie *Wheels on Meals* (which was originally titled *Meals on Wheels*) and heavily influenced by wider Hong Kong action cinema conventions, Irem's slick, repetitive martial arts coin-op is widely credited as the progenitor of the scrolling beat 'em up genre, preceding the likes of *Renegade*, *Final Fight*, *Double Dragon,* and *Streets of Rage.*

The setup is ludicrously sketchy (beginning with the immortal scene setter: "Thomas and Sylvia were attacked by several unknown guys"), but also hugely influential. You are a kung-fu expert who must rescue your kidnapped girlfriend from the clutches of a gangster. To get her back, you fight through five floors of the pagoda-style Devil's

Temple, using the kick and punch buttons to dispatch incoming enemies. On the first floor, most enemies simply try to grab hold of you, necessitating a frenzied bout of joystick waggling. Later, there are leaping dwarf fighters, fire-breathing dragons, and deadly . . . moths. More important, each floor ends in a boss battle, ranging from a boomerang thrower to a magician, and bosses have their own energy gauges—a vital genre addition.

Kung-Fu Master is a beautifully crafted example of the genre it helped to define. The controls are amazingly responsive, allowing for superfast fighting, and the addition of leaping and crouching moves adds depth to the combat repertoire. Meanwhile, the driving soundtrack racks up the tension, and the roughly sampled yelps and cries bring some kung-fu movie authenticity to the proceedings. Numerous home-console versions followed, but it was the original that will be remembered— alongside the likes of *Karate Champ* and *Karateka*—as a groundbreaking martial-arts game. **KS**

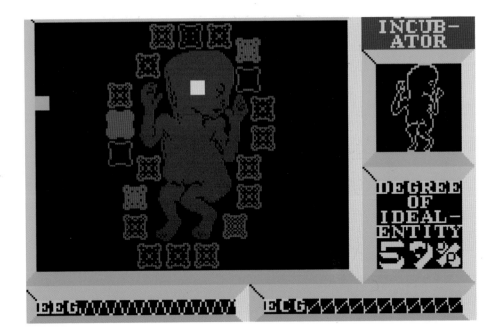

Deus Ex Machina

Original release date : 1984
Platform : ZX Spectrum, Commodore 64
Developer : Automata
Genre : Action

Not so much a game as a bizarre multimedia experience, *Deus Ex Machina* requires players to control the early development of a biological accident: a mutant born within the mechanistic confines of a computerized Orwellian society. The "action," such as it is, revolves around a series of abstract mini-games dealing with stages of the creature's life: Players must first weld DNA and safely incubate the fetus; as a "child" it has to be protected from the police, and, later, from the rigors of old age.

The on-screen activity tells only half the story, however. This ambitious project was conceived more as an enhanced concept album or prototypical interactive movie than a mere game. Coded by Andrew Stagg and scripted

by early computer game entrepreneur Mel Croucher, *Deus Ex Machina* shipped with an accompanying cassette containing an ambient synth soundtrack and dialogue spoken by *Doctor Who* actor Jon Pertwee, musician Ian Dury, and comedian Frankie Howerd. This was designed to be played in synchronicity with the game itself, providing a disembodied audio accompaniment. With lyrics merging adapted snippets of *As You Like It*'s "seven ages of man" speech with discourses on genetic experimentation and computer-age paranoia, it is a singular artistic endeavor, obtuse and self-indulgent, but also weirdly hypnotic.

Despite widespread critical claim and mainstream media interest, the game was a commercial disaster, in part due to Automata's difficulties with retailers who weren't sure how to deal with such a genre-defying product. Croucher was clearly undeterred by commercial difficulties: A couple of years later he came up with *iD*, a text-based curio in which the player converses with an entity living in their computer. **KS**

```
 Front of House, lying down                    Score: 10    Moves: 43
>get up
The bulldozer driver gives a quick chew of his gum and slams in the clutch.
The bulldozer piles into the side of your home.

Your home collapses in a cloud of dust, and a stray flying brick hits you
squarely on the back of the head. You try to think of some suitable last
words, but what with the confusion of the moment and the spinning of your
head, you are unable to compose anything pithy and expire in silence.

>s
You keep out of this, you're dead. An ambulance arrives.

>don't panic
You keep out of this, you're dead and should be concentrating on developing a
good firm rigor mortis. You are put in the ambulance, which drives away.

>pray
For a dead person you are talking too much. As the ambulance reaches the
mortuary a fleet of Vogon Constructor ships unexpectedly arrives and
demolishes the Earth to make way for a new hyperspace bypass.

We are about to give you your score. Put on your peril-sensitive sunglasses
now. (Hit RETURN or ENTER when ready.) >_
```

The Hitchhiker's Guide to the Galaxy

Original release date : 1984

Platform : Various

Developer : Infocom

Genre : Text Adventure

Douglas Adams's seminal sci-fi masterpiece, *The Hitchhiker's Guide to the Galaxy*, has taken many forms, from audio to books, to the small and large screens. When Adams teamed up with Infocom's resident funnyman, Steve Meretzky, to turn it into interactive fiction, he kept the key plot points. Moreover, he stayed true to its tangents, its self-awareness, and its cruel, absurd humor.

Hitchhiker's Guide mocks the expectations of gamers who have played Infocom's other hits. Negative feedback is brusque—"That's not important; leave it alone"—and even the minor descriptions are hilarious ("The floor acts like a trampoline on an ice rink"). The game will lie to you about how to exit a room or not let you look around a room unless you beg; if you die, it may keep going without you and chide you if you try to struggle. "You keep out of this, you're dead . . . ," it reminds you.

There are puzzles, too, like the legendary inventory puzzle that scores you the language-translating Babel fish. What's missing, however, are the characters—who fly by with little introduction—and the plot, which barely matters at all. It's as if Adams no longer had patience for retelling his tale and wanted to get back to messing with the parser and refusing to let you move aft unless you insisted half a dozen times. The game could be criticized as one of the few times Infocom let the puzzles and gags outweigh the story, but by 1984, the studio could get away with riffing on the genre it all but codified.

Unfortunately, a sequel based on *The Restaurant at the End of the Universe* was never completed—but Douglas Adams would go on to make more games before his untimely death in 2001, including Infocom's *Bureaucracy* and the graphic adventure *Starship Titanic*. **CDa**

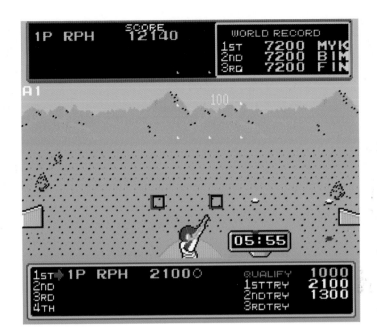

Hyper Sports

Original release date : 1984
Platform : Arcade
Developer : Konami
Genre : Sports

Konami's *Track & Field* proved to be an enormous arcade hit when it was released in 1984 thanks to massive novelty value and multiplayer appeal. It introduced the concept that button bashing translated into speed, pitted players directly against one another, and turned arcade gaming into a distinctly physical exercise.

It was all a bit *athletic*, though, an issue that the sequel, *Hyper Sports*, addressed by widening its scope and providing a much more varied range of events. It's still heavy on the button bashing, as illustrated by the opening swimming event, but then it gets into more gamer-friendly territory with a skeet shooting competition that's purely about twitch reactions, rewarding accuracy with faster and

higher-scoring targets, as well as fatter targeting reticules. Next comes a move to gymnastics with the long horse event, in which you're back hammering the buttons to turn somersaults while attempting a perfect landing, then it's a return to arcade shooting in the archery event. The *Track & Field* heritage is here in the way you hold down a button to set your elevation, but the moving target and accuracy bonuses introduce new layers of finesse. Finally, it's back to *Track & Field* territory for the final three events— triple jump, weightlifting, and pole vault.

It's a brilliant party game, and that's due to offering a broader range of events than its predecessor; if you can't win at the swimming event, you might still clean up at skeet shooting. If you're good at everything, you can showboat by going for the hidden bonuses and actually attempt to complete the pole vault, one of gaming's greatest tests. The game manages to combine mainstream appeal with hardcore hooks in a compact package—not a bad achievement at all. **JM**

Marble Madness

Original release date : 1984
Platform : Arcade
Developer : Atari
Genre : Action

Marble Madness used a trackball rather than a joystick and buttons, and it was the first Atari arcade cabinet to use a Yamaha FM audio chip, but it's a game that belongs in the history books for more than a simple string of design anomalies or firsts (and *Missile Command* beat it to the trackball, anyway). *Marble Madness* is colorful and loopy, a tense, often cruel action game that draws you back, defeat after defeat, with its wonderful levels and brilliant physics.

It *could* be described as a simple maze game, if there was anything remotely simple about its mazes. But we should remember that designer Mark Cerny drew much of his inspiration from the "infinite architecture" of artist M. C. Escher, and in reality the mazes become tortured chunks of magical geometry, the bright oranges, yellows, and blues hiding the fact that this is a truly brutal battlefield you're trying to navigate; each drop claiming hundreds of your glassy round brethren; each mean-spirited series of turns and loops tempting you to throw yourself into space with total abandon.

For those who successfully beat each course, working around sadistic chicanes, hairpin bends, slides, funnels, and even the odd enemy, the only reward is more of the same, Atari flinging another killing ground at you, ready to soak up a few extra lives and steal even more of your money. Although there are only six levels in total, the time limits imposed force you into regular mistakes, and the sheer variety of ideas on offer in each environment makes the game seem vast and unpredictable.

Proof that pretty, cartoony games often come with hearts as black as night, *Marble Madness* seems as good today as it ever has been, and its isometric style looks attractively retro, too. Track it down on one of Atari's many best-of collections. **CD**

Karate Champ

Original release date : 1984
Platform : Arcade
Developer : Data East
Genre : Fighting

The fighting genre can trace its DNA back to two titles from the mid-1980s. Konami's *Yie Ar Kung-Fu* takes the credit for introducing a range of characters with different fighting styles, and for giving each player a health bar that has to be gradually worn down. Data East's *Karate Champ* is responsible for pretty much everything else. Bonus rounds as an aside to the main fight attraction? *Karate Champ*. An array of far too many moves to immediately get to grips with? *Karate Champ* again. The opportunity to play against real people rather than computer-controlled characters? You guessed it.

Although *Karate Champ* contains the seed of a whole swathe of fighting games to come, it's a first attempt that packs features that were discarded by its numerous progeny. There are no buttons to push, only two joysticks. You launch an attack by pushing the two sticks in their own directions simultaneously—up on the left stick and right on the right stick for a flying kick, for example—and then, if your timing and placement are spot on, your opponent goes down instantly. If not, then you're wide open to him flattening you with his own counterattack. This game is *not* about wearing the other guy down. It's about precision and daring, being able to make the right attack at the right time so that the sensei awards you a full rather than a half point.

Karate Champ has more to do with real martial-arts contests than street fighting, especially in its original Japanese incarnation. A US-focused remake transplants it from the dojos to a series of exotic locations, and has you fighting to win the girl instead of a karate competition, but the fights themselves (and the bull-punching bonus round) remain the same. In some ways it's a historical curio, but in many others it's the definitive template. **JM**

KARATE

HISCORE
20000

00

TIME 27

1ST
1PT
½PT

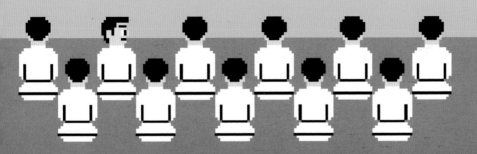

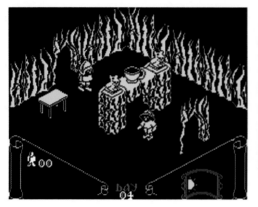

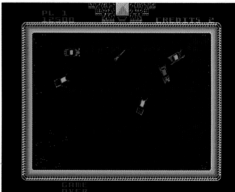

Knight Lore

Original release date : 1984
Platform : Various
Developer : Ultimate Play the Game
Genre : Action

Demolition Derby

Original release date : 1984
Platform : Arcade
Developer : Bally Midway
Genre : Driving

Equipped with the Filmation three-dimensional graphics engine, *Knight Lore* was a groundbreaking British platform adventure. While isometric perspectives were not new to gamers, *Knight Lore* kicked off an avalanche of similarly styled titles, some of which were highlights of the genre.

This is not to say that *Knight Lore* was lacking in highlights itself. Having been cursed by a "werewulf," Sabreman—now in his third adventure—is beset by lycanthropy. He has forty days to work through a maze of chambers and corridors in search of the dying wizard, Melkhior. Along the way, Sabreman must collect the ingredients necessary for his cure. If he fails, he must forever remain a werewolf.

Knight Lore presents a hearty challenge. In addition to the strict time limit, Sabreman must also endure his nightly transformation into beast form, making the game an action adventure that requires not only thought and good platforming skills, but decisiveness, too. At a time when gaming was all about homemade maps and tips traded in the playground, *Knight Lore* was a defining title. **MKu**

Demolition Derby captures the stripped-to-the-bare-bones nature of its inspiration (drive around, smashing the heck out of others' vehicles until only one remains operational) with no small amount of enthusiasm. It doesn't overstretch itself in the visuals department, but it doesn't need to: This is a game about cars ramming into one another (while keeping an eye out for damage-repairing screwdrivers and other bonuses), rather than negotiating complex tracks of curves and chicanes. The action is viewed directly from above, and the controls consist of a steering wheel and the ability to drive forward and backward.

Successful play is all about hitting opponents with the rear of your car. What feels unusual to begin with quickly becomes second nature, and the appeal of this unique twist persists throughout.

The game exists as a dual-control upright cabinet and as a four-player option. With friends taking part, personal grudges and alliances get brought into the game, but then ganging up on individuals feels almost par for the course in an activity as brilliantly lawless as this one. **TB**

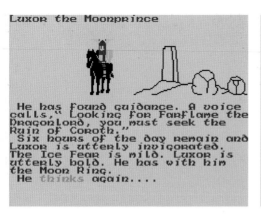

Lords of Midnight

Original release date : 1984

Platform : Various

Developer : Mike Singleton

Genre : Strategy / Adventure

In the early 1980s, Mike Singleton was writing fantasy role-playing games. When he set out to develop a similarly epic computer version, there were no orthodox methods of displaying the vast worlds he imagined. So he decided to invent one. *Lords of Midnight*, a vast adventure set within a fantasy realm, featured a groundbreaking graphics technique called "landscaping." It enabled the player to depict his surroundings from a first-person perspective.

The plot follows Prince Luxor as he seeks to defeat the armies of the evil Doomdark. Skilled, strategic planning is needed as you prepare for each new engagement. At the end of each turn, darkness falls and Doomdark makes his move. The following morning, you receive a written report of the battles, victories, and defeats of the previous night.

This kind of game may not be to everyone's taste, but *Lords of Midnight* does make for an atmospheric and pleasantly cerebral experience. Amusingly enough, Singleton was said to have thought there was no way to defeat Doomdark: gamers, of course—as is their wont—proved him wrong. **KS**

Jet Set Willy

Original release date : 1984

Platform : Various

Developer : Matthew Smith

Genre : Platform

Matt Smith's follow up to *Manic Miner* is a deeply unnerving and, frankly, rather sinister game. It's a mysterious and darkly comic wander through a nightmarish mansion as Miner Willy is forced to tidy up his home before his furious wife will allow him to bed. The mansion itself is one of the greatest locations of any computer game. Starting in the bathroom, working through dining halls, kitchens, servants' quarters, and into the garden, it's memorable and oddly disturbing, filled with dancing razor blades, chugging saws, and nasty flying pigs. As in *Manic Miner*, Willy's sprawling, leg-flailing jump is an instrument of pure platforming torture, as likely to carry you over your target or past it as it is to land you where you want to be.

Due to a software bug in the original code, *Jet Set Willy* was actually unfinishable in its original format—a fact that seems genuinely to enhance the Kafkaesque brilliance of the game. Compared to most other home computer titles at the time—many of which were a bit nutty themselves—it's a strange and singular feverish dream, a frightening 8-bit nightmare. **CD**

Pac-Land

Original release date : 1984
Platform : Arcade
Developer : Namco
Genre : Platform

While playing *Pac-Land*, it's easy to envision an alternate history of video games, one where Namco's mascot maintained his unquestioned dominion over gamerdom. When it appeared in 1984, the world was still in the grips of Pac-Mania. But the little, yellow pellet gobbler would soon be upstaged by other mascots. The Pac-Man franchise didn't *quite* have the legs to maintain its success while making the jump to home consoles.

But in *Pac-Land*, Pac-Man *does* have legs—literally— and he does an awful lot of jumping around. It's a side-scrolling platformer that, in fact, came out a year before the debut of *Super Mario Bros*. And it prefigures that game in many other ways.

Make no mistake, *Pac-Land* is not as good as *Super Mario Bros*. There are no bosses, the level layouts lack verticality, and the controls aren't as satisfying. But it's still solid fun, and of all the proto-*Super Marios*, it's the *Super Mario*-iest. The titular character bounces from platform to platform with aplomb, sometimes encountering his wife and child, Mrs. Pepper Pac-Man and Pac-Baby. (Character design and theme song are lifted from the Saturday morning cartoon.) As he hops along, Pac-Man is besieged by endless waves of ghosts. Power pellets occasionally appear, allowing him to gobble his foes, but it's often easier to simply evade them and keep running and jumping.

The historical value of *Pac-Land* is undeniable: If we study the hand-drawn look of the clouds and mountains in the background, the foreboding music that plays in dungeon areas, and the appearance of a multi-jump mechanic that recalls Mario's underwater swimming, it's hard to believe that the developers at Nintendo didn't draw inspiration from several elements of the game. **CB**

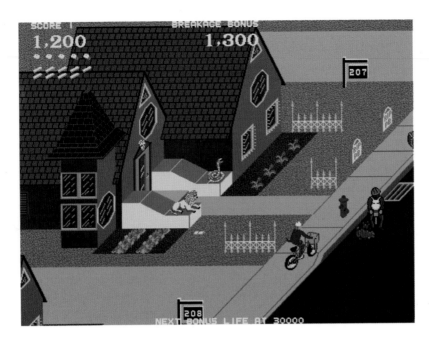

Paperboy

Original release date : 1984
Platform : Arcade
Developer : Atari
Genre : Action

An odd experience by today's standards, *Paperboy* is an ancestor of *Grand Theft Auto*: a game about a lone prole, struggling to stay afloat in a neighborhood turned treacherous. The player controls a hapless delivery boy who has to ride down the street delivering the *Daily Sun*—"the world's most throwable newspaper"—but to the right houses, and preferably without smashing any windows. The street is pushed all the way to the right of the screen, which makes it easy to miss oncoming cars until they're right on top of you. But it also affords you a better view of the neighborhood: robbers jimmy open windows, breakdancers bust a move where you're trying to ride, a kid with a remote-control car comes gunning for

your tires. The game is obsessed with death, or at least with Halloween, as hearses jerk out of the driveways in front of you and the Grim Reaper takes a stroll down the sidewalk. The lawns even sport tombstones with your initials on them. Feel free to knock them down for extra points.

With an actual pair of handlebars for controls, the arcade version handles much the same as the crappy no-gears bike that a kid his age would be dying to trade. But the game's biggest challenge lies in keeping customers happy. Following each day's delivery, angry customers will cancel their subscriptions; lose enough, and you're fired.

This idea of holding a neighborhood in the face of mortal danger would come back in games like *Saints Row* and numerous others in which a territory has to be maintained and defended. But, of course, the descendants of *Paperboy* swapped newspapers for handguns, and the price of losing became a lot bloodier than sitting on the curbside next to your wrecked bike, with a newspaper bag jammed over your head. **CDa**

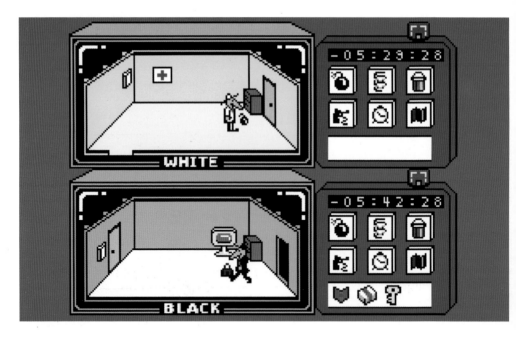

Spy vs. Spy

Original release date : 1984
Platform : Various
Developer : First Star Software
Genre : Action / Strategy

With this wonderfully devious multiplayer game from veteran designer Mike Reidel, the violent monochromatic nemeses made the transition from the ink-smeared pages of *Mad* magazine to 8-bit home computers. There's never been anything else quite like it: a title that makes ample allowances for direct combat between its players, but truly relishes indirect battle also, as two rival spies move around the same suite of rooms, laying traps for each other while collecting the necessary documents and money needed to flee the country via a small airstrip.

It's a brisk tactical challenge as players choose whether to carry all the items they've collected on their person—and subsequently risk losing them all if they get killed—or opt instead to stash their supplies somewhere, and booby trap the spot, gambling that their enemy will get his comeuppance while searching for them.

The traps themselves are lavishly comic affairs, with deadly buckets of water on doors, automatic guns tethered to furniture, plump anarchist bombs, and—best of all—a massive spring that, if deployed correctly, can propel the hapless victim through successive rooms. In a clever twist, each trap also has a weak spot that will allow a spy to sidestep the effects if they're carrying the correct item, so half of the fun comes from keeping an eye on your rival's screen and trying to remember which types of traps he has laid in store for you.

Comic and sadistic, *Spy vs. Spy* makes perfect use of the source material. It's a riotous, infuriatingly simple multiplayer classic that suggests a quirky direction that the genre has never really chosen to follow up. Remade rather elegantly for the Game Boy, there is also an Xbox update, but that is probably best avoided. **CD**

Bounty Bob Strikes Back

Original release date : 1984
Platform : Various
Developer : Big Five Software
Genre : Platform

In the family tree of video game genre, lines can be drawn from *Bounty Bob Strikes Back* to its predecessor, *Miner 2049er*, and to the vaunted Miner Willy series that took Big Five's passion project as its inspiration. Though *Bounty Bob Strikes Back* may be one of gaming's first true sequels, the real narrative lies in its development. Forged in the fires of the emergent 1980s technology that encouraged so much experimentation in video game development, the partnership of programmer Bill Hogue and designer Jeff Konyu caused a miniature media tidal wave, elevating the duo to temporary celebrity.

Meticulously traversing splintered platforms, lighting them up for points, and treading on a few enemy heads

along the way, *Bounty Bob* is filled with design ingenuity. Expositional details left behind by other miners pave the way for Bob's journey back toward the heart of darkness he faced in *Miner 2049er*: the lurking Yukon Yohan. They are cursory details not easily identified in the archaic engine, but it's a decision that belies a level of world-building coherence carried on by developers ever since.

The use of Bounty Bob's name in a sequel, and its underwhelming reception, leading ultimately to its studio's exit from the industry, could be argued as a small-scale harbinger of where the video game model would later lead. That isn't to deny *Bounty Bob*'s quality: more detailed, dense, and challenging across its twenty-five levels, it's superior to its progenitor in both looks and technical achievement. The implementation of vertical scrolling for level transitions was a minor revelation, and links sections into a singular chain, soldering coherence to Bounty Bob's underground quest. It also seamlessly nudges users into continuous play—and, of course, some manic mining. **DV**

Déjà Vu

Original release date : 1985
Platform : Various
Developer : ICOM Simulations
Genre : Adventure

Apple's computers have never enjoyed too much of a reputation as gaming formats, but rewind twenty years and the picture was at least a little different. *Déjà Vu* was the first of what was known as the MacVenture series—a collection of point-and-click adventures. In video gaming's evolution, the legacy of the MacVenture concept is its exploration of the WIMP (window, icon, menu, pointing device) interface in the context of gaming, thus paving the way for the likes of LucasArts's many adventure classics.

Déjà Vu is set in 1940s Chicago and draws heavily from film noir motifs, its bold, monochromatic presentation comfortably suiting the themes. As private investigator Ace Harding, you begin the game by awakening in a bathroom stall, faced with bloodstains, a gun, and fresh needle marks. Oh, and of course you can't remember a blessed thing. In fact, as hackneyed a device as it may be, your memory loss actually serves the interface well. Part of the joy of playing games is the expectation of the future, that sense of unknowing and subsequent desire to see what the next stage brings. Here, with each mouse click, another page in your story is turned over.

Unlike the text adventures that preceded it, *Déjà Vu* has game play that is mouse-driven, which makes it extremely simple to control, with no typing involved whatsoever. It's difficult to remember a time when a single button would be sufficient to complete an entire game and, for that, *Déjà Vu*'s simplicity is a quaint reminder for anyone overwhelmed by the amount of buttons that appear on all modern game controllers.

In fact, point-and-click adventures have been making a return in recent years, thanks to the rise of browser-based games that are a natural fit for the medium. **JBW**

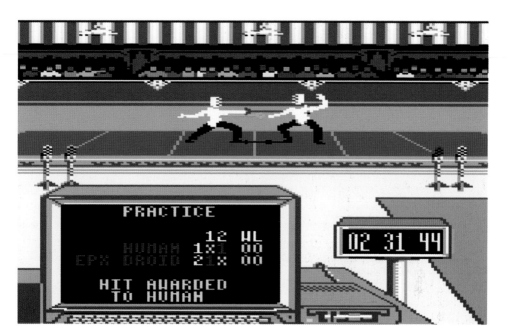

Summer Games II

Original release date : 1985
Platform : Various
Developer : Epyx
Genre : Sports

The world may have first encountered athletics in video game form via the arcade, but it was a series of games for home consoles that presented more deeply considered representations of such pursuits. Where Konami's *Track & Field* often focused on hammering buttons as quickly as possible in order to build up speed, Epyx's Games series tended to explore finer nuances of control.

Summer Games II represented an evolution over the original *Summer Games*, and included one more event, bringing the total to eight. The triple jump, high jump, and javelin throw hardly reinvented the sports game genre, but the rowing, equestrian, fencing, kayaking, and cycling events offered action that hadn't previously been seen.

While rowing requires rhythmic shifting rather than frantic waggling, it's kayaking that presents the more satisfying water-based challenge, negotiation of the various gates throughout its convoluted course requiring a good deal of paddling skill. Equestrian is a more novel inclusion, albeit a less successful one, while fencing pushes the envelope even farther, introducing a layer of strategy not normally associated with multidiscipline sports games. Finally, if it's a marathon challenge you're after, cycling will fit the bill, requiring you to repeatedly rotate your athlete's legs until you're convinced that something—either your wrist or the joystick—is going to expire.

The attention to detail in Epyx's animation gives terrific momentum to the various pursuits in *Summer Games II*, and, naturally, it's as a multiplayer game that it really comes to life. *World Games* and *California Games* developed and polished the central formula, but with a group of friends involved, this second sunny outing provides ample challenge and reward. **TB**

A Mind Forever Voyaging   Commando

Original release date : 1985
Platform : Various
Developer : Infocom
Genre : Text Adventure

Original release date : 1985
Platform : Arcade
Developer : Capcom
Genre : Shoot 'Em Up

At the height of its powers, Infocom took a chance on its boldest game: an interactive story about the power of politics to crush lives, a personal story told from inside a computer, and a game with almost no challenge. *A Mind Forever Voyaging* casts the player as a sentient artificial intelligence in a laboratory. The government is about to roll out a radical set of policies called the Plan for Renewed National Process, and you are tasked with exploring a simulation of the future to assess how the Plan plays out.

Across five decades, Perry, the human form inhabited by the AI, visits the fictional town of Rockvil, South Dakota, and tries to live an ordinary life: He buys some clothes, talks to pedestrians, and stops home to see his wife. But every decade, everything he sees gets worse. Perry can record his experiences and bring them back for evidence, but not everyone likes his report—and that's when the game's only challenge appears. But for most of the game, players explore Rockvil with nothing standing in their way, and the act of gathering research is as compelling as any riddlish Infocom puzzle.

As a point-by-point critique of conservative policies released at the height of the Reagan era, the game makes a radical political statement: writer Steve Meretzky essentially warns us that the policies of the right will destroy the human race.

A Mind Forever Voyaging never quite managed to raise the firestorm Meretzky had hoped, and today it's remembered more for the richness of detail woven into Perry's simulated world. The game forces you to witness cruelties both large and small, affecting those most precious to you. And even without a puzzle, the process of asking you to document these moments hooks you in a way unique to the medium. **CDa**

A chopper lands in hostile territory. Sandbags and rock outcrops shelter the enemy troops, and a formidable gate lies ahead. An endless army waits with guns, grenades, and even mortars, but the hero—Super Joe—is ready to take them on. Granted, he has an advantage: The other side fires the world's slowest bullets, which are easy to dodge in moderation. The enemy grunts are also predictable and single-minded, while Joe can whirl around and fire in all directions to clear his way forward. Still, he does have eight stages to get through on one coin.

A pioneer of its genre, Tokuro Fujiwara's *Commando* is a top-down run-and-gun game, where the hero is always charged with advancing, but can also backtrack a little and spread fire at the enemy that tries to surround him. With bunkers and sandbag covers protecting your targets, the game introduced more tactics than previous shooters. Crucially, it incorporates secondary fire in the form of grenades that can be flung over the tops of bullet-stopping enemy barricades.

The terrain and the challenges keep changing, and while the wartime setting is presented in a safe, blood-free manner, you will come across POWs waiting to be freed—as well as grueling trench warfare. And instead of giving you finite waves to beat, *Commando* keeps the attackers coming at a pace that's just short of frantic: Your only job is to keep pushing on to the end.

It was a winning formula that inspired many ports, sequels, and knock-offs. *Commando* was followed by *Bionic Commando*, which was marketed as a sequel (even though, as a side-viewed platform-based game, it is very different in style), *Mercs*, and, in 2008, by *Wolf of the Battlefield: Commando 3*, which failed to make anything like the mark of the explosive original. **CDa**

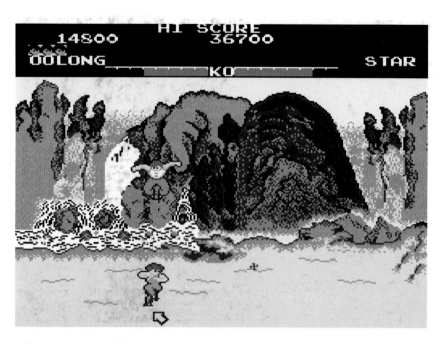

Yie Ar Kung-Fu

Original release date : 1985
Platform : Arcade
Developer : Konami
Genre : Fighting

Although the more naturalistic *Karate Champ* preceded *Yie Ar Kung-Fu* by a year, it is Konami's gaudy, quick-paced offering that many view as the archetypal fighting game. Wannabe martial-arts legend Oolong is pitted against a series of eleven progressively tough opponents, each with their own signature moves and weapons—from chains and clubs to razor-sharp fans and nunchaku (the latter wielded by a figure in a yellow tracksuit—a neat homage to Bruce Lee). It is this outlandish menagerie of characters, rather than *Karate Champ*'s austere sportsmen, that would influence the likes of *Street Fighter* and *Fatal Fury*.

This was not the game's only contribution to fighting game lore. *Yie Ar Kung-Fu* (or "One Two Kung Fu" to

translate from Chinese) also popularized the use of health bars for each fighter, rather than hit points, and it brought in the use of bright, detailed scenic backdrops: The first five fights take place in front of a waterfall; the final six in the grounds of a temple. Furthermore, Oolong is able to make extravagant leaps around the game area—another staple element of fighting game design and a vital tactical maneuver.

The player can call upon a range of attacks, accessible through combining the eight-way joystick with the kick and punch buttons. Each opponent relies on a different combination of attack patterns that must be studied and memorized to discover weak spots. The game's weakness is the inaccurate collision detection, which leaves players vulnerable at close range; and with no way to control the length of jumps, bouts descend into glorified leaping contests. But then, this was 1985, six years before the momentous debut of *Street Fighter II*. *Yie Ar Kung-Fu* may be a limited fighter, but its impact is uncontestable. **KS**

Gauntlet

Original release date : 1985
Platform : Arcade
Developer : Atari
Genre : Action

Long, long before the ravenous zombie hordes of *Left 4 Dead*, the ghillie-snipers of *COD4*, or the purple extraterrestrial pleasures of *Halo*, multiplayer gaming was all about *Gauntlet*: a top-down dungeon crawler, heavy on potions, keys, and ghoul battering, and satisfyingly light on just about everything else. It wasn't bad, as it happens.

Actually, it was amazing: a frenzy of shooting, magic attacks, treasure raiding, and—if played right—regular griefing—that could turn close friends into bitter enemies on the way from the entrance to the exit of each short level. Choosing from a range of familiar fantasy characters, players would band together in teams of four, then go pillaging assorted brown and gray rooms, unlocking doors

to progress to the next chamber, and, very occasionally, stopping to lend someone a helping hand. It was brutal, unforgiving, and fairly simple stuff, but it was also magical in its immersion and immediacy, the atmosphere heightened by the game's booming audio accompaniment: a series of somber musical pieces overlaid with the muffled tones of an unseen dungeon master offering such invaluable tips as: "Remember: don't shoot food."

An arcade classic from Atari's resident genius Ed Logg, numerous ports allowed you to relive the excitement on home platforms, but it was never quite the same as when you were battling together with friends in the confines of a dingy arcade. Modern-day sequels have tried to recreate the magic, but the rowdy, cussing brilliance of *Gauntlet* is at its best in its original form, a happy accident of simple design and limitless mutual recrimination. These days, games have evolved to become prettier and more complex, but clunky old *Gauntlet* is still admirably fresh and immediate. **CD**

Ghosts 'n Goblins

Original release date : 1985
Platform : Arcade
Developer : Capcom
Genre : Action

It takes more than mere courage to cross the six realms of *Ghosts 'n Goblins*, over bottomless pit and grasping claw, into the waiting arms of Princess Guinevere. It takes patience, a fistful of change, and a preternatural ability to leap while you look, if not before. Tokuro "Professor F" Fujiwara's platformer, in which the gallant Sir Arthur has to rescue his beau from the evil Goblin King, is notorious as one of the hardest coin-ops ever made.

Whenever you press the button to make Arthur jump, legs askew and arms akimbo, you're making a commitment. There's no midair adjustment or reversal, double jumping or ledge grabbing. Instead, you can be guaranteed that if your timing (or spacing) is the slightest bit awry, the least you'll lose is your trousers: one hit, and Arthur's armor falls off, leaving only boxer shorts to protect his dignity; another, and he'll disintegrate into a pile of bones: fall just a pixel short of a ledge, and you'll vanish into water, lava, or off-screen oblivion.

The game wants nothing more than for this to happen. While many of the harder side-scrolling coin-ops—notably fighters like *The Ninja Warriors* and *Vigilante*—have enemies flood in from the left and right of the screen, *Ghosts 'n Goblins* goes one step beyond. As birds swoop from the trees and coffins rise from the ground, your enemies come from *everywhere*—often right under your feet. Each of Arthur's weapons has a unique range and trajectory, some deliberately less favorable than others, meaning that even power-ups have to be dodged from time to time.

Alongside Capcom's emerging art style and penchant for epic boss battles, the difficulty of *Ghosts 'n Goblins* makes for a terrifically satisfying challenge, and one that also succeeds in its various home-conversion guises. **DH**

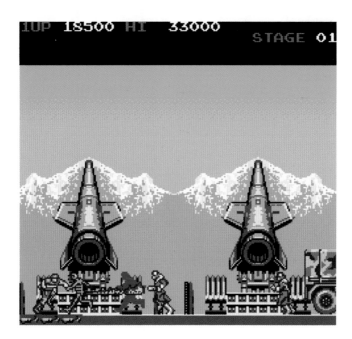

Green Beret

Original release date : 1985
Platform : Arcade
Developer : Konami
Genre : Action

The geo-political Cold War climate of the mid-1980s proved fertile ground for developers of action arcade coin-ops. With the threat of nuclear annihilation hanging in the balance, and one-man armies, such as Sylvester Stallone and Chuck Norris, on hand to save the day, rampant xenophobia was a theme that resonated just as well with audiences on the big screen as it did in dark, smoky amusement arcades. No surprise, then, that *Green Beret* was a big hit when it was released.

Most military-themed coin-ops were to consign their commie bashing and POW rescuing to nonspecific foreign locales. *Green Beret*, however, was far less tactful; a gratuitous antidote to prevailing platform-game cuteness.

Upon inserting a coin, the player is granted a glimpse of four squirming POWs roped up on enemy posts, soon to be served bullets for breakfast. Our green-clad hero proceeds to run horizontally through enemy military compounds, stabbing an advancing hivelike army of trench-coated bad guys with a knife. Along the way he picks up handy enemy weapons—flamethrowers, RPGs, grenades—to help sustain the frantic murder-thon.

As a precursor to *Contra* and other run-and-gun experiences, *Green Beret* is a twitch game par excellence— and a challenging one. Instead of cheap tactics, though, the game relies upon a constant barrage of enemy soldiers that eventually cause the player to lapse in concentration, each level's onslaught climaxing with an ever-greater number of hell-bent adversaries. As such, *Green Beret* is unselfconsciously one note, an orgiastic killing spree tempered only by its crudely animated 8-bit facade.

Green Beret enjoyed even greater mileage in its (slightly more parent-friendly) home computer editions. **JB**

Gradius

Original release date : 1985
Platform : Arcade
Developer : Konami
Genre : Shoot 'Em Up

In 1985, arcade fans—who were thoroughly used to chunky, garish 8-bit graphics—could have been forgiven for feeling something akin to religious rapture upon witnessing *Gradius*. Like having laser eye surgery of the pixel variety, game worlds suddenly emerged as beautiful beyond the imagination—and Konami's artists were among the very best in the business.

Although *Gradius* was the iconic shooter that rode this initial wave of transformation, its qualities were far more than just superficial. Above all, it has the distinction of introducing a weapon selection bar: By collecting glowing amber capsules that allow the player to cycle through the bar, new weapons are chosen by a power-up button on the cabinet itself. Individual weapons can also be powered up several times, and only the speed-up poses any kind of problem when activated in excess—as players would discover after getting too close to an erupting volcano.

The key power-up among the five available is probably the "option" (or "multiple," as the fuzzy announcer calls it), a yellow orb that follows behind your Vic Viper ship, unleashing the same force as its carrier. A series can be strung together in snakelike fashion, providing concentrated firepower with diligent positioning—particularly useful when dealing with boss enemies that require players to "shoot the core."

Above all, *Gradius* afforded players the newfound luxury of being able to select what power-ups might suit the moment—a feature that would influence the entire shoot 'em up genre—while providing a previously unseen level of aesthetic and aural sophistication. Successive titles in the series naturally took this formula and ran with it, and the 1988 sequel—*Gradius II*—in particular shines brightly in the pantheon. **JB**

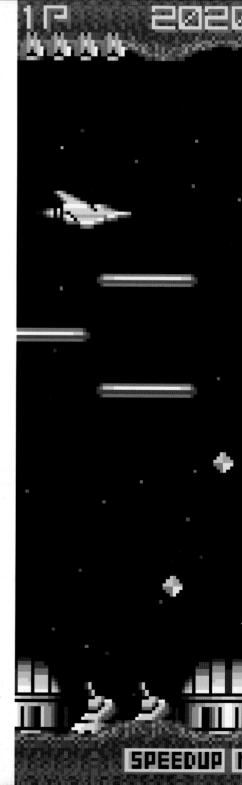

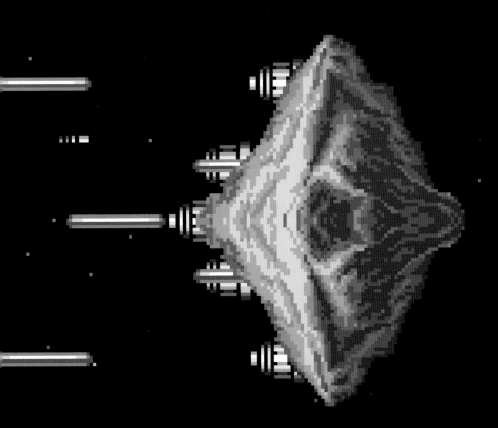

57300

DOUBLE LASER OPTION ?

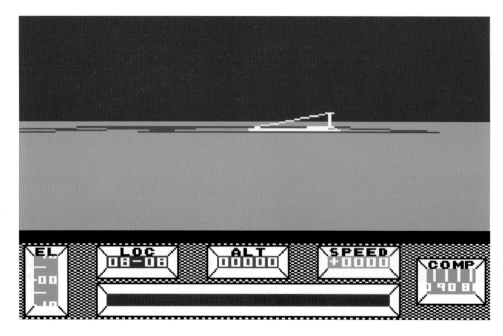

Mercenary

Original release date : 1985
Platform : Various
Developer : Paul Woakes
Genre : Action / Adventure

It is commonplace nowadays to hear developers boasting about fully explorable environments in which players are free to wander as they please. More often than not, however, these worlds are given their form and didactic function via an array of background narratives, cut scenes, mandatory objectives, and action choke points. *Mercenary*, on the other hand, builds a world and crashes the player on it. Everything else is up for grabs.

The game has no options screen and no introduction. Instead, it begins in a damaged spacecraft hurtling toward the planet Targ. Postcrash, players emerge into a minimal world sparsely populated by wire-frame buildings and symbolic scenic objects. The programmer, Paul Woakes,

constructed a fully three-dimensional environment with these basic graphical tools, even including a vast underground labyrinth of tunnels and rooms. Slowly, information is fed to the player via a computerized personal assistant named Benson: Two races are fighting to establish control of the planet—the peaceful indigenous Palyars and the invading Mechanoid army. As a soldier for hire, the player is able to take on missions for either side in order to save enough money to buy a spaceship and escape.

Mercenary is loaded with modern video game elements: a duplicitous mission structure, multiple endings, and a functioning economy. There's also a sly sense of humor at work—the player is rewarded for destroying the Atari sign in the Commodore version (and vice versa). The game was an enormous critical success, dazzling reviewers and contemporary game coders alike with the completeness of its universe. For vision, technical brilliance, and sheer gall, it wouldn't be significantly bettered until *Deus Ex* appeared fifteen years later. **KS**

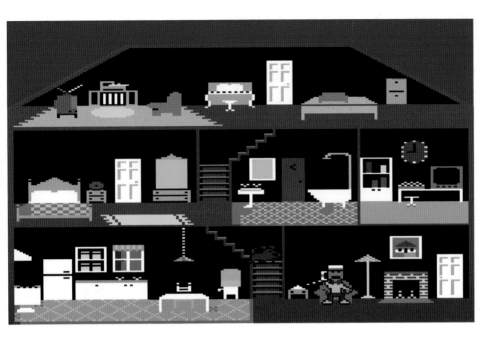

Little Computer People

Original release date : 1985
Platform : Various
Developer : Activision
Genre : Life Simulation

Little Computer People is endlessly credited as the inspiration for The Sims, but it is extraordinary in its own right, especially within the limitations of its technology. It presents a cross-section view of a three-story house populated by a little man, who goes about the rather mundane business of living—eating, drinking, sleeping, watching TV, shuffling around with his canine companion—and leaves the player largely to their own devices.

Besides sending enough food and drink to keep man and pup in good health, the player's role is marginal. So long as they're phrased politely, the computer person might listen to suggestions ("Please play piano!"); he might occasionally write a letter to express his satisfaction with his current state of affairs, or he might challenge the player to a game of cards. Most of the time, though, he's just puttering about doing nothing in particular. Little Computer People is a digital goldfish bowl, expecting nothing more from its players than calm and patient inquisitiveness. For some, that's too much to ask. What is unique and fascinating to Little Computer People's fans is boring and pointless to its detractors.

The game is based on the premise that these computer people do actually exist inside your machine, and the software is just a lens through which to view them—the game's manual and packaging are adorably stubborn in their commitment to the illusion. It is true, though, that no two computer people are the same. Each copy of the game generates its character uniquely, giving every player a slightly different experience—except the unfortunate souls stuck with the severely maimed cassette versions, which conjure a new character with every start up, removing all meaningful continuity from the game. **KM**

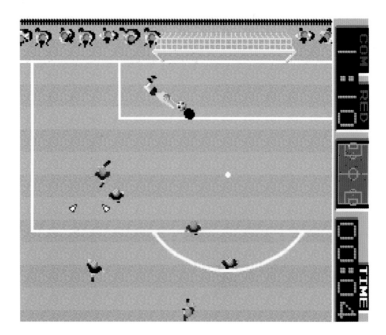

Tehkan World Cup

Original release date : 1985
Platform : Arcade
Developer : Tehkan
Genre : Sports

Some games create entire genres while others merely help to define them. *Tehkan World Cup* belongs in the latter category, but its significance shouldn't be played down simply because it wasn't the world's first soccer game. There had been numerous soccer simulations before Tehkan's game took to the field, but none that matched it in excitement for the gamer.

Presenting a view on the action from directly above, *Tehkan World Cup* doesn't get bogged down by convoluted animation or overcomplex controls. Instead, it's all about translating the dynamism of soccer at its most free-flowing, an objective it achieves with the aplomb of a thirty-yard strike driven into the top corner of the net.

The overhead perspective ensures that you're never left in any doubt as to the precise position of the ball, and it also allows for a quicker pace than the often snail-like side-viewed football games of yore.

Tehkan World Cup's view on the action necessitated a "tabletop" design for its cabinet, encouraging rivalry by allowing two players to compete head to head rather than side by side, which enhances the game's credentials in delivering the intensity of real-life sport. The distinguishing element its fans will hold up highest, however, is its trackball controller, allowing for considered and smooth-flowing manipulation of the players. Here, dribbling around an opponent in order to set up a goal-scoring opportunity can be a silky art, indeed.

On the downside the competitiveness triggered by the game, coupled with its control scheme, has resulted in countless playing injuries over the years in the form of skin pinched by madly spun trackballs, but to its legion of devoted fans, such mishaps are a small price to pay. **TB**

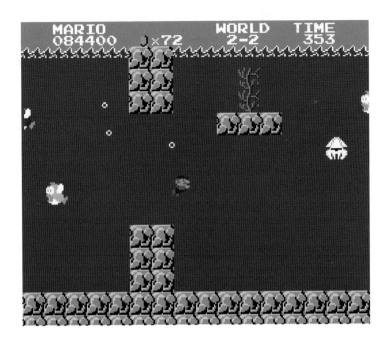

Super Mario Bros.

Original release date : 1985
Platform : NES
Developer : Nintendo
Genre : Platform

The problem with classics, by and large, is that they're old. They usher in great changes and they redefine the landscape, but less influential games perfect the trends they started and end up being a lot more fun to play. For example, *StarFox* isn't as ground-breaking as *Asteroids* as space games go, but anyone stuck in an elevator would undoubtedly prefer it as a means to pass the time.

And yet, while *Super Mario Bros.* (originally an arcade game but consequently a title that became synonymous with Nintendo's NES) did so much to define the side-scrolling platformer, twenty-odd years on it's still one of the best there is. Its colors may seem a little muted by today's standards, and its iconic plumber's moustache lacks definition, but this has excellent enemy design; tricky, secret-packed worlds; and an unforgettable Caribbean-flavored soundtrack as Mario—and brother Luigi in two-player mode—set off to rescue their princess from the clutches of hunch-backed, twiddly-toed Bowser.

Most of all, *Super Mario Bros.* has a sense of believable physics—something still missing from a lot of modern-day platformers. Set Mario running, and you'll need time and space to get him to slow down; attempt a big jump, and you're going to have to get a running start; bounce on an enemy, and you may well need to fine-tune your landing while still in the air. All of which gives the game the precision necessary to allow for a cluster of tightly paced underground and overworld levels, with their gloriously destructible environments and famous power-ups—like the growth mushroom and the fire flower. *Super Mario Bros.* is venerable, then, but not remotely rickety: a simple delight that can still give far more complex games a comprehensive run-around. **CD**

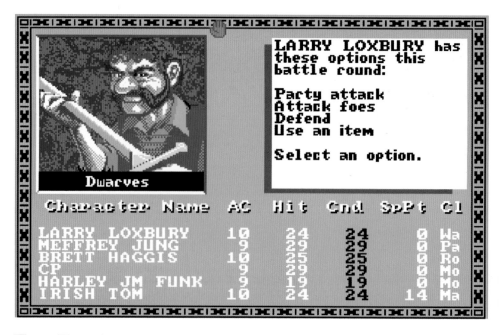

The Bard's Tale

Original release date : 1985

Platform : Various

Developer : Interplay

Genre : Role-Playing

In most role-playing games, bards are a niche class, a callow mix of rogue, healer, and play-enhancement dispenser, prone to flowery dialogue and over-the-top bravado. They're never as clever or as crucial as they think they are, but in *The Bard's Tale*, they're an essential piece of a party and one of the last lines of defense in a city plagued by an invasion. Skara Brae is suffering under the minions of the wizard Mangar, and it's up to the last lame adventurers left within its walls to save the day.

While the entire game takes place inside the city, Skara Brae offers streets, sewers, catacombs, and even a wine cellar. Diligent players mapped it all with pen and paper, exploring it in a straightforward dungeon crawl that competed head-on with major franchises like *Wizardry* and *Ultima*. Like *Wizardry*, it gave most of the screen to the player stats and commands, with a small window displaying the view a few steps in front of you. Ten different classes (including four kinds of magic users) brought depth to the character customization, and, in a cheeky move, the game even let you import your characters from its competitors. But the conceit of a bard who sang your triumphs and guided naïve young adventurers to victory gave the game more color and wit than the straight looting and boss battling of other role-playing games.

The Bard's Tale inspired two sequels, and in 2004, InXile Entertainment even produced a complete re-imagining that brought the drunken bluster of the titular hero to consoles of the era, mocking the clichés of the genre without adding any new ones of its own. Meanwhile, Interplay, the game's original developer, would redefine the role-playing genre in the late 1990s by publishing the first two *Fallout*s and *Planescape: Torment*. **CDa**

Fairlight

Original release date : 1985
Platform : Various
Developer : Bo Jangeborg
Genre : Adventure

With the release of *Knight Lore* in 1984, British game development studio Ultimate Play the Game raised the bar by such a margin that it immediately made all other home computer games look like antiques. How was it possible for hardware as seemingly primitive as Sinclair's ZX Spectrum to cast such magical three-dimensional imagery across the screen? Surely this was the pinnacle of achievable software engineering feats on 8-bit systems.

It wasn't, of course, but it took another year for *Fairlight* to arrive and show Ultimate's programmers a thing or two about graphical fidelity and associated game play complexity. Swedish programmer Bo Jangeborg had already built a reputation for pioneering work in the realm of home computer graphics by creating a powerful utility entitled The Artist, and his attention to visual finesse (along with the efforts of collaborator Jack Wilkes) furnished *Fairlight* with extravagant detail.

An adventure played out in isometric perspective, the game sees you exploring an extensively proportioned castle in a bid to retrieve the Book of Light. Key to *Fairlight*'s appeal is its handling of objects. Unlike in other adventures of the era, many different types exist, they have their own physical properties, and they can be manipulated relatively freely within the game's environments.

Such excesses naturally come at a cost. It takes a moment for the game to conjure up its locations as you move between them, for example, and the action can slow to a crawling pace when everything heats up. Meanwhile, the combat, which involves a variety of enemy types, is basic. But such issues shouldn't overshadow *Fairlight*'s triumphs. That few other 8-bit games attempted similarly ambitious agendas in its wake tells its own story. **TB**

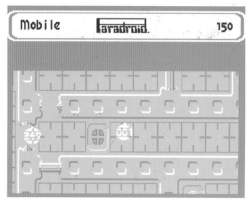

Paradroid

Original release date : 1985
Platform : Commodore 64
Developer : Graftgold
Genre : Action

A masterpiece of creative endeavor over the technical constraints of the Commodore 64 system, *Paradroid* enjoys a simple premise: You are in control of a robot beamed aboard an errant spacecraft whose crew has gone insane. The ship must be destroyed.

Two key design elements lift *Paradroid* beyond the wealth of multidirectional shooters on offer at the time. First, enemy droids are only visible when in the control robot's line of sight, leading to incredible tension with every freshly opened door or turned corner. Second, the player may gain control over any robot by ramming it, accessing its CPU, and overcoming its defenses via a circuit-busting minigame. In this way, participants become desperate robotic body snatchers, always scouring levels for new, more powerful hosts.

Visually, *Paradroid* is filled with numerous beautiful and subtle presentational flourishes. And to complete designer Andrew Braybrook's vision of an entirely robotic environment, the soundtrack comprises discordant bleeps and blips—a binary symphony for mad machines. **KS**

Skool Daze

Original release date : 1985
Platform : ZX Spectrum
Developer : Microsphere
Genre : Action

Like *Little Computer People*, *Skool Daze* is a predecessor of less "gamey" software. A school simulation, it casts you as the mischief-making scamp everyone secretly pretends they were, and tasks you with retrieving your school report from a safe in the headmaster's office, thus avoiding expulsion. Rather difficult when you've got to get a little bit of the safe's code from every other teacher in the school, all of whom have a beady eye out.

The entire school is on-screen, viewed as a cross-section that makes it resemble nothing so much as an ant farm. The teachers and other pupils walk about independently and have their own routines, which you have to learn and exploit. But the teachers will notice when you don't turn up to classes or misbehave in the corridors, so a good deal of time is spent pretending to be good while planning your assaults and raids. It might be the first game that demands you act rather than just play.

Limited in its objectives but expansive in how they are achieved, *Skool Daze* amused many, but failed to inspire a glut of similar games. **RS**

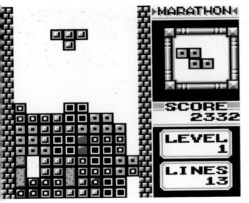

```
                    ▶MARATHON◀
```

Long Water
cool expanse of the river Serpentine.

A charming statue stands nearby.

There's a broken perambulator here.

A gleam overhead catches your eye.

Oh, dear. A missile is hanging motionless in the sky.

>look at missile
The missile isn't completely motionless. It's falling very, very slowly towards
the Long Water.

Your eyes follow the missile's trajectory downward, where you notice another
peculiar phenomenon. It looks like a white door, suspended just above the
surface of the water.

A flock of ravens glides into view! They circle over the Long Water and
disappear through the open white door.

The missile continues its slow descent.

>

Tetris

Original release date : 1985

Platform : Various

Developer : Alexey Pajitnov

Genre : Puzzle

When it comes to a game that practically anyone, in any corner of the globe, is likely to enjoy, Alexey Pajitnov's falling-blocks classic is hard to better. To see *Tetris* in action is to understand instantly what has to be done—tidy everything up and clear whole lines of blocks before the distinctively shaped pieces fill the screen. Playing on the compulsion to make order from chaos, which appears to be hard-wired into the human brain, a quick five-minute round can so easily turn into a three-hour session. Games come and go, but few have the power to haunt both waking hours and dreams quite like *Tetris*.

Designed by Pajitnov at the Academy of Science in Moscow, *Tetris* found itself embroiled in an international bidding war involving America, Japan, Britain, and the Soviet government. When Nintendo chose it as the ideal title for the launch of its new handheld console, the Game Boy, its place in the annals of video gaming was assured: We can equally imagine that Nintendo's little gray box might have found its way into fewer homes without this simple blocky pleasure wedged in the cartridge slot. **CD**

Trinity

Original release date : 1985

Platform : Various

Developer : Infocom

Genre : Text Adventure

One of Infocom's boldest experiments, *Trinity* is a puzzle game with elements of fantasy, concerning one of the darkest periods of modern history: the creation and testing of nuclear weapons. At the start of the game, the player is happily wandering through Kensington Gardens, among the mothers and prams. Suddenly a missile bearing a hammer-and-sickle motif hangs in the sky: World War III has begun, and everybody's about to die. But before that happens, a roadrunner leads you to a mysterious white door—a way out and an opportunity to change history.

The rich, florid writing contrasts with the gravity of the situation. You end up trading origami with a little girl seconds before the bombing of Nagasaki, or wandering in woods so confusing that words begin to turn backward.

Reality and fantasy, terror and laughter are contrasted: the dread of a freshly built bomb shelter, and the brilliantly dark humor of a coin found in the mouth of a corpse that bears the words "Not transferable." A mix of the wondrous and the horrifying, this is a thought-provoking and literary accomplishment. **CDa**

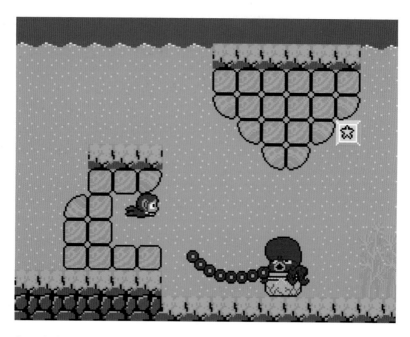

Alex Kidd in Miracle World

Original release date : 1986
Platform : Master System
Developer : Sega
Genre : Platform

If you had a sleek black Sega Master System instead of a bulky old NES in the late 1980s, Alex Kidd was probably your Mario—or at least you told yourself he was. And yet, while this perky hydrocephalus may not have left the mightiest imprint on posterity, for a certain kind of social outcast, the very mention of Miracle World is enough to thrust one back into the smoky depths of Proustian reverie.

While it's certainly no Mushroom Kingdom, Miracle World isn't a bad playground: There are bikes and aircraft to ride, shops to visit, octopode to fight—when it comes down to it, Alex Kidd can grow a fist every bit as large as his head, which is extremely handy for taking on the local wildlife—and a surprisingly wide range of environments,

from rocky canyons to magma-filled volcanoes, to explore. The music that chugs brightly from the Master System's limited sound chip is among the best the platform ever delivered. There's even a band of hand-headed foes ready to pop up at unlikely moments and engage you in fierce bouts of Rock, Paper, Scissors (and intrude into your nightmares from that point onward)—a horribly random piece of game design that, luckily, you can cheat your way past if you remember the special combination of button presses to reveal your enemies' thoughts.

It's all very colorful and fast-paced, and while it doesn't have the same sense of inertial physics that makes Mario and his gang such a pleasure to throw around, it's still got some nicely designed levels and a wicked difficulty curve. But as an example of 1980s platforming craftsmanship, *Alex Kidd in Miracle World* is charming and zippy—if ever so slightly forgettable. As a rare glimpse into Mario's forgotten competitors, however, it's a brilliant find, and well worth tracking down. **CD**

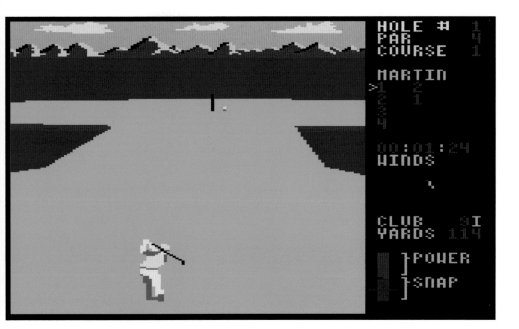

Leader Board

Original release date : 1986

Platform : Various

Developer : Bruce Carver, Roger Carver

Genre : Sports

Golf just isn't sexy. And yet some golf games are without question the best and most appealing sports sims in existence. Why? It's all because of *Leader Board*, a game whose appeal lies principally in its presentation.

Abandoning the top-down view forced on other games by hardware limitations, *Leader Board* renders its course in minimalist three dimensions. It's slow to draw on a Commodore 64, but that's a small niggle; the beauty of it is that it puts you right in the game instead of viewing it from overhead. Watching your ball sail into the distance, praying that the wind won't catch it too hard, quietly punching the air when it plops down right next to the pin . . . It's something that works so much better in three

dimensions—even the most basic 3-D. It really *is* a step toward virtual reality and the feeling of being there.

Besides its three-dimensional appeal, *Leader Board* is also notable for setting the standard for the way in which golf games are still played today, with its power bar and snap meter adding an arcade-style touch to what is an intrinsically pedestrian game. Press the joystick button to start your backswing, press it again to set your power and begin your forward swing, then make a third press to set the difference between straight down the middle and hooked or sliced into the rough. It's simple and brilliant, and has influenced every successful golf game since.

Eventually the game spawned numerous sequels down the line, incorporating replicas of the world's most famous golf courses. But there's something special about the original's island courses and the constant threat of losing your ball in the water. Vitally, it's a title that lends itself equally well to both intense multiplayer competition and absorbing single-player sessions. **JM**

Alter Ego

Original release date : 1986
Platform : Commodore 64, Apple II
Developer : Activision
Genre : Role-Playing

Billed as "a role-playing game about life," *Alter Ego* is the apotheosis of idiosyncratic 1980s gaming development. Released in both male and female versions, the goal is to guide a virtual human personality through the seven stages of life, achieving emotional, vocational, and physical balance in the process—or just experimenting in order to create the most psychotic monster the process allows.

Alter Ego could be viewed as a glorified Myers-Briggs psychometric questionnaire. At each stage of life, the player is presented with a map of icons representing experiences in various categories; clicking on these produces a series of multiple-choice questions designed to gauge the moral proclivities of the developing persona. As a baby there are the fundamental building blocks of social interaction—should you cry to get your mother's attention or gurgle contentedly? In those awkward teen years, what do you do if a group of friends want to get drunk on a school night? And what of the balance between work and love? Notions of sex, suicide, and drug abuse are also deftly explored. The game keeps a life score based on the player's choices, and the pithy commentary following each moral vignette hints at the wisdom (or otherwise) of the selected actions, proving intriguing insight into theories of human development. Critically lauded at the time (though not a commercial success), it was an interesting attempt to bring "realism" to the text-based adventure format of the day.

The field of social and psychological simulation would later reach the mainstream via EA's massively successful *Sims* series. But since *Alter Ego* is now available not only as a fan-produced online game but also an iPhone app, those reared on Will Wright's vision of an interactive soap opera can now discover *The Sims'* altogether darker, more troublesome progenitor. **KS**

Arkanoid

Original release date : 1986
Platform : Arcade
Developer : Taito
Genre : Action

Audacious makeovers of classic arcade games were big business during the mid-1980s, giving life to *Blasteroids* (*Asteroids* with power-ups and a boss battle), *Pac-Mania* (a colorful isometric *Pac-Man*), and, most notably, *Arkanoid*. Atari's *Breakout* had done much of the legwork, putting a 90-degree twist on *Pong* and building a wall of destructible bricks above the player's bat. But *Arkanoid*, coming a decade later and during the popularization of scrolling shoot 'em ups, had all kinds of new ideas.

First was the preposterous notion that the bat, now a rather posh affair with flashing tips and a metallic sheen, was actually a spacecraft called the Vaus, flung from a doomed mothership (Arkanoid) into a parallel dimension full of—you guessed it—destructible bricks. Lurking behind thirty-two screens' worth of those was DOH, a fortress resembling a Moai statue from Easter Island .

Enough of a hit to warrant more than a dozen ports and three major sequels, *Arkanoid* was a game for the power-up generation. Striking certain bricks would yield a capsule which, if caught, might widen the Vaus, equip it with lasers with which to simply shoot bricks, bring multiple balls into play, or make the existing ball "stick" (the player could then catch and launch it at will). Opposing spaceships would wander into play, diverting the ball at their own expense. And the multicolored bricks had different values, some awarding more points, others indestructible.

Like *Breakout* before it, *Arkanoid* used an analogue dial to control the bat. Unwieldy to the first-time player, it was vastly superior to the home alternative: digital movement via keyboard or joystick. The Nintendo Entertainment System devised its own solution, a bespoke "Vaus Controller"—a knob connected to a potentiometer—only supported by one other game: *Chase HQ*. **DH**

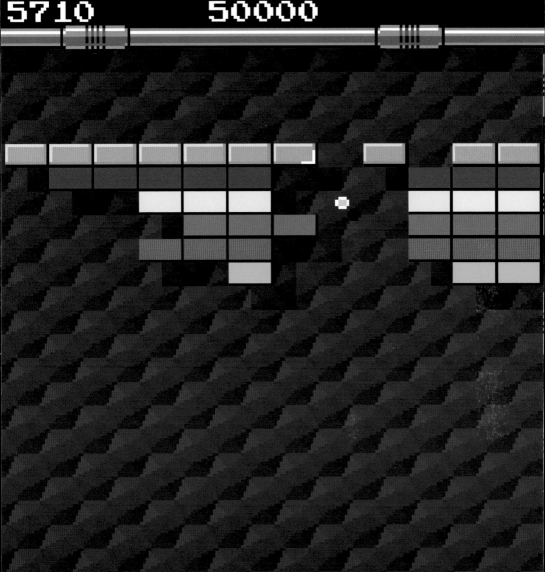

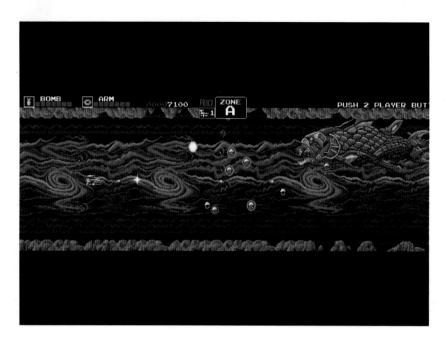

Darius

Original release date : 1986
Platform : Arcade
Developer : Taito
Genre : Shoot 'Em Up

"WARNING! A huge battleship is approaching fast!" To the underwater explorers of *Darius* that signals the arrival of something large, scaly, and probably very hard to kill . . . and agony if you've just lost all your power-ups.

By 1986, state-of-the-art visual gimmickry was seen as the most effective way to draw in the coin-op punters. Beyond just cranking out bigger and faster sprites than the 8-bit titles of previous years, the focus was now on offering experiences so sophisticated they would be impossible to recreate in the home—short of wheeling heavy arcade cabinets into the living room.

Taito's aquatic side-scrolling game arrived in an oversized cabinet that housed not one, but three monitors.

And because they were cleverly overlapped and reflected onto vertical mirrors set far back, the effect was a vivid widescreen panorama framed by expanses of blackness. This impressive sight was bolstered by a stunning attract mode that promoted its simultaneous—not to mention coin-gobbling—two-player mode, and a punchy electro-synth soundtrack (by Zuntata, Taito's cheesy in-house game Muzak band).

Those who succumbed to *Darius*'s slippery charms encountered the shoot 'em up equivalent of an extreme boot camp. Equipped with only missiles, bombs, and an energy shield, the player's Silver Hawk ship might look the part, but its default firepower is rudimentary and power-ups are slow to accrue. Which becomes especially acute when dealing with the game's coup de grâce—an entourage of ingenious robotic fish bosses.

Taito may have lacked ambition with its core mechanics, but *Darius*'s submerged parallax worlds and bizarre cast of inhabitants remain deep-sea wonders to this day. **JB**

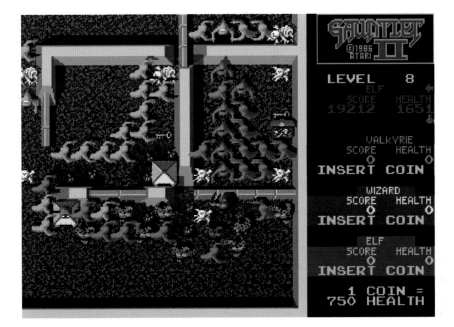

Gauntlet II

Original release date : 1986
Platform : Arcade
Developer : Atari
Genre : Action

Despite its many levels and an insatiable appetite for coins that meant your game was only over when you ran out of cash or the arcade-owner pulled the plug, 1985's dungeon romp *Gauntlet* left gamers hungry for more.

Arriving just a year later, *Gauntlet II* was unusual for a coin-op in terms of how successfully it shook up the mechanics of the original without weakening its essence. The crucial change is that instead of selecting one of four fixed characters, players in *Gauntlet II* can choose to be any character class they like, with multiple instances differentiated by color. You and your friends can head into battle with red, blue, and green wizards and an elf if you want, but you'll need to work even more tightly to defeat

hack-and-slashing Grunts without any comparable heft in your party as you have configured it.

Gauntlet II also toys with team balance by introducing "It" levels, which see tagged players attract all of the enemies on-screen. Among harmonious parties, a nimble elf might take on the role of It and rely on well-placed peers to defeat the enemies he lures away—but on a Saturday night with strangers, anything can happen. The game's fire-breathing dragon demands teamwork to overcome, however. Other notable additions include ricocheting shots, invisible walls, acid blobs, and more magical potions that permanently upgrade your character.

The tension between life-force, on-screen action, and pocket money is, of course, inevitably absent in the home versions, with their generous continues, as is the interaction with passersby. Ironically, for a game that anticipated the team-based possibilities that emerged with networked PCs, the quintessential *Gauntlet II* remains marooned at the end of a pier in a previous decade. **OB**

Salamander

Original release date : 1986
Platform : Arcade
Developer : Konami
Genre : Shoot 'Em Up

Salamander is a peculiar, troublesome sequel. Conceived as a follow-up to Konami's *Gradius*, it takes the staples of power-ups, core-destroying boss battles, beautiful and intricate level design, and a quite intimidating difficulty level, and does its own thing with them in such a way that it becomes more a spin-off than a sequel.

At first it looks like a straightforward follow-up, but then you chain your first enemy wave and are rewarded straight away with a multiple; you realize that *Salamander* has dispensed with the *Gradius* power meter and simplified the upgrade system, relieving you of the need to keep an eye on the meter and hit the "select" button to grab what you want. This makes it relatively easy to quickly tool up, surrounded by multiples and laying waste to everything ahead of you.

Then in the blink of an eye you make a mistake, and it's all taken away. No restart; the level surges inexorably forward, and a new ship spawns instantly, giving you a second's window of opportunity to grab dropped multiples, but with your weapon upgrades lost.

This happens a lot. *Salamander* is tough and exacting, often surrounding you with hazards and forcing you to learn each level by heart if you're to get to the end with anything more than a single cannon. You can force your way brutishly through the entire game by adding credits that translate instantly into extra lives, but with practice it is possible to weave your way through the insanity on a single life. It's a brilliant innovation that inspired the whole Danmaku/bullet-hell genre.

Gradius quickly returned to its original template, occasionally borrowing *Salamander*'s features, but in the history of the shoot 'em up it's *Salamander*, the troublesome spin-off, that's had the farthest reach. **JM**

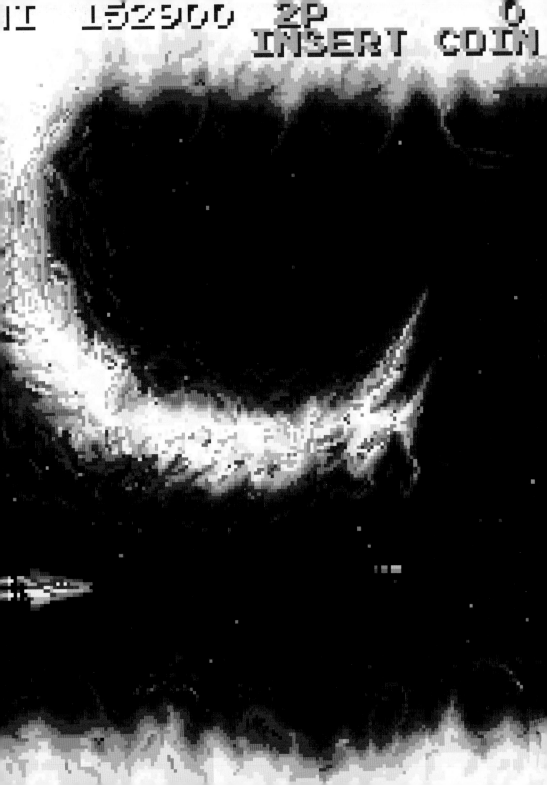

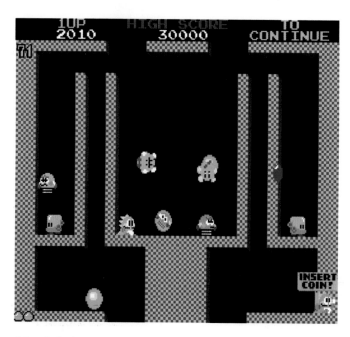

Bubble Bobble

Original release date : 1986
Platform : Arcade
Developer : Taito
Genre : Platform

Before *Super Mario Bros.*, there was plain old *Mario Bros.*, a game in which the brothers jumped around a static screen of vertical platforms, dodging enemies and occasionally working together to clear the screens. Nintendo and Shigeru Miyamoto soon left this design behind to revolutionize the platformer, but Taito didn't forget it. In 1986, *Bubble Bobble* took the basic idea of *Mario Bros.*—which was a pretty decent game in its own right—and made a classic out of it.

The premise is delightfully simple: two dinosaur brothers, Bub and Bob, have to clear each screen of enemies by trapping them in bubbles, which can then be popped with a touch. As every good boy knows, of

course, this not only kills an enemy but converts them into point-scoring fruit. If it isn't done quickly enough, then the baddies will escape in an enraged form.

There's no more to *Bubble Bobble* than this, taking place over a variety of different levels. But the push-and-pull dynamic created by its capturing, popping, and running wasn't only distinct from the period's usual offerings, but could be shared simultaneously with another player.

The spritework is simple but characterful, and the surreal world it creates is a big part of *Bubble Bobble*'s charm. It also masks the difficulty: This is an arcade game, and after a few easy screens, it lets you know exactly what that means (although the later console conversions would tone down the challenge somewhat).

For all that it's a *great* game inspired by a merely *good* one, *Bubble Bobble* was not, in itself, hugely influential—with the possible exception of the magnificent sequel *Rainbow Islands*. Between them, perhaps, they simply managed to perfect the formula. **RS**

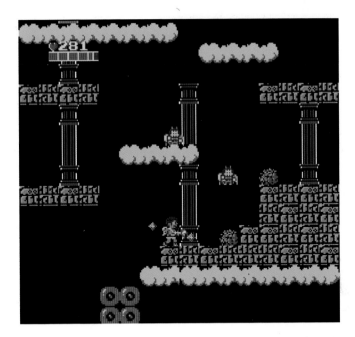

Kid Icarus

Original release date : 1986
Platform : NES
Developer : Nintendo R&D1
Genre : Platform

At a time when every game from Nintendo was destined to become a multidecade franchise, *Kid Icarus* was something of an aberration. Although the platformer had a half-hearted quasi-sequel on the Game Boy in the early 1990s, bow-wielding angel Pit was essentially a one-hit wonder, left behind while Mario, Link, Samus, and the rest went on to greater things. That says more about the fickle fortunes of the game business than it does about *Kid Icarus*, which deserves a place in the pantheon of 8-bit classics. But the main reason that *Kid Icarus* has fallen short of icon status can be attributed to one simple factor: Its extreme difficulty. Only an elite minority of players manage to make it past the first of four worlds.

The story: Palutena, the Goddess of Light, is losing her war against the evil Medusa. Her only hope is Pit, who, on the surface at least, doesn't seem well suited to the job. With his semifunctional wings and puny arrows, he seems outmatched by the Eggplant Wizards, Pluton Flies, and Sirens sent to dispatch him. The game demands a virtuoso performance. If you kill too few enemies or fail to explore all of the rooms in *Kid Icarus*'s nonlinear levels, you can miss out on crucial upgrades, making the rest of your journey that much more difficult.

Whispers of secret passwords—like "Icarus fights Medusa angels"—spread quickly after *Kid Icarus* was released, granting players quick access to souped-up weaponry and later stages. These passwords won't work on the modern Wii port of the game, though, and maybe that's for the best. Because *Kid Icarus* surely ought to be hard. If Pit can't be memorialized on cereal boxes and Happy Meals, he can at least be remembered as the hero who has to defy impossible odds on the path to victory. **JT**

Spindizzy

Original release date : 1986
Platform : Various
Developer : Paul Shirley
Genre : Action

The 1984 coin-op *Marble Madness* inspired a short-lived craze for rolling-ball adventures, and this beautifully minimalist example is one of the finest—even if programmer Paul Shirley claims to have been more influenced by Ultimate's isometric three-dimensional adventures, including the likes of *Knight Lore* and *Alien 8*, rather than Atari's trackball favorite.

As a trainee cartographer working for a galactic exploration firm, the player is thrown into space to map a newly discovered planet, Hangworld. The terrain is not encountered in person, though; a remote-controlled vehicle—GERALD—is instead sent in. What follows is a 386-screen isometric puzzler in which GERALD must be carefully navigated along narrow pathways, steep slopes and ramps, avoiding water hazards and long falls, and running across picture icons to open up new pathways. The controls are subject to inertia and momentum, making accurate navigation a tricky counterplay of acceleration and reverse movements. And, with a timer ticking down, speed and accuracy become paramount.

The level design is ingenious, providing a range of spatial challenges, within the tight construct of an effectively figurative landscape that the player experiences one screen at a time. The addition of trampoline and lift spaces adds to the range of movements on offer, as does the ability of GERALD to switch between three physical states—pyramid, gyroscope, and ball—all of which handle slightly differently.

The *Spindizzy* experience is ultimately more austere and cerebral than *Marble Madness*, and its witty scenario recognizes and renders explicit something important about the nature of adventure gaming: It is, in a sense, all about cartography. **KS**

Ikari Warriors

Original release date : 1986
Platform : Arcade
Developer : SNK
Genre : Shoot 'Em Up

The Sylvester Stallone blockbuster *Rambo II: First Blood* was arguably a step in America's healing process after the debacle in Vietnam: the beefy action star, shirtless and sporting a bandana wrapped around his head, tore through Southeast Asia with a machine gun on a quest to save the POWS that America forgot. *Ikari Warriors* openly copies the characters and even the look of *Rambo*, but reimagines it as a light-hearted buddy action flick. Two players can work together to charge their way through the jungle, avoiding slow-moving enemy fire and tossing grenades to clear the way. Water hazards, bridges, and bunkers complicate your path, and blowing up enemy emplacements can reveal POWs—and, more important, weapons caches allowing you to rearm for the fight ahead.

One of the many games inspired by Capcom's *Commando*, *Ikari Warriors* supports co-op play between two pals at the same cabinet, and the rotary joysticks allow you to move and strafe in different directions. The game limits your bullets as well as your grenades, forcing you to ration your mayhem. The obstacles and sharp corners throughout the levels give the enemy more hiding spaces, but players get a special weapon in the form of tanks, which are bulletproof and can wreck ferocious havoc on the enemy—at least until they run out of fuel.

Wisely, the game downplays the political context, remembering *Rambo* the way that kids of the day did—as a wicked awesome action flick in which tons of dudes get wasted. But the team behind this game was more radical than you might have suspected: SNK followed up *Ikari Warriors* with the game *Guerilla War*, which starred Che Guevara and Fidel Castro—though, sadly for English-speaking Marxists, the names were cut during localization for the West. **CDa**

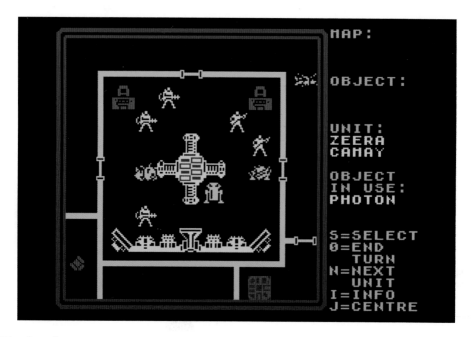

Rebelstar

Original release date : 1986
Platform : ZX Spectrum, Amstrad CPC
Developer : Julian Gollop
Genre : Strategy

Ranked the "second best game in the world ever" in 1992 in a list of the top one hundred Spectrum games published by *Your Sinclair* magazine, *Rebelstar* is the second title in a long-lived series that began with *Rebelstar Raiders*. Designed and programmed by Julian Gollop in machine code, it adds a single-player mode and greater depth to its BASIC-coded, two-player-only predecessor.

The aim of *Rebelstar* is to break into a moon base and destroy a computer intelligence before your opponents— who are computer-controlled defensive operatives—can locate and destroy your squad of raiders.

While the game could be criticized as short—it features only one map—it more than compensates with its design.

Offering play that couldn't be recreated by any tabletop war game, along with a clean, sci-fi graphical style, it sees your units struggle with morale, interact with their surroundings, and use terrain for cover. In an important twist, too—and one that would come to define Gollop's subsequent titles—units are also be able to "opportunity fire" during their opponent's turn.

As one of the first turn-based tactical games *not* aimed at the war-gaming community, *Rebelstar* marked an important milestone. With a well-designed interface and AI offering eight possible levels of difficulty, the game helped introduce the format to a wider audience, and would grow in popularity with Gollop's subsequent titles— before being overtaken by the vastly different lineage of Japanese-developed turn-based tactical games.

Rebelstar remains a very playable tactical experience in both its single- and multiplayer modes. It also serves as a great reminder of the clarity of some of the classic designs from the 8-bit era. **MKu**

OutRun

Original release date : 1986
Platform : Arcade
Developer : Sega-AM2
Genre : Driving

The fanfare accompanying the launch of some classic games may be difficult to comprehend several decades later. *OutRun* is most definitely *not* one of these titles. Boasting unforgettable design and expertly tuned game balance, AM2's assured masterpiece is *the* consummate exhibit in an oversubscribed genre.

A technical showcase of its time, *OutRun*'s sprite-scaling abilities have aged gracefully while its aesthetic—vibrant, colorful renditions of fifteen uniquely themed routes that fly past at triple-figure speeds—is yet to lose its appeal. It's a similar story when it comes to the game mechanics. The routes are arranged in pyramid fashion, so that any successful journey passes through five stages. The overall

route is controlled by the player, the road splitting in half at the end of each stage. This is an interesting feature as the two options offer different levels of intricacy—the left always proving to be the easiest segment. This means that the player takes dynamic control of the game's degree of difficulty, which when racing against the clock becomes a vital strategic aspect. Not that anyone of sane mind would ever resent having to persist in trying to conquer *OutRun*'s many twists and turns while weaving wonderfully between its heavy same-way traffic and keeping the Testarossa away from the treacherous roadside obstacles (and, in doing so, ensuring the happiness of the blonde babe in your passenger seat).

Supported by what is undoubtedly the best soundtrack to grace a driving game—who hasn't hummed "Splash Wave" or "Magical Sound Shower" during a rare traffic-free section of their daily commute?—AM2's title combines all of its supreme elements to deliver one of the purest and most joyous experiences in video gaming. **JDS**

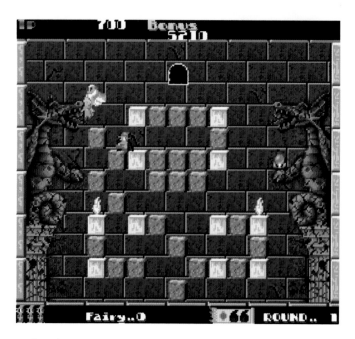

Solomon's Key

Original release date : 1986

Platform : Various

Developer : Tecmo

Genre : Puzzle

Solomon's Key is a particularly vicious wolf in extremely fluffy kitten's clothing. It looks like a simple enough platform game with an utterly straightforward mission—grab the key, avoid the monsters, nab the gems, get to the exit—and it even seems determined to make things extra-easy for you, giving you the ability to create your own blocks to jump on. You can destroy blocks, too—especially handy if there are monsters on top of them, because they'll immediately fall to their death. How hard can it be?

How hard can it be, indeed. The first screen is an easy introduction, giving you the opportunity to get a feel for how it all works, encouraging you to build staircases to get to the key, revealing that some blocks have bonus gems

hidden behind them and releasing a fairy that becomes a one-shot weapon if you catch it.

After that, the gloves come off, and *Solomon's Key* reveals itself as an especially sadistic puzzler. While you have impressive capabilities, each level is constructed to make using them effectively as difficult as possible. Some monsters destroy any blocks that are in their way, some follow the contours of whatever blocks they come across, and some just sit there and spit out fire. When you mix them all together, you get a game where each level's a minefield of split-second timing and lateral thinking. And just to make things extra-exciting, it's all done against the clock. You might need time to think and get your head around a level, but *Solomon's Key* isn't giving it to you.

It's rock hard and cruel and capable of tricking you into a position where you can't actually complete a level, but the design is solid and brilliantly executed. Better suited to home formats than the arcade, it's not impossible—it just doesn't suffer fools gladly. **JM**

Dragon Quest

Original release date : 1986

Platform : NES

Developer : Enix

Genre : Role-Playing

Even if you have never played the original *Dragon Quest* (known as *Dragon Warrior* outside of Japan), you have surely felt its influence. Any console role-playing game—or any game that boasts "RPG elements"—owes an enormous debt to *Dragon Quest*, which took the core design of tabletop RPGs like Dungeons & Dragons, and translated it to the TV screen. Hit points, experience points, random enemy encounters, leveling up—*Dragon Quest* may not have invented all of these mechanics, but it established them as video game standards.

Your character, who can be named anything you like as long as it fits within four letters, is a descendant of the great hero Erdrick. Just your luck, that means you're the only

guy who can retrieve a Ball of Light from the Dragonlord and save the kingdom. As usual, you'll fight increasingly difficult monsters to make it to the final boss. In *Dragon Quest*, though, the fighting is different from anything that had come before. Split-second reflexes are irrelevant. When you're choosing battle commands from a menu, it's careful strategy and calculated risk that come to the fore. And while the baddies get tougher, so do you, through the leveling system that slowly invests your hard work in a battle-toughened character.

This is a homely game. Its interface is simplistic, its story is clichéd, and its world is tiny. Yet when it was released, it was a revelation. With complete freedom of movement across the land and potential for danger at every step, the adventure offered a boundless thrill. It may be difficult for modern gamers to understand how fresh and exciting *Dragon Quest* seemed in the mid-1980s, but playing this game, which grew the roots of an entire genre, remains a rewarding rite of passage for any RPG fan. **JT**

Defender of the Crown

Original release date : 1986

Platform : Various

Developer : Cinemaware

Genre : Strategy

Released before Commodore's Amiga hit mass-market penetration with the release of the A500 model, *Defender of the Crown* was the first title released by Cinemaware, a company that would—as its name implies—become known for its heavily cinema-inspired titles.

A simple *Risk*-style game that is set in the Middle Ages, *Defender of the Crown* casts the player as one of four Saxon lords attempting to conquer England by marching armies across the country to capture counties, raise funds, and ultimately wipe their opponents off the map. The title distinguishes itself by offering home computer graphics that were astonishing for 1986: Though not fully utilizing the Amiga's power, it was the first home title to feature colorful, highly detailed graphics with a consistent art direction. This helped to transform action features, such as jousting tournaments and castle raids, into near-cinematic experiences for the home gamer.

Though a landmark title, the original release of *Defender of the Crown* was marred by being rushed to completion, several near-finished features—deeper strategic options, more locations, and different catapult ammo for castle siege sections—being dropped. But following its massive popularity, these omissions would find themselves reinstated in many of the game's ports—most fully in the Atari ST version.

While *Defender of the Crown* is childishly simple to play and offers—even in its most fully featured version—fairly limited replayability, the title began a drive toward productions that were conspicuously not *only* about game play, but equally about creating an interactive cinematic experience—an aim that would reverberate from one end of the industry to the other. **MKu**

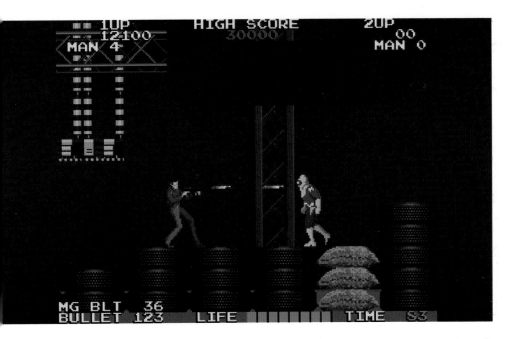

Rolling Thunder

Original release date : 1986
Platform : Arcade
Developer : Namco
Genre : Shoot 'Em Up

For a game that's all about marching from left to right while slaying scores of identical enemies, *Rolling Thunder* has a surprising edge. Not the shameless viscera of the original *Ninja Gaiden*, perhaps, where the abandoned hero is disemboweled by a descending circular saw, but a cut above the usual bad dudes and hoodlums. With stylized anime characters, sinister music, and a damsel in obvious distress, it's a standout from a time when Namco and Sega jostled for control of the world's arcade floors.

Rolling Thunder is the undercover arm of Interpol's secret espionage units. You take control of agent Albatross; your mission, to locate and rescue a missing female operative, Leila Blitz, who has been captured by

Geldra, an evil, criminal society trying to conquer the world from a secret New York base. Headed up by Maboo—part shaman, part hobgoblin—Geldra's private army has an endless supply of troops to defend against any slick moves that Albatross might have up his sleeve throughout the ten mighty levels of the game. Should he fail, the fate of the world is left to the imagination—unlike Leila's, which flashes across a giant video screen between levels.

Explicit by even today's standards, this was many gamers' introduction to the sometimes salacious world of Japanese anime. Beating the movie version of *Akira* by two years, it was more than just an 1980s equivalent of *Jet Grind Radio* or *Killer7*, taking unsuspecting Westerners by storm. Culture shock aside, *Rolling Thunder* owes a lasting uniqueness to its transitional game play, its ammo closets, not to mention its immense difficulty—a hangover from 1983 hit *Elevator Action*—and its controls and looks, which inspired a whole new generation of propulsive, accessible action games. **DH**

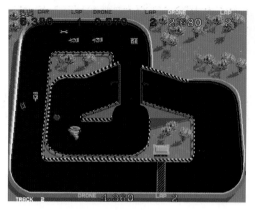

Super Sprint

Original release date : 1986
Platform : Arcade
Developer : Atari
Genre : Driving

You know you're not dealing with a serious racing game when you're offered only one pedal with which to control the speed of your vehicle. In fact, you wonder why Atari bothered to build *Super Sprint's* cabinet with an expensive steering wheel rather than simply going for a joystick—but then you take the wheel in your hands and start throwing the game's cars around the tracks, and it all makes sense.

Super Sprint is a supremely fluid driving game, its Formula One–styled machines smoothly tracing lines through each complex track layout like ice cubes propelled across a glass tabletop. The steering wheel is a key factor, but the game's carefully engineered animation and keen sense of speed is what keeps you feeding in the coins. You can also soup-up your car by collecting loose spanners laying on the track—these can be exchanged for performance-increasing boosters, such as improved traction and acceleration.

If you're after a racing game that will get the competitive energies flowing, then you need look no further than *Super Sprint*. **TB**

720°

Original release date : 1986
Platform : Arcade
Developer : Atari
Genre : Sports

The first skateboarding game didn't just offer tricks and half-pipes: It encouraged players to stick around and try to build a career. Racing from one skate park to the next, dodging traffic, players had to make enough money to reach the next level.

Where a home game expects you to linger, searching for hidden secrets, the intention of *720°*, as a coin-op, is to keep you moving. Take too long, and you'll hear the game's famous catchphrase—"Skate or die"—followed by a pack of killer bees that will sting you to death unless you scramble to the next skate park. And if you don't have the cash to keep going, it's game over.

The game benefits from a simple but effective control system. With just two buttons and a joystick, gamers tackle four different events, pulling off tricks on the halfpipe, threading through the gates on the slalom, or setting a speed record on the downhill course. The moves are simple next to today's byzantine skate titles, but the action is thrilling, and the concept was proven: *720°* gave birth to the extreme sports genre in gaming. **CDa**

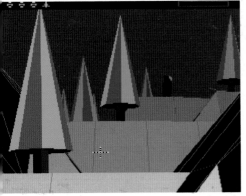

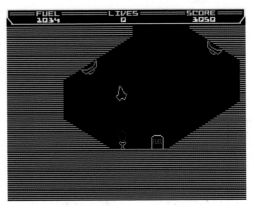

The Sentinel

Original release date : 1986
Platform : Various
Developer : Geoff Crammond
Genre : Strategy

Chess with added paranoia is how some think of Geoff Crammond's unique strategy game. A mysterious being known as the Sentinel is rampaging through the galaxy, landing on worlds and absorbing their energy until nothing remains alive. To fight back, a synthoid robot is created, also capable of sucking energy from environmental objects. It must seek out and absorb the terrible Sentinel, and then move on to the next ailing world.

Crammond used mathematical skill rather than design flair to create the game's endless, stark, flat-shaded, polygonal landscapes. The Sentinel itself is also suitably eerie, towering above like an Orwellian CCTV god. If it senses your presence, it begins to drain your synthoid of energy, so you need to stay out of its line of vision.

For some, The Sentinel is an early antecedent of the stealth adventure. By coincidence, the 1998 sequel—The Sentinel Returns—appeared the very same year as Metal Gear Solid. By then, however, gamers were no longer interested in abstract studies of surveillance state paranoia: They wanted to hide in boxes and blast soldiers. **KS**

Thrust

Original release date : 1986
Platform : Various
Developer : Jeremy Smith
Genre : Shoot 'Em Up

While a student at Imperial College in London, Jeremy Smith created one of the most important titles in the history of physics-based gaming.

The plot is typically brief for an 8-bit home computer title. Players must pilot a small craft through a series of cavernous alien landscapes, stealing fuel pods that will be used to power fighter ships in a galactic rebellion. The visuals are beautifully minimal; just solid cave walls and planet surfaces combined with the vector-based ship and enemy gun turrets. The hook is the precise physics modeling—the craft is subject to inertia and momentum and is piloted though simple controls enabling thrust and rotation in either direction.

Thrust is a game about concentration, forethought, and the ability to react with measured grace to the physical challenges thrown at your tiny ship. The game has inspired dozens of fan-made adaptations and was a crucial prelude to Smith's later project, Exile, a more comprehensively modeled physics-based arcade adventure and among the finest 8-bit games ever made. **KS**

Space Harrier

Original release date : 1985
Platform : Arcade
Developer : Sega
Genre : Shoot 'Em Up

Space Harrier looks as psychedelic today as it did when it first landed in the arcades. Back in 1985, it created plenty of surprise with its innovations. It's all about creating a *big* experience: The player climbs into the hydraulically powered cabinet, takes a seat, and immediately becomes immersed in a wild third-person shooter.

You are a Flash Gordon–like figure who flies through the so-called Fantasy Zone on a multipurpose rocket slung under his arm. Usefully, it doubles as a gun, which fires at the surreal characters you find zooming in your direction. Armored UFOs, flying rocks, one-eyed mammoths, and other outlandish flora and fauna fill each of the eighteen levels on the way to some seriously epic boss fights.

To the modern eye, the strangest feature of *Space Harrier* is the pseudo-three-dimensional graphics system that struggles to give it a convincing sense of depth. Driven by Sega's patented Super Scaler technology—the same kit that also powers *After Burner* and *OutRun*—it presents flat sprites that get larger the closer you get to them, while a checkerboard landscape emphasizes your velocity. Simply hitting a tree will knock you out, and you steadily earn points simply for staying alive. With each wave, the player gets a better handle on the game's odd perspective. The only way to fend off an enemy is to get right in front of it and shoot, even as the enemy fire flies straight for you.

Space Harrier is to the three-dimensional shooter genre what the zoetrope is to the motion picture: awkward and nostalgic, but the splendor of the images and the pace of the action merit another look. (And be sure to do so in its original arcade form, because the various home conversions, though often cleverly programmed, are poor reproductions of the real thing.) **CDa**

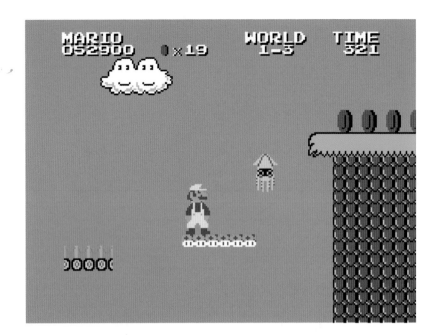

Super Mario Bros.: The Lost Levels

Original release date : 1986
Platform : NES
Developer : Nintendo
Genre : Platform

Familiar and mysterious at the same time, *Super Mario Bros.: The Lost Levels* was the secret sequel to the original *Super Mario Bros.* that wasn't released outside of Japan during the reign of the NES. The reason for this is simple: it was deemed too tricky for non-Japanese audiences (but we did get the lovely *Super Mario Bros. 2* to make up for it).

The Lost Levels is hard. But more precisely, it's simply rather unfair. The game may use the same sprites, tiles, and control scheme as its magical predecessor, but somewhere along the lines it's learned a handful of dirty tricks, too, which whittle away at some of the enjoyment. Mushrooms come with a new poisoned variety, which has to be evaded as it skates along the ground, magic invisible blocks are more than typically necessary to get through some of the game's more dastardly challenges, and the wind has a nasty habit of playing up on occasion to ruin your careful precision jumping.

The levels are also often gratuitously cruel in their layouts: Piranha plants abound, sudden drops are often dauntingly wide, and the enemy count has been massively dialed up. It's still fascinating, however, not least because there's a weird thrill to be found in seeing the game's familiar faces and locations twisted to such evil ends, and, inevitably, it's a rare player who gives up in frustration without fighting their way through to the final castle.

Unavailable in the West until its inclusion on the SNES's *Super Mario All-Stars* compilation, the black sheep of the family is increasingly being welcomed into the fold, a sign, if nothing else, that Nintendo's innate sense of balance and fairness hasn't always been quite so rock solid. Pick it up now on the Wii's Virtual Console, but don't complain if it makes you cry. **CD**

Buggy Boy

Original release date : 1986
Platform : Arcade
Developer : Tatsumi
Genre : Driving

Although ported to various home formats, the best way to experience *Buggy Boy* is via the original deluxe arcade cabinet and its panoramic three-screen display. The colorful graphics, exotic locales, and genuine sense of speed were a challenge to *OutRun*, and while *Buggy Boy* isn't revered in quite the same way as Sega's classic of the same year, it remains a key title in the racing genre's timeline. Introducing jumps and banked curves, *Buggy Boy* doesn't tether the player to the track like other racers, and the vehicle's constant bouncing reinforces the sense of driving off-road, not just on different-colored tarmac.

Five tracks are available, of which all but one are point-to-point. A clock ticks down to as you drive, but time can be added by completing the stages that make up each course or driving through the buggy-width time gates.

While racing lines are important, they are confounded by a litany of obstacles along the way: colliding with smaller detritus will send your vehicle skyward or onto two wheels; crashing into anything larger will result in a tumble, and the need to shift from "Hi" to "Lo" gear in order to pick up speed again.

Players yearning for even more to think about can attempt to collect flags. Each one yields a few points, but when picked up in a specified sequence, bonus points are earned for a short period. A hidden football, if found and hit, pushes the score even higher.

Tracks mostly consist of three lanes, but are occasionally constricted by tunnels or bridges. Thankfully, roadside signage provides *just* enough warning to get in lane. But *Buggy Boy* couldn't be farther from freeway delays, and thanks to its diversity, responsive handling, and focus on fun, is far more than just another racing game. **BM**

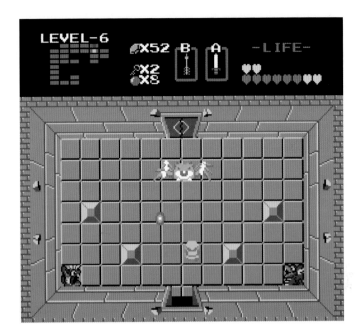

The Legend of Zelda

Original release date : 1986
Platform : NES
Developer : Nintendo
Genre : Action / Adventure

The Legend of Zelda has its own legend, as it so happens; a story that suggests that Shigeru Miyamoto came up with the idea for Link's epic adventure while opening and closing the drawers of his desk, and daydreaming that each one contained a separate tiny garden. We should probably be grateful, then, that he didn't have a staple gun or hole punch handy, or else the history of gaming might have turned out very differently.

Regardless of whether the anecdote is apocryphal or not, it certainly makes sense of Zelda's wonderfully simple structure. An action RPG in which brave adventurer Link, clad in green and wielding a sword and a shield, must venture into dank dungeons, defeating bosses and finding helpful items on his quest to rid the land of the evil Ganon, Zelda has a map divided into an orderly arrangement of individual game screens, each one holding a cave entrance, a rocky maze, a bundle of enemies to smack about, or some other delightful treat. Players progress through the dungeons in turn, picking up health hearts and the gadgets they'll need to defeat the bosses, and that will, in turn, open up more of the map for them, allowing them to explore farther into the world of Hyrule.

From this one title—delightful and balanced as it is—would spring one of the richest founts of tradition and lore in modern gaming: a series of polite yet gripping and intricate adventures, each one adding a handful of new elements while reveling in the structures of the past. Over the years, Zelda titles have become renowned as the cleverest, most beautifully crafted adventures in all of gaming, and it's dazzling to see so many of the series' finest ideas present in this first title—however Miyamoto came up with the idea. **CD**

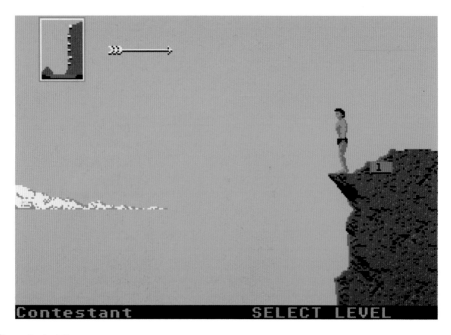

World Games

Original release date : 1986
Platform : Various
Developer : Epyx
Genre : Sports

The third original title in the immensely successful *Games* series, which includes *Summer*, *Winter*, and *California* flavors. Just like the titles that preceded it, *World Games* is a selection of mini-games playable in their entirety sequentially, as a bespoke selection, or individually (usefully, practice is also an option). But whereas its forebearers offer a fairly predictable selection of events from their respective seasons, *World Games* collects a surprisingly disparate group of disciplines, each of which represents a different country of origin.

The events on offer are: Russian weightlifting, French slalom skiing, Canadian log rolling, German barrel jumping, American bull riding, Mexican cliff diving, Scottish caber tossing, and Japanese sumo wrestling. The game really shines when played with friends, and up to eight can compete, choosing the country they wish to represent at the beginning before taking turns to go for gold. The only exceptions to the turn-based structure are sumo wrestling and log rolling, which pit two players against each other simultaneously. The different disciplines require mastery of various methods of control, and players must remain on their toes if they are to win across the board.

The imagination with which the sports were chosen is equally applied to presentation, every stage introduced with a short history of the event and a culturally themed tune (the bagpipes are particularly worthy of note). And the graphics are brimming with charm: fail at the caber toss, and the heavy log will hammer your Scotsman into the ground; fall into the water in Canada, and a shark's fin will circle your anxious lumberjack. *World Games* has lost little of its appeal in the years since 1986 and can still give modern party titles a run for their money. **BM**

Super Hang-On

Original release date : 1987
Platform : Arcade
Developer : Sega-AM2
Genre : Racing

When *Hang-On* appeared in 1985, it represented Sega producer Yu Suzuki's coming-of-age as a video game designer, an almost unconscious decision to become a fearless forward thinker in the arcade game space—with immersive cabinet and game designs—and even the home game space (with the sadly ill-fated Shenmue series). In light of this, *Super Hang-On* may feel like a footnote in Suzuki and gaming's history—a mere sequel to his breakthrough title two years before.

Indeed, *Super Hang-On*'s arcade mode looks almost exactly the same as the original *Hang-On*, but does feature racing tracks of varying lengths, located in different continents. Split up into stages (passing each adds time

to the in-game countdown clock), Africa is the easiest and shortest with six stages; Asia features ten; the Americas fourteen; and Europe is the hardest course with eighteen. Each track is a tightly designed course that also features a variety of backdrops to keep things visually interesting. As with Suzuki's 1986 hit *OutRun*, players have a choice of four musical tracks that will play during the race, and each stage has an individual ending.

So far, so typical for a time and market that had already been greatly expanded by Suzuki's work in the field. But detractors overlook the importance of iteration. By taking the lessons learned by the original *Hang-On* and *OutRun*, *Super Hang-On* was arguably the definitively playable Yu Suzuki racer until *Virtua Racing* appeared in 1992. The title also benefits from some of the best home ports of any of Sega's racing titles, with the Sega Mega Drive in particular featuring the ability for the player to upgrade bikes between races. *Super Hang-On* may be a footnote, but it leaves a lasting impression. **Mku**

Blasteroids

Original release date : 1987
Platform : Arcade
Developer : Atari Games
Genre : Shoot 'Em Up

The history of Atari is a tale of numerous, different companies selling the brand name among one other in a long and convoluted gaming relay. The part that we're interested in here is the Atari Games of the mid- to late 1980s, the arcade division that passed from pillar to post until an employee buyout provided the opportunity to reclaim the initiative and again become an arcade powerhouse. This was an era that oversaw the production of a succession of hit titles, including *Gauntlet*, *Super Sprint*, and *Marble Madness*. And *Blasteroids*.

Notable in being a rare title in the Atari Games stable to be based on a game from the brand's first golden age, *Blasteroids* closely observes the feel of the original *Asteroids* classic and then heaps innovation on top of it.

Minimalist vector outlines are thrown away in favor of great, huge chunks of digitized rock, tumbling through space. Your ship can morph between three different configurations—from slow and mighty through to speedy and weedy—and flying saucers drop power-ups when destroyed. But it's no longer enough just to survive; you now have an energy meter that drops when you fire your thrusters or take a hit, and you're dead when it hits zero. You get a small energy boost when you complete a level, but you'll also have to find red asteroids that'll release power crystals once destroyed.

Throw in boss battles, extra asteroid types, a strategic map-based approach that enables you to choose your battles—not to mention a two-player mode in which both ships can dock to become a turreted mega-ship—and you have a potentially overloaded game with all the tricks in the book applied to it. *Blasteroids* never feels like that, though. Sure, it's tough, but it reveals its secrets slowly and gives you a chance to settle into them. **JM**

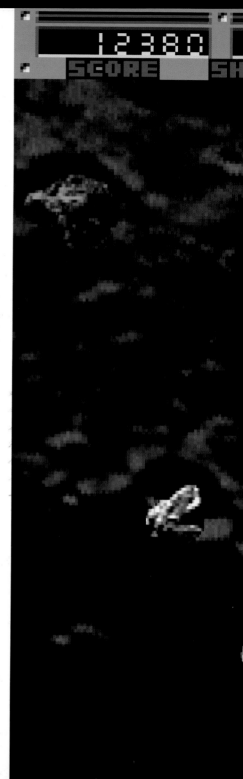

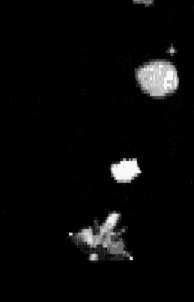

CREDITS 0

NetHack

Original release date : 1987
Platform : Various
Developer : Various
Genre : Role-Playing

NetHack may have started off as a simple version of the classic ASCII-graphics title *Rogue*. Players set off to explore a series of randomly-generated dungeons, fighting monsters and collecting items—but over the years it has become something much more elaborate and fascinating. A true ghost of the Internet, *NetHack* has been knocking around the web since 1987. During that time, everything from its appearance to its feature sets have been in a state of constant flux, but that same core feeling to the experience has never changed.

After selecting a character from a range of archetypes, players descend into *NetHack*'s fifty-level dungeon (viewed from a simplistic top-down perspective), on the trail of a glitzy trinket—the Amulet of Yendor—which lurks, allegedly, on the final floor. What happens next depends on you, as the game slowly reveals its tactics and secrets. (Although it's safe to assume that it'll probably involve monsters and potions at some point in the proceedings.)

Although *NetHack* is well over twenty years old, it's precisely because of its open-source nature that it's still being worked on, both by groups of isolated enthusiasts making their own versions in the equivalent of a board game's house rules, and, more thrillingly, by the NetHack DevTeam—a loose collective of coders and secret geniuses who release regular updates for the official version itself. With two decades of accumulated lore, inside jokes, and tips piling up in the darker corners of the Internet, *NetHack* is definitely one of a kind: both a huge world of magic and murder to discover and a fascinating and complex community to engage within. Tracking it down today isn't difficult—the dungeons are waiting, a mere Google search away. Getting yourself out again may prove a lot trickier. **CD**

A.P.B.

Original release date : 1987
Platform : Arcade
Developer : Atari
Genre : Action

Cop dramas have always been popular on TV and at the movies, so it should be no surprise to find the format transfer happily to the games console.

You begin your career in *A.P.B.* as Officer Bob, a rookie whose boss doesn't trust him to arrest anything more dangerous than a traffic cone. Get through basic training, and you'll soon have your daily quota of perps to pull over—mainly the regular riffraff and litterbugs. Life is good (the donuts are easy to find), but then you get your big shot: a chance to catch a drug-trafficking hippie, the target of an actual all points bulletin. And that's where the game really takes off, because as corny as *A.P.B.* may look to today's *Need for Speed*ers, it really knows how to pull off a high-speed chase.

Coming well after the end of the arcade craze, *A.P.B.* used a lengthy career mode and a flashy cabinet, replete with flashing police lights, to lure kids away from their Nintendos. The characters come straight out of a bad cop show, with nemeses, like Sid Sniper and Freddy Freak, and a boss who literally breathes fire at you if you rack up too many demerits. Casual offenders can be stopped by aiming a reticule at them and hitting them with your siren, and it moves farther out the faster you go, making it easy to pick off perps while you're racing down the road. Your reward, however, is that if you do a good enough job, your boss will let you carry a gun.

The driving experience is certainly breathtaking. Making full use of the tall, vertical-scrolling display, roads split and run parallel, with shortcuts and sharp turns everywhere. Bang into too many innocent cars, and you'll lose your job. Catch your target, and you can take him back to the station and "beat" out a confession. Your education as an officer is complete. **CDa**

Dungeon Master

Original release date : 1987
Platform : Various
Developer : FTL Games
Genre : Role-Playing

The computer role-playing game has gone through many phases of development, but it made a leap to real-time three-dimensional action as early as 1987, with the release of *Dungeon Master*. The Atari ST version came first, but it was soon converted to almost every platform of the day. The game has inspired many imitators, and is regarded as perhaps the era's finest accomplishment in the RPG genre.

Presenting the player with a small window into the game world, *Dungeon Master* is played from a first-person perspective. Action is delivered frame by frame, rather than being a real-time-mapped three-dimensional space as in the post-*Doom* era. Nevertheless, this design represented a colossal leap forward in presentation and interaction—

particularly in the way that the mouse drives the action through clicking on various icons (representing everything from movement to the various powers the characters have in their inventories). This influential approach was to remain popular until technology enabled gaming platforms to freely render 3-D environments in the mid-1990s.

Dungeon Master is notable for being remarkably free-form in the way it allows players to approach the action. The game takes place in a series of dungeons or underground tunnels, but the route through is nonlinear. Players are able to go away and explore other areas if they encounter monsters that are too dangerous or puzzles that are too difficult. This kind of open-ended design was incredibly fresh in 1987, and it remains significant today.

Perhaps the most important thing about *Dungeon Master*, though, is the way in which it changed the thinking behind how RPGs should work, moving away from text-based commands and stats and into an era where the user interface became the engine for interaction. **JR**

Servo   Ocean Pacific   01:20

California Games

Original release date : 1987

Platform : Various

Developer : Epyx

Genre : Sports

In the dreary, backward Britain of the 1980s, when the most exciting thing imaginable was either a computer game or a trip to the sandy beaches of the United States, Epyx's *California Games* was a ray of genuine sunshine: a brace of cool, West Coast sports to be enjoyed by players living under the gray skies of British resorts and industrial towns, combined with a generous chance to bask in the rays of sun that burst forth from the computer monitor.

Compilation games being in vogue at the time—Epyx had already released collections entitled *Summer Games* and *Winter Games*, while action titles like *Beach Head* and *Raid Over Moscow* would often play out as a series of levels each with their own bizarre mechanics and rules—*California Games* allowed players to indulge in a little rollerskating, BMX riding, and half-piping, as well as more traditionally Californian activities, like surfing. Other offerings were a little stranger—the entertainment factor in a good old round of "footbag" can be rather disconcertingly hard to isolate, regardless of where you happen to be in the world at the time—and suggest that the ideas might have been a little thin on the ground when the idea of this particular games package was pitched.

This is still a very generous title, though, and a few of its sports—surfing, in particular—are among the best included on any Epyx compilation. You're most likely to play *California Games* today as a middle-aged character searching for a doorway back to your wasted youth, and, the truth is, between the *Mario & Sonic Olympics* titles and Electronic Arts's fare, there are now far more competent selections available for those not riddled with melancholy nostalgia. But where were they back in the 1980s, eh? **CD**

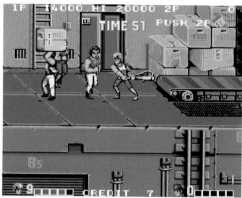

International Karate +

Original release date : 1987
Platform : Various
Developer : Archer Maclean
Genre : Fighting

The original *International Karate* was a polished but rather uninspired take on the fighting game genre. Indeed, it was so similar to 1984 arcade hit *Karate Champ* that Data East attempted to sue for copyright infringement.

On the surface, *International Karate +* is nothing out of the ordinary. The sequel does, however, feature some very useful innovations. Foremost is the superfast joystick scanning, coupled with some wonderfully smooth and exact animation, a combination that provides fast and responsive combat. Programmer Archer Maclean famously set about creating the game's dynamic backflip animation by physically tracing the movements of a background dancer from a video of the film *Grease*.

The game's coup de grâce, however, is the addition of a third fighter, either controllable by the computer or, better still, another player. Suddenly, there's a whole new group melee feel, upsetting the traditional one-on-one dynamic. And for the first time since Datasoft's 1984 platformer *Bruce Lee*, two friends could gang up on the AI fighter—a surprisingly therapeutic experience. **KS**

Double Dragon

Original release date : 1987
Platform : Arcade
Developer : Technos
Genre : Fighting

Taking their cues from Hollywood, the arcade brawling games of the Reagan era packed as much camp villainy, swift justice, and superhuman muscle into their action as a few thousand pixels would allow. *Double Dragon* has all the key ingredients: the hard-working American heroes, the invasion of home soil by a predatory force, and a winsome civilian caught in the crossfire. It has comic-book kingpins and chain-wielding thugs, who between them resemble a tryout for a seventh member of the Village People.

A spiritual sequel to *Renegade*—an earlier Technos beat 'em up—*Double Dragon* introduced features like beating an enemy with their own weapon, beating an enemy being grappled by your friend, and just beating your friend to waste money. "Friendly fire" in this two-player co-op game was an instant hit while the ability to turn grapples into throws and combos would create an appetite for games like *Ninja Gaiden* and *Final Fight*. Hugely popular, *Double Dragon* produced two arcade sequels and numerous ports. Just don't mention the movie, or its immortal line: "Eat some fist, butthead!" **DH**

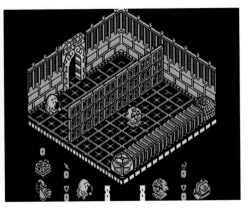

Head Over Heels

Original release date : 1987
Platform : Various
Developer : Ocean
Genre : Action

A genuine curiosity, *Head Over Heels* is a fabulously challenging isometric mind boggler. What's more, it's an idea that's barely been revisited since its first flush of unlikely success on 8-bit home computers in the 1980s.

The adventure begins as we meet the two quirky lead characters, Head and Heels, who are interplanetary spies, sent on a dangerous mission to free the prisoners of a mysterious space emperor. The task is a difficult one, but the spies aren't entirely powerless: Head has a mean jump and can shoot enemies with donuts, while Heels can climb on furniture and carry objects. To succeed, however, the two must work together.

What emerges over the course of this tricksy little game is a kind of single-player cooperative mode of action, as Head and Heels combine, often literally, to navigate a range of tricky environments. It's as bizarre as it sounds, and just as brilliant, and while the original game is hard to get running these days (at least without some very old gear) the coding collective Retrospec has developed a freeware remake to run on most operating systems. **CD**

Nebulus

Original release date : 1987
Platform : Various
Developer : John Phillips
Genre : Platform

Way before tower defense games became the strategy puzzler of choice for the casual gaming crowd, the 8-bit world was wowed by tower destruction. One odd little alien named Pogo is to blame. A bug-eyed, froglike critter of indeterminate origin, Pogo destroys the tower if he reaches the top of it. Two major obstacles stand in his way: weird enemies and the clock. Pogo makes his way up these vertical towers by hopping up ledges, disappearing through doorways to avoid enemies or to find a new route, and steadily gaining altitude with each move.

In a flash of design inspiration, Pogo remains positioned in the center of the screen and the circular tower itself rotates as you "move" left and right. The illusion of Pogo moving is matched by expert use of parallax scrolling, adding a three-dimensional depth to the tower that makes the overall visual quality a huge standout, given that the core creature and tower designs are very simple.

The Pogo concept has been recreated on numerous platforms, but always retains the core game play challenge that has proved enduring and endearing. **RSm**

Oids

Original release date : 1987
Platform : Macintosh, ST
Developer : FTL Games
Genre : Shoot 'Em Up

In many ways, FTL's *Oids* is much more than just an exceptionally playable gravity-based game. It's one of the last bastions of a different gaming age, one in which game ideas seemed more innocent, unconcerned with the commercial considerations so prominent in today's titles.

A much-loved creation, yet barely known outside of the ST and Mac fraternity, *Oids* requires you to pilot a V-wing starfighter, using thrust and direction change alone, within the perilous confines of a series of planets. Your mission is to rescue an enslaved android race, who have been scattered across the galaxy and forced to work in far-flung galactic factories.

As if negotiating the landscape isn't tricky enough—anything other than a carefully executed landing on flat ground will result in death by explosion—the factory owners have installed nasty defense systems. Luckily, your ship comes equipped with guns and a shield. (Watch out, though—the shield consumes fuel, and if you use too much, you'll have to waste valuable mission time searching for more.) Once the enemy threat has been dispatched, a single bullet will destroy the factory where the Oids are being held. Happy to see you, once you've found a safe place to land, they'll climb aboard. Take off, rejoin your mothership, and then it's on to the next planet.

The concept is as simple yet accomplished as the gorgeous, economical visuals, presenting you with an irresistible game mechanic that cleverly contrasts careful and considered navigational sections with moments of intense action. It's a powerful mix, and one that delivers a supremely addictive experience. In a particularly welcome touch, once you've exhausted the game's challenges, the built-in level editor effectively guarantees a lifespan as infinite as the universe. **JDS**

Galaga '88

Original release date : 1987
Platform : Arcade
Developer : Namco
Genre : Shoot 'Em Up

Take an old title, rework it with improved audiovisual content and refined game play, and then repackage it for a different audience. It's a popular idea nowadays, but hardly a new one: *Galaga '88* is an early example of this principle, a game from 1987 that takes a six-year-old vision and enhances it in just about every way.

Thankfully, Namco doesn't tinker too much with the nuts and bolts of the player's craft: You can still move only left and right, and your only offensive option is a single fire button. However, at the game's outset, you're given some interesting options. You can take a single ship into play, or use up two of your lives and take a pair of them into battle in tandem—thereby ramping up your firepower (although simultaneously providing the enemy with a bigger target). It's even possible to transform into a supersized version.

The action plays out against backdrops that contrast with the original game's simplistic starfields by presenting attractions such as nebulae, planets, and space stations. But it's what happens in front of them that makes the *real* difference. A broader range of enemies assembles before you in each wave, and although they are more colorful and cuddlier-looking than before, they also prove to be deadlier. The sequel also introduces scrolling levels, featuring asteroids and destructible crystal formations, and an ultimate boss enemy whose defeat brings the game to an end. Yes, *Galaga '88* is considerably more of a challenge than the original.

It really *is* difficult to dislike any game whose bonus stages involve their enemies maneuvering on to the screen in time with a neat little tango number—"That's galactic dancin'!" we're told by the on-screen text—but *Galaga '88* has much more to offer gamers than cheesy Latin music and synchronized aliens. **TB**

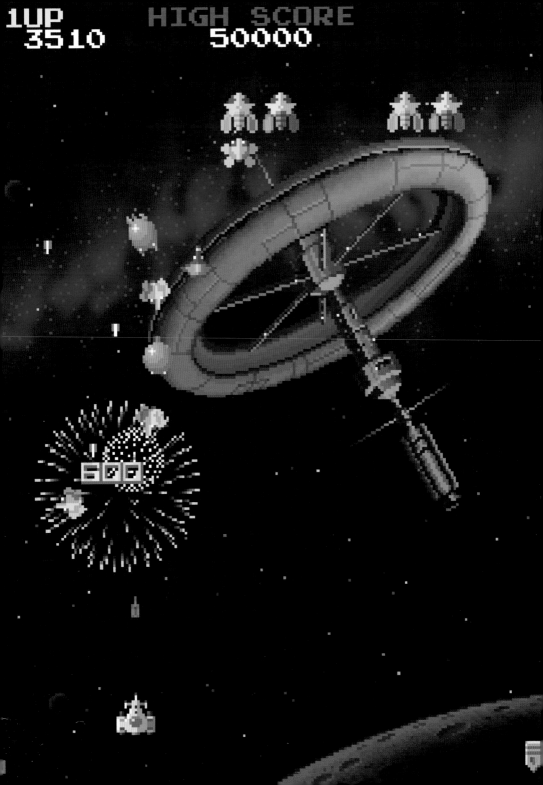

Maniac Mansion

Original release date : 1987

Platform : Various

Developer : LucasArts

Genre : Adventure

Maniac Mansion ushered in a new era for adventure games. It was the first title to make use of the venerable SCUMM (Script Creation Utility for *Maniac Mansion*) engine, the scripting language developed by LucasArts that enabled designers to create large parts of the game without having to write in the same language as the game's source code. This helped to create a more visually attractive game and friendly gaming experience.

Maniac Mansion was also a significant influence on the development of the adventure genre by daring to suggest that such games did *not* have to be solemn, worthy, and plodding. In fact, they could be witty, personable, and rich with smart pop-culture references. Heck, they could even

mimic haunted houses from teen movies and feature japes involving chainsaws and mysterious hamster deaths.

Local hero Dave Miller has been drawn to a strange spooky mansion on the outside of town to rescue his kidnapped cheerleader girlfriend, Sandy Pantz. But he's unaware that mad scientist Dr. Fred is inside, struggling with his own deranged family and a mean alien meteor with an attitude problem. So Dave explores the house trying to uncover its secrets—and trying *not* to get killed by members of the grotesque cast, such as Fred's lovable son, Weird Ed. Furthermore, the only way he can reach Sandy is by answering a series of neat—often rather smart—lateral-thinking puzzles.

Witty, clever, and filled with odd little secrets to discover as you explore, *Maniac Mansion* may not be as openly hilarious as the *Monkey Island* series that followed, but remains a very significant step in the history of the adventure game genre, and is as evocative and atmospheric today as it was back in 1987. **CD**

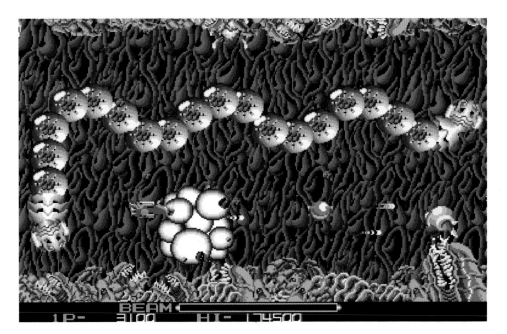

R-Type

Original release date : 1987
Platform : Arcade
Developer : Irem
Genre : Shoot 'Em Up

R-Type is one of the most enduring shoot 'em ups for one simple reason: People don't just play it to shoot things. Never shy of a little transdimensional mischief, it makes time and space for the things most others leave out: story, character, and themes. Loved by game historians more than players—it's mercilessly hard and fundamentally flawed—each level is a landscape work of art.

To survive, the player must learn to fight fire with fire. The Bydo, a biological weapon abandoned in space, has evolved into an empire bent on our destruction. With a simple order to "strike off and defeat" the threat, your job is to pilot two units: the R-9 Arrowhead, a curvaceous space fighter, and the Force, a chunk of Bydo flesh encased inside

a loyal sphere. Detachable, indestructible, and matched to the player's up/down movements, this iconic specimen is the center of the entire series. In fact, it's so important that later levels leap in difficulty if you die, leaving you to claw back your arsenal despite waves of enemies and obstacles. Some of the formations are deceptively intricate, others frighteningly so, while most favor a single route and plenty of trial and error. Weather the storm, though, and the rewards are everywhere. Form and function combine beautifully in *R-Type,* whether in the deadly hypnotic tail of the Dobkeratops, or a third stage focused entirely on the dodging and dissection of a Bydo battleship.

R-Type also features one of the video game genre's greatest soundtracks, full of percussive effects and chiptune anthems. But its genius lies in its use of screen space and resources, the parallax-scrolling backdrops, choreographed sprites, and bouncing neon lasers giving every pixel a chance to shine. In a gaming version of the Louvre, it'd be first upon the wall. **DH**

Gemini Wing

Original release date : 1987
Platform : Arcade
Developer : Tecmo
Genre : Shoot 'Em Up

When was the last time you approached a waterfall and were confronted by a giant, green, mutated walrus that proceeded to spit what looks like pulsating Maltesers at you? It's the sort of encounter that only belongs in video games, and it feels quite at home in *Gemini Wing*, one of the most distinctive and vividly realized shoot 'em ups of the mid- to late-1980s arcade scene.

A title that could be described as a "cooperative shooter," *Gemini Wing* allows two players to pilot their slightly portly-looking planes through a series of vertical-scrolling levels filled with strange creatures. Your enemies appear in forms that bring to mind elements from the natural world, such as woodlice, trilobites, and even the egg shells of skate fish (but in color schemes that give them a distinctly alien appearance).

Unusual for a game of its mechanical styling, *Gemini Wing* offers only one type of primary armament, but it goes some way toward compensating with its approach to dealing with secondary attacks. You collect one-use attacks from the playfield by maneuvering over them, causing them to chain behind your craft. Use one up and the next one moves into position. Stacking up a chain of significant length is an empowering sensation, and it's quite a wrench when you take a hit and see your precious baubles disperse in all directions—especially when your supposed comrade quickly moves in to suck them up.

Today, for raw action thrills *Gemini Wing* doesn't stack up so well against the superfast delights of, say, *Geometry Wars*, but then *that* doesn't have a weapon that works like some kind of windscreen wiper constructed of fire, nor a giant blue airship whose rear section spews forth a spinning skull with three eye sockets. If only all games had such personality. **TB**

1943

Original release date : 1987
Platform : Arcade
Developer : Capcom
Genre : Shoot 'Em Up

The year that the war ground on may have been 1943, when rationing continued to bite down hard, construction work on the Pentagon was completed, and the Japanese forces were driven back from Guadalcanal, but it's a whole lot more enjoyable if you think of it as this snappy little vertical-scrolling blaster from Capcom, released for the delight of the arcade-going public in 1987.

The sequel to Capcom's cracking *1942*, *1943* is set in the Pacific as the player fights off waves of oncoming enemies to take the battle to the heart of the Japanese fleet. Once again, victory depends on mastery of standard and special attacks, as you take down spinning, cycling, warping, and flipping waves of oncoming aircraft and ground troops, fighting elaborate boss battles and collecting brilliant power-ups. The health system has been modified somewhat, but the game remains as challenging as ever, and overall success is still as unlikely. (Although the introduction of two-player cooperative action evens out the odds a little, especially during the larger boss confrontations.) Like its predecessor, *1943* is now considered one of the kings of the one-credit play-through challenge, popular among a particularly hardcore group of the game's enthusiasts.

Having created the arcade iteration, Capcom handled a home version for the NES, but a vast and unwieldy range of ports across different platforms range wildly in terms of quality and degrees of fidelity. Faced with such a compromised muddle, if you're itching to restage the Battle of Midway in entirely unrealistic terms today, you'll probably want to hunt down the mighty *Capcom Classics Collection*—a generous PS2 and Xbox compilation—which features this game, along with many other greats, and has some rather delightful menus to boot. **CD**

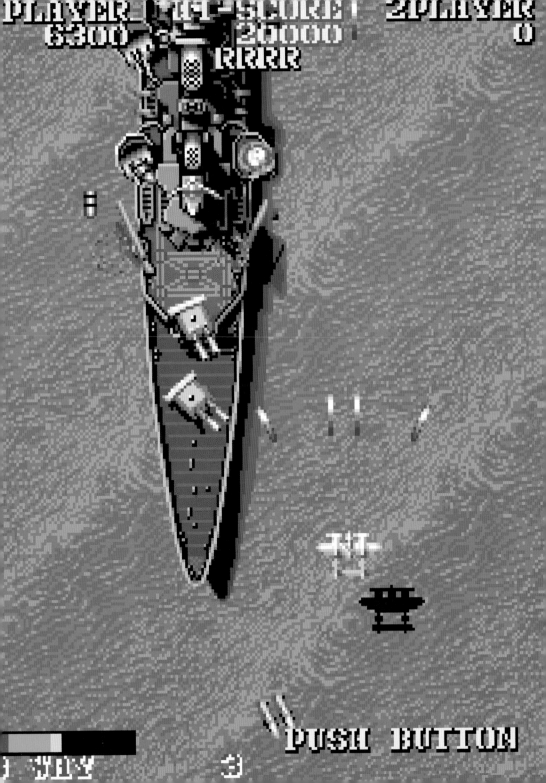

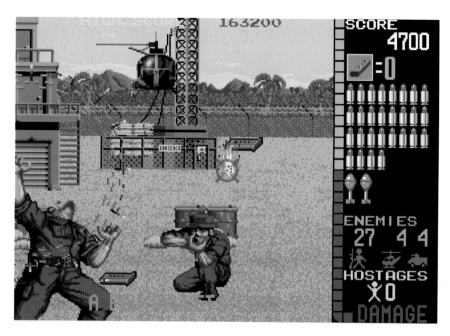

Operation Wolf

Original release date : 1987

Platform : Arcade

Developer : Taito

Genre : Shoot 'Em Up

To clear up a common misconception, *Operation Wolf* is not a light-gun game. A gun game, yes, but not one with any real connection between the barrel and the screen. It's the mount on the cabinet that does the work, using the gun's spatial positioning to determine the path of the crosshair. The two get mistaken because *(a)* no one honestly cares how a gun game works so long as it shoots where it's supposed to, and *(b) Operation Wolf* feels so damn right when you're anchored to the machine.

The first of four games in the series, *Operation Wolf* bears the closest resemblance to the god of 1980s action, *Rambo: First Blood Part II*. Tempting as it is to say you shoot guys, lots of guys, there's a tiny bit more to it than that. Following your attempt to free hostages from a South American POW camp, it scrolls sideways through six environments as countless goons assault the screen, coming at you with knives, helicopters, rockets, and rifles. Along with a handy grenade button on the controller, however, you have plenty of support items to level the odds. Well, almost . . . The instructions tell you: "Main items—magazine, mortar rocket, and power drink—appear by hitting coconuts, condors, chickens, etc." Needless to say, the "etc." tends to be those nasty armed foreign chaps.

With a fierce recoil action on the gun controller itself, the novelty of *Operation Wolf* in 1987 was huge. Add the bonus of big, detailed, fast-moving sprites, and you have a game that consoles and home computers simply couldn't copy, even if just about all of them tried.

(Incidentally, if you thought that blowing away ill-defined bad guys was a strictly 1980s phenomenon, you might want to check out 2008's *Rambo* coin-op, with its "computer graphics and real movie pictures.") **DH**

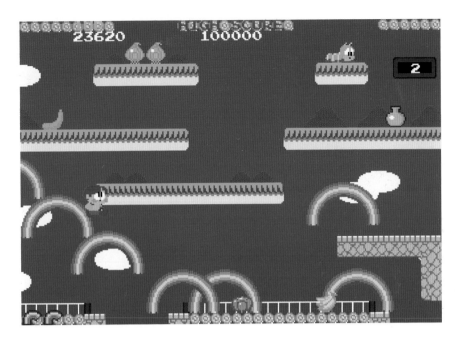

Rainbow Islands

Original release date : 1987
Platform : Various
Developer : Taito
Genre : Platform

Following the success of the brilliant *Bubble Bobble*, Taito's Fukio Mitsuji produced an even finer sequel. *Rainbow Islands* is one of those games that has helped define what people think of when they picture vintage platform games: blue skies, bright colors, elaborate bosses, and cute animals. This was jumping and running at its best, and it's as much fun to play today as it was back when it was released.

Game play takes place on a series of islands, each of which is sinking rather swiftly into the sea. This is vertical platforming taken to extremes, and there are a few neat twists thrown in, besides the direction of the scrolling. Much of the fun revolves around the player's ability to generate the titular rainbows, solid platforms of color that

can then be used either to access hard-to-reach spots or triggered to fall on enemies. Besides that, the game's ten islands—three of them are hidden and don't appear until you have completed the first seven—are riddled with secrets and power-ups, meaning that while the waters may be constantly rising beneath you, you're constantly being tempted to investigate strange areas and pull off elaborate platforming stunts to reach anything that looks even remotely promising.

Bright and goofy, such was the success of *Rainbow Islands* that a number of further *Bubble Bobble* arcade games appeared in the 1990s, such as *Bubble Symphony* and *Bubble Memories*. Taito also ended up porting it to just about any format on which it might run, and continues to squeeze the last drops out of the license to this day, with DS sequels that mess around with the basic concepts. If you're after the original, however, it's probably best to sit back and hope that it turns up on the Nintendo Wii's Virtual Console at some point. **CD**

Shinobi

Original release date : 1987
Platform : Arcade
Developer : Sega
Genre : Action

On the surface, *Shinobi* looks like just another example of the video game industry doing what it does so frequently—repackaging proven formulas; in this case, wrapping up Namco's *Rolling Thunder* in ninja outfits, replacing the bullets with shuriken. Scrape beneath the veneer, however, and what emerges is one of the finest action games of the mid-1980s arcade scene.

As Joe Musashi, you're out to rescue kidnapped children from the sinister Zeed organization. The game takes place over five areas of side-scrolling action, each broken down into individual levels and rounded off with show-stopping boss encounters. What makes *Shinobi* better than other similarly themed games of the era—*Ninja Spirit* and *Ninja Gaiden*, for example—is the variety of its enemies and environments, and its play mechanics, which are as sharp as one of Mushashi's throwing stars.

You set out in cold fear of getting anywhere near your adversary, relying on launching projectiles and hiding behind crates. But slowly, as you begin to learn their techniques and movements, your confidence grows, and you begin to get up into their faces and unleash killing blows at close quarters. Over time, the assassin's garb comes to fit you more comfortably.

Crucial for an arcade game, *Shinobi* has great over-the-shoulder appeal, never more so than when you let loose ninja magic, creating a kind of smart bomb that eliminates nearby threats while filling the screen with dizzying visual effects. Strictly rationed, the temptation is to save such attacks for boss encounters, but a true Shinobi master will make no use of them at all, preferring instead to let the traditional tools of the trade do the talking. It's that kind of game, all about showing what you can do, and therefore a natural fit for the proving grounds of the arcade. **TB**

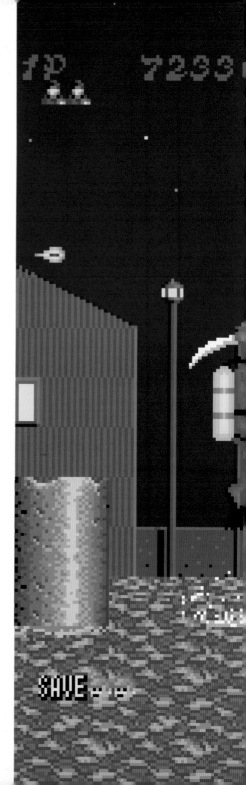

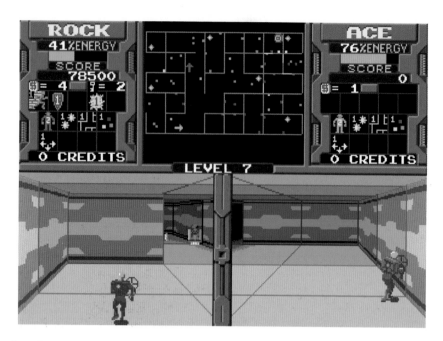

Xybots

Original release date : 1987

Platform : Arcade

Developer : Atari Games

Genre : Action

The grandfather of all modern third-person shooters, the sci-fi-themed *Xybots* offers three-dimensional mazes for one or two players to explore, with an unusual control scheme that, in its arcade setting, features joysticks that can be twisted left and right to direct the player's viewpoint.

Thanks to its unusual interface, *Xybots*'s play isn't as flowing as contemporary third-person shooter gamers would expect, with the game trading on the fear its clunky controls would engender. Designed by Ed Logg, the legendary designer behind the *Gauntlet* franchise, *Xybots* was originally intended as a *Gauntlet* title, and it retains many of the aspects for which the fantasy series is known, from confusing mazes with keys and hidden paths to the stress of a health bar that is constantly being depleted. As in *Gauntlet*, this—combined with unorthodox controls—creates a game where speed and decisiveness are all important, and one that is best played cooperatively, so that two adventurers can watch each other's backs. Of course, with two players taking part, the valuable coins strewn across the maps can become flashpoints for disagreements, as can the big bonus awarded for being the first to exit the level.

Maybe too advanced in design for its time, *Xybots* suffers from a cluttered layout in which each play window takes up only a quarter of the screen (the rest given over to the map and player information). This feels especially limiting when only one player is taking part. There's also a harsh requirement on skill that can feel like a cheap attempt to get more of your money. But when played with two, this is a much-refined take on the *Gauntlet* design that heralded the joy of co-op shooters such as *Gears of War* long before three dimensions became a standard. **MKu**

Sid Meier's Pirates!

Original release date : 1987

Platform : Various

Developer : Microprose Software

Genre : Action / Adventure

Billed as an "action adventure simulation" *Sid Meier's Pirates!* has everything from sea battles and swordfights to trading and treasure hunting. Along the way, the player's character, who starts life as a lowly privateer, must buy a ship, build a crew, and set out to make a fortune on the open sea. As the character ages, retirement looms—the open-ended goal is just to earn as much money and as many titles and honors as possible before dropping anchor for the final time.

For a game of its era, the sheer variety of activities is dazzling. One moment the player is controlling a small sloop following the winds around the Caribbean islands, the next minute the action moves onboard a rival ship, for a two-dimensional beat 'em up-style sword fight with its

captain. As with all Sid Meier titles, the setting is copiously researched and packed with historical detail. Players can select from six periods, beginning in 1560, with the Spanish in full control of the region, and culminating in 1660, with the Dutch, English, and French in ascendance. Each features different ships, based closely on craft of the time, and all present different challenges to the player.

Importantly, the game includes several elements that would later provide the foundations of Meier's magnum opus, *Civilization*. Notably, the game world is effectively randomized at the start of every session, ensuring that players must always spend time exploring the geographic, economic, and political natures of their new environment. Furthermore, the four nations represented in the game are—like the tribes of *Civilization*—in a constant state of diplomatic flux, shifting from peaceful relations to war and back again in an unending political dance. But *Sid Meier's Pirates!* is a key Meier title in its own right; absorbing, varied, and historically fascinating. **KS**

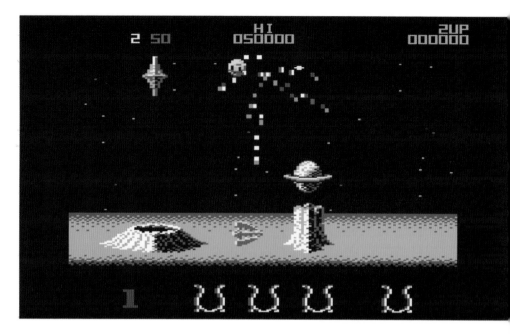

Wizball

Original release date : 1987
Platform : Various
Developer : Sensible Software
Genre : Shoot 'Em Up

Wizball has one of gaming history's least promising introductions, throwing you into a world where you appear to be a bouncing anthropomorphic cabbage (the titular Wizball) whose only controls are rotation and fire. Your only way to get around seems to be to change the angle of your bounce by your rate of spin—and that's maddeningly hard. Even with static adversaries in place at the start, it's still horribly easy to spin too fast and smash into the enemy, wasting one of your three lives. A little practice, and you'll soon be good enough to get those first two vital power-ups that enable you to actually control your ball properly, which makes it easier to get the Catellite power-up you need to actually play the game. It's a trial by

fire, but at least it ensures that you have a feel for the game before you get properly into it.

Once you're past that first hump, however, *Wizball* reveals its purpose and shows itself as a unique piece of gaming. Your task is to restore color to a number of monochrome worlds by combining the forces of Wizball and Catellite. You hunt down herds of colored blobs, shoot them, and then send out the Catellite to capture their released sploshes of color. Each world, however, only features one blob of color, so you need to travel around to gather other hues that can then be mixed up in the right quantities to create the color you need. That's all well and good, but your task is plagued by waves of more typical shoot 'em up bad guys. And they can ruin everything for you with a single shot.

It's hellishly tough, the stuff of smashed joysticks, but it's easy to forgive *Wizball* because it's such a neat concept, beautifully presented. It tests your patience and skills to the very limit, and rewards you in abundance. **JM**

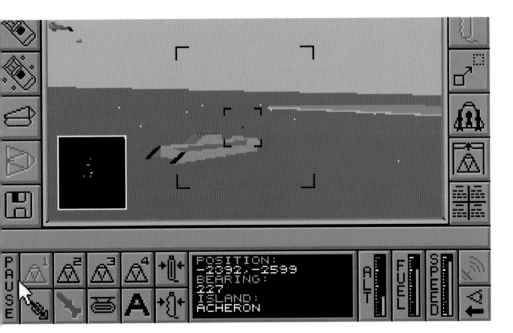

Carrier Command

Original release date : 1988
Platform : Amiga, ST
Developer : Realtime Games
Genre : Strategy

A vanguard of both three-dimensional graphics and real-time strategy, *Carrier Command* is a lasting highlight of the 16-bit era, a time when genres were as fluid as the sea.

The year is 2166, and nuclear weapons tests have created an island chain full of untapped energy. Hailing this "economically miraculous discovery," scientists build two robotic aircraft carriers to deploy command centers on the islands, using fleets of land, sea, and air vehicles to defend them, if necessary. The scenario no one predicts: that they'll be defending them against one another.

The technically superior ACC Omega has fallen into the hands of STANZA, a terrorist organization, its software hacked in order to conquer the archipelago. With neither

time to pay the ransom nor a viable nuclear option, the good guys order the ACC Epsilon to take its own territory, turning the area into a warzone. Facing a technologically superior enemy, success in *Carrier Command* means more than just a direct confrontation, so at your disposal you have a number of amphibious Walrus vehicles and Manta planes that can be deployed against the enemy.

Carrier Command was revolutionary in 1988, stressing the unique values of units and territories in real-time against a relentless AI opponent. With an interface well up to the task, controlling not just the field units but the Epsilon's weapons and repair system, it gave direct control over all its three-dimensional vehicles. Its most delectable feature, though, besides the topical premise, remains the ominous presence of a genuinely superior foe, stalking the game without handicap or respect for the lazy or impetuous. And, as ever, victory over a more powerful enemy always tastes sweeter. When it comes to the speed chess of the RTS, *Carrier Command* is a grand master. **DH**

Forgotten Worlds

Original release date : 1988
Platform : Arcade
Developer : Capcom
Genre : Shoot 'Em Up

You could say that "forgotten world" pretty accurately sums up the scrolling shoot 'em up genre, where so much effort has gone into such unfashionable areas as spaceships and science. *Forgotten Worlds*, though, is fondly remembered for bucking that trend at almost every opportunity, thus dooming itself to be a whimsical one-hit wonder. Taking a handful of ideas from 1985 shooter *Section Z*, it rapidly became known as "the one with bosses as big as the screen"; an empire built on sand if ever there was one. But when it's designed by the artists at Capcom, it's a gimmick that you'd rightly line up to see.

As much a flagship for the newly released CPS arcade board, the game ditches the spaceships of other games, instead having its heroes fly unaided, buoyed only by their obscene muscles, daft haircuts, and giant shoulder pads. These Nameless Ones face a wild array of enemies and environments, from Egyptian gods and temples to a dragon reclining in the sea. Unhindered by cockpits or reality, the Ones can, in the arcade version, fire using an eight-way joystick.

Much was made of the eight bosses, such as the mighty War God—"even BIGGER than the screen!" went the ads. Yet they are the easiest parts of the game to master. Exploitable and artificial, they're about as animated as the average theme park dinosaur. But they do award Zenny points for a quick win, and these come in very handy at the game's most significant novelty: a shop. It's here, courtesy of an oddly out-of-context female shopkeeper, that your skill is rewarded with a colorful selection of new weapons, peaking early on with the all-powerful napalm launcher. Quickly adopted by numerous shoot 'em ups on computer and console, this is the game's real legacy. **DH**

Ghouls 'n Ghosts

Original release date : 1988
Platform : Arcade
Developer : Capcom
Genre : Platform

How do you follow up something like *Ghosts 'n Goblins*, a hit arcade platformer from 1985 most notable for its monstrous difficulty? If you're Capcom's Tokuro Fujiwara, the answer's obvious: You wait a couple of years and remake it—bigger, better, and more difficult than ever.

The familiar opening level suggests straight away that you can expect more of the same. Like its predecessor, *Ghouls 'n Ghosts* never ever tires of finding new ways of killing you. It gives you that one armor-shedding chance before you're stripped to your boxers; one slip, one mistimed jump, one glance in the wrong direction when there's something erupting directly beneath you, and it's instant skeletal death.

It gleefully presents you with treasure chests that *might* contain special treats, but it's more likely to be a spectral magician who'll turn you into a duck or a wizened old man if you don't kill him quickly enough. It teases you over and over again, letting you *nearly* reach the end of a stage before idly swatting you from existence. It rewards you with new weapons and a special suit of gold armor that equips you with a charge shot, and then it slaps you straight back down again. And should you have the sheer dogged dedication necessary to reach the end, *Ghouls 'n Ghosts* has one final insult for you: It sends you right back to the beginning to find the ultimate weapon needed to even qualify for the final battle.

A gothic pantomime of cruelty, it's built to separate the men from the boys—and then mock them both, anyway. It demands perseverance and excellence; otherwise, it'll kill you over and over again, leading you to question your own gaming abilities. But think how sweet that victory will be should you reach the very end. **JM**

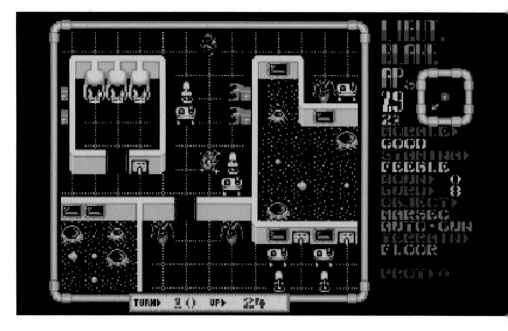

Laser Squad

Original release date : 1988
Platform : Various
Developer : Mythos Games
Genre : Strategy

The first installment in Julian Gollop's *Laser Squad* series came hot on the heels of the *Rebelstar* titles, appearing in the same year as the *Aliens*-inspired *Rebelstar II*. As a result, *Laser Squad* is visually quite similar to the designer's previous titles, expanding upon the concepts laid down by the original *Rebelstar* by adding three scenarios, each with its own difficulty levels and squad selections. A further four were available if you bought the expansion packs that were available by mail order.

As in *Rebelstar*, play is turn based and supports one or two players, with the use of an "action-point" system, allowing players to carefully allocate their characters' behavior across a turn via options such as moving, turning,

and shooting. Characters could also make use of cover, pick up items, and fire on their opponent during their turn.

While in retrospect *Laser Squad* suffers for its similarity to *Rebelstar*, gamers in 1988 saw it as further refinement to a great design. Ported at the time from the ZX Spectrum to a vast array of home computers—including the Amiga, Atari ST, Amstrad CPC—and in 1992 as an updated version for the PC, *Laser Squad* brought Gollop's action-point system to more gamers than ever before. Though the graphics remain starkly functional, the easy-to-use interface makes it feel more like an action title than a war game, meaning the tactical nuances of the title—carefully managing your action points to protect your squad while still driving toward your objective—could be picked up by osmosis rather than by reading the manual.

Laser Squad's highly playable range of missions represented the peak of the genre until *UFO: Enemy Unknown* five years later, and even today they offer up an addictive challenge. **MKu**

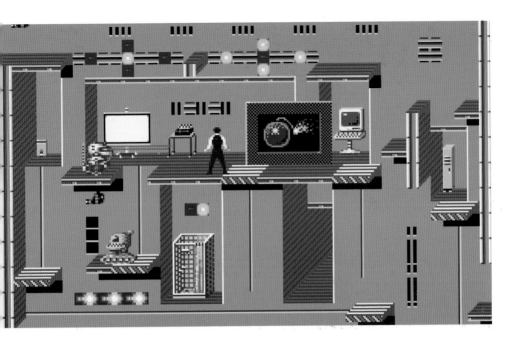

Impossible Mission II

Original release date : 1988
Platform : Various
Developer : Novotrade
Genre : Action

Programmed not by the original game's creator, Dennis Caswell, but by Hungarian code shop Novotrade (which would later create the *Ecco the Dolphin* titles), *Impossible Mission II* tinkers very little with the formula that ensured its predecessor's success.

Once again evil genius Elvin Atombender wants to destroy the world, and once again the athletic Agent 4125 is dispatched to stop him, a task that involves searching the objects in every room of Atombender's lair while avoiding the robotic home help. This time, however, the base is much larger, organized into a series of eight towers: The player must locate portions of a numerical code in each building before gaining access to the next; at the same time there's a musical sequence to collect and assemble to unlock the culminative control center. Additionally, rooms now contain an array of robots alongside the familiar security guards, including the clawed bot, which attempts to push the agent from platforms, and the "pestbots," which ride the lifts in each room, stalling the player's progress. The greater threat is balanced out, though, in the form of collectable bombs (which can also blow holes in the floor) and motion-sensitive mines. As with the original, a timer runs throughout the game, so success relies on quickly ascertaining the correct route through each room to search all possible items.

While providing a more significant—and graphically varied—challenge, *Impossible Mission II* lacked the sheer impact of its famous predecessor. The character animation was no longer revolutionary, and the memorable speech synthesis mostly gone—although the original's famous scream does make a startling return at the obtuse and rather abrupt finale. **KS**

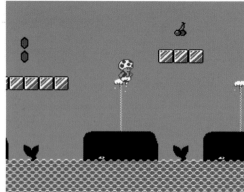

Power Drift

Super Mario Bros. 2

Original release date : 1988
Platform : Arcade
Developer : Sega-AM2
Genre : Driving

Original release date : 1988
Platform : NES
Developer : Nintendo
Genre : Platform

Power Drift was an attempt by Sega to create a cabinet as fast as the game inside it. At only minor risk of rectal injury or returning your lunch, players would be shunted in violent sync with the visuals of Sega's Y-Board hardware, which used advanced sprite scaling to create a sense of speed. And yet *Power Drift* is one of the less-remembered moments in the career of industry legend Yu Suzuki.

It deserves better. With all the motion-blurred trickery and heft of modern racing games, it's easy to forget just how fast and smooth *Power Drift* is. Running at an uncommon sixty frames per second, with cars that handle like they're driving on butter, it's a case of catching up with the action first and only then worrying about the race. (It also featured another of Sega's classic soundtracks, each game circuit having its own theme tune.)

Notoriously hard to emulate, *Power Drift* only properly arrived in homes with the near-perfect Dreamcast port. Part of the highly recommended *Yu Suzuki Game Works* collection, it's the only official release to capture both the frame-rate and full-screen tilt effect while cornering. **DH**

This is a bit confusing: *Super Mario Bros. 2* isn't really *Super Mario Bros. 2*. The *real* sequel to Mario's first side-scrolling adventure was deemed too difficult for audiences outside of Japan, and only appeared years later, as *The Lost Levels*. The Western *Super Mario Bros. 2* is actually a re-skinned version of the quirky Japanese platformer *Doki Doki Panic*.

And it shows: In the course of this beautifully drawn adventure, Mario rides magic carpets and fights a range of creatures who seem somewhat removed from the Koopas and Goombas of the Mushroom Kingdom. Gone, too, is Mario's ground-pounding attack, replaced with a system that sees him pulling vegetables out of the earth and hefting them at his enemies. It's an incredible journey, and one that can also be played as Luigi, Toad, and Princess Peach, each having their own special gimmicks.

Super Mario Bros. 2 might feel a bit unlikely as a *Super Mario* game, even if you didn't know its tortured history, but it remains a marvelous adventure, one that introduced its own cherished characters and mechanics into the established world of the Mushroom Kingdom. **CD**

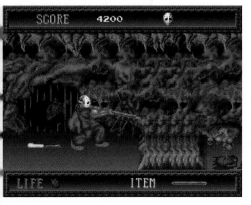

Splatterhouse

Original release date : 1988
Platform : Arcade
Developer : Namco
Genre : Fighting

Capturing all of the idiotic gore and nonsensical plotlines of the finest 1980s slasher flicks, *Splatterhouse* is the video game equivalent of renting *Friday the 13th Part VI*: tawdry, gruesome, but worryingly compelling.

Rick and Jennifer are two students who find themselves in the remote mansion of mad Dr. West. Jennifer vanishes; Rick awakes in a dungeon wearing a mask that gives him extraordinary physical powers. Rick must rescue his girl by exploring the house and grounds, kicking, punching, and slashing all and sundry. The horror styling is applied with exuberant Grand Guignol excess: rotting bodies hang from walls, vomiting gore; flaccid skeletons slouch, impaled on spears; hideous mutants crawl across the screen . . . And you can always pick up a meat cleaver to decapitate troublesome incoming zombies.

Like its movie inspirations, *Splatterhouse* was subject to moral hand-wringing when it transferred to the home entertainment market, and some elements were censored. But the plot retains its shocking sting in the tail, and, even watered down, it remains a horror favorite. **KS**

NARC

Original release date : 1988
Platform : Arcade
Developer : Midway
Genre : Shoot 'Em Up

With *Robotron 2084*, designer Eugene Jarvis created the twin-stick shooter, a subgenre of the action game that continues to be popular. Equally violent and fast-paced, *NARC* tapped into the start of another craze: the war on drugs that had begun to fascinate Reagan's America.

Ostensibly a simple side-scrolling shooter, in this game cool cops Max Force and Hit Man fought through varied ranks of street scum to take down drug lord Mr. Big. The game play was simple, but *NARC* looked unlike anything else at the time: a glossy urban shooter that reached unprecedented levels of violent realism.

It now seems rather charming, the game play's sheer delight in righteous slaughter giving the whole experience a pleasantly humorous kick. And it features a memorable final boss, as you whittle Mr. Big down to his skeleton before shooting out individual vertebrae.

NARC may have lost its power to dazzle, but it remains a brilliant example of 1980s arcade exuberance. If you want to play it now, avoid the loathsome 2005 PS2 and Xbox ports—these have little of the original's wit or aplomb. **CD**

Zak McKracken and the Alien Mindbenders

Original release date : 1988
Platform : Various
Developer : LucasArts
Genre : Adventure

Zak McKracken isn't the wittiest or most atmospheric of the early LucasArts point-and-click adventure games, but it's certainly the most ambitious. Indeed, it's no less than a globe-trotting new age mystery that takes its hero everywhere, from the streets of San Francisco to the temples of the old Mayan stomping grounds in Central America, and on to the shifting dunes of Mars.

A tabloid journalist whose regular gigs include choice assignments, such as interviewing three-headed squirrels and covering UFO sightings, Zak is an appealingly ordinary man. Togged out in his conventional 1980s regular-guy uniform—thin tie and tight slacks—he lives in a grubby apartment, has to remember to undertake the simplest domestic chores (like paying the phone bill and washing the dishes), and even has to keep track of his own finances while he jets about the game's world. That may not sound like much fun, but money equals freedom in the *Zak McKracken* universe, and if your cash card ever runs too low, the game has some uniquely entertaining ways of topping it up again—with a lottery win cobbled together by the most unlikely of sources.

Zak McKracken pulls together all manner of new age mysteries and conspiracy theories to create an exciting plot that omits almost nothing: the face of Mars gets a thorough exploration, as do African shamen and the Bermuda Triangle. An excellent game in its own right, while Zak never got a legitimate sequel, a cluster of fan projects have popped up over the years. Although the tabloid hack will never be quite as popular as Guybrush Threepwood and his pirate friends or *The Day of the Tentacle* geeks, Zak has a unique following all of his own. Mostly in Germany, as it happens. How curious. **CD**

The New Zealand Story

Original release date : 1988
Platform : Various
Developer : Taito
Genre : Platform

The arcade may have been a hotbed of innovation in the shoot 'em up and beat 'em up categories across its history, but it hasn't offered too much to fans of scrolling platform titles since the arrival in 1985 of *Super Mario Bros*.

This makes it unsurprising that *The New Zealand Story*, a cutesy platformer created by Taito in 1988 (following the success of single-screen platformers such as *Bubble Bobble*), would find most of its success in the form of home conversions. And yet the title is something of a wolf in sheep's clothing. Despite the generally held belief that it's simply a straightforward scrolling platformer, from the very first level *The New Zealand Story* proves to be something much stranger indeed.

Starring a small kiwi bird that has to rescue his kiwi pals, the game features floating enemies that spawn randomly across the screen, complex mazes of platforms and spikes that require pixel-perfect jumps (unless you steal floating enemy vehicles), and the ability to constantly shoot projectiles. It feels like a combination of an extremely hardcore shooter and an occasionally clumsy platformer, and the unusual design extends to parts of the game where death can transport you to levels set in heaven and an ice-encased boss who has to be killed from within his own gut after he's swallowed you up.

Almost anarchically strange—the kiwis are wearing sneakers, and one is seen puffing on a sly cigarette during the intro—*The New Zealand Story* gives the impression of a game developer messing about to see what would happen, but who somehow ends up with a superbly playable and challenging title. It's an unusually distinctive arcade game that shouldn't be overlooked in favor of Taito's better-known works. **MKu**

Exile

Original release date : 1988
Platform : Various
Developer : Peter Irvin, Jeremy Smith
Genre : Action / Adventure

Exile is a title that can be compared to Nintendo's *Metroid* series, as it presents the player with a system of alien caverns populated by unusual life forms to be explored through puzzle solving and combat. However, it's not quite that simple. While the *Metroid* games feature the gradual unlocking of new powers through the discovery of upgrades, carefully pacing and ordering the experience, *Exile* instead presents players with the full range of their abilities at the very beginning of the game.

Rather than create an ordered experience, *Exile* is a simulation disguised as a two-dimensional action-adventure. The world has its own consistent physics, requiring players to carefully navigate their surroundings using a jetpack that accurately struggles against gravity, wind, and its own inertia. Objects are just as physical, too: in one challenge you're required to put out a fire with a glass of water, but how to keep water in a glass when you're careening around on a jetpack?

As a simulation—and one that heavily taxed the powers of early home-computing hardware—*Exile* doesn't explain anything, expecting Newton's laws to speak for themselves through play. Though this means the game takes hours of work on the player's part to get to grips with, there is no significant penalty for reckless exploration and spontaneous experimentation; any deaths simply result in the game's protagonist being warped back to the last spot designated as a teleport location.

Though ported multiple times—with the definitive iteration considered to be the 1991 Amiga version, even over the graphically superior 1995 CD32 version—*Exile* is a title that deserves to have a spawned a legacy of action adventure titles in its wake, yet none materialized. Perhaps it was already simply too perfect. **MKu**

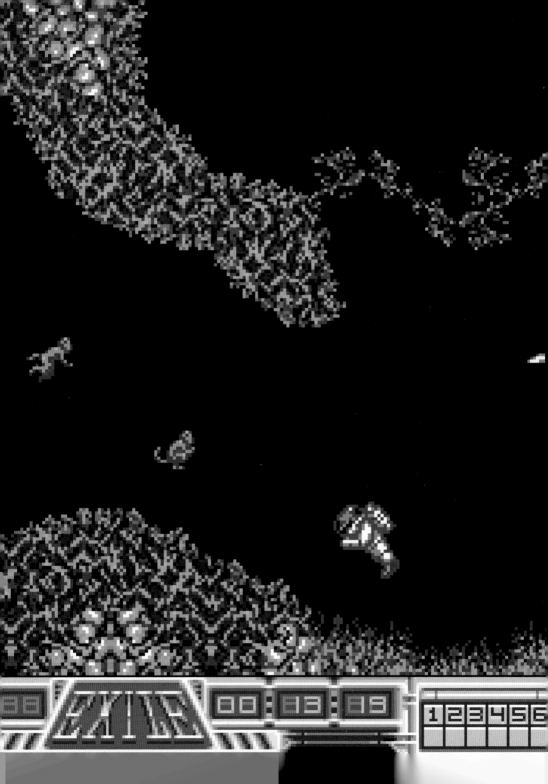

Fantasy World Dizzy

Original release date : 1989
Platform : Various
Developer : Andrew Oliver, Philip Oliver
Genre : Action / Adventure

The eponymous egg-shaped hero of the *Dizzy* series was, like Nintendo's Mario, a product of technical limitations. Developers Philip and Andrew Oliver wanted to create a character with which players could empathize, and that meant drawing one with big, recognizable facial features. But due to the sprite limitations of 8-bit home computers, this called for a model based *entirely* around the face—hence, an egg with arms and legs. As for animation, it was easier to make him somersault in the air rather than leap—hence the name Dizzy. A star was born.

By the time publisher Codemasters released *Fantasy World Dizzy*, the series was already a major success. Here we find Dizzy captured by an evil wizard and slung into a dungeon. He must escape if he is to rescue girlfriend Daisy from the sorcerer's tower. For this installment, finding and using objects is the focus of the game play, hence the design of the more robust inventory screen, which would remain intact for the rest of the series.

The Oliver twins, through their clever use of proprietary graphics techniques, were able to tease comparatively rich and detailed environments out of formats such as Sinclair's ZX Spectrum—everything from dank castles to leafy tree villages. At the same time, the daft text conversations with other characters, not to mention some bizarre design touches, continued the Pythonesque tradition of many British games of the 1980s. At one point Dizzy falls down a well and ends up in an upside-down version of the world; in another section he's able to pick up and use a hole—an allusion to the film *Yellow Submarine*.

This is Philip Oliver's favorite *Dizzy* title and, bursting with ideas and exhibiting a mastery of 8-bit hardware, its popularity extends far into the gaming world. **KS**

North & South

Original release date : 1989
Platform : Various
Developer : Infogrames
Genre : Action / Strategy

The American Civil War was surely not the most pleasant of wars. Wedged uncomfortably close to the nasty delights of industrialization, it was a muddle of shelling and gunpowder, in which people got their faces burned off, or were accidentally run through by their own side's sabers; it was a conflict in which troops were regularly trampled under horses, and that nice Kevin Costner almost had his leg lopped off and went to live with the Native Americans.

North & South tells a slightly cheerier story. A mixture of cold strategy and fast-paced battles, Infogrames's classic is based on a Belgian comic called *Les Tuniques Bleus*. This means that verisimilitude was never going to be *that* high on the agenda. That said, beyond the chummy cartoon faces and quirky animated asides (you can tickle the photographer on the main menu screen by goosing him with your mouse pointer), it's still a smart tactical challenge all the same.

North & South operates in two modes. There's the overworld view, in which you move troops around a map of the United States, staking out territory and pincering your enemy. There's also a battle mode that allows you to race through stripped-down skirmishes more personally, pushing around a range of infantry, cavalry, and cannons.

The story moves at a pace while excellent audio and visual presentation give the whole thing a sheen of polish missing from many other games of the era. The ending sequence, in which weary troops march home, the war over, set new standards for animation at the time of its release. Taken as a whole, North & South, while not particularly deep, makes for a pleasant arcade strategy experience even today—if you can track down an original and coax it back to life, that is. **CD**

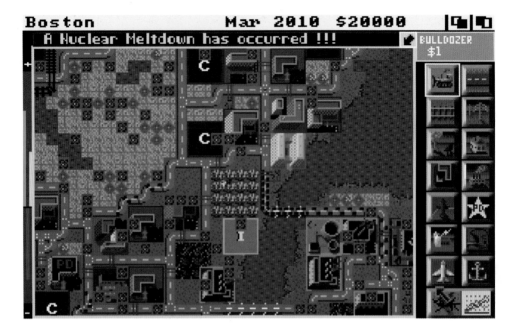

SimCity

Original release date : 1989
Platform : Various
Developer : Maxis
Genre : Strategy

Not yet a legend, Will Wright, was working on the environments for *Raid on Bungeling Bay*—Brøderbund's simple war zone shoot 'em up for the Commodore 64—when he had an epiphany: He realized that he was more interested in designing the cities than blowing them up. That urge led him to design a simulation program, where players could build and manage a city—*that* would be the game. At a party in 1987, Wright met producer Jeff Braun, who saw the potential in a game that, as he later told the *New Yorker*, would pull in "megalomaniacs who want to control the world." Braun and Wright founded development studio Maxis, and made millions from this simple "God game."

The most radical feature of the game is its most basic premise: You don't get to *win* at *SimCity*—but you'll derive constant satisfaction from playing it. The rules are clear and the results are immediate: build a useful road, and people will drive on it; draw a power line to your new industrial park, and the businesses will come. When things go wrong, it's usually easy to figure out why—and, of course, sometimes the player is the city's worst enemy. Taking a mature, finally tuned city and unleashing Godzilla on it is a rite of passage for many gamers. After all, you can learn as much from destroying something as from building it.

Maxis continues to ship sequels and expansions to the franchise, and *SimCity* paved the way for *The Sims*, by a wide margin the biggest seller in PC history. The latest editions of *SimCity* are so granular that they let you open espresso shops or tinker with universal healthcare. But newcomers should start with the original model: getting the fundamentals of a city right is still the most satisfying way to play God. **CDa**

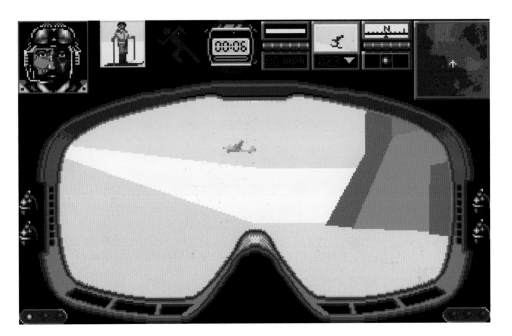

Midwinter

Original release date : 1989
Platform : Various
Developer : Maelstrom Games
Genre : Action / Role-Playing

Open-world titles might be in vogue today, but their roots go way back to games such as *Elite* and the legendary *Midwinter*. Mike Singleton's epic first-person role-playing game is remarkable. Set on a fictional island in the wake of a post-nuclear winter, the scale of the game is epic, covering hundreds of square miles. It also features thirty-two playable characters, all of whom have different skills and allegiances. Starting out alone on a snowmobile, the task for you as the player is to recruit all thirty-two into a network capable of preventing the tyrannical General Masters from taking control of the island of Midwinter.

The strategic breadth of the game is impressive by any standards, with a wide range of vehicles and weapons available. Sniper rifles, planes, skis, and bombs—there's a catalog of possible tools for your budding insurgency. The game itself, however, is low-key, and played in first-person through a set of snow goggles. It's a remarkably intimidating experience. And entirely unforgiving. You start out in the most dire situation: hunted, alone, and very likely to come to a sticky end. The chances are you would succumb to the treacherous environment, even if the enemy troops didn't get you. The game never really lifts from this moment-to-moment crisis management, even once you've begun to recruit your allies.

Everything about *Midwinter* is surprising, given its 1989 vintage. The eco-disaster plot; the human characters given to each of the agents; the cast of thousands that make up the rest of the island; the immense, fractally generated terrain—it is daunting, and inspiring. Few games have ever aimed this high, and fewer still have achieved such heights. "A modern *Midwinter*" is a phrase you hear regularly on the lips of wishful gamers. One day it will happen. **JR**

Minesweeper

Original release date : 1989
Platform : PC
Developer : Microsoft
Genre : Puzzle

Minesweeper is the video game that adults who have day jobs and responsibilities and families and mortgages and who really don't care for video games in the first place are likely to find horribly addictive. It's a classic Windows "Easter egg" that gives the player a simple task: to clear a small gray grid of a series of mines, deducing their various locations by reverse engineering the numbers written on adjoining squares.

If we're being totally honest, *Minesweeper* is not a particularly attractive game. Perhaps part of its appeal to nongamers is due to the fact that this potent little time waster looks a bit like a calendar or a calculator or some other legitimate productivity software. But it is nonetheless powerfully addictive: a gently taxing challenge with a near-instantaneous restart, meaning that you can be straight into your next game seconds before vowing to give up entirely and go to lunch.

Minesweeper is capable of providing enormous tension, each click of a square feeling as if you're clipping through a bomb detonation wire. But it's also kind of like doodling: something for your hands, and a peculiarly absent part of your mind, to do while you answer phone calls, browse spam e-mail, or print out those invoices for accounts. Furthermore, even though it's unlikely to win any awards for graphics, presentation, or plot, it's likely to keep you playing long after the most cinematic titles have started to gather dust in the cupboard.

A stalwart of every Windows operating system right through to Windows 7, whenever you turn on your computer, *Minesweeper* will be there, lying in wait for you; and whenever you prepare to shut the PC down for the night, you're never more than a tempting click away from a few more wasted hours. **CD**

Final Fight

Original release date : 1989
Platform : Arcade
Developer : Capcom
Genre : Fighting

History is full of decisions that may not have seemed momentous at the time but yet had untold ramifications. For example, Capcom electing to change the name of its side-scrolling beat 'em up from *Street Fighter '89* to *Final Fight* (after arcade operators argued that the game was quite unlike *Street Fighter*, which featured fixed locations and one-on-one battles) arguably opened the door for *Street Fighter II* to be developed—something that may never have otherwise happened.

Of course, that's not the only reason *Final Fight* is remarkable, because in its own way it revolutionized a genre. While the foundations of the side-scrolling beat 'em up were laid earlier in the 1980s, it was Capcom's decision to focus on simple controls (just two buttons: attack and jump) and concentrate on creating a title with dazzlingly large and detailed sprites that set *Final Fight* apart in the then-crowded arcade marketplace.

The plot sees Mike Haggar, ex-wrestler and now mayor of Metro City, on a quest to save his kidnapped daughter. Joined by her boyfriend, Cody, and his ninja buddy, Guy, we embark on one of the most celebrated—not to mention violent—two-player experiences in arcade history.

Make no mistake, *Final Fight* is simplistic in the extreme, and a progenitor of the defining design of many 1990s arcade games where skill isn't as important as your ability to put cash into the cabinet. However, with enough money on hand, it reveals itself as a slight but consistently entertaining video game version of the most popular action flicks of the time.

If you still question *Final Fight*'s importance, simply look at the dominance of the side-scrolling beat 'em up titles in Capcom's arcade output for the years that followed—all the way to *Battle Circuit* in 1997. **MKu**

Revenge of Shinobi

Original release date : 1989
Platform : Mega Drive
Developer : Sega
Genre : Action

The first outing for the *Shinobi* brand on the newly launched Sega Mega Drive platform following its popular appearance in arcades in 1987, *Revenge of Shinobi* wastes little time in slicing into the action.

You play ninja master Joe Musashi on a quest to save his kidnapped fiancée, Naoko, and exact revenge on Neo Zeed, the criminal conglomerate responsible. Its agents populate the game's eight environments liberally, only too keen to fall satisfyingly to your combat and shuriken-throwing skills, or witness, in awe, the devastating power of your ninjutsu magic.

The hour may be serious, but along the way you can't help but notice the graphical splendor as you run and somersault your way through the platform-based levels. An early example of 16-bit brilliance, the realization of the game's environments is both lovingly detailed and effortlessly distinct, beginning with a Japanese forest and progressing through memorable US-based locations before finally ending at Neo Zeed's marine stronghold.

Good as the visuals are, both for the hardware and the period, one element that has barely dated is the control mechanic. It's razor sharp, with Joe responding to every request in a consistently dependable manner while the apparent limitations of his offensive options—ninjutsu, attack, and jump—disappear without a trace upon play.

The action runs at a blood-pumping pace, with end-of-level bosses punctuating your progress in reassuringly predictable fashion. *Revenge of Shinobi* didn't revolutionize its genre—modern gamers will find little to surprise them here—but it does represent a finely honed example of its type, one that remains extremely capable in spite of two decades of breathtaking technological advancement. **JDS**

Herzog Zwei

Original release date : 1989
Platform : Mega Drive
Developer : TechnoSoft
Genre : Strategy

In 1989, before the emergence of *Command & Conquer*, *Warcraft*, or even *Dune II*, *Herzog Zwei* quietly invented a genre. Developed by Japanese shooter specialist TechnoSoft, the game arrived from nowhere, established the template for some of the most successful titles of the next decade, and then retreated back into the shadows. The obscure name didn't help the game's profile (it's a sequel to the equally inexplicably named MSX title, *Herzog*), but more than anything, it was authentically and counterproductively ahead of its time.

Herzog Zwei is remarkable for birthing real-time strategy almost fully formed. Red and blue armies battle for domination on scrolling maps filled with bases (three per side, including the all-important home base, and three neutral installations ripe for capture) by constructing and deploying a variety of fighting units. In contrast to later PC point-and-clickers, *Herzog Zwei* employs a central control unit to organize the battle, a transforming carrier jet for hauling regular units to their positions or back to base for repair, *and* it becomes a stand-up fighter robot on land.

At first glance this gives the game a deceptive action-blaster bent. The transformer re-spawns once destroyed, and it's tempting to rely on it as a central attacking force—something that no doubt confounded many players during *Herzog Zwei*'s poor initial reception. The groundbreaking truth of the game reveals itself slowly, a mix of strategy and resource management, in which players select not only units of differing costs and utilities but assign them tactical roles valued according to their complexities. Mix in variable terrain and a compelling split-screen two-player mode, and you have the silent inception of a gameplay revolution. **ND**

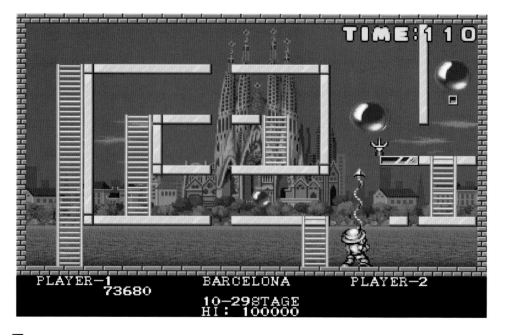

Pang

Original release date : 1989

Platform : Various

Developer : Mitchell

Genre : Shoot 'Em Up

Developed by Mitchell (better known as the developer of *Puzz Loop*), there's a strange quirk in *Pang*'s reputation as an essential video game. Its design is, in fact, identical to *Cannon Ball*, a 1983 Hudson Soft title for the Japanese MSX home computer format, right down to the distinctive twirling rope that follows the player's harpoon shot.

That means that *Pang*'s central conceit alone is not ultimately its distinction, though it remains remarkable that it is one of the few classic designs that has not been further aped. A combination of *Galaxian* and *Asteroids*—but featuring a pair of jolly, super-deformed heroes in safari suits, traveling across the world—play features a one-dimensional plane of movement (left and right across

the bottom of the screen) as you fire harpoons into the sky in an attempt to destroy falling balloons (seemingly of extraterrestrial origin) that are in the process of attacking famous world landmarks. To add a little spice into the mix, the balloons divide each time they are shot, one large balloon able to crowd the sky with eight smaller offshoots—each of which bounces lower and lower—if shots are not carefully timed and managed.

Pang's success is that it is as polished and accessible as an arcade game has any right to be. Featuring a bright, pleasant, and regularly interesting level design and play, in which failure is always the player's fault—often from simply trying to destroy too many balloons too quickly.

Pang really gets interesting when tackled in two-player mode. Like its spiritual predecessor *Bubble Bobble*, this is a game about working together—not just playing alone on the same screen—in order to succeed. It may well be inspired by an earlier title, but played with a friend, it comes into its own. **MKu**

Populous

Original release date : 1989
Platform : Various
Developer : Bullfrog Productions
Genre : Strategy

Populous, the ground-breaking sim that is *literally* about breaking ground, has a lot to say about God. It's not easy being God, apparently. You're hidebound by your followers, tied to their whims, and liable to run out of the juice you need to be truly godly if they get too heavily distracted or suddenly start dying. But it's also a lot of fun: lowering and raising the ground, shaping your minions' culture, and generally giving everybody a hard time.

If there had been "God games" before *Populous*, Bullfrog's offering made them all irrelevant. Reducing the Almighty's influence to a floating pointer hovering over the landscape, *Populous* was the perfect deity for the Windows generation: God as multitasker, middle-manager,

a being who monitors his manna levels and divides his holy wishes into discrete chunks. Much of the game suggested that a god's primary role was as a landscape gardener, in fact, who put considerable effort into smoothing out the peaks and valleys of his green and pleasant land to give his followers somewhere to build settlements.

It was a beautiful game for the time, too—real-time land deformation being an idea that has only recently come back into vogue as shooters like *Red Faction Guerrilla* and *Battlefield: Bad Company* look for something snappy to mark them out from the crowd. But the game's real legacy lies in the genre that grew up around it. Even before designer Peter Molyneux and his team threw genuine, if basic, morality into the mix with *Black & White*, the ideas developed in *Populous* were being tweaked and repurposed by a hundred other PC teams. Fittingly, given the subject matter, you may love or hate the results, but many would argue that the influence of *Populous* can be seen everywhere. **CD**

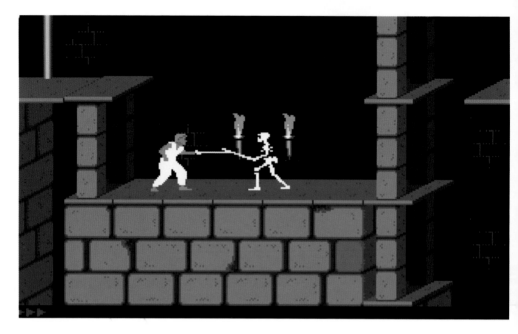

Prince of Persia

Original release date : 1989
Platform : Various
Developer : Brøderbund
Genre : Platform

Prince of Persia is an enigma. How could an unforgiving twitch platformer, one that arguably owed more to *Mega Man* than to *Super Mario Bros.*, cast itself as a romantic adventure? And what is the Prince of Persia doing at the bottom of a Persian dungeon? Is a time limit a boon or a curse? And just *how* do you kill a skeleton?

There's no doubt that the visual presentation of *Prince of Persia* seems dated, but the style remains: this was an early example of motion-captured animation in games, demonstrating the personality that could be projected through a few simple frames. The game's creator, Jordan Mechner, has since posted online the videos he took of his younger brother running,

leaping, and falling to help bring life to his creation—a beguiling look behind the scenes that's all the more astonishing for the fidelity of its realization in-game.

The task is simple: escape the dungeon, stop the evil vizier, and save the girl. It's a near-impossible quest that few players succeed in, thanks not only to the precision required for the game's most basic leaps and the learning curve for its daunting dueling system, but to the harsh time limit of one hour—always ticking, always unforgiving, nearly always ending the bravest of attempts.

And why do you keep on trying? Because in spite of the game's mechanical difficulty, the prince is at once the perfect cipher and a vivid personality, his stumblings and dashes as much yours as his; the blank face and anonymous white clothing an invitation to identify that few players would turn down; his daunting quest rendered all the more poignant by his all-too-human feats of exertion. The barest of narrative outlines but a simplicity of purpose that speaks to the most jaded heart. **RS**

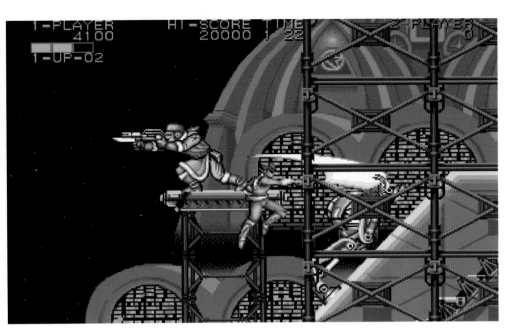

Strider

Original release date : 1989
Platform : Arcade
Developer : Capcom
Genre : Action

Not all of Capcom's mascots were destined for long and lasting careers. Some, like Strider Hiryu, were so bound to the world of two-dimensional games that three dimensions simply couldn't do them justice. A PlayStation game, a few cameos in all-star fighting games, and that was it—the legacy over. But like a self-destructive author or rock star, perhaps it's better that way. Strider, certainly, is too brilliant and virile a specimen to age with any dignity.

Able to hook onto walls and ceilings by mere touch, scaling them as quickly as if he were on foot, Strider—or Spider as he begs to be known—is a hard act to follow. In a memorable opening mission, he swoops from a robot glider, onto the rooftops of Kafazu (a fictionalized

USSR), while bright yellow searchlights probe a starry sky. The year is 2048, and Mother Russia has evolved into quite a spectacle. Metal Cossack dwarves patrol giant mosques, intruders are left to fight posing superathletes, and the Soviet parliament can more than fend for itself—ministers somersaulting out of their chairs to form a kind of ouroboros; in this case, a giant steel millipede waving a hammer and sickle. In a level as wide as it is tall, action rarely moves in the direction you expect.

So it continues through Siberia, the Amazon, and the skies, across flying fortresses and snow-capped mountains, and finally up to the enemy stronghold: the Third Moon. The levels are works of art, the enemies are works of art, and so is Strider, flashing his sword in a great arc, sliding under traps and cartwheeling over bullets.

To experience the game now, rather than *Strider II* (an unrelated European-made "sequel"), or even the decent *Strider 2* for the PlayStation, look for *Cannon Dancer*, the spiritual follow-up by creator Kouichi Yotsui. **DH**

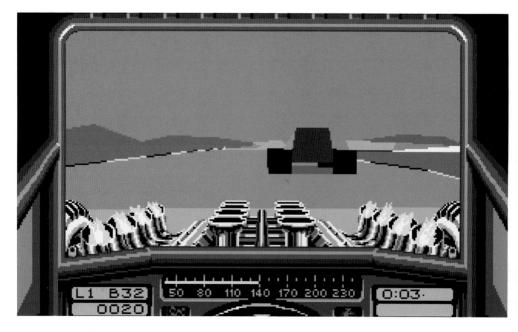

Stunt Car Racer

Original release date : 1989
Platform : Various
Developer : MicroStyle
Genre : Driving

An offbeat driving simulator, *Stunt Car Racer* is perhaps designer Geoff Crammond's most beloved game. It followed 1986's *The Sentinel*, his sole experiment away from realistic simulation.

This is a racing car game with a difference. Players drive on elevated race courses that are more akin to large rollercoaster tracks, except that there are no rails to keep their cars attached and there are dangerous gaps that need to be cleared. But unlike in other games based on precarious racing conditions, falling off the track isn't catastrophic, merely leading to lost time as a crane hoists the car back into place (although a succession of nasty falls, slams, and scrapes can eventually wreck your ride).

Featuring eight varied tracks and a full league mode, the game presents a captivating challenge, with clean, bright graphics only marred by the functional design of the opponent cars, which are little more than boxes on blocky wheels. Crammond's physics programming ensures that the car handling feels perfect, even when leaping over a hill at 230 mph, and the addition of a turbo-boost mechanic means that no race—even after a few spills—ever feels like a lost cause, remaining thrilling to the end.

Fast, fun, and endlessly playable, what keeps *Stunt Car Racer* in many gamers' minds to this day was the surprise inclusion of the ability to link up two Amigas (or Atari STs). Those with the drive to lug a home computer (and associated TV) over to a pal's house found probably the best two-player racing fun available until *Super Mario Kart* three years later. Even now it offers something special.

Crammond planned a 2003 sequel, *Stunt Car Racer Pro*, which sadly never saw the light of day, depriving a new generation of gamers a unique experience. **MKu**

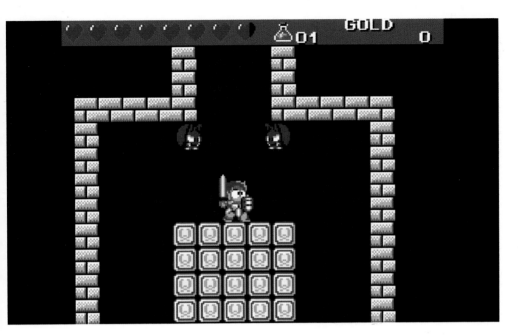

Wonderboy III: The Dragon's Trap

Original release date : 1989
Platform : Master System
Developer : Sega
Genre : Platform

Wonderboy was always thought of as the pudgy, oddly thuggish alternative to Link or Mario, a platforming—and sometimes light RPGing—cipher who struggled to cling to any sense of his own identity for too long.

Surprisingly, however, *Wonderboy III* was a genuine milestone in video game design. A vast rolling epic of an adventure, players could explore the outer reaches of a genuinely enormous map more or less as they wished, without sensing too many invisible walls or artificial barriers along the way. It was a triumph, all the more astonishing given the generally weak titles that preceded it.

For 1989, *Wonderboy III*'s scope was something of a revelation: a platforming game with the real depth and

persistence of an RPG. Fall into the sea, and you'd end up on the seabed; soar into the sky, and you might find a doorway nestled in among the clouds. The sense of freedom and exploration on offer is almost unrivaled outside of the rarefied world of the masterful *Zelda* series.

Wonderboy III carves up its world into areas that are only accessible once you've changed into the correct animal form. As part of the dragon's curse for defeating him in the previous adventure, Wonderboy has developed shape-shifting capabilities, and can now switch between lizard, lion, mouse, fish, and hawk incarnations, each one with its own set of unique skills.

Played today, the game's limitations and frustrations are a little more obvious: *Wonderboy III* is something of a slog, and its colorful fantasy worlds lack much in the way of character. That said, however, the sense of the future it promised is still there to be seen, each doorway promising to take you somewhere new, each wishing well beckoning you to plunge in and see what lays at the bottom. **CD**

- In 1991 *Sonic The Hedghog* increases the popularity of the **Sega Mega Drive**

- Increasingly powerful computers and cheaper processors usher in 3-D graphics in video games

- Real-time strategy games, such as 1992's *Dune II*, develop into a major new genre of video games

- Massively multiplayer online role-playing games (MMORPGs), such as 1997's *Ultima Online*, build international online communities

- Critics name *The Legend of Zelda: Ocarina of Time*, released in 1998, as the highest-rated video game of all time

- Consoles, such as the **Sega Dreamcast**, include a built-in modem for online play

1990s

The Secret of Monkey Island

Original release date : 1990

Platform : Various

Developer : LucasArts

Genre : Adventure

One of the sadder truths about video games is that not many of them manage to be particularly funny—or, rather, not many of them manage to be intentionally funny. Whenever comedy in games is being discussed, however, one title always comes top of the list: *The Secret of Monkey Island*. LucasArts's swashbuckling adventure game is repeatedly, elaborately, and inventively hilarious; a deviously plotted pirate romp with a twisty narrative, a memorable cast of idiots, and regular stabs from a rapier wit. It's not just the best comedy game ever made—it's the best by a couple of nautical miles.

Guybrush Threepwood has come to Melee Island, somewhere in the Caribbean, to break into the pirating trade—a quest that will lead him to partake of the famous Three Trials, gather together a crew, buy his own boat, and discover the eponymous secret that lurks on mysterious Monkey Island. Along the way, he meets some vegetarian cannibals, tetchy local saucepot Governor Marley, and LeChuck, the terrifying ghost pirate with a love for the governor and a fatal weakness for root beer.

From the insult-based swordfights to the asides poking fun at the limitations of computer games, *The Secret of Monkey Island* keeps the jokes coming thick and fast. More important than that, perhaps, is the game's sense of atmosphere. Few game worlds are as memorable as this, from the rickety boardwalks of Melee Island, trapped in a perpetual midnight, to the bubbling, lava-riddled underworlds of LeChuck's hellish HQ. Many years after its release, *Monkey Island's* status as a classic hasn't dimmed the edge of its wit, and serviceable updates—featuring an option to play with the original graphics—can be found on Xbox Live Arcade, the PC, and even Apple's iPhone. **CD**

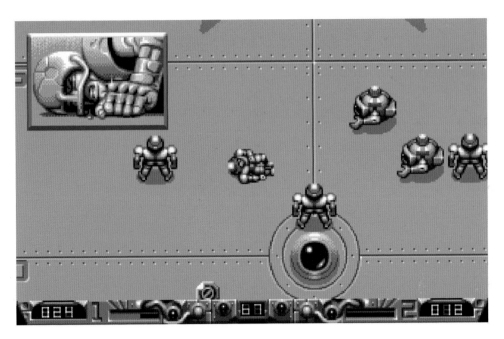

Speedball 2: Brutal Deluxe

Original release date : 1990
Platform : Amiga
Developer : The Bitmap Brothers
Genre : Sports / Action

Less controversial for its subject matter than for its title, which is coincidentally the name of an illegal drug cocktail, *Speedball* was a collision of ice hockey, Australian rules football, and Rollerball, the fictional blood sport from the 1975 James Caan movie. Two heavily armored teams would literally fight over a steel ball, bouncing it off the walls of an enclosed field until someone tossed it into their opponents' goal, often by hobbling the keeper. While the first game featured little else, most of its variety coming from half-time shop items, like bribing the officials, its sequel upped the game entirely.

The year is 2105 and a new version of *Speedball* has risen from the ashes of the original, which has moved

underground after descending into anarchy. The sport now occupies a gigantic colosseum hosting nine-person teams, with bumpers, rails, targets, and gates, like those of a pinball table. There's even a kicker that electrifies the ball, making it untouchable to opposing players. A points-based scoring system means you can win without scoring a goal; high points are awarded for crippling players and forcing on substitutes. Into this arena steps the Brutal Deluxe, the worst team in history. Your team.

A grandstanding effort from all concerned, notably pixel artist Dan Malone and sound designer Richard Joseph, *Speedball 2* forges an identity lacked by its predecessor. Its action is louder, faster, and even more violent, yet disciplined thanks to the Amiga's favored one-button control scheme. Matches move in unpredictable ways because of the different scoring methods, not to mention randomly placed coins that come in handy on the transfer market. Often described as one of the greatest multiplayer games ever, and not without reason. **DH**

ActRaiser

Original release date : 1990
Platform : SNES
Developer : Square
Genre : Action / Strategy

Sometimes a straightforward action game isn't enough. And sometimes, to really get to the heart of the fun, you have to blend a simple adventure game with the tenets of a city building god sim. *ActRaiser* may not be as famous as Square's other more traditional games, such as the successful and million copy-selling *Final Fantasy* series, but in its mixing of genres it ensures that there's nothing else quite like it.

Players are cast in the role of the Master and tasked with rebuilding an entire civilization by working through side-scrolling stages, lopping away at enemies with a sword and tackling bigger and bigger boss monsters. You also have to take a break now and then in order to switch to a top-down perspective, so you can convince tiny followers to build roads, houses, and other such important structures, and generally smarten the whole place up a bit.

It's tempting to see the game as *God of War* meets *SimCity*, but *ActRaiser* has a peculiar spirit all of its own, and one which, with its focus on deities and civilization, has landed the title in hot water with religious groups over the years. More of a curio than a smash hit, *ActRaiser* also confused as many players as it delighted. It's easy to see why this occurred; as much fun as the whole thing is, the mix of genres is not handled in the slickest of manners.

That said, this particular muddle of distinctive game types must have had something magical to it. The sequel, which dropped the city building aspects, has little of the original's charm and appeal. Whether *ActRaiser's* the kind of thing that you'll lap up or spit out is something you can discover with ease these days. You only need to spend a few moments downloading this strange and willful title through the Wii's Virtual Console service to experience the game for yourself. **CD**

Klax

Original release date : 1990
Platform : Various
Developer : Atari
Genre : Puzzle

A conveyor belt of dominoes tumbles toward the foreground, ripe for the picking by those willing to harbor the color-coded "klaxes" and rack up points by storing as many as possible. *Klax* is a cocktail of genre influences, closest in its one-hundred level, scroll-and-conquer structure to *Space Invaders*, but with an overall tempo that whiffs of a stern solution mixed from equal measures Connect Four and *Columns*.

Klax's stop-and-start momentum is a microcosm for the means of overall progression, with users able to skip levels in variables of five and ten—a neat ploy promoting replays and enticing gamblers and egotists into the fires of a delineated learning curve. The currency of *Klax* is the high

score rivalry of classic arcade leader boards. Dissipated though it is in home versions across a variety of systems, the essence of its addictive mechanics remains intact all the way to Nintendo's Game Boy and even to Microsoft's Xbox (it is a part of new licensee Midway's *Treasures* collection). Viewed as retro classicism, the block colors of the Commodore 64 era paint *Klax's* backdrops as nostalgic portraits of artistic, indulgent reveries.

The variety of the settings—from forests to the hands of God himself—are the hook for the game play's line and sinker. Such visual flamboyance is a symptom of the period but here plays a more important role, transfiguring the arcade cabinet into an ethereal kaleidoscope wherein the rigid rules of David Aker's programming are instigated.

Influential beyond its years, glimpses of *Klax* can be spied in everything from Tetsuya Mizuguchi's *Rez* to Jeff Minter's *Space Giraffe*. The psychedelic effects of depth of field—however illusionary—are a legacy the game can claim with pride. **DV**

G-LOC: Air Battle (R-360)

Original release date : 1990
Platform : Arcade
Developer : Sega
Genre : Shoot 'Em Up

When the book comes to be written about contributions to the world of arcade gaming, one company's achievements will stand above all others. Though it is known to many as the creator of countless console games, Sega has been committed to the coin-operated amusement market since the 1970s, and its innovations over the years are among the most notable in their field, from the sprite-scaling hardware that powered revolutionary 3-D games in the '80s to the networked game centers populated by many thousands of dedicated players across Japan. And, though it has a lower profile than many of Sega's famous productions, *G-LOC: Air Battle* deserves credit for its innovation—or at least it does in one incarnation.

Like many arcade cabinets, *G-LOC: Air Battle* was manufactured in several different iterations in a bid to appeal to arcade owners with varying budgets, but it's only the superdeluxe version of *G-LOC: Air Battle* that earns a place within these pages. Designed by Yu Suzuki, the genius behind so many Sega hardware innovations (such as *Hang-On*'s full-sized motorcycle), the *R-360* model of the game is the most ambitious coin-operated video game ever conceived, and, as a result, is closer to a fairground attraction than it is to its pixelated contemporaries.

Climb into the cabinet, carefully (and securely) strap yourself in, and prepare to be spun through the 360 degrees implied by the name. Other Sega machines tilt you left and right and spin you around; the *R-360* version of *G-LOC* changes the rules completely, flipping and rotating you in accordance with your joystick inputs. Underneath it all is a limited update of the *After Burner* games, but when you're having so much fun just trying to hold on to your breakfast, such concerns matter little. **TB**

Pilotwings

Original release date : 1990
Platform : SNES
Developer : Nintendo
Genre : Flight Simulator

Dreamy and beautiful, serene and well-mannered, *Pilotwings* is the SNES launch title most likely to see you drifting off into a strange, damp-eyed reverie at the merest mention of its name. It wasn't as colorful and perfectly poised as *Super Mario World*, and it didn't have the huge monsters of the imported *Ultraman* brawler, but it was a genuinely different kind of experience. A game that, even two decades after its release, remains frustratingly hard to classify, and has a strange magic that is irritatingly difficult to explain.

It's not *strictly* a flight simulator, even though it's almost exclusively a simulation of flight. Flight sims are engineers' games, filled with dials and switches and vectors and difficult landing approaches to Chicago O'Hare with low visibility and a cloud bank moving in. While *Pilotwings* has all of these elements in its own way, it doesn't feel like an engineer's game, but rather a poet's. A dash through the clouds, looking at the scenery—a wonderful, technically amazing introduction to flight that has been built for delight rather than precision.

Whatever it is that makes this title special, there's a lot of it to enjoy, with all manner of different challenges involving plenty of different planes. Rocket packs join more traditional aircraft on the runway, and there's even a mode in which you drop out of the cockpit for a little target-based parachute jumping.

Updated once for the N64, *Pilotwings* seems so perfect for the playful software lineup of the Wii that it's hard to believe that there's nothing in development over at Nintendo's HQ. Whatever happens, we'll still have *Pilotwings* on the SNES, a wonderful way to lose an afternoon or two, even if it's still hard to decide exactly what type of game you're really playing. **CD**

Out Zone

Original release date : 1990
Platform : Arcade
Developer : Toaplan
Genre : Shoot 'Em Up

Though better known as the developer of *Zero Wing*, inspiration for the infamous "All Your Base" Internet meme, Toaplan was one of the great shoot-'em-up studios from the late 1980s until its bankruptcy in 1994, at which point it spawned further shooter genre specialists such as Cave (*DonPachi*) and Takumi (*Giga Wing*).

Out Zone is one of Toaplan's more unusual releases. Though it is a vertically scrolling shooter, with its eight-way directional shooting it has more in common with run-and-gun games, such as *Commando* and *Ikari Warriors*. However, players can pick up a three-way shot that locks their character's view forward, changing the title into a more traditional shooter—albeit one in which the screen only scrolls if the player moves forward (players are driven onward by a constantly depleting energy bar refilled by collecting power-ups). This dual nature allows tactics to be switched while playing. Since the situation on the screen can change rapidly, it's an important consideration and one that puts *Out Zone* well above its predecessors.

Featuring Toaplan's renowned graphical style—full of incidental details and brightly colored brushed metal that make otherwise mechanistic enemies and locations feel warmly organic—*Out Zone* is a strikingly gorgeous experience, one that keeps you playing even in the face of its extreme difficulty. It features complex and mazelike levels that require careful maneuvering while simultaneously avoiding enemy attacks.

Out Zone often rewards memorization more than raw skill, but a variety of Easter eggs (such as cameos from other Toaplan games) offer rewards. It is a superlative shooter, and its maker deserves a place in gaming history more for its work here than as the studio behind a particularly awkward piece of mistranslation. **MKu**

Powermonger

Original release date : 1990

Platform : Amiga

Developer : Bullfrog Productions

Genre : Strategy

Powermonger was both the spiritual and the technical successor to Bullfrog's breakthrough title, *Populous*. It uses the same engine as Peter Molyneux's original god game, but here to more earthly effect. Gone are the earthquakes, volcanoes, and terraforming, sacrificed for a more intimate experience that sees you conquering 195 lands by amassing and expanding an army led by captains you recruit by pillaging.

And what a land. Molyneux may have been inspired to invent the god game genre by wreaking havoc on ants' nests as a child, but here he and his team took care to make the world's inhabitants seem human. They go about their daily lives as fishermen, farmers, and foresters oblivious to you, but you can click on them to discover their name, sex, age, allegiance, and even their hometown, a decade before *The Sims* popularized the convention. So engrossing was the world that it was easy to overlook some developer trickery. Like *Populous*, the three-dimensional terrain occupies only a limited portion of the screen, with the rest given over to the extensive user interface. The camera view features eight levels of zoom and can be rotated by ninety-degree turns, remarkable for the game's era.

While you command troops and need to secure ongoing food supplies, it would be a stretch to say that *Powermonger* invented the real-time strategy genre, but in ordering your captains to march around the land securing villages, it's another missing link. One lovely touch is that your orders to distant captains are delayed according to how far away they are by carrier pigeon.

Powermonger, something of a forgotten classic and a pioneering title, even supported a two-player mode via a null cable. The path to *Black & White* begins here. **OB**

DUNCAN   XENA

VIPER   MORGUL

TAGHOR   KEIRGAR

VIPER USES THE POWER TO TURN UNDEAD!   CAMP

Eye of the Beholder

Original release date : 1990
Platform : PC
Developer : Westwood Studios
Genre : Role-playing

Dungeon Master got there first, but *Eye of the Beholder* was bona fide Dungeons & Dragons. Fresh from the success of its Gold Box games, publisher SSI commissioned Westwood Associates in a bid to emulate the immersive atmosphere and critical success of *Dungeon Master*. Taking the first-person perspective of *Dungeon Master*, *Eye of the Beholder* applied it to the official Dungeons & Dragons rules and the *Forgotten Realms* campaign setting.

Compared to the *Gold Box* games, the campaign in *Eye of the Beholder* is light on story, with just the flimsiest of yarns sketched out. The story begins in the seminal *Forgotten Realms* city of Waterdeep, where our party of four intrepid adventurers (generated from the official selection

of statistics, races, and character classes) are hired to investigate some sewers, only to find themselves trapped by a landslide and forced to find an alternative way out.

This shortfall in narrative was more than compensated for by the unprecedented levels of action that followed. Compared to the staid, statistic heavy, turn-based affairs of the Gold Box games, the *Beholder* series (or Black Box games) were characterized by frantic, real-time point-and-click combat that was perfectly suited to the game's hack-and-slash, dungeon-looting adventure.

The ending might have been an anticlimax (later versions added an actual ending animation), but the authenticity of the Dungeons & Dragons rules, the *Forgotten Realms* setting, and the first-person perspective made the quest an epic one. It also paved the way for subsequent first-person Dungeons & Dragons games such as *Dungeon Hack*, *Ravenloft: Strahd's Possession*, and *Menzoberranzan*, all equally interesting in very different ways, if not quite as excellent as *Eye of the Beholder*. **DM**

Bomberman

Original release date : 1990
Platform : PC Engine
Developer : Hudson
Genre : Action

With more than sixty titles under his belt, *Bomberman* still might not boast the recognition factor of *Mario*, but he's come a long way, especially for a character with such inauspicious roots. Unlike most classics that have a foundation of originality or brilliance lurking at their core, the original was surprisingly bereft of genius at birth.

Conceived back in 1983 as a simplistic Japanese MSX title and then ported to the ZX Spectrum as *Eric and the Floaters*, the game later found a home on the NES. But with fifty repetitive, find-the-exit levels, and no multiplayer mode, it didn't amount to much. In fact, without multiplayer, many would later argue this wasn't really *Bomberman* at all.

That would all change, however, in 1990 when the bright sparks at Hudson Soft and NEC collaborated on a multitap adaptor for the trailblazing PC Engine console. Plugging the peripheral into the console's only joy pad socket allowed up to five players to compete, unleashing the game's potential and generating a sense of steadily mounting panic and fun that the original title simply lacked.

Subsequent iterations of the series have grown ever more complex—some to their benefit, others not so much—so it's refreshing to consider the simplicity of PC Engine *Bomberman*. Navigate labyrinth-like maps, drop bombs, take out your opponents, and try to be the last *Bomberman* standing. There are obstructions to be demolished and power-ups to be collected (such as speed-ups and the ability to kick bombs in the direction of opponents), but the rules were pretty simple back then.

While *Bomberman* fans might squabble endlessly over which version offers the most engaging action, the simplicity and purity of the PC Engine original is where it all began. **JB**

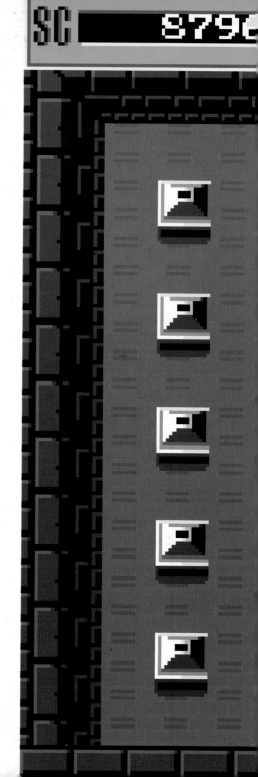

Dr. Mario

Original release date : 1990
Platform : Various
Developer : Nintendo
Genre : Puzzle

In Nintendo's rush to create a *Tetris* clone unencumbered by the legal disputes of the original, it seems nobody stopped to ask a few fundamental questions. For example, when did this world-saving plumber type find the time to acquire an MD? Perhaps the reason no one raised such pressing issues is that they were too busy playing *Dr. Mario*.

Instead of the blank slate that begins most *Tetris* games, each level of *Dr. Mario* is contaminated with red, yellow, and blue viruses. Mario attacks them by way of double-sided capsules, each half colored either red, yellow, or blue. Stack like colors atop or next to one another to eliminate them; match four or more in a row and they disappear.

One major difference between *Dr. Mario*'s capsules and *Tetris*'s tetrominoes is that the coins of *Dr. Mario*'s realm are much more maneuverable. The result is a greater focus on agility: if you want to succeed, you'd better master split-second reactions. For a *Tetris* knockoff, *Dr. Mario* is remarkably original. The game spawned a thriving branch of the falling block puzzle genre, and without it there might have been no *Lumines* and *Bejeweled*. **JT**

Columns

Original release date : 1990
Platform : Various
Developer : Sega
Genre : Puzzle

While *Columns* bears all the hallmarks of a *Tetris* clone—the narrow well of the game's playing field, the endless rain of falling blocks, and the fondness for abstract, arty backdrops—the final product actually works very differently. It relies on color matching, spatial awareness, and pattern rearrangement, and brings physics into play as unused tiles collapse to fill empty spaces. To Sega owners in the early 1990s this was their *Tetris*, and the good news is that it's a decent game in its own right. It may have lacked the frosty austerity of Alexey Pajitnov's masterpiece, but it had new features and managed to feel like a panicky, brightly colored kind of cerebral challenge.

Match-three titles have a history all of their own and the basic mechanics remain a cornerstone of the puzzle world, but *Columns* will always be special, its sparkling game pieces serving as a living embodiment of the glitzy sheen Sega employed, while its somewhat unpredictable high score rushes keep players tapping away into the night. *Columns* ended up ported to just about everything, so you should have no real trouble tracking it down. **CD**

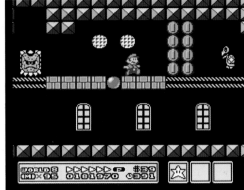

John Madden Football

Super Mario Bros. 3

Original release date : 1990
Platform : Mega Drive
Developer : Park Place Productions
Genre : Sports

Original release date : 1990
Platform : NES
Developer : Nintendo
Genre : Platform

Hustling a sport as complicated as American football into the limitations of a late-1980s 16-bit console may seem a daft idea, but that didn't stop Electronic Arts. Admittedly, this wasn't the first such representation of the sport, but the decision to display the action as though looking down from behind the quarterback position was a masterstroke.

It enables a beautifully economic method of displaying the hundred-odd plays, while doubling up as a masterful triple "passing window" option that shows the various receivers once in play. The clean menu-driven system is a control method that has been tailored to incorporate just three buttons, and an attention to the core elements of US football that guarantees levels of depth that you don't associate with the jerky yet undeniably charming visuals.

An exciting facet of one of the most successful video game series of all time is the action that takes place on the field. Although clearly basic by today's standards, the first *Madden* still plays a mean game of American football. It might be more of a history lesson nowadays, but it's hardly a boring one. **JDS**

After the strange dreamscapes of *Super Mario Bros. 2*, the third installment in Nintendo's greatest series is a sprawling adventure. And this is one of the NES's most ambitious games, a beautiful nonlinear platformer in which you're often given a choice of which levels to explore next.

It's full of surprise power-ups, too, from the frog suit, which allows Mario to leap farther than ever and swim smoothly underwater, to the racoon suit, which allows for a nifty tail attack and a short burst of flight. Even when it isn't doling out unexpected treats, the game bends its own rules, sending you off on levels that scroll up and down as well as left and right, and chucking in gigantic enemies like the hideous gulping fish. If you survive, you'll be rewarded with one of the most menacing final acts of any *Mario* game before or since.

Facing off against Bowser's entire family before taking the fight to the big man himself, this is a colorful journey where a new idea lurks around each corner, and the perfect 8-bit primer for the series' staggering leap into the 16-bit age with *Super Mario World*. **CD**

Rampart

Original release date : 1990
Platform : Arcade
Developer : Atari
Genre : Strategy

"Ready! Aim! Fire!" Three words that lie at the heart of so many video games, but delivered by a speech sample before battle in *Rampart* in such a way that for a moment you feel like you can detect the whiff of gunpowder in your nostrils. This is a game centered on the old-fashioned method of blowing things up—with cannonballs. *Rampart*'s setting isn't the thing for which it'll be remembered, however, because it is a delicious and inspired fusion of *Tetris* and strategy war gaming.

In single-player mode you first pick a castle, and then place cannons beside it. Then the game advances into its attack phase, and you move your crosshairs over the approaching ships, attempting to rain enough blows upon them to ensure that they don't make it ashore. All the while, they're returning fire, knocking holes in the walls of your battlements, and it's only when the round is over that you realize how much work is to be done. It's here that the *Tetris* element comes into play as you're given a succession of randomly selected blocks of different shapes and sizes with which to patch up your compound, and even expand farther to encapsulate other castles and increase your presence on the battlefield—if you're quick enough. More castles equals more cannons to play with, after all.

Rampart is a game of juggling. Do you focus on shoring up what you have in order to consolidate your position or do you instead go for territory, running the risk of not completing a boundary around your position, thus losing it? A fine diversion for one, it comes into its own with (up to three) multiple players, its mix of controlled aggression and fast-moving defensive tactics making it a unique and addictive strategy game. Though it has been ported to many home formats, the trackball-driven original is the definitive iteration. **TB**

Raiden

Original release date : 1990
Platform : Arcade
Developer : Seibu Kaihatsu
Genre : Shoot 'Em Up

Shoot 'em ups have always had a problem with identity. As a genre in which games rarely have more plot than casting the player as the one remaining spaceship against an invading fleet, it becomes hard to distinguish them for anything but their mechanics. Perhaps the reason vertically scrolling shooters have in recent times resorted to more and more extreme bullet hell trials.

Raiden, produced in 1990 by Seibu Kaihatsu, a Japanese developer unknown other than for creating the series, does not distinguish itself with its wafer-thin plot. Nor does it distinguish itself by its graphics, which are clean, functional, and attractive, but hardly remarkable even when compared to its contemporary competition. When taken as a straightforward challenge to get to the end, it can be assumed to be the same as any pocket-change devouring title from the arcades in the early 1990s.

However, for players who are willing to put the effort in, *Raiden* offers a lot. While *Raiden* is difficult, it is a perfectly balanced difficulty. Never needing to shower the screen with bullets, it's a glorious treat for high score chasers since it doesn't rely on the complex mechanics of the shooters that followed; no bullet shaving or careful combo management here. Instead it simply required that it be played well and cleverly, with bonus points to be found in hidden medals and by avoiding the use of bombs. Any risks the player needs to take are amply rewarded, and though the title features a small number of weapon power-ups, they are among the most satisfying in shooter history.

So perhaps *Raiden* doesn't obviously distinguish itself in the long list of arcade shoot 'em ups for its graphics, its background story, or its mechanics. However, its design is a masterpiece, a thoughtfully balanced experience for the discerning player. **MKu**

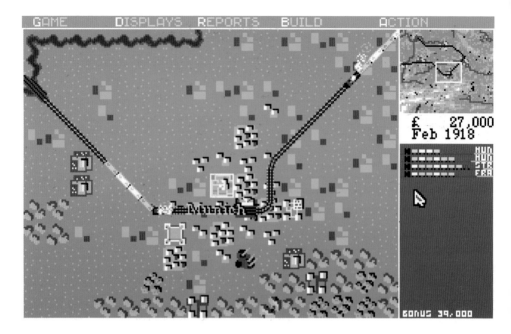

Sid Meier's Railroad Tycoon

Original release date : 1990
Platform : Various
Developer : Microprose Software
Genre : Management Simulation

Popular since the "carpet railways" that followed the rise of steam engines in the mid-nineteenth century, model railways are an enduring pastime for railroad enthusiasts, but since legendary game designer Sid Meier published *Railroad Tycoon*, you have to wonder why.

While this 1990 title is graphically basic, even for the time (and admittedly a fetishistic level of detail is a requirement for the average model railway builder), the game provides something no model railway could—a well-designed representation of the competition between companies in the early days of the railroad.

Like Sid Meier's other famous designs (most notably *Civilization*), *Railroad Tycoon* doesn't restrict the player

to a certain scenario. Instead, you are able to choose your individual difficulty level and location, including the United States, England and Wales, and continental Europe. Via the process of carefully laying your tracks and stations to maximize your profit (paying attention to the rule of supply and demand) and the buying and selling of stock, *Sid Meier's Railroad Tycoon* offers a light take on the reality of running a business, but it's continually captivating without ever overwhelming the player.

Though the title suffers from a highly dated interface, even those with no interest in the rise of locomotion can quickly find themselves playing the role of a railroad tycoon with aplomb. Perfectionists can work on improving their stations while those looking for glory can attempt to have the fastest trains going the farthest distances first. The ultimate pleasure of the game is in building a successful rail network, perhaps crushing opposing companies in the process, and then simply watching your own model railway work with clockwork precision. **MKu**

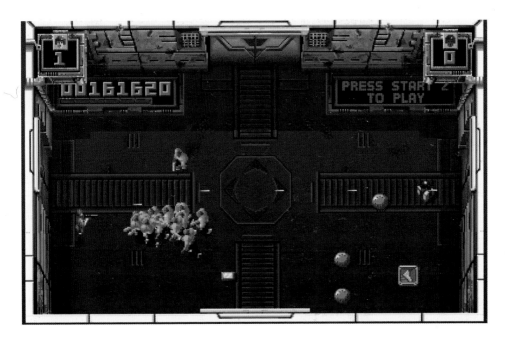

Smash TV

Original release date : 1990
Platform : Arcade
Developer : Williams
Genre : Shoot 'Em Up

For a game with a single, simple premise—kill everything on-screen—*Smash TV*'s components can be evaluated in a surprising number of ways. You can, for instance, ponder the satirical message in a setting that presents a futuristic game show in which contestants are locked in a sequence of studios and asked to win their freedom by blasting whatever enters each room. You can discuss the game's flippant attitude toward its presentation of violence, which shocked a not-inconsiderable number of parents upon release (how times change). And you can certainly consider *Smash TV*'s astonishing ability to directly target a primal, kill-or-be-killed mentality at the heart of any player. Or you could grab the controls to shoot first

and ask those questions later. Shooting is all you need to know about *Smash TV*. You're either on your own, picking up power-ups and weapons to gun down your foes, or you bring a friend along for the ride. In either scenario you're guaranteed a brutal orgy of frantic, merciless killing.

As the levels progress, so does the massacre, and it doesn't take long for the screen to be drowning in enemies, with you following the momentary path carved by your bullets while desperately hoping for a respite in the assault. This only really comes once you reach the end or—more likely, considering the game's level of difficulty—run out of lives.

Both outcomes matter little because you will find yourself returning to *Smash TV* purely for a dose of non-stop, fully focused fun. Sure, the sprite-based aesthetic hasn't so much lost its charm—because it never really possessed any—as aged considerably, but you'll have to search long and hard to find as addictive and rewarding a game mechanic these days. **JDS**

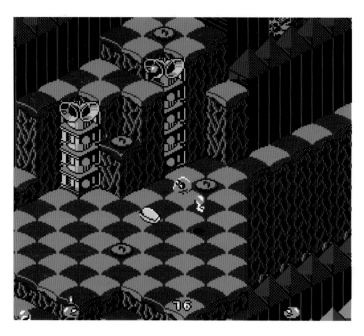

Snake Rattle 'n' Roll

Original release date : 1990
Platform : Various
Developer : Rare
Genre : Platform

In 1954, Atlantic Records's first president, Herb Abramson, told rhythm-and-blues musician Jesse Stone to write a song for blues shouter Big Joe Turner. One of *Rolling Stone*'s 500 greatest songs of all time, "Shake, Rattle and Roll" was a hit whose fiery facade overlaid a highly sexual anthem about a man who has "been holdin' it in, way down underneath." It's hard to say where that song's lurid nature plays into this title. Perhaps it's the snakes. There are two of them, Rattle and Roll, and they have to eat Nibbley Pibbleys to make themselves grow longer.

Okay, so there's nothing sexual about *Snake Rattle 'n' Roll*. It's pitched somewhere between *Marble Madness* and *Q*Bert* as you navigate a checkered, multilayered game environment, dodging bad guys and collecting power-ups. But there is a touch of the blues: The game's composer, David Wise, would later do the thumping percussion of *Donkey Kong Country*, and in this game it's Wise's ragtime riffs that give some musical bombast to an otherwise anodyne game.

Nowadays, Rare may be most famous for its original properties such as *Banjo-Kazooie*, *Killer Instinct*, and *Perfect Dark*, but the late '80s were not always kind to the UK studio, its output from the period including lackluster licensed titles such as *Who Framed Roger Rabbit?* and *Double Dare*. *Snake Rattle 'n' Roll* was one of the few original titles produced during the period and a sign of the off-kilter perspective the company would later bring to the Nintendo 64, on which it enjoyed some of its biggest successes. Just a year later the studio created one of most memorable, strangest, and trickiest games of the period in the form of *Battletoads*, but *Snake Rattle 'n' Roll* is the more innovative title. **JBW**

Super Tennis

Original release date : 1991
Platform : SNES
Developer : Tokyo Shoseki
Genre : Sports

The best tennis game ever? A contestable claim now, perhaps, but back in 1991, at a time when the competition was considerably more straightforward, it's a statement that couldn't be easily challenged—even if things had obviously moved on since *Pong*.

Mirroring the simplicity of the era, *Super Tennis* is magnificently pure, brilliantly simple. You get to choose between singles, doubles, or circuit play (in which one player goes through tournaments with the aim of climbing up the world rankings), then you select one of the twenty charming, caricatured players, each offering different attributes, and finally you select the court to play on (clay, grass, or hard). In play, it's the precision of the control method that most impresses, with players responding beautifully to directional input while the button-based moves allow for as comprehensive range of shots as even the most demanding of digital tennis players will require. Add in an opponent (or partner) and the full pace of the action reveals itself, with remarkable, titanic rallies serving up one of the best two-player console experiences to be had, regardless of the system.

Where progress has taken its toll is most evident in some of the game's technological merits (the SNES's Mode 7 has long lost its ability to inspire awe, for instance), but it's not affected the game's mechanics. If it no longer is the best tennis game ever made, it unquestionably prepared the court for the fine releases that followed. If you were to put it up against them now, *Super Tennis* certainly still has the ability to take a couple of sets, pushing things to a long-fought, very close tie. As such, it should be no surprise that, despite its age, it remains an immensely playable and addictive example of the genre. **JDS**

Kill it while you still can, Atropos!

Loom

Original release date : 1991
Platform : Various
Developer : LucasArts
Genre : Adventure

Loom is the LucasArts adventure that slipped through the cracks. It was the esoteric, rather serious fantasy title that didn't have crowd-pleasing comedy elements like insult swordfights, tabloid reporters, or talking meteorites. In fact, it was all pretty calm and cerebral: a haunting tale of another world, told in a way that made it both more imaginative and more unwieldy than its famous siblings. It doesn't even have the SCUMM engine's most distinctive feature, the verb list that traditionally dominates the bottom half of the screen.

Loom presents its players with a musical stave before sending them off on an epic quest as Bobbin Threadbare—amazingly not a name selected for its comedic potential—

in a struggle to save his whimsical fantasyland from an unknown shadowy menace. That's where the stave comes in. Most actions in *Loom* are achieved by playing simple pieces of music, each with their own power to affect the game world, instead of piecing together object-oriented sentences for the on-screen avatar to then enact as with other LucasArts titles.

The system is not entirely dissimilar to that which Nintendo would employ in *The Legend of Zelda: Ocarina of Time*, but it's far more complex in *Loom*, and rather than provide a rhythmic backup to a standard adventure control scheme, it pretty much replaces it wholesale.

A fascinating experiment, *Loom* may be more famous for its sales pitch inserted into the opening bar scene of *The Secret of Monkey Island*, but it's well worth tracking down in its own right. While it's almost inevitable that all of LucasArts's back catalog will one day make its way to the iPhone in some legitimate sense, the best means of playing this today is by downloading it via Steam. **CD**

Monkey Island 2: LeChuck's Revenge

Original release date : 1991
Platform : Various
Developer : LucasArts
Genre : Adventure

Although the first three *Monkey Island* games—boy, did the series lurch downhill after that—hardly represent your typical blockbuster trilogy, this second installment conforms to the "darker second act" pattern of series, like *Star Wars*, *The Matrix*, and *Indiana Jones*.

Washed up in yet another rickety pirate burg, Guybrush Threepwood, still not quite the mighty pirate he wants to be, is off in search of the treasure of Big Whoop. It's a journey that will take him across a delightfully broad sweep of buccaneering clichés, solving devious puzzles and meeting quirky eccentrics along the way, including his very own parents. Inevitably, Guybrush has done what every lonely, insecure male does at a certain age:

He's grown a beard, making him look a little like Kenneth Branagh, and it's a good match for the slightly more adult tone of this second adventure. The voodoo elements are dialed up for some gentle comic horror and the puzzles grow in intricacy; with one example involving a telescope and a picture of a parrot requiring some prolonged effort and rumination, while others—getting a bucket from a man whom, it turns out, doesn't actually own it in the first place—simply revel in the series' delightful tendency toward elaborate wordplay.

Using beautiful hand drawn artwork for the backdrops and featuring some of the best animation in any adventure game of the era, *LeChuck's Revenge* is a fascinating and sneaky puzzle game. It may not have the memorable challenges and classic structure of the first installment, or the rubbery cartoon exuberance of the third, but it's another winner all the same. It's yet more proof that if you want something done properly, don't get anyone named Guybrush Threepwood to do it for you. **CD**

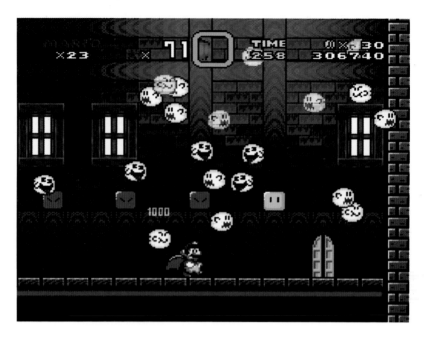

Super Mario World

Original release date : 1991
Platform : SNES
Developer : Nintendo
Genre : Platform

If there are cigars and then there are Montecristo cigars, you could argue that there are two-dimensional platformers and then there's *Super Mario World*: a decoction of everything Nintendo's brightest stars had learned or invented in the world of 8-bit consoles, transformed for the increased scope of the 16-bit world.

With the Sega Mega Drive starting the next generation console race early, Nintendo found itself on the back foot, and its heavily hyped SNES needed an absolute belter of a launch title to show that it was still the company to beat. *Super Mario World* was on hand to fulfill all expectations. It was a beautiful redesign of the Mario universe with gigantic sprites, hundreds of enemies, new backgrounds,

superb bosses that utilized the console's Mode 7 graphical effects, and a suite of new power-ups. One of these, Yoshi the dinosaur, popped out of a colorful egg early on in the game and would become both a staunch ally, a weapon, and a killer ride in the process.

With Mario's cape allowing him to take to the skies, the stage was set for one of platforming's most vivid and expansive adventures ever, delivering a wealth of different continents riddled with myriad memorable secrets. Finding yourself on the spectral Star World for the first time is an enthralling experience, while the addition of stages with more than one exit, each leading to different lands, builds on the nonlinear breakthroughs of *Super Mario 3*.

With the series' best music and most of its greatest single levels, everything that has happened since—even the glorious madness of *Super Mario 64*—can occasionally feel like a step backward. Mario had always been a wonderful adventurer's companion, but this was never going to be an easy act to follow. **CD**

Another World

Original release date : 1991
Platform : Various
Developer : Delphine Software
Genre : Platform

Another World is one of the great 16-bit video games, wildly experimental and a feast for the senses. Having worked as an artist and animator on point-and-click adventure *Future Wars*, creator Eric Chahi became captivated by *Dragon's Lair*—specifically, its port to the Commodore Amiga.

Visuals made possible by LaserDisc were being faithfully reproduced on floppy, albeit at the cost of huge memory consumption. Believing he could avoid that pitfall by using vector lines, Chahi imagined a science fiction game that fell somewhere between two of his favorites: *Karateka* (the first game by *Prince of Persia* creator Jordan Mechner) and *Impossible Mission*. In a process he describes as "educational improvization," he spent two years fulfilling his vision.

An intensely cinematic game which features no dialogue or in-game text, *Another World* is beautifully established by its intro, which Chahi completed without any real idea of how the game should actually play.

On a stormy night, physicist Lester Knight Chaykin arrives at his underground laboratory, the heart of which is a giant particle accelerator. He passes a routine full-body scan, sits himself down at the computer, and sets his experiment in motion. These details are important, because never had a game portrayed its story with such evocative full-screen animation. As the particles begin to collide, a bolt of lightning strikes the lab, causing an accident that sends Lester to a barren alien world full of strange and dangerous creatures.

Lester is abducted and most of the game charts his escape. With surprisingly varied action, involving perilous jumps and a multifunction firearm, *Another World* is inventive at every turn. More important, though, its art and animation get more enchanting with time. **DH**

Super Castlevania IV

Original release date : 1991
Platform : SNES
Developer : Konami
Genre : Platform / Action

The specter of Count Dracula looms over every *Castlevania* title, but the best games in the series understand that we're really there to visit his house. When *Castlevania* games fail, as in three-dimensional installments like *Curse of Darkness*, it's because Dracula lives in a boring old stone castle. In better installments, Castle Dracula is itself the enemy, a terrifying and disorienting house of horrors that only stout men of courage dare to enter. *Super Castlevania IV*, one of the series' stone cold classics, is quite brilliant.

Its most indelible sight is the vertigo-inducing spinning hallway, in which Simon Belmont hops from one free floating block to another while the castle's cylindrical walls rotate around him at a dizzying speed. The visuals come at a cost, however, as the Super Nintendo hardware strains to keep up, and when an enemy appears on-screen, the action slows to a crawl. But the stakes are clear: In this castle, nowhere is safe for you to venture.

Other areas are less flashy, but equally as diabolical, from a muddy underground cave with falling stalactites to a sprawling clock tower with gnashing gears that can help or hinder Simon. *Super Castlevania IV* is a buffed-up version of previous games. Its linear levels are marked with ghoulish big and mini bosses that are a who's who of classic movie monsters. Simon can now crack his whip in eight directions, which is helpful against the series' most vexing recurring foes, the disembodied Medusa heads that travel along the trajectory of a sine wave and are way too good at knocking Simon into pits. There are power-ups that strengthen and lengthen the whip.

After this game, *Super Castlevania IV* was due for a shake-up, which came in the form of *Symphony of the Night*. But it's not to say that *Super Castlevania IV* is stale, only that Konami could never top it. **MK**

Civilization

Original release date : 1991
Platform : PC
Developer : Microprose Software
Genre : Strategy

Want to make a PC gamer of a certain vintage cry? Whisper "*Civilization*" in his or her ear. There are any number of reasons why the tears might flow, but it's likely because more sleep, weekends, jobs, and relationships have probably been lost to *Civilization* than any other game.

This seminal strategy experience is vast. Beginning with just a settler wandering a hostile world 4,000 years before Christ, you found first a city and, through your choices, a civilization capable of defeating all its rivals or of sending a spaceship to distant Alpha Centauri. Blocking your path is terra incognito, barbarians, and rival civilizations, and the tools at your disposal run the gamut from trade and diplomacy to all-out hostilities.

You decide what civilization you'll play, choosing from the Mongols, the Romans, and other past and present contenders for the title of global superpower. Your choice affects trivial matters such as the names of your cities or the colors of your forces: *Civilization's* genius is that this decision does not determine the paths your people follow.

The technology tree does that; a brilliantly conceived flowchart of human progress that has been copied by most strategy games in *Civilization's* wake. By researching, for instance, the wheel, you can unlock further related technologies, such as transport or vehicular combat units. Few areas of human endeavor are ignored, but since you can only research one thing at a time, your civilization is shaped by the order of the choices you make.

With day-to-day tasks ranging from war to farming to transport planning to developing the Wonders of the World, the demands on the player are immense. What's incredible, then, is how the game manages to make time disappear as you play. If you've a fortnight to kill, then set it aside to play *Civilization*. **OB**

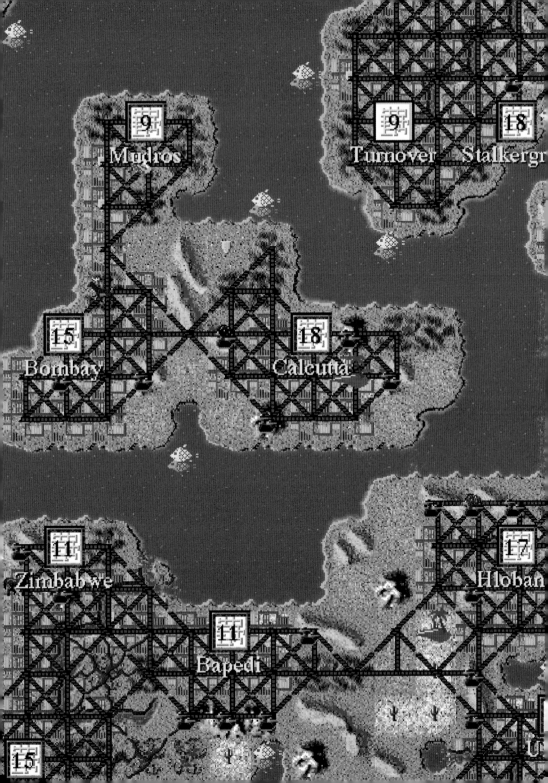

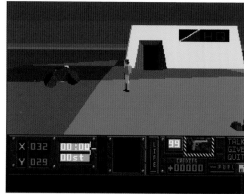

Cruise for a Corpse

Original release date : 1991
Platform : Various
Developer : Delphine Software
Genre : Adventure

The French development community was in its element on the Commodore Amiga, and few companies were keener than Delphine. Despite being keen to adventure beyond the point-and-click title, this Paris outfit went on to create a trilogy of such games that ended with its distinctive but flawed seafaring title *Cruise for a Corpse*.

Powered by the second evolution of Delphine's Cinématique engine, it follows the exploits of Inspector Raoul Dusentier, a guest aboard a 1920s cruise ship who becomes embroiled in a murder investigation. His host has been killed and each of his fellow guests has a potential motive. So, in the finest tradition of Agatha Christie, he has to learn their stories and test their alibis. *Cruise for a Corpse*'s clock advances as you stumble upon items and conversations, few of which you'll find through obvious signposting or logical deduction, but never mind . . .

The game is known for an interface that traded a verbal parser system for a contextual cursor, and for its early use of vector technology. The climax, meanwhile, is one of the best early displays of polygon-based game graphics. **DH**

Hunter

Original release date : 1991
Platform : Amiga, ST
Developer : Activision
Genre : Action / Adventure

Paul Holmes's game was generations ahead of its time, and is rightly considered the granddaddy of the increasingly fashionable sandbox genre. Taking place on a series of islands occupied by a dictator, the player is cast as the eponymous hunter, a behind-the-lines espionage expert with nothing but his wits, and whatever can be commandeered, to rely on.

Bicycles, jeeps, trucks, boats, helicopters and even a wind-surfing board can be appropriated and used against the enemy. The buildings dotted around the islands can all be entered, and often yield items of value (as well as the occasional washing machine mid spin cycle), while larger hangars might conceal a tank with which to wreak havoc. Destroyed landmarks remain that way, providing a possible tactical advantage later on; enemy uniforms can be stolen and worn; and the local residents will often give up useful information if bribed. The game provides a story, and even missions, but the real joy here is using your own tactics, improvising on the fly; and knowing that your experience is distinct from other players'. **BM**

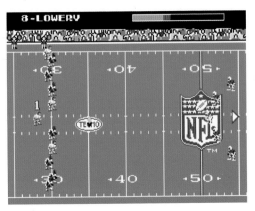

Tecmo Super Bowl

Original release date : 1991
Platform : NES
Developer : Tecmo
Genre : Sports

For a small, dedicated subculture of fanatics, video game American football begins and ends with *Tecmo Super Bowl*. Boasting a full complement of twenty-eight NFL teams and a customizable playbook, *Tecmo Super Bowl* was a revelatory upgrade of the crude gridiron simulators that preceded it. Yet the game play was still simple enough to allow a casual football fan to catch on after a few minutes.

Thanks to a fast pace, it's possible to play four quarters of football in about twenty minutes and, given the game's ability to simulate an entire pro season, the allure of a marathon session is strong. Before every down, both players secretly choose from a menu of eight plays—four runs, four passes—furtively cupping their hands over their controllers to keep the other guy from peeking.

The one aspect of football that *Tecmo Super Bowl* captures perfectly is gamesmanship. The action on the field may not be realistic but the psychological warfare is spot-on. That's why loyal communities continue to play *Tecmo Super Bowl* online, hacking the original cartridge data each year to reflect present-day NFL rosters. **JT**

Mega Lo Mania

Original release date : 1991
Platform : Various
Developer : Sensible Software
Genre : Strategy

The birthplace of Sensible Software's famous "little people" graphic style, *Mega Lo Mania* is a surprisingly reserved title from the otherwise madcap developer. A real-time strategy, or god, game in the vein of *Populous*, *Mega Lo Mania* allows the player to select one of four deity-type figures and battle against other gods for control of twenty-eight islands across ten epochs of time. Technologies range from rocks and sticks to flying saucers and laser turrets. Though the player is unable to control units directly, *Mega Lo Mania's* play is cleverly nuanced and highly strategic.

With a clear and succinct design, bolstered by a streamlined and intuitive interface, *Mega Lo Mania* is still playable in a way that many other real-time strategy titles fail to be, making it unfortunate that the game's planned sequel, *Mega Lo Mania II*, never saw the light of day.

Though it's never likely to be visited again (Sensible Software was absorbed by Codemasters in 1999), *Mega Lo Mania* is an intriguing dead end in the god game genre that deserves to be played by both fans of Sensible Software and real-time strategy games. **MKu**

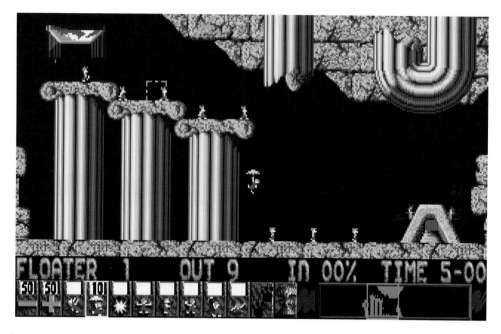

Lemmings

Original release date : 1991
Platform : Various
Developer : DMA Design
Genre : Puzzle

Few games other than *Tetris* can claim to have appeared on as many formats as this historic action puzzler. Dave Jones, the founder of DMA Design, claims to have lost count at twenty, and that was before the numerous PlayStation and mobile iterations were added to the list.

Famously, the idea was conceived almost by accident, when artist Mike Dailly was experimenting with the animation of tiny characters in an 8 x 8 pixel grid. Programmer Russell Kay saw the results and pronounced: "There's a game in that." And there certainly was.

At first glance, perhaps, *Lemmings* looks like a standard late-1980s platformer, its sparse yet neat visual style presenting teeny, teeming sprites. But it is, in fact, a

masterpiece of sandbox design, allowing players endless ways to complete each level. Over a vast series of levels, the player must guide a set number of tiny lemming characters from the entrance to the exit, avoiding hazards such as lava pools and large falls. Instead of directly controlling the critters, however, there is a range of eight skills that can be designated to individuals via a point-and-click interface.

The builder skill, for example, allows a lemming to construct a staircase across a chasm, while bashers, miners, and diggers all create differently angled holes in platforms to create new routes. It is up to the player to decide how the available skills should be used to solve each level.

Press coverage at the launch was very enthusiastic, and 55,000 copies flew from shop shelves on day one (impressive at the time). The ensuing conveyor belt of sequels and conversions led to subsequent sales of more than fifteen million units. Alongside contemporaries such as *Worms* and *Populous*, it's a defining work in the British game design canon. **KS**

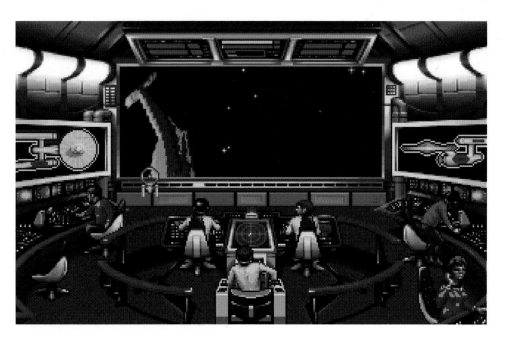

Star Trek: 25th Anniversary

Original release date : 1991
Platform : PC
Developer : Interplay
Genre : Action / Adventure

Here's a made up but patently true statistic: Eight out of ten *Star Trek* fans prefer the formularized soap of *The Next Generation* to Captain Kirk planting kisses and cardboard rocks on badly costumed aliens. Shame on them, really, and the hardware dominated video games they inspired— all first-person shooters and space combat sims. Not even 2009's hormonally charged movie reboot has rekindled interest in the original series, leaving a pair of outdated point-and-click affairs, *25th Anniversary* and *Judgment Rites*, as the finest *Trek* games to date.

One of the first games released as a CD-ROM "talkie," *25th Anniversary* arrived at just the right time to feature the voices of William Shatner (Kirk), Leonard Nimoy (Spock),

and the late DeForest Kelley (McCoy). Gaudier than even a Blu-ray version of the show's velour jumpsuits, it's hard to imagine a broader use of 256-color VGA graphics.

Faithful from the start, it divides its time between the captain's chair and away missions, even finding room for disposable cadets and their fateful red uniforms. Split into seven clearly defined episodes, it toyed with TV conventions long before *Alone in the Dark*.

Celebrity voice-overs are often hit or miss affairs. The good: *Ghostbusters*, *Heavenly Sword*, and later the *Grand Theft Auto* franchise; the bad: Connery in *From Russia With Love* and Eliza Dushku in *Wet*; and the ugly: Henry Rollins in *Mace Griffin: Bounty Hunter*. But the crew of the *Enterprise* clearly relish their return to duty, restoring the chemistry the game can't put on-screen. The script strikes just the right balance of jeopardy, comedy, and diplomatic hand wringing that makes up for an awkward interface. *25th Anniversary* is a giddy delight for fans, not to mention anyone tired of gaming's trend toward sobriety. **DH**

Sonic the Hedgehog

Original release date : 1991
Platform : Mega Drive
Developer : Sega
Genre : Platform

It's easy to write off good old Sonic as Sega's simple response to Mario—fast where the tubby plumber is plodding, filled with impatient attitude where Nintendo's mascot is cheerily serene—but Yuji Naka's original design has since proved to be something of a classic.

Spiky and blue and decked out in a snappy pair of running shoes, Sonic is a legitimate video game behemoth in his own right, powering through the famous checkerboard hills of the Green Zone without a care in the world. He has become something of a video game icon.

Even now, the speed can be astonishing at times. All Sonic needs is a gentle nudge and he's off, disappearing into the far edge of the screen, and momentarily out of sight, as he bounces through elaborate levels that have more than a little in common with pinball tables. One level, in fact, even appears to have been built inside an actual pinball table, and it's telling that Sonic feels entirely natural pinging off buffers and disappearing down metal tubes only to pop out somewhere else a millisecond later.

When the action slows down, as in the more thoughtful Marble Zone, with its deadly pools of lava and gentle block puzzles, or in the watery mires of the crystalline Labyrinth Zone, things inevitably begin to drag somewhat. However, a suite of hidden features, plus excellent boss battles, and some irritatingly catchy theme music more than make up for any slow spots in the game.

In fact, Sonic has never been better than he is here, right back at the beginning of it all, before his charmless family and friends began to intrude and the advent of 3-D gaming knocked the confidence out of him. Play *Sonic the Hedgehog* today on Xbox Live Arcade, or in dozens of different collection sets, to get a real taste of yesterday's idea of the future. **CD**

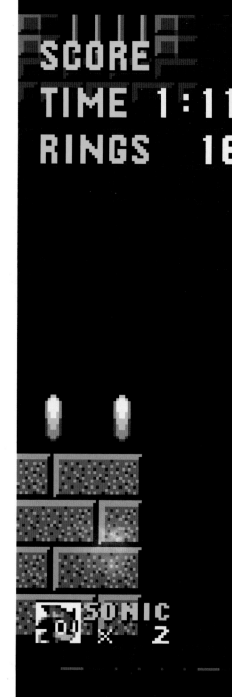

The Legend of the Mystical Ninja

Original release date : 1991

Platform : SNES

Developer : Konami

Genre : Action / Adventure

A series with a long and varied history in Japan, *The Legend of the Mystical Ninja* remains a strange rarity in the West. It's a beautiful and funny action/adventure game that emerged with the birth of the SNES and remains a shining example of everything the 16-bit era promised, and eventually delivered upon.

The Legend of the Mystical Ninja is a two-player cooperative title that incorporates platforming, fighting, and exploring elements that deliver a truly entertaining gaming experience. Each stage is broken down into a series of different events. The first is a town exploration mode that is usually followed by a platform adventure section. However, variations abound with lavish bosses

intruding into the environments and certain levels performing almost like piggyback vehicle speed runs. Weapons and moves are also brushed up generously throughout the riotous course of the tumbling adventure.

At the time of its release the sheer number of activities that players could engage in was quietly astonishing. Putting your head through funny statues served little game play value, but made the world feel richer and more interactive. Touches like these are what make a game so much more memorable. Even the music is among the best on the console, a series of lilting, Eastern-flavored tunes that will stick in the memory long after the ageing cartridge has been consigned to the attic.

The Legend of the Mystical Ninja is a great game for those enjoyable moments when gamers reminisce about the good old days of video gaming. *The Legend of the Mystical Ninja* is vivid, silly, and great two-player fun. And, of course, if you really enjoy it, there's always eBay as a means of tracking down the rest of the series. **CD**

The Legend of Zelda: A Link to the Past

Original release date : 1991
Platform : SNES
Developer : Nintendo
Genre : Action / Adventure

The reason the SNES has such a towering reputation among gamers—even those who were too young to have bought one originally—is because Nintendo's most treasured franchises all received updates that count among their respective series' best. Mario was arguably never greater than he was in *Super Mario World*, Samus Aran never beat *Super Metroid* for either style or substance, and *A Link to the Past* remains one of the most complex and confidently constructed *Zelda* games of all time.

Awoken in the middle of the night, young Link makes the perilous journey to Hyrule Castle, where he witnesses a staggering cataclysm that threatens to reopen an ancient door between two worlds. The boyish hero finds his homeland shattered into two separate dimensions: a light world—where the grass is green, trees are cute little bulbs of leaves, and the villages are neat and tidy—and a darker world, made from deserts and gnarled clumps of rock, where hideous malformed monsters trample the earth, and the smart little royal castle has been replaced by an ominous-looking pyramid.

These two realities fit together like clockwork, the game's best puzzles relying on a manipulation of both environments to progress. *A Link to the Past* is filled with simple genius: complex dungeons that are a high watermark for the series, dazzling bosses, and a superb lineup of useful gadgets.

From the world-shattering eruptions of the main plot to the sleepy discovery of the traveler camped beneath a bridge, *A Link to the Past* has so many moods, and so many brilliant ideas, that it's almost impossible to beat. *Ocarina of Time*, the long-awaited sequel, would just about manage that feat, but it remains a very close call. **CD**

NHL Hockey

Original release date : 1991
Platform : Mega Drive
Developer : Park Place Productions
Genre : Sports

For most essential sports games, the defining factor that makes them so interesting is simply that they were first, or best, at representing their chosen sport in the video game format. Not so for Electronic Arts's 1991 entry into the otherwise underrepresented ice hockey genre.

What sets *NHL Hockey* apart from its peers is a perfect implementation of a feature that would come to dominate the multiplayer sports game experience for the fiercely competitive player—the instant replay. No game has made the instant replay as integral and as exciting.

Scoring a goal in ice hockey is a challenge. With a crowded rink and large goal keepers, each goal—followed by that iconic siren—is a thrill that you want to experience again and again. You only have to watch one of the most famous scenes of the 1996 independent film classic, *Swingers,* to observe the power of *NHL Hockey's* instant replay on the male competitive dynamic. A bold Trent (Vince Vaughn), having scored on Sue's (Patrick Van Horn) beloved LA Kings, forces him to watch the goal again and again until the argument explodes into physical violence. The power of the replay is undeniable.

Though the original *NHL Hockey* was awkwardly localized outside of North America as *EA Hockey* and offers little in the way of options, other than playing single games or playoffs, the title remains as playable as it always was. The movement of the players on the ice was the first to feel right, and frequent fights ensured that every match was full of action (fights would be removed by *NHL '94*). Like *Sensible Soccer, NHL Hockey* is a peerless two-dimensional representation of its sport. Even if you have to unpack your Mega Drive to play it, the instant replay of the first goal you score against a friend is going to be worth it. **MKu**

Micro Machines

Original release date : 1991
Platform : NES
Developer : Codemasters
Genre : Driving / Racing

Before the arrival of the eponymous video game, Micro Machines were tiny model cars designed to be bought cheaply and then repurchased fairly regularly when the originals got sucked into the guts of a passing vacuum cleaner or lost, tragically, down the murky back of the sofa. Many people don't remember that now, and are far more likely to equate Micro Machines with Codemasters's brilliant little racing game for the NES platform.

And "little" is, rather suitably, the operative word for this particular outing. *Micro Machines* takes the toys' diminutive statures and sets races in a range of delightfully Swiftian settings, all riddled with the familiar trappings of domesticity. There are garden paths, with huge tufts of grass and rocks to skirt around, breakfast tables with tracks marked by lines of cereal crumbs, and even school desks, where notebooks and pens are waiting to trip you up. Add to this a range of different vehicles that allow you to experiment in ways that you might not have expected, and you have a hugely entertaining title.

Smart art design wouldn't have been enough if the game wasn't up to the challenge, however. The racing experts at Codemasters also crafted a smart and visceral racer, where your forward momentum is as likely to steer you off route and into disaster as it is to carry you over the finish line, while devious courses are just itching to trip you up as well as simply look cute. The idea stuck, and *Micro Machines* would be a feature of the gaming landscape long after the NES had been filed away in the attic, with titles—including the Europe and Australia-only *Micro Machines Military*—for everything from the Sega Mega Drive to the N64. All of those are very playable today, of course, but none of them, somewhat inevitably, have quite the freshness of this original 8-bit classic. **CD**

Final Fantasy V

Original release date : 1992
Platform : Super Famicom
Developer : Square
Genre : Role-Playing

It was ten years before the fifth *Final Fantasy* received an official English language release, although fans painstakingly did the work of translating the game's thousands of lines of dialogue themselves years earlier despite the threat of litigation. Their efforts show the affection fans of the series, and its associated genre, have for this Super Famicom title, which is still widely regarded by many employees of Square Enix (as Square is known today) as one of the best *Final Fantasy* games.

After the plot-heavy previous game, *Final Fantasy V* shifted its emphasis on to the battle system, giving the heart of this Japanese role-playing game (RPG) a severe overhaul. Principal among the game's innovations was the introduction of the Active Time Battle System, which, in measuring the amount of time you take to input a command during a battle, intensified the pressure at the core of the Japanese RPG experience. Its influence can be seen in almost all subsequent *Final Fantasy* games, including the thirteenth title on the PlayStation 3.

Moreover, the game radically broadened the scope of the job class system, allowing players to set up their band of warriors in whatever way they saw fit, making for far more dynamic and flexible battles. With twenty-two job classes, each with its own strength and weakness, the game can be played as offensively or defensively as players desire. So successful was *Final Fantasy V*'s job system that it went on to inform many other esteemed Square Enix titles, most notably *Final Fantasy Tactics*.

While part five's story may be far more simplistic than that featured in the games immediately preceding and following it, it's a functional tale that drives players toward the jewels of the experience—its battle system and associated character development trees. **SP**

Dragon Quest V

Original release date : 1992
Platform : Various
Developer : ChunSoft
Genre : Role-Playing

Dragon Quest V brandishes many of the tropes that make the Japanese RPG so divisive. With traditional random battles that punctuate every journey across the game world, and a simple fairy-tale story of a mysterious baby who the player guides through boyhood to maturity in a series of sequential chapters, the game's framework does little to broaden the scope of the genre. But despite this, the fifth title in Japan's favored RPG series fizzes with creativity. In part this is due to the delicate balance of humor and tragedy that infuses the story, courting cliché at all times, yet somehow evading it by way of thoughtful twists on well-worn themes.

Perhaps most significant, however, is the game's monster-hunting submechanic, an idea that directly begat *Pokémon* and its legion of imitators. By the midway point of the game it's possible to recruit almost any monster encountered in a battle, bringing them into your four-man-beast party to do battle against their own kind. Every monster in the game has its own elaborate development tree, ensuring that even the smallest, most insignificant foe can, in time, be turned into a powerhouse. The freedom the system affords players was unrivaled at the time of release and, even today, it represents one of the high points for a flexible party system.

While playable on Nintendo DS through a recent remake, complete with a graphical overhaul, there is no escaping the game's maturity, and many of its choices in style and design will seem anachronistic to contemporary players. But for those to whom J-RPGs are stories as much as anything else, *Dragon Quest V*'s breezy approach is both fresh and deserving of ongoing attention. The game was popular upon release, spawning a manga comic, and even scoring a release for Kōichi Sugiyama's soundtrack. **SP**

Alone in the Dark

Original release date : 1992
Platform : Various
Developer : Infogrames
Genre : Survival Horror

The fixed camera, the early 3-D graphics, the dreamlike sense of only partial control—the origins of survival horror can indeed be traced to *Alone in the Dark*. While it's true that *Sweet Home*, a 1989 movie tie-in for the NES, had just as direct an influence over *Resident Evil*, the use of polygonal characters over prerendered backdrops was even greater. This technological breakthrough, one of the first and most important of the 3-D era, would, in one way or another, come to define Capcom's series for more than fifteen successful years. Even *Resident Evil 5*, a game that promised a break from the so-called "tank" control scheme, feels haunted by it.

The similarities begin early, players choosing one of two characters, a man or a woman, before braving the game's story. Edward Carnby is a private investigator sent to recover a prized piano from an antique dealer's loft. Emily Hartwood is after it too, but only to recover a hidden suicide note from her late uncle Jeremy. Both paths lead to Derceto, a haunted mansion in rural Louisiana, where the truth is protected by monsters, booby traps, and hidden manuscripts, all inspired by the Cthulhu Mythos, the universe created by American horror writer H. P. Lovecraft.

The mix of zombies, mutant wildlife, escape scenario, and puzzle solving will strike an even louder chord with *Resident Evil* fans—as will the game's promise of "a paralyzing sense of personal danger"—though the lack of military themes gives it a more domestic weapon set. The lack of textures for its polygons, meanwhile, creates what's rightly been called an "origami" look, its models evolving from those of *Flashback* and *Prince of Persia* and never quite blending into the backgrounds. The years have been kindest to the fixed camera system, a gimmick made convention by its use elsewhere. **DH**

Pinball Dreams

Original release date : 1992
Platform : Various
Developer : Digital Illusions CE
Genre : Pinball

Pinball Dreams appeals to two different types of nostalgia at once. Obviously, it's catnip for pinball wizards who grew up on the machines of the 1970s, when the tables were simple and digital video displays were unheard of. But the game also stirs fond memories among the many fans of the Commodore Amiga, a home computer platform whose salad days were the late 1980s and early 1990s. The original *Pinball Dreams* was so popular on the Amiga that Commodore packaged a copy with some of its later models. Alas, the Amiga is dead, but *Pinball Dreams* is timeless, with ports on a slew of other platforms—most recently Apple's iPhone and Sony's PSP.

The game consists of four different machines—*Ignition*, *Steel Wheel*, *Beat Box*, and *Nightmare*—each of which mimics pinball design from the early arcade era. Some of the designs have aged better than others. The neon graffiti and clumsy lingo ("rock da house!") of the music-themed *Beat Box* feels awfully quaint nowadays, while the primary reds and blues of *Ignition*'s rocket launch still look as sharp as ever.

Navigating the terrain—ramps, spot targets, and, of course, that maddening gap between the flippers—is no picnic on these punishing tables, but with a little persistence, you will discover yourself making surprisingly accurate shots. Of course, the success of any pinball game ultimately rests on its physics, and *Pinball Dreams* gained fame largely because it was the first game to feature a ball with some realistic heft. No, it's not quite the same as playing at the arcade, but it comes mighty close. And given the impracticalities of lugging an actual table on the subway (not to mention it's murder on your back), *Pinball Dreams* is a solid option for the pinball fan with a long commute. **JT**

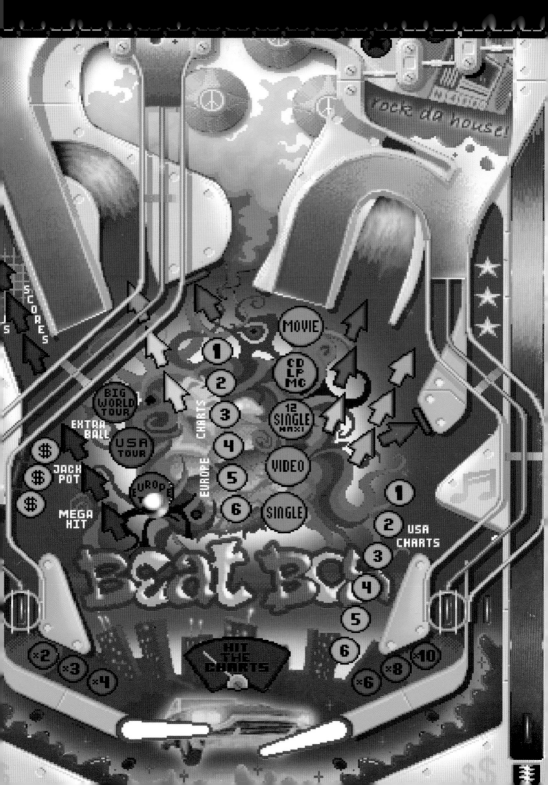

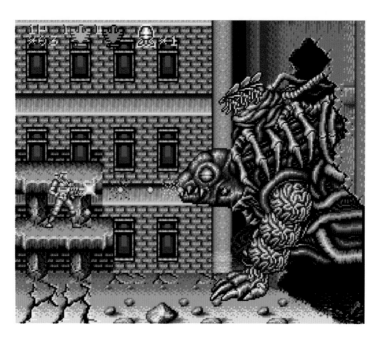

Contra III: The Alien Wars

Original release date : 1992
Platform : SNES
Developer : Konami
Genre : Shoot 'Em Up

Praise the lord for fans of rather banal testosterone-soaked side-scrolling shooters, because with the third game in the *Contra* series, Konami finally made something special out of its tired old merc stereotypes. Still playing as Lance and Bill, the bulging offspring of Steven Seagal and John Rambo, *Contra III: The Alien Wars* tossed away the previous games' human enemies and Reagan-era politics in favor of a balls-out cosmic battle of death rays, with an entire alien invasion force lining up to be wasted by the simple combination of running and gunning.

It's still a side-scrolling shooter for the most part, but now you're as likely to be jumping from rocket to rocket, blasting something ugly and green as you are to be on a

jet bike or even, on the odd occasion, in your own size-16 standard-issues. Occasional top-down sections provide opportunities to show off the SNES's Mode 7 graphics, with enemies barreling into and out of the screen toward your psychopathic grunts, as well as introducing a puzzle edge to the environments—but only a very slight one.

It's not the longest of games (a runthrough takes no more than two hours), but within its limits *Contra III* does everything it can to knock your socks off, as well as your head. There are bosses that take up half the screen, entire levels involving climbing huge structures, fast and deadly vehicles, and a brilliant assortment of alien-slaying guns that constantly interchange. It tells its own story that more than a decade later, when Konami finally decided to make *Contra IV*, its developer, Wayforward Technologies, ended up including so many ideas from the *Alien Wars* that the follow-up feels more like a tribute than a sequel. Not the smartest game you'll ever play, but a hell of a lot more fun than most. **RS**

Desert Strike: Return to the Gulf

Original release date : 1992
Platform : Various
Developer : Electronic Arts
Genre : Shoot 'Em Up

Ah, the good old days. In *Desert Strike* you're briefed by Stormin' Norman Schwarzkopf about a "psycho madman" called Kilbaba, who the artists didn't even try to make unlike Saddam Hussein, and then let loose in a digital version of Iraq with an Apache attack helicopter. *Desert Strike* took at least one idea straight from *Defender*, but its isometric perspective and tactical weapon set, not to mention the latitude in how to approach mission objectives, created an action game that verged on the strategic.

Its greatest touch is the momentum of the helicopter itself: The controls are intuitive and responsive, but the vehicle has its own mass and has to be shepherded as well as sent in with guns blazing. A central objective is always

to rescue stranded soldiers, which sees you tipping back and forth above them, lining up your ladder and silently begging for the little trooper to grab it, before slamming the nose down and speeding away with GI Joe hanging on for dear life. You're a savior as well as a destroyer in *Desert Strike*, a one-man army waging an entire war as well as a rescue mission.

Electronic Arts would go on to make four sequels to *Desert Strike*, which crescendoed from *Jungle Strike* in 1993 to *Nuclear Strike* in 1997 (a follow-up titled *Future Strike* has been hinted at for some years), but despite their competence, none approached *Desert Strike*'s simplicity of attack and rescue: tilt forward, tilt back. Its forbidding orange landscape populated with helpless sprites and SCUD missile launchers was pop warfare at its early '90s finest: low on politics and as iconic as it is dumb. If there's a place in heaven for old war games, *Desert Strike* lies peacefully under a headstone inscribed "Best game that never featured Wagner in its soundtrack." **RS**

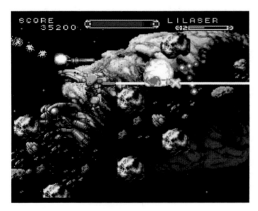

Cybernator

Original release date : 1992
Platform : SNES
Developer : NCS
Genre : Shoot 'Em Up

Cybernator was the kind of game that gave Western game developers sleepless nights. It captured everything Japanese designers did so right: futuristic, robotic space warfare featuring an inspired synthesis of platforming, shooting, jet-packing, and robotic fisticuffs.

The hybridized game play included some truly novel features. Star of the show was undoubtedly the player's mecha—a lumbering war machine endowed with realistic weight, gun recoil, and inertia. With a machine gun, flamethrower, fist, and shield on hand, lesser designers could have overwhelmed the player. But thankfully NCS had the foresight to lock the directional gun (or shield) of the mech so that it's possible to jump in one direction while firing in another.

Cybernator's Western translation was tainted by a butchering of its original content, and as a result it lacks some of the gravitas of its Japanese counterpart. But the game still stands as a testament to progressive arcade game design, and only its lack of levels detracts from what is a much-underrated classic. **JB**

Super Mario Kart

Original release date : 1992
Platform : SNES
Developer : Nintendo
Genre : Driving

Imagination has always been a cornerstone of the Mushroom Kingdom, but it took a special flight of fancy to create *Super Mario Kart*. Taking the chirpy Italian plumber out of side-scrolling levels and thrusting him into the competitive world of the racetrack was a brave decision and one that had serious—mostly positive—repercussions for the franchise. *Super Mario Kart* was the moment that Mario became a jack-of-all-trades, a mascot who could be slid into any kind of game.

And yet Mario looks very much at home in a kart, and that is perhaps because he's brought so much of his world with him. From the piranha plants popping up in the road to official race starter Lakitu and the other racers riding alongside Mario (including favorites such as Luigi, Yoshi, and Donkey Kong), this is an intelligent and creative use of the Nintendo world. The game is also a genuinely great racer, with the SNES's trademark Mode 7 graphics allowing for environments that rotate smoothly around the vehicles and a tidy range of power-ups available to alter the outcome of the race. **CD**

Axelay

Original release date : 1992
Platform : SNES
Developer : Konami
Genre : Shoot 'Em Up

Axelay was the first classic Nintendo 16-bit shoot 'em up. Whereas early SNES shooters, like UN Squadron and Gradius III, had been full of slowdown due to embarrassing technical issues, Axelay was a star performer from the outset: a shooter engineered from the ground up with a complement of speed, special effects, and coin-op-quality aesthetics to win over doubters of the SNES platform.

While its power-ups were fairly conventional, Axelay is perhaps best remembered for the pseudo-3-D distortion on its vertical levels, as well as an array of detailed side-scrolling space stations, futuristic cities, and snugly configured underwater caves. There was also a full suite of impressive bosses—such as the memorable ED-209–inspired robot walker—and an atmospheric soundtrack punctuated by trademark Konami commentary samples.

Axelay's only real flaw is that there simply isn't enough of the game—just six levels—to sustain longevity. But as an example of early '90s home gaming ascending into the realms of arcade quality, most would agree that it is an experience well worth savoring. **JB**

Flashback

Original release date : 1992
Platform : Various
Developer : Delphine Software
Genre : Action / Adventure

Reportedly the best-selling French game of all time, Flashback was a phenomenon when it debuted on Commodore's Amiga in 1992, and it remains a fascinating experience today. It's a science-fiction action adventure set in the year 2142, viewed side on, like traditional 2-D platform games, and is in a sense "realistic" as the character explores the world in a manner consistent with him being a normal human being.

Flashback is not a game where the skills of platforming are the payoff, however. The rewards here are in carefully exploring the rich environments and figuring out what you need to do in order to progress. As in traditional point-and-click adventure games, the solutions are often obscure, meaning that patience and experimentation are rewarded as much as skill and finesse with a joystick. All this technical and game design cleverness would be for nought if the game didn't have a decent story at the heart of it, and Flashback's tale of alien infiltration and forced amnesia is superb. It juggles action with atmosphere and delivers a game that is both intriguing and tense. **JR**

Indiana Jones and the Fate of Atlantis

Original release date : 1992

Platform : Various

Developer : LucasArts

Genre : Adventure

While Indiana Jones's return to cinema languished in development hell for nearly twenty years until *Indiana Jones and the Kingdom of the Crystal Skull* was released in 2008, the series received what many consider to be his "true" fourth adventure in the form of *Indiana Jones and the Fate of Atlantis* in 1992, a mere three years after the good doctor rode off into the sunset at the end of *Indiana Jones and the Last Crusade*.

Designed by Hal Barwood (who had previously worked with Steven Spielberg on *The Sugarland Express*) and Noah Falstein, the game has everything an Indy fan could expect—double-crossing Nazis, international travel, mysterious artifacts, and, of course, a love interest who at times proves more trouble for Jones than his enemies—wrapped up in LucasArts's SCUMM adventure engine while it was at the height of its powers.

Unlike other graphic adventures of the time, which tended to offer one static solution, *Indiana Jones and the Fate of Atlantis* gives players the choice of following the Fists path (a lighter, more action movie–like experience), the Wits path (lots of problem solving), or the balanced Team path (which features love interest Sophia Hapgood throughout). This allows you to tailor your game to how you see Indiana Jones—a lover, a fighter, a mild-mannered archeologist—as does a well-written story with a wide variety of dialogue options, giving the player a strong sense of authorship over their play, though it is possible to get stuck (and even die) on some of the trickiest puzzles.

Indiana Jones and the Fate of Atlantis is the rare example of a game that succeeds where installments in the original film series failed, and is a glorious and still-playable tribute to a character who endures. **MKu**

Mortal Kombat

Original release date : 1992
Platform : Various
Developer : Midway
Genre : Fighting

It may be one of the most popular arcade games of all time, but the biggest myth about *Mortal Kombat* is that it's a classic. This is a game that rode a wave of notoriety like few others, and despite its manifold flaws, manages to retain devotees even now. And, to be fair, *Mortal Kombat* does have a little substance beyond the gore.

The "photorealistic" visuals were pioneering, though their impact was rather spoiled by the fact that all seven fighters move and attack in very similar fashions. The fighting system was the first to include "juggling," by which opponents can be repeatedly struck while in the air, and this was the first fighting game with an unlockable secret character, Reptile.

Then there are the fatalities. At the end of the fight, when your opponent is beaten, they stagger in front of you waiting for the coup de grâce. What shall it be? Liu Kang turning into a dragon and eating them? Sub Zero freezing their body to shatter it with an uppercut? Sonya's deadly kiss? To teenagers at the time of the game's release, the combinations were the key to bragging rights. To Senators Joseph Lieberman and Herb Kohl, who headed a US government inquiry into "video game violence and the corruption of society," they contributed to all future video games being rated in the region via the formation of the Entertainment Software Rating Board.

In terms of violence, it's a silly game rather than a bloodthirsty one, and the character design stands the test of time in a way that the combat doesn't. Despite its limitations, *Mortal Kombat* retains a certain charm today, but it is a cultural landmark rather than a classic video game. For a brief while in the autumn of 1992, though, it seemed like the most important game in the world. **RS**

Sonic the Hedgehog 2

Original release date : 1992
Platform : Mega Drive
Developer : Sega
Genre : Platform

Mario games tend to be wildly different from one outing to the next. Sonic, although speedier on foot, has had a far more gentle evolution, and *Sonic the Hedgehog 2* is everything a well-handled sequel to a hit game should be: more of the same, a little bit prettier, a little bit bigger, and a little bit more intricate.

If several of the first Sonic game's levels seemed like out-of-control pinball machines, *Sonic the Hedgehog 2* only takes that further, with a couple of zones that act more as spectacle, in which the player can steer a little bit but often has to rely on luck. The game is staggeringly fast and a whirling, complex delight to watch. Areas feel bigger and more inventive, and boss fights, although fitting into the

same basic mold, often feature a clever twist or two. The bonus stages have gotten perhaps the biggest graphical upgrade, turning from a spinning headache-inducing 2-D maze to a kind of psychedelic 3-D-effect luge in which Sonic runs into the screen, collecting rings as he goes. Granted, it looks a little outdated today, but in the early '90s, it presented the serious prospect that 16-bit graphics might simply struggle to ever improve on it.

Then there's Tails, Sonic's ally, a fox with two tails. On the plus side, he allows for two-player action, which the game handles with remarkable assurance, and barely a drop in the ever-important frame rate. On the minus side, Tails opened the floodgate for the influx of Sonic's loathsome extended cast, the absolute nadir of which is Shadow the Hedgehog, who inexplicably got his own wretched game on the GameCube, PS2, and Xbox. For the time being, however, with the first of many sequels, it was just Sonic and Tails—the world was in balance, and all was good, clean, fast-moving fun in Greenhill Zone. **CD**

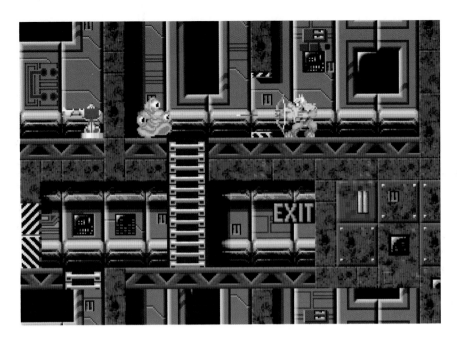

The Lost Vikings

Original release date : 1992
Platform : Various
Developer : Silicon & Synapse
Genre : Puzzle / Platform

The company behind *The Lost Vikings* might not sound familiar, but that's because it changed its name shortly after the release of this title. Silicon & Synapse had turned into Blizzard Entertainment by the time of the release of what is considered its breakthrough hit, *Warcraft: Orcs & Humans*, beginning the inexorable journey toward *World of Warcraft*.

However, Silicon & Synapse is arguably the more interesting company. Counter to Blizzard's later tendency to plagiarize setting and design from the likes of *Warhammer* and *Dune II*, *The Lost Vikings* is an entirely original idea. Starring Erik the Swift, Baleog the Fierce, and Olaf the Stout as a set of Vikings who find themselves

kidnapped by an alien race and lost in the mists of time, the player's aim is to use each of the trio's unique abilities (Erik can run and jump, Baleog can fight enemies and shoot arrows, and Olaf the Stout can use his shield to block attacks, or as a platform or parachute) to complete levels.

As a puzzle/platformer that has rarely been cloned, *The Lost Vikings* has much to offer interested gamers. While too often mistakes can lead to the death of one of the Vikings (each has only three hit points) and thus require that the entire level be restarted, each stage is an intriguing challenge in and of itself, similar to the *Lemmings* titles. Once the solution is found it can be a little trying to move each Viking toward it—the characters have no personal agency—but players are regularly rewarded with humorous back-and-forths between the three in their in-game dialogue.

Level themes never stray too far from platform game classics, but *The Lost Vikings*'s continually intriguing puzzle design enshrines it as a still-captivating treat. **MKu**

Virtua Racing

Original release date : 1992
Platform : Arcade
Developer : Sega
Genre : Driving

To play *Virtua Racing* is to understand why 3-D gaming was never merely a possibility, but an inevitability. Although it wasn't the first racing game to attempt three-dimensionality (that honor goes to Atari's *Hard Drivin'*, released three years earlier), it was perhaps the first to treat polygons not as a graphical gimmick but as an opportunity to expand the boundaries of traditional driving games. *Virtua Racing* employs technology in service of the game play, not at the expense of it.

Consider one of the game's many innovations, the "V.R. View" system, which allows players to switch between four different camera angles on the fly. It sure looks neat, as your perspective swoops from behind the wheel, all

the way back to a high and wide shot, all in one smooth motion. Which viewpoint you choose impacts how you drive. Inside the car, you get the best sense of your car's handling, but less time to react to the course and to other racers. Up high, you can see more of what's ahead and what the other cars are doing, but you're disconnected from the tactile feel of your vehicle. You may prefer one perspective to the others, or switch between them depending on the situation.

Virtua Racing was advanced for its time and played on the 16-bit Sega Genesis via special polygon-pushing hardware called the Sega Virtua Processor soldered into the cartridge itself. The home version was expensive when first released, though today it can be had cheaply from various online resellers, while an even more faithful version for the ill-fated Sega 32X includes two brand-new tracks. The arcade version is definitive, but play *Virtua Racing* in any flavor and you'll understand everything that follows it. It's like witnessing the discovery of fire. **MK**

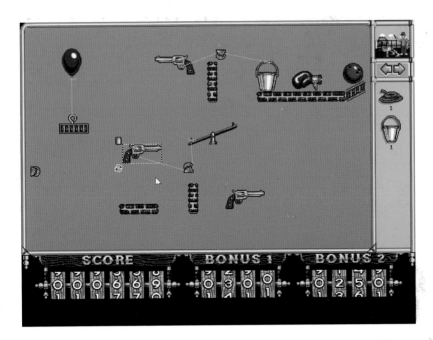

The Incredible Machine

Original release date : 1992
Platform : Various
Developer : Dynamix
Genre : Puzzle

Emergent game play and physics-based interactivity may seem like fresh concepts, but it was *The Incredible Machine* that really introduced these major game components almost twenty years ago.

Without doubt inspired by the ridiculously elaborate contraptions imagined by cartoonists Heath Robinson and Rube Goldberg, *The Incredible Machine* tasks players with inventing their own devices to carry out a series of simple actions. On each level an objective is given, ranging from popping a series of balloons to launching rockets to re-housing goldfish. A range of "useful" components is provided in an inventory box, and these can be dragged and dropped onto the game space to construct the relevant machine. Basketballs, torches, and pulleys all figure—as do mice, cats, and monkeys on bicycles—and all can be variously combined to complete the tasks.

The beauty of the game is its accurate simulation of gravity, inertia, and other vital physical processes. Just as important, there is no one way to complete each level, an emergent approach that encourages endless experimentation. The game also comes with a sandbox mode in which users are free to construct their own machines from scratch.

The game was a huge success on the PC (later appearing on the Mac and 3DO console), and creators Kevin Ryan and Jeff Tunnell would carry on to oversee two sequels, as well as a range of spin-offs, before their company, Dynamix, was dissolved in 2001. The series would surface again in 2007 as a mobile adaptation, courtesy of Vivendi. Two years later, Tunnell bought back the rights and further titles are planned. After a decade-long hiatus, the machine is finally being switched back on. **KS**

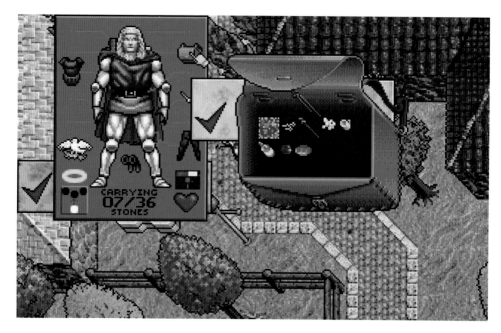

Ultima VII

Original release date : 1992
Platform : PC
Developer : Origin Systems
Genre : Role-Playing

Ultima VII marks the last game in Richard Garriott's series that could be called a success. Once again, the player visits Britannia as the Avatar, hooking up with old friends, like Iolo and Katrina. Once again, Lord British is in trouble and the land needs saving. But *Ultima VII* improved the interface and offered a more fluid experience than previous editions. As soon as players enter the game's world, they must use the mouse for almost every action. They are tasked with investigating a murder scene—a messy, ritualistic affair—and every object in the stable, however mundane, is clickable. From there, the same continental landmass and major cities of the past *Ultimas* will greet you, but the improvements give you a fresh perspective.

With a mystery to solve, players spend much of the game hunting for clues and secrets, and talking to everyone in sight. On top of the main plot lies a philosophical debate: The player learns about a Fellowship that is undermining the Avatar's teachings and pushing the values of unity, trust, and worthiness. You discover that the Fellowship is a cult that perverts the values it teaches; but it's a thoughtful cult, and it fits Garriott's tendency to bring abstract values to his stats-based role-playing.

The game sold and reviewed well. But for Origin, the writing was on the wall: The company was sold to Electronic Arts, and jabs at the parent company abound. For example, the names of two traitors in the game begin with the letters E and A. *Ultima VII* saw two expansions and a part two (*Serpent Isle*), but the next chapter, *Ultima VIII*, was glitchy and incomplete, and critical bugs frustrated what should have been a triumphant end to the franchise with *Ultima IX* in 1999. Technical problems are unfortunately one of the legacies of Origin's great fantasy series. **CDa**

Harkonnen Quad.

PALACE
DMG
REPAIR
LAUNCH

Dune II

Original release date : 1992
Platform : Various
Developer : Westwood Studios
Genre : Strategy

While it does a decent enough job of pleasing fans of the source material, history probably won't remember Dune II for the ease with which it threaded itself into the terrifyingly complex science-fiction world established in Frank Herbert's weighty bestseller. Its worth to gamers— even those who would have trouble picking a genuine sandworm out of a police lineup—is as a title that helped solidify an emerging genre, establishing the framework for the games that would follow.

The genre in question was real-time strategy, the hugely popular PC-centric war games in which the player acts as a commanding officer, building up forces and then dispatching them across the battlefield. Like almost all the RTS games that would swarm and multiply in its wake, Dune II revolves around harvesting resources (spice, in Herbert's fiction) to building the battle units necessary to lead one of a handful of opposing factions—galactic houses in this case—to victory in separate campaigns.

It's easy to point out the things that Westwood Studios did first: Dune II was the first RTS to use full mouse control, to have elaborate tech trees, and to put such a prime focus on resources. But harder to classify are the things it simply did better than anyone else. Mostly, it comes down to the maps themselves: Dune II's battlefields are tight, varied, and built for replaying, encouraging both unimaginative players and gifted strategists to experiment and discover the most interesting ways of examining situations.

Command & Conquer might be Westwood's most successful series, but so much of the good stuff started here, and even if you simply view it as an unofficial opening skirmish in the endless war between the Nod and the GDI, Dune II is well worth tracking down today. **CD**

Street Fighter II Turbo: Hyper Fighting

Original release date : 1992

Platform : Various

Developer : Capcom

Genre : Fighting

In 1991, Capcom released *Street Fighter II: The World Warrior*, and fighting games would never be the same again. With charismatic protagonists; grade-A audiovisual standards; and tight, supremely nuanced game play that married traditional combat with extravagant special moves, it went on to become a worldwide phenomenon. And, like so many phenomena, it spawned sequels. *Street Fighter II Turbo: Hyper Fighting* is the most intriguing of the permutations that Capcom's one-on-one beat 'em up would see before it was finally given a major update in the form of *Super Street Fighter II: The New Challengers* (1993).

Shortly after the release of 1992's *Champion Edition*, the hunger for *Street Fighter II* products was so great

that Chinese pirates had begun to operate sidelines in black-market upgrades to Capcom's arcade boards, their most infamous work being *Street Fighter II: Rainbow Edition*. Greatly increasing the speed of play and adding many additions, such as homing projectiles and fireball walls, these illicit reworkings reduced game play to an unbalanced mess, but still they found lucrative audiences.

Hyper Fighting was Capcom's attempt to stem the tide of such unlicensed modifications, increasing the speed of vanilla *Street Fighter II*, offering a new range of alternate colors for each character and, most notably, tweaking characters to fine-tune their abilities, as well as add new special moves, such as Chun-Li's fireball and Dhalsim's teleport. The game represents the peak of the *Street Fighter II* series, offering a selection of speed options and unparalleled level of balance that made unlicensed products, such as *Rainbow Edition*, essentially obsolete. Such considered updates mean that *Hyper Fighting* remains hugely enjoyable to this day. **MKu**

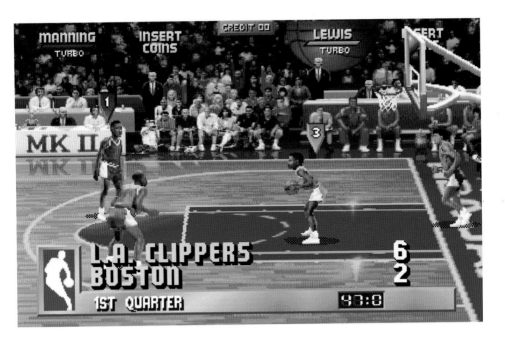

NBA Jam

Original release date : 1993
Platform : Various
Developer : Midway
Genre : Sports

The catchphrases are legendary: "He's on fire!" "Is it the shoes?" "From downtown!" You're apt to hear all these and more during a single game of *NBA Jam*, and if you need proof of the game's cultural currency, walk up to somebody, say any one of those statements, and see how they react. Most likely, they'll respond with the immortal, "Boom shakalaka!"

NBA Jam is the game of basketball as seen through a funhouse mirror. It uses real NBA teams and superstar players, such as Charles Barkley and Patrick Ewing, although that's about where similarities to the real thing end. (One notable omission is Michael Jordan, whose likeness was too pricey for Midway to license.) Teams take each other

on in games of two-on-two, which leads to fast-paced, high-scoring games without a lot of passing or strategy.

The game's true inspiration is to exaggerate the sport's traits beyond the limits of credulity. When a player hits three buckets in a row, he's said to be on fire, and from that point until the other team scores, he won't miss a shot, and the ball will scorch the net. The centerpiece of the game is its monster dunks—players can jam it in with a variety of long-distance tomahawks, behind-the-back moves, and aerial somersaults that take them outside the frame, each one lustily narrated by a Marv Albert soundalike.

NBA Jam's sense of fun knows no bounds. Fourth-quarter dunks have the effect of shattering the glass. A bevy of unlockable secret characters creates hilarious match-ups. Between the various arcade and home versions of the game, it's possible to play as actors, mascots, athletes from other sports, and even President Clinton. Slick Willie throwing down a baseline jam on Hakeem Olajuwon's head? Boom shakalaka! **MK**

Myst

Original release date : 1993
Platform : Various
Developer : Cyan Worlds
Genre : Adventure / Puzzle

The empty and enigmatic game *Myst* emerged into a world filled with noisy platformers, side-scrolling shooters, and brawlers, and clearly had other things on its mind from the beginning. This was a game about exploring rather than simply progressing to the far right side of the screen, about musing over scenarios rather than memorizing combos, and it was a lonely adventure suited to late evenings spent in front of the PC, perhaps with a printed-out FAQ to help when the whole thing got a bit too obscure.

Critics said *Myst* was nothing more than a vaguely interactive slide show, and on the surface, at least, their attacks have a point. Players explore the game's mysterious island setting by clicking on a series of beautifully rendered vistas, selecting their next location, interacting with many of the dormant machines, and piecing together—or failing to piece together—a complex backstory that leaves plenty to the imagination. By tightly controlling the interactivity, *Myst*'s developers ensured that they could put as much of their time as possible into making the game look good, and, for a good while, *Myst* appeared to be a bright shining gift from the future: a serene, poised, and complex vision compared to the pixelated firestorms that were taking place on other consoles.

The years have not been particularly kind, however. *Myst*'s brand of gentle interactivity have turned out to be something of a creative cul-de-sac, and despite the success of sequels like *Riven*, the game's developers eventually closed down their operations. Fortunately, this does not diminish the strange power of the original—a curate's egg, albeit a real money spinner at the time, and a journey to a land that games will probably never return to again in such a grand and openhanded manner. **CD**

Cannon Fodder

Original release date : 1993
Platform : Various
Developer : Sensible Software
Genre : Strategy / Action

Back in the early '90s, Sensible Software was a true maverick of the UK development scene, churning out 2-D classics like *Sensible World of Soccer* and *Mega Lo Mania*, all loaded with anarchic humor. With its pinpoint level design, detailed visuals, and tasteless jokes, *Cannon Fodder* provided the quintessence of the developer's approach.

Combining elements of the shoot 'em up and real-time strategy genres, *Cannon Fodder* requires gamers to guide a group of up to eight soldiers through seventy-two areas, shooting enemy soldiers, blowing up buildings, and rescuing hostages. Soldiers are directed via a point-and-click interface rather than direct control, and can be split into three separate squads in order to complete more

tactically demanding levels. The group management elements are deceptively complex, allowing the sharing of key weapons between squads and tactics, such as holding areas or surrounding enemy emplacements.

The brilliance of the game lies its nondidactic sandbox design, where players could roam at will. Players are given the tools to complete each level (including grenades, rocket launchers, and various vehicles, as well as the odd "supa dupa" power-up), but there are multiple routes to victory, echoing the emergent, open-ended approach of contemporaries such as *Lemmings* and *Dune II*.

But *Cannon Fodder* will also be remembered for its singular sense of humor. Beginning with a theme tune entitled "War Has Never Been So Much Fun," and ending each level by showing the graves of fallen comrades, the game is a sniggering satire on the glorification of war, with an underlying pacifistic message. Acclaimed by critics, *Cannon Fodder* is also revered by fans as one of the defining 16-bit computer games. **KS**

Maniac Mansion: Day of the Tentacle

Original release date : 1993
Platform : Various
Developer : LucasArts
Genre : Adventure

Ron Gilbert's *Maniac Mansion* of 1987 was an enjoyably atmospheric point-and-click adventure game with a lovely B-movie feel. *Day of the Tentacle*, its brilliant sequel, is an absolute A-list smash. Dazzling, 1950s-styled artwork and some wonderfully elastic character animation helps propel a team of hapless nerds through some of the most elaborate, fiendish, and satisfying puzzles of any LucasArts game before or since, and there's a joke—generally brilliantly played—lurking around almost every corner.

But *Day of the Tentacle*'s main trick isn't leveraging the familiar characters and setting. Rather, it comes from the game's time-travel plot, with temporal fluxes (characters travel back and forth through the future, sitting on top of toilets as they race to stop the purple tentacle from ruling the planet) providing some mesmerizingly brain-blasting puzzles, often requiring you to manipulate the same locations in a handful of different eras, trying to keep track of any possible repercussions your actions might lead to in other time periods. Cut down a tree in the past, for instance, and you'd best be prepared for it to zip out of existence in the future; change the design of a statue while it's still being carved and, years later, you can perhaps twist the dusty results to your own ends. With a cast that features mummified corpses and addled teens, as well as finding enough room to cram in cameos from America's Founding Fathers, every few minutes of progress herald a new surprise, and every fresh twist sends the story somewhere you hadn't expected. Long before LucasArts succumbed to the dark side and devoted itself to exploring the fringes of the *Star Wars* universe, it's worth remembering the studio was capable of stuff like this: intricate, colorful, and endlessly original. **CD**

Doom

Original release date : 1993
Platform : Various
Developer : id Software
Genre : First-Person Shooter

It may surprise you, but modern video games owe a lot to *Doom*. No, really! A few years ago a report concluded (in a masterful stating of the obvious) that the first-person shooter was the "most attractive" genre for publishers, based on revenue opportunities (ie, the likelihood of making money), and it certainly feels like every other game today is some variety of first-person shooter: *Halo, Call of Duty, Resistance, Far Cry, BioShock,* and *Battlefield 1942* are just some of the best. *Doom* was the first best. It wasn't the first, of course, but it was the first to feel like a shot of adrenaline, straight to the heart.

Banished to a marine base on Mars, the nameless hero soon finds himself the last man standing, battling hordes of demonic enemies. The object of the game was simple: shoot everything that moves and keep moving through wave after successive wave of every variety of infernal evil; survive a nightmare voyage to hell and back. Its appeal was visceral and obvious, from the increasingly bloodied face of your character avatar to the BFG, the weapon at the apex of the food chain. It's kill or be killed.

"If only you could talk to these creatures," concluded one early review that missed the point. Or did it? *Doom's* great strength lay in its relentless pursuit of immediate thrills. It was a masterpiece of design that went straight for the kill with a relentless, sharklike efficiency. But the game's legacy is just as important as its predatory instincts. *Doom* popularized a perspective that has since been used for everything from cowboys and Indians to horror in space, from talking to people face to face, to shooting them in it. That *Doom* laid the foundations for games as fundamentally different as *BioShock* and *Modern Warfare* is perhaps its greatest and lasting achievement. **DM**

Gunstar Heroes

Original release date : 1993
Platform : Mega Drive
Developer : Treasure
Genre : Shoot 'Em Up

If it's a Treasure game, you can guarantee lots of bullets. *Gunstar Heroes* isn't the company's finest shooter, but it is a supremely accomplished side-scroller that's as much about adventure as it is about enemies, a blast 'em up that bothers with characters, and home to some of the finest spritework of the 16-bit era.

There are several types of weapon, all of which can be combined to create new types of gun, a nice idea that in practice means there are two real possibilities if you want the best armaments.

The basic enemies aren't particularly engaging in combat, though it is fun to hit them and watch them flee and panic. What makes *Gunstar Heroes* is the sensational design of some of its bosses—several of which can still surprise you with their ingenuity and tactics nearly twenty years on—and the general incompetence of the enemy army implied in the little vignettes of animation and asides that occur throughout levels. You'll blow up a train and it'll stay on the tracks as it bursts into flames, disappearing off the screen and reappearing with enemy grunts panicking and clinging on to their dear leader for dear life, only to be imperiously tossed aside as he makes his escape. Or you'll be in a ferocious battle with an impervious foe until you finally crack him and he sheepishly hands over his crystal, bursting into tears at his failure.

These details explain why *Gunstar Heroes*, even if it is not Treasure's finest moment mechanically, remains special for so many grown-ups who were once Mega Drive owners. It's a game that doesn't just want you to play with it, but laugh at it, and it has enough room in its structure for variations that ensure repeat playthroughs throw up things you won't have seen before. **RS**

Ecco the Dolphin

Original release date : 1993
Platform : Various
Developer : Novotrade
Genre : Action / Adventure

Stylish, painterly, and calm, *Ecco the Dolphin* was the cartridge you used to plug into your trusty black Mega Drive to convince naysayers that video games weren't all about shooting things, driving things really fast, or generally setting the world on fire. *Ecco the Dolphin* was everything most games weren't: graceful and rather mature, filled with tinkly ambient noises and a protagonist that, as a bottlenose dolphin, is probably an endangered species by now even if he wasn't back in 1993.

That's not to say *Ecco the Dolphin* was a mere sop to one's worried parents. Developer Novotrade International's game is an intricate platformer in its own right. Its tangled undersea spaces are probably best described as mazes,

with a fierce, often rather nasty, difficulty curve as players pilot their lithe avatar through rambling and evocative networks of tunnels, ramming enemies out of the way, uncovering secret passages, and keeping an eye on the air gauge so as to avoid suffocating. Beneath the astonishingly elegant animations lurked a bitterly addictive game design that revels in the cruelty and unpredictability of nature—or at least it certainly felt that way when you were ten years old and more used to the cute ice-cream worlds of most traditional action games.

Amazingly, *Ecco the Dolphin* was a success. Despite breaking most of the rules of what made a hit, Novotrade created one of the few Mega Drive titles to sell enough to put it up with *Sonic the Hedgehog*. And, as with the *Sonic* series, sequels and ports followed, some of which were pleasant enough, none of which captured the rare spirit of the original. Despite the sales, developers struggled to follow in *Ecco the Dolphin*'s wake, which is why this strange, gentle, melancholy game stands out all the more. **CD**

38

5 6 7 8 9 10

206mph

POSITION

32/40

TRAFFIC

Daytona USA

Original release date : 1993
Platform : Arcade
Developer : Sega
Genre : Driving

The first time you successfully drift around a turn in *Daytona USA*, it all makes sense. First, steer into the curve. Then hit the brakes—you'll learn how hard you need to push on the pedal—and correct against the turn *just so*. You'll find yourself sliding sideways at high speed, your car in a delicate equilibrium between spinning out and bolting off the course, poised to explode onto the straightaway. Realistic? Not exactly, but so natural that any other racing game you play afterward will feel stilted and awkward.

Among its many technical innovations, *Daytona USA* is credited as a pioneer of texture-mapped polygons, giving its 3-D models a more organic look than those of Sega's earlier efforts, *Virtua Racing* and *Virtua Fighter*, with their plain, flat-shaded polygons. Texture mapping is used to great effect here, framing the racetracks with lush greenery, imposing cliff walls, and varied cityscapes. Up to eight competitions can be networked locally for epic in-person battles, which is where drafting—riding the slipstream behind another player's car to create a slingshot effect out of turns—can really make a difference.

Daytona USA also has its share of infamy. During its attract mode and on the Dinosaur Canyon racetrack, you are subjected to a cheesy, lounge-style song called "Let's Go Away," sung in English by a heavily accented Japanese man. You won't be able to get it out of your head.

A disastrous home version for the Sega Saturn in 1995 is reviled for its choppy frame rate and flickering polygons. In 1996, Sega would rectify the situation with *Daytona USA Championship Circuit Edition*, which sports improved graphics, truer handling, and three new racetracks. More faithful to the arcade original—except for its instrumental-only version of "Let's Go Away"—the *Championship Circuit Edition* is the definitive home version. **MK**

Return to Zork

Original release date : 1993
Platform : Various
Developer : Infocom
Genre : Adventure

"You are standing in an open field west of a white house, with a boarded front door. There is a small mailbox here." So begins seminal 1980 text adventure *Zork*. Infocom followed up with two sequels and various related projects, but it wasn't until 1993 that loyal fans were able to venture into their beloved world more tangibly. *Return to Zork* begins behind the very same white house that adventurers encountered thirteen years earlier, but this time, instead of a description, the building is rendered on-screen by the game's charming painterly graphics.

Although somewhat overshadowed by *Myst* (which *Return to Zork* actually predates by a few months), the game was part of an early wave of titles that took advantage of the increased storage capacity of CD-ROM. While the DOS release resembled a first-person take on Sierra On-Line's adventures, albeit steeped in *Zork* folklore, the optical versions contain a great deal of the digitized actor footage and better-quality audio that was then fashionable. The performances themselves are rather cheesy, but this only adds to the surreal atmosphere the game so successfully conveys. The player is also able to specify their mood in order to alter the way in which they interact with in-game characters, an innovation way ahead of its time.

Zork's famously flexible text parser is transformed into a similarly open point-and-click interface, which allows a great many more actions than its contemporaries, and most adventures since. However, the game does nothing to prevent the wanton destruction of key items by the player (nor alert them to their significance), leading to unwinnable game states that will frustrate all but the meticulous. Regardless of this, the richly detailed world delivers a genuine adventure that is enhanced by the game's mischievous sense of humor. **BM**

Ridge Racer

Original release date : 1993
Platform : Arcade
Developer : Namco
Genre : Driving

In these days of commonplace high-definition displays, it's difficult to fully convey the impact *Ridge Racer*'s visuals had when Namco drove its creation into arcades around the globe. Simply put, it was the most graphically advanced video game the world had ever seen, with texture-mapped polygons moving at speeds the human eye had difficulty interpreting, and featuring a number of elements that have gone on to become driving game clichés (helicopters, jet plane, roadworks—*Ridge Racer* had them all).

While you were still trying to assimilate the graphics, the cabinet tugged incessantly at your leg, demanding your urgent attention. One look at the three-pedal setup signaled the inclusion of a clutch, handy for navigating the

six-speed gear stick next to the seat. It's difficult to think of many arcade games that scream "Play me!" as insistently as *Ridge Racer*, and fewer still that have made it impossible for young men to walk past and not slot in a coin, misguidedly hoping to impress their accompanying girlfriends.

Thankfully, the game is too demanding to enable a quick glance at your spectator's undoubtedly bored and grumpy face. Rendered using a first-person view (an unusual approach for the time), the experience is relentless, even if its limitations seem pronounced nowadays, with little in the way of handling nuances, intrusive AI competitors, and nonexistent crash dynamics.

That said, one area that remains mostly intact is the power-sliding mechanic, which, although absurdly exaggerated, is still able to convey much of the original thrill and exhilaration felt by those who experienced the remarkable intensity of *Ridge Racer* the first time around. As history lessons go, you're unlikely to find many that will prove this exciting. **JDS**

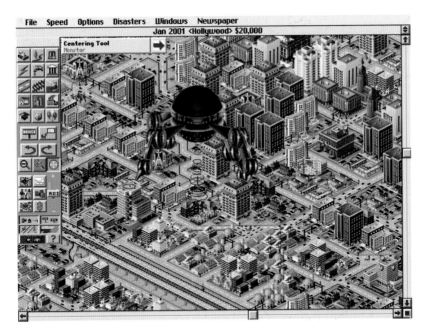

SimCity 2000

Original release date : 1993

Platform : Various

Developer : Maxis

Genre : Management Simulation

The march of technology might frustrate developers who have to keep reinventing the wheel and consumers who must periodically shell out for new hardware, but it sure makes game evolution pretty.

Consider *SimCity*. The debut title, released on PC in 1989, was a landmark—a cornerstone in showing what games could do, a missionary converting sceptical non-gamers to the cause, and a time sink without peer. But graphically, you'd think you were designing a circuit board.

In contrast, *SimCity 2000*, released just four years later, enables you to build a living, breathing metropolis that looks as good as it feels to create and manage. Instead of a top-down plan, you're given a diametric view of your growing city, which means skyscrapers tower over parks and older parts of town look quaint yet ripe for development. This pseudo-3-D perspective also enables the developer to add elevation to the terrain, so your exclusive uptown neighborhood really can look down on its neighbors. The attention to detail is fabulous, ranging from a factory's construction graphics to the run-down disrepair of urban decay.

The core game play, in which you designate and hook up residential, commercial, and industrial zones, remains in place, but you can now add special institutions, such as prisons, hospitals, and zoos. The transport options are more compelling, there are many ways to generate power, and there's deeper management of your city's fiscal affairs.

Like any good Will Wright game, there's also plenty of Sim silliness. Disasters range from fires and tornadoes to an attack from a monster. Newspaper stories vary from the useful to the bonkers. And if your arcologies are sufficiently hi-tech, you'll be rewarded as they blast off into space. **OB**

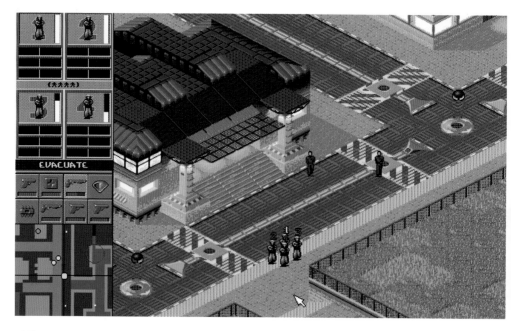

Syndicate

Original release date : 1993

Platform : Various

Developer : Bullfrog Productions

Genre : Strategy / Shoot 'Em Up

Peter Molyneux's Bullfrog Productions had made business sims before, but none were quite like this. Most featured spreadsheets and financial year reports. *Syndicate* had a heavier focus on nasty weaponry and industrial espionage. The game, created by Sean Cooper, is a gritty isometric future noir in which corporations fight one another for influence and market share, taking boardroom rivalries to the streets with a variety of brilliantly unpleasant guns and explosives, and bringing a new, rather literal, meaning to the phrase "hostile takeover."

Influenced by *Blade Runner* and the works of William Gibson as much as *Businessweek* magazine, *Syndicate*'s mix of urban grime and neon sleaze may initially remind players

of *Shadowrun*. Rather than a complex RPG, it's something a little harder to describe: a squad-based tactical game in which players run their own corporation and use a team of four characters to destabilize competitors, recruit the local populace, and generally cause futuristic chaos.

We did mention it involve guns—lots of guns—right? With weapons research and development being essential for players if they want to keep abreast of the rivals, *Syndicate* has the artillery to back up its obvious brains. Some of the game's weapons (the phenomenal Gauss Gun, for example) have found their place in gaming history, and allotting funds for research is just one of a series of ancillary factors players have to keep in mind while ruling the streets.

Syndicate was originally designed to have a multiplayer component that was, heartbreakingly, taken out at the last moment. What remains, however, is a beautiful night-time vision of a mean-spirited future. It is downloadable today for a reasonable fee via the PlayStation Network. **CD**

Sam & Max Hit the Road

Original release date : 1993
Platform : Various
Developer : LucasArts
Genre : Adventure

The number of scripted video games that reliably and intentionally make you laugh can be counted on one hand. That's one finger for *Maniac Mansion: Day of the Tentacle*, one for *Zak McKracken and the Alien Mindbenders*, one for *Maniac Mansion*, one that doubles for the first two *Monkey Island* games, and a thumb for the funniest of all point-and-clicks, *Sam & Max Hit the Road*. Made by LucasArts at the height of its powers, this was based on a comic by artist, author, and lead game designer Steve Purcell.

Known as the Freelance Police (which apparently frees them to uphold and break the law, often at the same time), Sam and Max are private detectives doomed to investigate the maddest corners of American society. Sam, a talking dog in a suit and tie, is a Philip Marlowe type with an ambivalent position on human suffering, especially when it's inflicted by his partner, Max, a "hyperkinetic rabbit-type thing." In *Sam & Max Hit the Road*, Bruno the frozen bigfoot has escaped from a local carnival, taking Trixie the Giraffe-necked Girl with him. With breaks for mini-games and trips to the toilet, the search for clues leads to tourist spots like The World's Largest Ball Of Twine, Gator Golf Emporium, and the Celebrity Vegetable Museum.

The strike rate of gags in *Sam & Max Hit the Road* at least compares to classic cartoons like *The Ren And Stimpy Show* and *The Tick*, its humor skewed equally toward adults and mature teenagers. Driving home the jokes are the wonderfully animated characters, the chemistry between its voice actors, a synchronized jazz soundtrack, and puzzles that actually relate to dialogue and situation. Surely the most quotable game of all time, it'll be remembered long after its recent comeback via a scattershot series of 3-D episodes has been forgotten. **DH**

UFO: Enemy Unknown

Original release date : 1993
Platform : Various
Developer : Mythos
Genre : Strategy

Many games struggle to make players identify with the digital puppets they're asked to play with, even if they're presented center stage, motion-captured, and voiced. And yet some of the most cherished characters in gaming are the randomly generated soldiers of *UFO: Enemy Unknown*. Each was merely a 2-D collection of pixels attached to a few basic statistics and a name drawn from a distinctive list of pan-European monikers, yet most players have heartfelt stories to tell of narrow escapes and last stands.

Giving you the role of commander of X-COM, a force devoted to combating extraterrestrial threat, *UFO: Enemy Unknown* is a combination of strategic resource management and turn-based tactical battling. On one

hand, you're building bases around Earth to shoot down UFOs, developing research capabilities, investigating spacecrafts, and creating more powerful weapons. On the other, you're directing small squads of soldiers to investigate crash sites and putting them in considerable danger while you're doing so.

With the difference between life and death a single turn, you quickly begin to value each and every one of your fighters, nurturing them into exquisitely skilled warriors capable of snap-shooting a gray in the head at fifty paces. When they die—and with no in-mission saves at your disposal, they will—you'll miss their talent badly.

Almost completely freeform, progression in the game is entirely in your hands. The objective of each crash-site mission is up to you, whether you want to capture a commanding alien for interrogation or gather materiel to use or sell for funds. It's this responsibility that's behind the strength of the bonds you form in *UFO*, and the reason why it remains a landmark in video games. **AW**

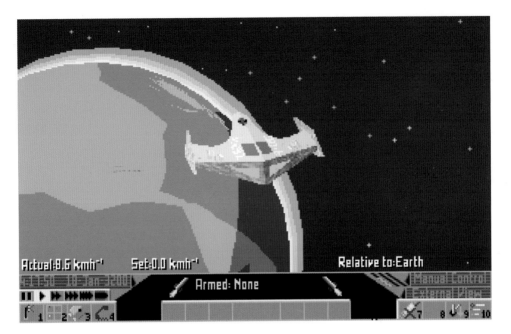

Actual:8.6 kmh⁻¹   Set:0.0 kmh⁻¹   Relative to:Earth
                              Armed: None   Manual Control

Frontier: Elite II

Original release date : 1993

Platform : Various

Developer : Gametek

Genre : Strategy / Shoot 'Em Up

Remember that thing about space being "really big"? Well, only a few games have managed to portray that with any kind of accuracy. One of these games is *Frontier*, sequel to the classic open-ended space game, *Elite*. Once again you are thrown in at the deep end of intergalactic adventure, with no plot, no quest, and no game-given direction.

You have to decide what to do with your spaceship, although money is mostly found in trade of one kind or another, legal or otherwise. There are a number of variables to consider as you formulate your approach, such as the Cold War state between two powers of the galaxy, and the political conditions of the planets you travel between. *Frontier* features an accurately modeled galaxy and physics

that are leaps beyond those of *Elite*. You start out in one of a handful of solar systems—including our own—and you are able to work your way out from there. The game's physics model means you're able to slingshot around the gravity wells of stars and large planets, just as real craft would do if they were navigating such spaces.

The level of detail is, for the time the game was released, utterly spectacular. You are able to take off and land on the surface of planets, seamlessly soaring through the atmosphere, into space and the beyond, even using hyperdrive for interstellar travel. Planets and space stations both provide for trade and ship maintenance, and you're no longer confined to a single, steadily upgraded craft as you were in the original game. A variety of different craft, suitable for different purposes, are instead made available. Newtonian physics mean that the game's combat is astonishingly complex—your craft and the enemy ship orbit each other until one manages to connect with lasers and destroy the other. Challenging stuff. **JR**

Plok

Original release date : 1993
Platform : SNES
Developer : Software Creations
Genre : Platform

The 1991 release of *Sonic the Hedgehog* started a stampede as companies competed to release platform games with cooler, more "radical" mascots than Sega's. By 1993, gamers were sick of it, meaning that a title like *Plok*—a "cutesy" 2-D platformer with a strong lead character—was doomed.

This is a tremendous shame, as *Plok* was—and still is—a fantastic platform game with great ideas that simply found itself in the wrong place at the wrong time. Designed by the legendary Pickford brothers, who had been working on their idea for more than five years by the time of release, *Plok* stars a strange hooded character with the ability to throw his limbs (used to attack enemies and even turn on switches). Plok finds his favorite flag stolen and embarks on a quest to get it back—a quest with a fair few twists and turns—and if that sounds odd, the game only gets weirder and weirder still.

A rare platformer with a compelling plot, albeit a totally bonkers one, *Plok* plays well despite its level of difficulty, and its unique graphical style pairs well with a highly impressive soundtrack by Tim and Geoff Follin. **MKu**

Secret of Mana

Original release date : 1993
Platform : SNES
Developer : Square
Genre : Role-Playing / Action

If *Final Fantasy* saw its developer Square raise the bar for what players would come to expect from turn-based role-playing games, *Secret of Mana* is the A-list company's subsequent assault on the realm of action-based RPGs. The result is a fast-paced, witty, and extremely beautiful adventure that blends frantic fights with careful exploration and some genuinely extraordinary 16-bit art.

The plot concerns a war between Earth dwellers and gods over control of resources, but the game is most famous for its interface: an elegant command system of menus that lets you cycle quickly through all of the options available to a selected character—an extremely influential design in the world of RPG.

Similarly trailblazing, the party system allows for extensive three-player dungeon crawls, an option that really brings the game to life. This is a title built with genuine cooperation in mind.

Aside from the glorious cover art, new standards were set by the dazzling soundtrack by Hiroki Kikuta and by Akira Ueda's masterful background art. **CD**

The Settlers

The 7th Guest

Original release date : 1993
Platform : Various
Developer : Blue Byte
Genre : Strategy

Original release date : 1993
Platform : Various
Developer : Trilobyte
Genre : Puzzle

The idea is simple: create a functional kingdom able to fund enough of an army to take over the map. However, where most real-time strategy games lean on the military side of the equation, reducing the financial side to mining some useful ores, The Settlers expands the economics into a main concern. It's easy to win when you have armies, but making an army is a process involving hours of play. It's not just ensuring you have enough miners, iron smelters, and blacksmiths to get your swords, it's about efficiency: working out a road system so that the workers carrying all the resources don't bottleneck hopelessly, creating catastrophic failure at the far side of your network.

The joy is the satisfaction of a well-balanced accounts book. It's much more fun than doing your taxes, however, because it sells the idea with charm (the characters are adorable) and scale—the 66,000 characters The Settlers can handle is still impressive. Later versions of the game sped up the pace somewhat, but for proof of what can be made entertaining in a game through pure craft, the original remains an inspiration. **KG**

Spearheading the "interactive movie" boom of the '90s, *The 7th Guest* coupled live-action sequences with pre-rendered 3-D. Rated as unsuitable for children for its horror and sexual innuendo, it was reportedly made with just $35,000, Super VHS cameras, and an improvised blue-screen technique. With sequel *The 11th Hour*, the game sold more than two million copies and earned over $100 million.

Welcome to Stauf Mansion, home of a reclusive toymaker whose dolls cursed their owners to horrible deaths. Six unknowing guests were invited to the stay the night, solving a number of fiendish puzzles and learning terrible secrets. None would escape, leaving the player's amnesiac character to retrace their footsteps in the game.

The game's pre-rendered nature leaves little scope for adventure. Instead, each location you visit features one of the aforementioned puzzles, such as a word puzzle hidden inside a telescope. Full-motion video clips, meanwhile, give detailed—and impossibly hammy—accounts of your ill-fated predecessors, each played by a real-life actor. Well, a real-life person, at least. **DH**

The Legend of Zelda: Link's Awakening

Original release date : 1993
Platform : Game Boy
Developer : Nintendo
Genre : Action / Adventure

A stranger washed up on a beach, a mountain capped with a giant egg, and a gentle quest to locate eight magical instruments—*Link's Awakening* is not just the first *Zelda* game to wedge its epic adventures onto the tight screen of a handheld, it is also the first to leave the rolling fields and forests of Hyrule behind, ditching the titular princess, the evil Ganon, and the beautiful Triforce. Link travels to mysterious Koholint Island, where he quickly discovers that he must awaken the slumbering Wind Fish if he can ever hope to escape.

Despite the superficial changes, it's another wonderfully comforting adventure, however, *Link's Awakening*'s overworld and muddle of dungeons quickly conforming to the eternally fertile *Zelda* template, with the rich cast of bosses and memorable items providing all the necessary adventure and threat you might expect. While the game features fetch quests a lot more heavily than other titles in the series, it also has its fair share of innovations, including a feather that allows Link to jump, breaking up the overhead action with some rare side-scrolling sections unseen since *Zelda II*, and—rather curiously—occasionally blending some of the minor characters from the expansive *Mario* universe into the mix.

Originally a standard Game Boy title, *Link's Awakening* was re-released for the color version of Nintendo's handheld in the form of *Zelda DX*, and those players who upgraded were rewarded with a special additional dungeon to hack through. Either way, this is a marvelous adventure, and although it's the first of the *Zelda* games on handhelds, it's also, in a strange way, one of the truest to the original source material. **CD**

Zombies Ate My Neighbors

Original release date : 1993
Platform : Various
Developer : LucasArts
Genre : Shoot 'Em Up

It's of little use having one of the best game titles ever conceived (although, disappointingly, silly censorship truncated it to just *Zombies* in Europe) if you haven't got the play experience to back it up.

But spend just a few seconds in either lead character's sneakers, and you'll know this B-movie-inspired cute and colorful parody is dangerously contagious. The structure follows standard run-and-gun principles, with levels requiring clearing of enemies (and, in this case, victims saved) before access to the next stage is allowed. However, as the title suggests so vividly, the content is far from standard fare, with the undead and their pals—werewolves, mummies, vampires, giant ants, and massive demonic babies, to name just a handful—liberally populating the game's fifty-odd stages.

If the enemies are far-fetched, just wait until you see the arsenal at your disposal. From plates to squirt guns to crucifixes, while also passing through more obviously offensive options, the zany selection is a key contributor to the cheeky humor at the (very human) heart of *ZAMN*.

The settings, too, reflect LucasArts' creative abandon, beginning with some generic examples of suburban life (backyards, a mall) rendered in the game's endearing visual style, before leading to more inspired and fiend-related examples that are best left discovered through play.

Regardless of the enemies, weapons, or environments, the core game mechanic doesn't falter, while the addition of limited puzzle elements brings a welcome dynamic into an already hugely entertaining package. Whether played alone or in co-op, it is brilliant fun and a 16-bit experience every gamer should unearth. **JDS**

Virtua Fighter

Original release date : 1993
Platform : Arcade
Developer : Sega
Genre : Fighting

Quarter-circle forward. Charge back for two seconds, then forward. Forward, down . . . down-forward? You almost need a PhD to understand how to play some fighting games. Even once you know the moves, you're still apt to be pounded into a fine paste by someone who has far more time to practice than you do. Sega's *Virtua Fighter*, by contrast, is simple enough for any newcomer to pick up. With only three command inputs—punch, kick, and defend—it relies more on timing and reflexes than mastery of joystick machinations.

Which is not to suggest that *Virtua Fighter* lacks depth. On the contrary, its eight combatants all possess different fighting stances and styles, rare for an era in which many games filled out their rosters with palette-swapped duplicates that were functionally identical. Winning a match with the burly wrestler Wolf Hawkfield requires a fundamentally different approach than it does with the lithe Sarah Bryant, and the beauty of the game is that you can begin to figure out why that is by the way it feels to move different fighters around the arena.

The combat is, by video game standards, realistic. Characters don't throw fireballs, or teleport, or spit acid. They fight hand-to-hand, probing for openings to deliver quick, devastating strikes. The special moves are there, such as counterattacks, combos, and parries, but they follow the flow of the fight, instead of dictating it.

As one of the earliest games to make the leap to fully three-dimensional graphics, *Virtua Fighter* looks downright primitive to modern eyes. The characters are blocky, and the backgrounds devoid of detail. But it all moves with fluidity, grace, and speed, and establishes the template that future 3-D fighters would follow. **MK**

You see a yellow potion.
You quaff the potion in one gulp.
You are healed.
Your plate leggings were damaged.
Your helmet was damaged.

Ultima Underworld II: Labyrinth of Worlds

Original release date : 1993

Platform : PC

Developer : Looking Glass Technologies

Genre : Role-Playing

How can a game with such broad horizons feel so claustrophobic? Sporting a 3-D first-person view that represented the technical pinnacle of the time, *Ultima Underworld II*'s free-form role-playing drama echoed that of *Doom* and provided the bedrock for the game series, which its developer, Looking Glass Technologies, would come to be celebrated for: *System Shock* and *Thief*.

Opening in a castle sealed in impervious black rock by the omnipresent *Ultima* antagonist, the Guardian, your task is to free the fortification and its inhabitants. Your only route is down into sewers and caves until you find a strange crystal that allows you to teleport into alternate dimensions. But as varied and ambitiously creative as they are, each is enclosed and confined, a reflection of both the castle's dark predicament and the technological limitations of the time.

In the Prison Tower, you must infiltrate a goblin-run jail in order to free its prisoners, while in the Pits of Carnage you enter a gladiatorial society in which you must duel to progress. The World of Talorus is an abstract but strictly hierarchical world of alien energy beings. In the Scintillus Academy, you must pass a magician's practical exam. Though each focuses on challenges such as puzzle solving, combat or exploration, the scenarios allow a variety of approaches. Locations of objects and conversations are subtly randomized and you usually have the choice to take your own approach, from talking to killing, looting to levitation. It's a freedom complemented by a magic system in which you construct spells using runes and language rules (for example, cause/life/matter casts Create Food). Like the rest of the game, it presents a logical and flexible system that rewards experimentation in spades. **AW**

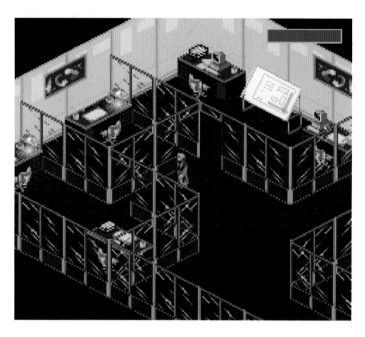

Shadowrun

Original release date : 1993
Platform : Various
Developer : Beam
Genre : Action / Role-Playing

FASA Corporation's cyberpunk RPG *Shadowrun* was once a pen-and-paper game, then it was an isometric action-RPG for the SNES, and then—sadly—it was a cruelly hobbled online-only multiplayer, first-person shooter for both the PC and Xbox 360. While there's no real disagreement over which version was the most disappointing, the SNES incarnation was certainly the very best of the bunch.

Thrusting players into a mysterious urban world of corporate overlords and renegade hackers, players find themselves in the natty leather boots and trench coat of Jake Armitage, a murky wheeler and dealer who has been double-crossed on a recent mission and awakens in a morgue with no memory. Quickly finding himself in the

thick of a murderous conspiracy, he has to find out who he is and why people want to kill him, while leveling up, getting better gear, and generally sticking it to The Man—whomever that might turn out to be.

Even by modern gaming standards, *Shadowrun* is an astonishingly stylish product, with moody character art, a great soundtrack, and a game world broken up into various pools of light shining out of the seedy and oppressive darkness. An excellent script and surprisingly unfiddly combat system that uses magic and more traditional forms of weaponry only add to the immersion.

Shadowrun, in all its forms, is a venerable RPG series with clever features and a real sense of depth, and while even the most recent game had its fair share of beleaguered fans lurking somewhere on the ravages of the Internet, it's the thought of one day getting a sequel to this SNES title—a complex narrative experience that revels in such a smartly realized universe—that is really enough to set even a nonhacker's mind on fire. **CD**

Breath of Fire II

Original release date : 1994
Platform : SNES
Developer : Capcom
Genre : Role-Playing

Breath of Fire II is an RPG great on a console crammed full of them. Released on the SNES, it joins the likes of *Secret of Mana*, the *Final Fantasy* series, *Chrono Trigger*, and the original *Breath of Fire* at the very top of its chosen genre. It takes place 500 years after the end of the original game to tell the story of Ryu Bateson, a blue-haired boy hero on a quest for justice, which is launched when his friend is framed for a crime he didn't commit.

The game picks up the day/night cycle from its predecessor, which sees the world and its inhabitants transform with every sunset, and it features the turn-based, random encounters that are a staple element of the Japanese RPG genre. Picking the right formation is a crucial part of combat strategy, while another key feature is each character's special ability, such as Ryu's dragon transformations or Bow's fusion form as a giant, cannonball-launching mech.

One of the best things about the game is the way the world is gradually opened up. Each party member has a unique skill that they can use outside of the normal course of play, so fishing and hunting skills, for example, unlock different mini-games. But the ability to swim or bridge chasms allows the party to access more of the increasingly vast game world, and it's pacing of exploration that is one of the game's greatest strengths. Another is the way the game prefigures the *Dark Cloud* series by giving you the ability to build your very own town, choosing its architectural style, and gradually filling it with non-player characters that can help you on the main mission—a mission with multiple endings, depending on how effectively you steer Ryu and friends on one of the classic quests of 16-bit storytelling. **DM**

Tekken

Original release date : 1994
Platform : Various
Developer : Namco
Genre : Fighting

In a time when 3-D fighting games were worldwide hits, *Tekken* grabbed the title of arcade, and, subsequently, console fighting champion. The first PlayStation title to sell a million units, the game continued the legacy of brawlers as a video game staple.

Part of *Tekken*'s appeal is its intuitiveness. Namco's commands are examples of great game design—simple to learn the basics, difficult to master over time. Each button corresponds to each limb of the figher, so understanding the relationship and appropriate command comes almost automatically. Using only a modicum of skill, it's possible to make a good deal of progress, which certainly makes *Tekken* a rewarding and extremely playable game.

In addition to the smooth finish of *Tekken*'s texture-mapped 3-D characters, the personalities of its characters give the game a distinctive edge. Namco infused each fighter with an elaborate backstory that contorted over time with each subsequent sequel. The plot revolves around Heihachi Mishima, the owner of a multi-national corporation and creator of the King of the Iron Fist tournament. His son, Kazuya Mishima, returns to defeat and humiliate his father for his attempt to test his offspring's mettle during childhood by throwing him off a cliff. Then there's judo expert Paul Phoenix, Kazuya's only equal, and King, a Mexican wrestler raising money to fund an orphanage. The plotlines have spun off in many directions since, but it was the initial decision to present such a charismatic roster of fighters that makes the game stand out. That, and its finely honed core game play, which has a realistic fighting style praised by the martial arts community. The reviews upon release were positive, and it has since spawned six sequels.

It is, as the announcer so definitively says, a "KO." **JBW**

EarthBound

Original release date : 1994
Platform : SNES
Developer : HAL
Genre : Role-Playing

EarthBound remains one of those titles that is name-checked by the video gaming cognoscenti more often than it's actually been played, and that's a crying shame, as the game behind the reputation is utterly brilliant. A quirky, comical RPG set in the real world rather than a mythical yesteryear filled with dragons and fairies, *EarthBound* is vivid, colorful, and consistently surprising, filled with memorable enemies and beautiful Americana-influenced backdrops, and centered on a brave band of backyard heroes setting off on the most unlikely of quests.

In Japan, the *Mother* series of games—of which *EarthBound* is the second installment—is a massive RPG franchise, up there with the likes of *Final Fantasy* and *Dragon Quest*. In the West, however, the titles have had a harder time making their mark. The first game was translated but never released—it lives on as a full-time Internet rumor, going by the name of *EarthBound Zero*—and the third, and most recent, game is available in a very gray sense via loving fan translation. Only *EarthBound* itself made it across intact, which is still something to be thankful for, as the series' oddball foibles (in the original *Mother*, the first enemy character to bring the player under attack takes the form of a humble table lamp) hardly make for bestseller material.

Which is strange, really, as the overworld is charming and interesting, the characters are utterly adorable, and the battle system is so refined that you have the option of dropping out entirely and letting the game handle all conflicts automatically. Regardless of its lack of success on Western shores, *EarthBound* continues to exist in some corner of the gaming landscape where it's always midnight in the suburbs, where aliens lurk in the darkness, and adventure awaits around every bend. **CD**

Doom II: Hell on Earth

Original release date : 1994
Platform : Various
Developer : id Software
Genre : First-Person Shooter

In *Doom II* there is a power-up that lets you punch something so hard that it explodes. Rarely has a sequel got it so right, but then rarely has a sequel had to do so little. The improvements over the original *Doom* are refinements, really: new weapons, including a magnificent double-barreled shotgun, more levels, and more monsters. *Doom II* also saw id's relentless experimentation at its best, creating levels that were all one big setpiece, battle royales that threw caution to the wind, and even moments of downtime amid the carnage—the first signs of what the FPS (first-person shooter) genre refers to as pacing.

It helped that it was built on the bones of the greatest FPS of the early '90s, and it also helped that it was made in double-quick time, id moving with the breakneck speed and effortless ingenuity of a developer not only at the top of its game, creatively, but at the height of its productivity. John Romero, one of gaming's lost, great, white hopes, was steadily alienating himself from the rest of id's small team, which culminated in his head being mounted on a stick behind the final boss, the Icon of Sin. When the player thought they were killing the final boss, they were killing Romero. Lead coder John Carmack, meanwhile, became fully absorbed in the stunning 3-D engine destined to replace *Doom*'s and make *Quake* possible.

By the time *Doom II* was finished, the seeds for id's destruction were sown. Yet the game itself wasn't just an immense successor to *Doom*, but the first FPS that could be played online. The LAN death matches of *Doom* were, thanks a peer-to-peer networking client known as DWANGO, now countrywide death matches. Next to that, the super shotgun is the least important aspect of *Doom II*'s legacy. Even though it does make a fantastic mess. **RS**

Earthworm Jim

Original release date : 1994
Platform : Mega Drive
Developer : Shiny Entertainment
Genre : Platform / Shoot 'Em Up

When he asked a man from Hong Kong for millions of dollars, David Perry was the hotshot programmer behind games like Disney's *Aladdin* and *Global Gladiators*, an award-winning platform game made for McDonald's. The man in question ran Playmates, a giant of the toy industry, looking to break into video games. Perry's Shiny Entertainment—a dream team of developers from Britain and the US—proposed something quite original.

Enlisting the help of Doug TenNapel, creator of acclaimed Nickelodeon series *Catscratch*, Shiny came up with *Earthworm Jim*, an American hero with a spacesuit and ray gun who, true to his name, was a great deal longer than wide. Sensing the opportunity to make a multimedia

juggernaut, Perry convinced Playmates and Universal Studios to handle merchandising and a cartoon show, solving the Catch-22 of needing one to justify the other.

Strongest of them all, though, remains the game. Animated using techniques familiar to TV rather than 16-bit console games, *Earthworm Jim* exploded with character. Jim and his fellow cast members—Professor Monkey-for-a-Head, Evil the Cat, and Bob the Killer Goldfish, to name but a few—were first drawn with pencils, then scanned, flood-filled with color and shrunk to create sprites. LaserDiscs of Tex Avery cartoons were used as inspiration, and the team was forced to express all its ideas as sketches.

The result is about as close to an interactive cartoon as you'll find, its action as smooth and exaggerated as its looks. Clearly made by people thinking on their feet, it has you launching cows into space one minute and riding giant hamsters the next, all while enjoying a responsive form of early run-and-gun. Not bad for a guy with no arms or legs. **DH**

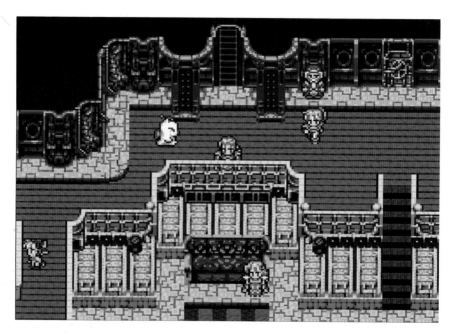

Final Fantasy VI

Original release date : 1994
Platform : Various
Developer : Square
Genre : Role-Playing

For a series often ridiculed for its predictability, *Final Fantasy VI* is a wholly surprising entry. Despite sharing many conceptual similarities to its namesakes—from its towns, dungeons, music, and battle system—in many ways the game bucks its own conventions.

Unusually for a J-RPG (Japanese role-playing game), the game features a large ensemble cast instead of a single protagonist, with your control switching between each throughout the game. Moreover, each of the controllable personalities you encounter has a completely distinct and unique way of behaving in battle, not to mention its own fully fleshed out back-story to uncover. Without doubt, *Final Fantasy VI*'s story is atypical of the series, crammed with visual jokes and witty one-liners. It suffers none of the bloated anime excesses that so often drag down other titles in the genre. Each character enjoys its own believable motivations, flaws, and quirks, which infuse the narrative with richness. The plot keeps the fantasy metaphysics to a minimum, instead focusing on politics and empire building, a decision that again helps the game to feel more grounded and earthly. The engaging setpieces, which walk a difficult line between profundity and comedy, push you onward, and the reduced emphasis on grinding your character through battles helps to keep the game interesting and exciting for those usually turned off by the genre's protracted play arc.

Battles, while more orthodox than the story, are still wonderfully inventive, individual character traits making the combat constantly exciting. For those who missed it on the SNES, Square Enix's Game Boy Advance re-release comes highly recommended, with a new translation that irons out some of the original's creases. **SP**

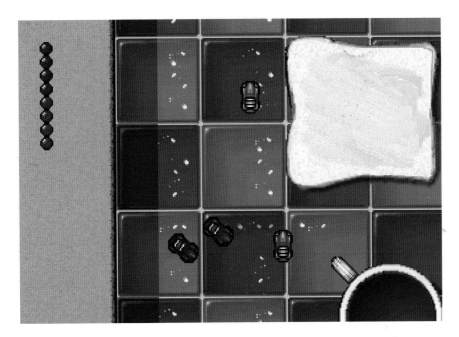

Micro Machines 2: Turbo Tournament

Original release date : 1994
Platform : Mega Drive
Developer : Codemasters
Genre : Driving / Racing

While the original *Micro Machines* established the winning high concept behind Codemasters' miniaturized racing series, it was *Micro Machines 2: Turbo Tournament* that tuned things to perfection, and drew a much wider audience.

Naturally, the game includes a new range of vehicles to race and household locations to speed around, with the level of scenic detailing raised considerably since the days of its NES predecessor. The toolshed table, complete with dangerously elongating drill bit; the sand pit scattered with discarded spades and dropped ice cream; the pinball table and its pesky flippers—all of these are rendered in Codemasters's once-trademark style, with chunky sprites and comic-book color palettes.

Although the sequel adds depth to the single-player experience via the new league and time trial options, the key appeal of the game remains its enthralling multiplayer mode, which sees participants being temporarily removed from the race if their vehicle falls too far behind the leader. Recognizing this appeal, Codemasters shipped the game with its J-Cart technology—essentially a customized cartridge complete with two extra joy pad ports, allowing four-player sessions and even an eight-player party mode. Mega Drive owners lapped it up.

Micro Machines 2 is a defining lesson in how to make a real game out of a children's license. It's all wrapped up in the cheeky humor that characterized Codemasters throughout the 8- and 16-bit eras (there's even a race around a toilet seat). The courses, superbly designed to reward skillful, experienced players, include shortcuts and neat little features, like the sponge ferry in the kitchen sink level that allows players to bash one another into the dishwater. There are no sponge ferries in *Gran Turismo*. **KS**

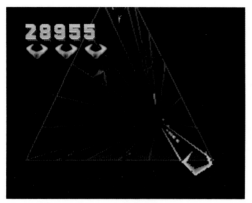

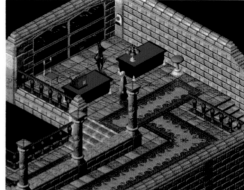

Tempest 2000

Little Big Adventure

Original release date : 1994
Platform : Jaguar
Developer : Llamasoft
Genre : Shoot 'Em Up

Original release date : 1994
Platform : Various
Developer : Adeline
Genre : Action / Adventure

Jeff Minter's updating of David Theurer's classic vector-based shooter took the basic elements of the original and turned them into something new. An audiovisual synthesis par excellence, pressure mixed with pleasure, and a basic core of blasting lots of enemies.

The visual style—everything from feedback to the spectrum of rainbow colors—sets the agenda. You're blasted with strobing lights, pulsing shades, and scattering particle effects. The soundtrack is a succession of relentless dance beats punctuated by sound effects that sync with the mechanical elements, helping you follow what your eyes can't quite glean from within the landscape.

For all the aesthetic pleasure, *Tempest 2000* is also the most finely honed shooter ever made by the man who makes nothing but finely honed shooters. Throughout the course of seventy levels, its difficulty spikes up and then smooths out, lets you relax a bonus round before throwing you back into the mix with maddening new elements. *Tempest 2000* remains a white-hot moment; it is no wonder that some still prize the Atari Jaguar today. **RS**

Developed in France but set in a vibrant world of pure imagination, this prototypical action-adventure title was like nothing else in 1994.

You play Twinsen, a Quetch whose nightmares see him labeled insane but will ultimately save his planet's inhabitants. This seemingly cute planet is effectively a police state, and its strange inhabitants include Grobos, who look like elephants; Rabbibunnies; and the ancient Spheroids with their distinctive ball shape. The world is rendered in isometric 3-D and is partially free-roaming as unlocked areas can be accessed at will. Standard stuff now, but radical at the time.

What endures more than *Little Big Adventure*'s technical achievements is the world itself. The essential polygonality of the characters is wonderfully realized in 3-D, the rich environments and music providing a palpable sense of place. Rarely have today's action adventures conjured the otherworldliness and drama of the innocuously titled *Little Big Adventure*, with its toy-town figures, charming sampled speech, and colorful environs. **OB**

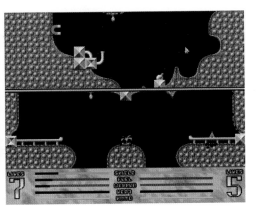

Gravity Power

Original release date : 1994
Platform : Amiga
Developer : Bits
Genre : Shoot 'Em Up

In a certain time and place, *Gravity Power* was the second greatest game of all time. Its time and place was on the dying Commodore Amiga format in the mid '90s, specifically in the readership of UK magazine *Amiga Power*. This specially commissioned version of *Gravity Force 2* takes the "Power" in its title from the magazine.

With *Gravity Force 2*, it wasn't about budget, it was all about the experience. You pilot a ship and attempt to fight your opposition while hindered by gravity. This element makes the twisted levels as much a threat as the bullets or bombs of your opponent. The strength is a simple core allied to a mass of levels, expanded by a function allowing you to design your own. Some stages marry high speed with perilous drops into lakes. Others are painfully intricate.

Gravity Force 2 was released via the shareware model, by which customers were able to upgrade to an improved version. *Gravity Power* is the full shareware version, with a few tweaks and extra levels. Sit and play it in two-player mode, and right there, right then, it won't be the second best game. It'll be the best. **KG**

Monster Max

Original release date : 1994
Platform : Game Boy
Developer : Jon Ritman, Bernie Drummond
Genre : Adventure

A dastardly human named King Krond has turned up on Max's planet and banned all music, which is the setup for more than 600 rooms full of the best puzzles this niche genre would ever see. Starting with nothing, you gradually acquire equipment for Max, incuding a pair of boots that let you jump, a force field, and lightning.

The locations are filled with spikes, conveyor belts, and blocks, and arrangements of these basic elements are the meat of *Monster Max*'s world. Within these considerable limits, *Monster Max* is nothing less than a mini-masterpiece. The variation it manages to squeeze from simple principles is remarkable, and the game rarely threatens to go stale.

A special mention, too, to Bernie Drummond's work on the visual style: the Game Boy was hardly what you'd call a processing powerhouse, yet Monster Max and his world positively ooze identity. The robots, traps, and monsters complement the daft plot perfectly, and even give an occasionally sinister air to its excesses, while few who made it to the end will forget the cathartic, exhilarating thrill that ended the adventure. **RS**

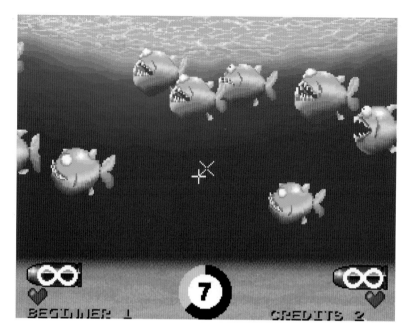

Point Blank

Original release date : 1994
Platform : Various
Developer : Namco
Genre : Shoot 'Em Up

In the '90s, light gun gaming was dominated by macho shoot-outs, like *Virtua Cop* and *Time Crisis*, featuring wide-shouldered gangsters and slick hyper-choreographed violence. And it was just then that *Point Blank* came along, unapologetically returning us to the campy, garish funfair roots of the genre.

Arriving first in the arcade before transferring to PlayStation, it's a frantic collection of shooting mini-games, none of them involving animated human targets (though the odd cardboard ninja is encountered). Players choose a skill level, then start blasting through myriad wacky stages, either alone or alongside a friend. (You have to love the fact that the guns provided with the coin-op cabinet are

blue and *pink*.) Some challenges are specifically designed to test speed, like having to blast a car with fifty holes or shoot all the bouncing balls within a time limit. Others concentrate on accuracy, like targeting a single leaf falling from a tree using just one bullet.

The defining element is the sheer and imaginative variety of the tasks. It's a surreal parade of daft ideas embracing everything from squawking chickens to leaping skeletons, all wrapped up in brash, kawaii visuals. And to provide uniformity, two bizarre characters named Dr. Dan and Dr. Don regularly appear, usually imperiled by incoming tanks or by tribesmen with flaming torches. In the PlayStation version and its sequels, this comedy duo take on a more central role, enlivening the cut scenes and intros with silly slapstick routines.

Recently exhumed for the DS, *Point Blank* is a formative example of the game that all the family can play, as enjoyable and challenging to hardcore Namco fanatics as it is to complete newcomers—a rare achievement. **KS**

Puzzle Bobble

Original release date : 1994
Platform : Various
Developer : Taito
Genre : Puzzle

A video gaming rule: Objects of the same color, when placed together in combination, will eventually reach critical mass and disappear. *Puzzle Bobble* is often described as a melding of various other puzzlers. In reality it is an original. A mass of colored balls descend relentlessly from the top of the screen. You control a cannon at the bottom of the screen, which fires colored balls that can be bounced off walls at angles, and stick where they hit on the approaching mass.

The genius of *Puzzle Bobble* (aka *Bust a Move*) lies in the player gradually building their own doom. It's rare that the screen fills with balls, thanks to simple gravity. It's your own missed shots and bad calculations that leave strange cornices hanging where there should be none, creating new obstacles as you try to rid yourself of the old ones. All *Puzzle Bobble* players can remember experiencing that moment when the anger became too much and, in a fit of desperation mixed with pique following a bad shot, they fired several volleys of balls in a desperate and foolish attempt to improve their situation.

It never does. A neat touch lets you get rid of any number of balls by removing their connection to the mass, meaning that bad shots can, with enough patience, turn into good ones. But this is a game where calmness is in short supply, captured in the little figures of Bub and Bob near the cannon, who become panicky as the mass of multicolor frog spawn inches closer and closer. It will always hit bottom, and it will always be game over, because that is how puzzle games work. But somehow you just can't help returning to them again and again. Needless to say, playing head-to-head against a friend delivers the maximum opportunity for delight and frustration. **RS**

Sensible World of Soccer

Original release date : 1994
Platform : Various
Developer : Sensible Software
Genre : Sports

Originally released for Commodore's Amiga in 1994, *Sensible World of Soccer* took the already amazing match play of its predecessor, *Sensible Soccer,* and wrapped it up within a more comprehensive management game than had ever been seen before.

It was the sheer size and scope that immediately impressed. For the first time, there were thousands of real-world teams, populated by even more thousands of real-world players, and an inexhaustible range of tactical options for virtual managers to pursue during the course of their twenty-year careers—from sitting back and shouting from the sidelines (well, the sofa) to getting hands-on and taking control of matches. Compared to the photorealistic

fakers and divers of today's football games, *Sensible World of Soccer* has a certain retro appeal, but in truth it isn't much to look at: tiny little pixely blobs pass for players who speed around simple 2-D fields that are basic blocks of brown or green. The great strength of the game lies in its speed and attention to detail: the way those pixely blobs move around the field with real intelligence, the way the ball bounces and moves realistically, the way you can curl shots into the top corner with a sweet dab of after touch. And all this via just one button.

It is a credit to the game's programming that the flat, unadorned rectangles that pass for fields actually take on real-world handling characteristics with surprising subtlety. Soggy fields hold the ball up, while the ball skids and bounces across freshly laid turf. And it is nothing less than remarkable how those tiny little stick men have the capacity to take over your brain and convince you that you are playing a real, live game of soccer, more so than in many fully 3-D successors. **DM**

Samurai Shodown II

Original release date : 1994
Platform : Various
Developer : SNK
Genre : Fighting

In the early '90s, arcade manufacturer SNK was set on besting *Street Fighter II* at its own game. *Fatal Fury* and *Art of Fighting* would be fussy, awkwardly different attempts, and each would fail to capture arcade-goers' imaginations.

SNK decided to try a different tactic, allowing an internal group of developers, known as Team Galapagos, to create a one-on-one fighting game that, rather than feature a contemporary street-fighting tournament, was set in feudal Japan, armed its characters with bladed weapons, and decreased the emphasis on special moves. That title was the original *Samurai Shodown*.

Though imperfect—and not just because of the egregious misspelling of "showdown" (the title is called

Samurai Spirits in Japan)—*Samurai Shodown* would become immediately popular. It had tense and deeply tactical play, attacks needed to be carefully timed to avoid revealing deadly weaknesses, and every single factor that made the original a success would be improved upon in the sequel.

Generally considered the peak of the series, *Samurai Shodown II*'s modifications—some new characters, a few more special moves and defensive options—are subtle, and the title retains the simplicity of execution that makes the *Shodown* games' weapon-based combat so satisfying. Featuring more detailed graphics and responsive controls, it is among the most accomplished fighting games of the mid '90s, with groundbreaking features, such as parrying, and a wealth of Easter eggs.

Indeed, the only thing that lets *Samurai Shodown II* down is its English translation, which is so bad you'd think it was intentional. Fortunately, a refined, balanced design can't be lost in translation. **MKu**

Uniracers

Original release date : 1994
Platform : SNES
Developer : DMA Design
Genre : Racing

The studio is now known as Rockstar North, but from its founding in 1988 until 2002, it was called DMA Design. The celebrated Scottish developer was responsible for a remarkably broad range of games, from puzzlers like *Lemmings* to open-world action games like *Grand Theft Auto*. Less famous, however, is its first game for console and Nintendo, *Uniracers*.

Not because it wasn't good. Known as *Unirally* in the UK, *Uniracers's* side-viewed unicycle-racing-cum-platforming moves both fast and beautifully smoothly, set on glossy, colorful tubular tracks that curve and cross like Möbius strips in abstract space. *Uniracers* also features a stunt system, which grants speed boosts for chains of twists and turns that you try to get your eager little unicycle to land correctly. Played in two-player split-screen mode, it's riotous, each contender desperately attempting to eke an extra stunt out of each jump.

The unicycle is displayed using pre-rendered CGI sprites—the in-vogue style of the time, since it came out around the same time as Rare's *Donkey Kong Country*—and it displays enormous character, wobbling in place before the start of each race, leaning forward as you boost, the seat looking back as a competitor approaches from behind, and bowing when you win.

But that very character would be the reason why *Uniracers* isn't as well known today as it should be. In 1994, Pixar was still to release *Toy Story*, the film that would push it to mainstream acclaim; already wielding considerable power, Pixar made a legal claim alleging that *Uniracers's* unicycle had plagiarized the star of its 1987 animated short, *Red's Dream*. DMA Design and publisher Nintendo lost the resulting court case, and Nintendo never created more than the game's initial run of 300,000 carts. **AW**

Sub-Terrania

Original release date : 1994
Platform : Mega Drive
Developer : Zyrinx
Genre : Shoot 'Em Up

Alongside asteroids and invaders from space, another threat to gamers throughout the years has been inertia. *Gravitar*, *Thrust*, *Exile*, and *Bangai-O* all task the player with metering out power and piloting their ship through a contorted maze of tunnels (often while wresting control from gravity's inexorable pull). Zyrinx produced one of the best examples of the genre in *Sub-Terrania*, a game that makes no concessions to underprepared players, delivering a sizeable challenge over its ten atmospheric levels.

The plot concerns an attack by aliens on an underground mining colony. You are the lone pilot tasked with defeating the aliens, using an experimental attack ship. While the game borrows many elements from predecessors (gravitational effects, finite fuel supplies, and the need to rescue stranded miners, for instance), it also innovates, adding features like fuel-saving mining rails to ride and submodules that allow your craft to travel underwater. But even with these aids in place, the game's difficulty surprised players and critics alike, making *Sub-Terrania* a perfect envoy for Sega's positioning of the Mega Drive as the console of choice for the hardcore gamer.

The game's fairly perfunctory visuals serve as a simple mechanism to communicate feedback to the player and compare unfavorably to some of the bolder graphical experiments of the era. They do have a charm of their own, though, evoking the biological horror school of game art made popular by Psygnosis. And, accompanied by the moody in-game music, players determined to beat the game will not soon forget them (much as they may wish to on failing level eight for the umpteenth time). One for the brave, then, but the rewards are proportionally increased for those willing to put in the extra effort. **BM**

FUEL

MEGA

1M

P.O.W.D ▯ ▯ ▯ ▯

SCORE   0002685D

Super Punch-Out!!

Original release date : 1994
Platform : SNES
Developer : Nintendo
Genre : Sports

Perhaps only Nintendo could have turned boxing into a funny cartoon and created such an evocative title with mangled English. *Super Punch-Out!!*'s greatness is in making fighting predictable, basing its entire system around the moment in boxing when one participant figures out the other, and so boils pugilism down to basics.

Simplicity of attack: one button punches with the left, one with the right, aiming for the head if you're pressing up and to the body if you're not; plus, a separate button for a superpunch. Simplicity of defense: to block, high push up; to duck, press down; to swerve, press left or right; to defend the body, do nothing. Simplicity of purpose: learn your opponent's attack patterns and how to counter.

To some, *Super Punch-Out!!* is a glorified series of quick-time events: Once you know how an opponent works, they can't touch you. To others, that's the whole point. You might know exactly how to put Bear Hugger, a fat lumberjack with an invulnerable gut, flat on his back, but you'll still get in the ring and do it again. You know what Mr. Machoman's going to do every time his trainer shouts, exactly how to alternate the blocks when Piston Hurricane tries his Hurricane Rush, and when to hit Bald Bull to put him down in one.

In part, *Super Punch-Out!!*'s attraction lies in its colorful personalities, their little tics and taunts as they try to outfox and outpsyche the coldest opponent they'll ever face. And the comic moments when they cheat outrageously, followed by the surprised expression when, realizing that the game's up, they crumple in defeat. But more than all of that, it's something that goes right to the heart of why victory feels so good in any field: because you've put the hours in to be this good. You've earned it. **RS**

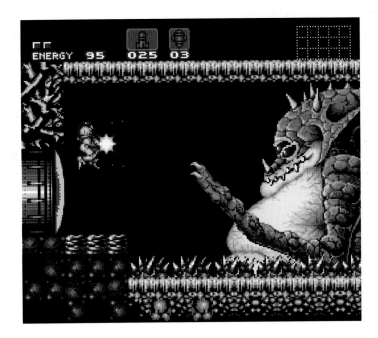

Super Metroid

Original release date : 1994
Platform : SNES
Developer : Nintendo
Genre : Platform / Shoot 'Em Up

While Mario and Zelda generally head off on chirpy, colorful adventures filled with allies as well as enemies, the *Metroid* series plumbs darker reaches. Taking its inspiration from deep-space horrors rather than the squishy delights of Saturday morning cartoons, the *Metroid* games provide a bit of balance to Nintendo's first-party catalog—complex, rather frightening stories that hinge on a feeling of being lost or trapped.

As with so many SNES updates to classic NES series, *Super Metroid* retains the basics—the moody exploration, the unfolding game world, the backtracking, the upgrading and transformations into the morph ball—and adds such a layer of imaginative polish and graphical beauty that the whole thing becomes completely transcendent. Plunged into adventure on the mysterious planet Zebes, where Samus must hunt for a stolen Metroid larva, *Super Metroid* conjures some of the spookiest, loneliest, and downright frightening platforming levels ever created. The sense of being deep underground and far from help is palpable, and, despite the vivid design, the game's sense of creeping dread can be overwhelming at times. The map is huge and complex, filled with secrets and hidden corners, while the power-ups constantly change the feel of the game. This is a completionist's dream, a trek to the hundred percent mark coupled with a rich, involving story.

It's also become something of a speed-run favorite, as players race to complete the epic adventure in as short a period as possible, harvesting as few of the game's power-ups as they can. But if this is your first time on Zebes, you should probably take your time. Slow down, check out every dingy corridor, and revel in one of video gaming's most completely immersive fantasies. **CD**

Beneath a Steel Sky

Original release date : 1994
Platform : Various
Developer : Revolution Software
Genre : Adventure

Of all the games produced by UK studios year upon year, the most quintessentially British might forever be *Beneath a Steel Sky*. Simultaneously delicate, sophisticated, campy, and melancholic, it's also a great interactive comic book. Its point-and-click action, peppered with cut scenes by *Watchmen* artist Dave Gibbons, make it one of the most fondly remembered and revisited of the early '90s adventure games.

Set in a bleak vision of tomorrow's Australia, it tells the story of Robert Foster, a plane crash survivor raised from childhood by tribesmen in the Outback, known here as the Gap. A smooth talker trained in robotics and survival, he's abducted by stormtroopers sent from Union City, a domed metropolis run by an omniscient computer. His tribe is annihilated, leaving him with no one for company but Joey, a robot companion he keeps stored on a circuit board. Fleeing his captors after their helicopter crashes inside the city, his escape takes him through a web of factories and skyscrapers, with the city's eccentric population giving him few of the answers he's looking for.

With its Yorkshire-accented jobsworths and Americans lumped with UK slang and references to *Doctor Who*, Douglas Adams, and Joy Division, *Beneath a Steel Sky* is as incongruous a game set in Australia as you're likely to find. But its inspirations, which range from Fritz Lang's *Metropolis* to dystopia fiction and Nietzsche, are universal. The same can be said of its backdrops, which represent Union City in the same painstaking detail as anything from LucasArts or Sierra On-Line. Though the game was made freeware in 2003, the 2009 iPhone version is an essential purchase, featuring excellent touch controls, preserved dialogue, remastered music, and "motion comic" cut scenes that refresh this early Revolution gem. **DH**

Killer Instinct

Original release date : 1994
Platform : Various
Developer : Rare
Genre : Fighting

Nintendo has long been known for its family-friendly attitude. Its participation, therefore, in the mid-'90s struggle for head-to-head fighting game supremacy was unexpected, the competing titles of the time generally vying to be as gratuitous and outlandish as possible. Rare's *Killer Instinct* remains something of an anomaly for the company—a no-holds-barred fighting game that lists among its cast of characters: a salivating werewolf, a shape-shifting alien, a sword-wielding skeleton, and, of course, a scantily clad lady of exotic provenance, all committed to beating the pulp out of one another.

Lacking the chesslike depth of *Street Fighter II* and the shock tactics of *Mortal Kombat*, *Killer Instinct* distinguishes itself in two ways. First, with its pre-rendered graphics, which lend its visuals a fullness and heft that real-time 3-D games would spend years trying to match. Characters look Plasticine-like and shiny, akin to moving action figures, which is oddly fitting given their caricatured designs. They fight against backdrops that have depth and detail, not like the uninvolving barren and static arenas found in *Killer Instinct*'s contemporaries.

Second, with the inclusion of nearly endless combos, each one celebrated by an announcer who sounds like a proud parent, *Killer Instinct* positions itself as a flashy crowd-pleaser. Combos aren't accomplished on a one-to-one basis with the player's actions. Instead, a relatively simple control input can unleash an absurdly long string of attacks. It is actually possible to start a fighter's devastating "ultra combo" and walk away from the cabinet for high-fives, your character pummeling some poor sucker all the while. Hey, what good is a fighting game if it doesn't let you humiliate your opponent? **MK**

Theme Park

Original release date : 1994

Platform : Various

Developer : Bullfrog Productions

Genre : Management Simulation

Theme Park is yet another management sim, but one that comes with a vital difference: what you're managing is actually quite interesting. Bullfrog's classic game puts you in charge of your own pocket Disneyland equivalent, a nexus of cotton candy and lines. Starting with a free plot of land and a few hundred thousand dollars, it's up to you to start laying out paths, placing concessions, hiring staff, and saving up for the best rides as you work your way steadily toward untold riches. So while at heart you're working out profit margins and trying to tilt the supply/demand curve in your favor, it all feels a little more fresh and exciting than if you were nudging out rivals in the garment industry or controlling the assets of an enormous international bank.

Bullfrog's skill with amusing little features helps: Entertainers waddle around your grounds, dressed as giant animals; fast-food stalls look suitably sugary and slick; and the rides, which, if you're playing one of the more advanced iterations of the game, you can click on for a quick cinematic, are suitably preposterous in their loops and dips and sudden curves. Or you might prefer the bouncy castle, the tree house, or the Ferris wheel.

Ported to almost everything—a recent version landed it on the DS, with mixed results—and as influential in the management genre as Bullfrog's own *Populous* was for god games, *Theme Park* is clever and colorful, streamlined and quietly sardonic. When Electronic Arts bought out Bullfrog, the publishing giant inevitably rode this rather charming slice of Britishness into the ground, but if you've got a yearning to plug through some spreadsheets and yearly accounts, and a sharp desire to calculate just how much salt to put on your fries, *Theme Park* is definitely the game you've been waiting for. **CD**

King of Fighters '94

Original release date : 1994
Platform : Various
Developer : SNK
Genre : Fighting

The first title in a successful, award-winning series of fighting games that would see yearly releases until 2003—and continue to see regular releases thereafter—King of Fighters '94 combines the fighters of SNK's Fatal Fury and Art of Fighting franchises (plus a few original characters) into a team-battle-based 2-D fighter that would become the company's flagship product.

Created to attract and combine the audience of SNK's differing fighting franchises, King of Fighters '94 was the first one-on-one 2-D fighter to feature team play. Players select a group of three fighters—each combatant battling after the other until defeated or victorious—to enter the game's fictional tournament. Unlike later King of Fighters titles, King of Fighters '94 restricts players to choosing preset teams that (supposedly) represent different nations and introduces players to characters that would become iconic in their own right, such as posterboy Kyo Kusanagi. Indeed, no matter what your taste in fighting games, you'll probably find something to like here.

Though the title is considered by many fans to be obsolete in the face of the many updates the series has seen since its introduction—and, as the first title in a crossover, it suffers some balancing issues—King of Fighters '94 is a highly playable fighter that presents a good introduction to the series for players who would be otherwise confused by the vast quantity of characters and fighting styles on offer in later versions. Featuring classic SNK art and music with some highly challenging AI, this is the title that finally distinguished SNK's street-fight-themed output from Capcom's, creating a popularity that would endure long after similar games were abandoned by most competitors. **MKu**

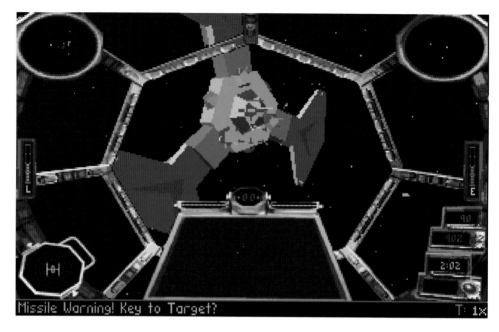

Missile Warning! Key to Target?   T: 1x

Star Wars: TIE Fighter

Original release date : 1994

Platform : PC

Developer : Totally Games

Genre : Shoot 'Em Up

It was perfect symmetry. Before making *Star Wars: TIE Fighter*, designer Lawrence Holland of Lucasfilm Games created a suite of World War II dogfighting games, including *Secret Weapons of the Luftwaffe*. For *Star Wars*'s space dogfights, George Lucas looked to *The Dam Busters* and *633 Squadron* for inspiration. When Holland was asked to think about creating a space combat game, he quickly realized that he and Lucas were already looking squarely at the same sources. The result was a series of games that represent some of the best film tie-ins ever created.

The secret is in the subtle blend of strict adherence to *Star Wars* lore and a willingness to design imaginatively on top of them. Immediately striking are the intense, twisting

dogfights against star fields streaked with beams of bright, green and orange laser fire, as well as the iconographic lines of *Star Wars*' distinctive spacecraft. But the meat lies in one of gaming's most beautiful mechanics: your craft's power system. Demanding that you delicately balance your finite energy supply between lasers, engines, and shields, you are continually asked to think about how to approach each situation. Dump all your power into engines for speed, and you'll risk running out of lasers and having no protection when you meet trouble.

Star Wars: TIE Fighter, which has you fight for the Empire, features smoothly shaded fighters and meticulously designed missions. And though you might assume you'd always want to fight for the plucky Rebellion, the game's vision of dark political intrigue oozing below a veneer of mundane bureaucracy is gripping. It remains a terrible thrill to pilot a craft as fragile and feather-light as a regular TIE. Showing *Star Wars* from the dark side resulted in one of the most enthralling visions of its universe. **AW**

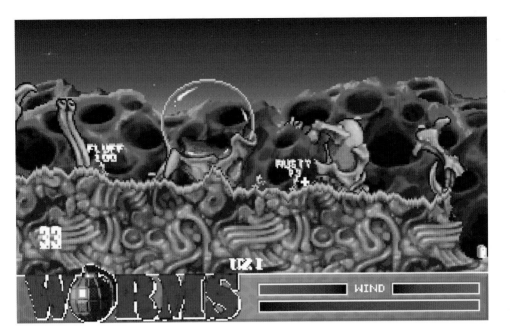

Worms

Original release date : 1995
Platform : Various
Developer : Team 17
Genre : Action / Strategy

Unassuming even by the standards of its own day, the basic visuals of *Worms* overlay a lot of big ideas. A turn-based combat game in which teams of four try to kill one another with an assortment of "wacky" weaponry, and a design that allows for utter chaos as much as it does for meticulous planning. It also features the Beatles in annelid form, a reverence for wind speed, a selection of close-combat moves perfect for bragging rights, and the option to commit suicide.

Four teams battle it out, with players taking their turn under a time limit, to prevent things from becoming too labored, and every game is different, thanks to the battlefield being randomly generated and fully destructible. Missiles create huge craters, players begin to cravenly tunnel out hidey-holes, and mines take out a good chunk of the ground, as well as worms. By the end of a round, the environment is always unrecognizable from its initial form.

The formidable armory is stocked with the typical missiles, grenades, and shotguns, but it's objects like the bungee rope, humiliating finishers like the dragon punch, and random nonsense like a bouncing, exploding sheep that make it memorable.

Unpredictability is the key quality of *Worms*, alongside colorful little touches, such as the ability to name your own team, push players into the water, or the gravestones that mark a fallen warrior. *Worms*'s greatness comes down not just to the combination of these elements, but to the simple fact it was designed to be played within half an hour with a few friends, a lot of chatting, and plenty of laughs. It may even be one of the first games to recognize just how social gaming can be. **RS**

Command & Conquer

Original release date : 1995
Platform : Various
Developer : Westwood Studios
Genre : Strategy

Widely considered the quintessential real-time strategy video game, Westwood Studios's epic used the latest PC technology to expand and popularize its predecessor, *Dune II*, laying the groundwork for more than just sequels and spin-offs.

The plot centers around Tiberium—a fiercely contested alien resource slowly infecting an alternate 1995. In the blue corner: the Global Defense Initiative (GDI), which with its real and hypothetical hardware is the game's United Nations. In the red corner: the Brotherhood of Nod, a bizarre but no-less-dangerous cult led by a charismatic terrorist called Kane. In a structure adopted by almost every RTS (real-time strategy) game since, each features its

own full-length campaign, encourages its own approach, and is crucially dependent on local Tiberium.

Most of *Command & Conquer*'s battles turn upon a well-prepared, decisive push that breaks the enemy line and ruins its mining operations, paralyzing its ability to repair and rearm. Nicknamed the "tank rush," it usually involves a large number of on-screen units commanded as one or more groups, a feature made possible by the game's greatly improved interface and performance, and competently defended by the opposing AI. Other missions involve just a single special-ops unit with a sneakier objective, or the survival of a group in which no one is expendable.

Sprinkled in between are the knowingly cheap and playful live action cut scenes that became a series hallmark, especially as it entered Cold War spin-off series *Red Alert*. The beloved cut scenes made a lauded comeback in 2008's *Red Alert 3*, with a quite stupefying and eclectic cast, ranging from Tim Curry and Jonathan Pryce to MMA legend Randy Couture and Jenny McCarthy. **DH**

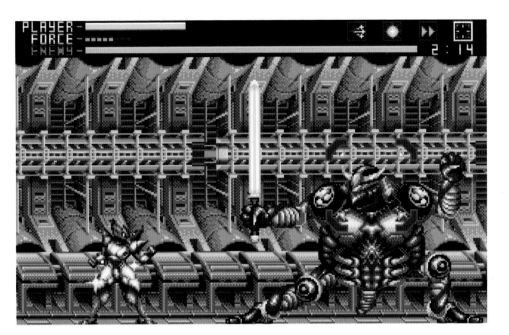

Alien Soldier

Original release date : 1995
Platform : Mega Drive
Developer : Treasure
Genre : Shoot 'Em Up

Treasure, so the story goes, once plotted a graph of the excitement a gamer experiences when playing one of their games, and discovered that the high points were invariably to be found during the boss battles. If that's the case, Japan's best-loved boutique developer concluded, then why not make a game that consists primarily of boss battles and not a lot else?

Alien Soldier was the prime beneficiary of this train of thought, being a side-scrolling run-and-gun shooter that, in many ways, represents the pinnacle of Treasure's exemplary work throughout the Sega Mega Drive era. With thirty-one bosses spread throughout its twenty-five levels, it's also one of the most exciting and intense experiences in the canon, a machine-gun volley of sprites that the hero, Epsilon Eagle, must dodge through and shoot down.

There are only two levels of difficulty in Alien Soldier—Supereasy and Superhard—but the truth is that the game is extremely challenging no matter which is picked. The principle difference between the two is the loss of soft saves and continues in the latter option. Far less accessible than Treasure's earlier classic, Gunstar Heroes (1993), Alien Soldier nevertheless features a similar multiple-weapon combination system, one that must be carefully learned and mastered if you're to have any hope of making it through the game.

Released toward the end of the system's life, Alien Soldier is now one of the Mega Drive's most expensive titles as it enjoyed only a small print run and never even made it to American shores. A few bugs were introduced into the English-language version, ensuring that the Japanese release is the premium edition. Today, it is also available to play on Nintendo Wii's Virtual Console. **SP**

Who are you?
How's it look?
I gotta get out of this town, fast!
Well, I'll let you get back to work...

Full Throttle

Original release date : 1995
Platform : PC, Mac
Developer : LucasArts
Genre : Adventure

The lure of the open road is a persistent theme in Western culture. Video games got in on the action with *Full Throttle*, one in a long line of superb adventure games from the LucasArts factory. Steeped in motorcycle culture and set in a cartoon version of the American southwest, it's a paean to rugged individualism.

Our hero, a barrel-chested, gravel-voiced biker named Ben, is cut from a familiar, antiheroic cloth. The leader of an outlaw gang called the Polecats, he rigorously follows his own code of honor and ethics, but when someone pushes him, he pushes back. The pusher, in this case, is a corporate executive named Adrian Ripburger. Ripburger frames Ben for murder as part of his dastardly scheme

to turn the world's last motorcycle manufacturer, Corley Motors, into a maker of minivans (the horror!), sending Ben on a quest to clear his name and find the true heir to the Corley throne.

As with all LucasArts adventure games, most of the game play in *Full Throttle* takes the form of (occasionally obtuse) puzzles, but, as befits Ben's bulldoglike attitude, they're more straightforward than usual. Empty gas tank? Siphon some fuel. Locked door? Kick it down. The game is also heavy on the action, with Ben partaking in motorcycle duels on desert highways and competing in a hilarious, fiery demolition derby.

The strong script, by Tim Schafer and Dave Grossman, and the sterling voice work, notably Roy Conrad as Ben and Mark Hamill as the slimy Ripburger, lend the proceedings depth, humor, and pathos. It's a quintessentially American story: After thwarting the moneyed elite, Ben turns his back on safety and security, and rides off into the sunset, because, baby, he's gotta be free. **MK**

BioForge

Original release date : 1995
Platform : PC
Developer : Origin Systems
Genre : Role-Playing / Puzzle

BioForge's original working title, *Interactive Movie 1*, should give you an idea of Origin Systems's cinematic ambition and the high hopes held for this game. Set in an unrecognizably distant future, where religious extremists believe mankind can only evolve through cybernetic implants, the player takes the role of a cyborg that wakes, suffering from amnesia, in a devastated research station on an alien planet.

While the setup—a ruined location where everyone who isn't dead is insane, and the player has to piece the plot together through reading notes and logs—has been used before and since, *BioForge* remains unique in its decision to tell its tale via specifically cinematic presentation, using third-person controls paired with fixed camera angles to carefully direct the player's experience.

Playing a Frankenstein's monster, the game's tanklike controls and clumsy combat feel more like intentional touches than awkward side effects of the technology, and though the game suffers when experienced nowadays, due to its fixed 320 x 200 resolution and mere 256-color palette, it featured many unique graphical touches for the time, such as single-skin texture-mapped characters with skeleton-based animation.

No longer technically stunning, *BioForge*'s strengths lie in its intelligently designed play, where the player joins the amnesiac protagonist in not knowing what to do. Rather than being led by the hand, the game encourages players to explore and experiment and find their own solutions to most puzzles. Unlike the majority of "interactive movies," *BioForge* told its own story in its own unique way, expecting players to use their individuality. What better definition of an interactive movie could there be? **MKu**

MechWarrior 2: 31st Century Combat

Original release date : 1995
Platform : Various
Developer : Activision
Genre : Action / Strategy

Hailing from the line of popular BattleTech tabletop games, *MechWarrior 2: 31st Century Combat* not only had to satisfy hardcore fans of a decade-old franchise, but, as a marquee PC game for publisher Activision, it had to make the case for two relatively unproven technologies: 3-D graphics and Internet play. *MechWarrior 2* succeeds on both counts, balancing an accessible control scheme with the deep customization that devotees demand, all packaged in a sterling presentation.

You play a soldier for one of two warring clans, Wolf or Jade Falcon, fighting in armored vehicles called mechs. Mechs are nominally humanoid in appearance, and pack devastating firepower. As fantastical as the conceit is, it's grounded by the mundane portrayal of mechs. In a world exhausted by war, conduits of destruction operate like old jalopies. Mechs can only carry limited ammunition. They overheat. They lose limbs, and stagger along like cripples.

All this makes victory in *MechWarrior 2* more a matter of strategy than of reflexes. Players need to carefully consider their builds before each mission. Whether battling another player on a direct connection or fighting several foes in the single-player campaign, it's most important to neutralize your opponent's strength. Against a fast-moving, high-jumping mech, take out its legs. Against a slow-moving, high-powered mech, try to destroy its weapon pods.

When faced with a mech on the brink of destruction, players will automatically eject, but a manual override gives you the option to go down with the ship. Though game play is unaffected either way, pride keeps many a pilot flailing in a broken, smoldering mech, even after all hope of recovery is gone. **MK**

Tactics Ogre: Let Us Cling Together

Original release date : 1995
Platform : Various
Developer : Quest
Genre : Role-Playing

The place of *Tactics Ogre: Let Us Cling Together* in gaming history is assured. Hironobu Sakaguchi, the chairman of Square at the time, was so impressed by the developer's work on this game that he hired the entire team to come and work on *Final Fantasy Tactics*, a game with which it naturally shares a number of similarities. A chess-like tactical RPG, *Tactics Ogre* also launched the career of designer wunderkind Yasumi Matsuno, who went on to create other classics in the canon, such as *Vagrant Story* and *Final Fantasy XII*.

The seeds of this success are all clearly visible in this game, which debuted on the SNES and combined a grand historical setting, full of Shakespearean knights and political intrigue, with a deep and involved combat system. Battles, played out on an isometric field, were innovative for deciding each character's turn, based on their speed statistic (in the past, each side would take turns to move all of their characters at once). And, for the first time, *Tactics Ogre* introduced a full branching storyline to the tactical RPG genre, with multiple routes through the narrative that ensure the player always feels as though their successes and failures play a vital role in the story's progression.

Thanks to its ingenious story; grand, evocative soundtrack; and some groundbreaking mechanics that updated and upgraded a somewhat crusty template, *Tactics Ogre* frequently makes the Hundred Best Games of All Time lists, and was voted the seventh greatest game of all time by readers of Japan's leading gaming magazine, *Famitsu*. *Tactics Ogre* should be considered nothing short of a masterpiece, even disregarding the fact that it was the catalyst for so many great titles in subsequent years. **SP**

Descent

Original release date : 1995
Platform : Various
Developer : Parallax Software
Genre : Shoot 'Em Up

The shameful secret of many early 3-D games is that they didn't actually take place in three dimensions. Oh, they gave the illusion of depth of field, but it was a ruse. In the early days you could never aim along the Z axis, or walk beneath where you'd been before. The arrival of Interplay's *Descent*, a dizzying corridor shooter that brought full 3-D to the masses, was like receiving a radio signal from an alien civilization: It changed everything we thought we knew.

In *Descent*, players pilot a small hovercraft through complex tunnel systems, attempting to eradicate a computer virus that has infected automated mining equipment and turned it hostile. The tropes are familiar for first-person shooters of the era: floating icons represent weapon and shield upgrades for your craft, hostages can be rescued by touching them, and advancing through the levels is mostly a matter of finding colored key cards and their corresponding doors. There's no sense of an in-game narrative unspooling or that the player's actions have consequences that will be felt later.

What *Descent* does have, in spades, is dizzying and devious level design. The tunnel networks are disorienting, to say the least. With environments composed largely of monochromatic walls, and a ship that can turn and spin in any direction, it's challenging enough to keep track of which way is up, never mind which way you're going. At the end of each level, players trigger an autodestruct mechanism and must race against a timer to escape the mine. This is not easy. Fortunately, the play control is excellent (as long as you're using a joystick). Ships drift and tilt with a naturalistic feel, which led to possibly apocryphal tales of vertigo and motion sickness among early players. Perhaps that was intended as praise. **MK**

Wing Commander IV: The Price of Freedom

Original release date : 1995
Platform : Various
Developer : Origin Systems
Genre : Shoot 'Em Up

Wing Commander is like TV's Battlestar Galactica played out through the eyes of fighter pilots, only with more World War II-style dogfights.

Capital ships are the cities, aces their champions, and the vacuum in between is where the fate of the galaxy unfolds. Plots are uncovered, patrols are ambushed—it's always "quiet, too quiet"—and deaths are avenged by Gatling guns and missiles. The narrative is unbroken throughout, the banter moving from the cockpit to the mess hall and back again, creating a sense of camaraderie amid the drama.

Over the next nine years each of the games marks a turning point in noninteractivity, be it the groundbreaking animated cutscenes of Wing Commander II: Vengeance of the Kilrathi, or the real-life actors and blue screens of Wing Commander III: Heart of the Tiger. The format stayed the same but the balance of resources shifted, the player needing ever-greater hardware while games demanded spiraling budgets. At a then-unheard-of $12 million, Wing Commander IV's topped the lot.

Set during the aftermath of the Terran-Kilrathi War that preoccupied games one to three, The Price of Freedom is the second to star Mark Hamill and Malcolm McDowell. Filmed at broadcast quality using actual sets, its B-grade drama spanned six CD-ROMs and had to be down-sampled (until a later DVD release) to play on hardware available at the time. It's a remarkably literal attempt to bring games and movies together which, like many of the interactive movies of the '90s, learns the pitfalls the hard way. It's actually hard to suspend disbelief when so much of what you're seeing is real, and even harder to withhold judgment of its writing and direction. **DH**

Wipeout

Original release date : 1995
Platform : PS1
Developer : Psygnosis
Genre : Racing

It's easy to forget that *Wipeout*, a PlayStation launch title in the West from Liverpool studio Psygnosis, entered the slipstream of popular culture two whole years before the first *Grand Theft Auto*. An elegant and sophisticated racer in its own right, it gained added lift from a seminal licensed soundtrack and cutting-edge look, courtesy of now-defunct design studio the Designers Republic. The futuristic setting and challenges of races like Silverstream (made in Greenland out of manmade crystal) and Terramax (on Mars) were accompanied by radical, contemporary tracks by the Chemical Brothers, Leftfield, Orbital, and others. Cutting edge music paired with fun, original, sci-fi concepts contribute to making this a pure adrenalin rush shot through with electronica.

The game was so slick, in fact, that even an early concept video was enough to feature in *Hackers*, the Angelina Jolie movie about high-school cyberpunks and Internet terrorists. Even without the mock-consumerist imagery plastered over its billboards and cover art, the sense of movement in *Wipeout*—racers piloting needle-like hovercraft which skimmed corners as if on a breeze— was unmistakable. Its 3-D ships and raceways, grounded in pseudoscience and real-world locations, defied comparison with that previous example of the antigrav racer, Nintendo's *F-Zero*.

Not even fourteen years' worth of sequels and imitators have rendered the first game entirely obsolete. While its soundtrack remains the series' best, its status as a weapons-free game of breakneck races and time trials has made it the envy of its successors. Now full of modes, power-ups, and visual experiments, there's no going back for Sony's loyal series—which gives its 1995 debut a unique and lasting purity. **DH**

Virtua Cop 2

Original release date : 1995
Platform : Arcade
Developer : Sega
Genre : Shoot 'Em Up

The citizens of Virtua City don't need a police force, they need an army. Due process? Not in a town where heavily armed gangsters are outnumbering civilians three-to-one. Criminals lean out of windows, swarm on motorcycles, and swoop through the air on jet packs. Law enforcement is about who can fire the most bullets. As one of three members of Virtua City's finest, your job is simple: pull the trigger until peace is restored.

The light gun shooter has always been a popular arcade genre, but until *Virtua Cop* came along, they were staid affairs, creeping along predetermined paths, with cookie-cutter enemies popping up in predictable places. *Virtua Cop 2* doesn't rewrite any of the rules—you still fire offscreen to reload and find weapon upgrades inside breakable crates and barrels—it just polishes them to a diamond-like shine.

Virtua Cop 2 whisks players through a series of thrilling action sequences. The camera never stays in one place for too long, whooshing down city streets and up the sides of buildings. Swiftly moving set pieces aboard a subway train and on the highway are the closest you'll get to starring in an action movie. Particularly rewarding is blasting the tires of an enemy sedan and watching it flip end over end.

Though the game is short, with only three levels, plus a Proving Ground mode, a few smart design decisions keep each play through feeling fresh. Every level offers branching paths, so you won't see the same sights over and over. And because the enemies react dynamically, depending on where you hit them, you get a real sense of immersion in the game world. Shoot a baddie in the knee, and his leg buckles. Shoot him in the arm, and he drops his weapon. Shoot him in the crotch, and—well, you'll find out for yourself. Everybody aims for the crotch. **MK**

The Dig

Original release date : 1995
Platform : PC, Mac
Developer : LucasArts
Genre : Adventure

A strange and demanding puzzler to rival *Loom* or *Myst*, *The Dig* is LucasArts's most divisive game. Based on an idea by Steven Spielberg, with effects by Industrial Light & Magic and dialogue by writer Orson Scott Card, it frequently breaks out of the orbit of the world of the point-and-click, gravitating toward "hard" sci-fi and Hollywood production. To critics it's muddled, humorless, and distracted, while fans agree that you would think that if you lacked the required attention span. As ever, the truth lies somewhere in between.

Opening with that classic shot of a stargazing observatory, the game sends a team of astronauts to investigate Attila, an asteroid on a collision course with Earth. Cracking it open with nuclear warheads, the unlikely trio of Boston Low (by-the-book survival expert), Ludger Brink (laconic superstar geologist), and Maggie Robbins (feisty reporter and linguist) venture inside, only to discover a starship that blasts them back to its distant home world. As weird and wonderful as anything in recent groundbreaking games or movies, this utterly alien planet gives little away, requiring close inspection and lateral thought to explore and escape.

Most of *The Dig*'s puzzles are of the lock/key variety, but with the locks and keys strewn about in the form of odd geometric treasures, murals, and machines. Symbols demand meanings and connections must be made, but the usual signposts are nowhere to be found. Voiced by Robert Patrick, an actor who excels at playing deceptively hardboiled servicemen, Low is no Indiana Jones, while this new world is no Monkey Island. There's a straightness to *The Dig* that jars with its wondrous music and scenery, much of which you'll visit a few times too many. Nevertheless, it's a bizarre and courageous oddity. **DH**

Yoshi's Island

Original release date : 1995
Platform : SNES
Developer : Nintendo
Genre : Platform

If you want to know just how staggeringly confident the 16-bit era *Mario* designers had grown in their own magical abilities to mint fun from simple pixels, look no further than *Yoshi's Island*. In this *Mario* "prequel" the plumber himself is restricted to the role of babbling infant, while Yoshi, the series' trusty dinosaur companion, restores kidnapped babies to their rightful parents long before the real adventures have even begun.

Just as the *Mario* series was settling into its delightful conventions, then *Yoshi's Island* came along to offer perhaps the most imaginative platformer yet, a charming kind of relay race in which each chubby little bulb-nosed dinosaur takes a turn piggybacking Mario and Luigi through one of the game's brilliantly imaginative stages, before passing them on to the next participant. Levels include ski runs, glittering mines, and the requisite fiery dungeons, and new gimmicks are thrown in to keep you on your toes and the action entertaining, such as destructible lumps of clay, squishy ground that will suck you in if you're not careful, giant enemies that swoop in from the background, and Yoshi's main skill, the ability to eat most smaller foes and transform them into eggs to be subsequently used as ranged weapons.

It's a visual departure for the series, too: a hand-drawn paper-and-crayon affair that makes the game look like a magical pop-up book filled with butterflies, strange watery demons, and glinting cardboard coins. And, sadly, it's a dead end. While the game received a streamlined sequel of sorts in the form of the N64's *Yoshi's Story* and the DS's brilliant *Yoshi Touch & Go*, the original was never bettered, and never, truly, advanced upon. Check it out now by tracking down the Game Boy Advance version, or look out for its appearance on Wii's Virtual Console. **CD**

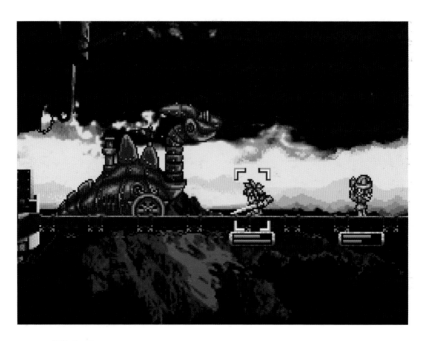

Chrono Trigger

Original release date : 1995
Platform : SNES
Developer : Square
Genre : Role-Playing

Chrono Trigger leverages that most underutilized of gameplay mechanics—time itself—to create a tightly controlled RPG that feels expansive, imaginative, and genuinely era defining, and the result, although one of the most strangely organized of all classic RPGs, is also one of the most widely loved. *Chrono Trigger* is, quite simply, a slice of genuine magic: one of the best Japanese role-playing games on a platform—the SNES—that was hardly short of fantastical brilliance in that department.

It all kicks off at the Millennial Fair with a disastrous test-run for a crackpot inventor's teleportation device. From this humble opening, a massive time-hopping adventure quickly unfolds, traveling back to the distant past, and forward to the irradiated future with its dusty raceways and empty factories.

Today, players are as likely to name check the game's many quirks—most notably the fact that the final boss was accessible from a fairly early point in the game, should the player be interested in trying their luck on a battle—but *Chrono Trigger* is actually all about the moments: the first sight of the grim future of a land you've already explored in its vibrant glory days, a trip to a mysterious church where some very sinister nuns are knocking around, and a devastatingly moving conversation with a little robot. Everyone leaves *Chrono Trigger* with their own favorite memories, of course, and it's the charm of the game that it manages to balance the epic with the intimate so well. After several sequels, add-ons, and even unofficial fan-made remakes, the good news is that following the release of the DS version, a title that was once an import-only experience for European players is now to be found on the shelves of your local game store. **CD**

The Logical Journey of the Zoombinis

Original release date : 1995
Platform : PC, Mac
Developer : Brøderbund Software
Genre : Edutainment

In the '90s, educational games were defined—for the worse—by a suffer-through-dinner-to-get-your-dessert style of game play epitomized by the *Math Blaster* series: The game would walk students through the same kind of math or spelling problems they struggled through in school, while bribing them with a reward of simple action games. Other educators rebelled at the scheme, and *The Logical Journey of the Zoombinis*, designed by Chris Hancock and Scot Osterweil, works off a completely different lesson plan.

Players meet the Zoombinis, a race of fuzzy creatures who lead happy lives until they're enslaved by their nemesis, the Bloat. They escape and make their way to a new homeland, and getting them there entails solving logic puzzles that are presented with almost no clues; players have to experiment their way through matching and grouping puzzles that get harder with every level. For example, a given rope bridge is allergic to Zoombinis who have a certain characteristic—say, the ones who wear rollerskates—but only through careful observation will you figure out which ones. The kid-friendly visuals coated puzzles that grew mind-boggling as you advanced through the levels, but every time the fun lay in the learning—and teamwork in the classroom was always encouraged.

The game was a hit that spawned two sequels, but even today, few others have followed its lead. Educational games have yet to get a serious foothold in schools; the *Math Blaster* paradigm remains common, and grown-ups and kids can both see through it. But video games can still teach problem solving, deduction, and teamwork, suggesting that the genre has potential—and classics like this game provide the case study. **CDa**

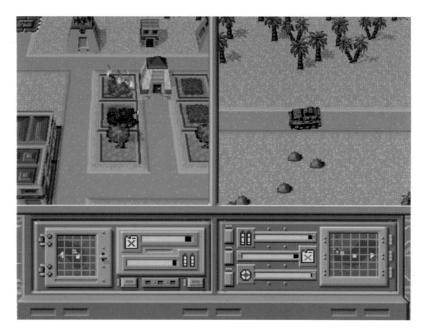

Return Fire

Original release date : 1995
Platform : 3DO
Developer : Silent Software
Genre : Shoot 'Em Up

There's something particularly curious about how the use of Wagner's "Ride of the Valkyries" in a game immediately lends it an added sense of substance. Given that *Return Fire* also throws in Rossini's "William Tell Overture," Grieg's "In the Hall of the Mountain King," and Holst's "The Planets," you'd expect the game disk and accompanying documentation to be made of uranium.

Aptly, there is weight—in a historical context, at least—to Silent Software's experience, which essentially offers a vehicle-based game of "capture the flag" set within a number of increasingly complex landscapes. Focused almost exclusively on a two-player dynamic (a single-player mode does exist, but the lack of genuine AI opposition makes the experience not worthy of great exploration), opponents have four units of varying abilities—helicopter, tank, support vehicle, Jeep—and must use these to scour the land, locate the enemy flag, and return it to their camp (alternatively, the annihilation of their rival also works). The appeal comes from working out strategic approaches that will outclass those of your counterpart, and adapting your machinery to whatever your preferred tactics are—not necessarily a common feature of games of the era.

The aforementioned exclusively classical soundtrack (delivered in surround sound), combined with once-impressive camera work and explosive two-player split-screen action, ensured *Return Fire*'s status as a must-have 3DO title upon release. Fifteen years of game evolution and the necessary distance and detachment from an ill-supported, struggling format results in it being difficult to conjure up quite the same excitement over the game, but it retains a simplistic appeal. A decisive strategy game in grand, stirring trappings. **JDS**

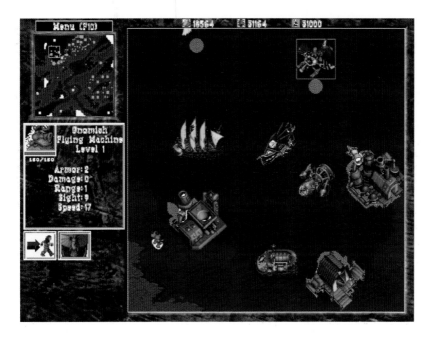

Warcraft II: Tides of Darkness

Original release date : 1995
Platform : PC, Mac
Developer : Blizzard Entertainment
Genre : Strategy

Warcraft II: Tides of Darkness won't be the most advanced RTS title a fan of the genre has played these days, but it may be the most fondly remembered. It will also be among the funniest. Where its main rival, *Command & Conquer*, was partly renowned for its live-action cut scenes, *Warcraft II* was better known for its protagonists' corny one-liners. This humorous bent extends to the game visuals, with the orcs in particular having an endearing cartoon quality, somewhat reminiscent of the Games Workshop *Warhammer* franchise that allegedly inspired the series.

That influence, plus *Dungeons & Dragons* and a splash of Tolkien, is writ large across the plot, which involves an almighty scrap between humans and orcs, and their allies, such as gnomes, elves, trolls, and goblins. Blizzard tells a decent story, but in terms of game play, the races make no real difference. Each side's units are almost entirely identical aside from visuals, with only a few spells setting them apart. Similarly, a few hero characters turn up as the campaign mode rolls along, but while they're almost all tougher than the common arrow fodder and help develop the narrative, they're not a big feature of battle.

The upside to this simplicity is that *Warcraft II: Tides of Darkness* is arguably the best-tuned RTS game of its vintage, especially in multiplayer. All the genre staples are here—gold and wood as resources, successively more advanced buildings and units as you traverse the technology tree, and fights that easily degenerate into a mob rush—and done with bags of charm. The naval and airborne units are a particular treat.

Without the success of this game there'd be no *World of Warcraft*. For that fact alone it deserves our respect or admonishment, depending on how your last raid fared. **OB**

The Beast Within: A Gabriel Knight Mystery

Original release date : 1995
Platform : PC, Mac
Developer : Sierra On-Line
Genre : Adventure

Full-motion video ushered in an exciting new era of game making, taking advantage of CD-ROM technology and providing a new outlet for actors to display their craft. The concept of bringing Hollywood into homes with full player interactivity sounded a death knell for traditional movies. This was the future. For about five minutes.

As quickly as they were heralded as the next big thing, FMV games became the butt of jokes. Still, after the phenomenal critical success of the first Gabriel Knight adventure, the second game jumped on the FMV bandwagon and gave the format credibility with a compelling game experience, supported by excellent performances from the cast. Filmed using blue screen

technology, the actors—notably Dean Erickson playing Gabriel and Joanne Takahashi as his research assistant, moral compass, muse, and sounding board—were then superimposed on static backdrops that the player interacts with to search for clues and information.

The game has budding novelist Gabriel traipsing to his ancestral home in Germany after reports of a werewolf attack. But this is no simple monster hunt as Gabriel's investigation and Grace's research leads to revelations about King Ludwig II and the composer Wagner. Heady stuff. But also smart and engaging stuff, wrapped as it is in a game play mechanic that manages to invoke a real sense of danger and trepidation.

This game's tremendous storytelling, exposition, and true adventure blend with excellent use of the era's hardware, for an experience that, for reasons that remain unclear to adventure fans, went out of vogue. The game further elevated designer Jane Jensen's profile as one of the most creative storytellers in the industry. **RSm**

Sega Rally Championship

Original release date : 1995

Platform : Arcade

Developer : Sega

Genre : Driving

In *Sega Rally Championship*, you may be racing other cars to the finish line, but your toughest opponent is the road itself. Narrow, winding streets challenge your reaction time with sudden hairpin turns. Shifting road conditions affect your car's handling as you go from slipping and sliding across a slick, muddy off-road section to screaming over the cobblestones of a European mountain town. There are small jumps, too, but instead of giving you an aerial thrill, they're terrifying hazards. Take one at anything but the perfect angle, and upon landing you're liable to spin wildly out of control, or worse.

The cars—your choice of a Toyota Celica or a Lancia Delta—have a real sense of weight and momentum. At times they feel like a willful steed, one you need to wrangle and finesse to get it to go where you want. Drifting is key, but it's a matter of constantly correcting against your car's inertia throughout the turn rather than locking it into the optimal angle at the start. For an arcade game, this is surprisingly deep.

Because the game follows the rally circuit model, it progresses through linear segments instead of repeating laps around perfectly maintained professional raceways. You'll zip through several distinct stages, each overstuffed with challenges. To help navigate is your co-pilot, heard but not seen, who calls out each upcoming curve in a chipper tone of voice: "Easy left!" "Medium right!" Occasionally, he seems unsure of himself, and, worryingly, adds the word "maybe" to his directions, although it sounds for all the world as though he's calling you "baby." Nonstop and demanding, *Sega Rally Championship* is a more rigorous and exacting racing experience than Sega's prior efforts, *Virtua Racing* and *Daytona USA*. **MK**

Broken Sword: The Shadow of the Templars

Original release date : 1996
Platform : Various
Developer : Revolution Software
Genre : Adventure

Straying from the tongue-in-cheek LucasArts heritage of the point-and-click genre, Revolution Studios fabricates a tangible world of mystery rooted in historical fact with the *Broken Sword* video game series.

Everyman protagonist George Stobbart leads an immersive narrative that draws threads of classic crime stories into a tapestry of animated adventure, journeying from thriller to character drama with ease. The physical travels of Stobbart and journalist Nico Collard, as they race to solve a murder shrouded in conspiracy, underpins the title's other main draw: its locales. The interactive backdrops of *Broken Sword* create both an intricate sense of place and the lure of the unknown. The Paris opening, the most layered and attractive, awash with autumnal hues, sets a bar that subsequent scenarios cannot quite reach, though. Additionally, for all the faithfulness to architecture and nuances of the picturesque, the puzzles themselves occasionally verge on incoherent (using a cat to obtain an essential object, for example)—an inherent foible of the genre, perhaps, but no less a confounding frustration.

The high level production values aren't limited to visuals. Television and film composer Barrington Pheloung's score punctuates *Broken Sword's* slow burn with sparks of orchestral grace. It's the juxtaposition of the quiet, contemplative investigation and creeping, cued diegetic sound that conjures the conspiratorial atmosphere and makes it stick long in the memory.

More than a puzzle quest for answers, *Broken Sword* is a key example of informed, engrossing virtual tourism to be filed alongside the likes of *Myst*. Visually stimulating in motion and rewarding in practice, it is a measured, captivating story intelligently and beautifully told. **DV**

Super Puzzle Fighter II Turbo

Original release date : 1996
Platform : Various
Developer : Capcom
Genre : Puzzle

Don't let the name fool you. Not only is there no un-Super or non-Turbo version of *Puzzle Fighter II*, there isn't even a *Puzzle Fighter I*. It's a riff on Capcom's endless Hyper, Turbo, and *Championship Street Fighter II* variations throughout the 1990s. It may have started as a goof, but *Super Puzzle Fighter II Turbo* is a genuine achievement, fusing gem swapping puzzle mechanics with an innovative head to head battle system as deep and rewarding as the fighting games it happens to lampoon.

Super Puzzle Fighter II Turbo is even presented like a fighter. When play starts, you and an opponent choose to play as a highly stylized, anime-inspired version of a combatant from Capcom's *Street Fighter* or *Darkstalkers*

series. Each player has a grid on either side of the screen, into which pairs of colored gems drop. To clear a gem, place a same-colored crash gem adjacent to it. It will not only destroy that gem, but all gems of the same color that it touches. The loser is the one whose part of the screen fills with gems first.

The fun starts when you realize you're not simply racing to clear your own screen faster than the other guy. Clear your gems, and you'll drop some onto your opponent's board, as your characters slap each other in the middle of the screen. Place like colors in rectangles of two-by-two or greater, and they'll form devastating power gems.

The bigger the power gem, the more counter gems it will drop on your opponent when you destroy it. A *Puzzle Fighter* match is a series of back-and-forth maneuvers, with players teetering on the brink of destruction before unleashing an endless chain that drops a screenful of gems on an opponent. Rematches are mandatory. A joke? Please. *Super Puzzle Fighter II Turbo* is serious business. **MK**

Duke Nukem 3D

Original release date : 1996
Platform : Various
Developer : Apogee Software
Genre : First-Person Shooter

By the end of the 2000s one of the biggest legends, and one of the biggest jokes, in gaming lore was *Duke Nukem Forever*. This was purported to be the latest chapter in a historic franchise, and is now a game that nobody expects ever to see the light of day. Why did anyone care in the first place? Blame the nostalgia on *Duke Nukem 3D*, one of the first classics of the first-person shooter genre and a lighter, crasser alternative to the clenched jaws and hellspawn of *Doom* and *Quake*.

Duke's opening quip sums up his philosophy: "It's time to kick ass and chew bubble gum. And I'm all outta gum." From the seedy side of Los Angeles to a riff on *Mission: Impossible*, he scours the streets for aliens, shooting up a porno store and fighting bad cops, who actually look like pigs, and when he runs out of bullets, a boot in the butt works too. But Duke's world is more than a shooting gallery. There are secret locations and weapons hidden throughout the game, requiring a measure of forethought and some interest in exploring levels thoroughly. Don't miss the RPG that's hiding in the first scene.

Duke Nukem 3D was also an early favorite for multiplayer deathmatches over LANs and the Internet. Shortly after the game's release, the Total Entertainment Network service matched players up online for a fee, and it was enormously popular. The game offered up inventive and entertaining play, and levels like "Spin Cycle," with its moving walls and confusing surfaces, still hold up well against modern titles.

Reissues on the iPhone and Xbox 360 keep the legend alive, and Duke was arguably an influence for 2009's *Eat Lead: Matt Hazard*, a send up of action franchises that last beyond their prime. Even with its dated graphics, it's still worth a yuck. But act fast: You'll definitely want to get caught up before the sequel comes out. **CDa**

HEALTH ARMOR
78 54

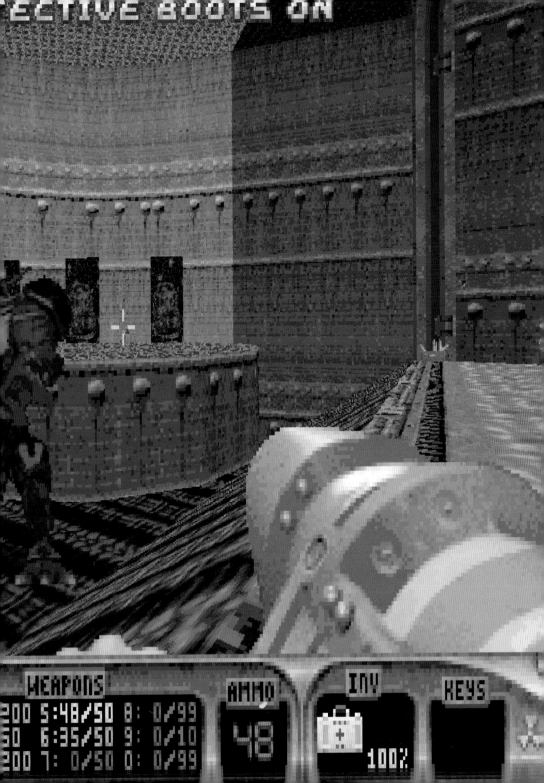

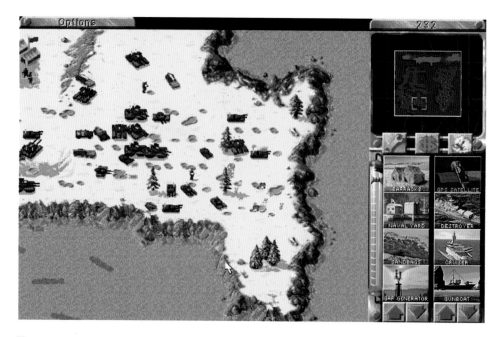

Command & Conquer: Red Alert

Original release date : 1996

Platform : Various

Developer : Westwood Studios

Genre : Strategy

Real-time strategy games tend to be fairly serious sorts of experiences. They're about war, for one thing, which is already serious enough, and they're generally enormously taxing and demanding, requiring players to take in an entire battlefield's worth of information, to isolate threats very quickly, and react to devastating changes on the fly.

So it's no surprise that *Command & Conquer* is a fairly serious real-time strategy game. Series offshoot *Red Alert*, however, really isn't. *Red Alert* is a counterfactual real-time strategy, turning on the notion that Einstein went back in time to kill Adolf Hitler when he was still a nobody (already, things are becoming fairly unserious), only to return to his own time to find the Allies hard at war in Europe, fighting

against a massive Soviet war machine that has sprung up in the absence of Nazi Germany. It could happen. What's less likely to happen, however, is the development of some of the units that *Red Alert* lets you mess around with. These include science-fiction standards like Tesla Coils, capable of zapping troops in a flurry of electricity. Subsequent games would take this concept further until, in *Red Alert 3*, you were firing armored bears at enemies or dispatching tanks that transformed into jet fighters.

That said, despite the wobblier sets and campier acting, *Red Alert* remains serious about being a game. Factions and units are well balanced, maps are clean tactical spaces, and the user interface sets the genre's standard. With the series getting loopier and loopier with every installment—the cover for the third in the series presents the prospect of Russian shock troopers in hot pants—*Red Alert* remains a necessary antidote to the glum world conflicts of the main *Command & Conquer* plotline, providing an explosion of color in a heavily cratered landscape. **CD**

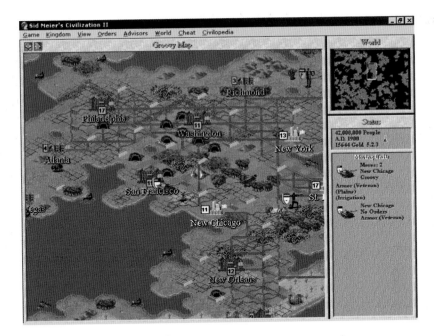

Civilization II

Original release date : 1996

Platform : PC, Mac

Developer : Microprose Software

Genre : Strategy

Civilization might have been the game with which Sid Meier made his name, but he wasn't involved in the creation of the sequel. Nevertheless, it built on the foundations laid by his groundbreaking original to make the march of human progress even more absorbing and addictive. Once again players negotiate the tricky waters of human history by taking a single tribe of near-savages and turning them into a technologically advanced civilization, ready to leave the planet and depart for outer space.

If *Civilization II* can be said to have a goal, it is to either subdue all of your competing empires or to launch a spaceship to Alpha Centauri by the year 2020. But, as ever, the journey is more interesting than the destination,

and the real objective is to simply manage the many, and sometimes conflicting, demands of growing a civilization from scratch. You have to deal with combat scenarios; learning diplomacy; the development of technology; managing the geographical expansion of your empire; the ever increasing size of the population; and ensuring the happiness of your people. In short, you have a lot of balls to juggle and they're all in the air at once. It's both compelling and demanding, a unique combination that makes the game completely addictive.

One of the brilliant things about *Civilization II* is the ease with which the scope of your struggles shifts, from the small scale and local at the outset, to planet spanning problems by its end. Early in the game your concerns are exploring the planet; by the end you are managing its conservation. Indeed, while the educational aspect of the game can be overplayed, its environmental message seems sound enough: The game deducts points from polluters. If only the real world were quite so civilized. **DM**

Mario Kart 64

Original release date : 1996
Platform : N64
Developer : Nintendo
Genre : Driving

The N64 version of *Mario Kart* has had more than its fair share of detractors, but while it may not have the pixelated charm of the original entry in the bestselling series, it's still a genre classic in its own right. This is a game that is all too possible to lose entire evenings to, even now.

Leaving behind the flat Mode-7 driven tracks of old, *Mario Kart 64* features full three-dimensional graphics delivering fantastical hills, bumps, jumps, and even the odd tunnel as you speed around the twisting courses. While giving the game a pleasantly bouncy feel, such features also play with your visibility, meaning that it's more important than ever that you learn the routes and pin down the hazards and shortcuts as quickly as possible.

The tracks themselves are a great haul. Toad's Turnpike marked the first appearance of other nonkart traffic in a *Mario Kart* game while the beautiful Royal Raceway let you duck out of the main course to explore Peach's castle. Each level has a bundle of features for players to enjoy along with a lovingly detailed design to back it up. Not all roads are classics, however. Rainbow Road is smartly crafted but a bit of a slog, while the less said about Yoshi Valley, with its confusing mess of alternate pathways, the better. Overall, though, these levels offer up a new and exciting dimension to this successful franchise.

The most important new addition comes in the form of four-player support. The screen is divided into quarters, so all players can see themselves and their opponents simultaneously, leading to some of the most heartfelt video game cursing of all time as Mario's colorful world turns dirty as the power-ups go off. All of them are a treat to use, but a well-timed lightning bolt when a competitor's about to take a jump can be particularly effective. If you're looking for hours of racing fun, look no further. **CD**

The Neverhood

Original release date : 1996
Platform : Various
Developer : The Neverhood
Genre : Adventure

Point-and-click adventures exist in an odd space in the video game universe. Some of the most beloved and appreciated games of all time reside under that banner, yet few of them achieve the kind of commercial success that their innovation and quality deserves. Count in that number *The Neverhood*, an original, inventive adventure starring Klaymen on a journey through a weird and wonderful world, accompanied by a funky soundtrack.

Designed by artist and animator Doug TenNapel (who also created *Earthworm Jim* for Shiny, and boasts an impressive résumé packed with popular graphic novels), the claymation art style provides a distinct backdrop for the puzzles and story evolution. Finding a way to each new location by pointing and clicking through puzzles is a reward in itself as you work to reveal the next part of a story in which Klaymen aims to awaken Hoborg, the creator of the Neverhood itself.

All good yarns need a compelling villain, and in Klogg, *The Neverhood* has a doozy. Klogg has wrested the crown from Hoborg and it's up to Klaymen to recover it. What he does with the crown, however, is a choice that leads to one of three different endings. The journey is packed with interesting locations and getting to know the ducklike Klaymen and his sidekicks all adds to the charm. And charm really is a big factor in *The Neverhood's* appeal, with well-written gags that buck the impression that the game is more suitable for kids. It's not; it's a truly imaginative journey through a world in which Klaymen has to understand his own origins and purpose. That's achieved by playing disks on TVs dotted around the world, each narrated by a character called Willie Trombone. It's easy to get lost in *The Neverhood*, which makes that final, concluding decision that much more compelling. **RSm**

Guardian Heroes

Original release date : 1996

Platform : Saturn

Developer : Treasure

Genre : Fighting

Japanese-style factory Treasure isn't short on beloved games, but few have captured the imaginations of the studio's audience quite as thoroughly as *Guardian Heroes*, a side-scrolling beat 'em up with colorful character designs, a great fighting system, and some very special additions to the format. Fan sites dissect the game's characters, fights regularly break out over the best tactics for winning its battles, and the art work is among the greatest that Treasure has ever created. Colorful and complex, it often seems to stand as a symbol for the company as a whole.

Guardian Heroes tells the story of four warriors who stumble upon a magical sword filled with ancient powers, and the Golden Warrior it subsequently wakes from the

dead. Foremost among the game's many innovations is the inclusion of this nonplayer/undead hero who will fight alongside you as you plow through the game, covering your back when you need it the most. Elsewhere, *Guardian Heroes* includes smart additions from other game styles, such as experience points, which can be spent to evolve your character, and a bizarre multiplaned battlefield, which means that the game blends three-dimensional and two-dimensional spaces in its combat. If that wasn't enough, the story itself throws up branching paths, offering a great deal of delicious replayability.

Released for Sega's 32-bit Saturn, a console whose peculiar innards have proven rather hard to emulate consistently, *Guardian Heroes* today may prove an expensive chore to track down. *Advance Guardian Heroes*, a sequel—in itself something of a departure for Treasure's willful iconoclasts—was released for Nintendo's Game Boy Advance, but, as smart as it is, it can't hold a candle to the original game. **CD**

International Track & Field

Original release date : 1996

Platform : PS1

Developer : Konami

Genre : Sports

Sometimes the things from which we expect the least are the ones that most surprise us. On paper, a remake of Konami's 1980s Track & Field games for the PlayStation generation doesn't seem worthy of much attention. Excellent as those early arcade hits were, gobbling up pocket money almost as quickly as players became able to tap those two run buttons, by the mid-1990s the focus had sprinted to the brave new worlds afforded by the arrival of three-dimensional gaming.

Not one to buck the trend, International Track & Field hopped, stepped, and jumped toward it, keen to embrace the three-dimensional space along with its contemporaries. The irony is that there are few examples from the era that do so as confidently and as competently as this reworking of a classic coin-operated title that few people cared to revisit. Aside from convincing animation and the atmosphere of a full stadium, multitap compatibility enables a crucial element: four-player action.

On your own, the game's eleven events will hold a certain appeal for as long as it takes to break most of the world records. But add in three competitors—previously not possible in the game's earlier incarnations—and mix in head-to-head events such as the hundred-meter sprint alongside traditionally individual challenges (javelin, long jump, etc.), and International Track & Field transforms into one of the most intensely competitive arenas.

While the graphics were reworked in line with the increased processing power of new hardware, Konami wisely refrained from updating the three-button setup of the original Track & Field. This means the focus on the game experience is uncommonly pure. The only drawback is the number of joy pads you'll go through. **JDS**

Nights Into Dreams

Original release date : 1996
Platform : Saturn
Developer : Sonic Team
Genre : Action

If you've ever dreamed that you could fly, then playing *Nights Into Dreams* will feel instantly familiar. You control an impish figure named Nights, who dresses as a court jester and soars through the air with a casual grace. Capturing the freewheeling sensation of flight, not as it is in real life but in the imagination, *Nights Into Dreams* is more about the joys of the immediate experience—swooping toward the ground, turning a loop-the-loop—than about pursuing ordinary video game objectives.

Those objectives are there, of course. They're just not the focus. To advance, Nights must collect a specified number of orbs from each level within a time limit. It's easy enough for anybody to progress from one level to

the next, but at the end of each stage, players are given a letter grade based on the speed and style with which they completed their goal. By linking together stunts and flying through floating gates in pursuit of the orbs, Nights can rack up style points while advancing through the story. What little challenge there is comes from trying to achieve that elusive A ranking.

The story's frame, about two children, each of whom experiences humiliation at school and then falls asleep to troubled dreams, provides the impetus for each level. Through the avatar of Nights, they will learn to overcome their fears—after the obligatory boss fight, that is. The game's insistence on the treacly narrative is a misstep, but one that's easy to overlook amid the pleasure of flying.

A shortened, Christmas-themed version of the game, with a Santa-styled Nights dashing through the snow to collect holiday ornaments, is rare but not impossible to find. The Yuletide makeover suits the game so well, it's just a shame that it's only two levels long. **MK**

GTI Club Rally Côte d'Azur

Original release date : 1996
Platform : Arcade
Developer : Konami
Genre : Driving

For a game that introduced something of a revolutionary concept to the already crowded driving game genre, GTI Club Rally Côte d'Azur had a surprisingly short-lived appearance in the arcade circuit of the late 1990s. But while it might have burned through its tank of gas faster than most, it nevertheless left a lasting impression on those who witnessed its cheeky, screechy arrival on the scene.

Who could forget the colorful (and then excellent) visuals depicting a small but feisty selection of European hot hatches and the tight, twisty, atypically busy nature of the game's Mediterranean setting? Not to mention a game cabinet that's the size of a small shop and includes a hand brake for negotiating those pesky 90-degree turns.

As important as those elements proved, they merely provide support for the game's central premise of a free-roaming environment that leaves you the choice of chancing new routes in the hope of discovering the shortcuts that will enable you to beat your seven opponents. Combined with the necessity to avoid civilian traffic (or else witness some great crash sequences) and the devilishly strict time limits of checkpoint-based play, the game experience emerges as an intense cocktail of constant frantic steering and countless near-misses.

What it isn't is a lesson in vehicle dynamics. Even for its era, the handling model is surprisingly basic, offering little in terms of player feedback other than exaggerated (but thoroughly artificial) body roll and an almost imperceptible level of road holding. In this particular case, however, that really doesn't matter. Because as proof of the importance of delivering a carefree, universally enjoyable, and charm-ridden central concept, GTI Club Rally Côte d'Azur still takes some beating. **JDS**

Harvest Moon

Original release date : 1996

Platform : SNES

Developer : Natsume

Genre : Role-Playing

Who do you want to be in a game? A spaceman? A soldier? A knight on a perilous quest? Okay, how about a farmer? You know, tilling the land, tending the livestock, looking after crops, and basing your life around the relentless ticktock of the passing seasons and trudging through the wintery snows to milk cows. Not so keen? Are you sure?

Harvest Moon is a farming simulation, but a farming simulation in which the nasty bits of farming, such as wrenching chicken's heads off and putting bolts through cows' brains, are dialed back a bit to make way for a gentle anime depiction of the countryside lifestyle in all its buttery glory. In this delightful title you get to feed and look after your animals, water your crops, milk your cows—and

talk to them while you're at it—and other such farming activities in the most timely manner imaginable in order to maximize your farm's potential.

Unlikely as it sounds, this calm and pastoral agenda will inevitably weave a strong spell until you're so gripped by the game that you can't escape it. A time management exercise at its heart, *Harvest Moon* is capable of dressing its bare clockwork up in such an entertaining manner that you don't really mind being rushed around or sent on a series of what are, essentially, some rather thankless tasks.

Fans certainly don't seem to care as they buy handfuls of very similar sequels by the bucketload and ensure that, even today, every season of the gaming calendar has a *Harvest Moon* release or two. While recent games are perhaps only for the hardcore pretend farmer, however, the original was a strange treat anybody could enjoy, and it's now available, inevitably, on the Wii's Virtual Console service. So, before you shrug off the idea of becoming a farmer, why not give this unusual game a try? **CD**

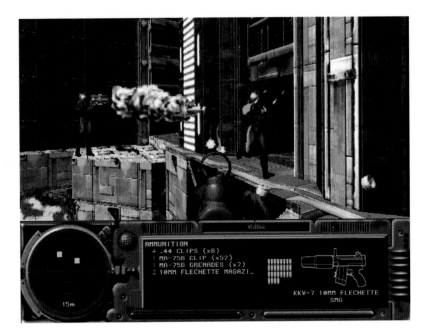

Marathon Infinity

Original release date : 1996
Platform : Mac
Developer : Bungie
Genre : First-Person Shooter

Long before Master Chief's fight began, Bungie was focused on another titanic struggle. The *Marathon* trilogy shares some of its mythology with the *Halo* universe (and indeed with the previous release, *Pathways Into Darkness*), but allusions are subtle, as mysterious as the alien races they reference. If any relationship with *Halo* is certain, it is the shared attention to detail with which both series' realities are constructed. *Marathon Infinity*, the final part of the story, is widely considered to be the pinnacle.

While sharing an engine with the second game, *Marathon Infinity* transformed the first-person shooter with its nonlinear, branching framework. The convoluted plot (best understood by playing through the first two games in advance) involves a search for a reality in which the chaotic and malevolent "W'rkncacnter" entity is not released. To achieve this, the player explores several different timelines, some of which contradict the events of earlier games, and each of which is followed by a dream sequence. The actions you take in the dream determine whether you find yourself in a new timeline or return to one already visited. These existential considerations are far in advance of the more typical "shoot everything" first-person shooter narrative.

Multiplayer games are fought on bespoke maps rather than emptied single-player levels, and a variety of play types are offered in addition to the basic death match. But it's the democratic stance on creation that most impresses—Bungie includes Anvil (a physics-and-graphics editor) and Forge (a map editor) with the game. Due to its Mac exclusivity, this astonishing series was somewhat overshadowed by its PC-focused peers, but now that freeware versions are available on Linux and PC, there is no excuse for anyone not to attempt a *Marathon*. **BM**

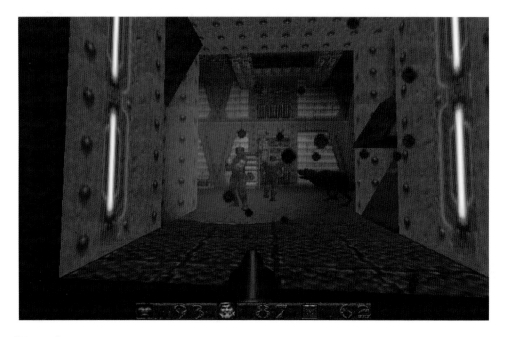

Quake

Original release date : 1996
Platform : PC
Developer : id Software
Genre : First-Person Shooter

Despite being a pioneer of full three-dimensional graphics in the first-person shooter genre—or perhaps because of it—*Quake* is a master class in level design. It's brightly confident in its grasp of space and solidity; even the difficulty and episode selection is its own memorable environment. The game crams in jumping puzzles, a secret area, and is also capable of moonlighting as an unlikely death match arena. In fact, if you pick any of *Quake's* two dozen or so levels, you'll find the critical path is less a line than a rabid dance lesson.

Chiseled into rock or beaten out of metal, *Quake's* forbidding angles remain unique, haunted by the ghosts of the games it could have been as id's hotheaded designers quarreled between dark, fantasy role playing and science-fiction shooter. Though it was the instigator of the "brown corridor" visual treatment, there's art and intention to the oppressive monotone. Its disconnected areas are thick with a sense of place, of eye-catching incidental detail, stranded in crushing blacks: vaults hemmed with silver crosses, the massive embossed metal Jesus, charnel house window settings for apocalyptic stained glass.

All anchored by one of the great pre-music game collaborations between developer and composer. Nine Inch Nails' frontman Trent Reznor's bespoke soundscape is at turns deafening, oily, and pitiless, and never less than part of *Quake's* texture. Aural cues sound out environmental hazards and forewarn of enemies well enough to play blind—or in a blind panic from the frenzy of its eldritch cage matches, its too close combat. In a *Quake* level, Always Run isn't a toggle, it's a commandment, and the numerous strengths within this title turn a game that should have been a "what if?" into a "this is." **BS**

Resident Evil

Original release date : 1996
Platform : Various
Developer : Capcom
Genre : Survival Horror

People have argued for a long time about where and when the survival horror genre got its start. Some stretch it as far back as the esoteric claustrophobia of *Impossible Mission* on the Commodore 64, while others would argue that games had to get clever before they got scary, and that Irrational's *System Shock 2* is the first game really capable of generating fear as well as simple surprise. But for most, the genre begins here, in a big scary mansion with some ropey full-motion video acting.

A haunted house story wrapped up with an unlikely tale of corporate wrongdoing, *Resident Evil* is almost a shooter. A couple of things stop that from feeling like the most accurate of classifications, the first being the cumbersome controls, making moving about a bit of a chore and aiming accurately a panicky frustration. On top of that, the game flings both enemies and ammunition at you in a far more limited manner than a standard action title would. This game is about staging fights and enforcing the hording of resources rather than allowing players to let rip with everything they have.

It's also about making you jump. From the sudden appearance of a zombie when you least expected one, to the moment that dogs leap through a window at you, *Resident Evil* is heavily scripted, certainly, but it has the power to shock you at least once. It may have taken until the fourth installment for the series to get really clever, but so much of that promise is already evident at the start of the franchise, despite the hackneyed story, horrible voice work, and simplistic puzzles. Like a zombie film that's past its prime, *Resident Evil* might be more endearing than frightening these days, but those strange, shuffling zombies have cast long shadows indeed. **CD**

Pilotwings 64

Original release date : 1996
Platform : N64
Developer : Nintendo / Paradigm
Genre : Flight Simulator

The serene world of *Pilotwings* got a cartoonish makeover for this much-loved sequel, with the full force of Nintendo's new N64 console thrusting the dreamy flight simulation into the new era of three-dimensional graphics. With a lovable cast, a sharpened structure of challenge missions, and medals to give shape to your progress, this is certainly a more focused game.

The missions return to the special mixture of different vehicle challenges that made the first *Pilotwings* so endlessly replayable. While there's a decent range of different objectives, from photographing certain sights to even blowing up targets with missiles, the bulk of the game hinges on the greater possibilities for exploration that came with the improvement in hardware. Mountains now rise out of the ground, and the landscape dips down from the hills to the sea's edge.

Another sequel would be lovely, but it doesn't seem to be much of a priority for Nintendo at present. However, it is more likely that *Pilotwings 64* may finally joins its SNES predecessor on the Wii's Virtual Console service. **CD**

PaRappa the Rapper

Original release date : 1996
Platform : PS1
Developer : NanaOn-Sha
Genre : Music

This unlikely game did much to shape some of the bestselling genres of today. It's a pioneering rhythm action title in which players beat each level by matching on-screen prompts while music dictates the pace.

With utterly lovable visual stylings by the renowned artist Rodney Greenblat, NanaOn-Sha's strange little game tells the story of PaRappa, a hip-hop dog who longs to win the heart of his best friend, Sunny Funny. The cast is a memorable collection of freaks and nerds, while PaRappa's musical mentors, from Chop Chop Master Onion, owner of the local karate dojo, to Instructor Mooselini, PaRappa's long-suffering driving coach, are some of the best characters in all of video games.

The songs are utterly perfect. PaRappa will leave you humming its rhymes unexpectedly, years after you last fired it up, transporting you back to this truly unique world. Sequels were forthcoming but nothing can compare to the first time you see PaRappa's flimsy world in motion, and nothing can compete with the first time you pick up the controller and ace a song: U Rappin Good. **CD**

Time Crisis

Original release date : 1996
Platform : Arcade, PS1
Developer : Namco
Genre : Shoot 'Em Up

Light gun games are inherently limited, but that doesn't mean you can't be innovative. *Time Crisis* took the genre forward with a blindingly simple idea that is now a standard. It let you take cover. Previous games in the genre simply demanded you be quick enough at shooting enemies that they couldn't shoot you.

Time Crisis's cabinet has a foot pedal that, when depressed, causes your hotshot secret agent to duck behind the scenery and reload. Of course, with this being a coin-operated game, that's where the *Time* bit of the *Crisis* comes in. You're subject to an initially lax, but increasingly punishing, time limit that's topped up in fractions as you clear each area of bad guys.

The plot's a classic: shoot lots of guys wearing sunglasses as they try to shoot you, then shoot their bosses when they turn up. And thanks to its innovations and unfussy presentation, *Time Crisis* remains a excellent blast today, though sadly its sequels don't quite have the same purity of purpose. An excellent conversion to the original PlayStation sealed the game's breakout success. **RS**

Saturn Bomberman

Original release date : 1996
Platform : Saturn
Developer : Hudson Soft
Genre : Action

With beautifully produced anime sequences and intricate visuals, *Saturn Bomberman* proclaims a new generation of fun for the 32-bit era. Graphically, this is the apotheosis of the two-dimensional *Bomberman* titles, boasting a wonderful selection of highly detailed maps and the playable character roster straying from the usual colored bombermen to a selection of cult Hudson Soft icons.

The game is based on a story that entails players traveling through a series of stages and face a number of boss battles. The addition of two-player cooperative play is a neat extra, and there's the standard battle mode, supplying eight stage designs and the usual chaos in which everyone attempts to incinerate everyone else.

The key addition for the Saturn release, however, is the legendary ten-player battle option, which utilizes two multitap peripherals and a widescreen display format. When the game was launched, Japanese and US players were able to compete online thanks to Saturn modem add-ons. As for the rest of the game, timeless more or less sums it up neatly. **KS**

Tomb Raider

Original release date : 1996
Platform : Various
Developer : Core
Genre : Action

It's all too easy to pin the initial success of *Tomb Raider* on the unlikely physique of the game's heroine, upmarket explorer Lara Croft but, in reality, sex had been used to sell video games—largely with mixed results—for some time before her appearance in the mid-1990s. *Tomb Raider* succeeds because it is, quite simply, a wonderful platformer with a genuine sense of adventure. It is an era-defining classic that did a lot to move running and jumping into a convincing three-dimensional world, while reveling in the kind of intricacy many two-dimensional action titles couldn't incorporate all that easily.

Rich girl Croft is a modern-day Indiana Jones, a seasoned adventuress with a fondness for motorbikes, crop tops, and shooting the legs off endangered species. Although she heads off on her outings with a gun strapped tightly to each thigh, in reality *Tomb Raider's* always been about quiet exploration rather than lining enemies up in your sights. This is a good thing, as it happens, because the shooting is pretty primitive. Instead, Croft's missions to locate mysterious artifacts play out in massive underground spaces, where ancient machinery needs coaxing back to life, and secrets lie around every corner.

The first installment was arguably the best—a fast-paced jaunt taking in jungles, Egyptian sphinxes, and the creepy pyramids of Atlantis. Distinct enough in its quiet, lavish environments to ensure that nothing else felt like it at the time, this series has been tirelessly copied since its first release, but still rarely bettered. While Croft has certainly done her bit for its profile—getting the game, famously, on the cover of the *Face* magazine—in reality, creator Toby Gard and his team of designers are the real heroes of these legendary stories. **CD**

Metal Slug

Original release date : 1996
Platform : Arcade, Neo Geo
Developer : Nazca
Genre : Shoot 'Em Up

War is perhaps gaming's most visited theme, yet few titles approach the horrors of the battlefield with such style and humor as Nazca's seminal side-scrolling shooter, *Metal Slug*. The cartoonish sprite visuals, rendered with a craftsman's skill that makes other similarly themed, two-dimensional games of the time look primitive, show off the Neo Geo hardware's awe-inspiring capabilities. But it's in the colorful animation and character of the graphics, and the tight controls, that *Metal Slug's* wonder is to be found.

You leap through powdery ice caverns, drive bouncing tanks (the titular Metal Slugs) through rivers, and watch as European towns scroll by in glorious parallax behind the action. Shirtless, bearded hostages salute when you free them from their binding ropes and shackles, while enemy soldiers spring to attention from languishing against a lamppost when you stumble into view, before disintegrating into a pile of warm ash when lit up by a flamethrower. As a result, *Metal Slug* is arguably the most expressive and characterful war game yet made, balancing carnage and sight gags with rare success.

Slower and more deliberate than *Contra*, its inspiration, *Metal Slug* eschews predictable enemy patters for a more dynamic assault on the player. Born in the arcade, the game presents a near-insurmountable challenge to the first-time player, but as you hone skills and build muscle memory, learning to juggle grenades, weapons, and your melee knife, so comes mastery. The series would blossom, with multiple sequels of scaling ambition, but the first game is perhaps the most enduring, with its tight focus and masterful level design winning out over the gimmicks that would come to define the (many) later games in the series. It's a game still well worth playing. **SP**

Super Mario RPG: Legend of the Seven Stars

Original release date : 1996
Platform : SNES
Developer : Square
Genre : Role-Playing

Nintendo's mascot meeting Square's talented role-playing game superstars in the final Mario game released on the ageing SNES? *Super Mario RPG: Legend of the Seven Stars* was bound to be an epic undertaking, even before you consider that it represented Mario's first steps in a genre that seemed the ultimate antithesis of his happy-go-lucky platforming norms. Even before too many details had emerged, this was clearly going to be a fascinating experiment, and the results would have a lot to prove.

Happily, *Super Mario RPG* lives up to the hype. With its overworld playing out as a kind of isometric platformer, with the bright colors and familiar cast fans of Mario would come to expect, the battle system is a clever synthesis of turn-based moves and action elements that add a nice sense of twitchiness to the role-playing traditions. Things really start to get in gear once you've got a decent party journeying with you.

The kidnap-heavy plot of a typical Mario game has little problem coming across to the world of role-playing games, and neither does the mixture of outdoor sections broken up with the grim and gothic indoor environments.

All in all, it's rather a neat match, with only the somewhat ugly, rendered, three-dimensional character models showing the game's age, appearing shiny and rather synthetic to modern eyes. As an experiment in the transposition of genres and temperaments, *Super Mario RPG* is a roaring success. As a sign of what was to follow, Square's title opened the door for the likes of the *Paper Mario* console series and the handheld console's wonderful *Mario & Luigi* adventures—and for that fact alone we should probably be eternally grateful. If you haven't had the chance to explore this game, do it now. **CD**

Donkey Kong Country 3

Original release date : 1996
Platform : SNES
Developer : Rare
Genre : Platform

Donkey Kong Country was the first game that Rare developed using a Nintendo trademark character. It's a visually stunning platformer that set an extremely high technical standard that would become the developer's trademark. For a publisher as traditionally conservative as Nintendo was at that time, allowing a British development team to take one of its original icons and give him a three-dimensional makeover, an extended family of other Kongs, and a whole new platforming game was a radical move.

It was the sequel, *Donkey Kong Country 2*, that enjoyed the most profuse praise, but this is the biggest and most fully featured game in the series. Released just after the Nintendo 64's arrival, it suffered from a crippling lack of

attention at the time. It also pushed Donkey Kong well out of the starring role, making way for two of Rare's own creations, Dixie and Kiddy, which didn't exactly help the game to gain exposure in the market.

Its structure and control is superbly fluid, and it imbues its beautiful side-scrolling levels with adventurous spirit. An open overworld design allows you to deviate from the set paths and sequences of levels that usually constrain the genre, and gave *Donkey Kong Country 3* an excellent sense of place and individuality. That element of exploration carries over into the levels themselves as well. Instead of forcing the player to simply collect things, the game often puts a puzzle between you and the desired trinket.

Donkey Kong Country 3's looks are still striking now, thanks to the strange character design and, especially, the fluidity of the animation. It's a creative and unconventional two-dimensional platformer, and the series sparked a relationship between Nintendo and Rare that resulted in some of the best games of the following ten years. **KM**

Syndicate Wars

Original release date : 1996
Platform : Various
Developer : Bullfrog Productions
Genre : Strategy

Syndicate Wars is one of those games that begins with the player in a position of relative strength, before screwing it all up for you. Leader of the EuroCorp network, ruler of the world, and generally the smartest man on the futuristic street, you'll quickly find that your global network of dubious power is being threatened.

This threat is in the form of the emerging Church of the New Epoch, a rival group with very different designs on the future. All of which is an excuse for some pleasantly complicated double-dealing and corporate violence, of course—this being *Syndicate* and all. Keeping the four-man squad basics of the original game, *Syndicate Wars* provides all the tweaks you might imagine from the third—and,

for the moment at least, final—installment in the series. Maps are considerably bigger and substantially prettier than before, nonplaying characters flocking the streets are more numerous, and the animations and explosions look a lot more cinematic than before.

Vehicles are also incorporated into the mix, adding a little variation to the game's missions. And, following its omission from the first game, LAN (local area network)-based multiplayer makes its first appearance. Willing players could now lug their PCs to friends' houses so that they could face off in the name of Keynesian economics and corporate loyalty.

Cementing *Syndicate's* reputation as one of the gaming world's more moody and stylish cutthroat entertainments, *Syndicate Wars* is now a lot older, and rumors have been circulating that Electronic Arts, the entirely legitimate megacorporation that owns the license, is thinking of creating a sequel. Great days, indeed, as surely there's no time like the present to return to the future. **CD**

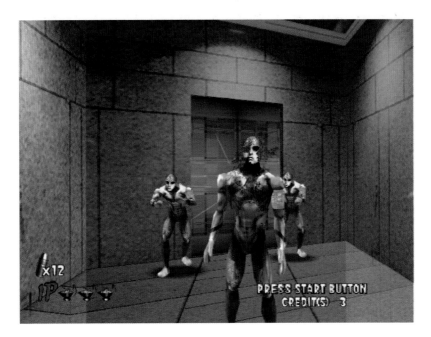

The House of the Dead 2

Original release date : 1996
Platform : Arcade
Developer : Sega
Genre : Shoot 'Em Up

There can be few things in life as thrilling as shooting a zombie in the face. What fortune, then, that Sega would bring to life an entire franchise around just such a premise.

An evolution of the on-rails light gun shooter format, *The House of the Dead* games differ most instantly from the more structured and controlled nature of their predecessors through considerably heightened levels of tension. Other than the obvious advantage of the thematic content, they do this by increasing the speed of play, along with the number of targets on-screen—so the typical attack structure of the genre is still employed, but the frenetic pace at which enemies appear creates a more natural flow to the action.

Rhythm, along with atmosphere, is something *The House of the Dead 2* manages better than most of its contemporaries. The relentless onslaught of shuffling rotten flesh intent on munching on your fine features, combined with suitably disturbing visuals, menacing sound effects, and swift camera work, engineers moments of genuine panic. Helpfully, stress is alleviated through unintentionally comedic interludes provided by dreadful cut-scene voiceovers. But the intensity of the action is such that one empty clip into the next level is all it takes for the soothing effect to have worn off.

A game of this type needs to provide an unflagging experience or risk losing a player's interest to a competing arcade cabinet. *The House of the Dead 2* is expertly built around the premise of commanding your attention from the first shot. It's unquestionably as shallow, as silly, and as short-lived as every example of the on-rails shooter genre before it or since, but when it comes to providing pure cathartic thrills, you'll find few able to match its calibre. **JDS**

Star Control 3

Original release date : 1996
Platform : Various
Developer : Legend Entertainment
Genre : Strategy / Shoot 'Em Up

Like any good interstellar battle, *Star Control 3* faced insurmountable odds. Outgunned by the intensely loyal fan base of the first two games and created without any input from original developer Toys for Bob, it was clear from the outset that the project would require bold helming. Despite the aforementioned devotees citing several misgivings (most notably with the pseudo-3-D space battles and digitized Henson-esque puppets used during conversations), the game was a critical success and is the most fully realised *Star Control* title.

Picking up roughly where the second game left off, you must lead an alliance in the fight against the Eternal Ones, a mysterious race who consume the energy of all sentient life every eon. To protect themselves from such a fate, the Precursors genetically modified themselves into six-legged cowlike creatures, but were trapped in this form when the robots they built to return them to their original form malfunctioned. Humans, in their quest to locate the legendary Precursors, have discovered this tasty beast and, unbeknown to them, are consuming their goal. The delirious plot belies a complex strategy game in which diplomacy is equally as important as maneuvering, with each new race you encounter a potential ally or enemy.

But there are also real-time space battles, a brilliantly involving adventure game, and a colony management side-quest with which you can feed your war machine. The combination of so many different genres is usually a bad idea, but here they gel into a coherent whole that can consume many hours of your life. The Hyper Melee mode, meanwhile, provides an opportunity to hone piloting skills against the computer or a friend. While the confrontation clearly resulted in casualties, *Star Control 3* is a worthy successor to its forebears. **BM**

Super Mario 64

Original release date : 1996
Platform : N64
Developer : Nintendo
Genre : Platform

Mario would seem to have come to the end of his natural life as games embraced the third dimension. Nintendo's mascot was getting on a bit, and he was so emphatically linked to the suddenly rather tired world of two-dimensional scrolling that many fans suspected either retirement or, worse, irrelevance awaited him on Nintendo's new console, the N64.

In fact, neither was the case. Mario's first three-dimensional adventure saw the plumber as trailblazing and trendsetting as ever, showing competitors how it's done, and throwing analog controls into the mix (a little push forward to walk, a push all the way to run) to create an adventure no one would forget in a hurry—particularly Mario's rivals on other platforms.

Certain things had to change. Rather than a long travelogue quest heading from the left side of the map to the right, *Super Mario 64* introduced Peach's castle as a hub from which other levels would be accessible once enough stars had been collected from the game's various challenges. The means of entering these themed levels—leaping through paintings—is still a genuinely magical piece of design. The worlds found beyond, all of which have room enough for a handful of different tasks, are masterpieces of thrifty imagination, providing the space for a coin hunt one minute and a boss fight the next.

Like the hub itself, the levels become nonlinear arenas, and from the mountainous peaks of Cool, Cool Mountain to the tangle of pathways that make up Big Boo's Haunt, *Super Mario 64* almost feels more like a theme park than a series of themed courses. No matter where exactly it's getting its inspiration from, however, *Super Mario 64* remains one of the most influential—and one of the best—video games ever made. **CD**

Wave Race 64

Original release date : 1996
Platform : N64
Developer : Nintendo
Genre : Racing

Let's be honest, nobody ever fell in love with *Wave Race 64*. Despite hailing from the same stable as *Super Mario* and company, this Jet Ski racing game with its four identikit riders just doesn't have the personality for that. The annoying announcer and late-1980s arcade-style visuals don't help either. Superficially, *Wave Race 64* is even a bit—whisper it—annoying.

Yet the game made a splash on release and, unlike many other older games, it's still worth checking out on its own merits, irrespective of its historical value (which isn't much; the game spawned no great lineage of Jet Ski titles). It's all about the realistically modeled water, and the joy of steering your craft upon it. The N64's innovative control

stick had already proved that analog was the future, thanks to the fine control it afforded Mario in his N64 debut, but *Wave Race 64*, itself a very early game for the console, was an even more convincing demonstration. As you steer your bouncing craft across the choppy surf or pull a hairpin turn, you can almost see the old two-dimensional, on or off era sinking beneath the waves.

The game is structured as a conventional racing game, albeit all at sea. In most races, you need to beat your fellow skiers around an island in various weather conditions, while also steering your craft past navigational buoys. Correctly passing a buoy boosts your speed, and at maximum power you really fly. Championship, Time Trial, and Stunt modes round out the package, and the mandatory two-player mode is also good fun, despite the somewhat restricted view afforded by the split-screen implementation.

Wave Race 64 remains one of the best water-based games you can play—although admittedly that's a genre with limited competition. **OB**

Wipeout 2097

Original release date : 1996
Platform : PS1
Developer : Psygnosis
Genre : Racing

The second title in Sony's answer to Nintendo's *F-Zero* series, *Wipeout 2097* is arguably the best of the bunch. While the original was perfectly entertaining, it made its impact as much for its cultural baggage—clubby music and graphic design from the hip Designers Republic agency—as for its game play.

Wipeout 2097 retains the cool look and feel of the original, but the game is more fully developed, its weapons and courses more varied. Set 101 years on from the game's year of release, this is science-fiction racing that packs a punch. The race craft hover above the track and are rather delicate things, handling like a razor blade when you're in the zone and like a bathtub at sea when not. You're offered a choice of models with different attributes for acceleration, handling, and shield power. Finding and holding the racing line without bringing your speed down is made harder by the elaborate courses, which include vertiginous drops, jumps, ninety-degree bends, and tight tunnels that seem impossible to navigate when you first encounter them. Complicating matters are the weapons you and your opponents can deploy. The pick-up powered arsenal includes the likes of the Quake Disruptor, which sends a powerful shockwave along the track, and the hit-and-miss Autopilot. Craft can be completely destroyed if they take sufficient damage from either weapons or collisions—a particularly anticlimactic way to lose a race.

It's easy to forget how distinctive the *Wipeout* games were at the time. They represented console games jumping up a generation, even if the trappings look rather superficial against modern titles. But there's nothing shallow about *Wipeout 2097*'s game play, which remains perfectly and consistently playable today. **OB**

Vectorman 2

Original release date : 1996
Platform : Mega Drive
Developer : BlueSky
Genre : Action / Platform

Arriving late in the Mega Drive's life, the second *Vectorman* game found itself able to benefit from advancements in programming techniques for its host system and can therefore lay claim to being one of the better-looking examples of 16-bit technology. But with the majority of the gaming public having by that time progressed on to the subsequent generation of hardware, the audience that welcomed it was limited.

That explains *Vectorman 2*'s relative obscurity, but it says little about its merit as one of the finer platform games of its era. An obvious element is its aesthetic styling, with impressively crisp, detailed graphics and a level of animation rarely seen for its time (a benefit of

using prerendered 3-D models), but the visuals are also supported by suitably muscular sound effects and a score that ably matches the action.

And plenty of action there is too. The game drops you in it from the start—literally, because you parachute down to Earth's surface—and the pace never lets up as you blast through twenty-five meticulously designed levels populated by mutated insects, better firepower, inventive power-ups, and, predictably, a number of collectable items. Crucially, the controls are as accomplished as the action, responding perfectly to joy pad input and thereby making it difficult to blame the game for your mistakes.

The one shocking factor of revisiting *Vectorman*'s danger-filled world is its level of difficulty. Older games are generally more difficult than new examples, but in this case the experience is brutal, and until your brain adapts to the game's unforgiving nature, it can take considerable effort just to make through the first level. Persevere, however, because a terrific platforming experience lies beyond. **JDS**

Age of Empires

Original release date : 1997
Platform : PC
Developer : Ensemble Studios
Genre : Strategy

While advances in video games are typically characterized by leaps in technology or game play innovation, lateral crossover is also important. Like some novel technology concocted in one of its temples, *Age of Empires* crossed two existing game play templates and boiled down the result to produce a new branch in strategy gaming.

The first parent was *Civilization*, Sid Meier's brilliant 1991 title. Devotees loved it, but its complexity and turn-based mechanics put off many more. By the mid-'90s, real-time strategy offered a more accessible way for armchair generals to marshal their forces. The bestselling strategy games—*Command & Conquer* and *Warcraft* —and their copycats were science-fiction or fantasy affairs. What

Ensemble Studios (including designer Bruce Shelley, who worked on *Civilization* with Meier) did was meld *Civilization's* historical trappings and empire building idea with the genre's game play and pretty graphics.

The result, *Age of Empires*, was an approachable take on dictatorship with enough historical finery to satisfy all but the most bookish rulers. Assuming leadership of one of a dozen peoples, from the Greeks and the Babylonians to the Japanese Yamato civilization, you guide your race from being hunter gatherers through several transitions to create a dominant Iron Age culture. The twelve civilizations are divided into four main groups, each one with its own distinctive architectural style. The emphasis is on military progression, though victory conditions include building a Wonder, such as an Egyptian pyramid. On the fighting front, dubious artifical intelligence, later patched, let things down. Still, Rome wasn't built in a day, and *Age of Empires* launched a globe-conquering franchise that eventually sold twenty million units. **OB**

Blade Runner

Original release date : 1997
Platform : PC
Developer : Westwood Studios
Genre : Adventure

Westwood's *Blade Runner* proves that you don't have to follow the script to make an authentic movie tie-in. Not, at least, when the movie's better known for its looks and symbols than its words. The developer of *Command & Conquer* wasn't known for its point-and-click adventures, either, which perhaps explains its avant-garde approach to this one. A necessary approach, it would emerge, that captured not just the Los Angeles of 2019 but the leg work, paperwork, and luck required to police it.

Hero Ray McCoy, a rookie on the trail of mutinous android replicants, is a more spirited cop than Harrison Ford's Deckard. Working out of the same cylindrical skyscraper as featured prominently in the movie, McCoy's puzzle solving has more in common with a *Police Quest* game than the average point-and-click. Rather than find illogical key-and-lock pairings for random objects, he has to pixel hunt for clues, feed them into some familiar forensic tools, and ask the right questions of the right people. Leads turn into new locations on the map, suspects coming and going in nonlinear real time. What results is a game of lucky breaks and chance encounters that boasts a whopping thirteen different endings.

Blade Runner used a proprietary voxel-based engine to create stunning portrayals of locations such as Animoid Row and Hotel Bradbury, along with gadgets like the ESPER 3-D scanner and Voight-Kampff profiler. By rotating dozens of voxels to match actual polygonal data, the game legitimately claimed to use "real-time 3-D graphics," even though it made no use of three-dimensional hardware. Steep CPU requirements led to cutbacks in the game's character models, prompting many to complain that they lacked the detail of the world around them. **DH**

Castlevania: Symphony of the Night

Original release date : 1997
Platform : Various
Developer : Konami
Genre : Action

Even in 1997 *Castlevania: Symphony of the Night* was an anachronism. With the gaming world's eyes firmly focused on Lara Croft and her jaggy curves, few were interested in two-dimensional games whose sprites appeared antiquated when set against Sony's new three-dimensional horizons.

While *Symphony of the Night* represented the first time Konami combined the series' classic brand of side scrolling, occultish violence with character development, it was nothing that hadn't been explored by Nintendo's *Super Metroid* some years before. Yet *Symphony of the Night* remains today as one of the finest action-adventure games in the canon, a title that has far outlasted its contemporary

rivals of the day, thanks to its enduring core. Playing as Alucard, the conflicted son of Dracula, you work your way through a sprawling gothic castle, uncovering new nooks, crannies, and hellish bosses while in search of the arch vampire. The ingenuity of the design reveals itself slowly, as Alucard discovers new abilities that, in turn, open up whole new areas of the game. Slowly, previously unreachable places become familiar as you chase breadcrumb trails of rewards, revealing the full map of the castle as you do so.

Matched by one of the great orchestral soundtracks of video games, the visuals perfectly suit the theme. Konami's use of color and architecture lends every area of the game its own character and ambience, yet manages to maintain a coherent whole. The ingenuity of monster design is unmatched, either in the series' subsequent titles or its close rivals. And the game's final twist reward (unlocked after what you suppose to be the final boss), turning the entire castle on its head so every floor becomes a ceiling and each doorway becomes a ledge, is peerless. **SP**

Bushido Blade

Original release date : 1997
Platform : PS1
Developer : Lightweight
Genre : Fighting

Bushido Blade's great innovation was simply to make a fighting game seem more like fighting. This was the first game to face up to the truth that few people walk away from a *katana* strike to the stomach. It's perhaps understandable that this approach didn't catch on. But Bushido Blade chooses to embrace this physical reality, and, in raising the stakes of every fight so high, succeeds in raising the intensity of the combat to a fever pitch.

The need for caution is emphasized by the game's health system, which isolates each part of the combatant's body so that a glancing blow to the arm will render that limb limp and useless. Take a stab to the leg and you will be forced to fight on bended knee, unable to run or manoeuvre, and a blow to the head or torso will call forth a crimson fountain and end both the match and your life.

Bushido Blade's maverick approach failed to inspire other fighting game developers to follow suit, and, indeed, a lackluster sequel revealed that perhaps the idea had already seen its ideal realization. For that reason, it remains the tensest fight to be had in video games. **SP**

Final Furlong

Original release date : 1997
Platform : Arcade
Developer : Namco
Genre : Racing

In the late 1990s the coin-operated market was being eaten alive by the graphically powerful 32-bit consoles. Manufacturers increasingly turned to novelty installation machines to tempt gamers back into the arcades. This horse-racing simulation provided one of the most compelling and entertaining examples.

The player sits on a small plastic horse, grabs the metal hand rail, and rocks backward and forward to propel their on-screen steed. A whip button teases out a few extra bursts of performance, while the reins can vaguely steer the horse. Each steed has a limited amount of stamina, and players need to judge this correctly to avoid burning out before the final sprint to the finishing line. To add a little strategic depth to the experience, there are six horses to select from, each with a different racing style.

For several years, Japanese arcades were bustling with businessmen letting off steam by frenziedly riding Namco's plastic mares against one another. A Wii version was shown off at the annual E3 video game show in 2006, but has since failed to come to fruition. **KS**

Blast Corps

Original release date : 1997
Platform : N64
Developer : Rare
Genre : Action

Beatmania

Original release date : 1997
Platform : Arcade
Developer : Konami
Genre : Music

From a deceivably simple concept—that of clearing a path for a lorry carrying nuclear nitroglycerine with a tendency to detonate should the vehicle come into contact with any obstruction—bursts forth one of the highlights of the Nintendo 64's line-up, *Blast Corps*.

As a member of the team expected to level every obstacle in the payload's path, your role is to jump in a number of vehicles with wildly varying demolition abilities and rush around ensuring a clear and safe path. While there's undeniable fulfillment in the relentless destruction, you soon have to rely on brains as well as brawn, with later levels introducing puzzle elements that add disproportionately to the already tense challenge.

The game remains remarkably refreshing. Rare got the formula right first time. Sure, it can get repetitive, the controls take some familiarity, it's difficult, and a number of the vehicles can be frustrating, but there's very little about *Blast Corps* that requires fundamental changing. That's possibly why no other developer has really bothered to revisit the premise, much to the gaming world's loss. **JDS**

Konami's *Beatmania*, billed as a DJ game, was the first of the Japanese company's rhythm action games, closely followed by *Dance Dance Revolution*, *Guitar Freaks* and *Drummania*. In reality, the similarities between the game and the gear from which it draws inspiration are loose.

Players use their left hand to press buttons in time with the descending markers on the screen. Meanwhile, the right hand spins a sturdy turntable every now and then, usually to trigger a rewind or scratch sample in the music itself.

The *Beatmania* experience is a strange amalgam of turntablism and one-handed piano playing, a curious hybrid that had to carve out its own audience. As streams of tiny markers filter down the screen and you tap the keys to trigger the relevant samples in the music, the principle of the music game is visible in its most raw and telling form: Simon Says for a digital generation. Despite being in its thirteenth iteration in arcades, *Beatmania* has been superseded by music games that allow for more expression on the part of the player, but its legacy is visible in the success of every contemporary music game. **SP**

DoDonPachi

Original release date : 1997
Platform : Various
Developer : Cave
Genre : Shoot 'Em Up

Bullet hell. *DoDonPachi* exemplifies the term better than any other shoot 'em up, providing a snowstorm of fiery pixels to both simultaneously dodge and eliminate. It's a merciless assault on the senses and reactions, about as far from the careful, precise shots of the genre's formative classics as it's possible to travel. But nevertheless, the principle remains the same: shoot the spaceships while avoiding being shot yourself.

Where the *DoDonPachi* experience differs from its traditional inspirations is in the size and fury of the bullets traded between player and opponent. Here the emphasis is on pattern memorization and reactions, the game demanding its player to discern enemy from friendly fire, and react accordingly in split-second decisions. The effect is then heightened by power-ups that turn what starts off as a trickle of bullets (laser or scatter shot) into a flowing river of rapids. Neon splashes of color and a confetti of score tokens light up every enemy grazed by your bullet spray, resulting in a screen that is soon enveloped in a blaze of hot, mesmerizing pixels.

As a game born in the arcades, high-score play is encouraged. This is achieved via a simple combo system that records the frequency of your takedowns and matches a score multiplier to the stream of hits. Perhaps more than any other shoot 'em up, *DoDonPachi* has inspired the recording of thousands of high score attempt videos, circulated throughout Japan in DVD collections.

The constant barrage of shifting bullet mazes reaches its climax during the game's hulking boss fights, where the stream of patterned bullets shepherd you inexorably around the screen. *DoDonPachi* is the acme of bullet hell shoot 'em ups, a twitch workout to leave your thumbs blistered and your mind frazzled. **SP**

Intelligent Qube

Original release date : 1997
Format : PS1
Developer : Sony
Genre : Puzzle

Upon its release, *Intelligent Qube* (aka *Kurushi*) did something rare for a puzzle game: It felt important. That's unusual because so many video games with puzzles at their core often feel fanciful. You play them for challenges, but questions of larger importance—such as why we're performing a particular action at all—are fleeting.

Intelligent Qube dire and epic. Set on a gray, modular game board suspended in an infinite black space, the character you control must strategically avoid and remove cubes that approach in successive waves. The act of constant flight makes the game play harried. Even at rest, the man in green trousers at the center of it all bounces repetitively, either in expectation of the next round or in exhaustion from his constant flight.

But it's the other elements of *Intelligent Qube* that give the game its gravity. The soundtrack, from Takayuki Hattori (the composer of two Godzilla films), is haunting with its sharp vocal arrangements and triumphant brass. The cubes roll after you with a powerful and resounding thud as you flee. And most players will distinctly remember the authoritarian, disembodied voice that says "Perfect" or "Again?" at stages during the performance.

Even varieties of cubes, such as Advantage and Forbidden, add a particular seriousness to *Intelligent Qube*, placing you as the director of a moral compass where you decide which cubes should be captured and which should be banished to the dark space below.

The end result is something more akin to the many boss battles of the *Final Fantasy* franchise rather than something in the flighty genre of puzzle games. Many action-driven brainteasers were made for Sony's original PlayStation, and *Intelligent Qube* stands among the most memorable of them all. **JBW**

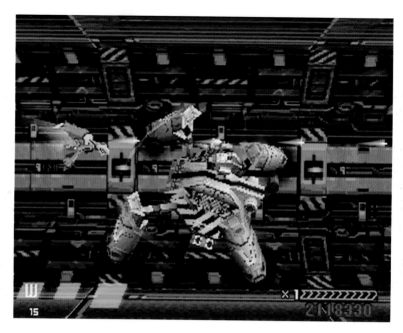

Einhänder

Original release date : 1997

Platform : PS1

Developer : Square

Genre : Shoot 'Em Up

Nobody expected much from *Einhänder*, a side-scrolling shoot 'em up on an unsuitable console at the wrong time, from a Japanese role-playing game developer with no prior (or subsequent) experience in the genre. As Japan's premier producer of fantasy role-playing games, Square was an expert at lavish, narrative-led epics, games just about as far from the twitchy, reaction-based arcade blaze of a futuristic shoot 'em up as it's possible to imagine.

Likewise, Sega's Saturn, while it was less commercially successful than the PlayStation, had already established itself as the genre's natural home. Few developers would dare release a shoot 'em up on Sony's console. Yet somehow Square crafted an exquisite, thoughtful,

rollercoaster ride of a spaceship game. It is a game that consists of hulking multipart bosses, enemies that must be taken apart piece by piece. The spectacle of these battles is heightened by a dark, brooding aesthetic with purple cloudy skies bisected by forked lightning, and dark tunnels punctuated by neon dots. Enemies jump from the foreground to the background and monsters are animated to look like oversized animals, their approaches and retreats defining safe areas of screen space.

The game takes its name from the grappling arm that hangs underneath your ship, which allows you to grasp at weapons dropped by downed enemies. These attachments have limited ammunition, a brave decision that introduces an element of resource management to the otherwise entirely reaction-based rhythm of play.

Following the game's release and modest success, the team was disbanded and redeployed to other projects, ensuring that *Einhänder*'s bright, brilliant excursion into new territory has never been repeated. **SP**

Dungeon Keeper

Original release date : 1997
Platform : PC
Developer : Bullfrog Productions
Genre : Strategy

It took two decades for PC developers to realize that fantasy role-playing gamers could be wicked too. Savvy pen-and-paper dungeon masters had known since the 1970s that designing dark lairs stuffed with evildoers to kill off their friends was at least as much fun as questing for treasure and maidens, but it took the ever quirky brain of designer Peter Molyneux to bring the concept to PC.

Dungeon Keeper was an inversion of everything gamers knew about subterranean adventuring, from Rogue to Gauntlet to Diablo. Instead of dark passages to explore and traps to avoid, in Dungeon Keeper your imps dig your tunnels or mine gold to fund your hero-impaling traps. Instead of slaying monsters, in Dungeon Keeper you lay out the floor plans of the perfect abodes to attract vampires or demon spawn to your underground realm. Get it right, and waves of adventurers will perish at your minion's hands (and then perhaps swell the ranks of your skeleton army).

Dungeon Keeper is first and foremost a real-time strategy game. You extract resources, breed chickens to feed your monsters, and move along a technology tree that unlocks ever more outlandish dungeon dwellers. It's the humor that really makes the game. From slapping creatures with your disembodied hand to the bemused narrator who can't fathom why anyone wouldn't want a River of the Damned for a High Street, Dungeon Keeper has black comedy by the bucket of blood load.

Some reviewers found its graphics dated while others thought the game peaked too early, but most are still waiting for an update. Molyneux later developed the idea of being evil in the Black & White games, but it is Dungeon Keeper that offers the purest, darkest, and certainly the funniest way to play as one of the bad guys. **OB**

Final Fantasy Tactics

Original release date : 1997

Platform : Various

Developer : Square

Genre : Role-Playing

Today *Final Fantasy* spin-offs are everywhere, but in 1997, the idea of a title bearing the family name that wasn't part of the mainline series was unthinkable. Not only that, but *Final Fantasy Tactics*, a historical and tactical role-playing game, bears few resemblances to its namesakes, save for a few Chocobos and oversize broadswords.

Nevertheless, it emerged not only as one of the best titles in the series, but also of all time. A beautifully balanced and executed turn-based strategy game that matches its grand narrative with deep, rewarding mechanics. Battles take place on three-dimensional isometric fields that are overlaid with a grid. For each unit's turn, you move a certain number of squares (depending on the character's class and

clothing) before executing an attack on an enemy unit. If your unit is a knight, you'll need the target to be in an adjacent square, but if you're controlling an archer or mage, you can use ranged attacks from afar. Every action, from a sword swipe to drinking a potion, earns experience points (to level up your character) and job points (to increase their abilities in their chosen specialization). It's a classic system the likes of which will be familiar to fans of *Disgaea* et al, but rarely have these mechanics felt as solid and workable as they do here.

Despite attracting widespread praise from the video-game press for its plot, soundtrack, deep and involving game play and intricate art from Akihiko Yoshida, the game was only a niche hit outside of Japan, not making it to European shores until the superlative PSP re-release, subtitled *War of the Lions*. For this remake the game's dialogue underwent a much needed re-translation from the original Japanese and, for this reason, the more recent version is recommended. **SP**

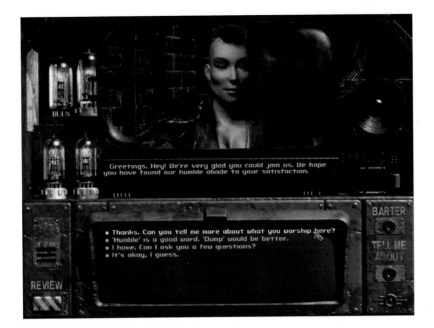

Fallout

Original release date : 1997
Platform : Various
Developer : Black Isle Studios
Genre : Role-Playing

Fallout casts the player as a young, naive adventurer born into an America that's been ravaged by nuclear war. When the underground Vault, where you grew up, loses its GECK—a chip that makes water drinkable and life possible in this wasteland—you're chosen to leave and search for a replacement. You have no idea what to expect and no one to guide you along the way.

It's easy to set off the wrong way and stumble into a situation far beyond your abilities, but poke around enough and you'll find clues in strange places. For example, a key clue in the story lies hidden in one of dozens of houses in the ruined part of a city. Character development and combat entail lots of numbers and painful trade-offs.

Unlike a fantasy game, where magic and swordplay are equal pursuits, investing in mental exercises, like science and diplomacy, makes you considerably weaker than if you bet everything on learning how to aim a pistol. Even then, mastering small arms doesn't transfer to the big guns you find later on. The turn-based battles, which use action points to allocate your moves, force you to consider each step and every blow. This doesn't get tedious because few of the battles are easy.

But just as memorable is the style, which harkens back to America in the 1950s, when the nation was at its post-war height while living in fear of a nuclear standoff with the Soviets. In *Fallout*'s future, of course, it's the Chinese who lob the bombs, and while the Geiger counters have settled down by the time the game starts, the people remain in anarchy. The image of the Pip Boy, the grinning, iconic figure who appears in your handheld computer, sums up the situation. You'd better smile, because how much worse can it get? **CDa**

Final Fantasy VII

Original release date : 1997
Platform : PS1
Developer : Square
Genre : Role-Playing

Final Fantasy VII may, apocryphally at least, be the most returned-to-the-store video game of all time, but there's no denying it's among the most important. Before its arrival on Sony's PlayStation, the Japanese role-playing game was a curious niche to many Western players—a weird, offshoot of the Tolkien-esque role-playing games that, themselves, were something of an acquired taste.

But Final Fantasy VII delivered one of the most technically arresting titles of the era, complete with 330 CG maps and forty minutes of full-motion video representing more than two years' work by more than one hundred full time team members at a cost of more than $45 million. With these record-breaking statistics, the world's attention

was grabbed, and the game's chosen genre was forcefully booted into the mainstream.

Set within a steampunk world threatened by the pollution of big business corporations, Final Fantasy VII's themes were previously untouched by the medium and maintain the series' advancing curve of maturity. In making the player's iconic character Cloud Strife complicit in a terrorist attack, the narrative finds a quick stride that is maintained over its course.

Today, the game looks dated. The shift between squat polygonal characters to prerendered movies is jarring, lacking the visual consistency of the simpler sprites of the former games in the series. But despite this, the iconic characters and evocative setting of Midgar have been resilient to the medium's ensuing technological advances, and the calls for a remake are loud. Players interested in a different point of view are encouraged to try the PSP spin-off Crisis Core, a game that helps to round out the narrative, albeit via an altogether different style of game. **SP**

Diablo

Original release date : 1997
Platform : Various
Developer : Blizzard Entertainment
Genre : Action / Role-Playing

If it's an Excel spreadsheet you're engaged with, clicking on things can be kind of boring. If it's *Diablo*, however, the same simple mechanic magically turns out to be utterly enthralling—possibly because, unlike with Microsoft's fine suite of productivity software, everything you click on in *Diablo* rewards you in some lavish, palpable manner.

Enemies explode in bursts of blood or collapse into rickety piles of bone, brave warriors race nimbly to the spot indicated and await your command, and loot—lovely, lovely loot—disappears straight into your inventory for another of *Diablo*'s unlikely sounding pleasures, stat comparison, and item management. *Diablo* isn't just a pretty isometric dungeon crawler, it's the best pretty isometric dungeon crawler. A simple—often almost gloriously brainless—trek through gloomy caverns filled with monsters and treasures, all of which you interact with through single stabs at the mouse and a few carefully timed hot keys. Blizzard's technicians spent a lot of time and money working on the procedural generation of the game's subterranean spaces, meaning that items, enemies, and geography would be different each time you loaded the game up, and the pleasures of exploration would, theoretically, never have to end. The result truly is a game that seems to keep on giving.

By today's standards, *Diablo*'s classes, characters, and teetering piles of rewards are actually rather shallow, but the game still exerts a wonderful fascination each time you return to its caverns. It's so simple that practically anyone can learn the basics, and so rich and textured that even seasoned pros will find themselves coming back for more. To this very day, its basic skeleton-smacking formula has barely been improved upon. **CD**

GoldenEye 007

Original release date : 1997
Platform : N64
Developer : Rare
Genre : Shoot 'Em Up

You could argue that the title of Best James Bond Game ironically sits with three games that aren't actually about James Bond: *Metal Gear Solid 3*, *Modern Warfare 2*, and *No One Lives Forever 2: A Spy In HARM's Way*. Less debatable, though, is the holder of the title Most Important Console First-Person Shooter. Before *GoldenEye 007*, an adaptation that played fast and loose with the 1995 movie, many would struggle with even the idea of such a thing.

Unlike contemporary *Turok: Dinosaur Hunter*, *GoldenEye 007* proved that joy pad controls were not a disability. Both games featured precision aiming thanks to the N64 analog stick, but Rare knew best how to use it. Reveling in the lack of hyperkinetic PC controls, it made a game in which every shot felt like something handmade. Hit a shoulder, and an enemy might pirouette to the floor; the groin—a natural favorite—and they'd fold and keel over; the head, and they'd drop as if hit with a polearm. Games like *Virtua Cop* got there sooner but, to borrow a phrase, nobody does it better than Bond.

In single-player mode, *GoldenEye 007* features a rarely emulated difficulty method that switches objectives at each level, making it highly replayable even now. But the game's split-screen support for up to four players, as much a testament to the N64's hardware layout, was the proof of concept for all console multiplayers. When games like *Halo* try to capture that feeling via Xbox Live, what they are referring to is the sight of your armchair buddy being dropped by the Golden Gun, one of umpteen weapons and modes that kept this game going for years.

Culling gadgets and characters from the entire Bond universe, *GoldenEye 007* pounced on every opportunity its license could afford. **DH**

Gran Turismo

Original release date : 1997
Platform : PS1
Developer : Polyphony Digital
Genre : Driving

Admittedly, at the time, part of the appeal of *Gran Turismo* was how recognizable the cars were. Other games would set you racing in souped-up monsters with elaborate spoilers and engines so tweaked they approached science fiction, but while *Gran Turismo* had plenty of that, it also had compacts and family hatchbacks.

It had the kind of cars your dad drove, as well as the kind of cars he wished he did. And while it didn't allow you to smash them up (damage modeling remains, to this day, something the *Gran Turismo* series won't go in for much), it would allow you to pop the hood and meddle with the engine. Prior to making the defining racer of the PlayStation era—apologies here to *Ridge Racer*—*Gran*

Turismo's developer Polyphony Digital made a cutesy bouncing cartoon racing game called *Motor Toon Grand Prix*. It was an enjoyable piece of fluff, but it was absolutely nothing compared to the game that would make the studio's name. Lavish, detailed, and rather grown-up, *Gran Turismo* would change the marketplace and give other developers something to aim toward for years.

A true driving simulation title in a world of arcadey racing games, *Gran Turismo* was still nippy around the track and handy in frantic multiplayer battles. The true addictiveness that really allowed players to get sucked in was the mixture of new cars you unlocked throughout the course of the game and the realistic way you could fiddle about with their engines and handling.

It also helped that at release, it was the best-looking PlayStation game ever made, a fact driven home by its dazzling replay mode. Play it today, and you can pick out the individual elements that transformed the way racing video games would be made forever more. **CD**

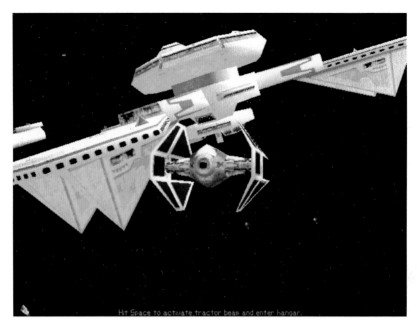

Hit Space to activate tractor beam and enter hangar.

Star Wars: X-Wing vs. TIE Fighter

Original release date : 1997
Platform : PC
Developer : Totally Games
Genre : Shoot 'Em Up

Upon release in 1997, *Star Wars: X-Wing vs. TIE Fighter* was undoubtedly one of the biggest disappointments of the year. For fans who had eagerly devoured both *X-Wing* and *TIE Fighter*, immersing themselves in those titles' strong campaign modes, to be greeted with a game that featured no campaign mode at all was a shock.

Of course, few can say they weren't warned, but the reaction was so immediate and so extreme that LucasArts and developer Totally Games quickly released an expansion (the ironically titled *Balance of Power*) in order to redress the situation. But by concentrating on what the game was missing, people overlooked what it had. *Star Wars: X-Wing vs. TIE Fighter* is a space combat game that

uses the well-respected design that powered the previous *X-Wing* titles, offering tactical nuance via the ability to switch power between shields, lasers, and engines, and exciting dogfight-based play. This format makes the game a multiplayer experience as accessible as the first-person shooter titles that ruled the online arena at the time, but that failed to convincingly mark out a place in history. The game ultimately represents a cul-de-sac in the multiplayer gaming space, one that titles such as *Crimson Skies* tried, but didn't quite succeed, in extending.

Players who ignore the game based on its legacy are missing out on some of the best multiplayer combat potential ever seen in a game. *Star Wars: X-Wing vs. TIE Fighter*'s flight model remains a blend of arcade-style thrills and simulation that nothing else has ever touched, and played against others it offers all the tension from the very heights of the *Star Wars* saga. Just ask the dedicated community who continue to play the game to this day via home-brewed game clients and other such hacks. **MKu**

The Curse of Monkey Island

Original release date : 1997
Platform : PC
Developer : LucasArts
Genre : Adventure

Guybrush Threepwood's third pirating adventure—the first to be made without the input of series veterans Ron Gilbert or Tim Schafer—isn't widely considered to be a classic. While it can't quite live up to the mordant wit of the original two games, it remains a sharp and pithy Caribbean adventure in its own right.

Threepwood's quest is to free his beloved, the generally furious Governor Elaine Marley, from the spell of a cursed ring that has transformed her into a gold statue. This sets in motion the charming idiot's most irreverent and wide-ranging adventure. This is a game that finds the time to parody everything from the foibles of Shakespearian actors to the intricate web of conspiracy theories surrounding the President Kennedy assassination—a brilliant sequence involving, rather predictably, banjos, flint-lock pistols, and a rubber tree. The island where the game's fabulously clever final act unfolds is as creepy and evocative as anything the series had previously created, while the very last sequence, which is set on a rickety rollercoaster moving through various animatronic dioramas depicting the great points from the series, was as fitting a close to the trilogy as could be realistically imagined.

The game is also the graphical highpoint for the series, employing a lavish cel-animated style that meant the finished product resembled an upmarket Disney cartoon, with elegant characterizations and trippy swirls of distant clouds. The game's final retail installment, the three-dimensional *Escape from Monkey Island*, would ditch this approach entirely, along with most of the series' elaborate punning brilliance. True fans of the series might want to draw the line after this outing—a witty send-off and a fond reminder of so many years of hilarious adventure. **CD**

MDK

Original release date : 1997
Platform : Various
Developer : Shiny Entertainment
Genre : Shoot 'Em Up

After playing *MDK*, you might ask why all games aren't like it. You'll almost certainly wonder why barely any are. The developer of *MDK* took the three-dimensional platform model introduced by *Super Mario 64* and went the opposite way of everyone else. Instead, Shiny Entertainment made a short, sharp, and hilarious shock trooper that might have been the vanguard for welding the madcap innovation of the 8-bit era with the three-dimensional intelligence demanded by the PlayStation generation.

Even at the time, *MDK* was misunderstood, often willfully. Did those three letters stand for "Murder, Death, Kill"; or "Max, Dr, Kurt" (the heroes); or "My Dear Knight" as emblazoned on the Japanese box art? Was it a platformer or a shooter? Was it serious or a joke? What did you expect when the game manual was an extract from the diary of a senile astronaut?

It isn't that complicated. Earth is being scooped up by giant Minecrawlers from space. As the hero Kurt, you parachute in from orbit, leap, drop, run, and gun your way through various bizarre arenas—all realized using a glorious software engine—destroy the lot, then ride the resultant energy stream back to base. If all you have to do is call in your dog to mount a bombing raid, or use the addictive sniper scope to shoot a grunt while he's picking his nose—a mode copied by every three-dimensional shooter that followed, but never to such amusing effect—then what is so complicated about the game?

MDK was only half a dozen levels long, but they are among the most inventive levels you'll ever experience. Perhaps other developers didn't follow *MDK* because, for all its wacky inexplicableness, they appreciated how high it set the bar. **OB**

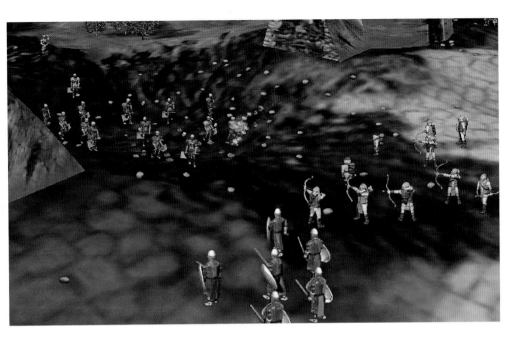

Myth: The Fallen Lords

Original release date : 1997
Platform : PC, Mac
Developer : Bungie
Genre : Strategy

The real-time strategy game blueprint is set in gaming lore. Third-person perspective, build trees, resource management, skirmishing, and then chucking everything you've got at the other guy. So how did a developer, better known in the ever decreasing circles of Macintosh gaming, approach a genre dominated by powerhouses like Westwood Studios and Electronic Arts? By self-publishing a tactical war game that wrote its own unique set of rules and was powered by a revolutionary new three-dimensional engine.

Dwarves lobbing Molotov cocktails is a good way to get your new game noticed. One precision strike can decimate an enemy army. But getting into position, aiming correctly, and assessing the current climate conditions are the strategies needed to manipulate this environment. Dwarves walk slowly, meaning you need to send them surreptitiously to their target, and hope they don't meet mean, melee-focused troops on the way. What if it's raining? It could douse the flames. What if the targets are wading through water? What if they're marching across a hill? The slope of that hill could send a lobbed bomb hurtling past a targeted enemy, only to fizzle in a puddle.

That's just a sliver of the new considerations that this original real-time strategy game evoked in the minds of gamers building personalized armies where every single unit can make a huge impact on the battle. On the face of it, the tightly managed unit numbers and small scale of the battles implies skirmish rather than vast battleground devastation. But the attachment you feel toward that lone pyromaniac dwarf and his cohorts adds a resonance to each encounter that focuses your tactical decisions on preserving each individual. **RSm**

Star Wars Jedi Knight: Dark Forces II

Original release date : 1997

Platform : PC

Developer : LucasArts

Genre : First-Person Shooter

Imagine the pressure. The original *Dark Forces* successfully coats a *Doom*-like first-person shooter with the veneer of the *Star Wars* universe, it delights gamers, sells well, and a sequel goes straight into production. The anticipation for the next installment of Kyle Katarn's adventures was through the roof, and LucasArts delivered a stunning shooter experience that integrated role-playing style, Jedi power progression, and story choices into a more traditional run-and-gun action product. And it introduced lightsabers. Oh, yes, the lightsabers.

Building a system that would fluidly switch to a third-person perspective when Katarn draws out the big stick proved to be a significant technical hurdle that was

executed perfectly. Katarn's story as a former Imperial officer turned mercenary takes a huge leap forward when he uncovers the Force. Now he can learn new Force powers and choose whether to follow the Light or Dark path on a quest to find his father's murderer.

It's a gripping progression that invests the player with an important role in this post-*Return of the Jedi* storyline. Even after the single-player plotline is exhausted, it's easy to replay, choosing different Jedi powers and experiencing the story from the other side. Then you can take those skills online in a multiplayer mode that pits Light against Dark Jedis in classic four-player match-ups.

This package set a new ambition bar not just for all future *Star Wars* games, but for first-person shooters in general. As three-dimensional graphics cards were gaining a foothold, this game was one very good reason to join the revolution, if you hadn't already. For fans of the series, all it takes is for that famous score to start playing, and the chills run down their spines. **RSm**

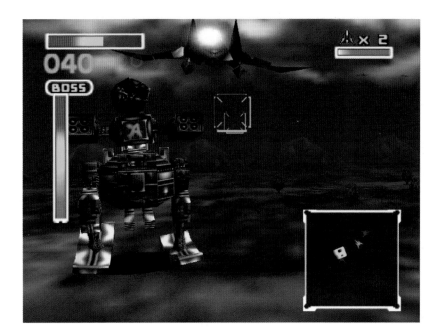

Star Fox 64

Original release date : 1997
Platform : N64
Developer : Nintendo
Genre : Shoot 'Em Up

The original Star Fox (known as Starwing in the West) was a proof of a concept for Nintendo's Super FX technology, a cartridge chip that allowed the aging SNES to throw around three-dimensional polygons in a way the machine's original designers never dreamed. The N64 sequel, however, had even greater ambitions. It wanted to take a band of furry pilots and create a space opera.

You can reel off influences, because the game isn't shy of doing so itself. The final level's a trench run straight from Star Wars, complete with a cheesy moment where Fox's father returns, while Independence Day provides the visual inspiration for a quite brilliant mothership battle. The original may have suggested a wider universe than existed

in its corridors, but Star Fox 64 goes there, moving from the bottom of the ocean to planets composed of lava, stopping off for dogfights in three-dimensional arenas and races through psychedelic wormholes. You'll be chasing down a train in a tank one moment and engaged in a laser ballet with robotic monkeys the next.

And of course it's made by Nintendo, so the list of brilliant little touches goes on and on; The camaraderie with the rest of your team, moaning about maneuvers one minute and diving into the heart of danger to help one another the next. The Rumble Pak, making this the first console game ever to include force feedback, now an industry standard. The multiple paths through the game, dictated by your successes and failures. The bosses that taunt you relentlessly, the distended plasticine face of ultimate villain Andross, and General Pepper's shocked "Whaaaaa?" when he received the bill for your services at the very end. Nintendo's band of furry pilots and their remarkable space opera have a place in many hearts. **RS**

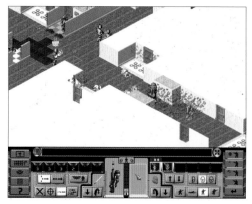

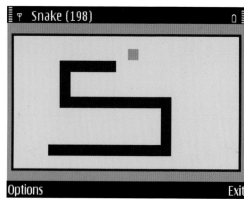

X-COM: Apocalypse

Original release date : 1997
Platform : PC
Developer : Mythos
Genre : Strategy

UFO: Enemy Unknown (aka *X-COM: UFO Defense*) is a valuable thing, a nexus of almost every traditional game genre. While first sequel *X-COM: Terror from the Deep* is essentially the same game with an underwater theme, follow-up *X-COM: Apocalypse* strives to be a true sequel, replacing the turn-based combat with real-time skirmishes. The core remains a tense, frightening hunt for an implacable, otherworldly foe through labyrinthine levels, with a backdrop of rapid technological progress aimed at finding a way to cut off this alien menace at the source.

The game is not as coherent as its predecessors, being a strange hybrid of action points and real-time combat that never quite finds a natural rhythm, but it still seems remarkably novel: a last gasp of offbeat invention before strategy games largely polarized into *Civilization* derivatives and *Command & Conquer*'s excessive spawn. *X-COM: Apocalypse* is a beautiful blend of base building, alien hunting, and science-fiction role-playing. Tantalizingly, Irrational Games, the creator of *BioShock*, is currently working on an official *X-COM* "reimagining." **AM**

Snake

Original release date : 1997
Platform : Various
Developer : Nokia
Genre : Puzzle

Snake falls into that strange category of games you don't really think of as games, titles you barely notice you're playing, and that hardly force you to really concentrate on what you're doing in the first place.

The premise is a staggeringly basic one: maneuver a snake around a blank space, without hitting the wall or running it into the folds of its own body, collecting various treasures along the way. The more treasures you pick up, the longer the snake's body grows, and the harder you have to work in order to keep it alive. It all works faultlessly, too; an effortless mix of simple ideas and mindless controls that mean you're almost always left with only yourself to blame when things go wrong. The genius lies with putting it on mobile phones, reigniting a basic game on a platform where mechanical and narrative directness are far more important than graphics, complex power-ups, and elaborate back stories.

Snake, like *Tetris*, will probably still be around in some form or another when the sun flickers out and Earth whispers off into the farthest corners of space. **CD**

Tekken 3

The Last Express

Original release date : 1997
Platform : Arcade, PS1
Developer : Namco
Genre : Fighting

Original release date : 1997
Platform : PC, Mac
Developer : Smoking Car Productions
Genre : Adventure

The first *Tekken*, thanks to an arcade-perfect conversion, was one of the titles that helped establish Sony's PlayStation as a new force in the gaming industry. Though all of the basic elements were there at the start, it was the series' PlayStation swansong, *Tekken 3,* which established a formula *Tekken* has retained to this day.

The initial roster of ten characters soon blossomed into more than double that number after a few plays and included characters that would become stalwarts. Then there were the multiple extra modes crammed into the package. *Tekken Ball* was beach volleyball played with punches and kicks, while *Tekken Force* was a side-scrolling beat 'em up that persists in the series to this day.

Tekken 3 also set a visual standard on the PlayStation that few titles could match, while luxuriating in the surreality of its characters and the King of Iron Fist Tournament itself. *Tekken 3* built on solid foundations in a way few expected and almost all of its additions became foundations for the later games. So much so that it's easy to forget that it remains a cracking fighting game. **RS**

Five years, $6 million, and one development studio at the breaking point (developer Smoking Car Productions was forced to close its doors directly after release), *The Last Express* is Jordan Mechner's magnum opus. An overlooked graphic adventure that deserves a place in the annals of video game history for its innovation rather than its status as one of the industry's biggest commercial failures.

The player takes the role of Robert Cath, a fugitive doctor on the run, who takes the train to meet with an old friend only to find the friend killed in his berth. Played in an accelerated real time, where events are constantly occurring and nonplayer characters use artificial intelligence to perform to their own agendas, *The Last Express* chugs along to one of several endings.

A gorgeous and complex experience, it features rotoscoped art inspired by the historically appropriate Art Nouveau style while the Orient Express is an accurate representation of how the train existed in 1914. Released with little publicity, and now out of print, *The Last Express* could be the greatest game never played. **MKu**

Grand Theft Auto

Original release date : 1997
Platform : Various
Developer : DMA Design
Genre : Action

Don't tell anyone, but *Grand Theft Auto*, the violent crime game that shocked parents everywhere, landed its Scottish designers in the tabloids, and even managed to get angry—not to mention entirely uninformed—questions asked in Parliament, is basically harmless, old pinball dressed up with some comedy cop murder.

It's pinball that makes sense of the top-down view and roadkill game play, and pinball that Dundee-based DMA Design fell back on when it was trying to make sense of the sandbox world it'd created. How to provide a sense of progression and an eventual target to aim for in a nonlinear game in which players can do as they please? Task everyone with earning a million points, that's how.

The murderous urban themes may have snagged the media's attention—and, in all truth, there is a slight shudder of delight to be found in running someone over with their own ride after you've yanked them out of it—but it was the delicate details that made the first *Grand Theft Auto* such a pleasure: the gentle differences between one vehicle and the next, the moment when you discover you can get on board the train and travel by rail (or blow it to pieces), and the way the music blaring from the radio depends on what kind of car you get into.

Even in such early days, Liberty City was a charismatic playground, with broken bridges to leap, skyscrapers to swerve between, and a chain of Hare Krishna to mow down for, perhaps, the gaming world's most unusual bonus. Subsequent games may have brought three-dimensional graphics, a sharper focus on character, and increasingly cinematic storytelling, but the two-dimensional debut was a surprisingly intoxicating mix. This rich and provocative game was a gangster version of *Marble Madness*, a *Goodfellas* with ball-bearings. **CD**

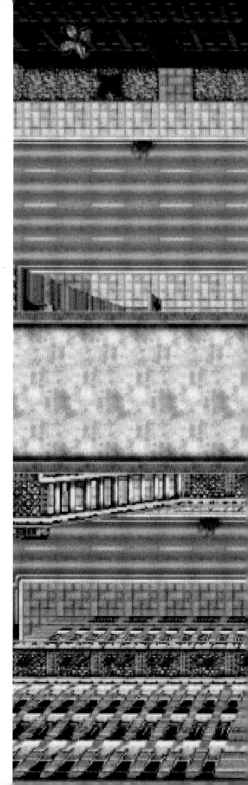

Ultima Online

Original release date : 1997
Platform : PC
Developer : Origin Systems
Genre : MMORPG

The history of online role-playing games starts with niche, text-only multi-user dungeons (MUDs) populated by early hackers and anyone else who could figure out how to get on Telnet. In the mid-2000s, the genre finally stormed the mainstream, thanks to *World of Warcraft*, which made rolling an elf and joining a guild as quick and easy as miniature golf. But somewhere in between, *Ultima Online* ruled the roost. Building off the franchise of Richard Garriott's two-dimensional *Ultima* games, *Ultima Online* brought thousands of players to the challenge of a massively multiplayer online role-playing game (MMORPG).

Griefers and gankers, cratering game economies, houses you could buy (or sell or break into), extreme role-playing, and emergent narratives—it all happened here, and informed every online game to come after it. The designers strove to make a living world, and skills like "forensic examination" and "begging" suggest the social interactions that are rewarded alongside the questing and the killing.

Compared to modern games, settling in to *Ultima Online* is about as easy as flying a bomber. Characters start weak and slowly improve their skills to the point where they can seriously tackle the world. Newer, friendlier software clients have launched and faded over the years, and while the standard top-down experience is cluttered and confusing, you'll have plenty of time to get used to it. Newcomers are encouraged to steer clear of combat and grind before they try anything risky.

Today, the game still claims about the same number of players as in its heyday, with a rich community and deep role-playing. Just as multi-user dungeons never really went away, *Ultima Online* fills a niche between the intimidatingly free role-playing of the old days and the glossiness of modern massively multiplayer online games. **CDa**

Quake II

Original release date : 1997
Platform : Various
Developer : id Software
Genre : First-Person Shooter

The most anticipated PC release of its day, *Quake II*'s nominal sequel status was merely a result of its developer's difficulties in trademarking preferred titles for the project. Sick of having alternatives rejected, id Software settled on reusing the *Quake* name. But aside from the genre and similarities between the arsenal and power-ups, the two games are unrelated. Instead of *Quake's* happily incoherent mash of dark fantasy and hi-tech, *Quake II* wields something resembling a narrative.

The player is in the role of Bitterman, the one surviving soldier of a disastrous counteroffensive on an alien homeworld. Though the game little troubles itself with this plot, beyond presenting a compelling impetus to gun down the cybernetic terrors known as the Strogg, it set a benchmark for the first-person shooter's advances in ambient narrative. The player clambers out of his shattered drop-pod into a ruined chamber. Electronics spark and smoke. Bodies of less successful marines slump in corners.

Though its atmospheric aspirations were shown to be relatively crude within a matter of years, *Quake II* was a marked step, introducing nonlinearity to its levels, which were structured around hubs (better explored by the revolutionary *Half-Life* less than twelve months later). The game shows its flair for gunplay, too, and it's the heft and sound of *Quake II's* weaponry that is its most lasting triumph.

Single-player mode was not its only draw. *Quake II* came with a slick netcode that, in terms of quality of service, remained unsurpassed for several years. Early patches brought bespoke death match levels, many recognized as classics today. Sustained by a lively modding scene, *Quake II* became the most popular online game of 1998. Though eclipsed by its successor, *Quake II* remains significant in the history of multiplayer gaming. **MD**

Interstate '76

Original release date : 1997
Platform : PC
Developer : Activision
Genre : Driving / Shoot 'Em Up

While games have done well at referencing their visual history to offer retro appeal, few offer the sense of cool that pulls from deeper cultural reference points than early 8-bit titles. Truly inspired or just lucky, *Interstate '76* draws from the deep well of creativity found in 1970s television shows and exploitation films, creating a game that succeeds in offering an authentic and thrilling experience, outstripping even the attempts of filmmakers such as Quentin Tarantino to recapture the vibe of the era.

Opening with TV series–style credits, with main characters assigned to fictional actors against bombastically funky music (the score, composed by Arion Salazar, is a consistently clever pastiche of 1970s funk standards), *Interstate '76* stars Groove Champion, a race driver turned reluctant vigilante after his sister is killed. Inheriting her 1971 Picard Piranha (the in-game equivalent of the iconic Plymouth Barracuda), Groove is guided by his sister's partner, Taurus, a vigilante with an Afro as large as his fondness for poetry, across Texas in a quest to discover what led to her death.

It's plotted (intentionally) like a B-grade road movie, but *Interstate '76* isn't theme alone. As the first vehicular combat game in full three dimensions, it defined a genre in which it has never been bettered. A full damage simulation system and well-designed weapons eased the difficulty of navigating a car while shooting at opponents. With tight game design and simple but clean graphics, it hasn't grown to look or feel archaic—something perhaps aided by the decision to render all of the game's characters using flat-shaded, untextured polygons. A striking look that anticipates the cel-shaded visuals of games such as *Killer 7*, it completes a title that feels dated in the right ways. **MKu**

Total Annihilation

Original release date : 1997
Platform : PC
Developer : Cavedog Entertainment
Genre : Strategy

The mid-1990s was the golden age of real-time strategy games. Sales boomed, and every few months saw a new challenger to the stranglehold achieved by Westwood Studios' *Command & Conquer* and Blizzard's *Warcraft*.

Stepping onto this battlefield—with little fanfare—came Cavedog's science-fiction romp *Total Annihilation*, with two largely identical armies scrapping it out in a 4,000-year-long war that players were lucky enough to be invited to. Savvy reviewers quickly realized *Total Annihilation* was a surprise treat, bringing graphical effects more usually seen in shooters to the genre, and adding several new innovations to its palette. The most important was the unsexy-sounding ability to queue commands

for units, such as patrolling via waypoints or constructing defenses. Stacking orders doesn't just free the player to do something more interesting, it fundamentally changes play, since complex bases with elaborate defensive structures can be planned out in just a few clicks.

Key to any battle is the commander unit, who can construct buildings and units, as well as fight in their own right. Starting with the commander, a game of *Total Annihilation* involves unlocking a standard real-time strategy technology tree, but one that is very well balanced so that advanced units don't dominate early ones, and any potential attack has a counterattack. Graphically, the game was a delight at the time, even if it did lag when things got hectic. An underlying physics engine enables units to explode into real pieces, and while the battlefield is two-dimensional, it does include height data. Despite eventually picking up a vast number of awards, however, the game didn't annihilate the competition. Perhaps it should have. **OB**

Shining Force III

Original release date : 1998
Platform : Saturn
Developer : Camelot Software Planning
Genre : Role-Playing

Released during the throes of Sega's Saturn, *Shining Force III* was delivered in three chapters, but only the first volume was released outside of its native Japan. Had the Saturn fared better, perhaps Sega would have published the rest of the story, but as it stands *Scenario 1* is still one of the most enjoyably accessible strategy role-playing games around.

The Shining Force series' distillation of more complex turn-based strategy RPGs like *Tactics Ogre* and *Final Fantasy Tactics* allows the player to focus purely on positioning and attacking, rather than become mired in stats, battle conditions, and defensive considerations. This means faster, tighter combat and more room for those coveted tactics. *Shining Force III* adds secret areas (which require strategic division of your potentially twelve-strong force), statistic boosts for favored weapons, and a brilliant friendship system. Any characters who unite on the battlefield, perhaps to attack the same foe, build a friendship that yields beneficial effects whenever they are subsequently in proximity.

The game introduces three-dimensional battlefields too, and while the Saturn is not known for its three-dimensional capabilities, the aesthetic is genuinely charming, full of bright colors and big-eyed, anime-inspired characters. It's not a purely cosmetic touch, though, since the viewpoint can be rotated and the battle-grid system freely navigated—both features that come into play during the campaign.

The localization is uncommonly good and even the somewhat flat voice acting can't dull the engaging plot's energy. A wonderful soundtrack (by Motoi Sakuraba, composer of *Star Ocean*'s) completes a package that deserved a far larger audience than it reached. **BM**

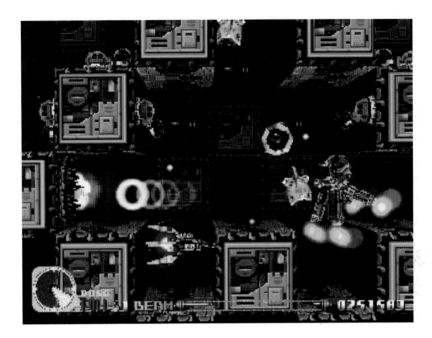

R-Type Delta

Original release date : 1998
Platform : PS1
Developer : Irem
Genre : Shoot 'Em Up

The core *R-Type Delta* experience, piloting the titular aerospace fighter along a razor's edge margin of error, has always been a little too brainy for its own good. Standing apart from contemporaries' increasingly arcane play styles and score multipliers, the series is defined by unflinchingly rigid pattern memorization. While the fourth installment retains the purity of its predecessors, it expands the width, if not the depth, of player agency.

Reading *Delta*'s fixed tempo and honing the *R-Type* player's sixth sense for anticipating that one innocuous bullet that costs it all is only half the game. The rest opens up to juggling and prioritizing weapons, superweapons and throttle, snatching back the moments between telegraphed oblivions. It's every bit a contemplative shooter, with austere production design pushing the series further toward an almost lyrical thematic density, a haiku 'em up fully realized in 2004's concluding *R-Type Final*.

R-Type Delta's stages are studies in isolation: abandoned cities, arctic stations, the frigid depths of water or space. Like a deep-sea nature documentary, it's more appallingly fascinating than attractive, with enough deliberate contrasts between metal and flesh, safety and mutation, to do Cronenberg proud. The game embraces polygonal 3-D with the same aloof genius, capturing the malicious momentum of obstacles plunging down underwater channels or spiraling in zero gravity.

Sinister and self referential—the moments leading up to its finale even twist back to the introductory ship's select screen—*R-Type Delta* stands alone, but enriches the entire sweep of its series. If 1987's exhortation to "Blast off and strike the evil Bydo Empire!" was once narrative enough, here *R-Type Delta* finds a context and delivery of its own. **BS**

Banjo-Kazooie

Original release date : 1998
Platform : N64, Xbox 360
Developer : Rare
Genre : Platform

The Nintendo 64 was the machine that saw Rare's last golden era, a time when it could pick a genre and make a masterpiece. *Banjo-Kazooie* may have been its boldest effort, nothing less than an attempt to outshine *Super Mario 64* on its own platform. It didn't, of course, but it got closer than it had any right to.

Banjo's a bear and Kazooie's a bird who lives in Banjo's backpack, and they've got to knock old witch Grunty for six by collecting jigsaw pieces ("Jiggies") as well as all sorts of subsidiary items, such as "Musical Notes" and "Mumbo Tokens," to aid them in their efforts (*Banjo-Kazooie* marked the start of a period when a platformer wasn't a platformer without a museum of largely pointless collectables to be

found). In truth, the character design is nothing special, but its bright and unthreatening world lent a particular charm in its smaller touches—the garbled gibberish of the characters' voices, for example, and the neat hints of exertion in Banjo's animation.

In size it certainly rivals Mario's most famous 3-D adventure and uses plenty of that game's ideas to good effect, as well as throwing in a smattering of its own. The nine nonlinear worlds are never short of ambition. There's the underwater Clanker's Cavern, the sprawling Mad Monster Mansion, and, along with the usual fire and ice worlds, the levels are always huge affairs, with intricate reworkings of their elements. In the hunt for Jiggies, the heroic duo, too, have plenty of surprising abilities that unfurl over the adventure's course.

Banjo-Kazooie falls short of *Super Mario 64* only in terms of imagination, which is no unforgiveable sin, and remains a monument to the days when Rare almost single-handedly carried the Nintendo 64's third-party offering. **RS**

Hangar Deck 0101

Burning Rangers

Original release date : 1998
Platform : Saturn
Developer : Sonic Team
Genre : Action

The irony of *Burning Rangers*, a game about high-tech firefighters, is that it showed up too late to save the Sega Saturn. The ill-fated console was running on fumes by 1998, having been crushed in the marketplace by Sony's PlayStation. *Burning Rangers* was a product of Sega's own Sonic Team development studio, the group responsible for the *Sonic the Hedgehog* phenomenon. If anything could rescue the Saturn, it would be this.

Burning Rangers is a fun and unique game, not least because of its premise. It plays like a typical third-person shooter in many ways, except that your opponent is a highly unpredictable and ravenous fire. Dousing the flames generates crystals, which are a resource that can then be

used to teleport victims to safety. As with the rings in *Sonic the Hedgehog*, crystals in *Burning Rangers* are your lifeblood. Getting scorched will cause you to lose all the crystals you're carrying, but you can scoop them back up. As long as you're carrying at least one, you won't die.

With only four levels, *Burning Rangers* is short, but elements of randomness keep additional play throughs feeling fresh, by positioning both victims and fires in different locations. Flames explode from unlikely places, signaled by a sound cue you will come to fear. Although navigation can be difficult in the absence of a mini-map, light platforming elements ease the pain somewhat, with acrobatic moves like double-jumps and air dashes. Plus, a split-screen multiplayer mode offers an entertaining change of pace.

Burning Rangers arrived to hype but few sales, and before long the Saturn would be dead and buried. That leaves *Burning Rangers* as just another historical footnote for a console rife with them. **MK**

Sid Meier's Alpha Centauri

Original release date : 1998
Platform : PC
Developer : Firaxis Games
Genre : Strategy

The game's tagline says it all: "The future of mankind." After *Sid Meier's Civilization* series had told the history of mankind and its struggle to reach the stars, *Sid Meier's Alpha Centauri* picked up where it left off, depicting the new colonial challenges presented by the human race's restless need to seek out new, ever more distant territories. In truth, mankind's future seemed eerily similar to its past. This is, in essence, old wine in new, space-age bottles.

The challenge is to settle a planet by exploring the world, gathering and managing resources, developing technology, and vying with rival factions by means of combat and diplomacy. The world is depicted in isometric view, overlaid with a grid that divides the terrain into units

to be controlled and exploited. Except now, instead of settlers and spearmen, there are terraformer modules and psionic warriors. Indeed, combat is one of the areas that expands on the original, allowing players to customize the default units, tinkering and tweaking to produce ever more cutting-edge battle technology.

Another area of expansion is the emphasis on social engineering, which, along with quotes from historical philosophers and artists as varied as Machiavelli and John Milton, perpetuates the creators' preoccupation with political philosophy. Any highbrow aspirations, though, are softened by the sci-fi setting, which comes complete with alien artifacts, mysterious monoliths, and a vast hive mind that makes possible a new victory condition to add to those from the *Civilization* games: In addition to subduing all of your rivals through conquest, economics, or diplomacy, colonists can also achieve transcendence, leaving their material bodies behind to reach a new plane of existence. **DM**

1080° Snowboarding

Original release date : 1998
Platform : N64
Developer : Nintendo
Genre : Sports

Video games offer experiences that are literally magical in that they allow you to try things out that you could never do in real life: shooting at cowboys from a speeding stagecoach, speeding through deep space with a talking frog for a wingman, or immersing yourself in the speed and splendor of snowboarding with no danger of caving your head in against a rock. For many virtual extreme-sports enthusiasts, snowboarding might begin and end with Electronic Arts's brilliantly exaggerated *SSX* series, but *1080° Snowboarding* represents a different approach.

Dialing down the elaborate caricature of the sport, *1080° Snowboarding* is a stylish downhill racer. Built by the team that made *Wave Race 64* and produced by Shigeru Miyamoto, the game benefits from some handsome frosty mountain ranges, a robust world that can zip by at a real pace, and a cluster of trick and race modes that bring real life to the limited range of slopes. At the time of its release, several reviewers became upset with the cheating AI, which was capable of blasting along next to you no matter how well you rode the mountain, but, in truth, the rubber-banding largely serves to keep a thrill of excitement alive when you would traditionally be on your own up front, with no particular sense of urgency.

Yet, despite playing it relatively straight when it comes to presentation, it's the tricks and stunts that carry the game. Watch a seasoned pro at work on the slopes, and *1080° Snowboarding* becomes a hair-raising spectator sport as riders chain moves together, using every inch of the environment to their advantage as they plummet downhill. Classy and lithe, the game is everything you want from a snowboarding experience—and, best of all, it won't land you in a Swiss hospital at the end of it all. **CD**

Dance Dance Revolution

Original release date : 1998
Platform : Various
Developer : Konami
Genre : Music

Up, down, left, right. Few contemporary video games manage to pare their interactivity down to four sparse directional inputs. But then, few video games are played with one's feet. Your first time with one of the formative and most enduring music games to come out of Japan's rhythm-action boom era is likely to be an awkward tussle of limbs, neither graceful nor particularly enjoyable.

Bundled with a plastic dance mat peripheral, the aim is to time your dance steps with the on-screen stream of instructions that move in rhythm with the music. Each input is judged for its accuracy—good, great, perfect— with the best scores reserved for those who manage both meticulous timing as well as physical dexterity.

As with all video games, with repetition comes muscle memory. The only difference here is that your whole body is the muscle that must be trained, especially challenging at the game's highest difficulty levels, accompanied with dizzying arrow indicators, which require you to move your torso in such a way to prepare for the next action.

The core mechanic is nestled within bright, neon Japanese presentation, with garish and loud visuals to match the sucker-punch electronic soundtrack. *Dance Dance Revolution*'s mechanics inspired a slew of real dancers to create routines around its songs, usually at lower difficulties, where the space between inputs is sufficient for freestyling. Conversely, others prefer to steady themselves on nearby furniture and let their legs flurry about beneath them, kicking at "perfects" in a dazzling display of speed sight-reading. Whatever your approach, when first starting out, be sure to clear away the ornaments and possibly draw the curtains. **SP**

Carmageddon II: Carpocalypse Now

Original release date : 1998
Platform : PC, Mac
Developer : Stainless
Genre : Driving

The idea of the car as a weapon has been punted about in both cinema and gaming for many years, but it reaches its logical apex in the *Carmageddon* games. *Carmageddon* means thinking of your car not as transport, but as a high-speed battering ram. The second game in the series is the best, being filled with both an astounding level of violence and some genuinely entertaining challenges. There are ten levels in total, and each is a race that can be won either by completing the actual race, killing all other cars, or killing all the pedestrians on a given level.

It is, of course, this level of violence that sets the *Carmageddon II: Carpocalypse Now* apart from its many peers. The streets through which the player races are filled with pedestrians, all of whom are viable targets. In many regions these were not people, but zombies, with one particularly sensitive market going as far as making them nonhuman aliens. A subsequent "blood patch" was distributed via the Internet, allowing people with the zombies version of the game to restore the original human pedestrians, and the red blood gore effects that went with them. The effect is a game that is comically hideous, with corpses bouncing and splattering around the simplistically rendered cities as you careen across the pavement, putting savage dents in your deformable ride.

It goes without saying that gratuitous violence gets boring if it's not tied to an interesting game, and it's certainly to the credit of this game's team that they managed to make the game a worthy challenge and fun to control. Jumps and stunts rely entirely on player skill, and hunting down zombies in the wide-open maps gives you the completist urge for replay that is common to so many games with open-ended objectives. **JR**

Cyber Troopers Virtual-On: Oratorio Tangram

Original release date : 1998
Platform : Various
Developer : Sega
Genre : Action

Before Capcom's *Steel Battalion* was released with a controller that made a mockery of practicality, the most complicated cockpit for virtual robot pilots was the twin sticks of Sega's *Virtual-On* games. Available for both the Saturn and the Dreamcast, they were the only way to replicate the complex, precise input required to master the controls of the gargantuan gladiators featured in the original coin-op. *Virtual-On* might have looked like a standard beat 'em up with robot fighters instead of humans, but the reality was very different, conjuring up a unique blend of tactics and action.

Oratorio Tangram is the sequel to *Cyber Troopers Virtual-On*, and its improved balancing makes it the more popular

choice among gamers drawn to the dizzying future-tech designs of the Virtuaroids that duke it out in Sega's robot arenas amid a riotous blaze of colors. Each Virtuaroid is a masterpiece of visual invention, from the MBV-707-G Temjin to the RVR-42 Cypher (those hard-to-pronounce names bolstering the game's pseudo-tech appeal). More than just decorating the game's sumptuous arenas, though, each Virtuaroid also makes very different demands on their pilots. Some are suited to keeping things on the ground; others are better in the air, and choosing the right Virtuaroid is the key to success in a game with a nearly vertical learning curve.

That learning curve and the complicated control scheme prevented the game from achieving mass market appeal, but its justifiable cult following was rewarded by the unlikely decision to re-release the game in 2009 on the Xbox 360 via its Live Arcade service; the only thing missing is the ability to save your color schemes on the Dreamcast's Visual Memory Unit, to use in the coin-op. **DM**

Body Harvest

Original release date : 1998
Platform : N64
Developer : DMA Design
Genre : Action

There was one game that all the staff at DMA Design wanted to work on—and it wasn't *Grand Theft Auto*. *Body Harvest*—a nonlinear, adult-themed sci-fi shooter—was developed and earmarked as a potential N64 launch title, which was a considerable honour.

Set in a nightmarish future, *Body Harvest* sees the player control an augmented supersoldier sent back in time to foil a series of invasions by man-eating alien insects that have destroyed humanity. The plot spans a hundred-year period and takes place in more than five countries. Employing a hierarchal system, the alien beings all have different roles that players must learn in order to knock out the attack waves as the invaders track their human targets.

Although each stage presents the player with set puzzles and objectives, the essentially nonlinear structure allows plenty of exploration and experimentation. The game's status as a prototypical open-world adventure is further cemented by the inclusion of various vehicles, which can all be attained and driven freely through the environment. Players are even able to shoot and/or run over human passersby. The fact that side missions can be picked up by conversing with locales would prove to be a highly influential addition.

Sadly, though, with its sluggish frame rate, poor draw distance, and frequent clipping issues, *Body Harvest* never quite looked like the revolutionary step forward it actually was. When Nintendo failed to comprehend the charm beneath the wanton destruction and decided not to handle the game, third-party publishers eventually released the title to a public who remained largely ambivalent, despite the good reviews and praise for its originality that it had garnered. **KS**

Xenogears

Original release date : 1998
Platform : PS1
Developer : Square
Genre : Role-Playing

A convoluted science-fiction project with a multi-million-yen budget or the most ambitious RPG ever conceived? When it comes to *Xenogears*, there are many who would argue it's both. With a back story stretching back for ten thousand years, penned by four scriptwriters and taking in untold forgotten battles, species, and technologies, the mythology is on a rare scale, contending with accusations of it being little more than a result of the awkward marriage of giant robots to overwrought philosophical posturing.

Xenogears is one of Japanese role-playing games' most interesting and challenging stories, its multiple battle systems and irresistible parade of set pieces outstretching most other games by their sheer creativity and spirit.

The game's cast is broad and fascinating, and protagonist Fei Fong Wong (named after the legendary Chinese hero Wong Fei Hung of Guangdong), who was abused by his surrogate mother from a young age, is a tortured and sympathetic lead. The game successfully marries the local with the intergalactic, examining how changes to the grand narrative of the universe affect those in small communities. By the game's end its themes have grown to encompass philosophy, religion, and man's relationship to the divine.

An exquisitely realized battle system and well-executed explorative elements give soul and purpose to the story. But this is a game brought to its knees by scale. Unfortunately, the second half of the game descends into extended cut scenes, limiting the amount of interactions as its developer desperately sought to tie up the loose ends of the story before the budget ran out. Despite this, *Xenogears* remains a triumph of world-building endeavor, a high point for both its developer and medium. **SP**

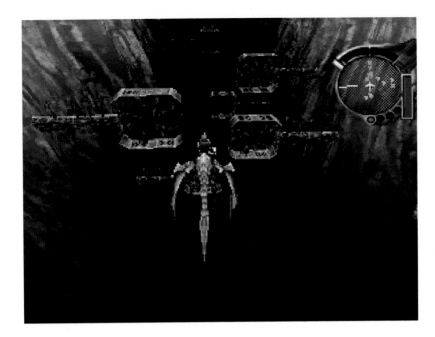

Panzer Dragoon Saga

Original release date : 1998
Platform : Saturn
Developer : Team Andromeda
Genre : Role-Playing

Following up "dramatic shooting games," as the first two *Panzers* were dubbed, with a four-disk RPG might not seem like a logical continuation. But in-house Sega developer Team Andromeda always had weighty aspirations for its ancient-futurist series.

The original 1995 *Panzer Dragoon* and its superb sequel, *Zwei*, had already done much to fabricate a rich and surreal universe, having the benefit of creative insight from esteemed visionary comic artist Moebius. However, the added game play depth that fans had craved all along finally crystallized in *Panzer Dragoon Saga*, particularly in terms of the story delivery, exploration, and its epic, sweeping battle system.

Compared to the cliché-ridden excesses of many RPGs, *Panzer Dragoon Saga*'s narrative unfolding is unusually restrained and surreally evocative, containing a huge amount of detail about the world—much of which could be accessed by simply targeting an object or person either while on foot or mounted on the dragon.

Visually speaking, *Panzer Dragoon Saga* is almost the stuff of legends. Sega's Saturn mostly fell short in its realization of 3-D worlds, but the expansive environments to be explored here are as huge as they are diverse, including canyons, forests, deserts, and subterranean ruins. Inevitably, only the prerendered FMV now seems crude by comparison. Audio was also an area that excelled, and the game features full voice acting for every character, as well as a memorable score. Many aspects of the game impress above and beyond even the best RPGs produced nowadays. English-language copies of *Panzer Dragoon Saga* are rare and often command extortionate prices on eBay. Such is the price of perfection. **JB**

F-Zero X

Original release date : 1998
Platform : N64
Developer : Nintendo
Genre : Racing

F-Zero X is racing at its absolute bare essentials: speed, tight handling, and the element of danger. Its courses aren't really racetracks at all, but rather looping, corkscrewing, abstract planes, suspended in space. The racers aren't hugely detailed vehicles with walls of stat screens and customization options. Instead, the vehicles are superfast hovercars comprised of no more than a few polygons. The aesthetic is spartan, the game play unforgiving. It's the racing game as a concept piece.

The learning curve is absolutely brutal. Surviving on the track with twenty-nine extremely aggressive racers is nearly impossible, until you get the feel of the very precise controls. The game constantly encourages you to flirt with

danger, to sacrifice some of your health bar for a speed boost or to bash another racer off the edge of the track. It wants you to tread the knife's edge between success and failure, between flying past the finish line or exploding on the guard rails after taking a corner too quickly.

That's assuming the course even *has* guard rails; racers frequently fly off into infinity on hairpin corners. Having so many opponents in view at once makes *F-Zero X* aggressively competitive; Death Race, one of the game modes, capitalizes upon this by turning the systematic destruction of everyone else on the track into a main objective. The AI encourages rivalries with particularly aggressive competitors. It's a generous game, too, with layers of difficulty levels, courses, and vehicle unlocks offering a perpetual challenge.

The lack of graphical detail on the racers and courses was necessary to preserve the game's frame rate and sense of speed, but this minimalism actually lends the game a strange, angular beauty. **KM**

RACE   0:08:59 LAP: 8 OF 9   LAST LAP: 1:09.71
FASTEST LAP: J. CLARK   1:07.73   BEST LAP: 1:08.01
9   D. GURNEY   LAG POSITION: 1   SPEED: 159 KM/H

D. GURNEY   TV 1
LIVE FEED   RATE: 0X

Grand Prix Legends

Original release date : 1998
Platform : PC
Developer : Papyrus Design Group
Genre : Driving

The late 1960s proved a magical era for Formula 1. Drivers had to delicately wrestle with four-wheeled vessels able to achieve speeds that far outran the mechanical tolerance of the components that created them. It was a time when changing gears required the use of the clutch and letting go of the steering wheel, and when losing control of the car and leaving the circuit would see you soon slowed down by a wall, a tree, or a crowd of spectators.

Few games capture that danger—and excitement— as convincingly as *Grand Prix Legends*. Still one of the highlights of the sim-racing scene, the game recreates the 1967 season and offers you a seat in one of the period's machinery—Lotus, Ferrari, Cooper, etc.—to pit your

skill against Clark, Brabham, and others as you tackle the likes of Monza, Monaco, and the infamous Nürburgring Nordschleife (in the days when it was actually lethal).

Unlike the cars, progress—even for those possessing considerable virtual-driving ability—is atypically slow. The handling model is sufficiently detailed to accurately portray the behavior of a 1967 F1 vehicle, meaning mere mortals will find initial stints behind the steering wheel hugely intimidating. More than almost any other sim-racing title before or since, therefore, *Grand Prix Legends* deflates egos faster than a blown Goodyear.

Then again, despite the spins, despite the crashes, despite the challenges, you'll keep putting the laps in. Because when you're sitting in the graphically simple cockpit, enveloped by the neck-hair-raising scream of a V12 at full throttle and battling nose-to-gearbox against historic adversaries while expertly executing four-wheel drifts around perilous strips of tarmac, there are few other virtual spaces you'll want to be in. **JDS**

Radiant Silvergun

Original release date : 1998
Platform : Arcade, Saturn
Developer : Treasure
Genre : Shoot 'Em Up

In *Radiant Silvergun*, Treasure sought to evolve the top-down shoot 'em up into something altogether different. There are no weapon pick-ups in the game; instead, all six of the craft's weapons are installed from the start, each triggered by a different combination of buttons and each with its own properties ideally suited to specific situations. As you defeat the swarms of enemies, the weapon you are currently using grows stronger, forcing a decision on whether to spread your power across all of the options or just focus upon your favorites.

Every enemy craft in the game is also assigned a color with score bonuses to be achieved by chaining together like-colored enemies or destroying them in particular orders. Underneath this high-level strategy, the game is also one of the finest shooters ever made, the relentless stream of exciting boss battles and dizzying graphical effects broadening expectations for what is possible in the genre. Pseudo-sequel *Ikaruga* chose to focus more fully upon the color-coded puzzle element, but for the more rounded package, *Radiant Silvergun* is essential. **SP**

Grim Fandango

Original release date : 1998
Platform : PC
Developer : LucasArts
Genre : Adventure

Manny Calavera is a travel agent in the land of the dead, a skeletal smoothie who provides his recently deceased customers with a one-way ticket to the Ninth Underworld. When he begins to suspect that there might be more than meets the eye to Meche, his latest client, he finds himself embroiled in a heady brew of dastardly corruption and connivance that will set him on an epic four-act quest.

Almost every aspect of *Grim Fandango* is refreshingly ambitious, from the snappy references you have to be cine-literate to grasp, and the elegant unspooling of smart plotting (which regularly hops forward leaving yearlong ellipses), to the fact that LucasArts was struggling with its first attempt to recreate the static world of adventure games in three dimensions, its characterful 3-D models moving against prerendered backdrops.

In every aspect it's a success, with smart design, devious puzzles, lovely art, and a truly memorable cast of characters. *Grim Fandango* is fashionable nowadays, but it is truly worth the love it gets—whether the people talking about it have genuinely played it or not. **CD**

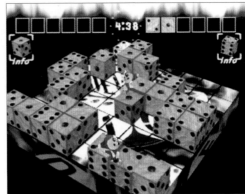

Half-Life

Original release date : 1998
Platform : Various
Developer : Valve Corporation
Genre : First-Person Shooter

In the first-person shooter world of biceps and crewcuts, one of the greatest heroes is a skinny twenty-seven-year-old physicist named Gordon Freeman. Freeman's a scientist, not a soldier, and that's how the game presents his world: calmly and analytically.

Deep in the Black Mesa Research Facility, an experiment has gone wrong, triggering a resonance cascade, rupturing the border between our world and a much scarier one. While the rest of the staff panic, hide, or die of their injuries, Freeman arms himself to make his way back to the surface, shooting his way through head crabs, barnacles, and other alien critters, as well as navigating the obstacle course left by the wreckage.

While *Half-Life* is a solid shooter, it shines most of all in its style. The game avoids cut scenes, because they would rob Freeman of the chance to make his own observations, scientifically critiquing and reveling in exposition.

From the surprises at the surface to Freeman's trip to the beyond at the climax, don't miss the chance to see Black Mesa, the incubator where a legend was born. **CDa**

Devil Dice

Original release date : 1998
Platform : PSI
Developer : Shift
Genre : Puzzle

The Yaroze initiative was an early and pretty much unprecedented experiment in user-generated content. It consisted of a cut-down development kit for the PlayStation, which allowed hobbyist programmers to create games for a fraction of the cost of a professionally developed title.

Most of those games were little more than rough-edged experiments. Some of them, however, were more successful, such as *Devil Dice*. Probably the best puzzle game on the PlayStation, *Devil Dice* was so successful that it spawned a couple of sequels, and would later be dusted off for the PlayStation 3 and PlayStation Portable.

Like all the best puzzle games, it is the essence of simplicity. It consists of a 3-D grid covered with dice. The object of the game is to flip those dice, one face at a time, in order to match the dots. Match the dots and the dice will disappear and the points will rack up. It's wrapped up in a structure that contains all of the play modes that you could possibly need, including a pregenerated puzzle mode and a frantic multitap mode. Diabolically addictive. **DM**

Oddworld: Abe's Exoddus

Original release date : 1998
Platform : PC, PS1
Developer : Oddworld Inhabitants
Genre : Platform

What a difference a save makes. *Oddworld: Abe's Oddysee*, lauded as much for its artistic vision as for extending the twilight of the 2D platform genre, had one crucial flaw in many eyes: It was difficult, and yet it had fixed save points. With the addition of a quick-save for this sequel—officially a bonus spin-off in the *Oddworld* mythology—everyone could love Abe without restraint.

The quick-save debate is a reminder that even games as concerned with setting and narrative as *Abe's Exoddus* can't drop the ball when it comes to mechanics; these are interactive experiences, not movies. Happily, in virtually every respect, *Abe's Exoddus* surpasses your expectations of platform gaming, drawing you into a world where you can perform a wide range of actions, yet you're far from invulnerable. Indeed, you're always a moment from death.

The back story and game play options are extensive. As Abe, you're freeing your fellow Mudokons from enslavement in a factory that uses their tears and bones to brew a potent drink. You can direct Mudokons using "gamespeak" to pull levers or attack enemies, or you can possess those enemies—Sligs, Slogs, Glukkons, and suchlike—to turn their weapons against them.

But this is to scratch the surface. Any game where you seize control of your farts to deploy them as an explosive device has hidden depths. In *Abe's Exoddus* it seldom pays to shoot first, and it's usually best to talk.

Abe's Exoddus has a depth of expression and a rich environment missing from most games of its ilk. Just as *Little Big Adventure* uses isometric 3-D to build a more vibrant game world, so the 2-D cartoonish *Abe's Exoddus* features harrowed faces and shrugging protagonists that make Lara Croft look like a mannequin. **OB**

Metal Gear Solid

Original release date : 1998
Platform : PC, PS1
Developer : Konami
Genre : Stealth

When designer Hideo Kojima brought his *Metal Gear* series to PlayStation, he did more than just kick-start the most popular stealth franchise in gaming history. He began a conversation that continues today, sharing his fears of nuclear holocaust, his distrust of the industrial-military complex, his love of movies like *The Guns of Navarone* and *You Only Live Twice*, and his sympathy for soldiers discombobulated by war. "Ghosts of the battlefield," he would call them, putting a fresh slant on the tired old cliché of the video game action man.

Retired special agent Solid Snake has been dispatched to Shadow Moses, a remote fortified island in Alaska. His mission is to quell an uprising staged by FOXHOUND, a terrorist cell in control of the island's secret: a walking nuclear doomsday weapon called Metal Gear Rex. Little does Snake realize that its mastermind, codenamed Liquid Snake, is actually his genetic twin, part of a government project to breed the ultimate soldier. His lieutenants, furthermore, are psychopaths and assassins with their own twisted agendas. The government calls them traitors, but can anything be that simple in this new world order?

If you think that sounds convoluted, wait until it gets going. Kojima isn't a man to use five words when fifty will suffice and didn't make a game to be played only once. The threads established here would multiply tenfold in games to come, as would the options for combat and stealth. Officially a "sneaking" game, *Metal Gear Solid* is fast and relatively forgiving; escape often as simple as hiding under a cardboard box. Intensely cinematic with its reaction shots and cut scenes, it's more fondly remembered for toying with that illusion: one boss's weakness being a quick change of controller port. **DH**

Street Fighter Alpha 3

Original release date : 1998
Platform : Various
Developer : Capcom
Genre : Fighting

Presenting characters from every iteration of *Street Fighter*'s main series that preceded it, along with many new ones and three different fighting styles for each, *Street Fighter Alpha 3* was arguably the definitive *Street Fighter* title until the surprise appearance of *Street Fighter IV* in 2008.

While purists might prefer the balanced nature of *Street Fighter Alpha 2*, and competition players overlook it in favor of *Street Fighter III: Third Strike*, *Street Fighter Alpha 3* offers an unprecedented variety of play for those who cherish the context of the *Street Fighter* universe as much as its design.

Players are able to choose between A-ism (based on the previous *Street Fighter Alpha*'s play style), X-ism (based on the simpler style of *Super Street Fighter II Turbo*)

and V-ism (a custom combo mode first explored in *Street Fighter Alpha 2*). With combos and special moves flashier than ever, matches are a sight to behold, though they never tip over into the sometimes confusing showiness of the *Marvel vs. Capcom* series.

Street Fighter Alpha 3 belongs in any fighting game fan's collection due to its perfect expansion on the backstories of many beloved *Street Fighter* characters. Fighters face various opponents with which they'll exchange story-driven dialogue, while an individual ending (which, unlike those of *Street Fighter IV*, tends to make at least some sense) rewards extensive play with all characters—even those who provide strange comic relief, such as female wrestler and Zangief fan, R. Mika. As a bonus, the worlds of Capcom's various combat-focused series are further intertwined, with the appearance of *Final Fight*'s main character, Cody, as a playable fighter, following the appearance of Guy and several other *Final Fight* villains from previous games. **MKu**

Resident Evil 2

Original release date : 1998
Platform : Various
Developer : Capcom
Genre : Survival Horror

Resident Evil perfected the survival-horror genre with a feeling of creeping dread quite apart from the grisly reality of the undead. *Resident Evil 2* had a hard act to follow, but did so spectacularly: Where else to go after a localized biohazard, after all, but the metropolis?

Raccoon City is as corridor-based as *Resident Evil*'s mansion, but it creates a flawless impression of something much bigger: Cars piled up to block side roads, doors are desperately barricaded with whatever was at hand, while every room reeks of abandonment. You blast your way to a police station full of undead employees, through it to a byzantine complex of sewers and industrial works, eventually ending up in the inevitable "other" secret lab.

Resident Evil 2 is a B movie in concept, but in video games that doesn't have to be a hindrance. There's a neat tale about the dangers of obsession buried beneath the groaning monsters you fight every step of the way, but this is about thrills: running battles with an encroaching horde; the lickers and their prehensile, stabbing tongues; and the hideous teeth-and-gristle mass of the bosses.

Your first play is only half of it: this unlocks a B game, which casts you as the character you didn't choose first time around. This scenario reuses the game's environments to spectacular effect: You missed all of the real action the first time around, it turns out, including the thudding, terrifying presence of Mr X., an unkillable beefcake in a trenchcoat, whose sole purpose is to kill you at the very first opportunity.

Resident Evil 2 became a best-seller and its focus changed the series for good: quiet scares were out, building-smashing pyrotechnics and huge globs of goo with fangs were in. Forget your brain—it'll only get eaten anyway—and lock and load. **RS**

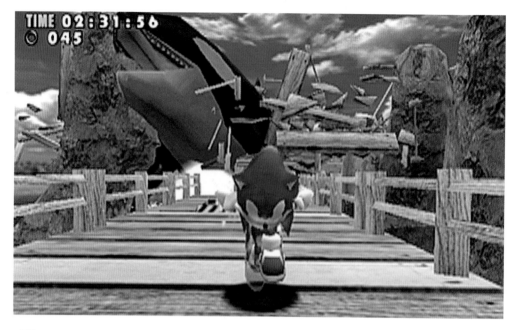

On the image: TIME 02:31:56 045

Sonic Adventure

Original release date : 1998
Platform : Dreamcast
Developer : Sonic Team
Genre : Platform

Designer and producer Takashi Iizuka went to Sonic creator Yuji Naka with a pitch for a new kind of game for Sega's hedgehog icon: a *Sonic* RPG with an expansive story, a wealth of characters, and, for the first time, 3-D visuals. It is the concept that would eventually evolve into Sonic Team's flawed masterpiece.

Sonic Adventure places the familiar platforming experience within a seamless action-adventure format, complete with exploration and narrative elements. Sonic still gets to charge around primary-colored landscapes at immense speeds, but players also gain control of other characters, such as Big the Cat (whose fishing mini-games divided the *Sonic* fan base) and a robot named Gamma.

On the periphery of the adventure, there are mini-games for different characters, and the Chao—cute critters that can be reared and cared for like virtual pets. *Sonic Adventure* is also one of the few titles to support Dreamcast's Visual Memory Unit with a dedicated game, *Chao Adventure*, through which the pets can be trained while the player is on the move.

But the highlights are found within the eleven action stages that take place in vast, twisting environments, loaded with trademark Sonic Team detail. From driving bumper cars in Twinkle Park to legging it down the side of a skyscraper on Speed Highway, the game brilliantly captures traditional Sonic elements. Some levels, especially Lost World, were rebuilt dozens of times as the programming team fought with transference to a 3-D world, and although the erratic camera shots pose issues, its dynamic setup, which cuts between views as Sonic runs, is a clever piece of engineering designed specifically to recreate the old feeling of speed. **KS**

Wetrix

Original release date : 1998
Platform : Various
Developer : Zed Two
Genre : Puzzle

A slant on the classic model of spatial puzzle blocks in both aesthetics and principle, *Wetrix* inspected the new era of three-dimensional space with a scientist's eye for conundrum and a trickster's eye for challenge. Both gift and curse, its isometric viewpoint lends the world-sustaining mechanics of holding your water (and then evaporating it for points) an element of informed guesswork.

The range of pieces the user juggles, from landscape-altering Uppers and Downers to earth-puncturing Bombs, leads to a game of climate—rather than riot—control. A calculating user can control and extend sessions in a way the twitch tactic immediacy of *Tetris* rarely allows for. The descending pieces coax a level of self-flagellation,

leading to a lesser-of-two-evils approach to progress that imbues *Wetrix* with a pervading sense of survivalist's dread. Challenge mode and handicaps take the concept a step further, forcing improvisation and prayers for Rainbows (world-saving gifts from the heavens). The split-screen multiplayer, however, allows the user to wreak vengeance with the very tools of destruction that have been the bane of the single-player campaign.

The game world itself, suspended as it is on an axis in wallpapered game space, allows the art to pepper the private oasis/hell with some stellar flourishes. Smoothly rendered textures and effervescent particle effects layer the often punishing risk-reward loops of interaction with a deceptive, attractive innocence.

Though ports were made—most notably to Sega's Dreamcast—*Wetrix* was never more at home than on the Nintendo 64. It showed that Nintendo's machine, both in physical design and theory, could challenge and change old systems of play. **DV**

Star Wars: Rogue Squadron

Original release date : 1998

Platform : N64, PC

Developer : Factor 5

Genre : Shoot 'Em Up

The Death Star trench run is one of the earliest and most thrillingly memorable video game experiences, thanks to Atari's 1983 vector-graphic coin-op classic. Fifteen years later, LucasArts enlisted Factor 5 to bring the attack on the Death Star back to life, along with Beggar's Canyon, the Battle for Hoth, and a host of other encounters drawn from the rich history of the *Star Wars* universe. The result is one of the definitive video game versions of that universe.

It follows on from the magisterial brilliance of the *X-Wing* and *TIE Fighter* series but tailors the experience for a console audience. For most of the game, it puts you in control of Luke Skywalker, sitting in the cockpit of his X-Wing—and A-Wing, Y-Wing, Snowspeeder, V-Wing, and, if you're skilled enough to unlock them, the Millennium Falcon, TIE Interceptor, T-16 Skyhopper, AT-ST, and (just in time for its first appearance in the movies) the Naboo Starfighter. One of the things that the game gets so right is the way it fulfills the wishes of *Star Wars* fans, serving up items, vehicles, technology, planets, and people drawn from the farthest reaches of the galaxy, raking through twenty years of detail and exploring beyond the celluloid edges of George Lucas's "lived-in" universe.

Every chapter opens with the famous opening crawl and continues to recreate, precisely, the sights, sounds, and action of all the major battles between the end of *A New Hope* and the start of *The Empire Strikes Back*. Thanks to the Nintendo 64's memory expansion pack, it also displays a higher resolution for the utmost graphical fidelity. More than anything, though, *Star Wars: Rogue Squadron* captures the feel and sensation of flying one of those Incom T-65s through a series of intense do-or-die dogfights. Saving the galaxy has never been so much fun. **DM**

Space Station Silicon Valley

Original release date : 1998
Platform : N64, PS1
Developer : DMA Design
Genre : Action / Platform

What about if, instead of talking to the animals, you could just take them over? *Space Station Silicon Valley*'s setting is a facility in the year 3000, filled with robotic approximations of Earth creatures—mice with wheels, foxes with rocket packs strapped to their underbellies, and steam-powered hippos. And you're a microchip that can control any of them—if they've been incapacitated. In essence it's a robotic recreation of the battle between hunter and hunted, with the delightful twist that here, at the right moment, you can switch sides.

This simple formula is the basis for a puzzling platformer that demonstrated the riotous imagination of DMA Design at its best. Gentle jumps might take you

to one objective, a sheep's coat puffing out to slow your descent, while in the next moment you're roaring up a ramp and then arcing over a lake (it's never a good idea for electronics to get wet, after all). You'll be zigzagging in and out of teeth and claws, but soon returning with teeth and claws of your own to exact revenge. Working out what to do is often the entire challenge, before crashing rudely into the ecosystem and actually pulling it off under the bewildered whiskers of those around you.

Leagues ahead of its time in concept, *Space Station Silicon Valley* suffers only from some basic failings in checkpoints and controls. For such a cuddly concept, it's brutally tough at times, and you'll be pursued throughout certain levels with the relentlessness only a mindless piece of programming can muster. But the bonkers, and genuinely amusing, plot helps keep your interest through even the worst of its excesses, alongside a quality you often don't find in more widely acclaimed games: You just don't know what lies around the next corner. **RS**

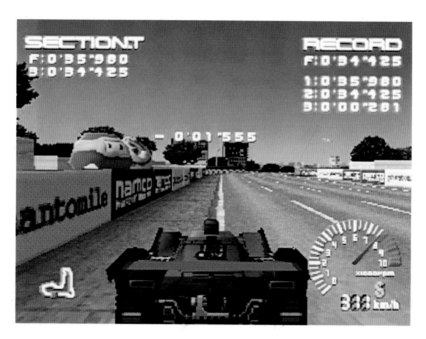

R4: Ridge Racer Type 4

Original release date : 1998

Platform : PS1

Developer : Namco

Genre : Driving

While the *Ridge Racer* series can be criticized for an overly controlled approach to handling and general game mechanics, it's equally important to recognize that the fundamentals of such an approach can create essential game experiences.

R4: Ridge Racer Type 4 is one such example. The game is a notable entry into the *Ridge Racer* lineage because, while adhering to Namco's passion for order and control, it manages to integrate its elements in an almost entirely harmonious manner.

From a technical perspective, the graphics are some of the best on the system (and their distinctive Gouraud-shaded look and delicate lighting continues to impress,

even if the darker setting is a little at odds with the typical *Ridge Racer* aesthetic), the eight circuits designed to showcase as many polygons as they can get away with. Further substance can be found in the game's main mode, which structures race meetings as a series of rounds, while, bravely, the handling model offers an option that provides an alternative to *Ridge Racer*'s signature power-slide-obsessed approach.

By today's standards the handling feels like something of an acquired taste, but there is a layer of depth and predictability in *R4: Ridge Racer Type 4* that is noticeably absent from the previous *Ridge Racer* games. What is consistent with the series is an exceptional sense of style and presentation, which, again, still stands up today. There are eight visually thrilling tracks and while the 300-odd cars available to unlock is a misguided excess on the part of the developer, *R4: Ridge Racer Type 4* can at least reverse into its garage, confident that it still delivers a thrilling and uniquely arcadelike four-wheeled blast. **JDS**

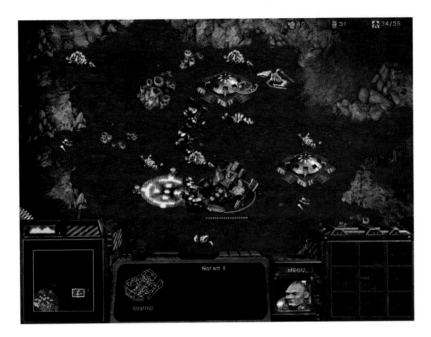

StarCraft

Original release date : 1998
Platform : PC
Developer : Blizzard Entertainment
Genre : Strategy

Defensive pop-culture creators often boast of being "big in Japan," but *StarCraft* was the first Western game to pin its success on South Korea. There was something about this real-time sci-fi strategy game that touched a nerve, making *StarCraft* a staple of the country's multiplayer PC cafés, which were emerging in the late 1990s, leading to the sale of 4.5 million copies in the territory. It also helped to establish Korea's professional gaming scene.

Of course, with more than 11 million sales worldwide, *StarCraft* is one of the best-selling PC games anywhere. Yet while initial reviews were overwhelmingly positive, it's fair to say that few commentators at the time, at least in the West, foresaw *StarCraft* being quite the enduring success

it proved to be. Despite the isometric graphics, the game isn't especially impressive, and less successful rivals have an edge in RTS innovation, particularly in terms of unit control and resource management.

But *StarCraft* has a very special trick up its sleeve: three completely distinct and playable races. The Terrans (humans), the Zerg (nasty, swarming aliens), and the Protoss (less numerous psychic philosopher warriors) all have their own units that don't just look different but play differently, too. For instance, as the Zerg you can burrow underground and attempt to overwhelm your opponent with sheer numbers, while as the Protoss you have fewer troops, but more powerful weapons at your disposal. Upon release, no race was blatantly overpowerful, and Blizzard has maintained this balance with occasional patches that address rush tactics and other foibles.

The combination of diversity and balance is extremely difficult to achieve, and it has underwritten *StarCraft*'s long shelflife as a multiplayer staple, in Korea and beyond. **OB**

Thief: The Dark Project

Original release date : 1998
Platform : PC
Developer : Looking Glass Studios
Genre : Stealth

It started as a communist zombie game. Then it was a *Dark Age of Camelot* game, based around a revisionist reading of the Arthurian mythos, with Mordred as the hero, Merlin as a time traveler, and Guinevere as a butch lesbian. The result is a proto-steampunk fantasy that's one of the most seminal PC releases of the late '90s and arguably the most important game in the development of the stealth genre.

Thief: The Dark Project splits such honors with its peer, *Metal Gear Solid*, but where Hideo Kojima's game provided the general techno-thriller tone and aesthetics for series like *Splinter Cell*, with a few exceptions, they all lifted mechanics from Looking Glass Studios's game. It was to the stealth experience what *Asteroids* was to the arcade

shooter: stepping away from the digital mechanics of its forebears and embracing a more analog system. So rather than simply offering cover opportunities in a binary fashion—on or off—the game overlaid its environment with layers of shadow and light. Due to the protagonist's supernatural thieving skills, the darker the shadow, the more invisible he is to the guards. The question swiftly becomes not whether you're hiding but whether you're hiding well enough. Add a series of tools to skew those odds—from water arrows to extinguish torches, to something as simple as crouching—and you have something from which you can hang an entire game.

It's telling that where *Metal Gear Solid* regularly turned to violence, *Thief: The Dark Project* kept faith in its core tenet: avoidance. It proved that you could make a game where the majority of your time was spent crouching in a darkened corner, scared to even look at the guard inching down the corridor, and still be as compelling as the most action packed of epics. **KG**

The Legend of Zelda: Ocarina of Time

Original release date : 1998
Platform : N64
Developer : Nintendo
Genre : Action / Adventure

An astonishing lifetime-spanning adventure, a reinvention of Hyrule that feels utterly new yet intensely appropriate, and a massive journey that returns, elegantly, to conclude where it began.

Reinventing *The Legend of Zelda* for the complex world of the N64 was a massive undertaking and from the moment Link takes his first melancholic trot through the thin mists of Hyrule Field, it's clear that Nintendo is more than up to the task. It is an adventure that rarely disappoints.

What's staggering is how much the development over-delivers, with a combat system that invented left-trigger targeting and puzzles that play out with a temporal twist as Link moves between time periods to progress the

plot in much the same way as he once dipped between light and dark worlds. It's a design choice that elevates the game into something truly moving, too, as the child becomes a man, and has to fit into a grown-up world in which everything has gone awry.

And then, of course, there is also Epona, the most wonderfully personal of all video game vehicles. Link's horse may be a necessary testament to the fact that Hyrule had become unwieldy and vast, but the relationship that's formed is so gentle, caring, and genuine, that she starts to feel like a real animal long before you realize just how useful she's become. And in a game that has so many wonderful moments—a massive ghost racing into the horizon, a spooky rider erupting from a gloomy painting—Epona's is perhaps the best at capturing the elation that only *Zelda* can provide, with that game-changing leap over the fence of the Lon Lon Ranch, sending you out to explore a world that—you can't help but suspect—will never be the same again. **CD**

Driver

Original release date : 1999
Platform : Various
Developer : Reflections Interactive
Genre : Driving

For those who grew up watching 1970s US cop shows on television—where cars with absurdly bouncy suspension lean their way around the streets and navigate ninety-degree corners by breaking into long, lazy powerslides—*Driver* is the embodiment of everything that made those programs so attractive. In short, it's all about screeching tires.

The star of the game, then, is not Tanner, the undercover NYPD detective trusted with bringing down the criminal gang he's infiltrated and whose McQueen-like demeanor you incarnate. Rather, it's the vehicles he's in—which include heavyweights of the era such as the Chevrolet Chevelle, the Dodge Charger, and the Ford Gran Torino, as well as a classic quartet of US cities: Miami,

Los Angeles, New York and San Francisco. What you do in those open-world environments doesn't alter massively. Whether you're driving a getaway car, tailing another, or providing a glorified taxi service, the action tends to follow an A-to-B or A-to-B-to-A pattern. Also consistent are the frequent police encounters, but unlike the missions, which can feel repetitive and suffer from unrefined, difficult spikes, being pursued around a landscape built as an homage to classic TV car chases (*Driver* includes a Director's Mode, enabling personalized replays to be savoured) rarely gets tiring.

Snaking masterfully through civilian traffic, throwing a muscle car sideways, hoping it'll make the turn, and noticing one of your hubcaps trying valiantly to overtake you, or charging down alleyways and smashing through cardboard boxes with an entire precinct hot on your bumper, *Driver* is the sort of experience that will bring a smile to the faces of all who play it, regardless of the decade in which they were born. **JDS**

Sega Bass Fishing

Original release date : 1999
Platform : Various
Developer : Sega
Genre : Sports

Messing about with maggots or making up doses of foul-smelling bait; reconnaissance trips that involve nothing more than baiting the water without any sight of a fishing rod; getting up in the dark early hours to sit in the rain for hours on end . . . Fishing can be a boring, pointless recreational activity. That much is beyond dispute.

And yet, thanks to a lucky historical accident that fused an obsessive preoccupation with fish with Sega's uncanny knack for making some of the world's best electronic entertainment, fishing forms the pretext for an experience that defies all logic and reason to provide some of the strangest thrills in the history of video games. *Sega Bass Fishing* ranks alongside the likes of *Seaman*, *Typing of*

the Dead, and *Samba de Amigo* as one of the marvelous oddities that the Dreamcast unleashed on a seemingly uncaring world. For anyone lucky enough to dip their rod into Sega's superbly teeming waters, it was all too easy to become hooked—unless you were playing with an unofficial rod. (Unofficial rods were generally rubbish.)

With Sega's official fishing-rod peripheral, however, fishing all of a sudden became fun. Showcasing amazing graphics and fluidity, this is a challenging and pleasurable experience. Pick your lure, cast your line, and then wrestle with whatever virtual freshwater denizen happens to swim your way. The art of landing those tantalizingly elusive big fish is all in choosing the right type of lure and manipulating it with just the right teasing motions before reacting to the superbly judged vibration feedback in your rod. It is to real fishing what *Crazy Taxi* is to real driving: a superb reimagination. And that probably was, and is, *Sega Bass Fishing*'s greatest achievement: the transformation of fishing. Still pointless, perhaps, but now less boring. **DM**

Aliens Versus Predator

Original release date : 1999
Platform : PC, Mac
Developer : Rebellion
Genre : First-Person Shooter

How ironic that the species best served by *Aliens Versus Predator* is the one left out by its title: us. The Colonial Marine campaign, set on the same planetoid LV-426 as Ridley Scott's movie and James Cameron's sequel, is one of the most terrifying survival horrors ever made, not to mention the best of more than thirty adaptations of Fox's towering franchises. Actually the second of Rebellion's stabs at the license—the first, a similarly structured game for Atari's Jaguar console, has long been considered a collector's item—it's no less effective today.

The monsters may be "coming out the goddamn walls," but the devil's in the details. The rattle of the pulse rifle, the urgent pop of the motion detector, the screech of the xenomorphs. By getting those right, *Aliens Versus Predator* wins half the battle right away. In fact, it's perhaps the only series entry after the movie *Aliens* to observe its golden rule: that you should only see the aliens in the seconds before the kill. In the utterly oppressive corridors of the isolated, desolate colony, it has you shooting at shadows the rest of the time.

The other two thirds of the game are pure role-play and wish fulfillment, adding two kinds of stealth to its feature list. The predator campaign, which visits three planets, including the third movie's prison colony, Fiorina 161, lets the weapons—the blades, plasma caster, and cloaking device—define the role, meaning you're always outnumbered but never outgunned. The xenomorph, meanwhile, lets you marvel at this ultimate killing machine from the inside. Its dizzying ability to climb every surface provides a liberating, demanding control system while its field of vision, complete with fish-eye effect, gives you a great impression of speed and a unique perspective. **DH**

Age of Empires II: The Age of Kings

Original release date : 1999
Platform : PC, Mac
Developer : Ensemble Studios
Genre : Strategy

Age of Empires II: The Age of Kings is a perfectly measured real-time strategy game that followed the success of Microsoft's first *Age of Empires* title. It's set in the Middle Ages, but it's inspired by the real thing rather than obsessed with it: the historical environment provides atmosphere and setting rather than a straitjacket. It offers a pretext for the thirteen playable nations, and for the technology progression within the game, allowing players to build towns, raise armies, and advance from one age to the next.

Those nations are drawn from all over the globe, from the Britons and Celts to the Goths, Mongols, and Japanese, and those ages range from the Dark Ages at the start of the game to the Imperial Age by its end. Throughout them all, across several single-player campaigns and potentially never-ending multiplayer contests, the object remains the same: gather food, wood, gold, and stone, and use them to build your civilization, harvesting enough resources to support a population big enough to sustain an empire.

Many of the game's innovations in interface design and streamlined control found their way into various subsequent RTS titles: being able to spot idle builders so you can set them to work, for example, or the ease with which units can be grouped together and put in formation to grant armchair generals more nuanced control over their armies. Such was the overwhelming critical acclaim and its popularity on the PC and Mac that the game was even the unlikely recipient of a home-console port, appearing on the PlayStation 2, and a handheld version on the Nintendo DS, as well as a spin-off released in 2000. But it is the 1999 computer game that is the definitive version, going down in history as one of the most outstanding examples of the RTS genre. **DM**

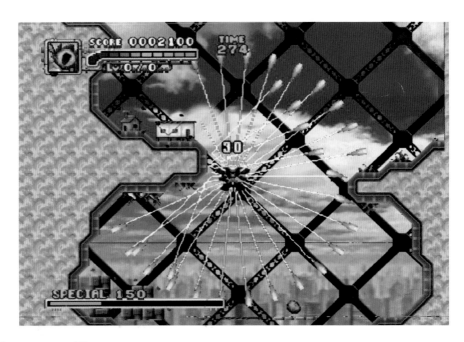

Bangai-O

Original release date : 1999
Platform : Dreamcast
Developer : Treasure
Genre : Shoot 'Em Up

When *Bakuretsu Muteki Bangaioh* was released for the N64—in extremely limited numbers and only in Japan—it was a unique fusion of tiny sprites, odd characters, and fruit, wrapped up in what was ostensibly a retro-styled shoot 'em up. But it was the game's worldwide Dreamcast release as *Bangai-O* that perfected its idiosyncratic blend of giant but tiny robots, millions of massive explosions, and unprecedented profusion of fruit.

At its core, *Bangai-O* is a frantically intense shooter in which players pilot the titular giant robot across forty-four levels, free to fire in entirely different directions, destroying scenery and picking up fruit for extra points. But it is a shooting game that plays like a puzzle. The first part of that puzzle is picking the right payload: firing off homing missiles in wide open spaces, but switching to bouncing bullets in narrow spaces or for firing around corners.

The second part is picking the right path through levels that are a smorgasbord of different designs, from bullet-hell bombardments to big boss battles and from complicated mazes to screens full of cascading blocks. There is one level in which you light a fuse and race it to the end of the level; others in which you encounter bosses that don't fight back.

But the final and most thrilling part of the puzzle is the explosion meter, and it was this that was changed from the N64 to the Dreamcast. In the N64 game, you charged your bombs by picking up fruit, whereas in the Dreamcast game you charged your bombs by unleashing explosions and flying close to them; the more explosions, the faster your bombs recharged. It opens up an entirely new dynamic of high-stakes risk and reward, an insane mixture of damage and speed, exhilarating and nail-biting in equal parts. **DM**

Ape Escape

Original release date : 1999
Platform : PS1
Developer : SCE Japan Studio
Genre : Platform

Hardly a video game colossus today, *Ape Escape*'s monkeys were briefly the closest thing Sony had to a Sonic or Mario—a mascot that made younger console fans very excited—and this charming and colorful platformer also belongs to the limited number of titles that have, over the years, brought about hardware innovations.

Ape Escape requires two thumbsticks to control—a design that is now standard (except on the rule-breaking Wii, of course, and the somewhat hobbled PSP, with its single analog nub), but back in 1999 it meant anyone who wanted to sample this game's peculiar charms had to buy a new controller, the DualShock. It was probably worth the investment, mind. Not only would the DualShock quickly become Sony's weapon of choice, but the game that ushered it in was masterful and distinctly clever.

An evil monkey in a brain-enhancing hat has traveled through time, sending out minions in a rather predictable bid to take over the entire world. It's the player's job, somewhat inevitably it must be said, to dash back and forth through the eons to capture all the evil monkey's agents and save the day.

Heavily caricatured historic periods, from the age of the dinosaurs through to the modern day, make for an elegant arrangement of levels, while the mechanics make good use of the controller's extra real estate, with the sticks divided between moving and aiming weapons.

Ape Escape is colorful, fast-paced, and fun, filled with humor and pop-culture references, and the structure mixes up the chasing down and catching of monkeys with the regular appearance of plentiful gadgets. The game's legacy includes some spin-offs and cameo appearances in everything from *Little Big Planet* to *Metal Gear Solid*. **CD**

Silhouette Mirage

Original release date : 1997
Platform : PS1, Saturn
Developer : Treasure
Genre : Action

It's not the first time that the struggle between light and dark had been literalized and used as inspiration for a game's underlying mechanics, as anyone who's marveled at the interplay between *The Legend of Zelda: A Link to the Past*'s light and dark worlds can attest. And in terms of Treasure's own output, *Silhouette Mirage*'s approach wasn't to be the last time the developer explored the idea, with *Ikaruga* using black and white to distinguish (and swap) between safety and danger in a potent shoot 'em up/ puzzle-game crossover. But *Silhouette Mirage* was perhaps the first platform game to apply the principle to its genre, and the resulting concoction of disparate influences is quite unlike anything else in gaming.

The core conceit is that every enemy is classified as either Silhouette (blue) or Mirage (red). When facing the right-hand side of the screen, your character, the diminutive world saver, Shyna, embodies all the properties of the Silhouettes, only able to damage the strength of an opponent, not its health. But when facing left, she's a Mirage, equipped to damage an enemy's health, but not their strength. By electing to use up a little of your own Spirit Gauge, you can switch the controls, so that facing right turns you Mirage and vice versa. And so a complex yet satisfying, directionally aware puzzle game emerges.

Unfortunately, while Shyna is a maneuverable avatar, the platforming element is uninspired, and the fussy rules can make for a slow-moving experience at first. But the boss battles bristle with creativity, and the game rewards those who can master its complexities. The game was tinkered with for its Western release, and the changes ultimately did more harm than good; therefore, the Japanese original remains the best option. **SP**

ChuChu Rocket

Original release date : 1999
Platform : Dreamcast, Game Boy Advance
Developer : Sega
Genre : Puzzle

Before online gaming involved millions of people around the world energetically shooting one another in the face while sprawled on their couches, it was this: the eternal fight between cat and mouse, played out on pastel-colored mazes where a single wrong decision could see your cutesy, squeaking charges delivered right into the maw of a strangely abstract orange death machine.

The Dreamcast came with a modem port, and, unless you were brave enough to face the space-age grinding and endless collegiate typing of *Phantasy Star Online*, you were probably going to end up playing this: a rather delightful puzzle game in which you place a handful of arrows on the ground to guide your mice to safety in a

rocket. Just like real life, then. The multiplayer mode was genuinely frantic, as everybody rushed to guide cats into rival paths while keeping their own whiskered friends safe, but lasting online interaction came in the form of sharing the devious new maps you'd built for yourself with the level editor. It was *ChuChu Rocket*'s major selling point, certainly, but the game remained sufficiently delightful to provide hours of fun, even with the phone unplugged.

Inevitably, however, broadband carriers blew open the barriers for the kind of games that could fit comfortably down a wire, and quirky oddities such as *ChuChu Rocket* were replaced with fragfests, death matches, and the endless delights of voice-chat griefing. While nobody's complaining too much when there's the likes of *Halo*, *Killzone 2*, and *Call of Duty 4* to enjoy, a look back at the online of yesteryear, especially when it's as cheeky and characterful as this, is still enough to give you pause (or perhaps paws). If your Dreamcast's in the loft, incidentally, you should still be able to track down the GBA port. **CD**

Street Fighter III: Third Strike

Original release date : 1999

Platform : Various

Developer : Capcom

Genre : Fighting

There's a reason for that subtitle. Capcom is well-known for milking its fighting franchises with remixed versions and re-releases, but talk of commercial considerations tends to overshadow the benefit to the games. They get better. *Street Fighter III: Third Strike* was third time lucky for Capcom and *Street Fighter*, proving to be the ultimate refinement of the game many consider the pinnacle of the 2-D brawler. Of course, those people are usually really good at it.

Whatever their relative merits and failures, there is one crucial difference between *Street Fighter III: Third Strike* and its illustrious predecessor: This one's not for beginners. The smooth, flowing animations are built for relentless combos and countercombos, with a new parry move introducing

a level of tactical depth relished by gaming experts (and responsible for the game's most famous moment: a seamless streak of fifteen parries from Daigo Umehara to survive a super combo from Justin Wong, before comboing into his own super—look it up on YouTube). Plus, there's a new roster designed to knock players out of their bad old *Street Fighter II* habits.

Few people wanted to kick the habit, of course, and *Third Strike* even lost a little of its resolve by restoring Chun-Li to the character select screen (only Ken and Ryu had originally survived the cull, and even then only after focus-group tests). By almost any standards *Third Strike* is a success, yet it falls short of its predecessor in terms of recognition and sales. But that only matters to Capcom. For players, it's an unquestionably brilliant 2-D fighter, capable of breathtaking beauty and brutality, and featuring character design of the highest order. It is a great game in its finest form, endlessly rewarding those with enough time on their hands to learn its dizzying intricacies. **RS**

Fatal Fury: Mark of the Wolves

Original release date : 1999

Platform : Various

Developer : SNK

Genre : Fighting

Perhaps the most highly regarded of fighting games on the hardware most highly regarded *for* fighting games, *Fatal Fury: Mark of the Wolves* is SNK's crowning achievement in the genre. Released late in the Neo Geo's life, it pushes its host system in ways previously thought impossible, painting the ballet and drama of the one-on-one fighting genre in tasteful yet exuberant 2-D visuals. A flock of pigeons scatters in a clapping of feathers at the toll of a giant bell in the background of one arena, while a train clatters past a sunset-drenched station in another.

Yet the game's primary innovation was not visual but mechanical, scrubbing away the long, exclusive move lists of the company's *King of Fighters* series, and giving all of *Fatal Fury: Mark of the Wolves*'s character roster the same set of inputs. By reducing and normalizing the vocabulary of interactions, players can easily switch between fighters, knowing that they can pull off the moves of each without the need to adapt inputs. Of course, being able to pull off a screen-filling special move is less important than knowing when to pull off the move in a match, so while the game is accessible, its depths, as with the very best fighting games, are near unfathomable.

Although it is an arcade game at heart, concessions have made the player's journey through the game more comfortable: defeat in battle gives the option to continue the match at a lower difficulty, with a full "special" meter, or with your opponent at a quarter of his or her health. While the original cartridge would have set consumers back hundreds of dollars, SNK has since ported the game to Xbox Live Arcade and PlayStation Network, from which it can now be downloaded at a bargain price. A rumored sequel is reported to still be in the planning stages. **SP**

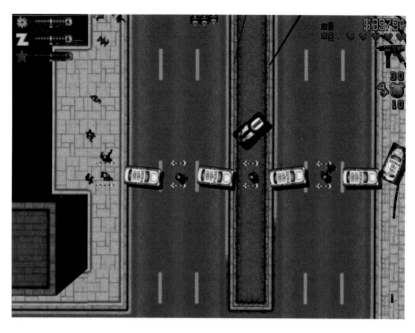

Grand Theft Auto 2

Original release date : 1999
Platform : Various
Developer : DMA Design
Genre : Action

Grand Theft Auto 2 has been unfairly marginalized by the success of both its predecessor and successor. Keeping the top-down view of the first Grand Theft Auto game, it has been judged by history as a minor iteration on an old formula, before the series' dramatic leap into 3-D—an evolutionary dead-end. But its innovations are far from insignificant. As with its forebear, Grand Theft Auto 2 launches the player as a free agent in a sprawling open city, full of lucrative criminal potential. Yet the sequel breathes life into its pedestrians. They get on buses, hail down taxis, and even get into fights with local gangs.

The gangs, too, present an important step, albeit not in a direction that Grand Theft Auto III would wholly follow:

Multiple missions are on offer from the three competing gangs in the area, and each one, when successfully completed, will increase the favor of that gang and decrease that of its competitors. The player must keep juggling the esteem of each so as not to get gunned down when straying into their territory.

Perhaps the game's greatest misstep was to set the game not in contemporary America but in a tongue-in-cheek near-future dystopia, the cyberpunk trappings of which undo some of the game's efforts at building a credible living city. Nonetheless, the game's world still exemplifies the developer's penchant for biting (and sometimes puerile) humor, with its cast of pervert scientists and vengeful Hari Krishnas. Save stations are churches with flickering signage, and they only work if you have the required donation of money. This is a city gone to seed, shot through with corruption—an atmosphere mirrored in the permanent dusk and gloomy neon lights of the graphically superior PC version. **MD**

Ferrari F355 Challenge

Original release date : 1999

Platform : Various

Developer : Sega

Genre : Driving

Yu Suzuki's love of Ferraris is evident throughout his notable career at Sega, and his devotion led to one of the most striking video game dedications to a single subject: *Ferrari F355 Challenge*.

Beginning with sweeping views of Ferrari's Maranello headquarters and the lustrous curves of the 355 Challenge itself, the game was built and tuned for the arcade. But *Ferrari F355 Challenge* also features a sensibility for simulation that few other arcade games have ever attempted. Indeed, next to *Sega Rally*, which converted the technicalities of dirt track driving into sweeping drifts, with the driving aids off (surely the only way to play) it feels almost impossible to master. Just finishing a race is

achievement enough. It's most certainly not about flooring the accelerator and pumping the brakes hard—you'll only spin out. There's even a fine art to simply launching the car well at the start of a race.

And yet *Ferrari F355 Challenge* maintains all the trappings of time limits and extends: the supremely cheesy Sega "Game over, yeah!" sample as you fail another checkpoint, and minimal options for play beyond single races and a championship mode. Indeed, you can't save during a championship in the console versions, and it's then that you start to see why the arcade game is actually a perfect fit for an exacting simulation. A three-screen cabinet version enables players to use the screens as side windows, giving them the sensation of driving in a real car. It's all part of a unique, intense experience. Arcade games don't hold your hand. They make you fight for their rewards, and as a result, you rarely regret failing to complete them. You're there more for the ride than the win. As good as driving a real F355 Challenge? Not quite, but near enough. **AW**

Chrono Cross

Original release date : 1999
Platform : PS1
Developer : Square
Genre : Role-Playing

The producers of *Chrono Cross* insist that they did not consider the game a sequel to 1995's *Chrono Trigger*, one of the most beloved RPGs on the Super NES. Yet *Chrono Cross* has always been overshadowed by its 16-bit forebear, which isn't entirely fair and doesn't do it justice. True to its makers' protestations, *Chrono Cross* is, indeed, an entirely different game. It inherits a fascination with time and scattered story elements from *Chrono Trigger*, but from there it crafts a distinctive, surprisingly emotional experience that deserves to be appreciated in its own right.

While collecting shells on the beach for his girlfriend, seventeen-year-old Serge falls into an alternate dimension. Serge learns that in this second reality, he's dead, having drowned ten years earlier. In fact, he's only alive because an interdimensional traveler rescued him from drowning, creating a time rift that allows Serge to complete a fated quest to save the world. And then it gets *really* confusing. Serge switches bodies, characters meet alternate versions of themselves, monsters spawn outside of time, etc. *Chrono Cross*'s complicated story does make sense, but it just might take a couple play throughs to catch it all.

The notion of repeat play might sound tedious, but *Chrono Cross* is less of a slog than most RPGs. There are no random battles—every enemy is out in the open, so you can avoid them if you want. And there's no need to grind, because character leveling is capped at reasonable levels. It's worth passing through the tropical world of *Chrono Cross* a second time, too, to bask in the game's moving soundtrack. It's a unique mix of Celtic, Mediterranean, and modern Japanese influences, exemplifying the fact that *Chrono Cross* isn't just unlike *Chrono Trigger*, it's unlike any other console RPG before or since. **JT**

Silent Hill

Original release date : 1999
Platform : PS1
Developer : Konami
Genre : Survival Horror

Don't even consider exploring the foggy town of Silent Hill if you lack the following: a desire to be genuinely scared, a strong heart, a fridge stocked with your favorite comfort food, and an economical energy tariff that means it won't be too expensive to leave all the lights on for a week after you play it.

This is one disturbing game. While other survival horror games make you jump, the hero usually comes packing a shotgun, which means that you rarely feel too threatened. In contrast, *Silent Hill* makes you feel almost physically as well as spiritually naked. This would be the game that *Resident Evil*'s monsters would play when they were of a mind to spook themselves.

The lighting plays a big role. Most of the time you can only see as far as your weakly powered flashlight allows, and using it creates more lurking shadows. (You can't even access the game's cheery tourist-style maps if the light's too bad.) Then there's the noise of scuttling beasts in the darkness, and the radio that emits static when monsters are nearby; a warning sign, but hardly a reassuring one. Your character, Harry, is physically frail (he pants for breath after running) and his ineptitude with weapons increases the sense of vulnerability.

The game environments are disturbing too, playing on residual fears of disease and death with old hospitals, abandoned wheelchairs, and a deranged nurse who inhabits both this world and its hellish flip side, known as the Otherworld. The plot pulling it all together is somewhat silly and overcooked, but it's a testament to the sense of loneliness the game induces that you'll actually feel sorry for the characters who have to live on in *Silent Hill* when you turn off the PlayStation and go outside for some fresh air and sunlight. **OB**

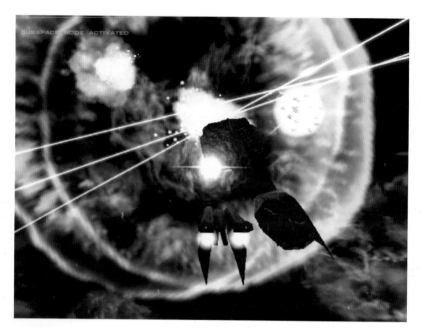

Freespace 2

Original release date : 1999
Platform : PC
Developer : Volition, Inc
Genre : Shoot 'Em Up

The subgenre of the "fantasy simulator" was once a quiet mainstay of the PC gaming scene, with numerous titles that approached science-fiction situations with the seriousness of intent associated with simulating real-world events. While its roots stretch back into the '80s and were more formalized with Origin's *Wing Commander* games, it only grew to full adulthood with LucasArts's *Star Wars: X-Wing*. It wasn't just fighting dogfights as you would in 1983's *Star Wars* arcade machine, it was controlling a "real" fighter, complete with throttle and shield controls. It was a genre about treating your fantasy worlds as if they were real, thereby allowing you to immerse yourself into them with sometimes alarming sincerity.

It was a niche whose development ground to a halt with the release of *Freespace 2*, which was rapturously reviewed and commercially ignored. Everything since has either stepped back toward being a plain arcade-style game or an attempt to recreate the freeform space-trading of *Elite*. To return to *Freespace 2* shows what we lost. It's a clear predecessor in tone to the reboot of *Battlestar Galactica* and the darker science-fiction of the *Mass Effect* games, putting you firmly in the middle of a genuinely epic intergalactic war. The key concept is scale. Battleships seem to fill the vacuum, exchanging supernova-bright laser beams, creating an undeniable spectacle.

In 1999 no one had seen anything like it, and no one has seen anything like it since. A sign of the depth of the game's influence lies in its still-existent playing community, who've been working on the source code since it was released to the public in 2002, keeping it up-to-date with the march of technology and, via modifications, bringing their favored science-fiction worlds to brilliant life. **KG**

Seifer
"Come out'n show your faces!
Don't leave me hangin' now!"

Final Fantasy VIII

Original release date: 1999
Platform: PS1
Developer: Square
Genre: Role-Playing

What do you do when you've just made the world's most successful RPG? Why, you make a sequel that has nothing to do with it, and then try out a new visual style for good measure. Such was the context for *Final Fantasy VIII*, which from the first released screenshots was subject to all sorts of criticism in Japan for its move toward more humanoid characters. Not only that, it had the temerity to be the most complex series entry yet, shifting focus from the ragtag army of *Final Fantasy VII* to a mere six characters and encouraging the player to craft the team they desired from a huge number of options. The basics are the same as ever—turn-based battling, leveling up, and traveling from place to place in a vast world—but on top of this is a

daunting web of skill trees and combat choices, far beyond *Final Fantasy VII*'s Materia system.

Final Fantasy VIII is also an epic story cramming in as much full-motion video as possible, following Square's rigid approach with its *Final Fantasy* series. All the emotional high points and even basic plot points are there for the player to look at rather than touch. It's hardly a ruinous quality, but it does represent rather a dead-end for the narrative possibilities of the medium.

Nevertheless, *Final Fantasy VIII*'s production values are such that it's one of the few PlayStation titles to stand up today. Square's secret isn't the performance it eked from Sony's aging machine, but the beautifully vivid world it created using it: universities with glass-blown arches and vast gardens, cherry blossoms cascading onto leather jackets, and space-age technology servicing atavistic ends. The story of Squall, Seifer, and Rinoa is a long and winding one with plenty of digressions—just how the game turns out, funnily enough. **RS**

Jet Force Gemini

Original release date : 1999
Platform : N64
Developer : Rare
Genre : Action

Despite Rare's legendary technical mastery of Nintendo systems, which gave us some of the best-looking games of their era, nobody would deny that the developer's art direction and character design can be a bit hit and miss. For every likeable Banjo the Bear there's a wild-eyed, staring Tiptup the Turtle; for every garden full of almost edible, lovable piñata animals, there's a bland, Vaseline-coated nightmare like *Perfect Dark Zero*. *Jet Force Gemini* is one of the developer's real artistic triumphs, set in a strangely gorgeous, abstract, and mature sci-fi universe painted largely in purple, green, and blue.

Splitting the action between run-and-gunners Juno, Vela, and their armored dog, Lupus, *Jet Force Gemini* borrows from the third-person shooter, platformer, and occasionally the first-person shooter, commanding all three genres with skill and obvious experience. The three threads of the story are eventually woven into one, leaving the player to explore each level with every character to reach previously inaccessible treasures.

That Rare humor is there, too: The two main players in the universe are called King Jeff and evil Prince Barry, and Rare's unofficial mascot, Mr. Pants, is hidden tastefully on a hard-to-find wall in one of Juno's levels.

Unfortunately, *Jet Force Gemini* is hampered by a genuinely terrible endgame. It is late-'90s kleptomaniacism of the worst kind, forcing the player to collect far too many spaceship parts and rescue every single one of the cuddly Tribal natives hidden within the level before allowing any progress to be made—a task made especially arduous by the fact that a stray laser blast could accidentally murder the cute little fellas. But such faults can be forgiven on the strength of what comes before. **KM**

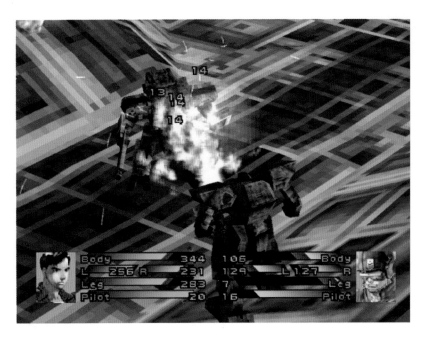

Front Mission 3

Original release date : 1999
Platform : PS1
Developer : Square
Genre : Strategy

The *Front Mission* series takes a genre that Japan has made its own and ties it to a Japanese-invented future technology. It's a turn-based strategy game, in which big bipedal robots duke it out across mostly urban environments, overlaid with grids that show you how far you can fire and move.

Front Mission 3 was the first game in the then-five-year-old series to get an English-language release, and if you can manage to stop sniggering at the decision to call the giant robots "wanzers" (taken from "*wanderung Panzer*", the German phrase for "walking tank"), you'll find a staggering amount of tactical strategy here to sink your teeth into. In keeping with all of the games in the *Front Mission* series,

that strategy is enveloped within a complicated storyline featuring the fractured politics of militaristic and futuristic nations vying for supremacy.

Set in 2112, *Front Mission 3* depicts events as a lowly test pilot gets caught up in a national conspiracy and a branching campaign that recounts events from both sides of the story. A fictional e-mail system and websites that prefigured games like *Grand Theft Auto IV* and *.hack* allow players to unlock various secrets while learning more about the fictional world in which the game is set.

Beyond the Byzantine diplomacy and richly imagined game world, however, part of the pleasure is in fiddling with your wanzer's parts: tailoring the payload and optimizing its construction before missions by fitting legs, arms, body, shoulder weapons, backpacks, and so on. But the main thing is the battles themselves, in which your newly decked-out behemoths blast the enemy's wanzers, destroying them entirely or simply disabling their weapons and forcing them to surrender. **DM**

EverQuest

Original release date : 1999
Platform : PC
Developer : Sony Online Entertainment
Genre : MMORPG

In the 1990s, role-playing games already had a solid and devoted fan base, with opportunities to imagine great fantasy worlds while acting out the life and times of any class, race, or even sex of choice. By late in the century, multi-user games of increasingly cutting-edge visuals were braving the fledgling Internet. It wasn't until the arrival of *EverQuest*, however, that the entire experience of online role-playing was elevated and thrust into the true 3-D age.

Requiring a quick, consistent Internet connection and an expensive 3-D graphics card, *EverQuest* occupied a niche of a niche in 1999. But such technology is used to its full potential, the classic fantasy world of Norrath coming to life in a way that captured gamers' imaginations and kept them coming back for more … and more … and more for a surprisingly long time.

Oh, sure, the svelte elves aren't outfitted to survive sprawling plains, mountains, and cavernous dungeons, but hell if they don't lure leering players to unload a few precious gold pieces to aid a fawning damsel in undress. Or you can take on a noble paladin role, vanquishing this and dispelling that; or skulk with the rogues; or cast with the mages; or so many other options that the world experience appears endless. You explore, learn trades and skills, as well as languages and even a whole new shorthand vocabulary (including the oh-so-appropriate moniker, EverCrack).

No doubt building a world and game mechanic from scratch brings attendant teething problems, imbalances, and even straight-up breakages, but between the zone exploration, the ambition, and opportunity for socializing with fellow gamers, the overall experience compels any RPG fan to commit for a long, long haul. **RSm**

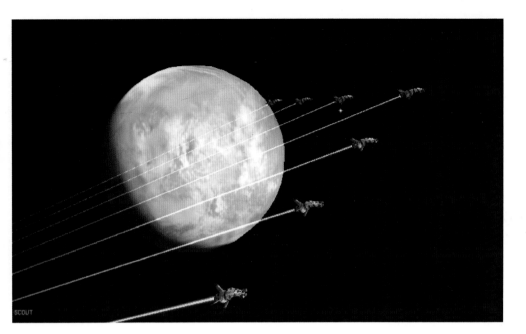

SCOUT

Homeworld

Original release date : 1999
Platform : PC, Mac
Developer : Relic Entertainment
Genre : Strategy

Homeworld occupies a unique position in the PC canon. Rarely has a game—let alone a studio's debut—unified innovations in game play, storytelling, graphics, and even music, to create such a compellingly playable package.

The big idea was to send the point-and-click mechanics of a real-time strategy into orbit—and the outcome is as initially daunting to play as it surely was to develop. Stripped of the familiar 2-D baseline of terra firma, you attack and defend from any direction, feeling your brain expand as you grasp the basics of three-dimensional tactics. It's not just that the battleground has expanded in volume. Without an earthly landscape of rivers, hills, and ruins, the clashes are all about the fleet's ships and their

position, down to the arc of fire of a particular turret. Think naval warfare, only with frigates that can fly and dive.

Players who master the initially daunting game play are rewarded with a brilliantly structured storyline where action and plot dovetail as in a great movie. Combined with traditional genre mechanics of extraction, construction, and researching new technologies, Homeworld feels far more personal than the typical rape-and-pillage RTS .

It also looks just as good as it plays. Without all that mud and mountain to draw, the engine can be devoted to ships and special effects to create scenes from a space opera that were unmatched for years to follow. The New Age soundtrack backs up this unearthly action perfectly.

Few games can boast equally excellent single- and multiplayer modes, but Homeworld's online play was strong enough to attract thousands of players in the early days of broadband. Even after official online support was discontinued, die-hards have continued to explore this uniquely different RTS. **OB**

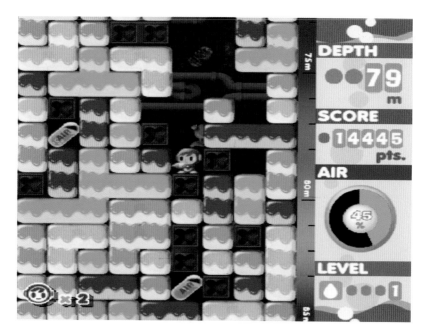

Mr. Driller

Original release date : 1999
Platform : Various
Developer : Namco Bandai
Genre : Puzzle

If *Mr. Driller* wasn't quite so colorful, cute, and friendly, it would be hard to avoid the realization that this is basically a game that revolves around the quite morbid and nasty concept of being buried alive; a game about fighting for every last breath as your air runs out.

It certainly doesn't feel like it, though. The game's relentless descent as you forge ever deeper into the ground might bring a slight twinge of claustrophobia to some of the more sensitive players out there, and, undeniably, a certain kind of panic inevitably sets in when your oxygen meter starts to run perilously low. But such murky horrors are masterfully undermined by the art department on a regular basis as you blast through layer upon layer of what looks like syrup, icing, custard, and sorbet. *Mr. Driller* might freak you out if you're the sort of person who prefers to take the stairs rather than the elevator, then, but it's probably the players on diets who should really watch out.

A race to get as deep underground as possible, *Mr. Driller* is effortlessly simple and addictive, each new game inching you a little bit closer to your goal as you duck falling debris and cut your way through the puzzly shapes a little more efficiently than the time before. Over the years, Namco Bandai's unlikely mascot has seen himself ported to almost every console and platform under the sun, and from the chirpy delights of this first outing, it's not at all hard to see why.

It almost never came to be, however. Originally created unofficially, development was suspended amid higher priority projects. Eventually the game, known then as *Dig Dug 3*, won through with its charm and innovation, and a miniature (and renamed) classic was born. **CD**

SNK vs. Capcom: Card Fighters' Clash

Original release date : 1999

Platform : Neo Geo Pocket Color

Developer : SNK

Genre : Strategy

The Neo Geo Pocket Color is as cult as a game system can get, and with good reason. Despite being released at exactly the wrong time—directly before manufacturer SNK was purchased by Aruze, and drastically remodeled—the system was streets ahead of the contemporary Game Boy Color. Although only eighty-five games were released for the system, no more than a handful were anything less than very fine indeed.

The crowning achievement of the Neo Geo Pocket Color system is undoubtedly the *SNK vs. Capcom* titles, with *SNK vs. Capcom: Card Fighters' Clash* being one of the earliest video game representations of the collectible card game (CCG) popularized in the 1990s by Magic: The Gathering. It's also one of the most successful because, rather than try to replicate the complex and lengthy rules of a physical CCG, it takes its cue from the Pokémon series and has the player on a quest to be the best card fighter around by winning tournaments and playing pick-up games, via a simple RPG where frequent card battles allow you to win new cards and fine-tune your deck.

The rules of the core card game are simplistic: Players have up to three cards to use to attack, defend, or perform special attacks. It is imperfectly implemented (certain cards are far more powerful than others), but battles remain captivating thanks to the amazing range of cards, with characters from both SNK and Capcom represented through gorgeous "superdeformed" artwork.

Due to the quick length of card battles, it's perfectly designed as a pick-up-and-play title, and arguably the only NGPC game more essential is its sequel, which was never released outside of Japan—though a fan translation can be found by the dedicated. **MKu**

Mario Golf

Original release date : 1999
Platform : Game Boy Color
Developer : Camelot Software Planning
Genre : Sports

As Mario's unlikely shadow career as the world's most versatile sportsman evolved with the gloriously playable *Mario Kart* games, golf was perhaps the most likely candidate for further expansion. The rolling hills of the Mushroom Kingdom would be an ideal location to sink a few holes. Golf games already had an established formula to riff on—Nintendo had already made a couple of stand-out entries—and Mario's crazy cast of friends and enemies would probably look delightful in plaid slacks, polo shirts, and funny little hats.

Who knew it would turn out as well as this, however? Camelot's game has (exceedingly light) elements of an RPG as you explore the local clubhouse, learning the ropes, setting up matches, and making friends, but it's also a smart, calculated golf sim for one or more players. It may be easy to play but *Mario Golf* is filled with variables that affect play, as well as charming, rich details, such as a suite of brilliantly structured courses; nice physics and ball effects; and a lovely, comprehensive leaderboard made for keeping track of your best shots and bragging about them to your friends. Visual and aural feedback is absolutely great too, as you might expect, and the whole thing basks in the warm glow of the *Mario* universe—even though you spend rather a large part of the game unlocking a range of characters who aren't the famous plumber.

Some of Mario's later excursions into sports have seemed a little tired at times as the branding, special moves, and general gimmickry became increasingly desperate and shrill, but here, on the Game Boy Color, the whole thing meshes perfectly together, and Mario is as at home on the emerald greens with a putter and sand wedge as he is dressed as a racoon and soaring over a gaggle of Koopa Troopas. **CD**

Outcast

Original release date : 1999
Platform : PC
Developer : Appeal
Genre : Action / Adventure

Outcast is another fallen soldier in the pantheon of excellent games that flopped on release. In this case the failure was sufficient to eventually bankrupt its developer, which ran out of money before it could finish the sequel. Chalk another one up to the great video game-buying public's lack of discernment? Not quite. *Outcast*'s main problem was of its own making.

The developer employed a technically brilliant software rendering engine instead of relying on the 3-D hardware acceleration that was just coming into its own. The payoff was the beautifully realized world of Adelpha, with its undulating hills, villages teeming with alien citizens, and visuals festooned with bloom effects, lens flare, translucent and reflective water, and much more that was impossible in concert on the 3-D cards of the day.

The downside was that you needed to have bought a new PC with a top-of-the-line Intel processor in the past month or two to run the thing. Those who hadn't couldn't confidently buy it. Given that PC games had about six weeks to prove themselves, the game was doomed.

Ironically, if you try to run *Outcast* on a modern PC, you'll need patches to slow it down, which means even today few people experience this engrossing adventure. As former US Navy Seal Cutter Slade, you travel to a parallel universe as an escort for three scientists, only to become separated and drawn into the ongoing civil war of the Talan—humanoid creatures with manifest spirits (called "essences") that shape their talents and their culture.

Outcast's cities bustle with life, the AI is fantastic for its vintage, the flora and fauna plausible, and the weapons are to die for. Well worth the effort, both for the doomed developer and for anyone who samples its creation. **OB**

Planescape: Torment

Original release date : 1999

Platform : PC

Developer : Black Isle Studios

Genre : Role-Playing

Planescape: Torment was created using BioWare's Infinity engine, and presents a drama that, though epic, is fundamentally human in scale. Quite an achievement when you consider that the game straddles entire dimensions as it follows its heavily tattooed, blue-skinned, amnesiac, immortal, and sometimes amoral protagonist. This Nameless One—his quest being for identity and understanding—is the entire point of the game. He is the focus of a much more intimate portrait of humanity than the simple conflict-resolution of other RPGs.

If he dies during the course of the game, he is simply sent back to a slab in the mortuary with no further consequence other than the sacrifice of another being

from the multiverse to sustain his unnatural lifespan—although their return to haunt him provides a very poignant reminder that this is a game in which every choice might have unexpected consequence. But the immortality of its protagonist is more than just an inspired piece of game design on which to hang a fiendishly clever quest structure. It is also an inspired narrative element, used to pose provocative questions about how life should be lived. *Planescape: Torment* confronted the player with moral choices well before it was fashionable to do so in gaming.

It is also full of wit and invention, from the magical tattoos that power up the Nameless One, to the creative interpretation of the normally half-redundant alignment system. Evocatively named locations, like the Fortress of Regrets, house remarkable sights and sounds, such as the Nameless One's sidekicks: talking skulls, succubi, pyromaniacs, and even a stranded fragment of a hive mind—a perfect metaphor for how this most cerebral of games defied convention and refused to follow the crowd. **DM**

Quake III Arena

Original release date : 1999
Platform : PC, Mac
Developer : id Software
Genre : First-Person Shooter

Nothing says "I killed you" like the rail gun in *Quake III Arena*. Introduced in *Quake II*, this weapon takes a long time to charge and then spends it all with a single shot, drawing a perfect line from the barrel to the center of the crosshair. If there's a body in the way, it explodes, and a smug little icon appears on the HUD. Two bodies: too bad for them. Of course, everyone else knows exactly where the user is and that their weapon's now empty, but it's a small price to pay for such a show of perfection.

It's also one of several reasons why the game is such a mainstay of the professional multiplayer scene. Happy to be the one minimalist, geeky (typical map name: Q3dm17), exclusively hardcore shooter left in the world, it's also one

of the most balanced. Responsible for grooming e-sports thoroughbreds like Jonathan "Fatal1ty" Wendel and John "Zero4" Hill, it promotes frightening levels of expertise and has, over a decade, rewarded them with lucrative prize tournaments.

Not just a perfectionist's game, then, but a game demanding perfection. Touted as the ultimate refinement of the death match, it must be the only sequel to dump its predecessor's single-player mode and even then keep its multiplayer largely unchanged. Beyond some famously efficient netcode, its biggest advance is its engine, one of the first to usher in complex, rounded environments and immensely popular among games of the time, going on to power several classic RPG series.

And the refinement continues. Having returned with even subtler upgrades in *Quake IV*, these classic modes and weapons are the cornerstones of *Quake Live*, the free-to-play browser-based version which, as ever, focuses purely on the game play. **DH**

Rocket: Robot on Wheels

Original release date : 1999
Platform : N64
Developer : Sucker Punch Productions
Genre : Action / Platform

Rocket: Robot on Wheels is not the only game to have sunk without trace in the vast sea of 3-D platformers around the turn of the century. It works clever physics-based puzzling into the usual template of large, colorful, collectible-filled worlds adjoining a central hub. It displays inventiveness in the sheer quality and variety of its challenges, but lacks the cartoonish visual flair of, say, *Banjo-Kazooie*.

Playing a uni-wheeled maintenance robot in a theme park gone wrong, the idea is to collect enough tickets and machine parts to get things up and running again. As more and more of the theme park is restored, rides and giant machines gradually open up to interact with. The fairground theme allows for some cute little mini-

games to show off the game's physics engine: throwing balls to knock colored cats off shelves, playing tic-tac-toe with a chicken, lobbing things into targets. Building your own roller coaster—and then riding it, in first person—is far more ambitious than what most platformers of the day were shooting for.

There's the usual steadily expanding arsenal of abilities, bought with liberally scattered trinkets. Rocket's tractor beam can grab and grapple objects and enemies in puzzles, which gives the game its unique feel, rather than the setting or more traditional platforming. It has ideas that are ahead of its time, such as hauling blocks around to make stepping stones and ladders, for instance, and a generous helping of vehicle challenges.

Rocket: Robot on Wheels is a technically excellent, energetic platformer, but oddly it lacks the personality and spark of later Sucker Punch games. Nonetheless, it deserves to be more than a curiosity. With more of a marketing push it might have been one of the N64's real successes. **KS**

Samba de Amigo

Original release date : 1999
Platform : Arcade, Dreamcast
Developer : Sega
Genre : Music

While gaming remains in the midst of an epidemic of peripherals—plastic guitars, drum kits, skateboards, and DJ turntables—it's worth remembering that this trend first showed its head back in the glory days of Sega's ill-starred Dreamcast console. Back then, the whole thing was a little more unpredictable and lovable: bass fishing games gave us rods and reels that could also be used for *Soul Calibur* matches, endless on-rails shooters dished out elaborate weaponry, and the fun-loving *Samba de Amigo* created a game that was controlled entirely with a pair of maracas.

The result is one of the most joyful games in Sega's extensive and cheery catalog, a classic, primary-color rhythm-action title that unfolds hilariously as you guide

Amigo through a suite of classic—and frankly not-so-classic—Latin standards by shaking high, low, and in the middle of the screen in time with the pumping, shimmying music. It's exhausting, but when played in a party atmosphere, it's also utterly brilliant. *Samba de Amigo* is a shyness-shattering smart-bomb capable of getting even the most nervous of performers to make glorious fools of themselves in front of their friends.

Samba de Amigo turned up again in a few other games over the years due to Sega's love of the back-catalog cameo, and the original title was remade for the Wii by FPS specialist Gearbox (the studio is home to long-term fans of the game, making it something of a labor of love), but Nintendo's Remotes are not precise enough to make the experience entirely workable (and, besides, they aren't maracas). All of which means that the original version is also the best: a rare synergy of game and hardware that cannot help but raise a smile. Track it down on eBay before inviting some friends over. **CD**

Shenmue

Original release date : 1999
Platform : Dreamcast
Developer : Sega
Genre : Action / Adventure

For better or worse, *Shenmue*'s most prominent legacy is probably the Quick Time Event. Is there any big-budget action video game today that doesn't feature one? But *Shenmue* broke so much new ground, it's difficult to know where to begin. Perhaps with Yu Suzuki's decision to create an RPG to be released on the Sega Saturn. Somehow, during its convoluted development, it morphed into the groundbreaking notion of an RPG set in the real world, and was released on the Saturn's successor, the Dreamcast.

It took some of the most cutting-edge currents in gaming and created many of its own: the day/night cycle and variable weather (based on actual weather records); vending machines and convenience stores that dispense all sorts of in-game power-ups and collectable geegaws, from dried squid to *Sonic the Hedgehog* key fobs; copies of real-world coin-op cabinets that house entire games such as *Space Harrier*; a multitude of mini-games, from playing darts to racing forklift trucks; the chance to trade items and compare scores over the Internet; and the winding roads and small parks of a convincingly realistic Yokosuka.

Now that our eyes have been spoiled by the polygonal perfection of today's software, it is impossible to convey how closely these crude and blocky approximations approached reality. *Shenmue* recreated the real world with a graphical verisimilitude that has since been eclipsed, but contains an attention to detail that has never been rivaled. It was all too easy to find yourself overawed by modern technology, amazed that a game could contain so much. If that sounds strange now, it is a measure of *Shenmue*'s paradigmatic impact on the entire video game industry and the alluring depths of Ryo Hazuki and his strangely unhurried quest to avenge his father's murder. **DM**

Seaman

Original release date : 1999
Platform : Dreamcast
Developer : Vivarium
Genre : Life Simulation

As Microsoft seeks to usher in a new era of interaction via the speech-recognition capabilities of its Xbox 360 peripheral, Natal, it's easy to forget that Sega pioneered the technology at the beginning of the new millennium. Its approach was to give players a fairly grotesque fish with a man's face to converse with, one who was eager to discuss everything from politics to reproduction to the relative merits of gangster rap.

In terms of its systems, *Seaman* works a little like a Tamagotchi, a virtual pet for you to nurture and care for from gurgling infancy as a tadpole right through to cynical middle age. The *Seaman* experience is measured in days and weeks, not hours. To begin with, you merely interact with the temperature and air quality of the water tank, until the egg inside hatches to release a clutch of molecular creatures. Eventually, after another couple of stages of evolution, the formative Seaman begins to create syllables of speech and, as you interact with him via the bundled microphone attachment, starts to form commands and sentences, with every stage of progression detailed and explained by Leonard Nimoy's voiceover.

As the experience progresses, you raise insects with which to feed your Seaman, but the Tamagotchi element of the game always plays second fiddle to the conversations it facilitates. While not without its foibles, the speech recognition is enormously impressive and, through your conversations, the illusion that your Seaman is gaining intelligence and understanding about your tastes is maintained. Best played in short bursts, to avoid ennui or repetition, *Seaman* ably demonstrates the wonders and limitations of nurturing a virtual conversationalist. For that, it is to be celebrated, if not mimicked. **SP**

The Longest Journey

Original release date : 1999
Platform : PC
Developer : Funcom
Genre : Adventure

The Longest Journey throws players into the deep end immediately. The scene opens, and an old woman tells two peasants in funny hats about "the Balance." A girl in her underwear dreams of standing on a precipice, haggling with a tree to save a dragon's egg. The dream ends, we find that we're in the future, and nobody tells us what's changed. But we do know that we've met our star, April Ryan, and that she'll keep a level head and snarky wit no matter how fantastical the journey.

The Longest Journey marked the end of an era: it's the last of the great, brain-busting graphic adventure games, a genre thought dead until Telltale Games and the casual space resurrected it in a simpler, more accessible form. The challenges that players will noodle through are considerable, but the story that rewards them is worth all the sweat (or cheating): *The Longest Journey* is the first in a planned trilogy set in a sci-fi/fantasy fusion dreamed up by Ragnar Tørnquist, who swears he'll finish the story even if he has to resort to pen and paper to do it.

April Ryan is a starving student in the hip neighborhood of Newport. But we come to find out that she's also a Shifter, charged with maintaining the balance between the world of technology and its magical counterpart. Tørnquist isn't the first to mix magic and science fiction, but his particular vision is dark, contemporary, and full of memorable characters. He and his team deserve praise for making a world that's edgy and contemporary, but still charming; April and her Newport pals use adult language and have adult conflicts, but one of her sidekicks is a talking crow. This mix of charm and despair propelled the game to a sequel, *Dreamfall*—a simpler and less satisfying experience, but one you'll be impelled to play, just to see what happens next. **CDa**

...eption with a game of cups? There are prizes to be won...

Space Channel 5

Original release date : 1999
Platform : Dreamcast
Developer : United Game Artists
Genre : Music

Space Channel 5 is another of those games (see: *Dead Rising*) perhaps better described in court. In an action that would ultimately cost her more than $600,000 in her opponent's legal fees, Lady Miss Kier, singer of '90s retro-funk band Deee-Lite, accused Sega of stealing her image to craft Ulala, a ditzy Barbarella type with smooth moves, fabulous outfits, and a penchant for making other people jive. Both personas wore pink hair, platform boots, knee socks, miniskirts and distinctive makeup, and appeared in works depicting "vivid graphics, groovy dance moves, a futuristic setting and an overall party feel."

Protected by the First Amendment, Sega won the case.

"female casual" market, *Space Channel 5* introduces Ulala as an outer space news reporter armed with two ray guns and a microphone. The guns fire "groove energy," which is useful when a race of diminutive aliens, the Morolians, invade the galaxy and start making everyone dance—badly. Rather than control Ulala, players have to follow her directions to keep the party going, using direction controls to copy her moves and press buttons to shoot. Do well, and Ulala's troupe gets bigger; don't, and it gives up.

With nothing to fall back on but Simple Simon Says, Ulala's numbers throw it all at the screen and speakers. The soundtrack is as uplifting as they come, using Ken Woodman's "The Mexican Flyer" as a launchpad before blasting off into joyous instrumentals. Its sets and characters take that famous Sega palette—something the Dreamcast hardware seemed designed to reproduce—back to the '60s for a kitsch makeover. And, as for its queen of the galaxy, she makes you wonder if the plaintiff had a

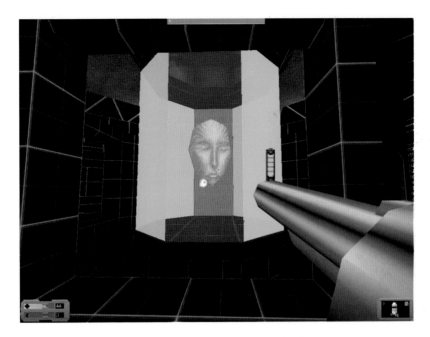

System Shock 2

Original release date : 1999
Platform : PC
Developer : Electronic Arts
Genre : First-Person Shooter

They don't want to hurt you, the twisted freaks that rush at you aboard the deserted spaceship *Von Braun*, but their will is no longer their own. Their bodies have been hijacked by a malevolent alien life-form called the Many, and they retain only enough of themselves to be horrified by what they see themselves doing. So they wail, "I'm sorry!" They beg you to kill them. And they're just about the only company you have in the whole dismal place.

System Shock 2 pushes a lot of the player's buttons, not least in the suffocating sense of isolation it imposes. You awaken on the abandoned ship with no friends and no hope, surrounded by ghouls and a trigger-happy automated security system. When a lone voice comes across your radio, asking for help, you give it unquestioningly, for the human connection if nothing else. This is a theme that *System Shock 2* designer Ken Levine would revisit in *BioShock*, and the reveal in this game is no less shocking—just less famous.

System Shock 2 purposely hobbles the player. Prior to the action, you can choose to play as one of three classes of character: the resilient soldier, who's only good with guns; the hacker, who can reprogram the ship's security systems for his own ends; and the psychic, whose telekinetic abilities can be devastating if used correctly. Each has his usefulness, though you'll more often find that each has critical weaknesses. Weapons and equipment break down as you use them, which leads to one quandary after another: Should you use your most powerful weapon now and risk being without it later, or try to find a less obvious solution? It can get a little complicated, but the result is a highly influential FPS horror game—unrelenting, unforgiving, and unforgettable. **MK**

Faselei!

Original release date : 1999
Platform : Neo Geo Pocket Color
Developer : Sacnoth
Genre : Strategy / Role-Playing

Released mere weeks before the untimely demise of SNK's outstanding Neo Geo Pocket Color handheld, very few copies of *Faselei!* actually reached the shops. As a result, this military-themed strategy RPG is one of the most collectible titles for the system, its value compounded by scarcity and, perhaps more important, quality.

Drawing some inspiration from Square's *Front Mission* series, *Faselei!* gives its player control of a handful of mechanized soldiers, the hulking bipedal combat mecha familiar to any fan of Japanese esoterica. These Toy Soldiers, as the game colloquially refers to them, must be maneuvered around a gridded, chesslike environment as you work to take down enemy military squadrons.

The game's unique feature is in charging players with anticipating enemy moves by programming their units before each turn. Each mecha has a limited number of command chips that can be taken into a match, such as "walk forward," "turn left," "turn right," "fire primary weapon," and so on. The command chips you take into each battle must be chosen beforehand, meaning that you have to balance offensive and defensive options carefully, ensuring that you will be able to move and attack in the desired ways. Want the ability to fire a secondary or tertiary weapon? Then you may need to do so at the expense of being able to move backward.

Since each unit can be equipped with diverse and unique additions on top of their programmable chips, the game provides generous scope for customization, a crucial component in making the player feel as though their choices are meaningful in any SRPG (strategy role-playing game). A unique, inspired take on a classic genre, *Faselei!* is well worth the considerable effort it may take to hunt down a copy. **SP**

Threads of Fate

Original release date : 1999
Platform : PS1
Developer : Square
Genre : Action / Role-Playing

Threads of Fate has the distinction of being perhaps the only video game to be renamed for English-speaking audiences because its original Japanese title, *Dew Prism*, sounded anti-Semitic (try saying it aloud). A bright, colorful game, there are few dark themes in this, Square's most gentle-hearted action-RPG of the PlayStation era. Its story is told through the intertwining lives of two young protagonists, Rue and Mint, whose distinct personalities and abilities provide the necessary friction for both the game's mechanics and storyline.

Rue's strength is primarily channeled down the shaft of his ax, but it's in his ability to assume the form and traits of defeated foes that the game's designers drew keenest inspiration for *Threads of Fate*'s puzzles. Choosing the most appropriate form to overcome an obstacle or greater foe constitutes the basis for most of the game's distinct challenges. By contrast, when playing as the treasure-obsessed princess, Mint, you can interact with the world by manipulating her twin hoop weapons and choosing from a selection of spells.

The visuals play to the PlayStation's strengths and, released late into the system's life, Square uses color and stylization to great effect, making this one of the best-looking titles of its time. The platforming and combat work in concert through the game's exquisite 3-D environments, and while the journey can feel almost roller coaster-esque in the carefully considered use of camera direction, it's one worth taking. Indeed, the manner in which the storyline carefully entangles the threads of its protagonists' separate journeys is masterfully handled, and the joyful tone and humor that peppers the broader narrative make this one of Square's best stories, one that delights in the telling as much as the tale. **SP**

ISS Pro Evolution

Original release date : 1999
Platform : PS1
Developer : Konami
Genre : Sports

Until the release of *ISS Pro Evolution* in 1999, the history of football games at Konami was tangled and complex. Early home system efforts led to the development of the *International Superstar Soccer* series for the SNES at Konami's Osaka studio, KCEO. *ISS*, as it was known, first appeared in 1994 as a like-for-like competitor to Electronic Arts' *FIFA Football*, and was built on a similar combination of accessibility and fast-paced arcade action.

While *ISS* was a success, Konami's second series not only eclipsed its previous effort but went on to set the standard for football games for a decade and more. A year after the release of *ISS*, Konami instructed its Tokyo studio, KCET, to develop what became *Winning Eleven*. The intention was to offer a more realistic experience than its sister game, more concerned with tactics and passing than crowd-pleasing spectacle.

For Western gamers, it took some time for the difference to become obvious. While the two series ran side-by-side in Japan (as *Jikkyou World Soccer* and *Winning Eleven*), in the UK they were marketed as confusing crossbreeds, with *Winning Eleven* games branded as "Pro" versions of their *ISS* counterparts. Even so, by the time *Winning Eleven 4* arrived on UK PlayStations as *ISS Pro Evolution*, KCET's more measured and challenging game was so superior to everything else on the market that gamers responded by dropping the "ISS" and referring to the game simply as "Pro Evo," a change Konami would later make official. In addition to the crisp tactical game play (one-two passing, faked shot cutbacks) that set the series apart, the game features the first appearance of the Master League manager mode, a triumphant time sink of transfer windows and team-building that ensured *ISS Pro Evolution* remained in a different league to its competitors. **ND**

Vib-Ribbon

Original release date : 1999
Platform : PS1
Developer : NanaOn-Sha
Genre : Music

Vib-Ribbon proves that less is more, coaxing a staggering amount of character out of a handful of skittish white vectors on a black backdrop. It manages to take the simplest of mechanics and spins them into a game that feels incredibly immediate and intense. Sony's game is tiny (so small, in fact, that it can be loaded in its entirety into the original PlayStation's miniscule onboard memory in one go), but it's a title you'll play again and again, an aging classic that you'd be wise to ensure is always within reach of your control pad.

The game is simple: *Vib-Ribbon* comes with a number of songs, all of which translate into basic assault courses for Vibri, the game's rabbit hero, to navigate. Each kind of obstacle, generated from the music track itself, is overcome with a press of one of the controller's buttons. Simply put, *Vib-Ribbon* is a test of recognition and reflex skills—and one that gets distinctly tricky as obstacles start to blend two different kinds of attack. You suddenly realize that you really must learn your control mappings.

It's much more entertaining than it may sound, and the real brilliance kicks in when you realize you can remove the original disk and insert your own CDs. A world of possibility opens up with the ability to sculpt courses from pop classics, blues standards, and even—although the results always turn out to be rather weird—classical music. If you're after a challenge, try hard rock.

Subsequent games tried to take *Vib-Ribbon*'s strange charms and apply them to other art forms, but the results have never been as coherent and delightful as they are here, and their presentation never quite as ingeniously understated. An underground classic with a genuine mainstream appeal, *Vib-Ribbon* is so slight, and so utterly perfect, that it could well prove to be timeless. **CD**

Team Fortress Classic

Original release date : 1999
Platform : PC
Developer : Valve Corporation
Genre : First-Person Shooter

Every legend begins somewhere, and before *Team Fortress 2* there was *Team Fortress Classic*. The game began its life in 1996 as a modification for id Software's *Quake*, but John Cook and Robin Walker's design finally felt at home as part of the fledgling Valve Software empire. In a quirk of history, *Team Fortress 2* was actually in development before *Team Fortress Classic*, but in the process of making development tools for *Half-Life* mod-makers, Valve chose to test its tools by making *Team Fortress Classic* entirely within them.

As in its better-known sequel, *Team Fortress Classic* pits two teams against each other in a battle to capture the flag, control territory, or escort an objective (in this case a very vulnerable VIP). Each team has a range of classes—

scout, sniper, soldier, heavy weapons guy, demo man, medic, pyro, spy, and engineer—and each of these has at least one unique weapon.

It's here that *Team Fortress*'s most iconic level, the capture-the-flag-based 2fort, made its mark. With two mirror-image bases facing each other and separated by a moat, it presented clearly all of the potential of team-based multiplayer. Multiple entrances to each fort are suited to different classes and tactics, and, by being heavily weighted toward defense, the level required incredible team coordination to pull off a win.

As a modification—and one without the eight-year development process—*Team Fortress Classic* is less tight in both design and play than its sequel, with classes featuring redundant weapons and less finely tuned differences. But to many it remains supreme—so much so that dedicated fans have remade it using *Half-Life 2*'s engine with the name of *Fortress Forever*. To this day it remains one of the ten most-played *Half-Life* mods of all time. **MKu**

The Typing of the Dead

Original release date : 1999
Platform : Various
Developer : WOW / Smilebit
Genre : Action / Edutainment

The House of the Dead is, of course, Sega's visceral, bloody, light gun horror series. Hammy voices and superbly stilted dialogue sustain the B-movie atmosphere as you frantically pepper the screen to survive Sega's relentless zombie slaughterhouse. Who'd have thought that one of the franchise's most successful and memorable entries would consist of watching gobs of undead flesh and blood spatter across the screen while you blow apart the shambling hordes of zombies by typing out random words and phrases on a keyboard?

And they really are random: "I'm dating the head cheerleader," you might type while playing The Typing of the Dead, before digressing into an extended discourse on

health and safety measures or financial prudence. At times these phrases are thought-provoking—"Don't blame yourself" ("For what?" you might think before casually reducing another reanimated corpse to a pile of blood and guts with your rapid-fire sixty-words-per-minute delivery). Most of the time they're just plain surprising. Pretty much all of the time, however, they are even more insane than the seemingly randomly thrown together nonsequiturs that passes for the actual cut-scene script. These cut scenes are almost exactly identical to the light gun originals, except that instead of carrying guns, our intrepid undead eliminators are now carrying keyboards.

Whoever it was who took the decision to convert Sega's zombie-filled slaughterhouse legend into an extended touch-typing tutorial is a genius of a particularly unhinged sort. Apparently untroubled by logic or judgment, they have come up with one of video gaming's most unexpected, idiosyncratic—and yet still utterly compelling—forays into entertainment. **DM**

- *The Sims*, first released in 2000, becomes the best-selling PC game ever

- Released in 2000, the **PlayStation2** (PS2) becomes the world's best-selling game console

- *World of Warcraft*, released in 2004, becomes the world's most popular MMORPG with more than 11.5 million subscribers

- *Call of Duty 2*, released in 2006, is the first **Xbox 360** game to sell 1 million units in the US

- Nintendo's **Wii** console, with its wireless, motion-sensing, handheld pointing device, is released in 2006, enabling sporting and other physically interactive games

2000s

Perfect Dark

Original release date : 2000
Platform : N64
Developer : Rare
Genre : First-Person Shooter

As the spiritual sequel to *GoldenEye 007*, a title that forever changed the direction of first-person shooters on consoles, things were never going to be easy for *Perfect Dark*, especially taking into consideration the absence of the official James Bond license. Add the departure during production of many of the talents who made *GoldenEye 007* great, and a protracted development period, and *Perfect Dark* felt like a failure even before it was released.

There are several aspects of *Perfect Dark* that make it seem like an ill-fated mistake. A plot that featured a war between alien races, masked as an industrial-espionage conflict between research companies on Earth, was dull—even to an audience that had just suffered the trauma of the trade-dispute-heavy *Phantom Menace* in the cinemas. The characterizations, from Lara Croft–alike Joanna Dark to comedy alien sidekick Elvis, meanwhile, are misjudged.

But to concentrate on these flaws would be to miss out on one of the most technically impressive titles available on the N64. Offering high-resolution graphics and Dolby Surround Sound, if at the cost of requiring a memory expansion pack, the title pushes the hardware to its limits and, sometimes uncomfortably, beyond.

However, *Perfect Dark* beat the PC-based *Deus Ex* by a matter of months in offering locations that actually felt like the real world, creating a complete and compelling experience that made up for the deficiencies of the plot.

Later in the year 2000 a version of *Perfect Dark* was released for Nintendo's new Game Boy Color. While there is some crossover in characters and locations, the two games are very different entities. Far more engaging is the 2010 Xbox Live Arcade revival of the original game, which delivers a smooth frame rate that enhances the imaginatively engineered multiplayer modes. **MKu**

Baldur's Gate II

Original release date : 2000
Platform : PC
Developer : BioWare
Genre : Role-Playing

In 1988, SSI's Gold Box series redefined the Western idea of the RPG genre. They took the single most important set of pen-and-paper rules—Advanced Dungeons & Dragons—and tied them to an epic series of campaigns that spanned entire continents and several games, breathing life into Gary Gygax's legendary creation. Running out of steam in the early 1990s, however, the *D&D* franchise was left to languish. Until, that is, BioWare created *Baldur's Gate*. The effect was like stepping through the rainbow, like moving from black-and-white to color.

Baldur's Gate was teeming with life in a way that no other RPG had ever been. Where the Gold Box games had provided hack-and-slash gaming supported by blocky graphics, *Baldur's Gate* offered would-be adventurers an abundance of quests and meaningful interactions across huge playing areas; across intricately detailed, beautifully rendered isometric recreations of a completely convincing fantasy medieval world.

The transition between *Baldur's Gate* and *Baldur's Gate II: Shadows of Amn* was every bit as pronounced. The sequel may have streamlined the interface, but it bulked out the playing experience. Like the Gold Box games, players could import their characters and items from a previous game, and as those characters grew in power, so the game changed to reflect their newfound influence. Building up their own strongholds and followers, they were free to lead their own way through a labyrinthine plot that weaved together divergent and mutually exclusive subplots and quests—indeed, some subquests were as weighty and complex as the entire first game.

As far as gaming goes, it's a satisfying complexity that has yet to be eclipsed. Indeed, *Baldur's Gate II* is probably still the pinnacle of the Western RPG. **DM**

Banjo-Tooie

Original release date : 2000
Platform : Various
Developer : Rare
Genre : Platform

Banjo-Tooie is one of the biggest, best-looking, and most representative examples of the 3-D platformer boom at the end of the 1990s. It may not be the best: its predecessor, *Banjo-Kazooie*, has imagination and new ideas that *Banjo-Tooie* does not. Instead, it builds on established foundations, booting the player into even larger, more colorful, self-contained 3-D worlds stuffed with even more trinkets, shinies, and treasures to assault your peripheral vision.

That's not to say it isn't an ambitious title. Thanks to its bewildering melange of different game play elements, moves, and collectibles, *Banjo-Tooie* is a much more expansive game than *Banjo-Kazooie*, often to the point of overcomplication. The levels themselves are large enough

to need warp pads to navigate, but are more sparsely populated than those of its predecessor. Each contains a bizarre shoot-'em-up section that seems to exist purely to show off Rare's muscle with the N64's technology, as if the sophisticated lighting effects and vast open levels left anything to be proved.

Banjo-Tooie might be bloated, but it's irrepressibly imaginative, full of mini-games, characters, and ideas. It handles with clout compared to Mario's tight, agile acrobatics, and the game's world is drawn in broader, more colorful strokes. Each level hides a secret transformation, turning Banjo into a weird selection of alternative forms, from a detonator to a washing machine to a tiny dinosaur: *Banjo-Tooie* isn't exactly sophisticated humor, but it *is* unique—if not downright weird.

Banjo-Tooie has resurfaced on Xbox Live Arcade with smoother looks, although with operation slightly altered to fit with the Xbox controller. But it still retains the sheer oddity of the original. **KM**

Marvel vs. Capcom 2: New Age of Heroes

Original release date : 2000
Platform : Various
Developer : Capcom
Genre : Fighting

One of the best things about *Marvel vs. Capcom 2: New Age of Heroes* is its ability to literalize arguments. Captain America might look tough, but you know that one dragon punch would have him seeing stars and stripes. The Hulk? He can get angry all he wants, but there's no touching Mega Man. Hardly clever, but very big, this smooshing-together of comic-book heroes and video game's toughest fighters is light-years ahead of its predecessor for the simple reason that it fully embraces the concept, building a spectacular light show of attacks, tag teams, and hundred-hit combos that leave the ground far beneath.

The game advances the two-on-two action of its predecessor to three-on-three, with teams switching between their members to recover and surprise the opposition with assist attacks. It also introduces the ability to force an opponent's next character into the ring with a snapback attack that, if unblocked, sends the current opponent flying out of the ring, to be replaced. Of course, there's a fight system as deep as you'd expect from Capcom, but the combos and team-ups are always subservient to the spectacle—the comic pows and whams and that upwardly ticking combo counter are the MSG of fighting games, and they are poured on relentlessly.

Let's emphasize once again the sheer scale of *Marvel vs. Capcom 2*: There are *fifty-six* fighters on show, ranging from Ryu to Spider-Man and Dr. Doom to M. Bison, and even the arenas are wider than the original. The game itself is a blur of hypercolor and crashing blows, quick tags, knockbacks, and desperate escapes; in slow motion the depth of interplay and counterplay at its beating heart is clear.

Marvel vs. Capcom 2 is nothing less than the ultimate fighting game—for true believers. **RS**

Deus Ex

Original release date : 2000
Platform : PC
Developer : Ion Storm
Genre : First-Person Shooter / Role-Playing

When *Deus Ex* first arrived on the scene, much was made of its hybrid qualities. An unusual concoction for its time, the game combined RPG-style character development, first-person combat, and player choice. In the wake of *Fallout 3*, *BioShock*, and the like, it's hard to recollect the novelty of *Deus Ex*, which speaks volumes as to how it has continued to define and overshadow gaming.

You are J. C. Denton, a new nanotech-powered United Nations antiterrorist recruit. When a pandemic sweeps the globe, its cure in the hands of a select few, your suspicions become aroused. Are your pay masters really safeguarding the interests of the public? Where has this plague come from and who benefits from distributing its cure? *Deus*

Ex takes a kleptomaniac approach to conspiracy fiction, assembling a greatest hits of millennial paranoia: men in black, Illuminati, Templars, and dastardly corporations all tumble into the pot to boil alongside hushed-up alien landings, sinister gene-splicing experiments, the ruthless rise of cybernetics, and self-aware AI.

The route chosen by the player to navigate these issues is brilliantly problematic. The game remains a yardstick for branching narrative paths, avoiding the common good/evil polarity. Ironically, given the game's title, *Deus Ex's* near-future dystopia offers no easy resolutions, every decision a tragic compromise between deeply imperfect ideologies. The game also exemplifies self-expression, spoiling the player with different means of tackling any objective. But whether sneaking through air vents or blasting mechs with EMP grenades, it's really about how those little choices build into our larger fears of secretive oligarchies, tyranny, and anarchy—and, more terrifyingly, whether there is really any better alternative. **MD**

QUEST LEG

NEW SKILL

Diablo II

Original release date : 2000

Platform : PC

Developer : Blizzard North

Genre : Action / Role-Playing

The genius of *Diablo* was in the ransacking of the archives. It took the ASCII RPG classic *Rogue* and turned it into an isometric point-and-click adventure. And just as *Rogue* had spawned an entire genre (known as "Roguelike"), in which a solitary hero would go off in search of loot and reputation, so *Diablo* unleashed a stream of action-RPG clones in which *Rogue*'s turn-based dungeoneering was given a real-time makeover and fancy graphics.

Diablo reduces the RPG to its barest essentials: that lone hero trawling through ever deeper dungeons, clicking on things until they die, and then picking up the loot. There are essentially just three different combat strategies: magic, melee, and ranged combat, each one reflected by the three core classes in the original game (warrior, sorcerer, and rogue). Blizzard North took those basics and polished and pared them with supreme skill, from the easy and intuitive design of the interface to the judicious balance between progress and reward. *Diablo II* is constructed from these solid foundations.

Designed with multiplayer in mind—and executed with Blizzard North's customary online flair—*Diablo II* features a number of important additions: mercenaries and hirelings to help during missions; five new character classes to replace the old ones; and even a secret in-joke level, filled with hellish, halberd-wielding bovines—which was a reference to the spurious Internet rumors of a secret cow level when the original was launched.

In truth, *Diablo II* was a success, and it is cited by the *Guinness Book of Records* as the world's fastest-selling computer game, because of those things that made the original a success: the pared-down simplicity with which it retells the hero's quest. **DM**

Elasto Mania

Original release date : 2000
Platform : PC
Developer : Balázs Rózsa
Genre : Motorbike Simulation

It's hard to credit *Elasto Mania*'s continued popularity from a brief play. Graphically the kindest thing you can say about it is that it has a naive charm. Furthermore, the first play can all too easily prevent you from persevering. The controls are basic—accelerate, brake, shift your weight back and forward, change direction—and at first they feel ludicrously twitchy. Simply accelerating without flipping over backward takes some learning. And the game's physics are not so much real world as dream world. Everything seems to happen in an almost nightmarish slow motion, the air seems thick and soupy, gravity isn't quite right, and your bike has a certain unsettling *elasticity* to it. Initially, this is all quite off-putting.

Except that it works—and it works astonishingly well. The peculiar physics, married to levels that at first sight seem plain impossible, encourage you to explore the subtleties of the controls and take your bike beyond the limits of its expected capabilities. Soon you are confidently showboating away with wheelies, somersaults, and tricks that involve balancing a wheel on a platform. Ten years down the line, players are still finding new ways to shave precious milliseconds from the speed records through exploiting the peculiarities of *Elasto Mania*'s physics.

Until recently it was a genre unto itself; that is, until RedLynx seized the initiative with its increasingly popular *Trials* series, taking the concept and making it bigger and faster and shinier. But its pace and instant-restart mentality make it a complementary title rather than a replacement; *Elasto Mania* is more thoughtful, less linear, and a whole lot loonier than the brash young usurper. It's eccentric and hard to get to know, but if you put the time and effort in, it'll reward you magnificently. **JM**

Excitebike 64

Original release date : 2000
Platform : N64
Developer : Left Field Productions
Genre : Racing

The original *Excitebike* appeared in 1984 on the NES, a perfect piece of pixel simplicity. The sequel, released sixteen years later, bears almost no resemblance at all, except that both titles represent a straight-up dedication to entertainment in their respective eras. Looking back at both of them now, the geometrical precision of the original is a more obvious sign of genius than the muddy, fuzzy brown screens of the sequel, which owe more to the technical limitations of the host console than to the off-road environments of many of the racetracks.

It's only when you pick up the controller and start to play *Excitebike 64* that its virtuosity becomes apparent, thanks to a handling model that carefully blends the impression of real-world physics with the hyper-reality of exaggerated handling. The key to its brilliance lies in the perfect balance between the effect of terrain on bike handling, and the effect of the rider's weight as the bike barrels through the air as you steer, slide, and turbo your way to victory around twenty-odd off-road tracks.

There's more to it than that, of course. The game comes with a track editor that adds an almost infinite variety to the action. You can save your best times as "ghosts" to race against in the future, and you can unlock special bonuses, including a randomly generated desert level and the original, bare-bones NES game. And there is an entire stunt system that capitalizes on the game's perfectly weighted aerial handling characteristics.

Above all, however, the thing that stands out in *Excitebike 64*, just as it had done in the original all those years before, is Nintendo's customary polish. Perhaps for that reason, it remains the high point in the video game output of developer Left Field Productions. **DM**

Grandia II

Original release date : 2000
Platform : Various
Developer : Game Arts
Genre : Role-Playing

To anyone raised on the frequent moral choices, free-form questing, party building, and brown textures that typified the Western RPG, *Grandia II* must have seemed like something from another planet. Its vibrant cartoon-styled characters, contrasting against bright blue skies, probably resembled luminescent aliens, and its lengthy, often moralizing cut scenes might have been incomprehensible to anyone raised on dialogue boxes alone. It is a game that embodies the differences in design philosophy between the two schools of RPG thought: a linear story—often adolescent and twee—plays out in cut scenes punctuated by bouts of exploring that serve mainly to house a battle system that is both intricate and rewarding.

The original *Grandia*, on PlayStation and Sega Saturn, solved one of the most commonly criticized features of Japanese RPGs by including random encounters, but representing enemy presence before they appear, making it possible to avoid confrontation. It featured an equally dynamic set of combat rules. In all other respects, it was an archetypal Japanese RPG, as was the sequel, *Grandia II*. It took a similarly pioneering approach to combat, introducing a limited amount of movement that allowed far greater tactical complexity than the static schemes used by more traditional RPGs.

The game recounts the tale of pouty teenaged mercenary Ryudo, who is given the task of protecting the songstress, Elena, as she embarks on what turns out to be an unexpectedly perilous journey.

Quite rightfully, the game earned a much-coveted platinum award from Japan's weekly *Famitsu* magazine, and a legion of devotees. To anyone raised on a diet of Western RPGs, it's among the best places to begin sampling the delights of Japanese RPGs. **DM**

Paper Mario

Original release date : 2000
Platform : N64
Developer : Intelligent Systems
Genre : Role-Playing

Legend of the Seven Stars, Square's attempt at bringing the world of *Super Mario Bros.* into the format of an RPG, showed that there was sometimes more to the famous plumber than simply running and jumping. Nintendo returned to this idea with *Paper Mario*, showing there was sometimes *less* to him than three dimensions as well.

It's a dazzling conceit. Perhaps it was even some kind of Christmas present to everyone who felt Mario had lost something in the midst of his—admittedly almost flawless—transition to 3-D environments. *Paper Mario* sends our hero back—sort of, anyway—blending his chirpy two-dimensional form with a vibrant 3-D world and setting him off on a ridiculous and sprawling quest, this

time in search of mysterious Star Spirits, which he needs to defeat a strange artifact that has rendered his pesky, perennial arch enemy, Bowser, invincible.

The visuals are a confident treat—particularly given the often grim end products of Nintendo's 64-bit console—and developer Intelligent Systems puts on plenty of new spin as you explore a strange new *Mario* world, meeting new partners and fighting strange new foes in the game's turn-based battles. Beyond the novelty, though, this remains a rich RPG with all manner of interesting items to discover and stats to tweak.

Paper Mario was released on a cartridge and quickly became something of a collector's item. However, now it can also be played on the Wii, this time via the magic of the Virtual Console. Four years after *Paper Mario*, a sequel emerged for the GameCube platform. *Paper Mario: The Thousand-Year Door* is still relatively easy to find on secondhand websites and will work on the Wii if your GameCube has been banished to the attic. **CD**

Crimson Skies

Original release date : 2000
Platform : PC
Developer : Zipper Interactive
Genre : Flight Simulator / Shoot 'Em Up

It's not entirely fair that flight sims seem to be considered universally dull by the uninitiated, but neither is such a viewpoint completely without foundation. *Crimson Skies* breaks ground by injecting the flight simulation model with *adventure*, prioritizing entertainment over realism, and heart-in-mouth dogfights over the precise execution of landing procedures. It creates its own middle-ground between arcade aerial shooter and flight simulation.

Set in an alternate-reality version of the 1930s, *Crimson Skies* follows the roguish adventures of Nathan Zachary, lovable philanderer, sky pirate, and general scallywag; think of him as a 1930s version of Han Solo. It has great voice talent and an irresistibly fast-paced plot, well enhanced by

self-referential and period-appropriate wireless broadcasts and pilot chatter.

Crimson Skies is more concerned with pulling off improbable maneuvers and shooting down other planes than the limitations of aerodynamics, but that doesn't mean it's not satisfying and skillful to control. The planes are actually quite difficult to fly, especially in the constrained areas that the game encourages you to navigate in order to dissuade pursuing planes. The dogfights also allow players the opportunity to exhibit their handling skills. But no concessions are made to realism where it might detract from that essential feeling of daredevil showmanship.

The game also charmingly produces a scrapbook of your aerial achievements, rewarding every mission, stunt, and particularly daring exploit with an extra newspaper clipping or photograph. This feature, along with the extensive plane customization, encourages players to form the kind of personal relationship with the game that makes it stick in the memory. **KS**

Giants: Citizen Kabuto

Original release date : 2000
Platform : PC
Developer : Planet Moon Studios
Genre : Shoot 'Em Up / Strategy

Sometimes it's good to find a game that *can't* be summed up in just a few words. It usually means that despite being odd, it's still good enough to have earned a commercial release. This seems to be the case with *Giants: Citizen Kabuto*, a game that manages to cram huge variety into its three-part structure, and be massively entertaining while *still* managing to wrong-foot you with its strangeness.

Giants: Citizen Kabuto is unusual in that it is a third-person shooter that combines real-time strategy elements. In the game, you control a single character from one of three humanoid races—a different one in each of the game's three phases—either to complete the story or to participate online in multiplayer matches.

The first part of the game features tiny jet pack-equipped Meccaryns as they attempt to establish an island base, first through combating the local fauna and then through real-time base building and resource gathering. This mixture of gunplay and exploration is highly engaging—both fun and challenging.

The second phase of *Giants: Citizen Kabuto* focuses on the Sea Reaper. She has a different set of attributes, such as casting spells or summoning fireballs in combat. Completing this part of the game is necessary to take on the final role—Kabuto, the island's resident beast. Kabuto rampages across the island, eating animals to stay strong and wreaking damage in moments leading up to a surprising conclusion—and one that would be a shame to spoil.

What this description fails to capture, though, is the game's humor. *Giants: Citizen Kabuto* is filled with stupid jokes and brilliant ideas. From sniper rifles to giant body slams, it's rich with inventive game mechanics while also being lewd, beautiful, and highly engaging. **JR**

Jet Set Radio

Original release date : 2000
Platform : Dreamcast
Developer : Smilebit
Genre : Action

The tireless pursuit of realistic graphics was given pause by *Jet Set Radio*, an astonishing game that spearheaded the use of cel-shaded 3-D. With a name derived from the acetate sheets used in traditional animation, this complex process applies solid fills and black outlines to 3-D objects, creating a cartoon look that has continued to mature in games like *Street Fighter IV, Okami, Viewtiful Joe*, and *The Legend of Zelda: The Wind Waker*.

The kids are *not* all right in the game's day-glo version of Tokyo. From the nightclubs of Benten to the telegraph wires above bustling Shibuya, gangs of kids on Rollerblades fight an endless turf war. Their weapons, spray cans; their victims, anything flat enough to provide a canvas. Shop windows, construction equipment, playgrounds, buses, and even the back of Captain Onishima, the Magnum-waving chief of police—nothing is safe.

Switching between members of an up-and-coming gang, the GGs, the player has to master the art of the seamless grind, using the scenery to reach higher and harder tagging spots. And while all of this is going on, pirate DJ Professor K keeps the gangs jumping to exuberant local sounds. This medley of J-pop and electro-funk isn't the only upbeat thing about *Jet Set Radio*. With a carnival atmosphere that makes even storm drains look flash, the game is a love-letter to *shinjinrui*, Tokyo's real-life "new race" of hip young radicals.

The baffling mix of respect and defiance, fashion and rebellion is unmistakably Japanese, which may explain why the game flopped when released in America. For a more fitting US alternative, check out the violent, nihilistic, and ham-fisted *Getting Up: Contents Under Pressure*, the video game debut of fashion designer Marc Ecko. **DH**

Capcom vs. SNK: Millennium Fight 2000

Original release date : 2000
Platform : Arcade, Dreamcast
Developer : Capcom
Genre : Fighting

Though SNK's *King of Fighters* series has never quite gained the traction that *Street Fighter* managed, the concept behind *Capcom vs. SNK: Millennium Fight 2000* is still instantly understandable. This is *the* two biggest 2-D fighting game developers pitting the pick of their rosters against each other.

This wasn't the first game in the series, but it was the first to be an arcade game, which is, of course, its natural home. The big decision was to adopt the SNK control system of four buttons (light/hard punch, light/hard kick) rather than the six buttons used by Capcom games, but the collision system and physics resemble *Street Fighter* much more closely, so it's a hybrid rather than a choice. But the rival companies don't shy away from going toe-to-toe: At the start of the game you can choose which "groove" you want to play in, Capcom or SNK, and this will affect the kind of super attacks your characters can perform.

There was even a new structure for fights, one that remains unique: a team battle in which you have to fill four slots, with each character being worth a certain number of blocks. (Cammy is one block, for example; Ryu and Terry Bogard are worth two; Rugal is three blocks; Akuma or Iori are four.) It's a more obvious tactical leaning toward team battling than any other game allows, and it lets players state their intentions before the round has begun.

Does it need to be said that beneath all these layers, this is a brilliant fighting game? Bringing together the best of each company, with a refreshing lack of preciousness about their characters and systems, *Capcom vs. SNK: Millennium Fight 2000* is one of the very best in the series, and just a big beautiful rumble in its own right. **RS**

Metropolis Street Racer

Original release date : 2000
Platform : Dreamcast
Developer : Bizarre Creations
Genre : Driving

Development diaries for *Metropolis Street Racer* provide a unique insight into the rigors of pre-launch console development. Written throughout 1998 and 1999 by developer Bizarre Creations, months before the arrival of the Sega Dreamcast, they describe informal head-scratching sessions with fellow developer Argonaut, awkwardly timed demos for Sega VIPs, and the monstrous task of texturing a game set in three real-world cities.

Metropolis Street Racer was a massively ambitious game for its time, featuring enough urban real estate to host 262 tracks. Still released before *Grand Theft Auto III* and *The Getaway*, it maps textures from more than 40,000 photographs to its extruded 3-D cityscapes, creating more than fifteen square miles of London, Tokyo, and San Francisco. Fictional radio stations add cultural backdrops, but the challenge is actually to blank these out while navigating the freakish hairpins, roundabouts, and chicanes of races taking place in venues like St. James's Park, Admiralty Arch, Shinjuku, and Fisherman's Wharf.

Providing the blueprints for Xbox exclusive *Project Gotham Racing*, *Metropolis Street Racer* would bring a new philosophy to driving games: "It's not about how fast you drive; it's about how you drive fast." And this is how you earn kudos—a currency based on your style and precision that unlocks more cars and tracks. The *Project Gotham Racing* series would tweak it extensively, but what sets *Metropolis Street Racer* apart is its penalty system: When the race is over, kudos are *deducted* for mishaps; joker cards double your wins and losses, encouraging you to gamble on your own skill. Later *Project Gotham Racing* games weren't nearly so severe, but lost something as a result. **DH**

Resident Evil Code: Veronica

Original release date : 2000
Platform : Various
Developer : Capcom
Genre : Survival Horror

The *Resident Evil* series has experienced many false starts. A near-complete version of *Resident Evil 2* was junked, several versions of *Resident Evil 4* were abandoned, and *Resident Evil Code: Veronica* was originally intended to be the series' third title. Eventually it became an exclusive Dreamcast launch title. It may have missed the launch by a year, but it just might be the best "old" *Resident Evil* there is.

It inherits many flaws from the first three games, with plenty of backtracking and a definite clunkiness in combat. Within the template, though, it also adds a great deal: This is the first title in the series to feature environments rendered in real-time 3-D, while the ability to continue after dying (rather than depending on manual save points) is something the series always needed.

Still an attractive game in spite of its age, *Resident Evil Code: Veronica*'s scope and pacing also deserve a mention. It ties up countless loose ends from previous games, brilliantly pulls the rug out from beneath the player halfway through, and never stops pushing forward. The storyline serves up melodrama and sumptuous cut scenes, but with a surprising knack for horror. Suddenly finding yourself watching a home movie of two young children torturing dragonflies is a shuddering experience.

There's a whole lot more to be shocked by, too. Your zombie foes are all individualized and show up in varying states of decay. Hunters return as gorillas with claws. Your ally is transformed into a mindless hulk that has to be taken down. It's all harrowing stuff.

Resident Evil Code: Veronica shows the limitations of the original *Resident Evil* template, but also, at its frequent best, just how powerful it can be. **RS**

Final Fantasy IX

Original release date : 2000
Platform : PS1
Developer : Square
Genre : Role-Playing

Knights, castles, princesses, and a quest for honor: *Final Fantasy IX* was nothing if not a return to the series' formative themes. After two preceding titles set in steampunk fantasy worlds and one set within the ups and downs of a high-school drama, Hironobu Sakaguchi was keen to make the ninth game in his misleadingly titled series a celebration of its earliest days. For fans who grew up with the original Famicom games, the gesture was not unappreciated, with the lighthearted dialogue; bright color scheme; and light, fantasy tale modernizing the classic formula while retaining its charms.

For those players who came to *Final Fantasy* after the world-conquering popularity of the series' seventh title, however, the response was lukewarm, its cutesy graphics and superdeformed characters a far cry from the angsty teenage drama of the recent titles. The game may have been a graphical triumph, released as it was toward the end of the original PlayStation's life, but its whimsical visual style failed to wow audiences taken by the gritty realism of *Final Fantasy VIII*. It failed to sell as well as either of the preceding games in any territory.

Deviating from the customizable character options of the previous games, *Final Fantasy IX* returned to a stricter job system, defining characters in their roles without room for deviation. Ironically, then, its stylized approach means that the game has aged rather better than its more popular predecessors, retaining much of its charm and appeal but shunning realism. With a likable and enduring cast, a whimsical storyline, and a rich and vibrant world to explore, *Final Fantasy IX* remains an appealing proposition for contemporary players. **SP**

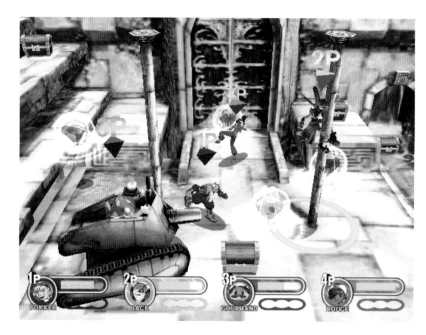

Power Stone 2

Original release date : 2000
Platform : Arcade, Dreamcast
Developer : Capcom
Genre : Fighting

One of the reasons that older gamers mourned the loss of the Dreamcast was that it signaled the demise of arcade gaming culture. Sharing the NAOMI hardware of its latest coin-ops, Sega's console gave hope that things were not about to change for the worse and that the tenets of fast fun and bright, attractive graphics were not about to sink into a brown and green bog of realistic war games. No matter how sober and pretentious things got, there would always be a place for *Power Stone*, right?

Wrong. While reports of fun's demise have been greatly exaggerated, *Power Stone* does represent a lost pleasure: a party game made with all the character and zeal of a "proper" triple-A title. Simply a game about killing your friends with toy weapons in amusement park locations, it now resides on the PSP in the shape of a largely forgotten port.

Making a swift transition from arcade to living room, *Power Stone 2* is a fantastic pick-up-and-play multiplayer game, supporting four participants over its predecessor's two. Choosing from such characters as Edward Fokker (boxer and fighter pilot) and Rouge (fire-breathing fortune-teller), players *can* rely on traditional fighting styles if they want, but it's more enjoyable to use the environment, pick-ups, and power stones; three of the latter will unlock special "power fusion" moves.

Of the ten stages, one delightfully features an airship that slowly disintegrates while coasting above the clouds. When the last of its platforms and turrets falls away, the fight continues in freefall, players swooping into melee attacks while keeping an eye for life-saving umbrellas. Crashing into the ground, it concludes in a multitiered temple with a respawning tank. Gimmickry all the way, then, but of the highest possible caliber. **DH**

Phantasy Star Online

Original release date : 2000
Platform : Dreamcast
Developer : Sonic Team
Genre : Action / Role-Playing

When *Phantasy Star Online* was released in 2000, it wasn't the first online console game. The Dreamcast itself had *Chu Chu Rocket* and *Quake III Arena*, while earlier consoles had embraced online gaming to varying degrees of success. But *Phantasy Star Online* was the first that felt like it really worked—and the first online game to adopt a console design sensibility, transforming it through the prism of online connectivity to create something truly original, something that probably couldn't have existed on a PC alone.

Taking inspiration from massively multiplayer online role-playing games (MMORPGs) that were in abundance on PCs at the time, *Phantasy Star Online* took the connectivity and community of the genre but brought a more tightly contained, console-style adventuring. It also provided superbly realized action-RPG mechanics: customizable characters in teams of four fought their way through sci-fi settings to battle colossal bosses and save the planet.

The real masterstroke, however, was the way in which communication and cooperation were set at the heart of the experience: selecting from a multilingual phrase book enabled gamers from all over the world to play together. (Finally realizing Sega's noble British ad slogan: "We all play games, why don't we play together?") Indeed, if you were lucky enough to play the game close to its release, before the cheats moved in, you could find yourself receiving tribute from high-level Japanese players, who would greet low-level newbies by simply dropping gifts at their feet. And that's the biggest difference between *Phantasy Star Online* and the po-faced competition on the PC: the game was actually fun—whether or not the lobby areas were decked out with huge hearts on Valentine's Day. **DM**

Tony Hawk's Pro Skater 2

Original release date : 2000
Platform : Various
Developer : Neversoft
Genre : Sports

Now and again, something comes out of nowhere and plants itself so firmly on the gaming landscape that it becomes difficult to imagine a time when it didn't exist. And this what happened with the *Tony Hawk* series.

Grinding their way from obscurity to a multiformat, multimillion selling phenomenon, the *Tony Hawk* games rolled in at just the right time, capturing—helping to push, even—a resurgence in skateboarding while riding the crest of the PlayStation wave.

Tony Hawk's Pro Skater 2 remains a series highlight, taking the core components of its predecessor —including the revolutionary control system that brilliantly transplants an infinitely complex pastime onto the eight-button,

twin-stick layout of a Dual Shock joy pad—and decking everything out with a "bigger, better, more" attitude.

Embarking on your newfound career as a virtual pro skateboarder, then, you get to enjoy larger play areas, a considerably extended trick repertoire, a greater number of mission-based objectives, and, perhaps most notably, an expertly refined set of game mechanics. It is this combination of enhancements that marks out *Tony Hawk's Pro Skater 2* as *the* skateboarding game of its generation and even, perhaps, the title that best encapsulates the all-encompassing nature of the PlayStation era.

Today, competition comes not from later versions of this game but from EA's rival *Skate* series. In such company *Tony Hawk's Pro Skater 2*'s more extreme, more exaggerated nature may jar. But the comparison is also unfair. More so than the titles that followed, this one embraces its arcadelike temperament with a view to providing an absurdly entertaining ride. And, judged on those terms, it's certainly a mission statement that still holds up today. **JDS**

Silent Scope 2: Dark Silhouette

Original release date : 2000

Platform : Arcade

Developer : Konami

Genre : Shoot 'Em Up

Some games lose little in the transition from arcade to home format; others fall so far short that you wonder why the decision was made to attempt the transfer in the first place. In the 1980s, many of the calamitous conversions could be attributed to home systems simply biting off more than they could chew. (Few who played games during the period *won't* have memories of the crushing disappointment of playing home versions that had little in common with the originals they'd loved so much.) In recent years, however, as arcade and consumer technology has converged, there is not a great deal that consoles cannot do. The exception is dedicated hardware such as the rifle used in the *Silent Scope* arcade series.

The story goes that one of Konami's designers had been playing with his video camera when the idea came to him to incorporate its viewfinder technology into the kind of light gun hardware that had a proven track record in arcades. And the concept he'd wrap it around? Sniping.

Shooting enemies from a distance using sniping tools had been seen in plenty of games before *Silent Scope*, but never as the sole focus and never with dedicated hardware. The result is a uniquely tense atmosphere as you scan a scene with both eyes and then nuzzle up to your weapon, squint into its sights, and make the shot.

Silent Scope II: Dark Silhouette (or *Fatal Judgement* as it was called in Europe) contains plenty of tongue-in-cheek humor (one exchange sees a character enthusing about playing "*Metal Gear* for real") across a series of atmospheric locations against typically restrictive time limits.

The home ports should be avoided at all costs, but the authentic arcade experience provides a sense of engagement with the enemy like no other game series. **TB**

Skies of Arcadia

Original release date : 2000
Platform : Various
Developer : Overworks
Genre : Role-Playing

Skies of Arcadia was Sega's answer to the Dreamcast's lack of a *Final Fantasy*. It eventually made its way to the GameCube after the demise of Sega's own console, but if you weren't lucky enough to play the original, you'd have missed out playing with the Dreamcast's tiny additional VMU hardware: a rather neat experiment in game design.

The game itself was an archetypal, if brilliant, Japanese RPG. As such, the game's strengths are those of the genre: strong characters, an engaging story, amazing worlds, and overblown boss battles. And similarly the flaws: too many random encounters—and overblown boss battles.

The Jules Verne–inspired story starts where most others end, with the rescue of a princess by sky pirates Vyse

and Aika and their band of Blue Rogues. The mysterious princess provides the premise for a heroic quest to defeat the evil empire and save the world.

Skies of Arcadia's most groundbreaking addition to the tried-and-tested Japanese RPG formula is how it handles the airship in which the sky pirates explore the world. Providing an excellent pretext for limiting the player's progress, rising above the airwaves or sinking beneath the clouds gives a very real sense of the epic scale of the game's world, while ship-to-ship battles bring another tactical dimension to combat.

While *Skies of Arcadia* doesn't revolutionize the genre, it works within its constraints to achieve near perfection: it comprises a blend of puzzles, intricate combat mechanics, fantastic environments, one of the longest boss climaxes in the history of climaxes, and some brilliant set pieces (a sequence played out from multiple perspectives, for example). Unsullied by the sulky teenagers seen in some of Square's games, this is blue-skies gaming at its best. **DM**

Sin & Punishment

Original release date : 2000
Platform : N64
Developer : Treasure
Genre : Shoot 'Em Up

Never released in the West first time around, Treasure's explosive and elaborate shooter *Sin & Punishment* was destined to become one of the most sought-after—and name-dropped—titles the cult developer has ever produced. Yet it has considerably more than chic rarity going for it. An on-rails shooter built from vivid colors and sharp controls, *Sin & Punishment* is an experience that no fan of fast-paced action extravaganzas should miss out on. Indeed, its relative obscurity is ultimately a crime rather than a selling point.

Sidestepping the forgettable, if timely, plot involving a near-future Earth in which mankind fights over dwindling resources, *Sin & Punishment* is a game in which control means everything, and although the "rail" nature means you're never at a loss for where to go next, there are still plenty of options dumped into the player's hands, from a choice of free aim and auto targeting for the target reticule, to a series of dodges and jumps that need to be perfected as you work your way through the game's ballistic set pieces without regular restarts.

And from the glowing orange limbo of the game's first stage to the crowded streets and mech battles of later environments, *Sin & Punishment* is a treat to behold, every new level throwing in an unexpected design flourish, each new boss providing an elaborate burst of eye candy the type of which only those chaps back at Treasure HQ in Tokyo seem able to create.

The best news of all, however, is that *Sin & Punishment* is now available on the Wii's Virtual Console service, which, given that the game's original cut scenes were already in English, means that there's no reason not to power it up and then power on through. **CD**

The Legend of Zelda: Majora's Mask

Original release date : 2000
Platform : N64
Developer : Nintendo
Genre : Action / Adventure

Arguably the most inventive video game ever made, *The Legend of Zelda: Majora's Mask* may have confused fans and divided critics, but it trumps the interdimensional puzzles of both *The Legend of Zelda: A Link to the Past* and *The Legend of Zelda: Ocarina of Time* with a story that blends the mechanics of a classic *Zelda* with a premise straight out of *Groundhog Day*. The results are as baffling, as fascinating, and as wonderful as that odd-couple pairing suggests.

It's very hard to come to grips with *Majora's Mask* at first. After the beautifully melancholy opening, Link finds himself in Clock Town, located in the strange land of Terminus, a kingdom living under a death threat from the leering demonic moon that threatens to crash into it

in just three days. Unlike most video game time limits, this one isn't just an empty threat: three days pass, the moon collides with the Earth, and Terminus is wiped out. And the whole thing starts all over again.

The game that unfolds is a real headache to comprehend at times, an adventure that plays out in three-day bursts of activity as you move the plot forward one stage at a time, warping back to the beginning of the story whenever the moon nears its impact once more.

Majora's Mask is as astonishing as it is clever, and although the dungeons may underwhelm, the overworld is built with such devious and thrifty skill that the game survives on the strength of that alone. With fascinating characters to meet, ingenious puzzles to solve, a cluster of shape-shifting masks to collect and use, and—best of all—that ominous and endlessly repeating threat lurking overhead, this is the dark nightmare shadow world of one of gaming's most reliably upbeat series, a frightening alternate universe to be explored at length. **CD**

The Sims

Original release date : 2000
Platform : PC, Mac
Developer : Maxis
Genre : Life Simulation

The year 2000 was feared for the millennium bug—at least by those who weren't worried about an apocalypse. As it turned out, we would instead become engrossed in domesticity. It was the year of *Big Brother,* a televisual human goldfish bowl that gave insight into the common banality of our actions and conversations. This obsession came as no surprise to PC gamers, who'd been addicted to the *Sims* since its arrival at the turn of the millennium.

The best-selling PC game of all time, *The Sims* confounded rival game developers who found they'd been designing castles and spaceships when what we really wanted was an in-game microwave oven. So out went the fantastical settings and in came the Sims—adults, children, and babies—each with a mind of their own and a need to stay not just well-fed but emotionally satisfied.

As far as the game is concerned, you don't direct your Sims' every action, but you do design their home and deck it out with furniture and playthings as their expanding budget allows. You can also encourage your charges to take jobs or get married. Otherwise the Sims will generally get on with life as they see fit, which can lead to depression, slumped in front of the TV, if you're not careful.

Sims can even die from starvation, electrocution, fire, or a virus, which can lead to a ghost Sim haunting its old house. Some players delight in finding outlandish ways to kill their charges, but most develop an eerie concern for their entirely algorithmic welfare.

Simsville is further fleshed out in various expansion packs, which bring more items, characters, and new locations into play, as well as a sequel. Indeed, we suspect we'll still be playing *The Sims* long after the Orwellian nightmare of *Big Brother* is finally over. **OB**

Vagrant Story

Original release date : 2000
Platform : PS1
Developer : Square
Genre : Action / Role-Playing

A brooding traipse through French medieval ruins; a story told in a weighty Shakespearean patois; a battle system whose depths are revealed over the course of days, not hours. *Vagrant Story* is an action-role-playing game that breaks the mold. Springing from the mind of Yasumi Matsuno, here is a game that seeks and succeeds in breaking free from the familiar constraints of genre, scenario, and setting.

Released during the PlayStation's twilight years, it is without question a technical marvel. But it's the animation and stage direction that turns still rudimentary polygons into something that breathes life and character. Camera moves are cinematic in a way few games achieve, a feeling matched by one of gaming's greatest scripts.

With a labyrinthine choice of armory, *Vagrant Story* revels in its RPG complexity, allowing players to tinker with its systems at the low level, while being pushed forward by the wider drama. A game that doesn't kowtow to expectations, it is the work of a true auteur, an approach that should be celebrated in the strongest terms. **SP**

Super Monkey Ball

Original release date : 2000
Platform : Arcade, GameCube
Developer : Sega
Genre : Action

Only Sega, purveyor of everything shiny and silly, could come up with *Super Monkey Ball*: a riff on *Marble Madness* that puts you in charge of a monkey trapped inside a transparent ball, and asks you to tilt and steer him toward the exit of each level as quickly (and painlessly) as you can.

If PETA ever opens a digital branch, *Super Monkey Ball* will quickly join the likes of *Manhunt* as games to hide away when polite society comes to visit. Each of the game's elaborate courses hangs spookily in midair, and one wrong move is enough to send your precious monkey plummeting horribly into the abyss. Close your eyes, and you can imagine the moment of impact.

There are plenty of other distractions on offer, too. Monkey Target is a ramped-up gliding simulator in which the ball opens to reveal a pair of wings; you then have to drop your monkey onto the highest-scoring target you can find—or, more likely, it will take a long plunge into the sea.

Cute and cruel in equal measures, *Super Monkey Ball* has something for everyone. A left-field classic, it's another one of Sega's grade-A triumphs. **CD**

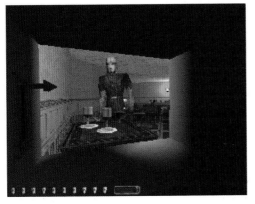

Thief II: The Metal Age

Sacrifice

Original release date : 2000
Platform : PC
Developer : Looking Glass Studios
Genre : Action

Original release date : 2000
Platform : Various
Developer : Shiny Entertainment
Genre : Action / Strategy

Thief: The Dark Project was strongly oriented toward stealth, but it had also played with other areas, such as *Tomb Raider*-style dungeon exploration. Most of these extras were removed from *Thief II: The Metal Age* in favor of seeing exactly what could be done with the core mechanics.

While *Thief II: The Metal Age*'s level design was a great improvement, arguably a little of the original's atmosphere had been sacrificed. Zombies had been a controversial component, the mere sight of the undead being enough to make most people want to turn to violence. With their removal, some of the supernatural dread disappeared. Perhaps that was appropriate. Thematically, the former game was all Dionysian pagan irrationality; This, with a plot based around the cult of the Mechanists, is about Apollonian newness.

Thief II: The Metal Age was Looking Glass Studios's swan song, and the gaming world remains all the sadder for the loss of the studio's formal invention and intelligence. That its games are still cited by contemporary developers is a telling monument to how inspiring they were. **KG**

If Hieronymus Bosch had been the art director of a video game, it might have turned out something like *Sacrifice*. A third-person action-strategy affair, this is a game about souls, wizards, gods, and bizarre visual design. You take the role of a dimension-hopping wizard, your tasks to settle a struggle between a pantheon of gods and to destroy other wizards. This curious group of celestials is beautifully acted by an all-star cast, including Tim Curry and Brad Garrett, whose superb efforts create an entertaining pantomime backdrop to a dark, magical world.

Visually, *Sacrifice* provides a landscape of floating islands and nightmarish visions in which you slay enemies to gather souls of your own. You are also given a selection of spells that take effect depending on the gods you side with through the conflict.

Sacrifice is as beautiful and weird a game as any published before or since, but it's also astonishingly well constructed. It is Shiny's offbeat masterpiece: a genuinely well-engineered strategy game that, despite its surreal and arty theme, hangs together as one of the greats. **JR**

Animal Crossing

Original release date : 2001
Platform : GameCube
Developer : Nintendo
Genre : Life Simulation

The Nintendo GameCube was armed with its own internal clock: a dull kind of feature, you might imagine, and something few people bothered to set properly before getting down to the likes of *Luigi's Mansion* or *F-Zero GX*. *Animal Crossing*, however, makes absolutely brilliant use of this inclusion, using the passage of time to brew its own powerfully affecting spell.

And it's all so simple: you switch *Animal Crossing* on at nine in the morning, and most of your animal friends will be wide awake and bustling around your cobbled village, chatting, trading items, and going about their whimsical lives. Switch it on again at nine in the evening, and the majority of them will be in bed—the town square will be deserted, and warm lights will glow from the windows of comfy little cottages. Turn it on in the winter, and it will be snowing; turn it on in the autumn, and you can watch the leaves turning brown. (And if you turn it on during Groundhog Day, a jokey letter from your mom will be waiting for you in your mailbox.) It's a very simple kind of magic, but one that ensures that *Animal Crossing* feels like very few other games.

On the surface, it's a bare-bones social simulator, plonking you into a village of strangers, lumbering you with a hefty mortgage to pay off and an empty house to fill with furniture, and pushing you out the door to make friends. In reality, however, it genuinely feels like a gateway to a different world: a bittersweet, somewhat capitalist fantasy land with quirky characters who are just as likely to sulk at you and move away as they are to shower you with gifts and empty pleasantries. The perfect example of a game rising above its core mechanics, then, *Animal Crossing* is smart, cynical, adorable, and worryingly capable of weaving its way into the fabric of real life. **CD**

Final Fantasy X

Original release date : 2001
Platform : PS2
Developer : Square
Genre : Role-Playing

A ragtag group of adventurers are brought together by fate and circumstance to confront an evil force that threatens the very existence of life on the planet. Quick: Which *Final Fantasy* game is it? If you answered "all of them," you're right, but the reason the series has stayed vital for more than two decades is the way it keeps finding new variations on its themes. Like expert jazz musicians improvising around a basic riff, the development team begin each entry with a few familiar elements before spinning something new and wonderful from it.

Final Fantasy X, the first game in the series for the PlayStation 2, stands apart by narrowing its focus. In truth, it's more about the inner lives of the characters than averting the end of the world. Our hero, Tidus—whose hair is spiky and blond, of course—is a professional athlete who nevertheless feels he's failed to live up to his father's expectations. And our villain isn't the all-powerful figurehead of an evil corporation or religious sect, but a lone wizard who simply wants to hide his existence from the world. These characters are fighting for their own souls as much as anything else.

That said, the fate of the world *does* nonetheless still hang in the balance, and *Final Fantasy X* contains its share of earth-rending battles. The graphical power of the PlayStation 2 lends dazzling color to magical spells, and fluid animation to brawling combatants. Our heroes' journey takes them through ice caves and up mountaintops—once again, types of locations that are common to the series, but that had never before been rendered like this.

Other titles in the series may contain deeper role-playing elements and more challenging worlds to explore, but few have the heart of *Final Fantasy X*. **MK**

Baldur's Gate: Dark Alliance

Original release date : 2001

Platform : Various

Developer : Snowblind Studios

Genre : Action / Role-Playing

When the original titles appeared on the PC, the *Baldur's Gate* games lasted for hundreds of hours, spanned an entire continent and occasional extra dimension, and contained almost the entire Advanced Dungeons & Dragons rule set. And they arrived on six disks—more if you count the side quests and stories included in expansions. There was just no way *Baldur's Gate* was ever going to fit on a home console, or be controlled on one, thanks to its menu-based, stat-heavy, mouse-driven interface.

That is until the creators of *Baldur's Gate: Dark Alliance* had a brainwave. They took the world and setting of the previous games and worked them into a *Diablo* clone, replacing the labyrinthine plotting and densely woven narrative with a cut-back, combat-driven action-RPG. Instead of a party of characters, you now controlled just one, picked from a choice of three at the start of the game. And instead of their abilities growing and developing according to the A D&D rules, players could use experience points to tailor their characters however they saw fit.

Like any good adventure, *Baldur's Gate: Dark Alliance* kicks off in the sewers, before graduating to a succession of fantastic environments, all superbly rendered by a groundbreaking engine that supported true 3-D graphics, dynamic lighting, and numerous other cutting-edge effects. Wading through the lustrous, velvety-surfaced sewer waters was never so much fun.

The final, crucial ingredient retained from the PC version was the fan service: D&D fans would have been delighted by the possibility of coming up against gelatinous cubes, kobolds, dragons, lizard men, and—best of all—the possibility of unlocking the legendary dark elf warrior, Drizzt Do'Urden, as a playable character. **DM**

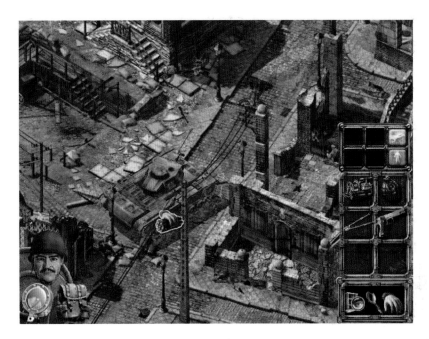

Commandos 2: Men of Courage

Original release date : 2001
Platform : PC, Mac
Developer : Pyro Studios
Genre : Strategy

A pack of Lucky Strikes dropped in a doorway attracts the gaze of a bored German sentry who ambles over and gets a knife in the back for his trouble. Moments later, the dead man's uniform is helping a strapping Allied commando infiltrate a naval base. Traversing a level in Pyro's World War II stealth-strategy magnum opus involves solving dozens of delicious, unscripted puzzles. Distraction techniques, disguises, athleticism, and concealment, plus good old-fashioned brute force, all play their part as players maneuver through the sprawling isometric, three-dimensional environments. Brazenly echoing movies like *The Guns of Navarone* and *Where Eagles Dare*, the absorbing action flits from island fortress to Bavarian Schloss to Far

Eastern river valley. The fact that these locations can only be viewed from four fixed perspectives hardly seems to matter, such is the exquisiteness of the art.

Character party pieces and map-specific hazards add further texture and challenge. In one typically colorful episode, the player's task is to steal an Enigma machine from an ice-bound U-boat, but danger comes as much from sustained exposure to the cold as a bullet.

For all of its richness and replayability, *Commandos 2: Men of Courage* didn't garner unqualified praise, critics rightly highlighting the limitations of its AI. While alerted guards may search areas methodically, they aren't as wary of corpse heaps as they might be. Friendly forces are also a little lacking in the self-preservation department, refusing to respond to attacks from unexpected quarters. Minor blemishes like these were partially addressed in the sequel, but *Commandos 3*'s shrunken venues and cropped operative roster meant it failed to measure up to the cloak-and-dagger masterpiece that is *Men Of Courage*. **TS**

Gran Turismo 3: A-Spec

Original release date : 2001
Platform : PS2
Developer : Polyphony Digital
Genre : Driving

By the time the *Gran Turismo* franchise sped on to PlayStation 2, powered by the pure-octane mix of a new console's then-unmatched graphical performance and a delicately tuned hype engine already revving higher than the average F1 car, it had amassed an unassailable lead.

Such an advantage ensured a commercial performance beyond anything a driving series had experienced before, but also placed considerable pressure on Polyphony Digital to keep its foot steady on the accelerator and refrain from drastic steering changes.

As such, *Gran Turismo 3: A-Spec* offers little in the way of surprises. Lift the hood and you find a refined handling system over the previous two games that effortlessly conveys most nuances of car behavior—in its day, the best of its kind on console—and successfully underpins a typically large array of vehicles to purchase and win as rewards for the many possibilities of on-track exploits.

The core structure, too, remains untouched. There is a clear attempt at broadening the game's appeal, but not at the expense of those already used to getting their hands coated in *GT*'s oil. At the heart of the experience is the continued concern with the RPG-flavored demands of obtaining and improving your vehicle before entering it into a series of eligible races, and collecting the subsequent winnings to spend on further upgrades or new models.

The lack of cosmetic damage and limited AI remain dents in *Gran Turismo 3: A-Spec*'s otherwise polished performance, and the corrosion caused by the passing of time is something even the remarkable content on offer can't mask. The game may no longer be the drive of your life, but there is enough mileage left in its engine to teach many of the newcomers to the racing genre a trick or two. **JDS**

Black & White

Original release date : 2001
Platform : PC, Mac
Developer : Bullfrog Productions
Genre : Life Simulation / Strategy

Willful and fascinating, *Black & White* sees the studio that practically invented the god game with *Populous* redesigning it from the ground up in the strangest of all possible manners. Morality occupies a central position, and babysitting comes to the fore as each player rules their people with a giant animal, which they must painstakingly teach to do their bidding.

It's a bit like living with a giant toddler at times, and it's the AI's quirky unpredictability that actually becomes one of the game's most enjoyable features. Commanding your giant turtle to attack your enemies only to see it wading into your own troops instead is frustrating, certainly, and probably counts as a bug, but it's a brilliantly strange sight

to watch unfold, and it's also a unique pleasure to learn the intricacies of the system.

The moral angle may be a little one-dimensional, but while such systems have become a feature of every genre since, from the creeping existential terrors of *BioShock* to the godlike chimney-hopping powers of *Infamous*, it was at its most groundbreaking here, when the basics of the idea were being so laboriously hashed out.

As with many games created by Peter Molyneux, there are frustrations, rough edges, and a couple of features that even the great man himself has admitted were unnecessary: the ability to draw real-time weather information into *Black & White* took a long time to implement and merely ensures that British players, at least, get to act godly under an endlessly overcast sky.

But the video game industry needs oddities like *Black & White* and always will—strange, massive, ambitious experiments; games that think, and subsequently act, on a larger scale. **CD**

Tribes 2

Original release date : 2001
Platform : PC
Developer : Dynamix
Genre : First-Person Shooter

While *Unreal Tournament* and *Counter-Strike* might initially spring to mind when thinking about large-scale multiplayer online first-person shooters, the originator of the genre was *Starsiege: Tribes*. Set in the same *Starsiege* universe, *Tribes 2* built on the original in every way and, though not able to boast the same following as its competitors, set a high-water mark for the genre. Perhaps the comparatively small audience for *Tribes 2* can be explained by its refusal to compromise.

Despite the tutorial levels, few concessions are made to the casual player, and surviving—let alone becoming good—takes a great deal of practice. The difficulty is in no small part due to the game's exploration of the Y axis; as well as running and gunning, players can launch into the air for limited periods using their jet packs, surveying the expansive maps as they do so, and taking potshots at the chaos below. Light, medium, and heavy armor suits provide the expected differentiation in abilities, and multiple classes within those create further subtle distinctions in play styles.

Due to the acrobatic nature of every aggressor, tactics slant necessarily toward splash damage. Forecasting an enemy's descent trajectory with a well-placed rocket is a unique skill, and one that is essential here. But vehicles abound, too, and some, such as the three-man bomber, require close cooperation with teammates in order to be used to maximum effect.

The danger of multiplayer-focused games is that their official servers will one day be closed down, and that was the fate that befell the *Tribes 2* community. Thankfully, 2009 saw fan-run servers spring up, and the game can be played again today. Whether you're brave enough to take on the experts, however, is another matter entirely. **BM**

IL-2 Sturmovik

Original release date : 2001
Platform : PC
Developer : 1C
Genre : Flight Simulation / Shoot 'Em Up

What's in a name? No whizbang marketing title to sell up this hardcore military flight sim; the developers went with what its target audience knows, which is—near enough—the name of a plane. The Illyushin Il-2 was mass produced by the Russian Air Force in World War II, when it served as a ground-attack fighter on the Eastern Front.

The name also serves to reinforce that this sim is not for the faint-hearted. The flight model is exacting, which means you need to understand pitch and roll mechanics, monitor speeds and altitudes, and more, just to keep them in the air. Then there's the Luftwaffe to deal with.

A robust mission editor allows you to plot your own targets and challenges, adding greatly to the long-term value of the package. Flyboys can also test their mettle online against other pilots, and with that kind of longevity potential we can forgive some of the functional, if not flashy, visuals. The unique setting, mission styles, and plane types, along with a well-designed, challenging flight model, all contribute to an original flight sim offering tons of variety to genre aficionados. **RSm**

Devil May Cry

Original release date : 2001
Platform : PS2
Developer : Capcom
Genre : Action

Sometimes you don't want to think too hard about what you're doing. Sometimes you just want to smash things up while firing off snarky quips. For those occasions, there's *Devil May Cry*, Capcom's gothic fun house, built from horror fiction's greatest demons and blended with the kind of things David Bowie probably dreams about when he has a high temperature.

Devil May Cry's blistering approach to combat sensibly values style above all else: whether blowing enemies to shreds or slicing them to ribbons, what truly matters in this game is how good you look doing it. Dante, the game's foppish protagonist, is a pleasure to throw around the various levels' numerous seedy environments, and when you're truly in the zone, the whole thing moves at such a staggering pace, your eyeballs may dry out just trying to keep up with the speed at which the action unfolds.

Other titles might have saner plots, deeper characters, or more elegant pacing, but if it's the death of a thousand cuts you're after, Dante and *Devil May Cry* are your first, your last, and your only real choice. **CD**

Frequency

Original release date : 2001
Platform : PS2
Developer : Harmonix
Genre : Music

Before turning its attention to the anatomy of rock, *Guitar Hero* inventor Harmonix chose a more natural subject for its rhythm games: electronica. The first and best of its PS2 games, *Frequency*, is an intricate, intimate journey into the genre's darkest corners.

Frequency adopts a multitrack approach to its music, splitting it into three-lane tracks for instruments and samples. With analog-controlled freestyle sections filling any empty spaces, it wraps this landscape into a tunnel, the player "locking down" tracks by matching notes with the PS2 controller, the idea being to build the song and maintain it to the end.

The "invisible" interface of the pad takes players to unexpected heights. Play for long enough, and muscle memory and reflexes unite with almost telepathic results, the notes streaming through the hands like punch cards through a nineteenth-century computer. Few games have made "the zone" of musical creativity such a readily accessible place, and a loyal community of online fans remains spellbound. **DH**

Stretch Panic

Original release date : 2001
Platform : PS2
Developer : Treasure
Genre : Platform

Linda has a magical possessed scarf that she must use to travel through the world, pinching people and freeing her sisters from their terrible all-consuming demons of vanity. Yes, it's Treasure, the boutique Japanese developer, famous for crafting imaginative mini-classics, heavy on clever mechanics, screen-filling explosions of color, and gaming's most elaborate bosses.

The great joy of *Stretch Panic* (called *Freak Out* in Europe) is the ability to tug at the delightfully stretchy environment with your mysterious scarf before yanking things around, snatching at rubbery clumps of the ground to propel you into the air or over ravines, and pinching the flesh of the game's bizarre bosses, twanging them where it really hurts. It's quite unlike anything else available.

Stretch Panic is not without its drawbacks: Some of the game play is frustrating and the navigation a little slow, but despite these issues there's something at the heart of the game that's so different, so gleefully unusual, that you may find yourself forgiving these faults and just losing yourself in the madness. **CD**

Mario Kart: Super Circuit

Original release date : 2001
Platform : Game Boy Advance
Developer : Intelligent Systems
Genre : Driving

Truly legendary games are few and far between, but *Super Mario Kart*, on the SNES, is certainly among their number. *Mario Kart: Super Circuit* borrows heavily from its template and pulls off the unexpected by being at least as good as the original. Bullishly confident in its thoroughbred pedigree, it throws down the gauntlet by including all of the first game's tracks (albeit with subtle changes) alongside twenty new ones, as if to invite direct comparison.

Presenting flat tracks, the game eschews 3-D bar a few graphical enhancements (the power-up boxes, for instance, hover above the track rather than constituting part of its texture) and is a delight for fans of 16-bit visuals. But it's the subtle mixing of the SNES and N64 *Mario Kart*

games' aesthetics that most impresses, the bright, bold colors working well to compensate for the original lack of backlighting of the Game Boy Advance. This fusion extends beyond the visuals, too, and some of *Mario Kart 64*'s mechanics make it into the game, perhaps the most amusing of which being the ability to become a mobile bomb when defeated in battle mode.

Players can number up to four, thanks to the GBA's link cable, and playing with others, whether racing or battling, sees *Mario Kart: Super Circuit* come into its own. The game takes advantage of the single-cart multiplayer functionality of the GBA by providing a pared-down party experience, even if only one person owns a copy, and thanks to the luxury of having your own screen, sneaking up on opponents is made easy. Some may lament not being able to keep tabs on competitors, but this seemingly small difference gives *Mario Kart: Super Circuit* a distinctive personality of its own and adds yet more depth to an already exceptional package. **BM**

Gitaroo Man

Original release date : 2001

Platform : PS2, PSP

Developer : iNiS

Genre : Music

Gitaroo Man was an unusual departure for Koei—the husband-and-wife publishing team behind several decades' worth of obsessively detailed, historically accurate simulation war games. But it wasn't the first. In fact, the company had tried stepping out of its comfort zone before, leaving feudal Japan behind to achieve some success in the field of romance strategy, notably in the shape of dating games like *Angelique*—a huge hit in Japan. But dating games and combat strategy have more in common than you might think. Certainly, they have more in common than *Gitaroo Man* and . . . well . . . anything.

In terms of the action, sure, there is a superficial similarity to *PaRappa the Rapper*: You press buttons according to on-screen instructions in time to music. But for *Gitaroo Man* those basics are just a launch pad, as it rockets off into the zaniest reaches of outer space, borrowing bits and bobs from the beat-'em-up genre along the way. Using a scratchy, neon art style, it tells a tale of talking dogs and a space-powered, magical-guitar-wielding hero called U-1, who is forced to defend himself against the Gravilians, led by Zowie. It was a perfect prefiguration of the sort of weirdness that was to come in later games from rhythm-action specialist iNiS, such as the *Oendan* and *Elite Beat Agents* series on Nintendo's DS.

But this isn't just weirdness for its own sake, and it's held together by game play that is an idiosyncratic fusion of beat 'em up and Simon Says—so keeping time is just one dimension of a game that is actually a succession of boss battles against Zowie's increasingly insane musical minions. *Gitaroo Man* is a one-off and, because relatively small quantities appeared outside of Japan, something of gaming rarity in the West. **DM**

Grand Theft Auto III

Original release date : 2001
Platform : Various
Developer : DMA Design
Genre : Action

Prior to its landmark third installment, the *Grand Theft Auto* series was an occasionally controversial oddity. Then it became a global phenomenon, a record-breaking hit whose irregular releases would become major events in gaming, with fans lining up at midnight outside stores all around the world, and coverage breaking out of the specialist press and on to daily news.

At least the game deserves it. Its transition to 3-D may not have led to the best-looking title, but this is a series that's all about the feeling—the night-time streets, the squeal of tires as you sling yourself into an unlikely corner, and the dull thwump of a policeman flailing over the hood and past the windshield. *Grand Theft Auto III*

nailed its murky *Goodfellas* atmosphere just as later games would capture the woozy citrus skies of Florida and the sunburned sidewalks of southern California. Liberty City is not just the setting but the main character, rising out of the ground with realistic architecture, its ragged arcs and streets a playground you'd revisit again and again.

And it's the little things that matter. *Grand Theft Auto III* may have been a step forward in terms of storytelling and mission structure—even though the series would always lag behind a little in the latter element, as it bounced against the endless opportunities of its sandbox—but the moment the game really starts to feel magical is when you slip behind the wheel of a car you've just stolen, casually reverse over the original owner, and then flick through the radio stations as you peel off into the distance. With a natural feel for pop culture and its excesses that's never quite matched in the game's more formal mechanics, *Grand Theft Auto III* made its world feel real, and that was often enough to convince you to come in and play. **CD**

Return to Castle Wolfenstein

Original release date : 2001
Platform : Various
Developer : Gray Matter Interactive
Genre : First-Person Shooter

Game franchises that go for long periods between installments have bigger problems to worry about than the question of their own relevance. With nearly ten years between the release of the original first-person shooter *Wolfenstein 3D* and *Return to Castle Wolfenstein*, technological progress demanded that the entire nature of the sequel be reconsidered: the original wasn't even three-dimensional at all, instead using techniques of ray casting and scaled sprites, so how could the sequel take onboard full three-dimensional environments powered by dedicated graphics chips?

Cleverly, single-player-mode developer Gray Matter Interactive took the "reboot" route, placing *Wolfenstein's*

hero B. J. Blazkowicz back into the castle's dungeons and from there into an entirely new situation. Blazkowicz then takes on the Nazis and the undead as he tries to prevent the SS Paranormal Division from resurrecting Heinreich I, an evil warlord of untold power from Germany's history.

For many, *Return to Castle Wolfenstein* removes one of the most important aspects of the original: You don't get to kill Hitler at the end. Yet it manages to update the franchise into a lively pulp adventure, recasting it as an Indiana Jones–style world of magic and mysterious powers sought after by the Nazis rather than simply a backdrop to an arcade-style three-dimensional shooter.

What makes the game *really* special is the multiplayer mode, in which Axis and Allies compete to complete objectives and win the round—or at least stop their opponent. With four balanced classes and well-designed maps, *Return to Castle Wolfenstein* influenced first-person shooters that followed, making it almost as relevant to its genre as its parent—not bad, given the ten-year gap. **MKu**

Max Payne

Original release date : 2001
Platform : PC
Developer : Remedy Entertainment
Genre : Shoot 'Em Up

With a name that sounds like a counterproductive suppository brand and a hero who looks like he's using one, it's hard to take *Max Payne* seriously. But its decision to use reference materials as textures, making it the first legitimately photorealistic 3-D game, meant it was taken very seriously by makers of early video cards.

Developed by Helsinki-based Remedy, the game originally looked like any other. But when its artists returned from a US field trip with hundreds of photos of New York City, revealing a landscape still as gritty as any in the *French Connection*, they knew what had to be done.

Told in a film-noir style, with grungy comic-book style cut scenes, *Max Payne* is a bleak tribute to Hollywood crime classics and hard-boiled archetypes. It opens with the destruction of Payne himself, a new father in the NYPD who comes home to find his family murdered. Addicts of a new street drug called Valkyr are responsible, and the search for revenge leads Payne from the bowels of Hell's Kitchen to the towers of the drug's creator, the Aesir Corporation. With his mind unraveling as the plot comes together, his journey is thick with nightmare and betrayal.

Introducing games to advanced particle effects and "bullet-time" gunplay, *Max Payne* was also a milestone for PC action games. Finally, they didn't have to feel like second-class citizens compared to traditional console genres. The game's mouse-and-keyboard controls bring precision to the combat; the textures are eye-popping at high resolutions. And with a New York winter inspired by Norse mythology, it brings an otherworldly quality to its crack dens and alleyways. Ironically, given its filmic homages, *Max Payne* was not well treated by Hollywood: The 2008 adaptation is a crushingly disappointing and depressing event in every sense. **DH**

Halo: Combat Evolved

Original release date : 2001
Platform : Xbox
Developer : Bungie
Genre : First-Person Shooter

Is it more shocking that the action game that would power Microsoft's unlikely transformation from spreadsheet facilitator and browser monopolist to the underdog savior of hardcore video gaming was originally a real-time strategy title? Or is it that it was originally intended for the Apple Macintosh? Regardless of which, clear heads prevailed, and the Xbox ended up with its first undeniably brilliant piece of software from day one of the console's life.

Halo: Combat Evolved is unapologetically epic space opera; its story concerns mankind's fight against the Covenant—a gaggle of religious fundamentalist aliens who want to wipe humanity from the stars. Stepping into the shoes of armor-clad supersoldier Master Chief, players explore a mysterious and ancient ring world—part shiny alien hardware, part lush, Alpine forests and mountains—engaging the enemy in exciting little clusters of combat, messing about with a near-perfect range of different toys, tooling around in the Warthog assault jeep, and generally saving the universe.

Touted for its famous "thirty seconds of fun"—the core game loop that comes alive with each encounter, blending a handful of carefully arranged enemy types with a choice of delightful guns—beneath the epic musical score and waffly, often rather windy, plot, *Halo* is simply about the eternal pleasures of tight and economical game design, as explosions, environments, and enemies come together in a thrilling muddle.

Halo: Combat Evolved has become the Xbox's own *Star Wars*, a pop-culture giant with increasingly elaborate lore. And while the hype surrounding each subsequent release is inevitably getting out of hand, when the games themselves are this effortlessly replayable, the marketing will never overshadow the series' true achievements. **CD**

Silent Hill 2

Original release date : 2001
Platform : Various
Developer : Team Silent
Genre : Survival Horror

The setup is the stuff of nightmarish J-horror. James Sunderland receives a letter from his wife, asking him to join her in Silent Hill, the rural town in which they once vacationed. One problem. She's been dead for three years. He turns up, anyway. So begins another slice of psychological survival horror from the Team Silent crew.

While the original title focused on external supernatural peril, the sequel is very much about internal demons. *Silent Hill 2* is shrouded in mist, effectively symbolizing Sunderland's emotional fogginess, and the characters he meets—a slutty dead ringer for his deceased wife, a possible serial killer, and a suicidal woman looking for her lost mother—all read as aspects of his inner torment. Sunderland has a secret: a tragic involvement with his wife's death, and it only gradually comes to light as he explores the abandoned town, getting ever closer to the hotel at the center of his torment.

Team Silent fills its dank, fetid universe with layer upon layer of grotesque imagery. The hospital walls smeared with blood, the toilet clogged with viscera, everything is rotting, burned, or broken. The monsters, too, are hugely disturbing. The deformed nurses, the stumbling shop window dummies, the horrific Pyramid Head—they're ugly yet weirdly sexual; real, but blurred and nightmarish.

As with all *Silent Hill* games, there are multiple endings depending on the actions of the player and what they discover throughout. None are particularly happy, although the two hidden spoof endings are an unexpected joy. Really, though, the best Sunderland can hope for is self-realization. It's a typically downbeat end to an intense adventure, loaded with the sort of psycho-sexual symbolism and Freudian imagery you'd expect from a Hitchcock movie rather than a horror game. **KS**

Shenmue II

Original release date : 2001
Platform : Dreamcast, Xbox
Developer : Sega
Genre : Action / Adventure

The second part of Yu Suzuki's unfinished symphony of video game storytelling expands the horizons of the first game and its spiky-haired protagonist, Ryo Hazuki. When Ryo steps off a boat to find himself in a compellingly realistic but dauntingly unfamiliar Hong Kong at the start of the game, it's clear that he's now in a much bigger place than the small, familiar streets of Yokosuka. It's a world in which the supernatural mixes with the mundane: brawling with giants one minute, shifting boxes or rolling dice in a desperate attempt to make some pocket money the next. Some parts of the game see Ryo rubbing shoulders with the grittily realistic gangs that compete for control of Kowloon; others see him retiring to monasteries and temples to learn near-mystical fighting techniques on his quest to locate Lan Di and avenge his father's death.

That quest contains more mini-games, more coin-ops, and more brawling than ever before, and it also contains more freedom, since Ryo's movements are no longer quite as curtailed by bedtime. It also streamlines many aspects of the first game; for example, allowing players to skip ahead instead of waiting around for appointments. But the two most important elements are the story and characters: There are new rivalries, and love interests, here, and a colorful cast of supporting characters, from the pirate-styled Ren to the ginger-haired Joy.

In terms of graphics and interactivity, *Shenmue II* sacrifices some of the finer details of the first game, but the result is a far wider geographical and thematic scope, reflecting the way Ryo's hunt has wrenched him from the cozy environments of adolescence to thrust him into the challenges of becoming a man. Maybe one day that hunt will reach its conclusion. **DM**

Serious Sam

Original release date : 2001
Platform : PC
Developer : Croteam
Genre : First-Person Shooter

As first-person shooter developers pursue an evolution of the genre, adding RPG elements, strategy, character development, cover mechanics, and evocative storylines, *Serious Sam* throws all that high-brow nonsense on the "not in this game" pile to focus on shooting stuff with big guns in crazy situations. The result is a mindless, unadulterated shoot-fest that gets increasingly improbable the farther you travel through its ancient Egyptian levels.

How Sam "Serious" Stone gets to ancient Egypt is ridiculous enough. He's sent back through time to defeat evil alien forces led by Mental (yes, you read that right) in order to change the course of history and prevent Earth's devastation in the present.

Every good shooter needs memorable enemies, and *Serious Sam* is full of them. The headless bomb-handed kamikazes are the standout, the game's powerful 3-D engine allowing for vast open expanses of sand dunes from which these guys can appear and home in on Sam before exploding in his face. Add marauding werebulls, aerial harpies, machine-gunning giant scorpions, and you can see that Sam will never want for a target.

When literally hundreds of werebulls appear out of thin air, you have to appreciate both the power of the engine and the manic action it delivers. By that point you'll be used to seeing monsters appear from nowhere, particularly when you pick up a desperately needed health pack or armor shard. Some of the sound effects are probably the cackles of glee from the developers striving for the unapologetically silly. At the same time, the hardened twitch gamer will have to be on his A game to meet and defeat the challenge, chuckling along the way at the ludicrousness of it all. **RSm**

Luigi's Mansion

Original release date : 2001
Platform : GameCube
Developer : Nintendo
Genre : Action

Nightmares and dreamscapes abound! GameCube launch title *Luigi's Mansion* is the *Mario* game where you can't jump or bottom-bounce off foes; indeed, it's the *Mario* game where you don't actually *play* as Mario. Instead, his lanky brother, Luigi, comes to the fore, the beanpole hero in green dispatched to a haunted house where his famous brother has been kidnapped by a mischievous gaggle of ghosts.

What unfolds is one of the strangest and most constantly surprising *Mario* titles ever—a room-clearing riff on *Ghostbusters*, with Luigi working as a no-nonsense exorcist, sucking the cartoony blobs of undead into his handy Poltergust 3000. Essentially a series of extremely quirky boss fights strung together with a spooky minimalist narrative, *Luigi's Mansion* is an absolute masterpiece of staging, each self-contained chamber featuring its own otherworldly gimmick, be it musical instruments that play themselves, a candelabra glimpsed bobbing down the hallway, a nightmare of mirrors and doors, or—best of all—the wood-lined observatory where a peak through the telescope takes Luigi on a brief, magical trip through a twinkling universe of stars.

It's a bold departure, and throughout it all there's the lingering sense of a seasoned development team letting go after years of expanding on a brilliant, but well-defined, template. Not only did *Luigi's Mansion* nail the slippery business of bagging ghouls far more convincingly than 2009's *Ghostbusters* game for the 360 and PS3, but it also managed to add valuable new material to the *Mario* canon itself, casting Luigi as the cowardly brother made heroic, bringing a dash of lasting characterization to a series that had plenty of personality, but relied, for the most part, on interchangeably cheery ciphers for the leads. **CD**

Jak and Daxter: The Precursor Legacy

Original release date : 2001
Platform : PS2
Developer : Naughty Dog
Genre : Platform

Jak and Daxter's own precursor was Crash Bandicoot, a character who became something of a mascot for the original PlayStation and an example of Naughty Dog's technical skills. *Jak and Daxter: The Precursor Legacy* is similarly demonstrative of the developer's talents when it comes to character design and the manipulation of Sony's hardware: players are treated to a high level of detail, charismatic animation, and a streaming world with no loading screen in sight. The game also paved the way for Nolan North's later proliferation of vocal appearances by casting Max Casella (an actor who nowadays also has *The Sopranos* and *Grand Theft Auto: The Ballad of Gay Tony* on his résumé) as the voice of Daxter.

As 3-D graphics had been well exploited for the previous generation of consoles, standing out from the crowd in the 128-bit landscape required new tactics. *Jak and Daxter: The Precursor Legacy*'s main innovation is the aforementioned lack of loading. Before this, games were predominantly discrete experiences lacking in holistic permanence, but here players could travel to locations visible in the distance, and challenges begun would remain in the state they were left, rather than requiring restarts. The stage props used by preceding platform games had been transformed into a living, breathing world.

That the mechanics of the game are heavily evocative of classics like *Super Mario 64* and *Banjo-Kazooie* is simply another reason to recommend it; the polished, fluid controls ensure that simply moving Jak around is a joy. Thought is also put into the reinvention of genre clichés: The collectibles here aren't abstract tokens but energy orbs, which make sense in the context of the plot, setting a new bar for consistency and motivation. **BM**

Maximo: Ghosts to Glory

Original release date : 2001
Platform : PS2
Developer : Capcom
Genre : Action

Maximo: Ghosts to Glory is a rare example of a Japanese game done justice by an overseas developer. Even more remarkable is that the game is *Ghosts 'n Goblins*, the arcade classic celebrated for its surgically accurate level design, magical characterization, and coin-gobbling difficulty. And most astonishing of all, this wasn't a mere sequel but a 3-D spin-off—a doom-laden prospect if ever there was one.

Thanks to a grueling approval process suffered while handling another Capcom game, *Final Fight Revenge*, Capcom invented *Maximo: Ghosts to Glory*, a self-contained brand with its own hero, art style, control system, and story. It's all about an intrepid knight named Maximo, who returns from war to find his kingdom cursed by an ancient

evil, the throne taken by his trusted advisor, Achille, and its princess abducted and forced into marriage. The four sorceresses that hold power over the land have been locked up in towers, each surrounded by legions of zombies and hellish beasts. With little more than a trusty sword, iron shield, three lives, and a spring in his step, Maximo must conquer all if he's to take the magic back.

The irony is that of all the 3-D updates to classic arcade games, one of the few really good ones should act under an alias. *Maximo: Ghosts to Glory* would have made a great sequel to *Ghosts 'n Goblins*, and has every right to bear the family crest. In its dynamic 3-D world, where soil transforms into lava as coffins rise up like elevators, jumps and swipes must be judged as if your coins depend on it. Which they literally do, since a continue means handing over a precious "death coin" to the Grim Reaper, and he loves to add inflation. Striking a delicate balance between risk, reward, strategy, and mischief, *Maximo*: *Ghosts to Glory* is anything but a loose adaptation. **DH**

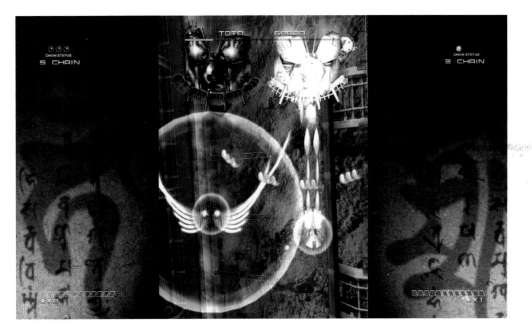

Ikaruga

Original release date : 2001
Platform : Various
Developer : Treasure
Genre : Shoot 'Em Up

Ikaruga wasn't the first vertically scrolling shoot 'em up that Treasure had made. It wasn't even the first to use a color-matching twist, building on a template created for the famously expensive eBay darling, *Radiant Silvergun*. But in its simplicity, its style, and its relentless pace, it's certainly the best: a game to cherish and replay, a tiny, perfectly designed slice of twitchy perfection that will live on whenever you close your eyes, long after your most recent run-through has finished.

At the heart of *Ikaruga* is a very straightforward idea: Enemies and projectiles are divided into black and white varieties, while you also have the power to flip your ship between the two polarities. Attacking an enemy with the opposing color fire will double the damage you inflict, but, while you can absorb incoming bullets of the same hue—it helps to power up your special weapon—you're extremely vulnerable to the opposite variety.

From such a simple framework, Treasure works its usual brand of elegant wonder, spitting out increasingly complex formations of waves, drenching the screen in projectiles as it swings toward the bullet-hell end of the shooter spectrum, and throwing a suite of vast alien bosses your way before you reach the finish line. And, as with all the developer's best games, of course, getting to the end is actually only just the beginning. *Ikaruga* isn't about surviving, but thriving, and the leaderboard of high scores is where the game's real battle will continue to grind out for years to come.

Outside of its triumphant arcade setting, *Ikaruga* was quickly issued on the Dreamcast and GameCube platforms. The best way to enjoy the game today is almost certainly via Xbox Live Arcade. **CD**

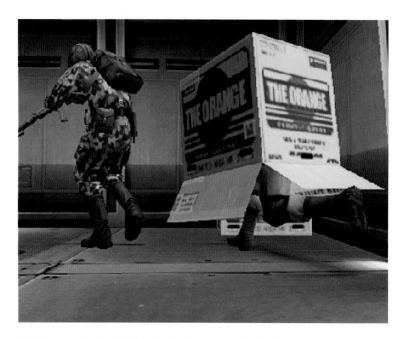

Metal Gear Solid 2: Sons of Liberty

Original release date : 2001

Platform : PS2

Developer : Kojima

Genre : Action

High expectations for *Metal Gear Solid 2: Sons of Liberty* reached fever pitch at 2000's Tokyo Game Show, where a returning Solid Snake was shown leaping from the George Washington bridge onto a passing oil tanker, ready to sneak again into a new adventure. Thanks to the hotly debated power of PlayStation 2, his latest mission promised a visual feast, his outfit in the trailer hammered by torrential rain, his face finally chiseled into something close to human. In hindsight, though, it probably wasn't the best way to demo a game about someone totally different.

Disguised as Iroquois Pliskin—the most overt reference yet to *Escape from New York* hero Snake Plissken—Snake is just a bystander for most of *Metal Gear Solid 2*, the limelight moving to a new face—FOXHOUND agent Raiden. After the demo's tanker prologue, this blond pretty-boy is sent to a hijacked oil rig called Big Shell to rescue the US president, held captive by rogue antiterror group Dead Cell. The nuclear threat this time is twofold, the platform hiding a monstrous weapons platform, Arsenal Gear, and a new type of mechanized walker: Metal Gear Rex.

In an indulgent and consciously divergent sequel, the arrival of Raiden was massively controversial. At worst seen as shameless bait and switch, it marked a new and lasting friction between designer Hideo Kojima and his fans. All of which makes *Metal Gear Solid 2: Sons of Liberty* a fascinating artifact. A sprawling treatise on government and the betrayal of democracy, it plays some superb mind games during its closing act, tying its story in knots while breaking the "fourth wall," even "crashing" the player's console with a nod and a wink. Adding characters, weapons, and tactics with abandon, it climaxes with a notoriously long cut scene lasting for almost forty-five minutes. **DH**

Operation Flashpoint: Cold War Crisis

Original release date : 2001
Platform : PC
Developer : Bohemia Interactive Studios
Genre : Shoot 'Em Up

There had been attempts across the years to create a definitive "soldier sim," but *Operation Flashpoint: Cold War Crisis* was the game that defined what the phrase actually means today. It's a fascinating piece of design, not least in its lack of concession to beginners. You either stick with it or you go and find something else to play.

At its heart there's an infantry experience that remains terrifyingly real. A few bullets will put you down, and your enemies operate with a ferocity that was unknown in shooters up till that time. In most games the enemies are there to be shot, and ultimately let you win. No such luck for players of *Operation Flashpoint: Cold War Crisis*, who face formidable challenges. The single-player campaign is

notable for forcing your character to spend long periods of time crawling around on his belly, as the only possible method to avoid getting gunned down by roving troops. As this campaign opens up, however, you begin to sense the enormity of the vision: an open island, with all vehicles interactive throughout. If you happen to find a tractor or a tank, you can drive off with it. *Operation Flashpoint: Cold War Crisis* is an ode to realism, and as such it is unlike almost anything other than its own sequel.

Where *Operation Flashpoint: Cold War Crisis* made the most ground, however, was in the way it facilitated the ambitions of a creative community. The game editor and mod system were open and flexible, allowing players to create diverse and often intricate multiplayer scenarios. This enabling of creativity ended up fostering an even richer community as new players flocked in to enjoy the fruits of their industrious peers. Had the game not supported this kind of activity, it may not have been considerably more than a curious footnote. **JR**

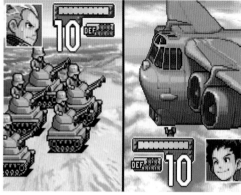

Pikmin

Advance Wars

Original release date : 2001
Platform : GameCube
Developer : Nintendo
Genre : Strategy

Original release date : 2001
Platform : Game Boy Advance
Developer : Intelligent Systems
Genre : Strategy

Shigeru Miyamoto, creator of *Mario* and *Zelda*, never has to look hard for a game idea: *Pikmin* was created after a bit of gardening. The result is something of an oddity—a real-time strategy game of sorts, albeit one like no other, and something that can delight and disturb in equal measure.

Captain Olimar has crash-landed on a mysterious planet, and needs to reclaim the various pieces of his spaceship. Marooned in a frightening environment, he enlists the help of Pikmin, funny little vegetable people who will apparently follow Olimar into the mouth of hell itself if called upon. What follows is an ingenious mixture of spatial puzzles, battles with local wildlife, and strategy, as you work out how many of the different kinds of Pikmin you need to handle each engagement.

Pikmin is an exercise in pure Darwinism. It really is survival of the fittest as the friendly space captain uses his new friends to keep himself alive, even if they die in the process. It's cute and disturbing at the same time, but that doesn't stop it from being a sublime piece of game design in its own right. **CD**

Advance Wars, like chess, suggests that global conflict doesn't have to be messy. It can be precise, thought provoking, tidy, and actually rather polite. If you're after a breezy tactical challenge with a story that unfolds in friendly commuter-sized chunks, built to fit into a space of fifteen minutes or so, this is the game for you.

The game's chummy tale of rip-roaring geopolitical shenanigans unfolds in bright, anime-styled cut scenes, peopled with a youthful cast who seem to treat the prospect of planet-wide warfare with all the gloom and terror one might summon for a playground game of marbles. *Advance Wars* may paint conflict in very cheerful colors, but to write the game off as childish would be to miss the fearsome tactical heart that beats at its core.

Gripping and unforgettable, it's elegant stuff. Indeed, a game as eternally enjoyable as *Advance Wars* suggests that Intelligent Systems (many of whose key staff had been part of Nintendo legend Gunpei Yokoi's Research and Development Team) might just be the most aptly named of all video game studios. **CD**

Golden Sun

Original release date : 2001
Platform : Game Boy Advance
Developer : Camelot Software Planning
Genre : Role-Playing

Camelot's *Golden Sun* is an engaging and storied RPG with one eye set firmly on the past. Its lush, colorful visuals and pseudo-3-D battle system may have pushed the GBA to its limits, but they aided in the telling of a fiercely traditional story, one with plenty of the genre's classic elements.

Set on a vast flat-Earth–styled fantasy world, *Golden Sun* follows the story of a band of plucky teens trying to safeguard the powerful Elemental Stars, which have kept the forces of evil at bay for generations, allowing piece and prosperity to reign.

Golden Sun benefits from beautiful art; a snappy yet intricate narrative; and a rich, melancholic soundtrack. It's a game that rewards experimentation, much of the fun coming from trying out new combinations during the game's fairly regular battles.

Earnest and epic by turn, *Golden Sun* is just the game for anyone who fancies a dip into the play styles of the past. While the original GBA game and its excellent sequel, *The Lost Age*, can still be found fairly easily at online auction sites, the series received its first DS installment in 2010. **CD**

RuneScape

Original release date : 2001
Platform : PC
Publisher: Jagex
Genre : MMORPG

While the grown-ups slap down their credit cards to pay the stiff monthly fees on games like *World of Warcraft*, there is an entire stratum of free-to-play games offering online role-playing that's just as massively multiplayer. *RuneScape,* the original leader of this tier, can be run on a web browser from any computer, and instead of demanding dollars a month, the game makes its money from banner ads or low-cost premium memberships. Written by two brothers, Andrew and Paul Gower, it was launched in 2001 as a basic, old-school adventure. Even after moving to 3-D in 2003, it still looks primitive, if cute and charming. But its simple-to-use character creation offers twenty-four skills, from fishing and woodcutting to thieving and summoning; the combat, on the other hand, is a little stiff and dated.

RuneScape faces stiff competition: It's more mature than *Club Penguin* but less dazzling than Sony's *Free Realms*. What other games can't offer, however, is the deep community, a (predominantly teenage) fan base in the millions, and the satisfaction of a rigorous, endless grind that could keep them busy all the way to adulthood. **CDa**

Super Smash Bros. Melee

Original release date : 2001

Platform : GameCube

Developer : Nintendo

Genre : Fighting

Super Smash Bros. is a fighting series with more than a little touch of sumo to it—although it would have to be a frighteningly complex, high-speed, side-scrolling variety of Japan's most famous grapple sport. Inflicting damage on your opponent by combining different moves is still important, but forcing players off the edge of the numerous themed stages is the real objective here.

The result is a fighting game in which tactics and technical approaches are crucial to success at anything other than the most basic levels, but which still has time for a rush of pure spectacle. Even if you are playing with balletic precision and attention to detail, the game will still look like an apocalyptic rumble taking place in the world's

least stable fireworks factory, as players sail through the air and land with concussive thumps, and overindulgent effects spit shiny particles into the sky.

Super Smash Bros. Melee, the GameCube's installment, was built on the success of the N64 original, with smooth animation; a suite of beautiful, themed backdrops; and even more of Nintendo's evergreen favorites with whom to get in a rumble. With twenty-six characters to choose from, the game has fourteen more stars than the original, and the gathering ropes in characters from *Zelda*, *Mario*, the *Fire Emblem* series, and the *Mother* RPGs.

With power-ups themed from numerous Nintendo games littering the playing field, and snatches of familiar faces and textures glimpsed whenever the battle slows down even for a second, *Super Smash Bros. Melee* is the kind of world-blending romp that could only exist in the video game. A blistering spasm of cartoon violence existing at the very point where precision meets popularity, the whole thing quickly descends into a hot mess. **CD**

The Legend of Zelda: Oracle of Seasons/Ages

Original release date : 2001
Platform : Game Boy Color
Developer : Capcom
Genre : Action / Adventure

The follow-up to the Game Boy's brilliant *The Legend of Zelda: Link's Awakening* was always going to have its work cut out, even before you consider that, for the first time, third-party developers were handling the most delicate of Nintendo's whimsical properties. And although Capcom can't compete with the master company's own designers, it does a pretty decent job of playing babysitter to greatness, with a couple of games that certainly cover very suitable territory and repeat all the right moves.

The Legend of Zelda: Oracle of Seasons/Oracle of Ages are a pair of complementary interconnected games. The two games, released simultaneously, interact via a Nintendo Game Link Cable, enabling the two titles to be played on two different Game Boys at the same time. Each game transports our hero Link to a different magical land, where a powerful local oracle has been kidnapped. While the larger story can only really be grasped once both games are completed, each title can still be enjoyed as a standalone adventure in its own right. And, helpfully, Capcom has been taking notes, with adventures that unfold in a familiar progression of item-gathering, over-world exploration, and dungeon crawling. It's not a bad copy of the previous games, and the development team manages to throw in enough new magical twists and ideas to keep you chugging along on a series of journeys that only just fall short of what *Zelda* fans traditionally expect.

With visuals and controls almost identical to *The Legend of Zelda: Link's Awakening*, the *Oracle* games never quite reach the heights of Nintendo's own work, though they still do a decent job. Heartfelt, varied, and often clever, they serve as a reminder that the right property has the power to lift everyone associated with it. **CD**

SSX Tricky

Original release date : 2001
Platform : Various
Developer : Electronic Arts
Genre : Sports

Wintry counterparts to the mega-popular *Tony Hawk's Pro Skater* series, the *SSX* snowboarding games were probably the best sports titles to come out of Electronic Arts during the PlayStation 2 generation. The varied stages of *SSX Tricky*, the sequel to the original, mark the height of the series' esoteric wackiness. (The third volume—*SSX3*—would shift to the grander, more unified setting of one monstrous peak.) In *SSX Tricky*, though, every track is a distinct adventure, each more impossible than the last: the snow-capped buttes of Mesablanca, the urban powder of Merqury City, the gravity-immune melting glacier of Aloha Ice Jam, etc. These landscapes, riddled with shortcuts and surprises, are the main characters of the game.

Of course, the actual characters aren't bad, either. You choose your rider from a cast of eccentrics, ranging from a Japanese schoolgirl to a British street biker, and work your way to the top of the international racing circuit. Smooth controls make it a pleasure to carve your board around the steep turns of each racetrack, but the real joy happens in midair, where you execute the twists, grabs, and backflips that give *SSX Tricky* its name. In fact, the game's Show-Off mode dispenses with the race premise altogether and simply rewards you for how many badass jumps you can pull off without face-planting in the snow.

Hip-hop and techno backing tracks remix themselves on the fly to match your progress, so when you're cranking out "Über Tricks," the beats are pumping. This audio legerdemain feeds the sensation that every part of the game is moving in sync, from your thumbs to the last pixel on the screen. Motion-controls interfaces are all well and good, but a gimmicky joystick will have trouble matching the kinetic thrill of *SSX Tricky*. **JT**

Star Wars Rogue Squadron II: Rogue Leader

Original release date : 2001
Platform : GameCube
Developer : Factor 5
Genre : Shoot 'Em Up

It's a measure of the brilliance of Factor 5's *Star Wars Rogue Squadron II: Rogue Leader* that it starts where most other games would reach their climax—with that paradigmatic trench run on the original Death Star, allowing players to *start* the game by re-enacting that seminal piece of cinema history and destroying the most powerful weapon in the galaxy. Where do you go from there?

Well, from there, you get to engage in ten missions that take you right up to the run on the second Death Star at the end of *Return of the Jedi*. It's like an enhanced remake of the original *Rogue Squadron*, extended to include all three of the original movies. That means it recreates the sights and sounds of the *Star Wars* universe with stunning fidelity,

from the shriek of TIE Fighters to the vast dimensions of Imperial Star Destroyers. Development studio Factor 5 gained a reputation for industry-leading technical achievements throughout its history, and this represents some of its finest work.

Though only ten missions are on offer, they pack pretty much everything in, from Hoth to Bespin; from womp rats to Nien Nunb. And there's plenty of replay value, thanks to the same mission-ranking system as in the first game, allowing expert pilots to unlock five bonus levels, granting them the option to play as Darth Vader or pilot all sorts of secret vehicles, including Boba Fett's space-snail, Slave I, and the sound designer's Buick Electra 225.

Perhaps the only disappointing aspect of *Star Wars Rogue Squadron II: Rogue Leader* is the rock-hard difficulty toward the end of the game, culminating in a final Death Star run that resembles the end of *Star Wars* on a dodgy DVD that keeps skipping at the end. But you already knew how it turns out, right? **DM**

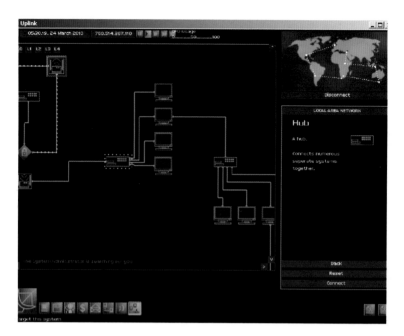

Uplink

Original release date : 2001
Platform : PC, Mac
Developer : Introversion Software
Genre : Hacking Simulation

Immersion is a highly sought sensation in the drive toward realism in games, but challenged by the natural narrative drive of game writers. It's hard to believe that you're part of the experience when you're controlling a hero who is—more than likely—more dashing and heroic than you'll ever be, even if he's as mute as a fish. Alternate-reality games have perhaps made the best inroads toward making players feel as if they're part of something big. But what if you want to be the chosen one?

Developed by the self-termed "last of the bedroom programmers" team at Introversion Software—who started the company while working from their homes, and in true geek-made-good style, apparently enjoyed early success by spending "£10,000 a week on speedboats and fast cars"—Uplink is a game where you are the hero and the setting is wherever you have your PC set up.

A hacker simulation that takes its cues from Hollywood's brief flirtation with computer-crime drama, Uplink offers a convincing and consistent front end that "connects" the player's computer to a gateway owned by the mysterious Uplink Corporation. After a short tutorial the player is using password crackers and other software to break into computers across the world to steal and sabotage for profit, but danger never feels too far away: Players must keep a keen eye out for traces on their machines and may even be caught through a slipup as simple as forgetting to delete access logs.

Uplink is both thrilling and scary to play, despite looking about as exciting as a spreadsheet, and the design is so immersive that you fear the trace is happening to your very computer and that the police really are about to come knocking at your door. **MKu**

Age of Mythology

Original release date : 2002
Platform : PC, Mac
Developer : Ensemble Studios
Genre : Strategy .

Ensemble didn't take risks. It didn't have to. From the moment the historical build 'n' bash *Age of Empires* launched in 1997, its course was set: It would be populist king of real-time strategy, absurdly successful regardless of whatever doomsayers might claim about the PC and Mac platforms. That owner Microsoft closed the studio in 2009 didn't seem to add up: No developer knew how to be a reliable money-factory quite as well as Ensemble.

Age of Mythology, the studio's first game for Microsoft, doesn't take risks either. It does quite the opposite, dragging the fantastical elements that less successful rivals tend toward into its own straitlaced but highly polished strategy structure: harvesting wood and stone, building

bases in an exact order, deftly making every unit a precise rock to some other soldier's paper or scissor. Ensemble took someone else's risk and made it into the most sensible thing in the world. It has minotaur and sphinx and valkyrie, but somehow they're not an outlandish presence among the more familiar cavalry and archers. Instead, they're smart, strategic high-end units, vital to tipping the game's mathematically precise balance in your favor. *Age of Mythology* knows *exactly* what it's doing, and being in the company of mythical beasts doesn't change the cast-iron formula one jot.

Age of Mythology may have played it safe, but it did suggest Ensemble might be a little more playful from thereon in. That didn't happen. Next in line came the button-downed *Age of Empires III*, and then *Halo Wars* as a confident dying gasp. That leaves *Age of Mythology* as an aberration: perhaps the only game where this one-time king of studios allowed its own character to appear alongside its unsullied strategy-design skill. **AM**

Battlefield 1942

Original release date : 2002
Platform : PC, Mac
Developer : Digital Illusions CE
Genre : First-Person Shooter

Battlefield 1942 put intelligence into multiplayer team-based shooters. PC players had been ganging up since *Half-Life Team Fortress*, and limited coordination was hinted at as early as *Starsiege: Tribes*. But by placing multiclassed team combatants within cunningly designed World War II arenas, *Battlefield 1942* forced the issue, making for an epic multiplayer behemoth that rolled over the opposition.

The core action takes place in loosely authentic theaters of war in the game's "Conquest" mode, which pits two historically appropriate armies against each other: the British versus the Germans in Europe, or the Japanese versus Uncle Sam in the Pacific. Each team is assigned control points, typically villages or islands, where the action

begins, from which fallen soldiers can respawn as one of several specialized character classes. Fighting side-by-side with other players—up to thirty-two in total—you battle to seize control of these strategic points, forcing back the enemy and depleting the tickets that end the game at zero. Every death reduces tickets too, neatly incentivizing players to fight for their lives rather than go for suicide missions.

The game also plays smart by dumbing down, enabling you to drive, pilot, or plunge to your death in dozens of vehicles—from jeeps and tanks to aircraft carriers and airplanes—but it eschews fussy control variations in favor of a cartoonlike equivalence. The graphics engine copes well, with ceaseless cinematic moments emerging from the random actions of you and your fellows.

It all conspires to unite far-flung and (often idiotic) online gamers to give the illusion of a cohesive fighting force locked in battle. Think *Wacky Races* meets *Medal of Honor*—and don't get too snooty, because the result is a blast, and it spawned a monster. **OB**

Burnout 2: Point of Impact

Original release date : 2002
Platform : Various
Developer : Criterion Games
Genre : Driving

Burnout opened up the throttle and snarled its way on to the video game motoring scene with all the youthful enthusiasm of a young Lightning McQueen and the destructive nihilism of *Mad Max*. At a time when the fashion in racing was for real-world physics, processional AI, and dull driving tests, Criterion's game opted for arcade-styled exuberance and hyperintense high-speed thrills, where the car-porn crashes were just as important as the right racing line. This is a game in which drivers are encouraged to live dangerously or die trying in slo-mo scenes of shearing metal and twisting, burning wreckage.

Sequel *Burnout 2: Point of Impact* picked up on the popular appeal of those collisions, making them even more prominent by introducing a Crash mode that plays like a demented, damaged version of bowling with cars. The main racing mode, though, remains, in essence, the same as its predecessor: roaring around busy roads, weaving slightly too close to the traffic, swerving round corners, and flying over jumps to charge your boost meter and secure the extra miles-per-hour needed to nose in front of the opposition. It does what video games do best: allow players to experience something that is impossible to experience in real life—and certainly inadvisable to even attempt, as so many pre-game warning screens soberly inform us nowadays.

Burnout 2: Point of Impact helped to free the entire racing genre from the shackles of realism, paving the way for the likes of Sega's glorious resurrection of *OutRun* and the muddy mayhem of the PlayStation 3's *MotorStorm*. There is, of course, a place for realism in gaming, but if that's what you're looking for, the risk-filled roads of *Burnout 2: Point of Impact* are most definitely not it. **DM**

Crazy Taxi 3: High Roller

Original release date : 2002
Platform : Various
Developer : Hitmaker
Genre : Driving

So, professions you initially think probably shouldn't be immortalized in video games—number 37: taxi driver. Taxi drivers follow orders, they don't blow things up, they don't fire sub-machine guns, and they drive about in tiny environments fulfilling a set of mundane objectives.

Wait a minute! Professions that, upon further reflection, are actually pretty much perfect for immortalization in video games—number 101: taxi driver. Taxi drivers follow orders, they make the most of small environments, they accept endless missions from dull quest givers, and they are rewarded each time they complete a task with a tiny amount of money. Also, occasionally they get to run someone over.

Taxi drivers understand the grind of most games, in other words, but *Crazy Taxi* isn't an RPG. It's a fast-paced arcade racer in which you drive clients between various locations, competing for hi-scores, racing the clock, and avoiding too many accidents. All *Crazy Taxi* games are actually pretty much the same title: The colors are intense, the characters are lovably ridiculous, the cars handle with wonderful cinematic looseness, and the sun shines in that Sega-patented manner. Often they even reuse a previous title's range of environments.

What makes *Crazy Taxi 3: High Roller* stand out in particular, then, is the inclusion of the new Vegas-styled Glitter Oasis environment, and the addition of a few nighttime levels. Not too much on the surface, perhaps, but it all mounts up to one of those titles that quickly becomes worryingly replayable: a glimpse into the grim cogs of compulsion, certainly, but a brightly colored glimpse, with a chugging rock score, bright lights, and beautiful weather—even during the night. **CD**

Dark Chronicle

Original release date : 2002
Platform : PS2
Developer : Level-5
Genre : Action / Role-Playing

Level-5's reputation is secure: *Dragon Quest VIII*, *Jeanne D'Arc*, and the *Professor Layton* games have established themselves as favorites around the world. When *Dark Cloud* (the precursor to *Dark Chronicle*) first appeared, however, the developer was unknown in the industry, creating an oft-delayed, experimental RPG for a console that had yet to establish itself as the most successful in history.

And it really was experimental: an unprecedented and slightly incongruous mix of world building and dungeoneering. It played like a cross between *SimCity* and *Diablo*, bound together by the rich character design and story—typical of the developer's subsequent hits. The idea was for players to fight their way through randomly

generated dungeons in order to find and bring back the parts to rebuild a succession of villages and cities. And there was a fishing mini-game for good measure. (No self-respecting Japanese role-playing game is complete without a fishing mini-game.)

It was met both by critics and buying public alike with the sort of bafflement reserved for an art-house curio, instead of recognition as a new RPG landmark. That weird premise and some rough edges simply seemed to obscure its paradigmatic brilliance. Until, that is, *Dark Chronicle* tidied up all of the rough edges, threw in some new mini-games, and made the switch to the cel-shaded graphics that have characterized many of the company's games ever since. In truth, it wasn't the most radical of makeovers, and the invention and photography mini-games are as inappropriate as the combination of world building, fighting, and fishing. But the game took the premise from the original and delivered on its unlikely promise, which was enough to persuade the critics. **DM**

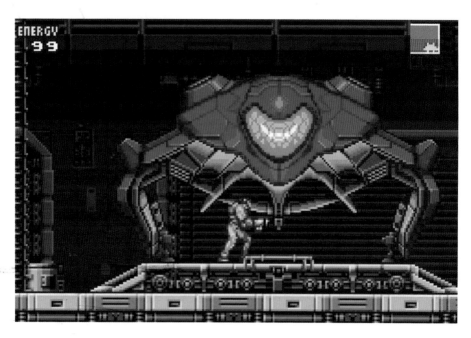

Metroid Fusion

Original release date : 2002
Platform : Game Boy Advance
Developer : Nintendo
Genre : Platform / Shoot 'Em Up

The translation of 2-D *Metroid* into 3-D *Metroid Prime* may have been one of modern gaming's great success stories, but at the same time there was something missing: claustrophobia. The 2-D spaces, and the restrictive axes that go with them, enable you to hem in a player much more effectively than would ever be possible in a 3-D world. And so with *Metroid Fusion*, the first 2-D *Metroid* since the superlative *SNES Super Metroid* (and so the first to be designed without the input of Nintendo legend Gunpei Yokoi), Nintendo returned to the mix of claustrophobia and fear that only 2-D corridors can give.

The twist this time is that Samus's suit, the source of her power, is killing her. Not only that, but the biological

nasty called Phazon that's doing it has somehow managed to clone her, creating a much more powerful version of Samus who exists in the same 2-D corridors with the sole purpose of destroying her. You can't face this until fully upgraded. It's a scripted hunt rather than a dynamic one, but it's wonderfully done: You'll be crouching in a duct, only to hear the intense thrums that herald fake Samus, and stay silent and still as she tramps mere inches above your head. When the final showdown comes, after many moments like this, it's as cathartic as it is spectacular.

Alongside this, place an excellent 2-D map design that no developer but Nintendo seems able to touch, and the ever-brilliant upgrade system that locks into it, opening up areas and revealing secrets in places you thought you were long done with. Its diminutive stature means *Metroid Fusion* will never be considered in the same category as the series masterpiece, *Super Metroid*, but certain converts—or let's call them "heretics"—might wonder whether it supersedes it. **RS**

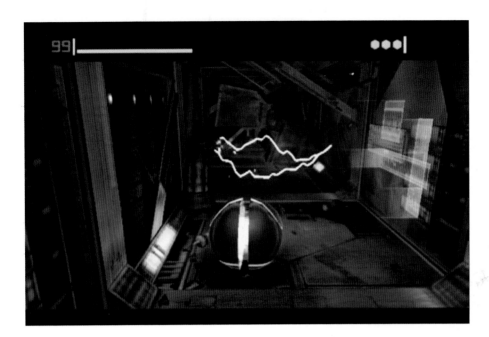

Metroid Prime

Original release date : 2002
Platform : GameCube
Developer : Retro Studios
Genre : Action / First-Person Shooter

Let's be honest. Nobody thought this one was going to work. First off, there was the fact that *Metroid* was being handled by Retro Studios rather than Nintendo itself. Could an external company (and an American one at that) understand the slow burn of Samus Aran's mysterious adventures? Worse still, the venerable platformer was going first-person. What? Was Nintendo about to let one of its more thoughtful action games turn into just another stupid corridor shooter?

The answer, quite obviously, was no. *Metroid Prime* is as sympathetic an update as any in gaming history. With its brooding, twitchy score, and lush, mostly deserted, environments, Retro managed to summon up the peculiar brand of melancholy and isolation that defined the 2-D originals, while finding an intelligent means to retain the manner in which your growing arsenal of weaponry and skills gradually opens up the complex environment the deeper you get into the game's spooky ruins. What's more, along the way, it still managed to blaze its own trail, creating a title that feels cut from the same cloth as the original titles, but without seeming like its best ideas are all borrowed.

It's colorful, too—a ceaseless riot of deep greens, rusting golds, and blinding white lights—and it crams a dazzlingly varied ecosystem into its handful of different locations. Subsequent adventures may have offered, very moderately, diminishing returns, but even if Retro were never to make another game ever again, the smarter action fans out there will always be thankful for this one. Sleek, thoughtful, and rather sad, *Metroid Prime* is a game that's as inventive and sharp and mysteriously alluring as the series to which it belongs. **CD**

Dungeon Siege

Original release date : 2002
Platform : PC, Mac
Developer : Gas Powered Games
Genre : Role-Playing

Dungeon Siege was touted as party-based *Diablo*. Why defeat evil alone when you can do it with nonplayer character friends? Gamers raised on traditional RPGs, and the frenzied button bashers that made Blizzard's previous RPG a smash, all drooled. That *Dungeon Siege* was from Chris Taylor, designer of the fabulous *Total Annihilation*, only added to the anticipation.

Yet on arrival *Dungeon Siege* featured almost none of the tactical party-based nuances expected of it. Sure, you assemble a group, with mages, archers, ax-wielding dwarves, and even a mule for carrying your nobly gotten gains. And everyone does their bit. But that's just it: You can play *Dungeon Siege* on autopilot. Most of the player's choices are concerned with inventory management: collect the fallen weapons and loot, throw the excess on the mule, and look out for a shop. Your party levels up no matter what you do. It is also very linear—like moving along some *Lord of the Rings* rollercoaster—which renders its innovative seamless loading rather moot. Quests are little more than plot developments. Perhaps the story is so predictable that they know you'll succeed.

So why are even discussing the game? Because judged on what it *does* rather than *doesn't* do, *Dungeon Siege* is superb. Upon release it was jaw-droppingly beautiful, and even today the detail is impressive. It's almost embarrassingly playable. And, rather like one of those movies that makes you feel clever by name-dropping, there's so much happening on-screen that you rarely consider you're just one hack from a slash.

A final twist: While the game rarely deviates from its one path, its excellent content creation tools spawned a plethora of mods. **OB**

Medieval: Total War

Original release date : 2002
Platform : PC
Developer : The Creative Assembly
Genre : Strategy

Medieval: Total War transplants the unexpected success of Shogun: Total War from the exotic campaigns of Sengoku, Japan, to the more familiar battlefields of western Europe during the Middle Ages—a period rich and fertile in terms of the conflict and strife needed to support a long and fruitful military campaign.

Here, military campaigns are conducted in two arenas: real-time tactics, which determine the outcome of battle, and turn-based strategy, which shapes the long-term fate of your kingdom or empire. Either could have been packaged and sold separately, and yet Medieval: Total War finds space for them both. It also grants players the freedom to automate battles or just to dive in and skirmish

without all the long-term turn-based politicking, if they wish to concentrate on just one aspect of the game. There are also historical scenarios, such as the Battle of Stirling Bridge, for those inspired by Braveheart, or the Hundred Years War for those seeking a lengthier challenge.

Battles represent the pinnacle of real-time tactics of the era: massed armies of authentically equipped knights and archers fight across 3-D battlefields, using authentic siege machinery. The turn-based campaign, meanwhile, brilliantly captures the essence of the dynastic and religious politics of the period. Family members can be used as pawns in your diplomatic strategy, while disobeying the pope carries the risk of excommunication. The battles and campaign combine to construct a quintessential recreation of a fascinating historical period.

There are other history games, there are other real-time tactics games, and there are other turn-based strategy games, but no other game combines all three to create such an original, enthralling experience. **DM**

Steel Battalion

Original release date : 2002
Platform : Xbox
Developer : Capcom
Genre : Action

There are plastic peripherals like guitars, drum kits, and fishing rods, and then there are plastic peripherals like *Steel Battalion*'s absolutely gigantic foldout robot controller. This was the game that promised to make you feel like you were really piloting one of its giant, hulking mecha walkers, and the add-on was an essential part of the experience. If you had room for it on your coffee table (and there certainly wouldn't be much room left *after* it was installed), it would turn your living room into the cockpit of an elaborate machine, providing access to all the switches, gauges, and dials a futuristic pilot could desire, with even a few joysticks crammed in.

It was financial suicide, naturally, but it's also the kind of thing that makes the video game industry so enduringly fascinating to follow. And the game that was wrapped around the inputs isn't at all bad either: a stylish in-cockpit mecha assault game in which you pilot your walking death machine through various scenarios, in a bid to take down the enemy in the most explosive manner possible.

Somewhat inevitably, it simply proved too much for too many players—in terms of complexity, financial commitment, and the sheer amount of room taken up playing it. And furthermore, a series of ingeniously brutal design decisions eroded even the most enduring of players' loves: fail to eject safely before your robot is destroyed, and the game will delete your entire save file, giving you a sense of what death might be like.

But let's put such ancient scars aside. In an era when video games scrabble over one another to become *more* casual, *more* caring, and *more* immediate, it's nice to know that there are still elaborate, delightful, disastrous follies like this in existence—even if they are now wedged in the back of the closet. **CD**

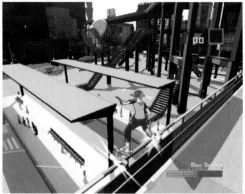

Eternal Darkness

Original release date : 2002
Platform : GameCube
Developer : Silicon Knights
Genre : Survival Horror

A horror set around several generations of a cursed family, *Eternal Darkness* saw Canadian developer Silicon Knights trying to send its audience conclusively around the bend.

It *really* isn't like other survival horrors. Sure, you still wander around a cluster of moody hallways, picking up grisly clues and fighting unspeakable foes, but *Eternal Darkness* has loftier ambitions: a complex plot that spans several millennia, a range of playable characters (almost all of whom meet ridiculously unpleasant ends), and some rather weighty Gothic fiction name-dropping. *Eternal Darkness* wears its brain on its sleeve, in other words, while other titles are happy just to splatter it over the walls.

But the game's real claim to greatness are the insanity effects that kick in as your character becomes more and more disturbed by what's going on. Some are simple visual effects, but the best of them target your worst fears as an actual gamer: the save file that claims to be deleting itself; the polite announcement—as zombie hordes rush you—that your controller is unplugged. Few games have so convincingly messed with their audiences' minds. **CD**

Jet Set Radio Future

Original release date : 2002
Platform : Xbox
Developer : Smilebit
Genre : Action

The task of providing a sequel to a game as singularly personable as *Jet Set Radio* was no easy task, and while Smilebit's follow-up struggled to sell more than a fairly dismal 30,000 copies, it's a title that sings with ideas: vivid, lovable, and effortlessly cool.

Kicking the action into a future of subculture quirks and break-dancing robots, *Jet Set Radio Future* pits you and your gang of skating graffiti artists against the sinister Rokkaku Group, who are trying to overwhelm your city. Tagging remains the key to your revolt, albeit returning in streamlined form, and with a new hardware generation behind it, the game's streets are filled with crowds of messy iconoclasts to barrel through and barge out of the way as you set about your mission. The game's greatest pleasure, however, comes in its intense verticality, as you scale the towering megastructures of the Skyscraper District, bouncing off satellite dishes and grinding the gutters, until you throw yourself back to the streets below.

Jet Set Radio Future is one of those rare titles that really transports you somewhere else. **CD**

Soul Calibur II

Kingdom Hearts

Original release date : 2002
Platform : Various
Developer : Namco
Genre : Fighting

Original release date : 2002
Platform : PS2
Developer : Square
Genre : Action / Role-Playing

Who'd have thought that the fairly anonymous arcade fighter *Soul Edge* would spawn one of video gaming's genre-defining beat 'em ups? But when *Soul Calibur* appeared on the Dreamcast, it was proof that home consoles had overtaken the coin-op: better-than-arcade graphics were nestled within the most comprehensive single-player campaigns ever seen in a beat 'em up.

Soul Calibur II retains the strengths of the previous games—the single-player campaign, the intuitive control scheme, the characters, the (sometimes skimpy) costumes, the weapons, the booming voice as you volley opponents "OUT OF THE RING!" It also adds three popular console-specific characters: *Tekken*'s Heihachi for the PS2; *Zelda*'s Link for the GameCube; and the twisted teen-hero Spawn for the Xbox version. All three console versions share cutting-edge graphics and feature a refined version of the fighting engine.

"WELCOME TO THE STAGE OF HISTORY!" the voice bellows at the start of the game. It sets the tone for what is still one of the best beat 'em ups of all time. **DM**

A merging of the crowd-pleasing worlds of Square's RPG catalogue and Disney's priceless cast of characters, *Kingdom Hearts* was perhaps inevitable—but that doesn't mean the end result isn't personable, colorful, and rather wonderful as well.

A complex RPG and a best-selling series in its own right, *Kingdom Hearts* tells the story of Sora, a young boy gifted with a magical weapon called the Keyblade, which he must use to fight off the Heartless, a sinister group of shadowy beings. Teaming up with the likes of Donald Duck and Goofy, Sora sets off on an epic quest to save his world from destruction.

With lavish art and an epic, rather grown-up storyline that regularly deals with themes of death and sacrifice, as well as finding room for a dizzying number of Disney cameos, it's hardly a shock that *Kingdom Hearts* was a massive hit when launched on the PS2. Since then, as is Square's way, it's spawned an unlikely muddle of genuine sequels and oddball offshoots, including a series of increasingly strange titles for the mobile phone market. **CD**

The Elder Scrolls III: Morrowind

Original release date : 2002

Platform : PC, Xbox

Developer : Bethesda Game Studios

Genre : Action / Role-Playing

The *Elder Scrolls* games are best known because of the fourth chapter in the series, *Oblivion*, released in 2006. *The Elder Scrolls III: Morrowind* is altogether more of a curate's egg, neither as commercially successful nor critically lauded. Perhaps because of that, however, it's also a much more interesting game. This isn't the traditional Tolkienesque fantasy of the later version; instead it is a weird blend of traditional fantasy with people and places that are characterized by an almost eerie otherworldliness.

One thing that *is* true of both games is the unparalleled freedom that their creators hand to players. More than many other similar games, *The Elder Scrolls III: Morrowind* contains entire societies and cultures that are completely convincing (and, by including the *Elder Scrolls* construction set, even allowed players to create their own).

In one inspired piece of design, the tutorial contains the entire character creation process as part of the narrative, with attributes and skills generated by the choices the player makes while describing their character's background to a prison bureaucrat. In another, character skills advance as players use them. If you want to become good at, say, swordfighting, you simply keep swordfighting.

For a set of rules designed to let gamers play without worrying about the numbers, this latter system is easy to exploit by anyone who wants to artificially inflate their character's abilities. In this, however, it is also a typically well-intentioned albeit flawed piece of design—but flawed in such a way that it actually enriches the experience: *The Elder Scrolls III: Morrowind* grants players the freedom to play it as an experience, absorbing the story and forging their own, or as a set of rules, to be ransacked with an obsessive-compulsive eye for exploits in a bid to "beat" the game. **DM**

Mafia: The City of Lost Heaven

Original release date : 2002

Platform : PC

Developer : Illusion Softworks

Genre : Shoot 'Em Up

Proving that an open world doesn't have to offer countless possibilities, *Mafia: The City of Lost Heaven* expects just one thing from its fictional city: detail. Period detail, to be exact; this gangster epic assumes the cars, streets, decor, and even laws of a city during the Prohibition. A little too sensational to be *The Godfather*, perhaps, but it does a damn fine impression of *The Untouchables*.

The story is told in flashbacks by Tommy Angelo, a member of the Lost Heaven mafia who quits the life of crime and rats out his "family" to a detective in a restaurant. In a bid for witness protection, his story goes right back to day one, when two gangsters jump into his taxi and "ask" him to outrun some trigger-happy pursuers. Made an offer

he can't refuse by the impressed Don Salieri, we see him rise through the ranks of the underworld and wage war on a newfound enemy, the connected Don Morello. Needless to say, the words "double-cross" feature prominently throughout the game from thereon in.

Mafia: The City of Lost Heaven's idea of exploration is to drive between waypoints and sniff out the best avenues for on-foot missions. It's immersion, really; a chance to live out the age of Tommy guns, Studebakers, speakeasies, and bootleggers. Radio sounds include Louis Armstrong and the Mills Brothers, while references to *Goodfellas* (not, admittedly, a 1930s saga) are everywhere.

Aside from an early emphasis on visuals, most remember the game's strict highway code, its police not taking kindly to you breaking the local speed limit. This suggestion that responsible driving could be just as enjoyable as pedestrian-mowing chases would be championed by games like *Driver: Parallel Lines* and *Grand Theft Auto IV*—but not for some years. **DH**

Disaster Report

Original release date : 2002
Platform : PS2
Developer : Irem
Genre : Action

It's a mystery why so few games, before or since, have attempted to appropriate the rubble-strewn trappings of the disaster movie. It's been an enduring cinema staple, from *The Poseidon Adventure* to *2012*, and one that you'd think would be particularly ripe ground for video game adventure: more destruction than you can fit in a first-person shooter; big, set-piece action; and the slow reveal of the intermingling motivations of an ensemble cast.

Disaster Report features the whole lot, and it runs the whole range of disasters: earthquakes, landslides, tsunamis, fires, and, as in any good disaster movie, other humans. And like all great disaster movies, the real mystery is the one at the heart of the game. That mystery concerns

the construction of a massive artificial island—or rather its gradual destruction, from which the game's hero must make his escape. The challenge isn't to find new and interesting ways of killing others, but to save yourself—for example, crawling slowly through a burning building, trying to avoid asphyxiation, or leaping your way to safety from a slowly crumbling bridge.

One of the most interesting aspects of the game is the way your character's constant thirst regulates his progress and ratchets up the tension. As each aftershock rumbles in, you're never sure how far you are from the next life-saving swig of water. But you're also never far from a bit of light relief, most notably in the shape of some excellently nonsensical collectibles, like an *R-Type* compass.

In the end, the conspiracy at the heart of the disaster is a bit unconvincing, but for a medium in which fighting people continues to be the default mode of interaction, *Disaster Report* is a breath of fresh air. Well, grit-filled, smoke-choking air, anyway. **DM**

Grand Theft Auto: Vice City

Original release date : 2002

Platform : Various

Developer : Rockstar

Genre : Action

More '80s than the '80s themselves, the follow-up to *Grand Theft Auto III* packed players into a pastel-colored time machine for a trip through the coke-fueled psychopathy of Florida gangster culture. Rockstar's remit, as described by president Sam Houser, was to prove that video games could go toe to toe with cinema—and aesthetically *Grand Theft Auto: Vice City* is a startling success.

The sun-kissed setting, the clothes, the cars and music recreate the 1980s in a condensed hyper-real form. There's a heavy dose of nostalgia in the triumphant eruption of Blondie's "Atomic" from the radio, as you scream down a beach-side boulevard in a convertible—but it's always undercut by a horror at the period's self-destructive decadence, its revolting avarice, and its terrible obsession with puffy shoulder pads.

As jailbird Tommy Vercetti, you arrive in Vice City, planning to sew up an easy coke deal. The deal goes south, leaving Tommy without the drugs or his money—and in debt to his overlords back in Liberty City. In the process of recovering the goods, Tommy rises through the ranks of the city's criminal elite, snapping up rivals' scams. He nicks many a car, of course, but he also plunders the archives of gangster filmography too. Isn't that the sniveling lawyer from *Carlito's Way*? Isn't that the mansion from *Scarface*? Wasn't that scene straight out of *Miami Vice*?

The game also marks the point when *Grand Theft Auto*'s template could be logically expanded without feeling overcrowded with features. Though Rockstar's ambition for its mission design had increased, it's the lurid mania of its place and time, rather than any unique aspect of play, which marks out *Grand Theft Auto: Vice City* as one of the series' dizziest peaks. **MD**

Medal of Honor: Allied Assault

Original release date : 2002

Platform : PC, Mac

Developer : 2015

Genre : First-Person Shooter

There was always going to be a point when the rest of the game industry caught up with what Valve had been doing with the original *Half-Life*, scripting events to seem more dramatic—not to mention more cinematic. It took until 2002 for *Medal of Honor: Allied Assault* to use the same idea in a World War II shooter, and it did so to startling effect.

The opening of the game would have been familiar to anyone who had seen *Saving Private Ryan*, as it was a direct video game reworking of the nightmarishly intense beach-storming sequence from Steven Spielberg's movie. The gate went down on the landing craft, and you struggled ashore, under fire from the beach. If you made it to the first sand dunes, then you proceeded with the assault on the

fortifications above, and then onward into the theaters of Europe and North Africa, set piece by set piece.

In the game you take the role of Army Ranger Lt. Mike Powell, who finds himself in a number of ugly situations. You assault German bases in Norway and Morocco, and also perform a number of rescue missions behind enemy lines in France during the invasion.

If there's a significant failing on the part of *Medal of Honor: Allied Assault*, it's probably down to the way the Allied soldiers only feature in very limited sequences of the game. Most of the time you are facing the Germans on your own, and the action therefore devolves into that of a more traditional shooter. The final level, in which you have to wear a gas mask, is also rather disappointing.

Nevertheless, *Medal of Honor: Allied Assault* was the first game to learn the lessons of *Half-Life*, and it can most definitely be seen as a major waypoint on the road to the major successful shooters of the past few years, such as the hugely successful *Call of Duty* series. **JR**

No One Lives Forever 2: A Spy in H.A.R.M.'s Way

Original release date : 2002
Platform : PC, Mac
Developer : Monolith Productions
Genre : First-Person Shooter

Prior to becoming synonymous with miserable urban horror games, Monolith Productions enjoyed a much richer palette, highlights being the laser-sharp franchise sequel *Tron 2.0* and a psychedelic trio of spy games in the form of *No One Lives Forever* and its sequel, plus *Contract JACK*, a spin-off. Indebted to shows like *The Avengers* and *Mission: Impossible*, these kitsch classics are from a time when 3-D gaming had yet to sink into the browns and greens of relentless modern warfare.

Reuniting players with heroine Cate Archer, an ex-cat burglar with more costumes than Lady Gaga, *No One Lives Forever 2: A Spy in H.A.R.M.'s .Way* sees uniform jumps in production values and scope, from character animation and

rendering to early experiments with Havok physics. It kicks off in a Japanese village where Archer, armed with one of many exotic gadgets, is spying on the head of H.A.R.M., a global crime syndicate. Stabbed and left for dead by an ninja assassin, she makes it back to England where, recovered, she's given her most preposterous assignment yet.

In cahoots with the Soviet Union, H.A.R.M. wants to turn the Greek island of Khios into a communist tourist spot. Following the trail, Archer battles deadly mimes, super soldiers, and some of the unlikeliest set-pieces devised for a first-person shooter, including a ninja swordfight in the midst of a trailer-tossing tornado.

Like fellow physics pioneers *Half-Life 2* and *Painkiller*, *No One Lives Forever 2* turns its landscapes into leading characters, featuring over-the-top action that mellowed in subsequent games. Monolith redeployed many of these themes in physics-mad horror game *F.E.A.R.* Now owned by Warner Bros., the studio shows no signs of looking back, leaving this period favorite trapped in time. **DH**

Tom Clancy's Splinter Cell

Original release date : 2002
Platform : Various
Developer : Ubisoft
Genre : Action

In the shadows, one man can be an army. In the shadows, perfection is about deathly silence and deadly force. And in *Tom Clancy's Splinter Cell*, the first installment of Ubisoft's celebrated espionage franchise approved by thriller writer Tom Clancy, the shadows are long and deep. Created using the Unreal 2 engine, its levels are a chiaroscuro landscape of warehouses and oil tankers, barely illuminated by strip lamps and the soft warm glow of computer monitors. It's a darkness in which only covert NSA operative Sam Fisher, dispatched to avert World War III, feels at home.

Tom Clancy's Splinter Cell didn't invent the stealth genre (*Metal Gear* got there first), but its boldly gloomy visuals were a remarkable innovation. Never before had wet work

seemed so tense and lonely; murky in every way. Fisher, speaking in the gravel-gargling tones of actor Michael Ironside, was perfectly suited to it; an aging veteran whose years in the gloom had turned him cynical and suspicious.

At its heart, *Tom Clancy's Splinter Cell* is a game about execution. Not just the snapping of your enemies' necks (although there *is* plenty of that), but decisions over how to execute each mission. Do you kill the guard or distract him with a thrown bottle? Sneak-walk through the shrubbery or shimmy overhead on pipes like a cat? The challenge lies in adapting your arsenal to each new scenario.

The techno-porn inventory is pure Clancy, yet the game's ability to induce nail-biting tension as you creep between pools of light surpasses any airport thriller. The aim is silent invisibility, slipping in and out without alerting guards or triggering alarms. And for all its high-tech gadgetry, *Tom Clancy's Splinter Cell* searches for an ancient, Zen-like harmony: that exhilarating moment when you become a true shadow warrior. **JRu**

Neverwinter Nights

Original release date : 2002
Platform : PC, Mac
Developer : BioWare
Genre : Role-Playing

No computer RPG can compete with the experience of playing a pen-and-paper campaign. No computer is as flexible or as creative as a human dungeon master, capable of creating characters and subplots and adjusting the rules on the fly to make sure his players are having just the right amount of fun. There are not enough variables inside a computer to compete with the infinite possibilities of the human imagination. So the argument went.

That is, until Neverwinter Nights came out, confounding the argument by giving human DMs as much control over a computer RPG as their pen-and-paper counterparts.

Following on from the Byzantine brilliance of Baldur's Gate II, BioWare's successor cut back the size and complexity of the single-player campaign, but didn't skimp on the ingenuity, with a story centered on saving the city of Neverwinter from a nefarious plague. That single-player campaign was just a tiny part of the whole game, however; Neverwinter Nights was designed from the outset to be enjoyed as a multiplayer experience. It was notable because it provided players with a suite of tools that allowed them to create their own game worlds and campaigns, turning the infinite possibilities of the human imagination into video game realities.

What's more, the same tools allowed DMs to referee those campaigns on the fly, adjusting them with just as much freedom as if they were playing with pen and paper. Except, of course, they didn't have to be in the same room as their fellow players. (Which, some might argue, made it a superior experience to the real thing.)

So Neverwinter Nights proved that computer RPGs are every bit as rich and varied as their predecessors. The only thing lacking is odd-shaped dice, beer, and pizza. **DM**

Panzer Dragoon Orta

Original release date : 2002
Platform : Xbox
Developer : Smilebit
Genre : Shoot 'Em Up

Panzer Dragoon appeared on the Saturn in a blaze of glory, reaching heights of hitherto unimaginable technical excellence and becoming a poster boy for the power of Sega's new processing powerhouse. And it is contained, in its entirety, in *Panzer Dragoon Orta*, demonstrating how far video game technology had come by the time the fourth game in the series burst on to the Xbox.

Although *Panzer Dragoon Orta* was created by a new development team, it was staffed by many of the people who had produced its predecessors. They retained the ability to shift between different dragon forms: base wing for all-round balance; heavy wing for increased firepower; and glide wing for better maneuverability.

By the time *Panzer Dragoon Orta* came out, the on-rails shooter had become a desperately unfashionable genre, even if *Rez* had recently given it a brief dose of dance-culture respectability. Compared to games in which you are free to shoot, rob, and steal, *Panzer Dragoon Orta*'s only concession to freedom was to allow you to steer your mysterious dragon mount around the screen as it progressed along its preordained path.

What a path, though! This is a game that serves up set pieces with remarkable ease. Some sequences recreate scenes from the original in high fidelity; others are wholly original, such as a level in which you are forced to steer your heavily damaged dragon across the floor as you attempt to destroy a gigantic manta ray undulating in and out of view alongside you.

There are plenty more bells and whistles. Multiple forking paths exist throughout the game, and Pandora's Box, which houses a host of secrets and collectibles, including additional missions and movies, can be opened up to provide plenty of scope for replayability. **DM**

Star Wars Jedi Knight II: Jedi Outcast

Original release date : 2002
Platform : Various
Developer : Raven Software
Genre : Action / First-Person Shooter

A run of *Star Wars*–themed games that failed to capture the kudos of the earlier *Star Wars: Dark Forces* games caused a rethink at George Lucas's game studio. The new philosophy was simple: get the most respected developers in specific genres and hand them the keys to the *Star Wars* universe. Who would turn down the chance to make a *Star Wars* game? For first-person shooters, Raven had a well-established history of quality games going back to *Heretic* and *Hexen*, and more recently, with *Star Trek Voyager: Elite Force*. The Wisconsin-based studio also had experience with the latest, greatest game engine from John Carmack at id Software, so it used the *Quake III Arena* engine to power the hugely anticipated sequel to *Jedi Knight*.

Picking up the story after the conclusion of the *Mysteries of the Sith* expansion pack for *Star Wars Jedi Knight II: Dark Forces*, it once again focuses on the adventures of Kyle Katarn, who has ditched the Force. He's quickly back on track after he believes his friend and sidekick, Jan Ors, to have been killed by the Dark Jedi Desann. It's a handy method of reintroducing the process of earning your lightsaber and powering up a choice of Force powers that many players will have already experienced.

The new engine coupled with Raven's experience from prior projects allowed the team to introduce fresh elements to the series, such as having characters occasionally fight alongside Katarn. It also powered flashy new special effects, adding more sizzle to the Force powers, as Katarn visits locations such as Cloud City—the home of Lando Calrissian, who we also meet in this game.

Raven lived up to its billing as a leading FPS developer, crafting an experience that fits capably alongside the other highly regarded games in the series. **RSm**

Suikoden III

Original release date : 2002
Platform : PS2
Developer : Konami
Genre : Role-Playing

Inspired by the classical Chinese novel *Water Margin*, *Suikoden* has always had a penchant for grandiose scale. When the time came to move the series to PlayStation 2, Konami ensured that this continued, creating an intricate and surprisingly mature plot that never strays too far from fantasy clichés, but imbues them with new depth and insight. Changes are also apparent visually: Moving to full 3-D, the game immediately impresses with its chunky art style, somewhat reminiscent of *Skies of Arcadia*.

But the aesthetic differences are negligible compared to the refit applied elsewhere. The newly introduced Trinity Sight system takes full advantage of the intricately woven story by allowing the player to experience initial events from three different perspectives, playing through early chapters as Hugo, Geddoe, or Chris Lightfellow. Brilliantly, they can be tackled in any order, and events from one will inform the others. Further viewpoints are unlocked as the game progresses, and the 108 heroes of the game's inspirational material can be used in battle as they are discovered. At release, those battles courted a little controversy as the six-strong party is split into pairs, meaning only three orders can be issued. But any loss of fine-tuning is compensated by slick, exciting encounters.

Party-focused, large-scale battles are complemented by a huge number of character-customization options. All characters can learn skills, but specialization is only possible for specific individuals, so no two players' parties are likely to be identical. Fortress building also returns, which, as well as housing your burgeoning army, provides ample distractions from the main quest with a generous selection of mini-games. All round, it's an appropriately accomplished tribute to its revered source material. **BM**

Shinobi

Original release date : 2002

Platform : PS2

Developer : Overworks

Genre : Action

They don't call ninjas "shadow warriors" for nothing. Just as the original *Shinobi* was followed in short order.by Tecmo's *Ninja Gaiden*, its reboot for modern consoles would be eclipsed two years later by its returning foe. Why? Partly because of the power gap between PS2 and Xbox, but more because of nostalgia: The new *Ninja Gaiden* makes itself at home in the living room; *Shinobi*, on the other hand, seems to long for the arcades.

It's a smaller and potentially older audience, then, that really appreciates Overworks's game. The first *Shinobi* in 3-D and the first in the series for seven years—the last was the poorly received *Shinobi X* for Sega's Saturn—it's a tricksy blend of efficient combat and arcade ritual, low

on checkpoints, high on sudden deaths, and played throughout at breakneck speed.

Picking up the story of the Oboro clan, it follows the exploits of a new ninja, Hotsuma. Having slain his brother in a fated duel, he leads the family as Hiruko Ubusuna, an enemy vanquished decades earlier, returns to seek his vengeance. In something of a Japanese action game tradition, a giant Golden Palace then lands in the center of Tokyo, filling the streets with hellish creatures.

No arcade game would be complete without a time limit, and Hotsuma's sword does the job perfectly. It literally thirsts for blood, sapping its owner's energy if it can't find it elsewhere. So Hotsuma, able to dash intelligently between mobs of enemies with just a button press, has to make every kill count. Multiple kills can be achieved in quick succession by performing a sequence of attacking moves for which you are rewarded with more soul energy, greater sword power, and, best of all, a real-time cinematic of your enemies falling to bits. **DH**

Resident Evil Zero

Original release date : 2002
Platform : GameCube
Developer : Capcom
Genre : Survival Horror

Cooperative play was a part of *Resident Evil* long before the online antics of *Resident Evil 5*. *Resident Evil Zero*, the last of its GameCube titles, bucks the trend for having two characters on two separate disks, and has them both on screen at once, a "partner-zapping" feature letting you switch between them. Each has unique strengths, be it the power to move heavy objects and sustain greater damage, or the frame to squeeze through tight spaces while mixing those life-sustaining herbs.

A day before the events of the original *Resident Evil*, Raccoon City police division STARS investigates a series of murders in the local mountains. A helicopter crash later, and its team is marooned in a remote forest. Alone, medic

Rebecca Chambers stumbles upon a zombie-infested train and a disgraced ex-Marine on the run, Billy Coen. Together they follow the tracks to an underground lab, home to the Umbrella Corporation and its marauding experiments.

The series was under great pressure to stir things up after the millennium, especially concerning game-isms like the magic storage trunk (where an item placed in one box would appear in every other) and mechanical puzzles. Originally planned for the Nintendo 64—few at Capcom believed a disk-based version would load fast enough— *Resident Evil Zero* arrived on the GameCube in relatively short order, with little of the epic prototyping that would soon shape *Resident Evil 4*.

You can tell: The AI that takes over the character you're *not* controlling makes a poor partner, and there are contrived work-arounds for when the cooperative puzzles clash with the refurbished inventory system. Still, *Resident Evil Zero* is one of the most beguiling games in the series, often bettering the looks of *Resident Evil Remake*. **DH**

Sly Cooper and the Thievius Raccoonus

Original release date : 2002
Platform : PS2
Developer : Sucker Punch Productions
Genre : Platform

The introduction of Sony's light-fingered raccoon was almost too perfect a heist for anyone to notice that it had happened: a mascot-driven pure platformer in the twilight of mascots, or even pure platformers. Though *Sly Cooper and the Thievius Raccoonus* leans toward action-adventure, and its subgames experiment with various play styles to varying degrees of success, at heart this is a game of running, jumping, and timing. If that's not apparent on the first play through, a series of unlockable time-trial runs reveal how tightly wound a machine the core levels truly are.

Visually, too, the game presents a double-take, with the dusky watercolors and expressive, flowing lines of a lost Sullivan-Bluth production. Those brushstroke looks are a foil for the absolute solidity of the game world. The key is physics and physicality, evident in that no opportunity for a fraught tightrope-walk or giddy carousel goes unmissed. Practically every object not already in constant motion bobs and sways with carefully judged cartoon gravity. Just the simple act of traversal is an obvious delight, abetted with a generous stickiness that focuses on show rather than forced restarts.

But much of the joy of movement is carried on Sly Cooper's wiry shoulders. A hugely expressive creation, every exaggerated action from tiptoe stalk to the twitch of his tail is a flourish of unspoken narrative. If his supporting cast can't quite compare, at once too shrill and too straight to fill the clown shoes of comic relief, the rogues' gallery rides its stereotyped excess to perfection. Given a hero, villains, and a canvas to spread them across, it's a playable Saturday matinee, with all the lightness of touch and the deftness of nuance that entails. **BS**

Hitman 2: Silent Assassin

Original release date : 2002
Platform : Various
Developer : IO Interactive
Genre : Action

Killing isn't easy, even for killers. Agent 47, the antihero of this sneak-disguise-assassinate-escape game, established himself as a killer with a conscience in the first title in this impressive series. This sequel sees him atoning for the sins of his previous employment under the guiding presence of Father Vittorio. But the forces that want Agent 47 back in the game know exactly how to lure him to the killing side. Vittorio is kidnapped and a ransom issued, and the hitman knows only one way to raise that kind of capital.

How you choose to approach each challenging, inventive, and truly original mission setup is limited more by your imagination than it is any artificial rules of engagement. Multiple solutions to each scenario ensure one player's experience can differ wildly from another's, and present excellent replay value as you try another tactic. Charging in with guns blazing is an option that usually ends in a swift restart—but it is, nonetheless, an option. Whether it's skulking past threats toward a target or taking out bystanders, hiding their bodies in a Dumpster, and stealing their outfits for a disguise, the variety is vast, but executing a plan is far from easy.

Of course, though this is about Agent 47's conscience being salved, these are still deadly strikes, and discovering that you're a pawn in a bigger global power play is a huge revelation that calls for reflection as well as retaliation. It's in these moral conundrums that *Hitman 2: Silent Assassin* reveals a depth and complexity that led to Hollywood calling to bring the exploits to the silver screen. Saving Vittorio is a noble goal that requires ignoble deeds. And, ultimately, you vanquish personal demons worthy of a name, not just a number. **RSm**

Pokémon Ruby/Sapphire

Original release date : 2002
Platform : Game Boy Advance
Developer : Game Freak
Genre : Role-Playing

The charm offensive was so intense, and the marketing so all-pervasive and brutally effective, that it can be hard to remember just how good *Pokémon* is as a game—how well its RPG mechanics work, how delightful its world is to explore, and, most of all, how memorable its cast of collectable critters is. A mixture of wonderful, imaginative visual design and smart, wordy names, every Pokémon is a delight to behold, and the game's great slogan is also the mantra that drives you through this long and complex adventure: You really will find that you gotta catch 'em all.

With a forgettable world-spanning narrative, *Pokémon* is really a simple story of exploration and collection, inspired by the bug-collecting fascinations of the game's creator Satoshi Tajiri. Wading through a *Pokémon* game's long grass is a treat, as random battles here become something of a pleasure; a chance to see a strange new breed of creature that might have eluded you until now, or an opportunity to tame, own, and then slowly learn to understand a new life-form.

While each *Pokémon* game is essentially the same, no matter the little kinks put in the story and slow shuffling of the cast, each has its own charms and features, and *Pokémon Ruby/Sapphire* is no different: moving the series on to the Game Boy Advance, the graphics have been spruced up, multiplayer has been expanded to a four-person cap, and double battles have been added.

Beyond that, however, if you can't track down *Ruby* or *Sapphire*, pretty much any game in the suite will do: there aren't any duds in this series, and you can't really put a foot wrong. Just remember that if you stay too long, you may find yourself coming down with collection fever too. **CD**

Ratchet & Clank

Original release date : 2002
Platform : PS2
Developer : Insomniac Games
Genre : Action / Platform

If you've ever wondered what it would be like to be a space-faring feline with a scientific expert of a robot strapped to your back, now you can find out. Just don't blame us if you have identity issues afterward.

Like Naughty Dog's *Jak and Daxter: The Precursor Legacy*—from which Insomniac borrowed both the game engine and the control system—*Ratchet & Clank* stars a double act, each with their own abilities. Most of the time you're sulky, teenage, catlike Ratchet, whacking enemies with your OmniWrench 8000 or exploding them from a distance with your Bomb Glove. Certain areas, however, require you to switch to Clank, who otherwise acts mainly as a backpack for Ratchet.

Besides hearing out the engaging story, the main attraction of *Ratchet & Clank* is the weapons and gadgets you pick up along the way. These include the Suck Cannon, which gobbles enemies and spits them back at others, and the Taunter, which distracts your foes, making them easier to dispatch. There's a certain amount of dutiful and mindless smashing and collecting of bolts, the game currency, so that you can keep stocked up on firepower using the game's shops, but a sensible save system means it's never too onerous.

Graphically, *Ratchet & Clank* is gorgeous. Each planet is visually rich and diverse, and the character animation is superb. For anyone who tracks down and plays Shiny Entertainment's *MDK* and then wants more, *Ratchet & Clank* is worth a try. Admittedly, Insomniac's game leans more toward *Futurama* than *MDK*'s Terry Gilliam zaniness, but in terms of comic sci-fi exuberance the two titles occupy a sparse branch in 3-D platform gaming. **OB**

Grow

Original release date : 2002
Platform : Internet
Developer : Eyezmaze
Genre : Puzzle

For all the game industry's discussion of sandbox worlds and open-ended play, as a player undertaking a task in a game you tend to achieve one of two results: you either complete it or you don't. Sure, the possible journey might be different in the most open of games, but what about games where the end result, imperfect or not, leads you somewhere interesting, anyway?

Grow, developed by an unknown Japanese Flash developer who works only under his company's name, Eyezmaze, shouldn't really work. You are given a red sphere, emblazoned with the word "Grow," and asked to place onto it twelve disparate objects—a plate, a section of ladder, a whirlwind—one after another, to see what

happens. After a couple of objects are dragged across, you begin to see what's happening. Based on the order you place them, they change form, becoming larger or turning into something different (a hill becomes a volcano) and begin to interact (the whirlwind begins to power a fan).

The aim is *broadly* to reach a maximum level with all of the objects you place. But if that's all that was happening, it would be a frustrating trial-and-error experience. It's not, for example, clear why or how placing a pipe would "evolve" into an egg. The game succeeds because every failure leads you somewhere interesting. Placing the pipe before the fan and the hill means that when it spits out some bubbles, they aren't blown away by the fan but instead rain on the hill, stopping it from becoming a volcano—but perhaps by doing that you weren't able to get the TV screen working or the robot built. So you try again.

It's easy to deride *Grow* as a toy, a Flash trinket, a time waster. But when every decision—even a wrong one—is rewarding, what's wrong with that? **MKu**

The Legend of Zelda: The Wind Waker

Original release date : 2002
Platform : GameCube
Developer : Nintendo
Genre : Action / Adventure

Link's first GameCube adventure launched into stormy seas, following a blustery Internet reaction to a sudden change of art style. Rather than being a 128-bit upgrading of *The Legend of Zelda: Ocarina of Time*'s distinctly melancholic fantasy world, *The Wind Waker* has a landscape drawn in broad, primary-colored strokes, with its hero transformed from brooding time-traveling teen to wide-eyed cartoon child, with stumpy legs, a determined frown sketched in a single uppity scribble, and a giant balloon for a head.

Fears were misplaced, however, as *The Wind Waker*'s sharp cel-shading has ensured: Besides *The Legend of Zelda: A Link to the Past*, it's perhaps the most timeless of *Zelda*s, a stylized and stylish romp through some of the beautifully

constructed dungeons of the series, with highlights including a temple designed around a giant turbine and a forest getaway where thick tendrils of thorny branches erupt from the ground to form impromptu mazes.

Burying the Hyrule of old under a rolling blue ocean may have seemed almost as sacrilegious as the shift toward a more childlike narrative, and, it's true, *The Wind Waker* lacks the intricate multidimensional structure of previous entries, but such audacious changes allow for a fresh kind of adventure filled with pirates, sun-bleached islands, ghost ships, and a mysterious frozen castle trapped beneath the waves. It's a fair trade in the end.

Some of the game's bosses may seem familiar to fans of the previous games, and there are obvious signs that the project was finished in a hurry, with entire dungeons hitting the cutting-room floor, but *The Wind Waker* remains a lovable addition to the franchise, offering an untold bounty of treasure, mystery, and drama to anyone who dares sail its shimmering foam-flecked oceans. **CD**

Super Mario Sunshine

Original release date : 2002
Platform : GameCube
Developer : Nintendo
Genre : Platform

After all that time spent rescuing princesses and generally saving the world, it was inevitable that Mario would need a vacation sooner or later—and it was equally inevitable that things would go comically awry pretty quickly once he jetted off for the sun. Minutes after landing in the tropical paradise of Isle Delfino, poor old Mario finds himself framed for vandalism, when it transpires that a mysterious shimmering blue Mario clone has been covering the resort in nasty, sticky gloop.

It's up to Mario to tidy things up, naturally, a task he must achieve with the use of FLUDD, a water spout on his back that also doubles as a rocket booster and, eventually, a turbo jet for powering him through obstacles. FLUDD is

there to handle the tricky matter of judging jumps correctly in 3-D games, as it enables a Harrier Jump Jet–style slow hover as he eases his way over obstacles. This is the centerpiece of one of Mario's most challenging games yet.

Super Mario Sunshine takes place in some of the most recognizably real-world locations throughout the entire series. Of course, we're not too surprised when we find the resort's hotel is filled with shape-shifting ghosts and has a maze on the roof, while the rocky cliffs tower above waters that contain a monster with a toothache.

The game is still imaginative and thrilling, however, with enough great moments—navigating the underworld grid of a lofty mushroom village, and being pursued by Bullet Bills along some basking beaches—to lift it to the terrific standards of the other games in the series.

A bold departure and one of the greatest summer games ever made, *Super Mario Sunshine* will play just as well on the Wii as it did on the GameCube, so there's absolutely no reason for you to miss out on it. **CD**

Warcraft III: Reign of Chaos

Original release date : 2002
Platform : PC, Mac
Developer : Blizzard Entertainment
Genre : Strategy

Though *Dune II* is credited with kick-starting the real-time strategy genre, it's the *Command & Conquer* series that came to define it. How different things could have been, though. In 1995, two RTS titles of note were released: *Command & Conquer* and *Warcraft II*. Both of them were brilliant, but while *Command & Conquer* went on to spawn what seemed like hundreds of sequels, *Warcraft* fans had to wait seven years for their next fix.

If *Warcraft* had been taking on its rival in an RTS, the situation would have been severe, with Blizzard's RTS swamped by weight of numbers. But *Warcraft* was biding its time, hoarding its resources for the end game: With the release of *Warcraft III* the definitive RTS had arrived.

Warcraft III: Reign of Chaos adds night elves and undead armies to the humans and orcs from the original game, and features a single-player campaign that works its way through each of them in turn. If you were to plot its progress on a graph, it would be a perfectly graduated incline pitched right on the sweet spot between simplicity and depth; between the pain of acquiring new skills and the pleasure of using them.

As in any RTS, the essence of the game is managing resources—gold, lumber, and food, in this case—and then using them to build an army to crush your opponent. What sets *Warcraft III: Reign of Chaos* apart, however, is that there is simply nothing to complicate that. Not the story, which is perfectly integrated into the action. Not the interface, which is the epitome of intuitiveness. Not the graphics, which prefigure the effortless excellence of *World of Warcraft*. And not the design, which manages to establish a perfectly measured progression from resource-gathering to military expansion. **DM**

TimeSplitters 2

Original release date : 2002
Platform : Various
Developer : Free Radical Design
Genre : First-Person Shooter

Balanced between a rough-sketch first game and a disappointing third installment, *TimeSplitters 2* exists at that rare moment when everything works: a first-person shooter with all the character, artillery, and general silliness that you could ask for, moving through a range of brilliantly caricatured video game clichés without ever becoming lazy or letting the jokes do all the talking.

Actually, it's the guns that do most of the talking. The brilliantly stupid plot, which sees you pursuing aliens through various points in human history, is the perfect excuse to dabble in a broad range of weaponry, from the six-shooters of the Wild West to laser guns from the distant future. With its opening sequence a heavy-handed homage to the beginning of *GoldenEye 007*, there's no forgetting that this is the product of the same people who first made the first-person shooter—a PC genre if ever there was one—feel truly comfortable on consoles.

The scenarios are vivid and action-packed, ranging from a campy *Star Trek* parody on an alien world through to demonic goings-on in nineteenth-century Paris, and the scenery is enhanced by the characteristic rubber-faced charm of your targets. But the main reason to dust off your copy today, as with *GoldenEye 007*, is for the brilliantly chaotic multiplayer, a series of pacy arena battles that move unlike any other game, with a rudimentary level editor included for even more hilarity.

TimeSplitters 2 has dropped off the FPS radar now—and following the disappointing *Haze*, Free Radical has shut its doors and been reborn as Crytek UK—but this is a relic from the days when the team seemed unstoppable; a seriously well-balanced shooter that always manages to keep its tongue stuck endearingly in its cheek. **CD**

The Mark of Kri

Original release date : 2003
Platform : PS2
Developer : Sony
Genre : Action / Adventure

Taking cues equally from Polynesian tribalism and Disney animation, *The Mark of Kri* is a reduction of the action adventure down to its thickest, broadest strokes. Any genre baggage that doesn't fit within its invented legend is eliminated and abandoned with the same casual force that animates and defines Rau, *The Mark of Kri*'s remarkably mute barbarian hero.

Though he has a narrator and a more talkative backup cast to color between his lines, Rau is a video game lead expressed entirely with action. Scaling ladders with such heft that you expect him to wrench out the rungs, he's a throwback to the medium's legends, when look and movement were all an avatar had to become iconic.

And, as it was then, it proves more than enough, lending his astonishingly violent journey a narrative maturity and instinctual savagery beyond *The Mark of Kri*'s flashier counterparts. An exercise in cartoonish restraint rather than the easier target of cartoonish excess, the "Disney" it channels is the foreboding of *The Black Cauldron*, the spirit of *Pirates of the Caribbean*. Like the latter, its one-track levels play out as a brutal theme park ride, masterful color theory and art design couching their LEGO-block structure in earthiness and sense of place.

That richness is drawn out by the measured pace of *The Mark of Kri*'s game play: predatory, premeditated, a study of the long moment before sudden death. It's palpable in the silent face-off as enemies warily encircle Rau—a figure so powerful that the only remotely fair fight is one where he's vastly outnumbered. The weighty, body-smashing combat itself is no slouch, but ultimately *The Mark of Kri* is an action game that prioritizes everything around the action, and in doing so makes it so mortal and memorable. **BS**

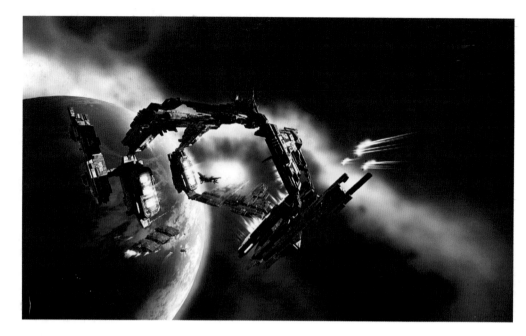

Eve Online

Original release date : 2003
Platform : PC, Mac
Developer : CCP Games
Genre : MMORPG

While *World of Warcraft* has seen the occasional in-game wedding, the community behind *Eve Online*, CCP's awe-inspiring MMORPG, is constantly embroiled in much grander, complex human interactions. Vast conspiracies, elaborate deceptions, bloody coups, embezzlement, and fraud on an interstellar scale—all of it driven by players.

Eve Online is a Machiavellian world of some 5,000 star systems, vied over by player-created corporations, each attempting to mine, trade, fight, and scam their way to dominance. The stories that emerge from this fray are startling. One renowned coup saw members of a mercenary group known as the Guiding Hand Social Club infiltrate another powerful corporation over the course of

a year, before seizing its assets, ambushing its lady CEO, destroying her unique ship, and collecting her ejected, frozen corpse for delivery to their vindictive client. The assets plundered from corporate coffers then amounted to a figure in tens of thousands of US dollars.

While exchanging the in-game currency into real-world money is forbidden by the user agreement, the sum is testament to the amount of genuine labor that goes into such dastardly plots. This is a game, after all, whose developer has hired its own economist to help shape and stabilize the market. Playing *Eve Online* isn't an easy job. It may be a job in space, but the awe of its setting does little to mitigate its notoriously overwhelming complexities and time-intensive labors. This is to say nothing of the actual act of space flight or combat, which is often abstracted to the point where you are staring at readouts and figures rather than sizzling laser fire. *TIE Fighter* this is not. It is, however, the most fascinating, organic, and utterly ruthless digital community ever born. **MD**

Beyond Good & Evil

Original release date : 2003
Platform : Various
Developer : Ubisoft
Genre : Action / Adventure

Rayman creator Michel Ancel's charming tale of deep-space whimsy takes a recognizable gaming template—in this case, the item-based advancement system and loose dungeon structure of the *Zelda* series—and uses it to spin out an action adventure that feels like nothing else.

Cast as the green-lipped, lighthouse-dwelling journalist Jade, the *Beyond Good & Evil* player uncovers a vast and menacing conspiracy that threatens the peaceful mining planet of Hyllis, while exploring a variety of dingy factories and spooky caves, snapping pictures of the local wildlife, and whacking enemies with a handy telescopic staff.

Yet what makes Ancel's game stand out is not the plot or action so much as the sense of place and character. The watery byways of Hyllis offer a distinctly European take on the future, while the moody palette of grays, silvers, greens, and blues lends the game a melancholy and sophisticated air. Jade is a surprisingly human lead compared to most games, while Pey'j, her porcine friend and accomplice, is perhaps one of the most endearing sidekicks in all of video gaming, despite a tendency to repeat the phrase, "Say when, Jade!" until you feel like pushing him over a cliff.

Mechanically, Ubisoft's *Beyond Good & Evil* isn't the most memorable of titles—although there's a certain pleasure to be had from gradually upgrading your nippy little hovercraft until it is ready to go all the way out into space—but this is one of those rare games where the tone is more important than the minute-to-minute activities.

Ubisoft continually proposes a sequel, which, given the reputation the original adventure has built up since its rather quiet release, would probably make financial sense, but it's yet to be seen if we *are* going back to this particular future any time soon. Just say when, Jade. **CD**

Disgaea: Hour of Darkness

Original release date : 2003
Platform : Various
Developer : Nippon Ichi
Genre : Role-Playing / Strategy

Confused by the vowel-heavy title? Put off by the spiky anime hair? There's only one thing you really need to know about *Disgaea: Hour of Darkness*, the first installment of Nippon Ichi's increasingly popular tactical RPG, and that's 9,999—the game's ultimate level cap.

Most RPGs engage in a little leveling porn: When it all goes right, the incremental improvements of hitting monsters and getting a little more powerful in return can be deliriously compelling; when it all goes wrong, however, it becomes a dreaded grind, a tireless slog to become powerful enough to move on to the next area, take on the next boss, or venture into the next dungeon. *Disgaea: Hour of Darkness* simply takes this idea of numerical progression

further than most would dare, presenting a nearly limitless road of character improvement that refuses to stop until players have leveled into almost five figures.

It's a testament to how good the game is that a lot of people actually bump their heads against that cap. The story of an unlikely rabble of Netherworld inhabitants and their cheeky adventures, *Disgaea: Hour of Darkness* is a staggeringly complex tactical RPG in which each new environment is turned into an isometric chessboard as you move your pieces about, attacking enemies, finding items, and teaming up on baddies to unleash devastating attacks.

The lush yet breezy art has already inspired manga and novels, while the bizarre soap-opera lives of the main characters are crazy enough to delight even the most jaded of battlers. Extreme, complex, and unforgiving, it's wonderful to consider that there's still scope within the world of games for a treat like this, and better yet to realize that it's successful enough to spawn sequels, and delightful portable versions for the PSP and DS. **CD**

Fatal Frame II: Crimson Butterfly

Original release date : 2003
Platform : PS2, Xbox
Developer : Tecmo
Genre : Survival Horror

Games are often compared to films, usually in the context of storytelling or emotional engagement. But *Fatal Frame II: Crimson Butterfly* shows that games are just as capable as any noninteractive form of entertainment when it comes to scaring people. And even a little bit more potent.

Building on the successes of its predecessor, the game eschews weaponry for a single camera obscura that the player, cast as young girl Mio, must use to locate and exorcize malevolent spirits as she searches for her missing sister, Mayu. It's *Luigi's Mansion* meets *Pokémon Snap*, but with a distinctly adult flavor.

Not all of the ghosts mean you harm, however, and many will offer guidance and help throughout. Good or bad, all are invisible to the naked eye, their presence only telegraphed by environmental "happenings" or when the filament built into your camera changes color. In order to see the spirits, the camera's viewfinder must be used, switching the viewpoint to first-person and forcing the player to nervously scan their environment, with the knowledge that *something* is already watching them.

Fatal Frame II: Crimson Butterfly's audio design is particularly effective. Tecmo cleverly builds associations of dread or safety with certain sounds and themes before taking advantage of the player's complacency and systematically shaking any sense of comfort from the nervous wreck now holding the controller. If you're feeling brave, however, subsequent run-throughs allow for the retention of collected items (special lenses, film types, and other upgrades), providing additional motivation to see the four different possible endings. That this added capability does little to degrade the sense of creeping terror says much for the game's horror credentials. **BM**

Call of Duty

Original release date : 2003
Platform : PC, Mac
Developer : Infinity Ward
Genre : First-Person Shooter

The first iteration of the famed *Call of Duty* series remains a tight, violent, and thrilling experience. Divided into three campaigns—for British, American, and Russian perspectives on the war—it was filled with ambitious set pieces and inventive combat scenarios, each designed to suit their protagonists. The opening of the Russian campaign, in which Red Army soldiers are transported, unarmed, across the Volga river into the besieged city of Stalingrad, via barges, remains one of the most intense experiences shooters have to offer.

Call of Duty's storytelling device—dividing the game up into the experiences of several different soldiers in entirely different theaters of war—remains at the heart of

the series today. The reason this model is so successful in *Call of Duty*, however, is down to the intensity with which the experiences of combat are delivered. The adapted and enhanced id Tech 3 engine, previously used in *Quake III*, is extremely efficient at portraying close-quarters combat, but it also enables the Infinity Ward team to incorporate a brutal shell shock effect from the impact of large-caliber weapons and explosives. While previous shooters had portrayed many of the same scenes from World War II, none had been able to make an MG42 roar with such violence or make the experience of cowering behind a dead cow for cover so terrifying. The Stalingrad sequences show the lengths to which the *Quake III* technology has been pushed, with hundreds of soldiers on-screen, and a huge cityscape displayed as the assault pushes forward.

It's rare that the first game in a popular series remains a contender with its sequels, but this is one of those special cases. *Call of Duty* remains undoubtedly one of the greatest shooters ever made. **JR**

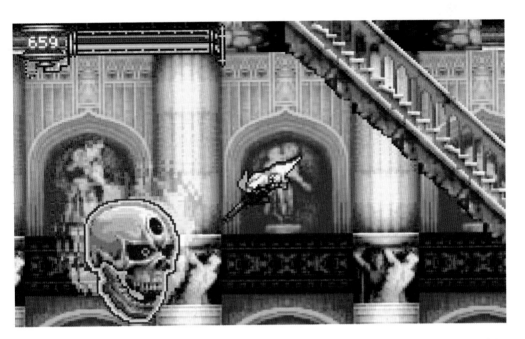

Castlevania: Aria of Sorrow

Original release date : 2003
Platform : Game Boy Advance
Developer : Konami
Genre : Action

It's been more than two decades and some twenty-five games since the release of the original *Castlevania* on Nintendo's Famicom Disk System. The series has since evolved, from simple scrolling beat 'em ups to explorative epics that combine RPG and platform genres to create a series of undead-hunting classics of absorbing complexity.

Until the arrival of the DS, *Castlevania: Aria of Sorrow* was the definitive handheld *Castlevania*. It picks up the plot of the series in 2035, to depict the future of the Belmont bloodline as it seeks, once again, to defeat Dracula. There ensues a typically outlandish series of metaphysical events and supernatural escapades, which take, as their model, *Symphony of the Night*—the PlayStation title that was the

first to fuse the *Castlevania* setting with a design inspired by Nintendo's *Metroid* series. So there is a similar blend of action and exploration, with unceasing bouts of combat facilitating the gradual acquisition of abilities that make it easier for players to navigate their surroundings. One of the best things about the later chapters in the *Castlevania* series has always been that sense of foreshortening: the way previously large distances are brought into perspective by your ever-growing supernatural powers.

The game's major innovation is the "Tactical Soul" system, which allows players to acquire new abilities by absorbing the souls of defeated enemies—thus layering a *Pokémon*-style gotta-catch-'em-all dynamic over the existing *Castlevania* template. In those heady, pre-Internet-enabled days, players were only able to trade souls using the GBA link cable, but it didn't make the results any less compulsive. Hailed upon release as the highest ever rated *Castlevania* game by leading Japanese gaming magazine *Famitsu*, it remains a classic. **DM**

Amplitude

Original release date : 2003
Platform : PS2
Developer : Harmonix
Genre : Music

Donkey Konga

Original release date : 2003
Platform : GameCube
Developer : Nintendo
Genre : Music

Despite being told by Microsoft that no rhythm game could succeed without a bespoke hardware controller, Harmonix secured enough cult appeal for the hypnotic *Frequency* that a sequel, *Amplitude*, preceded the switch to plastic guitars. With its predecessor's tunnel of notes flattened to more of a wave, this glitzier effort was—perhaps rightly—accused of dumbing down an entirely successful formula. But if the first game felt like being shot through the synapses of a euphoric clubber, the second is more corporeal, with the player zapping notes that pass beneath a hovering spacecraft.

Like *Frequency*, *Amplitude* is notable for providing the blueprint for the *Guitar Hero* and *Rock Band* games. Though it uses the PS2's native controller, the arrangement of songs into an unlockable playlist featuring encore "boss battles" is entirely familiar; so too is the use of power-ups to create a score-attack framework.

Fans who have devoted many hours to *Amplitude* will be delighted to know that Harmonix has expressed interest in continuing the franchise on PS3. **DH**

The best rhythm-action games have always been the games with the best peripherals, and following *Samba de Amigo*'s maracas, *Taiko no Tatsujin*'s drums, and the accessories of *Guitar Hero*, *Donkey Konga*'s bright orange bongos were a welcome addition to the band.

The skeletal plot involves Donkey and Diddy Kong discovering some mysterious bongos on the beach, with the power to grant them more bananas than they could ever dream of, and so they embark on a bout of beat-matching game play across some thirty-odd songs. The list features several of Nintendo's infectious soundtracks, including fan favorites from the *Mario* and *Zelda* series, alongside a variety of such bongo classics as "Hungarian Dance No. 5 in G Minor," by that chart-topping popstrel, Johannes Brahms.

Donkey Konga ticks all the boxes for a superb music game, with a tub-thumpingly great peripheral, but it was not a big hit, coming out near the end of the ill-fated GameCube's life—not such a problem now, of course, considering its compatibility with the popular Wii. **DM**

Bookworm

Original release date : 2003
Platform : Various
Developer : PopCap Games
Genre : Puzzle

With *Bookworm*, PopCap Games proved that it could even bring a sense of pacy fun to activities as dry as spelling tests, with a simple word search that proves remarkably hard to put down once you've got started.

Under the watchful eye of the bookworm Lex, players must unscramble the longest possible words from a set of randomized letter tiles, being careful to use only connecting pieces. Variously colored tiles can be used to improve a word's scores—as does finding longer words, of course—while nasty red tiles pop up now and then, only to burn slowly to the bottom of the screen, the point at which the game ends.

It's all strangely addictive, partly due to the quirky cartoon visuals and some lovely sound effects, and partly just down to the fact that there was always something rather likable about spelling tests back at school . . . unless dyslexia made them rather less appealing.

Bookworm is playable today in its original form as a downloadable title, available from plenty of online portals or as an iPhone game with a user-friendly interface. **CD**

Wario World

Original release date : 2003
Platform : GameCube
Developer : Treasure
Genre : Action / Platform

Before the frantic mind-warping nonsense of the *WarioWare* series propelled him to the upper tiers of Nintendo's royalty, the world's most successful game company seemed unsure as to what to do with Mario's evil counterpart. The first title in which he takes the lead, *Wario World* is a short but charismatic 3-D platformer and brawler—and it's pretty good, too.

Wario's treasures have been stolen, so he embarks on a quest across four themed worlds, getting his money back and sorting out his enemies in the process. Platforming is slick and rarely bogged down by undue intricacy, but the majority of the game is given over to Wario's handful of intensely satisfying fighting moves. Not the most complex of combatants, Wario focuses on bone-crushing rushes, grabs, and pile drivers, bringing a distinct hint of the WWE to the goofy monsters of the Mushroom Kingdom.

There are plenty of opportunities to be nice in Nintendo's universe, which is why we need Wario all the more: yang to other heroes' yin, a chance to explore the messier, more selfish aspects of life. **CD**

Freedom Fighters

Original release date : 2003
Platform : Various
Developer : IO Interactive
Genre : Shoot 'Em Up

Freedom Fighters features gaming's second most famous plumbers—Chris and Troy Stone, two regular working stiffs, trapped in a counterfactual world in which the Soviet Union ended World War II with the first nuclear blast, and then, inevitably, headed across the Atlantic to give the decadent Yankees a good shoeing. With the Red Army occupying New York City, Chris Stone joins a resistance movement and takes to the streets to undermine Uncle Joe's bullyboys in any way he can—generally by shooting people and blowing stuff up.

As a Tom Clancy–ish humorless rant, *Freedom Fighters* would be nigh on unbearable, but the developer IO Interactive—more famous for the excellent *Hitman* series—is smart enough to mix a tongue-in-cheek tale of working-man bravado with some excellent squad-based game play, and the result is one of the most fondly remembered action games of the PS2/Xbox era.

At the heart of the experience is the Charisma Meter, which grows as Chris performs heroic actions, allowing him eventually to recruit additional squad members—up to a limit of twelve. Squad members can be given basic orders as you fight through the shattered streets of Manhattan, sticking it to the man. In a devastating diversion from the norm, they're actually smart enough to look after themselves for the most part.

With a decent range of multiplayer options and a knockabout single-player campaign, *Freedom Fighters* worked its way quite deeply into a surprising number of people's hearts. A sequel would be a rather popular move at this point, and is regularly hinted at, but for the time being you'll have to keep your old consoles out of the attic if you want to enjoy this. **CD**

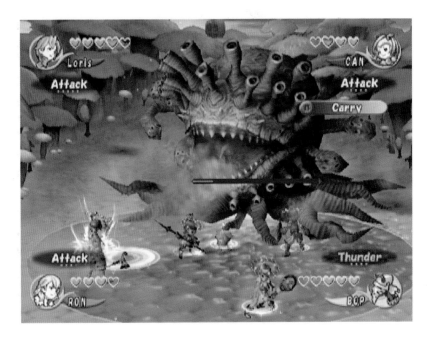

Final Fantasy Crystal Chronicles

Original release date : 2003
Platform : GameCube
Developer : Square Enix
Genre : Action / Role-Playing

The publisher of the world's most popular RPG series has never been shy about attaching the *Final Fantasy* name to other projects, in an often-quixotic effort to broaden its fan base. This has led to such misbegotten stepchildren as the dumbed-down *Final Fantasy Mystic Quest* and the execrable cart-racer *Chocobo Racing*. But don't let that stigma dissuade you from *Final Fantasy Crystal Chronicles*, one of the best multiplayer RPGs to grace a console.

After customizing your character from the usual menu (warrior/mage/healer, etc.) you set out to find the source of "miasma"—a cloud of nerve gas that has plagued the land since times untold. Since your hometown's antimiasma crystal (this is an RPG, so crystals can fix anything) has to

be recharged annually, you loop back home once a year—every couple of hours in real-world time. It may sound tedious, but it's not: The routine gives the story a tangible passage of time. The combat system is streamlined, with no random encounters or separate battle screen, so fighting and exploration happen in the same realm, with blessedly few interruptions.

Final Fantasy Crystal Chronicles can be played alone but is designed to shine with a partner or three. Team members can coordinate their attacks and pool their magic for a precision-timed burst of elemental smackdown. There is, sadly, the thorny matter of hardware. Multiplayer *Final Fantasy Crystal Chronicles* requires not only a GameCube but also a Game Boy Advance for every player—each with its own special attachment cable. But these gadgets aren't especially hard to find—long-serving Nintendo fans should have some lying around in the back of a cupboard. The extra hassle is worth it in order to experience this long, satisfying journey with some friends by your side. **JT**

Flipnic

Original release date : 2003
Platform : PS2
Developer : Sony
Genre : Pinball

Flipnic's original Japanese box art famously announces that it is "an enjoyable simple-action amazing pinball game for you." That claim's disappearance from the more conservative Western artwork could well have been a safeguard against false advertising lawsuits. It *is* enjoyable, if at times masochistically so, and with three-button input it *is*, technically, simple action. But then things get a little more complicated.

Even if pinball by nature is as much arbitrary as skill based, *Flipnic* is openly, willfully capricious. A delirious 8-bit-styled introduction sequence determines your luck for the session, unfavorable results daring you to reset the console in a cosmic tilt. The levels—too sprawling, too intricate, too video gamey to be called tables—toy with physics, gravity, and momentum as they see fit. There are mini-games. There are boss fights.

The truth is that *Flipnic* isn't a pinball game, but a video game concept album about pinball games—in a similar manner to 1988's miniature-golf-in-name-only *Zany Golf*. *Flipnic* revels in the haziness of pinball lounge memories: in unreliable nostalgia. Rather than dryly replicating the mechanics, *Flipnic* mythologizes the experience as a stream of altered consciousness: solar system menus and calypso soundtracks; superkitsch video footage; stoner philosophy voice-overs; bad-trip "game overs" drawled by hard-smoking anatomical skeletons; and levels that read like a set of high-school textbook spines.

It's a throwback to a time that may not even have existed, but *Flipnic*'s careening whimsy not only convinces you that it did, but that you were there. And for that glorious sleight-of-mind, if it's not an amazing pinball game, it *is* an amazing video game. Within such a personal bubble of eccentricity, *Flipnic* is just "for you" after all. **BS**

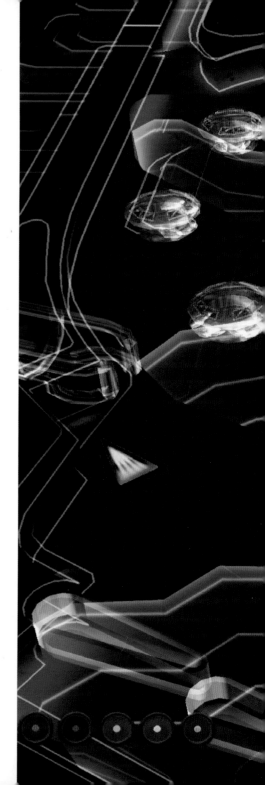

DANGER

Astro Boy: Omega Factor

Original release date : 2003
Platform : Game Boy Advance
Developer : Treasure / Hitmaker
Genre : Action / Fighting

Treasure's status as a legendary game developer is built upon its dedication to original, rarely duplicated titles, but the company's forays into licensed titles are equally created with love and dedication. The pinnacle of such efforts has to be *Astro Boy: Omega Factor*, a 2-D side-scroller that, as well as offering a carefully blended mix of the shoot-'em-up and beat-'em-up genres, is a densely packed love letter to the canon of *Astro Boy*'s creator, celebrated manga author Osamu Tezuka.

As the player progresses through *Astro Boy: Omega Factor*'s story mode, Astro Boy meets other characters from Tezuka's universe—such as the famous Black Jack and Kimba the White Lion—filling up an in-game encyclopedia

and gaining new powers via a simple upgrade system that ties knowledge with power. As the story loops back on itself through two episodes—"Birth" and "ReBirth"—by the time the player is pushed into the position where they must use all of their skills to save Tezuka's world, they know intimately why they must.

For gamers who fear Treasure's propensity for difficult games, *Astro Boy: Omega Factor* offers an accessible easy mode, which can be either button mashed through or used to learn the many quirks of the shooting/fighting design (despite being controlled with only four buttons and a D-pad, Astro Boy combos as well as a *Marvel vs. Capcom 2* character). This makes the normal and hard modes gleefully rewarding for those who wish to play it more than once, in a style reminiscent of *Gunstar Heroes*, Treasure's debut game from 1993.

Astro Boy: Omega Factor may not be the definitive introduction to Osamu Tezuka's universe, but it never forgets to be a superbly playable game. **MKu**

Midtown Madness 3

Original release date : 2003
Platform : Xbox
Developer : Digital Illusions CE
Genre : Driving

Released just prior to *Driver*, a game often credited with inventing the free-roaming driving genre, *Midtown Madness* staged a madcap series of races across a virtual Chicago. Creator Angel Studios was praised for its "living, breathing environment," full of abusive pedestrians, famous landmarks, destructible scenery, and angry traffic. Trading exotic supercars for hatchbacks and buses, it featured modes like Checkpoint, in which players could tweak the traffic to find their own difficulty level, and Cops & Robbers, a vehicular take on capture the flag.

Published by Microsoft, it was used to promote both the gaming potential of Windows and the MSN Gaming Zone, a user-friendly online multiplayer service. So when

power and connectivity again became the selling points of its first console, the Xbox, it knew exactly where to turn.

Developed by *Battlefield 1942* creator Digital Illusions CE, then known more for its ambitious racing games, *Midtown Madness 3* rises to that task. Switching venues to Paris and Washington DC, it's an early taste of what complex light and shadow can add to an open world, and a further example of what an open world can add to a racing game. Routes aren't mastered in *Midtown Madness 3* but discovered, the risk being an impromptu shortcut and the reward being that one doesn't end in a lake or bus station. Rather than learn corners, you have to study the ways of the city: how its cars behave in dynamic situations.

It's a game built to be played online, and with the plug-and-play simplicity of a modern networked console. The riotous party modes are one thing, but what sets it apart wasn't on the disk when it launched: regular, substantial updates via downloadable content, a feature that would revolutionize gaming in years to come. **DH**

WarioWare, Inc.: Mega MicroGames!

Original release date : 2003
Platform : Game Boy Advance
Developer : Nintendo
Genre : Action

WarioWare, Inc.: Mega Microgames!, although self-consciously slight, is the desert-island video game bar none: a title that breaks the full history of video games down into vivid pieces before firing them at you in endless five-second bursts. Wario (Mario's occasional nemesis) has started up his own video game company, producing some of the strangest titles ever. As the player, it's your job to beat them all, playing through assortments of the strange little things, divided into themed rounds, ending with a longer boss encounter, in a title that behaves like a kind of ADD's ludic jukebox.

Almost no game genre escapes some kind of ribbing, from RPGs and racing games to Nintendo's own venerated back catalogue. *Mario* is reduced to a game about jumping on things, while noble *Zelda* becomes an adventure revolving around walking into caves. Wario's memory is vast and exacting, too, poking fun at the time a much younger Nintendo made a game about vacuum cleaners, and wheeling out ROB, one-time NES robot mascot, for another spin at one of his own rather poor titles.

Beyond that, there are games about eyedrops, haircuts, eating apples, sneezing, and catching toast; games in which you slice into steak, catch tiny stickmen under glass tumblers, and help chickens out of the way of stomping feet. Each new title is as unlikely and refreshing as the last, with each building and riffing on expectations set up five minutes earlier, while reveling in its own aesthetic rules.

Vivid, hilarious, and strangely beautiful, *WarioWare, Inc.: Mega Microgames!* is nothing less than the game your entire life has been preparing you for. History is often put through the grinder in an industry as involuted as this one, but the results are rarely, if ever, quite this satisfying. **CD**

Viewtiful Joe

Original release date : 2003
Platform : Various
Developer : Capcom
Genre : Action / Fighting

With his squat, sinewy body wedged into a nasty skintight outfit, Viewtiful Joe doesn't present the most attractive of propositions, but that's until you see him move; racing, punching, and high-kicking through his game's distinctive 2.5-D environments, speeding up time until the screen's a blur, or slowing it down to a thick crawl as he knocks bullets back into guns, blasts robots into shiny chunks, and punches bosses so quickly that they promptly catch fire.

In an age when screenshots still sold video games, *Viewtiful Joe* was a difficult title to evaluate. It was hard, practically impossible, to even work out what was going on in most of the game's freeze-frames, with their Parisian boulevards filled with mechanical gunslingers, or their fat red fighter jets ducking elaborate transforming enemies. What *was* actually going on, however, was one of the PlayStation 2 generation's most imaginative brawlers, each new environment putting a fresh spin on the game's tight handful of mechanics, each new boss leaving you confused and pummeled by a mixture of quirky visual design and intense pattern-based attacks until you finally worked out how to chain the lengthy series of necessary moves together to achieve victory.

Viewtiful Joe is pretty and clever, then, but above all it's hard: The game's elaborate worlds, with their punishingly irregular checkpoints, ask a lot of their players; and its bosses, even on a second play through, can throw up frustrating roadblocks that can last for months on end. Despite all this, it's rare to start the game without one day getting to the end, just because of the sheer vitality of the delivery. No other titles explode across the screen in such a mindless blur of creative enthusiasm, and few have balanced frustration with spectacle so dazzlingly. **CD**

Hidden & Dangerous 2

Original release date : 2003

Platform : PC

Developer : Illusion Softworks

Genre : Shoot 'Em Up

Tom Clancy's Rainbow Six reminded virtual combatants that, in the real world, a single bullet is very, very dangerous. The biggest surprise, however, was how well *Quake*-bred death matchers embraced the idea. Tactics? Tangible danger from that single gunman? Backed by a brand name at its peak, it refreshed the shooter community and led to the inevitable stream of wannabes.

Illusion Softworks saw an opportunity to take a similar approach and place it in a World War II setting. With the original *Hidden & Dangerous*, the team crafted a boldly ambitious plot around four-man SAS teams getting up to military mischief behind enemy lines. Its ambition wasn't matched by its polish, but with the sequel the development team had the opportunity to refine its forthright ideas into a more cohesive experience.

In 2003, World War II was yet to wear out its welcome with gamers, and this time the SAS units traversed the globe, fighting Nazis as well as Japanese forces in Burma. The tactical element presents itself from the outset as you decide which four of your squad to take into a particular mission. It's all about horses for courses, not just saddling up the four sharpest-shooting thoroughbreds in your stable. Once on the ground, when you issue orders your team usually responds the right way. This level of interaction is required to maintain the tension since each situation, whether in thick jungle or across icy plains, presents its own original challenges.

This satisfying sequel is certainly no tightly tuned action spectacular, but its variety (including vehicles), sprawling levels, and attention to detail in everything from footsteps to gun sounds to the deadliness of a single bullet make it a standout shooter in a crowded marketplace. **RSm**

Jak II

Original release date : 2003
Platform : PS2
Developer : Naughty Dog
Genre : Action / Platform

Like Mr. Hyde to Dr. Jekyll, *Jak II* is the schizophrenic alter ego of predecessor *Jak and Daxter: The Precursor Legacy*. Protagonist Jak's breezy charm has been torn from him by two years of imprisonment, and the misanthropic gun fetishist that emerges is somewhat bitter. *Grand Theft Auto III*'s success clearly made a very big impression on Naughty Dog, but what initially appears to be a non sequitur actually develops into an enthralling experience.

After traveling through a portal, Jak finds himself in a dystopian future where he is promptly arrested by the Krimson Guards. He is handed over to the sinister Baron Praxis, who uses him as a subject for his Dark Warrior project, exposing him to Dark Eco. Thankfully, despite

being dropped from the title, Daxter successfully mounts a rescue bid, and you find yourself in a world torn apart by a three-way struggle between Praxis, the hybridized Metal Heads, and the resistance (which you subsequently join). Importantly, Jak can now morph into Dark Jak by collecting Dark Eco, a form in which he is far more effective at hand-to-hand combat.

Haven City acts as a central hub from which discrete levels can be reached via airlocks. *Grand Theft Auto*'s influence is keenly felt here, too, as the city is a bustling metropolis full of pedestrians and vehicles (which can be "borrowed" through force) and a menagerie of missions, side quests, and races doled out by its inhabitants. The story-progressing missions predominantly take place outside of the city, beyond the airlocks, and it is here that the game feels most like its predecessor.

Jak II is a bold rebuke to the "more of everything" school of sequels, choosing instead to redesign from the ground up and offer a unique experience that stands alone. **BM**

Harvest Moon: Friends of Mineral Town

Original release date : 2003
Platform : Game Boy Advance
Developer : Marvelous Interactive
Genre : Life Simulation / Role-Playing

Harvest Moon was originally created to communicate the goodness of rural life to millions of concrete-bound Japanese in the mid-'90s. This Game Boy Advance version, though, is the ultimate expression of creator Yasuhiro Wada's simple, idealized dream-version of the farming life. Set on a large, run-down farm on the outskirts of a busy village full of likeable characters, *Harvest Moon: Friends of Mineral Town* makes agriculture into something social. Farming is at the center of the town's existence, and everybody's lives revolve around the changing seasons.

Harvest Moon is a gentle, lovely cycle of investment and reward, sucking the player into a comforting, regular rhythm of planting crops, caring for animals, and harvesting produce. Like real life, much of the game is everyday toil, made fulfilling by the distant prospect of a house expansion, a wedding day, or the arrival of a new calf. But that slow pace is tempered with unpredictability: There's no way of knowing whether today's the day that something really exciting is going to turn up; perhaps a storm, or a visitor, or a surprise party in the village.

The characters are cute, but not vapid, and they are what sets *Friends of Mineral Town* apart from every other game in the *Harvest Moon* series. They have lives and personalities; potential brides have fathers and friends that need buttering up; and their relationships with one another play out in unpredictable hidden cut scenes.

It feels like a living world, a lovely alternate reality where hard work always pays off, and its incalculable depth means that even after years of in-game time, there's always something new to discover. The farming life might seem like a strange target for escapism, but *Harvest Moon: Friends of Mineral Town* makes it seem highly attractive. **KM**

Mario & Luigi: Superstar Saga

Original release date : 2003
Platform : Game Boy Advance
Developer : AlphaDream Corporation
Genre : Role-Playing

Mario & Luigi: Superstar Saga was not the first RPG in the *Mario* series by a long shot, but it's arguably the best, and almost certainly the most beautiful. A glorious romp through pretty pixel worlds drawn in rich purples and shining golds, this is an epic—and somewhat complex—journey that swings you through a dizzying range of cameos until it blasts toward its conclusion with the brilliant (not to mention hard-as-nails) multistage final boss.

The plot may be old hat for a *Mario Bros.* game—Princess Peach's voice has been captured by emissaries from a foreign land and the brothers have to get it back—but heading into the neighboring Beanbean Kingdom gives the designers a chance once again to embrace a totally different style of game play. Playing as both of the famous plumbers simultaneously (Mario and Luigi are mapped to different buttons but steered as one for the most part), just getting around the environments becomes more like a rhythm-action game, and the expanding arsenal of spins, drilling moves, and squashes only adds to the melody. But it's in the turn-based battles that the game really finds its groove: Timing is everything as you learn how to evade, and hopefully even counter, each of the game's delightful range of enemies, while power-up attacks bring an unlikely degree of twitch skills to the often fairly gentle world of cueing up attacks and deciding on spells that defines most RPGs.

The game is hilarious, too: a wonderfully scripted pantomime featuring memorable digs at Nintendo's most cherished properties that almost elevates it to the cackling heights of *WarioWare*. Lengthy, rich, and charming, *Mario & Luigi: Superstar Saga* was one of the best handheld titles—and one of the best RPGs—of its generation. **CD**

Geometry Wars

Original release date : 2003
Platform : Xbox 360
Developer : Bizarre Creations
Genre : Shoot 'Em Up

Geometry Wars looks like the past, but has always felt like the future. A love letter to the blistering clarity of vector graphics and to the total control of other twin-stick shooters like *Robotron 2084*, Bizarre Creation's fierce little arcade blaster was originally an Easter egg hidden away within *Project Gotham Racing 2*. Its success with fans led to its arrival early on in the days of Xbox Live Arcade's series of bite-sized downloadable games, and to this day it has continued to have a controlling influence on the service, standing proudly for everything that's bold, bright, and intoxicatingly slight.

It all sounds painfully simple: geometrical enemies move around the neon graph-paper arena, and your only task is to shoot at them with one thumb stick while slipping between oncoming dangers with the other. No, there's much more to it than that. Like *Robotron*, Bizarre understands the appeal of creating an ecology of enemies—symbiotic baddies whose quirks and charms snap tightly together. Black holes draw foes in if not blown to pieces quickly enough, and can eventually erupt into dozens of deadly homing missiles, while the green squares that flee from your shots can make you accidentally back into the homing rhomboids. Meanwhile, tiny little windmills flap brainlessly through the world on random paths, getting in your way when you least expect it. And the less said about the snakes—road hogs whose glowing tails take up valuable real estate—the better.

It's a simple pleasure, then, but one that is incredibly hard to put down. With the scramble up the leaderboard waiting for you every time you log in, and the thought that a few good seconds of play could really turn your fortunes around, there are few games as likely to keep you up on the sofa at four in the morning as this. **CD**

Pro Evolution Soccer 3

Original release date : 2003
Platform : PS2
Developer : Konami
Genre : Sports

It's rare for annually updated sports games to be recognized as classics. It's the nature of the beast, each shop-packaged installment representing a few extra blocks on an ever-growing tower. But if *ISS Pro Evolution* was the landmark game that distinguished *Pro Evolution* not just from Konami's parallel *ISS* series, but as the best soccer game in the world, then *Pro Evolution Soccer 3* is the series' next big step, an overhaul that required Konami to prove itself all over again with a new generation of technology.

It did so with a game that built extensively on what had come before. *Pro Evolution Soccer 3* retains the core realism on which the series is founded, a realism based on scores of animation touches (players opening their body to take free kicks or stretching their necks for headers) and an unspectacular passing system that, in comparison to the bombastic *FIFA* series, appears downright mechanical. But appearances are deceptive. There is extraordinary depth to the movement of the ball and the reactions of players—the essence of soccer, after all—that both reflects the reality of the sport and makes scoring a consistently rewarding challenge. In the contemporary versions of *FIFA*, scoring a goal is often a matter of weaving through defenses with stat-heavy superstars and thumping the ball. *Pro Evolution Soccer 3* is a more demanding mistress, forcing you to shift defenses and work openings, seducing her into giving up an opportunity.

Big changes take the form of an overhauled graphics engine and additions to the already essential Master League, which now features a European Cup competition. That's not, of course, the same as the Champions League— the lack of official licenses is still the game's major weakness, but the personality and exceptional quality of the game is such that these limitations hardly matter. **ND**

Mojib Ribbon

Original release date : 2003
Platform : PS2
Developer : NanaOn-Sha
Genre : Music

By the time *Mojib Ribbon* appeared, NanaOn-Sha had already established itself as the unhinged pioneer of the Japanese rhythm-action boom, tempering Konami's rigid reliance on polished sequels with quirky creativity. After a game in which a rapping dog teams up with an onion to win the heart of an attractive sunflower, a game in which an anthropomorphic lamb saves the world with the power of rock, and another in which a vector bunny sings her way through geometric obstacles, the makers could have been forgiven for making something a *little* more normal, but *Mojib Ribbon* is as weird as any of them. And it's practically impenetrable to nonJapanese speakers.

The aesthetic and game play are both based around the art of sumi-e ink painting and Japanese calligraphy; instead of interacting with the melody or the beat, the player paints the lyrics of songs with a giant ink brush, flicking it up and down between ink block and paper with the right stick. Mojibri, an aspiring rapper, struts across the screen with the brush as the lyrics scroll past, muttering them in his strange synthesized voice as they pass beneath his feet. The gorgeous ink-on-paper look stands in intriguing juxtaposition with the electronic music.

Two more characters with weirder synthesized voices and different handwriting join Mojibri later on, lending the raps themselves some musical variety. It's terribly sad that the language barrier prevents most players from being able to enjoy the actual lyrics; they're as deranged as *PaRappa the Rapper*'s. Another of *Mojib Ribbon*'s nicest features is the opportunity to construct your own custom raps and send them to friends, but that requires a PS2 online account (and, like the rest of the game, the ability to read Japanese). *Mojib Ribbon* simply couldn't work in translation. But you wouldn't really want it to. **KM**

Zoo Keeper

Original release date : 2003
Platform : Various
Developer : Robot Communications / Success
Genre : Puzzle

A free internet time-waster and then a quirky and colorful launch title for Nintendo's DS, *Zoo Keeper* is a pleasure to look at and a delight to play. It's hard to argue that there's anything particularly original going on under the game's charming cartoon hood, but the results are cute, swift-moving, and entertaining, and the whole thing moves along at a decent pace.

Replacing jewels and gems with cartoon animals, *Zoo Keeper* has an unmistakable blocky aesthetic, and, on the DS, extremely precise controls that help make the game's stricter time-based challenges more manageable. As your score steadily inches higher and higher, you unlock the ability to use a binoculars icon—a get-out-of-jail-free card—that helps you pick out tricky matches, and while all the game types boil down to variations on a theme, the theme itself remains an enjoyable one.

Rather than give you a target score for each level, *Zoo Keeper* tasks you with collecting a precise number of each animal in order to progress to the next stage, and while you hunt down that last elusive giraffe, any other matches you make will extend your time, thereby helping with the search. As the game grinds on and a new animal enters the game in its later stages, the possibilities for chaining become truly astronomical.

It's all very elegantly handled, and the hilariously bad translation from the Japanese original—in which the zoo keeper himself explains the reasons for his tough and rather brusque exterior in phrases so halting and mangled that it can be genuinely difficult to work out what he's talking about for most of the time—only enhances the fun. *Zoo Keeper* might not be the most complex of games, but it's direct, easy to get to grips with, and as worryingly addictive as any other example in the match-three genre. **CD**

Metal Arms: Glitch in the System

Original release date : 2003

Platform : Various

Developer : Swingin' Ape Studios

Genre : Shoot 'Em Up

In the voodoo science of predicting sales or judging sales potential by critical appreciation, games like the quirky, quality shooter *Metal Arms* make developers and publishers bang their collective heads against the wall. The people who gave it a chance reveled in an original, stylish action game crammed with good ideas. But it was a disappointingly small number, meaning many missed the adventures of Glitch, a 'droid with a 'roid-fueled attitude.

This colorful shooter packs in the weapon options for Glitch, from sniper rifles to shotguns to rocket launchers. It packs in the environments, as the adventure crosses some forty locations. It packs in a handful of vehicles and static turret emplacements. It even packs in some strategy and puzzling, both through the use of enemies to aid Glitch's cause and imaginative level layouts. Better still, the difficulty is skewed more toward hardened players than the cartoon-robot-visuals might suggest. Indeed, the game manages to retain a high quality bar across all of these devices and features.

A real standout in the strategy of achieving each level's objectives is the use of a tether utility that allows Glitch to take over opposing robots and use their abilities against other enemies and the environment. The robot theme, the action, and the tethering suggest the developers at Swingin' Ape were familiar with the classic Commodore 64 game *Paradroid*. It's testimony to *Metal Arms*'s fundamental fun factor that it deserves to be mentioned in the same breath as such a home computer gaming classic. It even packs in a four-player component that includes seven game variants and serves as further evidence that no part of this fast, furious—and certainly tricky—shooter was simply bolted on. **RSm**

NBA Street Vol. 2

Original release date : 2003
Platform : Various
Developer : Electronic Arts
Genre : Sports

Basketball has a tendency toward the brashly ridiculous when converted into video game format. Straight-faced simulations will always have their fans, but maybe a sport featuring players who are almost exclusively seven feet tall, and that seems to be all about dunking the ball as forcefully on your opponent as possible, is more likely to attract games that play fast and loose with its rules. *NBA Street Vol. 2* was the first title since Midway's 1993 arcade hit *NBA Jam* to successfully offer a pleasing combination of arcade thrills and basketball fundamentals.

Building on the original *NBA Street*, *NBA Street Vol. 2* consists of three-on-three basketball games in a street-court setting where the aim is not simply to win the game but do it as stylishly as possible. The controls enable a variety of ball-handling skills to be performed—from simple defender fake outs to more complex tricks such as passing between teammates using the hoop backboard. All of these are used to raise your Gamebreaker meter. A single-level Gamebreaker is an especially fancy dunk or long-range shot, which raises your score by two or three points and reduces your opponent's by one; if you can hold out by filling your Gamebreaker meter twice—which is dangerous because an equally skillful opponent can sap your meter—then enacting an unblockable, Earth-shattering dunk or long-range shot could reduce your opponent's score by up to four.

It doesn't sound fair, but once the controls have been mastered, a game between skilled players can turn into a major back-and-forth of out-of-control proportions, each attempting to outdo the opposition's last move. The plays seen in *NBA Street Vol. 2* might not be strictly legal, but rules are made to be broken, aren't they? **MKu**

Kill Switch

Original release date : 2003
Platform : PS2
Developer : Namco
Genre : Shoot 'Em Up

History reflects kindly on games like *Kill Switch* (or *kill.switch*, if you want to be picky about the title), a tactical shooter credited with inventing the *Gears of War* cover system. It may have failed to do anything particularly inspiring with it, letting down a more intriguing premise than Epic's alien invasion story, but that's academic. Critics and hardcore gamers like nothing more than giving credit where it's due—especially when it's overdue.

As the game opens, you're dumped on a battlefield under the familiar guise of an all-American hero, Nick Bishop, blasting hordes of identical enemies. But here's the meta-twist: You're actually an avatar whose clichéd looks are all part of the plan. Piloted by the nefarious Controller (the real you), this false flag terrorist is trying to pin his crimes on a global superpower, instigating a war from which his creators can profit. In what barely constitutes a plot, memories of family bubble to the surface while a mysterious ally, the Duchess, fights for control of his mind.

All of which invites you to read between the lines of the game's unremarkable mission briefings, only to find there's nothing there. As Nick Bishop's identity returns, the story surrounding it disappears, the game going native and becoming just a straightforward shooter. Straightforward, that is, but with a cover system that would reshape the entire third-person action genre.

Sharing the credit with Koei's *Operation Winback*, this is the game that turned "run-and-gun" into "stop-and-pop." Pillars, concrete barricades, and cars act as cover for Bishop, gaps in enemy fire allowing him to peek out and snipe or toss a grenade. It's a system that lives or dies by the AI's ability to hound the player from one cover point to the next, and the control scheme's ability to keep up—both of which were perfected in *Gears of War*. **DH**

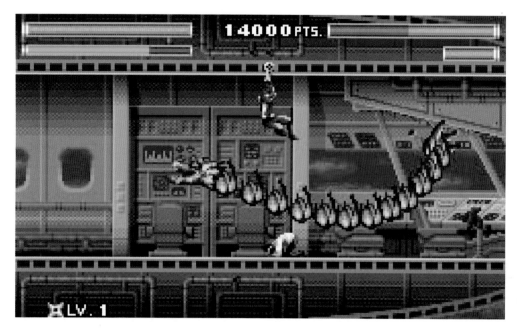

Ninja Five-0

Original release date : 2003
Platform : Game Boy Advance
Developer : Hudson Soft
Genre : Action

Now and then a game that could not look more formulaic comes along that takes you completely by surprise. *Ninja Five-0* (named *Ninja Cop* in Japan and Europe), the law-keeping adventures of a ninja named Joe, is one such title. What at first looks like an uninventively old-fashioned, nostalgic side-scrolling ninja game in the mold of *Shadow Dancer* or *Revenge of Shinobi* turns out to be an almost *Metroid*-like sprawl of explorable levels. It has brutally quick enemies, hostages, copious hidden nooks and keys, and an admirable eye for what made late-'80s side-scrolling action games so masochistically compelling.

What elevates *Ninja Five-0* from uninventive homage to inspired reinvention is the grapple hook. A step up from *Bionic Commando*'s retractable arm, it requires immense skill and timing to command; swinging up onto and around overhead platforms without sending Joe smacking unceremoniously into a wall makes you feel superhuman. It's a tough, tightly constructed platformer as well as a punishing action game; a rogue *shuriken* can easily kill a vital hostage, and other ninjas turn up from time to time equipped with as much agility and skill as your own. Furthermore, the bosses—sometimes screen-filling behemoths squished to fit the GBA's diminutive proportions—can usually kill in two hits.

Ninja Five-0 plays to nostalgic instincts. It can be completed in twenty minutes by an inhumanly talented player with no taste for exploration, but like the games from which it drew inspiration, it's punishing and replayable enough to extend that lifespan for anyone else. *Ninja Five-0* respects the core simplicity and appeal of its old-school inspirations, but rather than ripping them off, it imbues an old genre with new creative spark. **KM**

Prince of Persia: The Sands of Time

Original release date : 2003
Platform : Various
Developer : Ubisoft
Genre : Action / Platform

Very few classic properties survive the march of time in a technology-led industry. *Prince of Persia: The Sands of Time* is one of the very greatest exceptions; outside of *Mario*'s whooping leaps, it's perhaps the greatest 3-D game ever spawned by a 2-D title.

This is a world inspired by the mystical associations of Persia as much as the original game's pits and spikes. From both visual and gaming perspectives it's a tour de force. To give an example: You find yourself inside the very top of a cylindrical tower; you wind your way down by running along the walls, the colorful tapestries fluttering and giving way to your pattering feet as you descend, corkscrewing into the depths. It's a breathtaking sequence, the world

seeming to move around you rather than vice versa, and the game in miniature.

Then there's the wonderful idea that elevates *Prince of Persia: The Sands of Time* to the rank of the greats: You can rewind your mistakes. If there are any frustrating moments in the level design, you certainly don't realize they're there—you simply go back and try again.

Finally, there is the elegant story. The prince's journey is as much about tragedy as triumph, each victory tainted by the knowledge that you're only containing the evil you released. The narrative structure is simple but smart: The prince is telling you the tale as you play it. When you die, he catches himself and mutters, "No, it didn't happen like that," as you furtively jab for a restart.

A 3-D platformer with an inspired central mechanic, a work of artistic beauty, an evocative story told with restraint, and an inspiring journey, *Prince of Persia: The Sands of Time* is all of these things, and the combination creates a single, wonderful adventure. **RS**

PlanetSide

Original release date : 2003
Platform : Internet
Developer : Sony Online Entertainment
Genre : First-Person Shooter

In the first few years after release, online RPG sensation *EverQuest* had seen upward of 400,000 people paying roughly $10 per month for the privilege of prancing around Norrath. That's after forking out the purchase price for the retail box in the first place. Imagine what Sony Online Entertainment might achieve if it could nail the same come-back-for-more game play dynamics for the massive first-person shooter audience.

But handling massive, *massive* firefights is a whole new deal. So is balancing a game world in which committed players can earn levels that enhance their experience but that doesn't exclude potential newcomers. This is where *PlanetSide* scores so well from the start: The game's three

factions—Terran Republic, Vanu Sovereignty, and New Conglomerate—hit all the bullet marks of ingrained conflict, and players are spurred immediately to choose a side and get involved in the fight.

The distinct combat-themed roles provide varied game play, too: medics and engineers are as vital as assault troops at the sharp end of the action, and, as in the best online combat games, vehicles play a huge role on the battlefield. The core shooter game play works as any FPS veteran would expect, with open environments and tight choke points to focus the action. The earned experience spread across three areas (battle, support, and command) generates some kind of reward however you get involved: By ensuring the action is available to every player, rewards are distributed appropriately, and the most committed players earn status that positively impacts their experience.

PlanetSide never gained the popularity it was shooting for, but some of its achievements make it a landmark title in the evolution of online action gaming. **RSm**

Railroad Tycoon 3

Original release date : 2003
Platform : PC, Mac
Developer : PopTop Software
Genre : Management Simulation

The humble train set has long fueled the imagination of young children, but the ambitious network builder will soon come up against issues of affordability and space. Sid Meier must have felt similarly constrained when he created *Railroad Tycoon* in 1990. A critical success in its day, its commercial performance failed to live up to its now legendary status. Fortunately, it had dedicated fans at PopTop Software, which bought the rights and developed a sequel, although it wasn't until the third iteration that the series realized its wider potential.

Despite making the leap to three dimensions, *Railroad Tycoon 3* retains the distinctive, cheerful aesthetic of the first two games, managing to pack in nuanced strategy,

a complex business simulation, and a vast train set while remaining accessible for a title of such scope.

Unlike the first two games, passengers and mail are not generic commodities, paying out based on distance traveled, but preferential customers who must be ferried to their desired location. Conversely, raw materials for industry no longer remain fixed in position on the map, so trains needn't pick up at source—in the original, it was not uncommon to build a station next to a remote farm or mine just to provide a city-based business with its requirements. If you couple this with the option to connect to a competitor's track—thus sharing fares, but gaining geographical advantage—the strategic possibilities are dizzying. Trainspotters are well catered for by a long list of accurately modeled engines from the history of railway, and the game's passionate fan base has created a great deal of additional content, too. The game is best enjoyed with human opponents online or over a LAN, so perhaps the attic needn't remain empty after all. **BM**

Rise of Nations

Original release date : 2003
Platform : PC, Mac
Developer : Big Huge Games
Genre : Strategy

Rise of Nations is the kind of game that would be incredibly hard to sell to anyone doubting it. Superficially, it looks like another historical strategy game; indeed, almost every aspect of its interface and mechanics makes it seem just like another historical strategy game. But it really isn't: It's the canny editor who's been through the overlong, turgid book he's working on, filleted out everything worthless and tedious, and left only what's pacy and thrilling. *Rise of Nations* is exactly what it looks like, but its audacity is in its speed, its focus, and its tightness.

The key is that it takes the core model of turn-based strategy games—specifically *Civilization*, whose splendid sequel was cocreated by *Rise of Nation*'s lead designer,

Brian Reynolds—then implants it at the warlike heart of a real-time strategy game. The effect is profound: It's not a game of steamrolling the opposition into destruction or submission, but of territory and technology; of making your chosen faction territorially larger and industrially superior, not simply stronger. Workers manage themselves, resources don't deplete, and conquered settlements join you rather than render half the map suddenly pointless. It's about growth and speed, not dawdling around worrying about the little things. To that end, it's possible to complete a multiplayer game spanning all of human history within a lunchtime. Compared to the likes of *Civilization*, which requires the best part of a weekend for anyone to seize the globe, it's like the invention of fire.

Reynolds went on to join social game specialist Zynga, creator of Facebook favorite *Mafia Wars*. It may seem like a strange move, but his unparalleled understanding of strategic fun being applied to an entirely different field offers an excellent prospect. **AM**

Zone of the Enders: The 2nd Runner

Original release date : 2003
Platform : PS2
Developer : Konami
Genre : Action

Zone of the Enders simply couldn't match the impossibly unrealistic expectations heaped upon it by gamers starved of their *Metal Gear Solid* fix. Eager to get a glimpse of the next anticipated masterpiece from the brains behind *Solid Snake*, many gamers bought the title simply because it had been bundled with the first playable demo of *Metal Gear Solid 2*—the game that was being feted to showcase the PlayStation 2's capabilities. With many playing *Zone of the Enders* as little more than an afterthought, it was widely criticized for being short, simplistic, and niggly to control.

Unburdened by these concerns, Konami quietly fixed all those problems to produce an unfairly overlooked piece of action excellence. Like its precursor, *Zone of the Enders: The*

2nd Runner was produced by Hideo Kojima, and featured robot designs by Yoji Shinkawa. Game play consisted of a series of missions featuring third-person robot combat tied together by a typically tortuously plotted storyline.

The game resurrects the robot star of the first game, an "Orbital Frame" called Jehuty, and offers a much more engaging combat experience thanks to a tweaked combat engine and a dramatic increase in the number of enemies. Fighting is fast and graceful as you unleash screenfuls of pyrotechnics with your subweapons and hurl the smashed-up robot carcasses of your enemies into the ranks of their fellow warriors.

Zone of the Enders: The 2nd Runner also offers epic boss encounters, a one-on-one versus mode, and a host of unlockable mini-games—including a 3-D homage to Konami's *Gradius* (called *Zoradius*, just to make the parallels completely clear). It still falls short of the masterpiece that only ever existed in the imaginations of the *Metal Gear* fans, but, then again, that's probably a good thing. **DM**

Samorost

Original release date : 2003
Platform : PC, Mac
Developer : Jakub Dvorsky
Genre : Adventure

Built as a degree project while Jakub Dvorsky was still a student at the Prague Academy of Arts, Architecture, and Design, *Samorost* quickly established him as a major talent in the indie development scene. The committee marking *Samorost* as part of Dvorsky's thesis, however, were a little confused as to why he had created a computer game and awarded him a B grade. Little did they realize that it would resuscitate its chosen genre almost singlehandedly.

Released for free, the Flash game does little to tax the player. The objective—to stop the home of a space-faring gnome colliding with an incoming ship—is completed in swift measure, and the puzzles that punctuate its point-and-click play barely threaten to confound. But it's the way

these elements combine overall—the feverishly surreal landscape, the endearing cast, and the gentle intonations of ambient noise—that make *Samorost* such a memorable aesthetic experience.

The world itself is a sumptuous collage of macro photography and vector graphics, lending a quaint DIY tangibility to the surroundings that recalls Cosgrove Hall's stop-motion films or Oliver Postgate's *The Clangers*. *Samorost* speaks to that nostalgic combination of untethered imagination and innocence that is childlike without being childish—even the gnomish protagonist is brought to life with a charming naive energy.

A sequel continues the story with some elegance, and Dvorsky has since gone on to make *Machinarium*, solidifying a reputation in a genre thought to have peaked in the early 1990s. *Samorost*, though, has proven that a sense of beauty and ingenuity has a profound rejuvenating power—the game's charms outstrip any qualms with the limitations of interaction taking place. **MD**

SimCity 4

Original release date : 2003
Platform : PC, Mac
Developer : Maxis
Genre : Management Simulation

The neighbor towns in *SimCity* games before *SimCity 4* were mysterious entities. You could see the name of the city next door, yet in the end, you were stuck on your own parcel of land, left to wonder about what laid beyond. *SimCity 4*'s signature feature, region play, clicks the zoom out button and removes all mystery. In this game, you can build Catville and then start Dogville right next door, and build their neighbors, and so on. The expansive acreage invites you to build a humming megalopolis and makes past *SimCity* exploits seem terribly provincial.

The game's achievements on the macro scale are equaled on the micro level. The hordes of Sims that populate your cities have gotten more sophisticated, and they respond to small changes in their locale. If there's too much traffic at the corner, they might get fed up with the commute and flee your city. Widen the lanes a bit and they'll come flocking back. Traffic, smog, water quality, mass transit, land values—every one of them affects the disposition of your persnickety Sims. Attentive urban planners will delight in the unending potential for improvement in their digitized utopias.

SimCity 4's most brilliant stroke, though, was opening itself up for user modification. If you'd like to tweak the simulation, dive into the countless plug-ins created by the online *SimCity* community. Some mods are so advanced that they correct flaws in the original game. To wit: Sims often drive themselves mad in traffic, even when there's a subway station mere steps away; a user-programmed patch that knocks some sense into commuters has become an essential add-on. It's no surprise that *SimCity* users have proven so industrious: They love to build things, and *SimCity 4* provides the ideal construction site. **JT**

Star Wars: Knights of the Old Republic

Original release date : 2003
Platform : Various
Developer : BioWare
Genre : Role-Playing

After the success of the *Baldur's Gate* series, Canadian developer BioWare became one of the hottest properties in gaming. So when it turned its hand to one of the hottest intellectual properties in entertainment, it was a match made in heaven—or in a galaxy far, far away, at least.

Star Wars: Knights of the Old Republic represented the first time the *Star Wars* universe had been turned into a role-playing video game (although not the first time it had been turned into a role-playing game in other media). Like the *Baldur's Gate* games, *Knights of the Old Republic* is based on Wizards of the Coast's pen-and-paper rules. Thus, freed from the demands of devising their own game mechanics, the experts at BioWare were given the opportunity to tinker with the characters and campaign setting—the most crucial parts of all the best RPGs.

That campaign is far, far away in time as well as space, set some 4,000 years before the events depicted in the movies—another key design decision that granted the developer an extraordinary level of autonomy over George Lucas's universe. This unprecedented freedom allowed BioWare to devise a narrative equal to the *entire* double trilogy of movies in terms of dramatic scope and complexity—complete with a plot twist every bit as revelatory as the moment when Darth Vader reveals Luke's lineage. It also enabled it to create a new cast of characters, such as the Sith Lords Darth Malak and Darth Revan, both of whom rival their notorious descendants—Darths Vader and Maul—in terms of evil and menace. Above all, *Star Wars: Knights of the Old Republic* grants the players their *own* freedom—the ability to forge their own paths, choosing, by their actions, to ally themselves with the light side or the dark side of the Force. **DM**

Tales of Symphonia

Original release date : 2003
Platform : GameCube, PS2
Developer : Namco
Genre : Role-Playing

Namco's series of *Tales* video games, despite being hugely successful in Japan, has never really matched the popularity achieved by the RPGs of Square and Konami. Not only is this a great shame but also ironic since they feature some of the most accessible mechanics of any Japanese RPG. *Tales of Symphonia*, originally released on Nintendo's GameCube, is perhaps the most explicit demonstration of this long-standing franchise trait.

Set in Sylvarant, a place dying as its natural mana seeps from the land, the game casts the player as Lloyd Irving who, along with Colette Brunel, become the latest teenagers to shoulder a huge responsibility bestowed upon them. Taking up the controller, however, is far less

of a burden. Random encounters are now all but absent thanks to enemies appearing on both the 3-D world map and in dungeons, so most dangers can be avoided, although to succeed against bosses some voluntary grinding will still be required. Namco's Linear Motion Battle System returns, this time augmented by overlimit and unison attacks, customizable party AI, and the ability to summon elemental creatures.

In addition to leveling, titles can be earned for meeting certain conditions in battle to provide relevant stat boosts. These titles are far from permanent, though, and must be maintained by consistently performing well. Plot development is similarly persistent, with expositional skits occurring during travel or in the many towns and cities. The choices made here will have a subtle effect on the overall story arc. All of this is presented in a whimsically rustic cel-shaded style that suits the tone perfectly. Indeed, the overall package may just be enough to convert even the biggest J-RPG skeptic. **DM**

Manhunt

Original release date : 2003
Platform : Various
Developer : Rockstar
Genre : Action

James Earl Cash, executed in prison in *Manhunt*'s opening moments, wakes up in the middle of a nightmare, cast in the role of prey in a vivid mixture of snuff movie and game show, pursued by murderous gaggles of masked thugs and egged on by the mysterious Director. *Manhunt* is a fairly bleak tale, then, but it's also a terrifyingly well-constructed one: a brilliant piece of game design that pushes the player to greater and greater acts of cinematic sadism as they fight their way out of the Director's horrible maze, one death at a time.

Manhunt is about waiting, about lurking in the shadows and biding your time. Face your enemies head-on and you'll be quickly overpowered. Instead, it's much better to hold your breath in the wings, learning your quarry's movements, and then walk up behind to finish them off. Once you have a victim targeted, a button prompt appears, allowing you to kill them. The longer you delay the kill, however—and the longer you tease it out, the greater the risk of discovery—the more brutally satisfying the execution will be. It's frightening, frankly, to see just how long you're willing to wait for something you'd never choose to see in any other media.

Implicated in a real-world murder investigation—wrongly, since it was the victim rather than the teenage killer who had played the game—*Manhunt* has become a scapegoat for all manner of violence and excesses in gaming. While allegations of unpalatable grot may be true of the rather nasty sequel, for the original, it's a misplaced charge. Brutal and thought provoking, *Manhunt* is an elegant and poised game, one that forces its players to consider the nature of the link between entertainment and violence—a relationship that other, less controversial titles are willing merely to capitalize upon. **CD**

Max Payne 2: The Fall of Max Payne

Original release date : 2003

Platform : Various

Developer : Remedy Entertainment

Genre : Shoot 'Em Up

The title's a bit misleading. As long as you ignore the catastrophic downturns, things are looking up for the returning Max Payne. He's bagged himself a girlfriend, Mona Sax, who only briefly tries to kill him. Also, he's back on the force, albeit by the grace of a secretive crime family. Finally, he even has a new face: No longer that of Remedy staff writer Sam Lake, locked for whatever technical reasons in a constipated smirk, but of real actor Timothy Gibbs. It's fair to say that with a 600-page script—the first game's is a *mere* 160—*Max Payne 2: The Fall of Max Payne* can be regarded as an improvement in every respect.

Having avenged his family last time, the reinstated Payne has a new target in the sequel: the Cleaners, a group of contract killers tied to recent high-profile murders. Mona Sax, a hired gun in the first game and a fugitive in this one, has nowhere to run: The cops want her arrested; the Cleaners want her dead. Just as well, then, that Payne has nothing to lose. Igniting their feelings for each other, he joins her in battling the game's real villains: the Russian Mafia and the Inner Circle (a society of crooks, not the Jamaican reggae group).

Considerable support from Rockstar Games meant a leap in production values for Remedy's sequel, the casting of family members and visiting pizza boys being just one of the first game's numerous shortcuts. Gibbs's performance in the sequel is second only to that of the surroundings—Havok's physics engine giving your bullets *real* impact. A combo-driven active-reload system spices up the gunplay, while the story is more adventurous, even switching characters for later missions. To the delight of Remedy and its wider fan base, the console versions are also vast improvements on those of its predecessor. **DH**

Wolfenstein: Enemy Territory

Original release date : 2003
Platform : PC, Mac
Developer : Splash Damage
Genre : First-Person Shooter

One of the many happy side effects of PC gaming not suffering the same controls and restrictions as consoles is that it offers an avenue for new developers to emerge. *Wolfenstein: Enemy Territory* began life as a semi-amateur modification for Raven's *Wolfenstein* 3-D sequel, *Return to Castle Wolfenstein*. Fan acclaim for the fledgling British studio Splash Damage's map quickly led to a sack of cash from Activision, and a deal to make a free, standalone *Wolfenstein* game all of its own.

We may take unlockables, classes, and leveling up in multiplayer shooters for granted now, but *Wolfenstein: Enemy Territory* was way ahead of its time when it offered a ranking system back in 2003. Finally there was a reason

to play beyond winning for the sake of it, and the drip-feed of rewards for doing well. Making the maps about seizing, destroying, and defending objectives rather than simply a points-based scuffle boosts the thrill factor, turning every match into a capsule action movie rather than simply the strange, screen-based sports of its contemporaries.

Even today, there's a freshness and an urgency to this free release that the stodgy multiplayer modes of so many huge budget shooters can't creep close to. The creators' enthusiasm for team play and for high-speed yet strategic action burns brightly, and that's why *Wolfenstein: Enemy Territory* will be remembered for longer, and with greater fondness, than its parent game.

Alas, Splash Damage couldn't repeat its magic with the retail sequel, *Enemy Territory: Quake Wars*, that prize freshness being sadly smothered by overcomplication. Not that it could have really hoped to replace the still-popular *Wolfenstein: Enemy Territory*, of course, which is far too much of landmark game to die out anytime soon. **AM**

F-Zero GX

Original release date : 2003
Platform : GameCube
Developer : Amusement Vision
Genre : Racing

How fast is too fast? *F-Zero GX* comes perilously close to answering that question. Even on easier settings, this game moves at ludicrous speed: Imagine riding a rollercoaster that isn't tethered to the track, and you start to get some idea of what it feels like to zip along its undulating courses—and to soar off of them, repeatedly, prematurely ending your race in a fiery fashion. Mastering *F-Zero GX* is less about dexterity than about training your brain to process an onslaught of incoming information more quickly than evolution ever intended.

Epileptics beware: *F-Zero GX* is an overwhelming sensory spectacle. The aesthetic is pure junk food, all flashing lights and bright colors, backed by a pumping techno beat that never lets up. Even with thirty racers on-screen at a time, the frame rate is locked at a crisp sixty frames per second, animating the chaos with liquid ease.

Although *F-Zero GX* lacks anything that might ironically be referred to as realism, there are hints of strategy to keep things interesting—if, that is, you can stay on the track long enough to put them into practice. **MK**

R-Type Final

Original release date : 2003
Platform : PS2
Developer : Irem
Genre : Shoot 'Em Up

It's rare enough to find a shoot 'em up with a story, much less one that knows how to end it. Yet *R-Type Final* feels more like a funeral cortege than a military strike, full of listless enemies, solemn reprises of 1980s chip tunes, and dismal encounters with once-great opponents. The Dobkeratops, for one—a series icon and resident boss— sits wired to a life-support machine immersed in amniotic fluid; one level sees the soldiers of the Bydo Empire stretchered back and forth on conveyor belts; others begin with epitaphs and haiku, visiting bombed-out cities and autumnal forests.

The game—developed secretly for eighteen months by producer Kazuma Kujo—soon abandons its downbeat tone and shoots for the stars, taking its fleet of ships banking through time warps and into parallel dimensions and alternative levels, evolving play throughs and ending with spectacular boss fights. New titles may have been added, but as an action game, Kujo maintains that the *R-Type* series ended in 2004. For a highly regarded brand, *R-Type Final* is a fitting send-off. **DH**

Gregory Horror Show

Original release date : 2003
Platform : PS2
Developer : Capcom
Genre : Survival Horror

Its cubist, cartoon visuals immediately cast *Gregory Horror Show* as an atypical survival-horror game, but it's more disturbing simply because of its disregard for gore, shocks, and genre convention. Based on an equally discomfiting anime series, the game traps the player in a surreal purgatory, a run-down old hotel run by an old mouse named Gregory. Your only friend and ally is a zombie cat, once the pet of a hotel guest, whose eyes and mouth have been sewn up by the sinister proprietor. Gregory himself is a sadist, polite but menacing; his guests, driven mad by their incarceration, are deranged and violent.

The game itself consists of spying on the other guests, collecting enough information about them to steal the bottled soul that each keeps close, in order to trade them with Death for your escape. As time goes by, the game becomes so difficult and the puzzles so obscure that few players ever manage to escape.

Gregory Horror Show is ostensibly the most visually interesting game in the genre. It may also be one of the most effective. **KM**

Zuma

Original release date : 2003
Platform : Various
Developer : PopCap Games
Genre : Puzzle

Zuma is PopCap's take on Mitchell Corporation's *Puzz Loop*—a homage that briefly landed the famous casual-game developer in hot water. But while its origins are clear, PopCap has worked its strange magic in terms of style and delivery, turning a bead-matching game into the adventures of a bizarrely charming frog. It adds up to a reinvention of the core idea that towers above the original.

Zuma tasks you with shooting beads out of your frog's mouth to make matches with a long strand of other beads that constantly passes along a twisty-turny channel carved through the game world. If the strand manages to get to the exit, it's game over. It's excellent fun, and it's also decidedly hard for what is alleged to be a casual game, a sweaty scramble to beat the clock that can leave you howling in misery before your computer screen when victory is snatched from your grasp at the very last second.

Other PopCap video games may be more instantly entertaining or have sparkier characters, but *Zuma* remains unrelentingly addictive over time—a compulsive life ruiner if you allow yourself to get sucked in. **CD**

Pool Paradise

Original release date : 2004
Platform : Various
Developer : Awesome Developments
Genre : Sports

Despite enjoying the endorsement of Jimmy White, Archer Maclean's *Pool Paradise* needed to find a way to compete with the simulation accuracy of *Virtual Pool* and the official licensing of *World Snooker Championship*. Awesome Developments' answer was to set the game on a tropical island, provide an eclectic roster of opponents (including some knowing caricatures), and offer numerous distractions beyond the main tournaments. As if the game's irreverent tone might be missed, your buy-in for the tournament is funded by a loan shark (quite literally, a shark).

But this exuberant exterior belies a game that takes its pool very seriously, indeed. The accessible and intuitive analog controls allow players to take full advantage of the realistic physics: Everything is weighted perfectly, balls can be jumped, and trick shots set up and performed. The numerous available rule sets complement the various table shapes and sizes, and the AI scales to your ability. There really is little else to want for, and the game provides by offering customizable cues, baizes, and table themes, as well as unlockable mini-games. These include darts; a coconut shy played with a cannon; and, brilliantly, a full version of Maclean's 8-bit shoot 'em up, *Dropzone*, presented in an upright arcade cabinet on the beach.

Attention to detail is everywhere, from the day/night cycle and ever-changing cue ends in certain view modes, to the charismatically animated disembodied hands that represent competitors. *Pool Paradise* does for pool what *Dead or Alive Xtreme Beach Volleyball* does for its sport, providing an immersive and engaging world rather than a dry simulation. More important, the game is enjoyable regardless of your feelings toward pool, and may even convert skeptics. **BM**

Half-Life 2

Original release date : 2004
Platform : Various
Developer : Valve Corporation
Genre : First-Person Shooter

It's entirely reasonable to suggest that the greatest games of all should be the most influential. But sometimes they're not. Sometimes, a game will just set loftier goals, take greater risks, and wield stranger powers than anyone else can match. Put simply, it raises the bar.

Half-Life 2 is just such a game. Released in 2004 after five years in development, it continues the story of an alpha geek, scientist Gordon Freeman, as he deals with the aftermath of an experiment gone wrong. Placed back on Earth by the mysterious G-Man, he finds himself entering City 17, the cold and forbidding capital of a world now enslaved by aliens. The Combine, who snuck into our dimension, thanks to the events of *Half-Life*, have broken humanity's spirit and turned its cities into ghettos. Citizens wear rags and huddle next to tenement windows, waiting for the Civil Protection squads to abduct them to who-knows-where. There are no children.

Had the game been so vulgar as to mimic any movies, there'd have been a Hollywood version years ago. But the secret of its success is that, while full of historical parallels, it tells its story as if games were the only medium on Earth. There are no cut scenes, no paragraphs of exposition to read, and the closest you'll get to pop-culture references are Orwell and H. G. Wells. In their place, Valve's artists, technicians, storytellers, and sound engineers create a unique milieu: a distinctly Soviet metropolis being literally consumed by alien architecture. The work by art director, Viktor Antonov, with his background in conceptual vehicle design, is nothing short of visionary.

Proving that shooting virtual ragdolls doesn't have to mean cheap thrills for angry boys—not all the time, anyway—*Half-Life 2* is a master of the genre. **DH**

Bejeweled 2

Original release date : 2004
Platform : Various
Developer : PopCap Games
Genre : Puzzle

If you're collecting together a handful of games that really changed the face of the industry itself, you'd almost certainly have to include the *Bejeweled* series—simple and addictive, colorful and bright, and capable of selling a new copy somewhere in the world every ten seconds.

Bejeweled may be an endearingly straightforward match-three puzzle title, but it also proved that small games can be big business, shipping millions of copies—PopCap initially had a buzzer rigged up in its offices to announce a new sale, but quickly had to turn it off. The various sequels have only raised its profile and further cemented the series' legendary status. *Bejeweled 2* is probably the best of the lot, keeping the basic mechanics

of the first installment but throwing in a range of new game modes—like the gravity-bending Twilight, which changes the direction of gem drops, and other Easter eggs waiting to be unlocked. The sound and visuals are constantly refining until every session plays out in a shimmery clatter of delightful rewards. Most recently, *Bejeweled Blitz* has brought a little of *Bejeweled 2*'s magic to Facebook, providing a tight score-rush mode with a strict one-minute time limit and a brilliant breakdown of post-game stats. It is easily the best introduction to the wider game that anyone could ask for.

Selling to men and women, young and old, and keeping so-called "casual" gamers hunched over their PCs and Macs long into the night, *Bejeweled 2* is a far cannier product than many of its envious critics assume. Wonderfully balanced and perfectly realized, it's one of a few titles that have genuinely brought a new audience to video games, and then kept them there—often to the point when they're late for work the next day. **CD**

Cave Story

Original release date : 2004
Platform : Various
Developer : Studio Pixel
Genre : Action / Adventure

You probably have certain expectations about free Internet games—or rather, you probably have a careful lack of expectations of them. For a game to be free, it's probably hastily made, short, sloppy, and—increasingly—trying to sell you something, like a Coke discount or cheap sneakers. *Cave Story* couldn't be more different. A prolonged yet fairly random burst of pixelated generosity, it took five years for its designer to complete, and its old-school polish shines from every single screen.

It's massive, too, plunging its amnesiac—obviously—hero into a gigantic network of underground grottoes and villages, populated with the fluffy and adorable Mimigas. The Mimigas are being pushed around by the nefarious Doctor, and, still with no memories to speak of, you soon find yourself on a daring rescue mission that could turn around the fortunes of an entire species.

With a range of different endings and literally dozens of oddball secrets to hunt down and uncover, *Cave Story* could easily have passed for a classic SNES or GBA release from the glory days of action RPGs with no questions asked. That it's free only adds to the quirky sense of wonder the game constantly exudes. The game was extremely well received upon release, and has since been voted number one on a list of the best freeware games ever. Easy to track down online, where *Cave Story*'s many followers turn out artwork, fan fiction, and FAQs as they pick over the game's minutiae, Wii owners can purchase an updated version—with both the improved and original graphics included—for the platform's WiiWare service. There's a small fee involved, of course, but, after years of being recipients of such ceaseless generosity, is probably the least we can do. To the Mimigas! **CD**

City of Heroes

Original release date : 2004
Platform : PC, Mac
Developer : Cryptic Studios
Genre : MMORPG

Massively multiplayer online games (MMOGs) demonstrate the most obvious potential for fun out of just about any genre—offering gigantic, rolling worlds where hundreds of players can get together to write their own stories—but they often seem the most limited in terms of implementation. Fantasy features heavily, and it's almost always fantasy of the same kind: magical, medieval, and filled with wood elves and gruff orcs. That's hardly a crime, but it makes something like *City of Heroes* all the more admirable. Sure, we're still in the world of adolescent make-believe, but rather than the realm of the +10 Mace, it's capes and cowls, jet boots and doomsday devices that get to do all the heavy lifting.

City of Heroes is a comic book fan's dream: Developer Cryptic Studios has built a shiny metropolis to fly, race, or bound through, filled with robberies to stop, zombie outbreaks to subdue, and megalomaniacs to put behind bars, every activity beating to the well-trodden point-gathering and stat-leveling rhythm. It is ironic, to be sure, that in comic books there are generally only a few superheroes doing the rounds, whereas in Cryptic's world they almost outnumber the general populace. But the developer is so adept at giving you ridiculous quests and left-field challenges that you almost never stop feeling special. Plus, it is always surprising and pleasurable to see the kind of bizarre saviors that your fellow players have brought into play.

City of Villains proved perhaps the most obvious expansion of all time, but was no less successful for it. Cryptic's game may well be currently wending its way into late middle age, but there's still much to admire and lots to enjoy here—particularly in the recent Mac version. **CD**

Counter-Strike Source

Original release date : 2004
Platform : PC
Developer : Valve Corporation
Genre : First-Person Shooter

This total remake of the original *Counter-Strike* modification—an online team-based shoot 'em up of antiterrorist gunplay—came about when Valve rebooted its Source game engine for *Half-Life 2* and launched the digital distribution system called Steam. The *Counter-Strike Source* version is as much a commercial move as a necessary update for this ludicrously popular multiplayer shooter, because anyone who wants to play this new version of the game will need to install Steam to do so. It was this free game that made Steam the software-distribution platform of choice for PC gamers.

Counter-Strike Source is a peerless classic of symmetrical combat. Two teams, terrorists and counterterrorists, battle for control of a series of maps, each with its own objectives, such as planting or diffusing a bomb or rescuing and securing hostages. If one team is wiped out, then it's game over. Weapons are quasirealistic, including 9mm pistols, automatic shotguns, and sniper rifles. As players progress through a number of rounds, they earn money, which enables them to "buy" from the arsenal at the start of each round. Players may save their funds in order to buy a favored high-end weapon and some body armor at a later stage, dramatically improving their chances.

The remake reproduces most of the classic maps from the original, but it also adjusts a number of minor parameters, such as the significance of smoke grenades. These now propagate much more slowly, but with a more pronounced effect, using enhanced graphical tech to obscure visuals for affected players. The environments are more dynamic too, since *Counter-Strike Source* enables the inclusion of physical objects that can be knocked over or blasted across the map. **JR**

Donkey Kong: Jungle Beat

Original release date : 2004
Platform : GameCube
Developer : Nintendo
Genre : Platform

Though it's played with the bongo controller Nintendo developed for their *Donkey Konga* rhythm-action title, *Donkey Kong: Jungle Beat* is actually a platformer—and one of the most physical games of all time.

A follow-up to Rare's rather more traditional platformers for the SNES and N64, *Donkey Kong: Jungle Beat* was created by Yoshiaki Koizumi, who'd go on to direct *Super Mario Galaxy*. But it shines with its own invention— not least in the surprising delicacy of a knockabout and simple control system that prefigured the Wii's motion sensing. The whole thing works with just three inputs: bash the right bongo to run right, left for left, and clap to jump. The faster you drum, the faster Donkey Kong goes. It's not just about getting to the end of the level, it's about how many points you can obtain. Points, or "beats," are gained from grabbing bananas and performing combos.

The game is also a fine example of Nintendo's knack of repurposing its own heritage. There's *Donkey Kong* and the platforming, of course, but there's also *Punch-Out!!* with its boss fights, which are staged as boxing matches with a rogue's gallery of simian bruisers.

Though it hasn't many levels, depth is lent by a stern score attack, which is intensely challenging, even if you are just playing for bananas. Most sections are designed so that you can traverse them with chains of moves, such as wall jumps and vine swinging, which, as long as you don't touch the ground, will earn you higher scores. But what you'll remember are the ends of each level. If you were hoping for a moment to relax, forget it. The mini-game involves an extended pounding session in order to earn as many bananas as you can—leaving your arms and palms burning with the sheer euphoric effort of it all. **AW**

⊗ : Talk

Angelo
It's easy to let your guard down when victory's in sight. That's when you're most in danger of losing.

Dragon Quest VIII: Journey of the Cursed King

Original release date : 2004
Platform : PS2
Developer : Level-5
Genre : Role-Playing

Dragon Quest VIII: Journey of the Cursed King kicks off with a curse, inflicted by evil jester Dhoulmagus on the kingdom of Trodain and its king, Trode. Thus begins the journey of the title, as the game's nameless hero embarks on an expedition to restore king and kingdom. But in many ways the game itself is the culmination of a very remarkable journey: It is the perfect distillation of every current of design that has flowed through the Japanese RPG ever since the first *Dragon Quest* was released in Japan in 1986.

Dragon Quest reshaped the RPG genre for the Japanese market with amazing success. By the time the eighth chapter was released, the series had sold nearly 50 million units across every major piece of gaming hardware, and

each new game was a major event. In Japan *Dragon Quest VIII* sold 3 million copies inside a week. Since the series' inception, there has been a remarkable continuity in design, partly because the same key individuals have been responsible for the creation of every game. Series creator Yuji Horii has always been in charge of design, Akira Toriyama has always worked on the characters, and Koichi Sugiyama has always handled music.

The hallmarks of that design are the quest structure, turn-based combat, random encounters, slime—lots of slime—and the remarkable people and places that you meet on your travels, rendered in this installment with unbelievable cel-shaded flair.

Despite the popularity of the series, *Dragon Quest VIII* was actually the first installment to be released in Europe. Given the game's heritage, it is no surprise that the localization is superb, producing an experience that was described by one reviewer as *Monty Python* meets *The Princess Bride*. It's certainly as entertaining as either. **DM**

Doom 3

Original release date : 2004
Platform : Various
Developer : id Software
Genre : First-Person Shooter

Sales of more than 3.5 million copies make *Doom 3* the most successful game in id Software's history, but opinions differ over its worth as both an FPS and a sequel. How do you follow up *Doom*, exactly, when its repertoire of pixel-mush hobgoblins, cyborg cacodemons, BFGs, and Martian corridors feels every bit its eleven years old? The answer, as you might expect from the master of early 3-D graphics, was technological.

No matter how sophisticated their light and shadows, or how bleak their subject matter, most games know instinctively to use ambient light. Because without it there's nothing, not just impenetrable black but absolute black. The kind of black you see in horror movies, where the marine's flashlight goes out just as the monsters appear. The kind of black that scares are made of. With its pioneering use of dynamic per-pixel lighting and stencil shadowing, *Doom 3* turned off the ambient light, leaving players ultra-sensitive to its environment and scares, and reliant on a flashlight they had to holster before they could shoot.

Doom 3 overexploits this, and its own reliance on heavily telegraphed jump scares grows old very quickly. But as you learn macabre facts through abandoned personnel files, the game becomes an effective survival horror. Its venue, a military-industrial research facility on Mars, is a pressure cooker full of heavy machines, twisting conduits, and prison walls. Its airlocks offer false hope of escape, the surface of the Red Planet giving you seconds before you suffocate. And as you drive your anonymous marine toward an infernal endgame, the real devils of the story are, of course, the resident humans and their plans, which leaves one nagging question: Should it really have been a *Doom* game at all? **DH**

Halo 2

Original release date : 2004
Platform : PC, Xbox
Developer : Bungie
Genre : First-Person Shooter

After an initial showing that suggested *Halo 2* would carry mankind's battle against the Covenant to the cities and streets of Earth itself, many fans ended up ultimately disappointed. While Bungie's sequel did make a polite landing among the gray megastructures of New Mombassa—the effect is like wandering around an extremely violent modern university campus—it doesn't stay put in this hardware-intensive world very long before Master Chief and crew warp out again, bound for far more predictable territories.

While the chance to drive a Warthog up the side of the Eiffel Tower or through the burning ravages of Times Square would have to wait for another day—actually, we're still waiting—*Halo 2* is still a visceral follow-up to the Xbox's biggest game. It may lack the air of mystery and discovery of the first title—and its second half rehashes the weaker points of the first game's plot to a rather frightening degree—but it had enough innovations to carry the day. Such innovations include dual-wielding weapons and a delightfully overpowered Needler.

More important, it takes the game's original local multiplayer and puts it where it belongs: on Xbox Live. *Halo* online is nothing less than a phenomenon: fast paced and full of action, with a series of intricate maps, including the peerless Zanzibar, that bring out the best in the weapon set.

It all ends, unexpectedly, with a nasty and rather unsatisfying cliff-hanger, but the multiplayer alone was enough to ensure that gamers would still be playing *Halo 2* when the final game in the series came out. Besides, it's hard to begrudge any *Halo* game that loves the Needler as much as this one does. **CD**

EverQuest II

Original release date : 2004
Platform : PC
Developer : Sony Online Entertainment
Genre : MMORPG

EverQuest was a trailblazer in creating a 3-D-powered persistent world, so it shouldn't be a surprise if some of its design fundamentals came up a little short. Though the online format allowed for updates and patches to address issues of balance caused by overpowered items, spells, or abilities, a total reboot was the chance to learn from every experience and every note of feedback. So with *EverQuest II*, Sony Online Entertainment made significant strides in a number of key areas. For starters, the improved graphics engine totally revolutionizes the world of Norrath, adding incredible detail to every character and location and ensuring that each new encounter—even with familiar items, spells, or races—feels fresh.

Some time into the development process, the bold decision was made to apply a voice to every character in the world. The result was a reported 130 hours of dialogue recording, including cameos from Christopher Lee and Heather Graham. This backs a renewed emphasis on meeting and greeting characters in each city, and then completing the tasks they dole out. The shift in balance from hacking bats and rats to performing quests encourages more exploration across a Norrath some 500 years removed from the events in the original game. In that time significant upheavals have reshaped the landscape, even removing access to the moon of Luclin.

Though *EverQuest II* represents Sony's second major fantasy-themed massively multiplayer online RPG, it launched at a time when the genre was still in its growth phase. It was a balancing act of skill-tree progress, leveling, and item acquisition, with no hard and fast rules of what the potential audience would embrace. As such, it remains a work in progress, with new content continually added to flesh out the world and refine its game play. **RSm**

Gradius V

Original release date : 2004
Platform : PS2
Developer : Treasure
Genre : Shoot 'Em Up

A series of smart side-scrollers with a natty little power-up system that sees players advancing up a tiered set of perks, *Gradius* is a franchise that has launched very few disappointing games. *Gradius V* is often considered the very best, however; partly because it's clever and colorful and a constant visual bombardment, and partly because it's built by boutique studio Treasure, so was always destined to be a cut above the average.

In a not particularly coherent way the story concerns humanity's battle against the Bacterian and your role within it as a spaceship called *Vic Viper*. The fifth installment in the *Gradius* series retains the franchise's traditional power-up system and also allows for extensive weapons editing. It's also the first *Gradius* game (at least strictly by name) to make room for two-player simultaneous play. This innovative system allows Treasure to ramp up the heartbeat of the scrolling space battles to create some really ridiculous asymmetrical conflicts.

The glowing sunsets and explosions of light the developer is known for come together with the established rules of the *Gradius* universe very well, but what's really staggering is how fresh the series feels as it heads into old age. The game's difficulty levels were tweaked to make the traditionally extreme levels of challenge a little more appealing to players of all skill levels. This can be seen most notably in the fact that death merely scatters your power-ups around the screen, where they can be recaptured, rather than removing them entirely. *Gradius V* is one of those games you should really think about trying out, even if you're not a fan of the genre. The best of its kind, it has the power to rise above its own traditions, limitations, and stereotypes. **CD**

Grand Theft Auto: San Andreas

Original release date : 2004
Platform : Various
Developer : Rockstar
Genre : Action

With sales of more than 20 million copies since its launch in 2004, *Grand Theft Auto: San Andreas* is the biggest-selling PlayStation 2 game of all time, and not without reason. Though initially a game about gang bangers and turf wars in a fictional Los Angeles (Los Santos), channeling scenes from *Menace II Society* and *Boyz N the Hood*, it blossoms into an ode to the entire West Coast. Three whole cities—the others being San Fierro (San Francisco) and Las Venturas (Las Vegas)—create a game four times bigger than *Grand Theft Auto: Vice City*, home to just about every idea from Rockstar's whiteboards. Weight gain, pimping missions, robberies, drive-bys, swimming, clothes shopping, martial arts, casino games, horse racing—the list goes on.

The hero this time is Carl "CJ" Johnson, a Los Santos native who returns for his mother's funeral after five years in Liberty City. Chaos greets him, his neighborhood falling to gang violence while rivalries and suspicions break up his family. Blackmailed by the crooked Officer Tenpenny (a very game Samuel L. Jackson) and distracted by girlfriends, hippies, and everyone in between, he gradually unearths the secrets behind his mother's murder, following the clues to the far reaches of the map.

Just as important as the urban centers of San Andreas are the spaces in between: the rural retreats and vast open roads that turn the game into a road movie. No *Grand Theft Auto* before or since has let you point toward a random horizon and just keep on driving, capturing that post-Woodstock spirit of movies like *Easy Rider* and *Vanishing Point*. None has featured a more star-studded cast, either, or so many ways of getting from *A* to *B* via *X*, *Y*, and *Z*. Though it lacks an occasional dab of polish, *Grand Theft Auto: San Andreas* is an embarrassment of riches. **DH**

Far Cry

Katamari Damacy

Original release date : 2004
Platform : PC
Developer : Crytek
Genre : First-Person Shooter

Original release date : 2004
Platform : PS2
Developer : Namco
Genre : Action

Why hide when you're the hero? If you're the man with the plan (and, indeed, the heavy-duty ordnance), why should you be crouched behind a crate when your instincts tell you to get out there and unload the full artillery?

Far Cry doesn't force you into the shadows, but it does provide ample opportunity for stealth, its structural design open-ended enough to allow you to piece together your own method of play. Since the game is set on a tropical island, it's difficult to imagine it working any other way; the temptation to explore these beaches and jungles is a strong one, and you're rarely prevented from doing so.

The organic, vegetation-rich environments set new standards at release, and contrasted sharply with the browns and grays so beloved of the PC first-person shooter scene. The game is least effective when it takes the action indoors and those hackneyed hues come to the fore, along with some more sci-fi-focused themes. Nevertheless, this is one of the strongest debuts in game history, announcing Crytek's technical credentials with some flourish and marking it out as a studio to watch. **TB**

Playing as the Prince of All Cosmos, a tiny, noble creature with a head that looks like it's been caught in a mailbox, you move around a series of laudably messy game worlds, rolling objects into a huge sticky ball called a Katamari, in order to meet certain requirements set by your father, the king. The larger the object, the larger your Katamari will have to be to capture it, and so the game moves forward with a brilliantly cumulative structure, starting with you gathering up dust motes and paperclips and ending with the collection of skyscrapers and giant monsters.

The presentation is blocky, vivid, and refreshingly unique, but the real pleasure comes from the ephemera you'll find yourself gathering up: household goods, scientific curios, monuments from around the globe. The king, who accidentally destroyed most of the galaxy in a legendary drinking binge, is a wonderful mentor, managing to be sniffy, surreal, and distinctly sinister. The game's glorious soundtrack matches the chaotic game world track for track, unfolding as a jukebox of upbeat tunes, most of which are genuinely unclassifiable. **CD**

Mashed

Original release date : 2004
Platform : Various
Developer : Empire Interactive
Genre : Racing

Taking a rare top-down view, this is a knockabout kind of game with boxy vehicles and muddy, indistinct tracks. None of that matters, of course, because it moves at such a pace that you'd never get much of a chance to look at the surroundings, anyway. While other games worry about racing lines and gear changes, decals and procedural physics, all that matters in *Mashed* is getting ahead and then staying ahead, making sure that, at the very least, your car never drops out of view as the racers hurtle round the pack. Disappear offscreen and it's all over for you, at which point, in a brilliant twist that acknowledges that there's nothing worse than being knocked out of an event and watching your friends continuing to have fun, you become a floating disembodied cursor and get to spend the rest of the race comprehensively griefing anyone left in with a handy arsenal of explosives.

Sampled as a single-player experience, *Mashed* is more or less a total bust. But with a few friends around, this simple, budget-graphics title will take your evening and chew it up right in front of you. **CD**

Mario Power Tennis

Original release date : 2004
Platform : GameCube
Developer : Camelot Software Planning
Genre : Sports

Mario Power Tennis preserves the simplicity of classic pick-up-and-play games, but also introduces nuanced strategy typically reserved for more complex sims. Plus, you can clobber your opponent with koopa shells.

Players choose from a cast of classic *Mario* characters, each with their own on-court strengths. Lanky Waluigi plays a killer serve-and-volley game at the net, for instance, while slow, hard-hitting Bowser is better suited to the baseline. The "Power" part of the title refers to power shots that can be unleashed after building up a charge in your racket. Like the booby-trapped Gimmick Courts and numerous side games, the power shots are humorous crowd-pleasers that wear a bit thin over the long run.

Indeed, despite a panoply of entertaining bells and whistles, the enduring pleasure of this game is its pure tennis: the grind of a long volley, the science of a whizzing topspin, the careful dance of court position. Even players with no particular affinity for the famous Italian plumber will appreciate the care with which Camelot translated the game from racket to game pad. **JT**

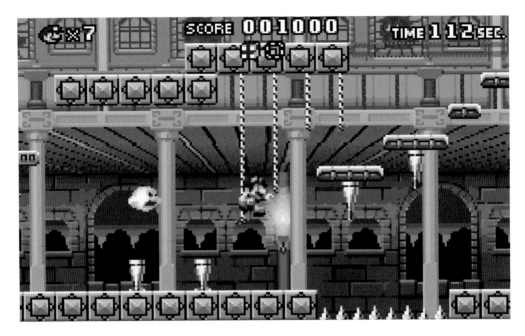

Mario vs. Donkey Kong

Original release date : 2004
Platform : Game Boy Advance
Developer : Nintendo
Genre : Platform / Puzzle

It took this—the quirky kind of off-shoot game made possible on handheld consoles like the Game Boy Advance—to reunite Mario with his oldest nemesis, Donkey Kong. This, the seventh *Mario* game on the GBA, is a clever puzzle platformer that borrowed a handful of ideas from other action strategy titles, but rendered them all beguilingly unique in a way that only Nintendo can.

The story is suitably whimsical. Adorable clockwork mini-Mario toys are taking the world's shops by storm, but on the eve of their big release, Donkey Kong, in a fit of gorilla-ish pique, steals them all, sending Mario on a globe-hopping quest to get them back. What this sad tale of industrial espionage translates into, however, is a

series of smart and vivid platform challenges, set around some familiar themed worlds, ranging from construction site to ghost house. Our handstanding, backflipping hero races through a landscape of 2-D platforms, sometimes simply picking up keys and collecting mini-Mario toys, at other times guiding the chittering little chaps to the exit indirectly, or engaging in a series of steadily evolving boss battles with the stubborn monkey himself.

It's a smart addition to the *Mario* universe, a game that manages to foreground preplanning without leaving out the pleasures of last-minute fiddling, and it's well worth tracking down on eBay. Colorful and seemingly slight, yet with a strong strand of steel running through the center of its challenges, *Mario vs. Donkey Kong* may not be the kind of epic adventure *Mario* fans would expect, but it's a pocket-sized diversion that perfectly fits its platform. Sequels, both for the DS and the DSi's downloadable DSiWare service, embellished the concept further with new mechanics and a smart Wi-Fi-enabled level editor. **CD**

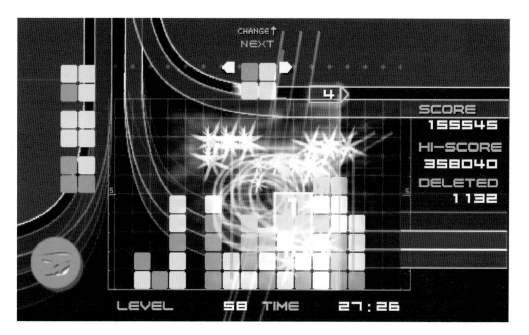

CHANGE↑
NEXT

4

SCORE
155545
HI-SCORE
358040
DELETED
1132

LEVEL   58   TIME   27:26

Lumines

Original release date : 2004
Platform : PSP
Developer : Q Entertainment
Genre : Puzzle

Block-rocking beats, or beat-rocking blocks? *Lumines* (pronounced "luminous") gives you plenty of both. The first game from Tetsuya Mizuguchi's Q Entertainment, this widescreen take on *Columns* and *Tetris* continues the tradition of his previous games, *Rez* and *Space Channel 5*, by using music and light to energize a classic game mechanic. More than just a vehicle for soundtrack and special effects, though, it's another synesthesic masterpiece that fits the PSP like a glove.

Two-by-two squares of blocks fall into the playing field, and the player is able to nudge and rotate them until they land and are locked in place. Each component block has its own color, and if four identical colors come together,

they're destroyed and points are scored. Further pairs of the same color will extend this formation in any direction: 2 x 3, 5 x 2, an unbroken *L* shape—all are valid if the colors match. Destruction only happens in the wake of a vertical line that moves slowly and continuously across the screen, giving you a few vital seconds to build these structures for giant combos. And because gravity makes the surrounding blocks collapse, colors often come together by chance. If they run out of space, of course, it's game over.

This would be enjoyable in a single nondescript stage, but *Lumines*, as much a game as a twenty-first-century mix tape, prefers "skins." If you clear enough blocks, the visual and sonic theme changes entirely, every input and explosion triggering new effects that layer on top of the backing track, creating a rolling, dynamic soundscape. The bebop one, the break beat one, the electro house one; that's how you'll remember its levels.

Other games may be glitzier, but *Lumines* is the essential PSP mix: portable, limitless, and incandescent. **DH**

Metal Gear Solid 3: Snake Eater

Original release date : 2004

Platform : PS2

Developer : Kojima

Genre : Action

Metal Gear Solid was a series of two halves after this third outing, torn between sermonizing future shock and sepia-tinted homage. To a lesser extent, it had also developed two audiences, each loyal to a different side of creator Hideo Kojima. Most agree, though, that '60s flashback *Metal Gear Solid 3: Snake Eater* is Kojima's masterpiece: coherent, personal, and breathtakingly romantic.

Tracing Solid Snake's family tree to his legendary "father" Big Boss, it begins in 1964, deep in the jungle of Soviet Russia. At the height of the Cold War, CIA agent Naked Snake is sent to rescue a defecting scientist named Sokolov, together with plans for a nuclear tank he calls the Shagohod. This opening "Virtuous Mission" is a failure; Snake's mentor, the Boss, turns traitor and hands everything over to the sadistic Colonel Volgin, who, with a single nuclear strike, brings the world to the brink of armageddon. A week later Snake returns as part of a new mission, Operation Snake Eater, to put things right.

Boasting an improved stealth system focused on outdoor environments and degrees of camouflage, *Metal Gear Solid 3* demands a bit more patience than earlier games. But it's no less propulsive, its cut scenes flashier and its characters more alive. Stealing the show is Ocelot, an ambiguous series villain with a passion for revolvers and spaghetti Westerns. Other standouts include the Cobra unit, traumatized soldiers with eccentric superpowers; and Eva, a smoking hot double agent and the game's femme fatale.

But the real star is Kojima himself. His rambling dialogue is awash with in-jokes, cultural pointers, questions and answers, while this latest (or, indeed, earliest) Snake feels more than any other like one of his own idols. *GoldenEye 007* be damned; here's your ultimate Bond game. **DH**

Metal Gear Solid: The Twin Snakes

Original release date : 2004
Platform : GameCube
Developer : Silicon Knights
Genre : Action

One hardware generation after *Metal Gear Solid* had defined a genre on the PlayStation, Silicon Knights was tasked with updating it—a rather thankless task, you might think. Not so. By 2004 standards *Metal Gear Solid* was beginning to look a little angular around the edges, and Silicon Knights brought an admirably self-effacing approach to the task. It remade the game, adding only those elements that would definitely improve it: new animations, a few story tweaks from Hideo Kojima, and a smoothing-out of any bits of mechanical clunkiness.

Metal Gear Solid: The Twin Snakes is thus the definitive version of a gaming touchstone. And the greatest compliment you can pay *Metal Gear Solid* is that it's a game done a disservice by the constant descriptions and explications that follow it. It's a brilliant game, first and foremost, but it's also a brilliant game about games, and about how players play games. Mentioning Psycho Mantis, Revolver Ocelot, and Shadow Moses to a fellow veteran is the prelude to hours of chat and anecdotes, no one else's interpretation quite seeming to match your own.

Alongside *Metal Gear Solid 3: Snake Eater*, this is the pinnacle of the series and is emphatically a game rather than a dissertation delivered in FMV form (there's still a huge amount of dialogue to wade through, but the excellent translation helps). Many games have intellectual ambitions, but few have the bravery to try to reconcile their loftier goals with the game itself, much less bring them to bear on the player through the player's own actions. Constantly surprising and kept fresh by the workmanship of Silicon Knights, *Metal Gear Solid: The Twin Snakes* is an uncompromising version of a classic, and as rich, detailed, and clever as games come. **RS**

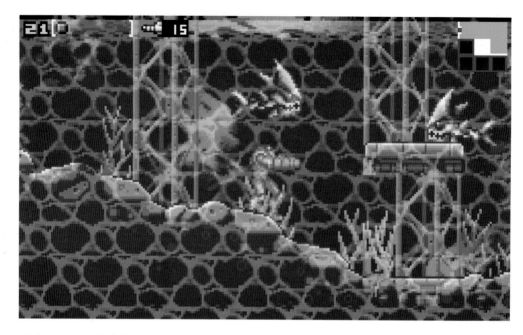

Metroid Zero Mission

Original release date : 2004
Platform : Game Boy Advance
Developer : Nintendo
Genre : Platform / Shoot 'Em Up

Samus Aran, perhaps Nintendo's most grown-up mascot, returns to her roots with the action-adventure *Metroid Zero Mission*. The result is a glitzy and typically atmospheric remake of her very first 1986 NES adventure, scaled up from the blocky 8-bit science fiction of the first outing to make the most of the elaborate opportunities brought by the 32-bit Game Boy Advance.

And the adventure is every bit as good as older gamers might remember it being: a claustrophobic and often frightening rattle through the interior of the planet Zebes, as Nintendo's fizzingly animated bounty hunter tracks down and defeats the terrifying and disgusting Mother Brain. A testament to an almost two-decades-old game

design, the original *Metroid* has lost none of its queasy wit or creepy charm in the transition, while *Metroid Zero Mission* actually rewrites the past in all the right ways by including a handy mini-map that makes the murky business of navigation a little less frustrating this time around.

That map is not the only welcome addition, either. In its journey from one piece of hardware to another, *Metroid Zero Mission* has also picked up additional bosses, fresh twists, an entirely new area called Chozodia, and a fan-favorite sequence in which players get to play as Samus out of the confines of her suit for the first time ever, after she is ambushed and left to sneak around with a single weak pistol and a stylish turquoise jumpsuit.

Some still complain that the end results are too short, but no one complains that they aren't considered or elegant. Thrilling, beautiful, and intricate, the *Metroid* series has rarely put a foot wrong. It's good to know that it was already getting the important things right all the way back at the start of the journey, too. **CD**

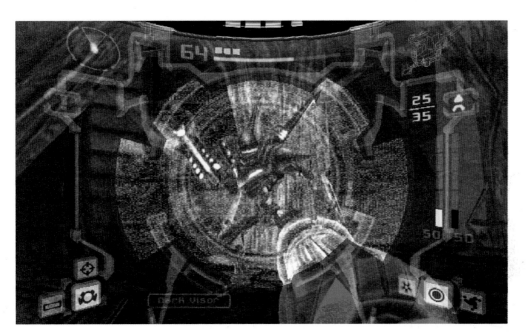

Metroid Prime 2: Echoes

Original release date : 2004
Platform : GameCube
Developer : Retro Studios
Genre : Action / First-Person Shooter

After *Metroid Prime* had proved the 3-D adventures of Samus could be as evocative and twisting as their 2-D incarnations, Retro Studios got ambitious. The concept of *Metroid Prime 2: Echoes* was to out-Nintendo Nintendo. Filching its key idea from *The Legend of Zelda: A Link to the Past*, *Metroid Prime 2: Echoes* is set in two worlds: one of light, one of dark—a feature that is responsible for the game's most basic weapons and enemies, its biggest successes, and the failures of design that almost spoil it.

The 3-D environments are open-ended, vast, and poorly signposted. Everyone who plays this game will get lost. There are other problems: respawning enemies, ridiculously tough bosses, and a key-hunt mission that defies belief. But

you accept these niggles as the price for what is otherwise an inspired experience, and even getting lost is mitigated by the quality of the game's sumptuous world.

From the light beam finding a dark creature to the differences between the same location in the two worlds, the art direction and realization is first class. The challenge is steep, puzzles often require you to flit between worlds, changing elements in one to alter the other, and it's undeniably satisfying to finally work them out.

The idea of light and dark is the focus of the game's narrative, and the plot that unfolds on Dark Aether is an intricate and coherent saga that stands as one of *Metroid*'s finest, even putting the Space Pirates and Metroids on the back burner (not totally, of course). And that portentous subtitle actually justifies itself. This *is* a game of echoes: Did I see that corridor before? Is that object in the dark world too? Where have I seen that glyph? That's why, despite the flaws, it's worth chasing the echoes of *Metroid Prime 2* down to their source. **RS**

Def Jam: Fight for NY

Original release date : 2004
Platform : Various
Developer : Aki Corporation
Genre : Fighting

Latecomers to the *Def Jam* series of fighting games might only know its disastrous finale, the hubristic and somewhat unplayable *Def Jam: Icon*. Before that, though, came two titles by Japan's renowned Aki Corporation, the maker of umpteen wrestling games. While *Icon* painted its gangsta stars as vulgar penthouse moguls, Aki saw them for what they really are: circus performers full of smack talk and testosterone. In other words, pro wrestlers.

First game *Def Jam: Vendetta* took the likeness literally, casting caricatures of acts like DMX, Ludacris, and Method Man in a largely straight wrestling game with eye-watering special moves. This drew unfavorable comparisons to existing wrestling games—specifically, how its match

types and rules stacked up next to Aki's landmark export, *WWF: No Mercy*. For the sequel the series switched stances.

Def Jam: Fight for NY is a unique brawler. Broadening its horizons without ever really choosing a direction, its cast includes actor Danny Trejo, singer and raconteur Henry Rollins, sex symbol Carmen Electra, and several familiar hip-hop luminaries, including Sticky Fingaz, Xzibit, and Busta Rhymes. Players create their own hero, choosing from fighting styles like kickboxing and wrestling, before prizefighting their way through a lengthy career. As hired goons for returning kingpin D-Mob, players have to take back the streets and clubs from shady hoodlum Crow (played by Snoop Dogg) and his lieutenants.

Some fights ask you to throw your opponent under a speeding subway train or through an upstairs window or perhaps into a parked SUV until it's totaled. Brutality is assured thanks to finishing moves like the Violator and the ominously titled Balls to the Wall. Games this crazy aren't meant to have sequels. **DH**

Ninja Gaiden

Original release date : 2004
Platform : Xbox
Developer : Team Ninja
Genre : Action / Adventure

Some games are tricky, some games are downright hard, and some games are utterly infuriating in their ceaseless brutality. Then, and only then, will you get to the special circle of hell occupied by *Ninja Gaiden*. Team Ninja's third-person action game—it's utterly misleading to call any title that demands such rigor a brawler—lured audiences in with its staggering visuals, but it kicked just as many out again pretty quickly with its insane level of constant challenge. As an indication of the horrors in store, the first boss, found at the end of the very first map, is such an overpowered freak that many players simply gave up and never loaded the disk ever again. Some probably snapped it in half, with tears running down their cheeks.

They were missing out, of course, because *Ninja Gaiden*'s seemingly interminable punishment cloaks a fighting system of brilliant refinement, in which lights, heavies, blocks, and dodges all come together in a graceful partnership in the hands of a truly great player, while the very best ninjas out there can make the whole thing look dazzlingly simple.

Sure, series protagonist Ryu Hayabusa looks like a bit of an idiot most of the time, clad in what looks like a body stocking, but he's a wonderful character to inhabit once you have his sword and spell attacks safely under control. As the game progresses, he cuts a swathe through some truly ridiculous locations, meeting—and subsequently skewering—some of gaming's more deranged characters. A treat for the eyes and, ultimately, the thumbs as well, *Ninja Gaiden* is a throwback to when games were merciless and often bleak, but also to when they had the power to make you feel that you'd really achieved something magnificent at the end. **CD**

Paper Mario: The Thousand-Year Door

Original release date : 2004
Platform : GameCube
Developer : Intelligent Systems
Genre : Role-Playing

A counterpart to Mario's handheld RPG adventures, *Paper Mario: The Thousand-Year Door* compounds its slick visuals with some of the most inventive mechanics ever seen in an RPG, even one as genre-bending as this one.

While trying to unlock the mysterious Thousand-Year Door that stands beneath the unexpectedly sleazy hub-world of Rogueport, Mario is sent off into a series of quests. Each chapter of this hilarious adventure usually involves very different mechanics and often casts the famous plumber in an entirely new kind of role. The story begins traditionally enough with a suite of side-scrolling levels leading to traditional boss fights, but Mario soon finds his skills put to the test in unexpected ways. For example, he sets off on a genteel train journey, playing detective, Agatha Christie style, and, in one marvelously inventive section, the challenge is to rise through the ranks of professional wrestling, while also exploring the seedier side of the ring.

There's a lot going on behind the scenes, too, with Princess Peach captured, stuck on a UFO, and exploring some deep philosophical themes with a sentient AI. Bowser rambles around disastrously, and Luigi goes off on his own equally ridiculous adventure, returning between chapters to update Mario on his progress—and sending him to sleep in the process.

It all adds up to one of the quirkiest and most lovable adventures available, a stylish game that pokes plenty of fun at RPG traditions, while conforming to the escalating powers and relentless leveling that made them great in the first place. This is one door that's definitely worth opening, perhaps more than once. **CD**

The Sims 2

Original release date : 2004
Platform : Various
Developer : Maxis
Genre : Life Simulation

What Maxis needed to deliver with *The Sims 2* wasn't more stuff for the little computer people to play with, but more personality. The Sims of the original are generic, angular, basic character models with few thoughts beyond their next meal, party, or toilet visit. The virtual people of *The Sims 2* have individual personalities, believable facial expressions, and lifelong aspirations.

These irrepressible cartoonized people are bursting with life, and have far more charisma than before. Their appearance can be tweaked to an exacting degree, though it's somehow impossible to make an ugly one. Sims can be left to their own devices, and, if anything, their individual traits are almost too developed. Watching your Sim sneak away from family obligations to play video games alone can be like staring into some twisted existential mirror.

With this added personality, heartbreakingly, comes added mortality. Sims grow old and die, and their little lives can be touched by tragedy. *The Sims 2* is the very definition of emergent game play; it's not so much the daily cycles of work and play that make it so compelling, but the spontaneous stories that arise from the everyday.

The Sims 2 channels players' creative energies as well as their obsessive-compulsive tendencies. Players have created a vast and bewilderingly inventive selection of items, houses, and people for other players to download, and YouTube is full of impressively complex machinima, from huge-scale choreographed dances to recreations of everything from *Star Trek* episodes to Britney Spears videos. It all proves that it's not just the modding hardcore who are capable of creating something awesome with a game engine. **KM**

Daigasso! Band Brothers

Original release date : 2004
Platform : DS
Developer : Nintendo
Genre : Music

A console's launch software exists primarily to cover bases: a sports title, a fighter, a shooting game, and so on, each entry ensuring that the new system appeals to as broad an audience as possible. As such, nobody expects much grand innovation at a piece of hardware's birth. But *Daigasso! Band Brothers*—released at the launch of Nintendo's DS—confounded expectations and delivered an innovative and unusual music game quite unlike anything else seen before.

Taking inspiration from Konami's *Bemani* series, the basic interactions are familiar: tap and hold the buttons indicated on-screen in time with a piece of music to trigger the audio samples. Where the game begins to depart from its tradition is in that each of its songs is divided up into its constituent instrument types. Multiple players can then pick up different "instruments," connecting to one another wirelessly to create an impromptu DS band or orchestra as they seek to play together in time.

Daigasso! Band Brothers was one of the first titles to investigate the potential for multiplayer music games in this way, and also to do it with instruments as diverse as harmonica, drums, piano, and guitar, and across multiple musical genres. Alongside the J-pop and anime theme songs, Nintendo fans are well catered for with *Mario*, *Zelda*, and *F-Zero* medleys to play along to. But the game's most valuable feature is perhaps its MIDI composer, a tool to allow songwriters to pencil in a multipart composition and then play the results back in the game itself. While the feature is somewhat hidden in the package as an unlockable extra, it turns the DS into an instrument itself, delightfully redefining the purpose of the console. **SP**

ソング　メドレー　　　　　　　　　　ブラス

BEST 8888 GOOD 8888 BAD 8888 MISS 8888

CONDITION ‖‖‖‖‖‖‖‖‖‖‖‖‖‖‖‖‖‖‖‖‖

COMBO

8888

練習

TEMPO
x8.8

採点

戻る

Second Sight

Original release date : 2004
Platform : Various
Developer : Free Radical Design
Genre : Action

More famous for turning out knockabout first-person shooters like the *TimeSplitters* series, where the plot comes a distant second to the headshots, Free Radical Design also made this rather more thoughtful title: a smart third-person action-adventure game with the studio's familiar rubbery-faced character design intact, but with a focus on a complex, if playful, narrative that saw the studio breaking new ground.

John Vattic wakes up in a strange military hospital, distinctly the worse for wear, but blessed, all of a sudden, with a frightening range of ESP abilities. Using telekinesis he is able to lob objects around with the power of his mind alone, and with projection he can peel off a ghostly

counterpart persona to scout ahead, sliding through obstacles that would keep his tangible body blocked.

What follows is a game that plays out both in the present, as Vattic moves about the installation, slowly uncovering his mysterious past, and in flashback sections that unfold in the form of his returning memories, allowing the player to change the outcome of history, rescuing colleagues who originally died, and generally putting right what went wrong in the past. Vattic's present is largely a mixture of clever puzzles and twitchy stealth as he eludes capture in his quest for knowledge, but the flashbacks are third-person shooting at its best, with lively weapons, a series of pacy objectives, and a genuine sense of growing intrigue as Vattic meddles with his own past.

Plotlines converge eventually in a brilliant twist that will send shivers down your spine. Although *Second Sight* has all the hallmarks of a smart team working on a tight budget, Vattic's adventures will live on in your own memory long after the game has been completed. **CD**

Psi-Ops: The Mindgate Conspiracy

Original release date : 2004
Platform : Various
Developer : Midway
Genre : Action

Before Midway's best action team began work on *John Woo's Stranglehold*, a brain-dead shoot 'em up that turned out to be a good deal better than anybody expected, it made *Psi-Ops: The Mindgate Conspiracy*, a brain-dead physics-based shoot 'em up that turned out to be a good deal better than anybody expected. And not that brain-dead, actually.

The year 2004 was an exciting time for gaming, with its generation of console platforms pretty well understood by developers, and physics quickly emerging as the next battleground as the hand-over-hand scramble for better graphics gave way to a more nuanced interest in richly detailed, developed, and interactive worlds; places that

felt believable and reacted to your presence in a range of interesting ways. *Psi-Ops: The Mindgate Conspiracy* might have a fairly disposable story—you're an amnesiac psychic-powered agent infiltrating a group of terrorists—but it wraps it all up in a series of environments that are fun to run around in, and its forgettable protagonist has some genuinely unforgettable mental abilities.

He has powers like mind control, which lets you take control over enemies with hilariously trigger-happy results, or telekinesis, which allows you to dangle unfortunates over ledges, and its evil twin pyrokenisis, meaning you can subsequently set them on fire before letting them drop. All of which ensures that the game rises above some fairly stupid enemies, its own ridiculous plot, and a few uninspired moments. Ignore the box art and the interchangeable title, *Psi-Ops* is really a simple physics playground with a reasonably entertaining game wrapped around it, and the results remain as ludicrously enjoyable now as they were when it was first released. **CD**

Sly 2: Band of Thieves

Original release date : 2004
Platform : PS2
Developer : Sucker Punch Productions
Genre : Action / Platform

The original *Sly* was enjoyable enough, but the sequel is better in every way. It's one of the high points in the PS2's excellent portfolio of platformers.

The toon-shaded art style is as gorgeous as ever, and the characterizations are even sharper. The rascally protagonist can now actually pick the pockets of his foes, and there's literally more life in him: The addition of a health bar means no more annoying instadeaths. Sly's sidekicks are now playable in side missions that are a marked improvement over the forgettable mini-games in the first installment—you'll find yourself eagerly anticipating your next tank battle as Bentley the turtle, or your next melee brawl as Murray the hippo. Even the hacking mini-games

of *Sly 2: Band of Thieves* are a hoot, casting you as a 2-D spacecraft weaving through mazes as you blast wave and after wave of foes. It's an arcadelike experience that puts *BioShock*'s hacking-themed plumbing puzzles to shame.

The game's greatest triumphs are unquestionably the cityscapes in which you carry out your heists. The locales, like Paris and Prague, are intricately designed playgrounds perfectly suited to the protagonist's gliding double-jumps, and his ability to effortlessly latch onto pipes and tightwires. One of the game's signature pleasures is scaling the highest building and gazing down on the sprawling explorable environment below. The cities become more and more fun to traverse as you get to know them better, though a few of them overstay their welcome. (This twenty-hour game would have been even better if it wrapped up around the fifteen-hour mark.)

On a side note, you'll want to hunt out that PS2 USB microphone, as *Sly 2: Band of Thieves* gives you the opportunity to distract enemies by hollering at them. **CB**

Ridge Racers

Original release date : 2004
Platform : PSP
Developer : Namco
Genre : Driving

Playing *Ridge Racer* games is like listening to your favorite album: You pick a track, wait for the laser to find its groove, and let the rhythm take control. A coin-op compilation full of age-defining sounds and images, it's an emotional ride for those who mourn the extinction—in the West, at least—of arcade gaming culture.

The greatest-hits collection *Ridge Racers* ported the games beautifully to the PSP, with all roads in the earlier games leading to Ridge City. A swirling paradise of tunnels, flyovers, coastlines, and closing straights, it's the perfect escape from all the violence of modern driving games. It has gravity, yes, but just enough to keep its cars in orbit around sweeping corners or bring them back to Earth after giant jumps. There's no damage, not a speck of dirt, and absolutely no benefit to even touching your opponents. Japanese to the core, it's about mastering your racing, not spoiling someone else's.

Perfection is an intimidating goal, and the series has twice been asked to aim for it on Sony's behalf. First it was about getting close to arcade perfection, the original *Ridge Racer* attempting to shrink a cutting-edge arcade machine into a home console. But with *Ridge Racers* it was something even more remarkable: PlayStation perfection, the transplanting of PS2-era tech into a machine the size of your pocket. With a clarity of purpose and presentation still rare on the PSP, this launch title sits firmly among its all-time top five. Nothing—from cars and tunes to the speed at which they load and run—feels compromised.

Ridge Racers celebrates the series' adventures, avoids its later misadventures, and thrives in its handheld format. Its breezy races, originally designed to eat coins rather than time, make for a surprisingly enduring package. **DH**

Red Dead Revolver

Original release date : 2004
Platform : Various
Developer : Rockstar
Genre : Action

Rome: Total War

Original release date : 2004
Platform : PC
Developer : The Creative Assembly
Genre : Strategy

Red Dead Revolver is a pure spaghetti Western, telling the tale of Red growing up to avenge his parents' brutal murder in the mostly lawless and wild frontier country. The hero grows up to be a no-nonsense bounty hunter, earning his living from eliminating criminals in stylishly constructed shootouts while getting ever closer to resolving his unfinished business.

Played in third-person, the game saddles up a very enjoyable adventure whose controls can, at times, be as rough around the edges as some of its unsavory characters, but it still holsters a decent, responsive shooting dynamic and, thankfully, isn't yellow-bellied when it comes to introducing one or two twists of its own.

Crucially for a production of this type, it also drips atmosphere as liberally as the red stuff coming out of your victims' bullet wounds, perfectly capturing the essence and feel of Sergio Leone's films and transporting players into a convincing, character-filled world consumed with revenge and retribution. The musical score, in particular, is as authentically note-perfect as you could hope for. **JDS**

Rome: Total War puts more emphasis on historical detail, such as battlefield terrain and troop morale, than almost any of its peers. It is a full strategy experience, complete with research, trading, spying, army deployment—more than enough to keep you occupied over a campaign spanning three centuries. If you want to play without muddying your feet on the battlefield, you can.

You'd be mad to, though. *Rome: Total War* saw the introduction of full 3-D to the *Total War* series, with spectacular results. Greek spearmen, Carthaginian elephants, and your Roman Triarii are made real. 30,000 men can be rendered at once, making for epic encounters.

The game is vast. Starting out as the head of one of three Roman families, you have to subdue not just the empires of Egypt, Carthage, and the primitive hordes, but also negotiate, tame, and ultimately conquer the Roman senate. Not to mention the epic multiplayer mode.

If you're after a deep, strategic challenge that's made immeasurably better by a near-peerless tactical battle game, all roads lead to *Rome: Total War*. **OB**

Pikmin 2

Original release date : 2004
Platform : GameCube
Developer : Nintendo
Genre : Strategy

In the original *Pikmin*, Captain Olimar, stranded on a distant planet and watching his life slowly ticking away, enlisted the help of some delightful vegetable people, the Pikmin, in order to gather up the scattered remains of his spaceship so that he could escape. In *Pikmin 2*, Olimar's back because his business is in danger of going under, and he needs the same Pikmin to help with his new scheme. All manner of scrap and junk needs to be collected to help him rebuild his fortunes.

Pikmin 2 is every bit as charming and cleverly built as the first game, with a handful of extra features to boot. Alongside the new objectives, there are underground cave sections and an option to team up with another captain for multiplayer co-op or challenge games. Two new Pikmin varieties are also introduced: the sinister, white, poisonous Pikmin, and the hulking purple Pikmin, which are slow but tremendously strong. Both provide more tools for you to mess around with. This is a game that has always done a lot with little and remains as engaging and lovable as its predecessor. **CD**

Puyo Pop Fever

Original release date : 2004
Platform : Various
Developer : Sonic Team
Genre : Puzzle

Pairs of colored blobs fall from the top of the screen. You move them left and right, and rotate them. When four or more like colors meet, they disappear. It's that simple. But it's the competitive mode that elevates the game. Playing the game in this manner sees every colored blob (or puyo, to give it its official name) you remove from your playing field transfer across to your opponent's in a translucent form, where it essentially creates a barrier until it is eliminated via the removal of any adjacent colored puyo. The competitive dynamic fostered by these mechanics can be fierce indeed, and there are few sensations as pleasurable as dumping a towering stack of troublemaking blobs on to your opponent's side.

The game concept has been explored in many sequels since, but *Puyo Pop Fever* attempts to take it the farthest, its "fever" mode introducing new, extended puyo formations and oversized varieties. Every iteration of *Puyo Puyo* offers at least a solid version of the game play that made the series famous, and anyone who hasn't tried it is missing an impeccable puzzler. **TB**

Star Wars: Knights of the Old Republic II

Original release date : 2004
Platform : PC, Xbox
Developer : Obsidian Entertainment
Genre : Role-Playing

The success of BioWare's *Star Wars: Knights of the Old Republic* made a sequel inevitable, and the task of developing it fell to Obsidian Entertainment. Like Black Isle Studios before it, Obsidian has long acted as a kind of goth little brother to BioWare, taking its established titles and game play engines and developing sequels that are darker, edgier, and usually just as strong.

For *Star Wars: Knights of the Old Republic II*, some of the key talent, including producer Chris Avellone, took the dramatic bravado of the original down a darker path. The game tells the story of the Exile, who sets out to recover memories of a lost connection to the Jedi order, and to the Force itself. Your closest associates are the ones you shouldn't trust, and the Sith that line up against you include some of the most forbidding villains in the *Star Wars* canon—like Darth Nihilus, who wears a white-and-red mask and communicates in whispers and warbles.

As with *Star Wars: Knights of the Old Republic*, the game play strikes an awkward balance between setting up tactics and then sitting back to watch the lasers fly. Hit pause and cue up a lightsaber duel, and your character will handle the action—satisfying neither deep strategy buffs nor real-time thrillseekers. But the real hook lies in the story and in the chance to take another trip back to the Old Republic, where you can enjoy the themes of *Star Wars* without getting mired in the films' continuity.

Unfortunately, the team at Obsidian ran up against their deadlines before development was complete, and Avellone has aired his regrets about cutting content to meet their schedule. Later, loyal fans would restore some of the missing pieces, recovering more of the content of this dark almost-classic. **CDa**

Chronicles of Riddick: Escape from Butcher Bay

Original release date : 2004
Platform : PC, Xbox
Developer : Starbreeze Studios
Genre : First-Person Shooter

The *Chronicles of Riddick* games force us to consider the term "role-playing game." Does it have to mean a game of quests, stats, and rolls of the dice, or can it be any that blurs the line between you and your character? Either way, you'll feel closer to Richard Riddick than you will most avatars; a little troubling, as he happens to be a psychopath.

Unlike most movie tie-ins, *Chronicles of Riddick: Escape from Butcher Bay* was a true collaboration between a star (Vin Diesel), a production company (Tigon Studios), and a developer (Sweden's Starbreeze Studios). It's an official prequel to the movie *Pitch Black*, featuring an original story that's not only faithful to the universe you see on film, but referenced within it. The hellish prison of Butcher Bay, we

discover, is where Riddick had his eyes "shined" to give him that all-important night vision. And, as the game depicts in gory detail, it's where he earned his reputation as the most dangerous inmate in the galaxy.

Much comes together to make you feel like this man. There's the venue: a dank, grievous cesspit full of men for whom death has been judged a luxury. The physicality: This is one of the few first-person games to render your entire character—legs landing jumps and biceps snapping necks. The script: full of deadpan monologues tailor-made for its star's performance. But above all there's the action: brutal melee combat using improvised weapons, later switching to taut gun battles and predatory stealth.

Bullets kill quickly in *Chronicles of Riddick: Escape from Butcher Bay*, as do screwdrivers and shivs. The game wouldn't be half as compelling if it didn't constantly remind you that Riddick, however skilled and dangerous, is still just a man. Its villains, meanwhile, with their pride and paranoia, are always too human for their own good. **DH**

RollerCoaster Tycoon 3

Original release date : 2004
Platform : PC, Mac
Developer : Frontier Developments
Genre : Management Simulation

There's no small degree of Schadenfreude in running a virtual theme park, what with the spiraling ticket prices, escaped balloons, endless lines, and terrifying rides. And the vomit, don't forget, which someone has to mop up to earn the pittance that you, the boss, call a salary. The constant, ubiquitous, gravity-defying vomit, none of which can touch you on your managerial perch.

Your public should be grateful. With their money, patience, and fear, the rides you can build in *RollerCoaster Tycoon 3* are unlike any others in the world. Coasters shaped like the lower intestines, which corkscrew through waterfalls into mountains carved into your initials, are probably the simplest thing you'll make.

A departure from the successful *Transport Tycoon* series, *RollerCoaster* was devised by industry legend Chris Sawyer in 1999. A sleeper hit, it would move to David Braben's Frontier Developments for its third game, with Sawyer acting only as a consultant. Far from derail it, Frontier would twist and elevate it, adding a host of entirely positive features. There's the CoasterCam, which lets you sit in the front carriage of your attractions, while the MixMaster lets you conduct your own firework displays. A day/night cycle affects the type and tastes of your customers, and scenic themes set up zones like Western and Science Fiction.

Like most great comedians, *RollerCoaster Tycoon 3* takes itself very seriously indeed. With later expansions adding more complex landscaping options and water behaviors, it goes deeper than mere customization. The God genre has always been more about ownership than management, and by taking that to an extreme, the feeling you get from this game isn't nausea, but pride. **DH**

The Legend of Zelda: The Minish Cap

Original release date : 2004

Platform : Game Boy Advance

Developer : Capcom

Genre : Action / Adventure

Like the *Zelda* games *Oracle of Seasons* and *Oracle of Ages*, *The Legend of Zelda: The Minish Cap* was developed for Nintendo by the best minds at Capcom. While the first two offerings were very fine photocopies of Nintendo's classic series, *The Minish Cap* actually has a little of the home-grown series' genuine and elusive magic. This is a pocket-sized adventure that's epic in scope, and with a little of the best titles' sense of unforced intricacy.

Much of the reason for the game's success comes down to the Minish cap itself, a chirpy, bird-headed hat that gives Link the ability to shrink down to the size of a few ragged pixels whenever the situation demands it. It's a promisingly *Zelda*-ish idea and Capcom takes it to the limits, at least in terms of charm, as Link stealthily sneaks along dusty rafters, tiptoes past hulking acorns, and explores the game's villages and dungeons. These vibrant realms are seen from two unique perspectives.

The game is unique and creative in every aspect. Link is aided on his journey by some great gadgets, the highlights being a pot that sucks in and then blasts out air, and mitts that allow him to dig through earth like a mole. The design work is top notch, particularly with the inspired dungeons; one, set in the air itself, sees Link punching his way back and forth through delightful cartoon clouds. These elements, along with a final boss as clever and multi-waved as anything the series has created before or since, all come together to make a wonderful adventure.

With the subsequent arrival of the DS, Nintendo took back control of the portable offerings of its most storied franchise, but while titles like *The Legend of Zelda: Phantom Hourglass* are polished and brilliant, *The Minish Cap* suggested that the series was already in good hands. **CD**

The Legend of Zelda: Four Swords Adventures

Original release date : 2004
Platform : GameCube
Developer : Nintendo
Genre : Action / Adventure

Compared to Mario, who can be sent out onto the greens to play golf, onto the dusty old diamond to hit speeding baseballs, and over to the track to zip around in carts when he isn't doing what he does best, the *Zelda* series is remarkably resistant to cross-genre tampering. The closest Nintendo's legendary RPG has gotten to an off-shoot is probably either *Link's Crossbow Training* (a pleasant but forgettable shooting gallery bundled with a rather abstract plastic gun peripheral for the Wii) or *The Legend of Zelda: Four Swords Adventures*. This game used a cumbersome hardware combination, which made it somewhat less than accessible, but did reward determined gamers with one of Nintendo's least appreciated masterpieces.

Four Swords Adventures takes the aesthetic from *The Legend of Zelda: Link to the Past* and opens it up for four players, either scrabbling around the landscape on their own or teaming up in formation to hit switches, lift rocks, and progress through an inventive series of artificial bottlenecks. It was ideally played on four GBAs connected to a GameCube, and such an awkward option stopped the game from being a retail hit. You can still have your own adventure alone and with the aid of three AI accomplices, but that misses the chaotic fun at the heart of the game.

And it is chaotic. While the series has traditionally been a model of careful order, *Four Swords Adventures* turns its Hyrulian landscapes into a series of crazy arena battles, where players fight one another for the jewels that pour from almost every in-game object. A meaty adventure as well as a depraved kind of game show, each round ends with a results screen totaling up the gems each Link has collected, and declaring the winner. Summed up quickly: expect fights to break out. **CD**

Torus Trooper

Original release date : 2004
Platform : PC
Developer : Kenta Cho
Genre : Shoot 'Em Up

As a designer of abstract, bullet-heavy shoot 'em ups, Japanese developer Kenta Cho (who publishes his titles online for free, as ABA Games) is a man who doesn't need a lot of words to explain his games. And *Torus Trooper*, which could be described as a reimagining of Atari Games's 1989 coin-op *S.T.U.N. Runner*, is described simply on his website as: "Speed! More speed!"

There's little more that really needs to be said about the title. Players pilot a ship down a tunnel that twists and turns—the titular "torus"—attempting to destroy enemies and bosses. The aim is to progress as far as possible before a constantly ticking timer runs out, with certain kills and high scores rewarding the player with more time. The

requirement that you kill as fast as you can to avoid losing via time-out propels you ever forward ever faster, and a well-played game can soon begin to exceed 5,000 km/h.

The torus is a constant web of bullets—powered by Cho's own BulletML scripting language—and sensible players would suppose the best way to play would be to maintain a steady momentum to simply keep the number of time-extending kills high enough to beat the clock, but there's no such easy answer. Speed with added speed is the only way to play, keeping the finger on accelerate and simply trusting that your skill will help you weave through the bullets and destroy everything in your way.

With the game's abstract wireframe graphics, pumping soundtrack, and tough demands on reflexes, *Torus Trooper* feels like a futuristic test for drugged-up astronauts. And while deaths can sometimes feel like unavoidable bad luck, they only cost speed and time. No matter, as there is always more time if you can get back up to speed. Speed! More speed! **MKu**

Unreal Tournament 2004

Original release date : 2004
Platform : PC, Mac
Developer : Epic Games
Genre : First-Person Shooter

While the *Quake III vs Unreal Tournament 2004* debate will rage for all eternity, it can be stated with certainty that the latter is the finest iteration of the *Unreal Tournament* template. Its 3-D engine is a masterwork of efficiency, so much so that even low-end machines from the year of its release were able to cope admirably with the game's huge maps and ambitious graphical effects. This flexibility and solidity arguably has not been seen again since, even in more recent iterations of the *Unreal Tournament* engine.

Perhaps *Unreal Tournament 2004* was meant as a demonstration of Epic's technology, but it's a brilliant game in its own right, and in terms of level design, a kind of master class. The standard, arena-based death match maps encompass everything from boiling furnaces to gravity-scrambled space stations, while other game modes introduce huge environments, ludicrous vehicles, and even moving levels, such as an assault on a speeding train. Nevertheless, it's the balance of play that really kept players connected. Epic fine-tuned this game to the point of perfection. The physics of the weapons immediately make sense, and even unskilled players will feel at home in the tight shooter logic of its world.

It certainly helps that the game arrived during the height of the first-person shooter modding craze, because it now boasts thousands of conversions, maps, and mutators. It might take hundreds of hours to tire of the core game, but it would take thousands more to even explore the surface of the materials forged by its fan community. This is a brash and brilliant combat game, but it is also a gateway to some amazing experimental experiences, such as the insane airship warfare of *Air Buccaneers* and the Mad Max apocalyptic death match of *Roadkill Warriors*. **JR**

WarioWare: Twisted!

Original release date : 2004
Platform : Game Boy Advance
Developer : Intelligent Systems
Genre : Action

The chunky, oddly shaped cartridge for this *WarioWare* sequel remains hard to come by in certain regions; it was never released in Europe, for example. This is a great shame, as this quirky addition to Nintendo's unlikeliest of killer franchises has plenty of smart ideas for you to enjoy and a dazzling amount of clever unlockables to chase after, such as records, figurines, and even musical instruments.

WarioWare: Twisted! has an in-built accelerometer, and most of its games—and all the UI and navigation—literally turn on the premise of tilting your GBA back and forth. With a good deal of precision built in and a delightful buzz of rumble feedback, the technology's come a long way from the rough old days of *Kirby Tilt 'n' Tumble*, but, more important, while the notion sounds gimmicky and limited, *WarioWare: Twisted!*'s ingenious and witty designers simply never seem to run out of ideas. This game, in fact, has some of *WarioWare*'s most inventive offerings yet, from a spot of scratchy turntable action to a stroll through the world of *Super Mario* reshaped as an endless, curving track. Every new unlockable takes you somewhere unexpected and strange, and the color and comedy available everywhere you look set new standards for the series.

With the Game Boy Advance long retired, a release in Europe seems distinctly unlikely at this point, making it all the more necessary for you to get on eBay as soon as possible and score your own copy of this strange and wonderful title. Whether you prefer this or the DS's charming *WarioWare: Touched!* offering as the best way to move the series forward is ultimately your decision, but whatever you do, you probably owe it to yourself to track this down and take *WarioWare: Twisted!* out for a spin. **CD**

Warhammer 40,000: Dawn of War

Original release date : 2004
Platform : PC
Developer : Relic Entertainment
Genre : Strategy

For a company that has fashioned entire worlds from tabletops across the planet, Games Workshop's video game output has been surprisingly earthbound. The great majority of video games based on Games Workshop's brilliant board games actually just tend toward mid-sized planet mediocrity. *Warhammer 40,000: Dawn of War*, though, is definitely one of the firmament's brightest stars.

Tying together the war-torn universe of *Warhammer 40,000* and the real-time expertise of Relic Entertainment, it streamlined the base-building aspect of most other RTS games and replaced it with a strategic system of battlefield control much better suited to the squad-based skirmishes of the board game. Instead of tank rushes and resource-gathering, *Warhammer 40,000: Dawn of War* is all about taking the fight to the enemy and making the right tactical decisions when you do so.

But on balance there's nothing groundbreaking about the way *Warhammer 40,000: Dawn of War* implements real-time strategy; its value lies more in its flawless polish. The game's strength lies in the way it ties those real-time rules to the richly imagined history of the board game universe, and in the way it distils the dystopian vision of the source material. All of the major races are present in the game: the religious combat fervor of the emperor's devoted Space Marines; the animal instincts and steam-powered mayhem of the Orks; the effete lethality of the space-faring Eldar; and the tainted evil of Chaos.

Warhammer 40,000: Dawn of War plays like an extended bout of fan service, which, given that the fans it is servicing are fans of one of the best tabletop war games in history, is probably the highest compliment you can give it. **DM**

Spider-Man 2

Original release date : 2004
Platform : Various
Developer : Treyarch
Genre : Action

In January 2010, Activision Blizzard CEO Bobby Kotick went on record saying: "Our *Spider-Man* games have sucked for the last five years. They are bad games. They were poorly rated because they were bad games." That's not particularly true of *Spider-Man 2*, and does it a disservice, seeing that it certainly wasn't bad and wasn't so poorly rated. But to Kotick, who's used to *Guitar Hero* and *Call of Duty* levels of critical and, more important, financial success, *Spider-Man 2* was an also-ran.

The game certainly captures more of the spirit of the web-slinger than its predecessor. Originally designed to be an open-world-style game, it makes some advances to Spider-Man's web-slinging abilities by allowing players to grapple on to solid objects rather than simply shooting webs into the sky, which is what happened in the first title. In fact, for a game that predates massive free-roaming hits and runs on previous-generation hardware, *Spider-Man 2*'s approach to creating a realistic Big Apple is quite convincing, and succeeds in giving players a bird's-eye view of the city that can be thrilling when you're exploring it at speed and with purpose.

The game's movie origins would normally count as a limitation, but then the source itself was an adaptation. You'd expect a clunky, derivative plot, but Treyarch's tale holds up well, with high-quality voice-acting from movie cast members Tobey Maguire, Kirsten Dunst, and Alfred Molina. It helps that the game doesn't attempt to follow events of its source too closely—Mysterio, for example, does not appear in Sam Raimi's film, but he turns up here as Spidey's archenemy. *Spider-Man 2* benefits from its looser approach, and is a much bigger success than the man who published it would have you believe. **JBW**

Transformers

Original release date : 2004
Platform : PS2
Developer : Melbourne House
Genre : Action

Hasbro's plastic goliaths have been in numerous video games over the years, but only in one truly good one. Rather than making a weak cash-in on an anime series or film (although it is based on the Armada cartoon), Melbourne House looked hard at the franchise to see what people would really want from a giant robot brawler.

The answer is something like this: a series of expansive—and rather beautiful—levels in which players, filling either the roles of Optimus Prime, Red Alert, or Hot Shot, fight their way through waves of Decepticlones, toward boss confrontations that can take up the entire space of the stage itself. The essential matter of transforming from vehicle to robot and back again is handled with the touch of a button, and plays out in a luxuriously beautiful animated sequence that will delight robot fans of every stripe, and the game that emerges is as much a fast-paced racer as it is a gruelling robotic fist fight.

Much of the rest of the fun comes from finding and equipping Mini-Cons (smaller robots that are capable of providing handy stat enhancements), better guns, or new powers. As you can only cobble on a certain amount at any time, every choice entails a sacrifice, and a deep tactical appreciation of your load-outs is essential for getting through some of the game's later stages.

The game diverges from the comic and anime storylines but manages to retain the DNA of a classic *Transformers* experience. Treating the venerable series with an unexpected degree of respect, *Transformers* is an extremely stylish and action-packed video game that would succeed even without the famous license. With it, however, it's a truly irresistible slice of pop-culture nostalgia and a gleaming piece of brand love. **CD**

World of Warcraft

Original release date : 2004
Platform : PC, Mac
Developer : Blizzard Entertainment
Genre : MMORPG

World of Warcraft is now so established that it seems almost destined to have come about; as if all the social RPGs that came before it would inevitably produce *World of Warcraft*'s heady mix of loot, lore, and leveling. But that's a notion that would discount the hard work and imagination that Blizzard has put into its development, both before its release in late 2004 and since, with the constant improvements, tweaks, and additions to its world.

To nonplayers, it appears anachronistically simplistic: mechanical battling between paper-thin avatars in a now-crudely realized and petrified virtual world with a veneer of social interaction slapped over the top. But it's an entirely different prospect for players who have sunk hundreds if not thousands of hours into playing it. They instead see avatars that embody their many adventures, wearing and wielding gear they've strived with skill, work, and deep knowledge to win. They see a profoundly complex and layered combat system, which rewards multitudes of tactics and playing styles, and which takes the full course of the game's current eighty levels to learn properly for each of its ten divergently designed player classes.

They also see a world rich in fantasy history, where every character and locale has a compelling backstory, profoundly enriched with the actions of thousands of other players. The world is a vibrant economic, social, and political culture, delineated by the game design that transfixes even those who have beaten and experienced everything *World of Warcraft* can offer them.

But Blizzard isn't standing still with what has become one of video games' biggest cash cows. With the new expansion, *Cataclysm*, the world is being made new all over again. *World of Warcraft*'s continuing domination of the realm of the MMORPG is surely guaranteed. **AW**

Clubhouse Games

Original release date : 2005
Platform : DS
Developer : Agenda
Genre : Adaptation

Most game makers return to their origins at some point. But for Nintendo, which started by making card games in 1889, the origins were more distant than most. *Clubhouse Games* (released as *42 All-Time Classics* in Europe) is a celebration of a pre-video gaming era, one expressed through the video game medium. It offers a compendium of classic card games, board games, and bar sports, all slotted into an engaging meta-game to encourage new generations of gamers to discover these jewels of yesteryear: blackjack, Texas Hold 'em poker, chess, Ludo, dominoes, solitaire, *Battleships* (awkwardly renamed *Grid Attack* for copyright reasons), draughts, *Othello* (aka *Turncoat*), darts, rummy, backgammon, sevens, and hangman.

The contents of *Clubhouse Games* are akin to a stack of dusty bar games, piled up beside the whisky bottles in an old country pub. Of course, mini-game collections are ten-a-penny in these post–Nintendo Wii days, so what enables *Clubhouse Games* to stand out from the crowd is the execution. In every case, Nintendo has managed to represent these classic games in a way perfectly suited to the DS touch screen, with a presentation and ease of delivery that is consistently engaging.

The AI is competent rather than accomplished (as will become clear to any practiced chess player who takes it on), but the creases in this package are few. All but three single-player games are available for online or local wireless play. There's built-in PictoChat, self-translating chat phrases for online use, and the facility to send any one of the games as a gift to be stored in the recipient DS's soft memory—features that ensure the game is just as engaging a communal pursuit as a solitary one. The result is a perfect match for its format, a compendium every bit as enduring as the classics it contains. **SP**

Dr Kawashima's Brain Training

Original release date : 2005
Platform : DS
Developer : Nintendo
Genre : Puzzle / Strategy

Math, memory tests, and reading might not sound like a recipe for long-term success in a market dominated by chunky robots with Gatling guns for elbows, and taciturn superspies brought back for "one last mission," but Nintendo has always tended to kick trends off rather than follow them. Certainly, no one could accuse the company of treading safely when it revealed its killer application for its DS handheld console.

The house of *Mario*'s latest mascot turned out to be the floating head of noted Japanese neuroscientist, Dr. Kawashima. The game itself, based loosely on the good doctor's best-selling book, promised a kind of gymnasium for your mind: a regular workout that would keep your mental faculties fresh, even charting the age of your brain on a handy, and rather depressing, graph.

There's a strong chance that the scientific grounding for all of this is largely spurious, but what isn't in doubt is the unique appeal of *Dr Kawashima's Brain Training* itself. With its boldly bland interface and friendly words of encouragement, it's a title that anyone can pick up and understand. The simple collection of mathematics puzzles, reading comprehension, and other brain teasing staples are as weirdly seductive here as they are within the battered pages of those magazines you find in dentists' offices.

Subtle mechanics encourage you to play a little every day, and even share the experience with your friends, while your brain age itself exerts the same kind of compulsions that many find in the leveling curve of a game like *World of Warcraft*. Dr Kawashima might turn his nose up at the software's success, but this brain game at least proves that Nintendo has its head screwed on properly. **CD**

Castlevania: Dawn of Sorrow

Original release date : 2005
Platform : DS
Developer : Konami
Genre : Action

The subtitle was presumably chosen because *Dawn of Sorrow* is the first game in the *Castlevania* series to be released on the DS. It takes the mechanics from the greatest Game Boy *Castlevania* game, *Aria of Sorrow*, and continues where the plot left off. It is several decades in the future, a year after Dracula's latest failed attempt at world domination, with the game's hero Soma Cruz still trying to defy his destiny as the reincarnation of Dracula. Not so easy when there's a bunch of cultists out to sacrifice you in a bid to bring the dark lord forth once again.

Thus ensues another perfectly pitched balance of platforming and exploration. The twisted topography of Dracula's castle is one of the stars of the show. The other is the Tactical Soul system, which returns from *Aria of Sorrow* and seems to find its true home on the DS as the game's mechanics assume greater relevance, thanks to the ease with which players can trade souls using the wireless functionality of the DS. They can also switch between different soul setups more easily, quickly accessing various abilities as the need arises.

The touch-screen functionality of the DS also gets a look in. The new Magic Seal system sees the use of the stylus to defeat bosses, and there is a handful of simple touch-screen puzzles (in truth, their inclusion feels slightly forced, but there aren't enough of them to really intrude). And the platform's mass-market appeal is acknowledged by the use of a new, more accessible, visual style, which some hardcore fans predictably denounced.

Dawn of Sorrow has since been followed by further DS installments, but it is the original and still the best *Castlevania* on Nintendo's dual screen handheld. **DM**

Battalion Wars

Original release date : 2005
Platform : GameCube
Developer : Kuju
Genre : Action / Strategy

Conceived as a console spin-off of Nintendo's brilliantly successful handheld *Advance Wars: Dual Strike* strategy games, *Battalion Wars* is a colorful and cartoony battler built by a British developer, Kuju, that doesn't really require any knowledge of Nintendo's original series to enjoy it.

Along with the shift to a more console friendly, third-person, three-dimensional perspective, *Battalion Wars* also dares to ditch the signature turn-based battling in exchange for some frantic real-time skirmishes. But it's real-time like little else out there, with the ability to hop from one delightful death-dealing war vehicle to the next in order to micromanage the game's multifront fights.

Switching around such core elements of the original series is probably the brightest idea the developer had. By kicking loose, replacing the chesslike rituals of the source games with something a lot more messy, and throwing out Nintendo's earnest cast for a range of caricatured sexpots, *Battalion Wars* is remarkably confident. If you're in the market for a brightly colored ruckus, track down the original GameCube title. **CD**

Battlefield 2

Original release date : 2005
Platform : PC
Developer : Digital Illusions CE
Genre : First-Person Shooter

Swedish developer Digital Illusions brought its mastery of online first-person shooter design into the modern era with this wisely judged sequel, *Battlefield 2*. Set around a thinly sketched twenty-first-century military escalation, players choose a side from three options—the United States, China, or the Middle Eastern Coalition—and fight their way through a range of fraught skirmishes. As with its predecessors, the emphasis is on the multiplayer Conquest mode, in which teams of up to thirty-two players seek to win and hold control points on a series of maps.

Players create squads of up to six players and take part in closely collaborative missions, spawning near one another and using the game's built-in VoIP system to communicate. The inclusion of military bureaucracy has fostered online battles of compelling structure and purpose. *Battlefield 2*'s bleeding-edge engine pushed the boundaries of the burgeoning sciences of ragdoll physics, destructible environmental objects, and material penetration modeling. Subsequent booster packs have added to the tactical depth of this immersive game. **KS**

Call of Duty 2

Original release date : 2005
Platform : Various
Developer : Infinity Ward
Genre : First-Person Shooter

Steven Spielberg's *Saving Private Ryan* has been slavishly copied by dozens of games, all seeking to be louder, more realistic, and more poignant than the game next door. *Call of Duty 2*, though, has a quality gamers crave even more: momentum. This World War II game is all about the storm.

Telling the stories of soldiers in three different theaters of war, it hops from the Battle of Stalingrad to El Alamein, Egypt, Tunisia, and finally the push from Normandy to the Rhine. There's barely a breath to be caught between them. Whenever you're not fighting, you're thinking about who to fight. Whenever you're not being shot, you're recharging. If you're comfortable behind cover, then a grenade will land in your lap.

Call of Duty 2 owes some of its success to timing. This Xbox 360 launch title was the first to match the experience of PC enthusiasts. Its sound is nothing short of a blitzkrieg, and its high-definition visuals add a layer of precision to match its large, tumultuous battlefields. Above all, it's happy to be nothing more than what a good soldier should be: a tirelessly efficient killing machine. **DH**

God of War

Original release date : 2005
Platform : PS2
Developer : Sony
Genre : Action / Adventure

Anyone who's read *The Iliad* or *The Odyssey* might be aware of the realization that—far from being po-faced and dusty—the ancient classics are actually knockabout fun, filled with regular beheadings and men with names like Pylon repeatedly putting their fists through somebody else's stomach. Taken in this light, the astonishingly visceral butchery of David Jaffe's *God of War* fits very nicely into such an ancient tradition.

God of War rewrites classical myths on a whim, zeroing in on the murder, monsters, and general mayhem, while cutting out anything that doesn't come up to snuff. The story of Kratos the Spartan going on a rampage across the ancient world, for reasons that probably don't bear up to much scrutiny, is vivid enough in its own right, but the delivery captivates from start to finish.

In the end, *God of War* is that rarest of beasts: a game that understands the true nature of its source material as well as the visceral needs of its players. *God of War* is a title that manages to be extraordinarily violent and effortlessly graceful at the same time. **CD**

Freedom Force vs. The 3rd Reich

Original release date : 2005

Platform : PC

Developer : Irrational Games

Genre : Strategy / Role-Playing

The superhero and the video game maintain a tempestuous relationship. More often than not they produce ugly, clumsy offspring, but on rare occasions they produce a beautiful thing like the tactical role-playing game *Freedom Force vs. The 3rd Reich*.

The *Freedom Force* characters are broad parodies of Golden Age comic book characters, all conceived by artist Robb Waters, who is also known for work on *Thief* and *System Shock*. Each of the heroes is an absurd caricature with over the top superpowers and, as they take on the Nazis and their allies, the group proves to be even more bombastic than in 2002's original *Freedom Force*. The villains are equally ludicrous, of course, with the German

blitzkrieg, Italian Fortissimo, and Japanese Red Sun uniting to take on the all-American *Freedom Force*. Sadly, the best character of all from the original *Freedom Force* game, Man-Bot, does not appear this time around.

Freedom Force vs. The 3rd Reich allows you to create some of your own superheroes, building them from a varied template of exotic powers and nonsensical costumes. The game is engaging because it presents its action in a third-person tactical view that can be paused at any time, allowing you to consider the best way forward for your heroics. The stars of the show have a wide range of powers available to them, and their superstrength and other abilities mean they're able to pick up environmental objects to use against their enemies.

Mind control, energy beams, flight, and area of effect powers also feature as you battle your way across a series of maps, before going toe-to-toe with boss characters. *Freedom Force vs. The 3rd Reich* remains as funny and compelling now as when it was released. **JR**

Civilization IV

Original release date : 2005
Platform : PC
Developer : Firaxis Games
Genre : Strategy

It's always tempting to rely on military might in a game of *Civilization*. In fact, you often think that it's the only way to play: pile into weapon-heavy research, build an army of thugs, and off on a rampage you go. The appearance of your first tank, therefore, is a moment of jubilation, celebrated by its first blooding. In *Civilization IV*, however, you'll cheer with as much gusto at the appearance of Elvis.

The concept of culture was brought into the series in *Civilization III*. By extending your cultural power through theaters and libraries, you can extend the boundaries of your empire and even take over other civilizations' cities without doing so much as looking at them funny. However, it took *Civilization IV* to embody this, along with

the deeply satisfying technique of having Elvis settle in a border city and seeing your territory instantly expand as his fame spreads across the land and people flock to see him.

Civilization IV also stripped out a lot of the drudgery that had lodged in the series—in particular, the punitive and boring penalties of having units far from the city that built them, and "corruption," which creamed resources from smaller, less developed cities. These simply evoked the awful bureaucratic horror of the reality of running an empire. *Civilization IV* instead brings the fun bits of ruling to the fore instead, such as marshaling large military forces and putting everything into constructing the Rock 'n' Roll Great Wonder, and it works wonderfully.

The real achievement of this tweak to a format that's otherwise remarkably faithful to the games that spawned it is that it always subtly keeps your mind firmly fixed on higher things instead of the minutiae of administration. And it's when you realize this that you also realize that *Civilization IV* is the best of the series, and its genre. **AW**

Chibi-Robo!

Original release date : 2005
Platform : Various
Developer : Skip Ltd
Genre : Platform / Adventure

Japanese developer Skip's biggest little adventure focuses primarily on its shift in perspective: taking video games' usual epic worlds and shrinking them into a single two-bedroom family home with its protagonist hardly more than two inches high. It does do this brilliantly, although so have a decade of games before it, including such titles as *Toy Commander* and *Mister Mosquito*.

Chibi-Robo's dirty domestic secret is that it plays out in a household rife with marital strife, not too terribly far off from a candy-colored, light version of *Who's Afraid of Virginia Woolf?* Mr. Sanderson, it turns out, has found himself out of work and has taken to whiling away his days watching cartoons and buying too-expensive gifts

for himself (say, for instance, two-inch-high robots) under the guise of presents for his daughter. Meanwhile, Mrs. Sanderson, at the end of her own tether trying to keep the budget in order and the household together, has kicked Dad to the couch at night, and all of the tension has driven daughter Jenny to act bizarrely, suiting herself in a frog-head hood and speaking only in "ribbits."

It's your job to keep these frayed ends from unraveling farther by helping out with small chores, such as collecting discarded candy wrappers, scrubbing up dog tracks with a toothbrush, and acting as a sounding board for each family member's troubles. This is all before you inadvertently stumble into a deeper plot involving a much larger cast of *Toy Story*–style characters, each of whom comes with their own sets of neuroses and personal problems.

Chibi-Robo is one of the GameCube's best-kept secrets, not just for making scalable mountains of its staircases, but also for weaving an adventure out of the tangled emotions of everyday family life. **BB**

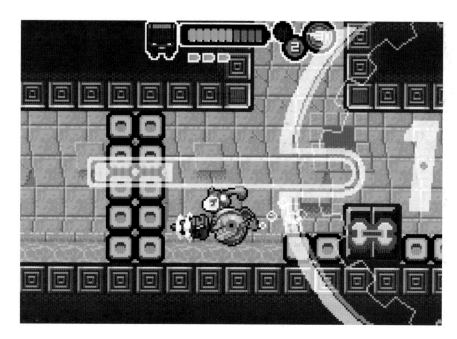

Drill Dozer

Original release date : 2005
Platform : Game Boy Advance
Developer : Game Freak
Genre : Action

This is the other game that the venerable *Pokémon* developer Game Freak built, and while it's not as popular—and hardly as famous—as its record-breaking, chart-topping brothers, it's just as smart, colorful, and charming as anything involving a Psyduck or a Chimchar.

Playing as Jill, prosaically named daughter of the leader of bandit gang, the Red Dozers, it's your job to infiltrate various museums and high-security facilities around the game world, defeating bosses and making off with a colorful range of diamonds. To do this, you must use the upgradeable Drill Dozer vehicle that Jill appears to have built herself into, bouncing off walls, grinding through rocks to locate secret areas, and even throwing the thing into reverse to unscrew vital parts of the enemies that get in your way. It's a perky, cheerful sort of adventure, and moves at a frantic pace.

But *Drill Dozer*'s unique selling point comes in the form of the game's oversized cartridge, which brings a much needed touch of rumble to the Game Boy Advance, elevating your juddery platform antics to a whole new level of earth-pulverizing glory. With its pastel colors, cheeky bandit gangs, and lengthy dialogue cut scenes, Game Freak's *Drill Dozer* is cutesy and inevitably a bit of a niche product, but the title is still charismatic and snappy enough to be worth some of your playing time.

The game's finale sets things up nicely for a sequel which, frankly, is distinctly unlikely to make an appearance given the original's modest sales. However, there's still a lot of fun to be had with this solo outing with some uniquely enchanting moments. Besides, it's nice to know that the company that often seems to be drowning in Pokéballs has a few other tricks up its sleeve. **CD**

Darwinia

Original release date : 2005
Platform : PC
Developer : Introversion Software
Genre : Strategy

Darwinia's story is inextricably linked to the biggest award it ever won: the grand prize at the Independent Games Festival (IGF) in 2006. That was the year the IGF gained momentum as a king maker, with winner *Wik: Fable of Souls* chosen as a launch title for the Xbox 360's Live Arcade, and rising indie stars Jonathan Blow and Jenova Chen taking home awards for *Braid* and *Cloud*, respectively. But the team at Introversion were the stars of the night, taking home three well-deserved awards.

But what about the game itself? Introversion earned a reputation for fast-paced, stylish strategy games, and *Darwinia* builds a campaign around a poignant cast of characters—the Darwinians, simple digital life-forms who

look helpless against the many horrors Introversion throws at them. These creatures live in the computer of a Dr. Sepulveda, who pops in via webcam to walk you through the campaign. Over a series of grid-lined landscapes like topographic maps, the player has to lead the Darwinians against an invasion of red viruses.

Special armored units take the brunt of the attack, and while the regular Darwinians take some micromanagement, they're noble, diligent, and brave. When they die, they release their spirits into the sky, a graceful suggestion that their souls may well remain within the bowels of your machine.

After *Darwinia*, Introversion also produced *Multiwinia*, a fast-paced multiplayer game that pits the Darwinians against one another. Fast matches turn chaotic as special weapons drop from the sky, turning the tide of battle in seconds. Originally developed for the PC, both games were packaged together in 2010 when Introversion released *Darwinia+* for the Xbox 360. **CDa**

Dead or Alive 4

Original release date : 2005
Platform : Xbox 360
Developer : Tecmo
Genre : Fighting

From its inception, the *Dead or Alive* series was as attractive as it was lethal. Unbelievably beautiful fighting girls and hunky muscled men tussled with amazing speed, unprecedented grace, and flawlessly depicted bodies. This is a series that probably featured more physics in the breasts of its female protagonists than most other fighting games managed to fit in their entirety.

But don't let the titillation and superficially glossy presentation obscure the fighting fundamentals. Though it never quite secured the affections of the frame-buffering obsessives that flocked to the *Virtua Fighter* series, this is classic beat-'em-up gaming. And since towering technical achievement is one of the hallmarks of the series, it found its natural home on the Xbox 360 in the shape of *Dead or Alive 4*. Speed and counters are the key to combat success; an intuitive control scheme and fighting flow can be forgiving for beginners, but fatal in the hands of experts. Microsoft's cutting-edge console transformed the game's tag-team dynamics and tiered environments, allowing them to be rendered with unprecedented panache. It also supports online play, implemented arcade style.

Dead or Alive 4 also sees the introduction of new characters to add to the roster of fighting styles: Kokoro's Bajiquan techniques, for example, now join Kasumi's ninjitsu. So strong is the appeal of the characters, in fact, that several of them have appeared in various spin-offs, from Zack and his island in *Xtreme Volleyball*, to Ryu Hayabusa and his quest for vengeance in *Ninja Gaiden*.

But it's the core *Dead or Alive* fighting series that remains Tecmo's greatest success. For the authentic *Dead or Alive* experience, avoid the movies, stick to the fighting, and enjoy *Dead or Alive 4*, the apogee of the series. **DM**

Animal Crossing: Wild World

Original release date : 2005
Platform : DS
Developer : Nintendo
Genre : Life Simulation

Animal Crossing: Wild World is not that different from the GameCube's own *Animal Crossing* title, but it marks the point at which the series suddenly leaped from much-loved cult treasure to all out platinum-selling mega hit. While the mechanics changed very little in the DS version, Nintendo's snarky little life-simulation title found its perfect ally. Soon, everywhere you looked—on the train, dawdling over coffee, wedged into a comfortable chair in the local library—people of all ages were tending their gardens, hunting for furniture, and accidentally hitting villagers with shovels when they turned too quickly.

There are a few changes to the basic formula. Along with the touch control that players would expect from a DS installment, *Animal Crossing: Wild World* sets the game's village on the rolling surface of a sphere, ditching the top-down view for an elegant scrolling plane in which trees and houses are constantly popping into view over the horizon. It also means that, for the first time, village inhabitants can look up and see a sky over their heads.

Speaking of the sky, one of *Animal Crossing: Wild World*'s most enduringly lovable elements is the addition of an observatory to the village museum. This allows players to spend some quality time staring into the heavens and—this being Nintendo—sketching their own constellations, which will then roll over their village at night. While the DS also allowed *Animal Crossing* fans to connect easily with their friends and go visiting in other villages, it's little touches like these—and the town's new coffeeshop, in which Brewster the owl will rustle up a lovely cup of Java while you listen to the saddest melody in the world—that make this such an unmissable treat. **CD**

Yoshi: Touch & Go

Original release date : 2005
Platform : DS
Developer : Nintendo
Genre : Platform / Puzzle

Although not recalled with the reverence associated with *Mario 64* or *Pilotwings*, *Yoshi: Touch & Go* is perhaps the purest example of Nintendo's ethos: that hardware must enable new experiences, and the software designed for it must take advantage of these possibilities. When releasing a console as groundbreaking as the DS, you need a title that concisely showcases its potential.

Stripped entirely of traditional controls, *Yoshi: Touch & Go* is easily misunderstood. While presenting the tropes of a classic two-dimensional platformer, it's actually a score attack game to be repeated and refined while maximizing points. When approached with this fact in mind, its genius becomes apparent. Split into two styles of level, each run begins with a vertical descent as baby Mario plummets helplessly through the sky. By drawing clouds on the lower screen, he can be guided to coins, and away from danger. Waiting below, however, is Yoshi (his specific color and abilities determined by the number of coins collected from the sky). Upon landing, he begins his inexorable journey to the right of the screen, baby onboard.

By drawing more clouds, gaps can be bridged, enemies trapped, and more coins collected. Tapping Yoshi makes him jump, while tapping elsewhere shoots an egg (useful for collecting coins in the upper screen). Charmingly, any extraneous clouds may be removed by blowing into the DS microphone, but just one enemy is all it takes to end a run. The whole thing is drawn in a painterly style that's evocative of SNES classic *Yoshi's Island*. As a demonstration of left-field innovation, *Yoshi: Touch & Go* is a powerful one, and it goes to show that sometimes blue-sky thinking can benefit from being a little cloudy. **BM**

Advance Wars: Dual Strike

Original release date : 2005
Platform : DS
Developer : Intelligent Systems
Genre : Strategy

Such is the clarity and vision of the *Advance Wars* series that Intelligent Systems doesn't really have to do that much when bringing out a new edition. Players just want another campaign, new maps, and perhaps a sexy new CO with huge headphones and a tinkly laugh. When the developer does add things, the result is often akin to the hateful pipes network of *Advance Wars 2*—artificial contrivances that bring nothing to the game.

A shift to the DS required a certain degree of innovation, however, and the developer rose beautifully to the occasion, providing a generous measure of additional graphical polish—setting the game's maps at an attractive angle and beefing up the transitions and presentation somewhat—while throwing in new modes and tricks to keep established COs satisfied.

The main campaign provides another cartoony romp through the hellish caldera of war, throwing in a few missions built around quirkier, more narrative led objectives like stopping missile launches, rather than the regular slog to the death the series usually trades in. The ability to double-team COs changes the strategic options somewhat too. Elsewhere a handful of new modes kept players busy away from the main campaign, Survival throwing out a gauntlet of matches and starting points, while Combat is practically a shooter, switching the game to real-time with oddball results.

Multiplayer users hoping to take the fight online would have to wait for the bleak follow-up, *Days of Ruin*, which irradiated the game's cheery color scheme and offered a slightly grittier plot. *Advance Wars: Dual Strike* feels like the more faithful title, and the more imaginative. **CD**

Golden Tee Live

Original release date : 2005
Platform : Arcade
Developer : Incredible Technologies
Genre : Sports

By the time *Golden Tee Live* began popping up in bars and airports, arcades in the West had long since sunk into decline. The idea of playing video games in public seemed positively quaint, a relic even, but this game, as part of a certain class of attractions that includes its light-gun based cousin, *Big Buck Hunter*, continues to persist as the last remnant of the arcade culture.

What's unusual about *Golden Tee Live* is its utter lack of bells and whistles. At a time when video game players were anxiously awaiting latest next-generation consoles, the graphics of *Golden Tee Live* were primitive. The concept is simple enough. You play golf against your friends. *Golden Tee Live* is also kind enough to hide Easter eggs throughout the various off-course regions of the game to reward players unable to keep their drives on the green. Importantly, it was also the first Western coin-operated game with Internet link-up play, allowing players to update their scores and compete in international tournaments.

At the heart of *Golden Tee Live*'s appeal is its trackball controller, which governs your swing and spin. Much like the original arcade version of *Marble Madness*, *Golden Tee Live* invites players into a type of performance, allowing for a variety of techniques to wind your golfer up and spin the trackball forward as quickly, and for as many revolutions, as humanly possible. This physical act, combined with copious amounts of beer and sprinkled with a dose of competitive spirit, makes *Golden Tee* the perfect activity for half time, and turns the strategy and finesse of golf into a demonstration of sheer brute force. Pity the poor engineers who repair pummeled trackballs after particularly long nights of *Golden Tee Live*. **JBW**

F.E.A.R.

Original release date : 2005
Platform : PC
Developer : Monolith Productions
Genre : First-Person Shooter

F.E.A.R. (First Encounter Assault Recon) was Monolith's highly successful attempt to cross three outgoing cultural fads—Japanese horror movies, like *Ring* and *Dark Water*; the slow-motion action of a John Woo movie; and cyberpunk anime, like *Appleseed* and *Ghost in the Shell*. The player takes the role of a special-operations point man sent to investigate weird goings-on in Fairport, a large US city.

Paxton Fettel, commander of a unit of telepathically controlled supersoldiers, has seized control of Armacham, the shadowy research company that created him. Worse, a troubled child called Alma, the subject of its cruelest psychic experiments, has been unleashed upon the nearby area. A little girl in dire need of a haircut, Alma conducts

a symphony of scares as you follow the game's clues. She appears in hallways that burst into flame, turns soldiers into spiraling body parts, and hijacks your point of view when you least expect it. At her most effective, she has you firing bullets at vanishing ghosts, leaving just smoking holes in the wall. So heavy on special effects that it crippled PCs at the time, *F.E.A.R.*'s production values are like those of a blockbuster action movie.

But while its psychic ambushes come violently and rarely, Fettel's Replica soldiers are a more constant threat. *F.E.A.R.*'s combat AI is some of the best in the business, and is brilliantly served by its environment. Office cubicles and crumbling warehouses aren't the most ambitious venues, but they can be the most exciting when you're ducking in and out of Reflex Time, and dodging bullets and enemies. With the smart use of banter to suggest team-based tactics, it appears intelligent even when it's not, and then finds a way to put a bullet in your back. This, more than any apparition, is its spookiest achievement. **DH**

Fahrenheit

Original release date : 2005
Platform : Various
Developer : Quantic Dream
Genre : Adventure

Quantic Dream is David Cage's French development house, and a team with a bold ambition—to make cinematic games that raise the level of storytelling for the game industry and to craft truly adult experiences with believable characters and motivations, with room for the player to make choices that will really make them think.

It's strange, then, that *Fahrenheit* should have such an enjoyably schlocky narrative. Released as *Indigo Prophecy* in the US, *Fahrenheit* is set in a New York terrorized by a spate of cultish murders carried out by seemingly ordinary citizens. From this intriguing premise, the plot steadily goes south, eventually breaking loose from all moorings entirely as it plumbs the depths of paranormal bizarreness.

Narrative aside, the game remains truly fascinating, an action-oriented adventure title in which the player switches back and forth between a handful of different characters in an attempt to uncover the truth behind the murderous mystery that wracks the city.

On top of that, the controls are distinctive for an adventure game, relying almost exclusively on thumbsticks, with one of them handling movement while the other is taking care of just about every other action in the game, from opening doors to disposing of murder weapons, to fighting, and even playing the guitar.

From the introductory sequence—a brief tutorial presented by Cage himself in full Hitchcock mode—*Fahrenheit* is bemusing and beguiling by turn. Quantic Dream hasn't made a masterpiece, necessarily, but it's certainly turned out one of gaming's most intriguing follies. A title that you owe it to yourself to track down, the Xbox 360's downloadable Xbox Originals collection is probably a good place to start. **CD**

Fable

Original release date : 2005
Platform : Xbox
Developer : Lionhead Studios
Genre : Action / Role-Playing

Xbox exclusive *Fable* is rustic, beautiful, epic, and charming, but the game is perhaps more famous for what it didn't include than what it did. One-man hype machine Peter Molyneux, whose Lionhead Studios designed and built the adventure, had a habit during development of announcing incredible innovations that players could expect to enjoy in a world that featured real and persistent consequence.

Some of these—plant an acorn one day, and years later the seed will have grown into a tree—didn't make it into the game, and so *Fable* launched into a tetchy sea of Internet agitation as aggrieved fans made their feelings known. Today, of course, this is how every game gets released, but back in 2005, it was still something of a

novelty. Disappointments and petitions aside, *Fable* is a magnificent game, a bold adventure that charts your own personal hero's journey from childhood, through dark tragedy, to unexpected strength and valor as you take on an evil blight that threatens to sour the fields and cobbled squares of Albion. If you don't feel heroic, you can be evil, murdering innocents, stealing and pillaging, and generally scaring the socks off some poor librarians. The game will keep track of your actions, transforming your character model accordingly as you head toward either light or darkness, and causing the town's people to treat you with fear, love, or even disgust.

Or you could ignore that entirely and just mess around, firing off magic spells, getting stupid haircuts, and engaging in a world rich with a singularly British kind of humor. Scaling effortlessly to your interests and proclivities, *Fable* is a fascinating experiment in ego and entertainment, a raucous journey that will feel different each time you embark on it. **CD**

Façade

Original release date : 2005
Platform : PC
Developer : Procedural Arts
Genre : Interactive Drama

Your old friends Grace and Trip have invited you over for dinner, and it doesn't take long before you wish they hadn't. Veiled jabs and passive-aggressive taunts fill their conversation, and a night with your friends gets awkward and ugly. You have to respond to the situation and, if you feel like it, play marriage counsellor. Your only tool is conversation—and you communicate in full sentences, just like you would in real life.

Co-designers Michael Mateas and Andrew Stern built *Façade* as an experiment in natural language processing, wrapped in the structure of a one-act play. Five years in the making, its engine can handle full sentences on topics that go beyond the usual "go north" or "pick up glass." You can

ask for a drink, talk about a holiday, or even make a pass at one or both of the stars. They'll also throw you out the door if you're rude enough, and the way Grace and Trip carry on, it's tempting.

Grace and Trip respond with 20,000 lines of spoken dialogue that run the gamut from anger to tears, and their actions are organized in story beats rather than a script. Until a gamelike exercise at the end, where you find out if you've helped or harmed the marriage, *Façade* strives to create a natural interaction between three people.

The graphics are basic, and the parser's not perfect; Grace and Trip often react to a suggestion they don't recognize with an awkward stare or a look of horror. Ultimately, *Façade* is an experiment rather than a finished game, but it's a mammoth work for a two-person team. This title points the way to how an interactive drama could work and how nuanced game characters can become, when you can interact with them in your own words. This is one title worth playing at least once. **CDa**

Guild Wars

Original release date : 2005
Platform : PC, Mac
Developer : ArenaNet
Genre : MMORPG

ArenaNet was brave to even begin developing a game on the scale of a massively multiplayer online (MMO) role-playing game (RPG) without the intention of charging people a monthly fee to wander in its world. NCsoft was brave to release it, and it was incredibly brave to stick with that subscription-free model, even when it became apparent that millions of people would gladly throw money at Guild Wars for years to come. Guild Wars isn't just a superb game, it's a massive multiplayer milestone.

Guild Wars's unconventional structure allows it to be a little more ambitious with its storytelling than other MMOs. Quests are instanced, meaning that each player or party is wandering around in their own unique version of the beautiful and vast game world. There are no lines of other players waiting to slay a dragon or collect or kill or craft five of something to bring back to the nearest village. Consequently, Guild Wars can weave its tale like a single-player RPG, with cut scenes, unexpected twists, and dramatic set piecing, without a whole universe of players around to ruin the atmosphere.

It's a full-bodied fantasy enriched by gorgeous art direction. Every player in Guild Wars looks like an ancient Grecian deity, a welcome novelty in a genre often populated by orcs, elves, and ogres. Tyria is a varied realm, at turns verdant, mountainous, or desolate. Some players find its instanced environments lonely but, thanks to its relatively low-level cap, Guild Wars is also mercifully free of the tiresome grinding for loot and experience points that can make those persistent universes such a chore to inhabit. Guild Wars is an innovative success story, giving players hundreds of hours of play. It's entirely deserving of its enduring popularity. **KM**

Fire Emblem: Path of Radiance

Original release date : 2005
Platform : GameCube
Developer : Intelligent Systems
Genre : Strategy

Intelligent Systems extended its hold on strategy games from the militarized futuristic warfare of *Advance Wars* to the world of fantasy and magic with its equally venerable *Fire Emblem* series. *Fire Emblem: Path of Radiance*, the ninth game in the series, is probably the strongest of the lot. This is a characterful and involving adventure with plenty of battles for tactically minded players to mull over.

With a narrative entirely unrelated to any of the preceding *Fire Emblem* games, *Fire Emblem: Path of Radiance* tells the story of a band of brave warriors seeking to repel an invading horde that threatens to swamp their proud nation, while restoring the rightful ruler to the throne. It's standard fantasy stuff, in other words, with lots of opportunities for battles on a large scale, but while the game retains the tone and spirit of the earlier titles—and many of the *Fire Emblem* series' standard tactical features— it does find room for a handful of tweaks.

From a presentation perspective, *Fire Emblem: Path of Radiance* is the first title with full voice acting throughout, and it also features sharp, cel-shaded visuals. In terms of content, the title also finds the room to introduce a new race of characters to wage war against, and creates a new battle preparation system to up the strategic ante.

Besides that, the series strong points remain the same. Party members leveled up over hours of game play will die for good if killed, while the new cartoon visuals retain a sleek Western influenced aesthetic that has always been a series hallmark. *Fire Emblem: Path of Radiance* is hardly the best-looking game to be released on the GameCube, but with tactics this deep and an adventure this wide, it's one that's still worth returning to again and again and remains a title that strategy fans should try at least once. **CD**

Garry's Mod

Original release date : 2005
Platform : PC
Developer : Team Garry
Genre : Role-Playing

Of all the games in this book, *Garry's Mod* is perhaps the one that strains the definition of the word "game" the most. When it started life in 2004, it was certainly nothing of the sort. It was a slightly kooky modification for *Half-Life 2*, which allowed you to place props from the game around an empty environment, tie them together with rope, and fire spinning aerial drones from the game's normal pistol. The subsequent twelve iterations have seen the mod gain support for any Source engine title that has a software development kit, and graduate from the mod section on Steam to a standalone game.

In the form that it arrives to the new user, unextended by further downloads, it's still hard to say that it's a game. Without any goals, win conditions, or predetermined experiences to explore, it's really more of a toy or a tool. *Garry's Mod* has a variety of functions, from a physics sandbox, in which you can experiment with welding propulsion systems onto melons or building tanks out of wheeled garbage bins, to a Valve-themed diorama creator, complete with photography kit. It's also communal, allowing players to come together on a single server and cooperate in building their elaborate contraptions or, more often than not, spend the time firing melons at the back of one another's heads for amusement.

The title is also a springboard for other mods, like the team multiplayer game *Zombie Survival*, in which one side survives six waves of increasingly powerful dead heads, or the extensive role-playing platform *DarkRP*, or *Super Mario Boxes*, a physics-based team game that locks play to the *X* axis and spoofs the chirpy, blocky graphics of the NES. *Garry's Mod* is as versatile as it is sometimes inchoate. It's testament to its creative potential that it is a game, but only if you want it to be. **MD**

Devil May Cry 3

Original release date : 2005
Platform : PS2
Developer : Capcom
Genre : Fighting / Action

The *Devil May Cry* series started out as just another episode of *Resident Evil* until the folk at Capcom realized that Hideki Kamiya's creative vision was simply too full of life for the shambling hordes of undead. Borrowing its structure from *Resident Evil*, but switching its inspiration from the zombie B-movie to the action blockbuster, the original *Devil May Cry* created an entirely new video game genre. It's difficult to imagine games like *Bayonetta* or *God of War* ever happening without *Devil May Cry* as their predecessor.

Devil May Cry 3: Dante's Awakening was chronologically the first in the series, and a welcome return to form after *Devil May Cry 2* disappointed fans of the first game. As in the previous entries, the star of the show is the game's diabolical leading man, Dante. This time he is united in combat with his brother, Vergil (also playable in the special edition of the game), to battle the mysterious Arkham and to explain the story behind the eventual creation of the *Devil May Cry* investigative agency.

The real star of the show is the effervescent action that fizzes out of Kamiya's original, inspired game design. *Devil May Cry 3: Dante's Awakening* is a return to that infernal blend of platform, puzzles, and superstylish combat—taunting enemies to sustain your ranking, and juggling them in the air to inflict massive damage.

As well as the numerous demonic transformations and upgradeable weapons of the previous games, there is the ability to select one of six different fighting styles, such as the self-explanatory Swordmaster and Gunslinger techniques (which help when it comes to defeating some of the hardest bosses in the whole series). Indeed, after *Devil May Cry 2*, part three represents business as usual, the business in question being the brutally elegant decimation of unceasing hordes of demonic villains. **DM**

Meteos

Original release date : 2005
Platform : DS
Developer : Q Entertainment
Genre : Puzzle

While falling block matcher *Lumines* brought a splash of stylish suavity to Sony's sleek PSP, Q Entertainment was also working on a puzzle game for Nintendo's more rugged and homely DS. The result was *Meteos*, a far noisier, more knockabout game than the classic that graced the PSP. It consists of simple colors, nice stylus controls, and a bizarre subplot about an evil planetoid that almost everybody, probably rightly, chose to ignore.

While you're still arranging blocks, this time there's a gravitational twist: You try to ignite specific stacks by matching their colors before launching them off the bottom screen and into space. Running the stylus over the game pieces to change the arrangement of the different hues is a beautiful use of the DS's hardware and particular capabilities, and it makes for a uniquely visceral and tangible puzzle game along the way. *Meteos*'s various planet-based levels, each with their own visual themes, also experiment with different forms of gravity, so you can never rest on your laurels with an old strategy for very long.

There is one problem, however, with the game's streamlined stylus controls. *Meteos* is almost too accommodating, and sneaky players quickly found that practically every single one of the game's levels could eventually be completed simply by scratching the stylus mindlessly up and down the screen until victory was assured. It's a brute force solution that, given the game's elegance, seems almost shameful, but it merely serves to add an element of morality to the title.

Playing *Meteos* the way it was intended to be played is great fun, and the knowledge that your progress is built on careful consideration and thoughtful action, rather than outright cheating, makes eventual success all the more pleasurable and satisfying. **CD**

Grand Theft Auto: Liberty City Stories

Original release date : 2005
Platform : PS2, PSP
Developer : Rockstar
Genre : Action

Everyone knows what's great about *Grand Theft Auto*. It is the original free roaming, go anywhere, do anything, crime simulation sandbox. Everyone knows that Liberty City is still the most memorable region from the many that have been created by those architects of crime at Rockstar. It's still the best—possibly because it was the original—and it holds fond memories of misdemeanors, felonies, and carjacking for millions of gamers who like their action edgy.

Grand Theft Auto: Liberty City Stories is a chance to return to the scene of those old wrongdoings and repeat them, but this time in a game that has been fashioned specifically for a handheld experience. Missions are more bite-sized than before, but no less morally ambivalent, and the game packs just as much devilish satire and sophisticated contrarianism as the original console games. As in *Grand Theft Auto III*, it gives players the freedom of the city, to whatever they please, no matter how morally dubious.

It also introduces motorcycles to Liberty City, along with a selection of new side stories and subquests, played out to the accompaniment of a soundtrack made up from the player's own collection, thanks to a custom audio feature. Added to the technical achievement of fitting the whole city inside the palm of your hand, it also introduces the series' first ever multiplayer mode, granting Wi-Fi equipped gamers the debatable pleasures of chasing one another on scooters while wielding chainsaws.

Rockstar's characteristic brand of nostalgia worked so well, in fact, that *Grand Theft Auto: Liberty City Stories* was eventually ported back to the PS2, and paved the way for a reprise of *Grand Theft Auto: Vice City*, also on the PSP. This title is a slice of video gaming history, an experience that everyone should have just once. **DM**

GT Legends

Original release date : 2005
Platform : PC
Developer : Simbin
Genre : Racing

With their throwback typeface and blue and orange color scheme, designed to evoke the famous Gulf liveried racers that dominated Le Mans, even the menus in *GT Legends* are infused with the spirit of 1960s and 1970s motor racing. This follow-up to the scintillating *GTR* benefits from a fresh engine that allows for more detailed, curvier cars and densely decorated scenery. Placing you in the snug Nomex overalls of a gentleman racing driver, *GT Legends* offers a choice of classic machinery to throw around a healthy selection of European circuits.

"Throw" is the right word. Unlike the hunkered-down, stiffly sprung modern racers of Simbin's debut, these vehicles roll and wallow through corners, requiring an armful of opposite lock when the rear end attempts to overtake the front. As a handling specialist, Simbin has ensured that the vehicle dynamics never feel anything less than utterly convincing. It's only the arbitrary unlock system, easily Simbin's biggest misstep, that keeps you from experiencing and comparing them all from the outset. Still, whether you're behind the wheel of the nippy Mini Cooper or the frankly terrifying De Tomaso Pantera, the racing is a fraught, high-speed jousting match.

In keeping with the broad range of performance and grassroots feel, *GT Legends* is also a showcase for club level circuits that will be unfamiliar to many players. Most of the tracks have shorter, national or junior configurations, and circuits such as Dijon-Prenois and Mondello Park are rarely seen in simulations based on licensed championships.

However, that's what makes *GT Legends* such a tantalizing morsel. These cars and tracks, which are so often overlooked and forgotten by others, are reproduced in loving and definitive detail. **MCh**

Guitar Hero

Original release date : 2005
Platform : PS2
Developer : Harmonix
Genre : Music

There had been guitar-based video games before *Guitar Hero* swooped onto the scene. Konami's *Guitar Freaks* also asked its players to strap on a plastic guitar and strum along in time with an eclectic soundtrack. But it wasn't until Harmonix captured the big hair essence of stadium rock and packaged the mechanics within bright primary colors that the idea finally settled into its rhythm. It's nothing like playing guitar, of course, as so many yawnsome, musically minded onlookers will be quick to point out. However, this game sure feels like playing rockstar, and the game's strict appraisal of its player's timing makes it a bona fide music tutor, no matter what the snooty naysayers claim.

In many ways, *Guitar Hero*'s onscreen readouts are a sort of musical notation. Notes move toward you down a stave and, when they pass a bar marker, you must hold down the corresponding button on your guitar and strum the note. Hit the timing, and the lick will play out, loud and proud above the backing. Miss, and there will be an awkward splang in the soundtrack, the musical equivalent of a gameshow's "nuh-uh."

The correlation between music and interaction helps cement the sense of important cause and effect between game and player, inspiring you to make every note or risk letting the rest of the band down. In this sense, *Guitar Hero* is a more faithful representation of being part of a group than its critics give it credit for.

Guitar Hero's aesthetic is more pastiche than a serious attempt at realism, but it is appropriate for a game that asks you to do something so ridiculous, inviting you to join in the joke, rather than sneer at it. But don't be fooled. *Guitar Hero*'s core was, and is, a serious business, a catalyst for a plastic instrument revolution that today threatens to kill the radio star. **SP**

Gunstar Super Heroes

Original release date : 2005
Platform : Game Boy Advance
Developer : Treasure
Genre : Shoot 'Em Up

Gunstar Heroes was the first game created by Treasure when the company was set up by a handful of ex-Konami employees at the start of the 1990s. It was the game that set in motion a sequence of playfully intertextual, usually brilliant, mostly shoot-'em-up classics that have so far lasted more than fifteen years, bringing us the likes of *Radiant Silvergun*, *Ikaruga*, *Bangai-O*, and *Sin and Punishment*.

But it wasn't until 2005 that it got a sequel. *Gunstar Super Heroes* is, of course, that sequel, and it appeared on Nintendo's Game Boy Advance. It's interesting, and slightly typical of Treasure, that both games were released on consoles that were just in the process of being replaced by technologically superior successors. The story picks up where the first game finished, but the action is almost a respectful recreation. A run-and-gun shoot 'em up that also finds time to pay homage to other (sometimes obscure) Sega classics, from *After Burner* to *Flicky*, and wraps it all up in some of the most spectacularly arresting visuals seen on Nintendo's handheld console.

There are some differences. The previous game's combinable weapons have been superseded by a more straightforward choice of three, allied with a meter that charges up a superpowerful attack; there is an increased range of melee options; and characters can now bat incoming bullets back toward the enemy (an idea that, thanks to Treasure's constant reharvesting of its best ideas, also appears in *Bangai-O Spirits* and *Sin and Punishment 2*).

The one thing that remains the same is the gleeful playfulness and inventiveness that characterizes all of Treasure's games. *Gunstar Super Heroes* might be just six levels short, but there is plenty to play and replay here for anyone that likes their entertainment slightly insane. **DM**

Fire Pro Wrestling Returns

Original release date : 2005
Platform : PS2
Developer : Spike
Genre : Fighting

The tragedy of the modern three-dimensional wrestling game is that realism is the key to only one kind of success: financial. In all other respects, the realities of professional wrestling make it impossible for a series like *WWE Smackdown vs Raw* to provide all the modes, characters, and techniques that fans really want. There's no time, thanks to the yearly update schedule, and no freedom, the wrestlers all split between fiercely political promotions.

So why bother, asks *Fire Pro Wrestling Returns*, when instead you can have a roster of 327 lookalikes, a crafty renaming option, and slots for 500 custom characters? With its wimpy two-dimensional sprites and isometric rings, *Fire Pro Wrestling Returns* is the Rey Mysterio of the sport, the underdog champion. A legend of the 1990s import scene across platforms such as the PC Engine and Super Famicom, it takes its grappling seriously. Its fans want dream matches with options that leave everything to the imagination. MMA takedowns and ground games, steel cages, barbed wire, eight-man tag-team matches, battle royals, and even the landmine matches of 1990s Japanese trash promotions are just the tip of the iceberg.

In place of the deeply unsatisfying button-mash grappling of the *WWE* games, *Fire Pro Wrestling Returns* uses a more complex system of timed button taps that promotes skill over attrition. Its counter and reversal system is so thorough that every move must be chosen according to the momentum of the match, starting with jabs and roughhousing before moving to slams, leaps, and finishing moves. Hit the buttons arbitrarily, and you'll be on the receiving end. Like *King of Colosseum* and *Giant Gram*, it's a game about the true reality of sports entertainment, which is as much about performance as victory. **DH**

Killer 7

Original release date : 2005
Platform : Various
Developer : Capcom
Genre : Adventure / Shoot 'Em Up

Killer 7 is one of the few games that is genuinely impossible to classify. Part rail shooter, part puzzle game, part light-gun gallery, part mystery, it's video game design at its most enjoyably idiosyncratic. The game offers a frightening babble of styles and ideas that works its magic by keeping you constantly on edge rather than conforming to chummy ritual.

The story alone suggests that it's going to be a bumpy ride. Harman Smith is an ancient and seemingly eternal being, capable of manifesting seven different versions of himself, all of whom he'll need—along with their respective special powers—when he tangles with a terrorist group known as Heaven Smile, deadly and invisible killers who appear to be living bombs. In game play terms, this amounts to a bizarrely hemmed-in action-adventure title in which the player switches back and forth between Harman's seven separate identities. Each of these identities walks either backward or forward along prescribed paths (occasionally stopping to allow the player to choose directions for them at junction points), with the aim of solving puzzles and taking down members of that dastardly Heaven Smile.

Compounding such a bizarre structure is an equally eccentric visual style, using sharp blasts of flat colors, bold outlines, and plentiful blood splatters. The character designs range from sadomasochistic gimps dangling from doors to sharp-suited wise guys and hot nurses. From the maniacal cackle that announces the start of the game right through to the maddening finale, this is fascinating and disturbing stuff. Here is a game that few players will genuinely love, perhaps, but everyone would be richer for at least trying it out. **CD**

LEGO Star Wars

Original release date : 2005
Platform : Various
Developer : Traveller's Tales
Genre : Action / Adventure

Very few games explain themselves so comprehensively in the space of their own titles, but *LEGO Star Wars* genuinely does exactly what it says on the box. It reduces George Lucas's much beloved space opera to the level of the village choir, restaging its climactic battles in simulated plastic, and flinging famous Jedi, 'droids, and stormtroopers into a world of knockabout platforming nonsense.

The results are enduringly hard to dislike. Boiling each film down to a handful of pantomime cut scenes and some elaborate, rather undisciplined, stages (the first game sullies itself with the largely embarrassing prequel trilogy, but the follow-up tackles the original movies), you'll eventually play almost every hero and villain in the series.

Wielding blasters, lightsabers, and the mysterious Force to battle an onslaught of brainless enemies, you negotiate the terrain and deal with an almost unprecedented array of collectibles and unlockables. While the backgrounds themselves are static, most of the more immediate furniture is made of LEGO blocks, and a huge part of the fun comes from simply smashing things to pieces and seeing what you'll find inside.

If style, warmth, and a cooperative system are the game's strengths, the various puzzles you'll encounter along the way are perhaps its weaknesses. Most of them are meandering and, considering the game is aimed at children, often really rather fiddly. That's not enough to undo the general sense of Saturday morning fun that Traveller's Tales's game can summon up, however, and once the whole thing's finished, you may find yourself playing through it again and again until you've found absolutely all of its secrets. And that, incidentally, will take you a long, long time regardless of how far away your galaxy is. **CD**

Mario & Luigi: Partners in Time

Original release date : 2005
Platform : DS
Developer : AlphaDream
Genre : Role-Playing

Following on from the charming *Mario & Luigi: Superstar Saga*, AlphaDream's DS sequel, *Partners in Time* sent the world's most famous plumbers on another role-playing adventure. This episode traveled into the dim past and very distant future of the Mushroom Kingdom in order to discover wacky characters and intricate mechanics, in a story of alien invasion in which flying saucers are piloted by mushrooms, and nothing is quite as it seems.

It's another colorful romp, then, filled with more of the same in-jokes, smart rhythm-based fights, and unlikely cameos. If the somewhat restrictive map means it's not quite as satisfying to explore as the original, it's still got enough bosses and battles to keep all but the pickiest players happy from start to finish.

Complicating matters on this outing is the fact that Mario and Luigi team up, Bill and Ted style, with themselves—on this occasion, their toddler selves, last seen properly in the magnificent *Yoshi's Island*—and the game wrings a lot of complicated fun from splitting the team up, slotting them back together again, and generally messing around with time and causality. Inevitably, there's quite of lot of crying along the way, too.

The temporal complexity never quite delivers on the overall promise and the very last boss fight is staggeringly hard, but *Mario & Luigi: Partners in Time* is a creditable follow-up to the Game Boy Advance's classic *Mario & Luigi: Superstar Saga*. The game is as charming an adventure as you could hope to find on the DS and as complicated a control scheme as you could dream of concocting without driving your own audience to drink. Both fans and newcomers to the series will appreciate it. **CD**

Mario Kart DS

Original release date : 2005
Platform : DS
Developer : Nintendo
Genre : Racing

Mario Kart had been around for at least a decade by the time it found its way on to the DS, but something magical happened when Nintendo's family friendly racer met the faddish handheld's new and expanded audience of moms, sisters, and granddads. *Mario Kart DS* sold and sold, and continues to sell even now, rarely out of the charts and almost never out of the "still playing" piles of DS owners around the globe.

And it's a solid version of an enduring classic, ditching the sprite-based presentation of the Game Boy Advance installment, *Mario Kart Super Circuit*, in favor of chunky three-dimensional models playing out on a series of quietly inventive courses, and roping in the spiral staircases of Bowser's castles, to the leafy seafronts of *Mario Sunshine*'s Isle Delfino. Unlockable vehicles and characters plumb new depths of weirdness as the game progresses, with the appearance of generally unkillable castle favorite Drybones on the racing roster, while heavy classes get a chance to take Bowser's hideous prop airplane for a spin. The power-ups have had their customary rejiggle to ensure that running into those tempting question mark boxes remains as fresh as always.

Online mode is more divisive due to the cornering for a boost mechanic that allows talented players to zigzag along straights to gain an endless nitro streak. Still this is a landmark title for Nintendo, embracing the online world in a manner to which it had always previously been reticent. All in all, then, it's not hard to tell why *Mario Kart DS* proved to be such a prolonged success. Perhaps emboldened by the surprise hit, the series would go on to even greater sales with the evergreen Wii version. **CD**

Jade Empire

Original release date : 2005
Platform : Various
Developer : BioWare
Genre : Action / Role-Playing

BioWare is the Canadian studio that, with titles like *Baldur's Gate* and *Neverwinter Nights*, made some of the best traditional Western fantasy role-playing games (RPG) of any generation. With titles such as *Mass Effect* and its sequel, *Mass Effect 2*, it's proved it can handle science fiction with the same po-faced ease it tackled the world of dwarves and armor.

Jade Empire is perhaps its most ambitious work to date, a role-playing title set in an Eastern-influenced game world, with the aim of providing a deep and unfolding story experience that's married to a solid martial arts combat system. With a tale involving a group of students tasked with recovering and protecting a mystical artifact known as

the Dragon Amulet, *Jade Empire* takes its Chinese-flavored setting seriously, turning in a narrative that wouldn't be out of place in a genuine Asian cinema epic. It's surprising, then, that the end results should somehow manage to feel so traditional at the same time.

With two overarching philosophies standing in for the moral alignments beloved of the developer, and a range of different fighting styles to unlock and evolve throughout the journey, there's still plenty of BioWare to see in between the lush environments and fast-paced battles. While the overall effect is perhaps not as consistent as the developer's more famous games, with a range of playable characters; a smart adventure; and an incredibly colorful, thoughtful presentation, this remains one of the most intriguing and distinct RPGs around.

Rumors abound of a sequel—which seems rather unlikely—but the original can be found, appropriately enough, on Xbox Originals, and is well worth trying out if you're looking for an adventure game with flavor. **CD**

Rogue Galaxy

Original release date : 2005
Platform : PS2
Developer : Level-5
Genre : Role-Playing

The Japanese role-playing game (RPG) marketplace is owned by the established franchise and after Level-5 demonstrated its skills by developing the well-received *Dragon Quest VIII: Journey of the Cursed King*, the studio chose to follow it up with its own original title, *Rogue Galaxy*. Featuring many of the enhancements to the genre seen in *Dragon Quest VIII: Journey of the Cursed King*, such as large, load-free environments and striking cel-shaded graphics, it departs heavily in most other respects.

Rogue Galaxy opens in a style that could be considered outright plagiarism of *Star Wars*. Protagonist, Jaster Rogue, is a boy abandoned by his parents on a sand planet who learns to fight from a mysterious stranger in the desert,

before teaming up with an effeminate robot and his jolly squat pal. However, it quickly opens up into a more complex plot, intertwining the story of Jaster with the seven characters who join his party across the game. It never quite manages to avoid referencing everything from the *Pirates of the Caribbean* franchise to even Disney's cinematic bomb, *Treasure Planet,* in its visual design.

Rogue Galaxy delivers via a wide variety of different locations and by simply being relentlessly bright and cheery. Dungeons might go on a tad too long, but a real-time battle system is accessible to those who enjoy both tactical planning or near mindless hacking-and-slashing, and an abundance of possible side quests and distractions means you can easily get involved with insect battling or working to create weapons if the main quest is too much.

Concentrating on the *Professor Layton* series, Level-5 hasn't shown interest in creating a sequel to *Rogue Galaxy*, making it a rare Japanese RPG, but one that joins *Skies of Arcadia* in the annals of often overlooked gems. **MKu**

Need for Speed: Most Wanted

Original release date : 2005
Platform : Various
Developer : Electronic Arts
Genre : Racing

Nestled amid the detritus of a difficult console launch, *Need for Speed: Most Wanted* is widely dismissed as a botched Electronic Arts (EA) cash-in on the Xbox 360. Flawed it might be, but it's also the most exciting of the series' urban street racing games, if more for fans of *The Blues Brothers* than *The Fast and the Furious*.

Arriving in the fictional US town of Rockport, the player gatecrashes a fight between the local race crews and Sergeant Cross, a simmering cop bent on putting them behind bars. This means catching the Blacklist, a fifteen-strong roster of the fastest, slipperiest racers in the district. Your goal, naturally, is to earn your place at the top. *Need for Speed: Most Wanted* pulls together elements of older games, like *Need for Speed: Underground 2* (a nocturnal racer in the *Fast and the Furious* mold) and *Need for Speed: Hot Pursuit II* (a gumballer's game, full of rural highway chases). Like *Burnout*, it also features a recharging nitrous oxide boost. Most of its career milestones involve point-to-point races against the names on the Blacklist, but it's the bits in between that stand out.

Earning enough bounty to challenge each racer means winning tollbooth time trials and other challenges and getting up the nose of the local constabulary. Tagging a police car will catch their interest, but it's a challenge in itself to rile them enough to promote you, then survive long enough to be on every police radio in the city. Before long you'll be hiding from helicopters, playing chicken with SUVs, scanning the airwaves for tactical banter, punching through roadblocks, and pulling handbrake U-turns. The longer you last, the more you earn, but you'll lose it all if they catch you. It begs the question of which is more dangerous: their driving or your ego? **DH**

Project Gotham Racing 3

Original release date : 2005
Platform : Xbox 360
Developer : Bizarre Creations
Genre : Racing

Want to know the most immediately impressive feature of *Project Gotham Racing 3* upon release? It wasn't the then-unrivaled high-definition graphics or the game's entirely convincing and quite impressively detailed (and functional) in-car view. Nor was it the extent to which Bizarre Creations managed to convincingly recreate Las Vegas, New York, Tokyo, London, and the dreaded Nürburgring in digital form. Although strong and mostly crucial, none of the above elements represent the most arresting element of the game upon release alongside the launch of Xbox 360.

That would be the side mirrors. Because not until the arrival of *Project Gotham Racing 3*'s fully functioning side mirrors did the concept of high-definition driving games truly manifest itself in a manner that was tangible. The emphasis on eighty high-performance cars away from everyday production models is welcome, as is the retention of the franchise's popular and proprietary Kudos system (where experience points are awarded for stylish driving). And the implementation of the online multiplayer modes proved commendable at a time when few developers were even thinking about let alone exploiting this area properly.

Elsewhere, the series' uniquely tuned arcade handling makes its usual impression, catering for complete beginners, regardless of their knowledge of turn-in points, apex clipping, or throttle phases. It remains a remarkable and mostly underrated feat. In many ways, the game can be considered a high-definition version of *Project Gotham Racing 2*, but its role as what gamers should expect from a new generation of driving titles deserves to be recognized. The game has since been overtaken by others, but at the time of its release Bizarre Creations enjoyed an enviable period of not having to look nervously behind it. **JDS**

Nintendogs

Original release date : 2005
Platform : DS
Developer : Nintendo
Genre : Pet-Raising Simulation

Everything's in the name. For generations of gamers the word "Nintendo," if it means anything, means "games." But with the addition of those two little letters, *g* and *s*, a portmanteau was born that changed that definition ever so slightly to something much simpler: play. *Nintendogs* doesn't describe a new type of game so much as a new type of animal, a piece of software that's about play for play's sake, that turns the most mundane of tasks into a touchy-feely thrill and makes work fun. Because *Nintendogs*, at heart, is an object lesson in transmuting basic interactions into gold.

The game convention is simple: You choose a type of dog, and then look after it. You walk the dog, feed the dog, clean the dog, and play around with the dog. There are no levels here, no fixed goals, no achievement points, and not even what could be called a structure. There's simply you and a remarkable simulation of an animal brought together in the game that, above all others, shows what Nintendo's handheld hardware can do in the right hands.

Everything is based on touch or sound. You stroke the dog, pull it along on walks, and teach it tricks by talking to it. The usual barriers of interface are simply removed, and the result is a connection that depends as much on your own sense of physicality as the algorithms behind the animal that you've chosen for yourself.

Your Nintendog responds to you directly, not to your pressing of a button, and so comes to feel almost alive. For many of *Nintendogs*'s players, the illusion becomes real. It feels as if the "Ninten" part of *"Nintendogs"* has simply faded away, leaving a machine in their hands that, through some kind of magic, contains nothing less than a living, breathing pet. It's almost as addictive and entertaining as the real thing, thankfully without the mess. **RS**

Tower Bloxx

Original release date : 2005
Platform : Various
Developer : Digital Chocolate
Genre : Strategy / Puzzle

Until the iPhone came along, there weren't many talked about mobile phone games, certainly not with the kind of quality and polish that meant they could measure up to regular handheld console titles. All of which makes *Tower Bloxx* very special.

A puzzle game by Electronic Arts founder Trip Hawkins's Digital Chocolate label, *Tower Bloxx* is everything a mobile phone game should be. This title is a tense, quick win, a no-frills time waster with an extremely simple control scheme, and the deepest of game play compulsions.

At the heart of the title's brilliance is the fact that, in a probable reaction to the dazzling array of different mobile phone inputs available, *Tower Bloxx* uses a single button for all of its actions. The aim of the game is to construct skyscrapers, from the vantage point of a swinging crane, by dropping one prefabricated floor after another onto the existing stack. Get the angle wrong too many times, and your wonky tower will start to fall and finally collapse; get them spot on, and you earn a combo multiplier you can build on with successive perfect drops. Lose three floors entirely—by missing the stack completely or letting them topple into oblivion—and it's game over.

There's a wider structure in which you redesign a bustling town center by building a series of different-sized skyscrapers but, pleasant and strategic as it is, *Tower Bloxx* was built for the simple brilliance of its endless mode, where the game is measured in the insane number of floors that you can chain together, while your wobbling megastructure inches past clouds, hot-air balloons, and the night sky, heading, ever upward, for the stars themselves. Still doing the rounds wherever decent mobile phone games can be bought, at the kind of price you're likely to pay there's simply no reason not to give this a try. **CD**

Trauma Center: Under the Knife

Original release date : 2005
Platform : DS
Developer : Atlus
Genre : Medical Simulation

As lead character names go, Derek Stiles lacks a little . . . something. You sound like a newsagent or a loss adjustor rather than a world famous lifesaving surgeon. But lifesaving surgeon you are, and Trauma Center: Under the Knife, Atlus's 2005 DS stitch 'em up, is an astonishing beast. A queasy heart-racing medical puzzle game, and a nutty apocalyptic soap opera all at the same time.

The game progresses through its rambly and rather insane narrative in a series of close-up operations, as you struggle to piece back together a range of patients, making as few mistakes as possible, within a strict time limit. Whether you're laser cutting or suturing, the game has a distinctly icky feel to it, even when the internal organs of your subject are drawn in such lovingly cartoon aspects. With vitals dropping and your tools fidgeting about in your hand, Trauma Center: Under the Knife can induce stress levels most other games can only dream about.

It works because it's primarily on the DS, and you will find it remarkably easy to look at the console's touch screen and pretend you're staring into a chest cavity, or to suddenly start believing that your plastic stylus—which lives, for the most part, down the back of the sofa—is a pair of gleaming sterilized forceps.

The difficulty level spikes a few times, as if the balancing team went into some sort of shock themselves while finishing the game, and the awards that pop up at the end of each level are rather hard to predict (decent surgeries scrape through, while a fluff often gets the highest commendation), but if you want something pleasantly disgusting to do on a train journey, Trauma Center: Under the Knife is society's only acceptable answer, really. **CD**

Rebelstar: Tactical Command

Original release date : 2005
Platform : Game Boy Advance
Developer : Codo Technologies
Genre : Strategy

With a gap of seventeen years since the previous Rebelstar title, the reappearance of the franchise as Rebelstar: Tactical Command was a surprise, especially on the Game Boy Advance, a format already crowded with Japanese-style tactical titles such as Final Fantasy Tactics and Advance Wars. Gamers who expected the varied play of the UFO: Enemy Unknown series found themselves the most disappointed, as the title featured none of the base building, research, or resource management features that those titles were known for.

Rebelstar: Tactical Command, outside of the Japanese-influenced art update and the inconsequential addition of experience point skill upgrades, is a pure return to the turn-based tactical action of the original Rebelstar series. Using Julian Gollop's lauded action point system, the game offers a wide variety of tactical possibilities, but at the cost of being incredibly demanding on the player's abilities. Perhaps gamers had just become soft by 2005, but Rebelstar: Tactical Command is as hard as its predecessor, requiring players to carefully manage their action points to ensure their squad is never left out in the open for a turn.

It's possibly thanks to this incredible difficulty that the game didn't take off the way the Advance Wars series did, but more likely a variety of frustrating flaws held the game back. A lack of polish in the front end and a poorly written plot make the game generally feel less complete than its predecessors, a shame in a title that requires so much concentration and thought from its players. Gamers who can stand its flaws will find a game that is unique in the handheld market and, as the last title produced by Julian Gollop, an unmissable artifact. **MKu**

Phoenix Wright: Ace Attorney

Original release date : 2005
Platform : Various
Developer : Capcom
Genre : Adventure

While popular enough a video game to secure four sequels, it's easier to think of *Phoenix Wright* as the best television legal drama never made. All the classic ingredients are here: confident ensemble cast, a "villain of the week" structure, epic underlying plot strands, and more comedy sidekicks than you could point an accusatory finger at. Regularly criticized for its stifling linearity, enthusiasm for its world and characters is enough to see the plucky lawyer through. Look to *Phoenix Wright's* popularity on the cosplay and fan fiction scene for the frightening evidence.

Phoenix Wright: Ace Attorney, or season one, sets the tone, the first in a trilogy of games charting Wright's rise from unconfident legal goof to slightly more confident legal goof. Joined by a hapless psychic—regularly possessed by the ghost of his dead mentor—the tone is wildly silly, grounded by some genuinely malicious murders and an earnest ongoing discourse on the professional relationship between defense attorneys and prosecutors. The latter spawns the series' strongest moments: Wright's nemesis is the suave Miles Edgeworth, whose cocky arrogance fuels blistering, fist-slamming confrontations throughout (and earned him his own spin-off game).

While much is owed to the original writers, *Ace Attorney* benefits massively from sensitive localization (the original Japanese games also contained English text to act as a reading trainer). Character names are pun-filled groaners—Wendy Oldbag, Will Powers, Sal Manella—and the dialogue is rife with surreal nods to television. One ambitious moment hides the lyrics to the *Fresh Prince of Bel Air* theme tune in a testimony. Worlds apart from the Capcom of old and its clunky *Resident Evil* scripts. **MC**

We Love Katamari

Original release date : 2005
Platform : PS2
Developer : Namco
Genre : Puzzle

Keita Takahashi's feelings about the surprise success of his artsy, experimental game, *Katamari Damacy*, seem to be of the distinctly mixed variety. Not only is *We Love Katamari* the only one of the game's increasingly tired sequels that he was involved with directly, its very story is a charmingly sour-natured reflection on the nature of dealing with fans. *We Love Katamari*, but it's not clear whether Takahashi did.

Maybe that's a step too far. While the sequel doesn't add too many new ideas to the mix, it's still crafted with care and attention and delivered with a brilliantly sardonic wit. The king of the cosmos has become famous, and the prince must now roll specific Katamaris to sate the whims of the king's many followers. What this translates to is a series of rather more varied missions. You're still rolling up everything you find, but your targets are different.

With the scope of the game growing grander and grander until you're effectively organizing cataclysmic events, *We Love Katamari* also spreads outward, with customizable costumes for the little prince, and a new cooperative mode to match the competitive offering of the original game. As expected, it's rather quirky (each player controls half of the same Katamari), but it's a distinct touch and gives the definite impression that there was still a bit of passion in development.

It's that passion that is harder to detect in the developer's more recent offerings. Takahashi has moved onto the odd pleasures of *Noby Noby Boy*, while Namco continues to milk this least likely of cash cows. A game that was a reaction to sequels is now a bi-annual event, and the little prince is starting to look rather tired. So would you be after pushing around such a heavy load … **CD**

Silent Hunter III

Original release date : 2005
Platform : PC
Developer : Ubisoft
Genre : Submarine Simulator

Few slippage announcements can have been greeted with more glee than the one that emanated from Ubisoft on July 6, 2004. To anyone with any interest in combat simulation, the news that *Silent Hunter III* was being held back for six months to allow the construction of a dynamic campaign was massively encouraging. In those two words lay the promise of freedom, replayability, and resonance.

By allowing submarines to wander the North Atlantic essentially at will, the game captures the essence of World War II U-boat operations perfectly. Randomly generated convoys and weather ensure every patrol is unique, every career unpredictable. Elastic realism and time-compression options mean the maritime cat and mouse can be as

grueling or as gentle as the player wishes. At one end of the difficulty spectrum, automatic torpedo targeting and a steady supply of fat, easily detected prey for the casual kapitan; at the other, long hours in the conning tower staring at an empty horizon, plus lashings of authentic trigonometrical calculations for the history minded masochist. However you choose to approach *Silent Hunter III*, the potent salt rimed atmosphere comes as standard.

Earlier installments of the series included a crew management dimension but here, for the first time, crewmen are presences in polygon form.

Not that any self-respecting submarine simulation lover would ever consider playing *Silent Hunter III* in its original state. Another reason the simulation has generated such a large and loyal following is its openness to tampering. The Grey Wolves' *"GWX"* mod—the most impressive expression of this malleability—augments and improves almost every aspect, turning an already accomplished simulation game into a genre crown jewel. **TS**

Shadow of the Colossus

Original release date : 2005
Platform : PS2
Developer : Team Ico
Genre : Action / Adventure

The follow-up to Team Ico's haunting, lyrical, unforgettable platform adventure *Ico* is another sparse, rather mysterious affair, retaining the desolate wind-whipped art style of the original, but turning the game play mostly on its head.

Instead of a spooky and deserted castle to explore in the company of a ghostly girl, *Shadow of the Colossus* immediately gives you a horse, places you inside a much larger open world, and tasks you with tracking down a number of wandering Colossi—massive, lumbering beasts with strange, mossy, partly mechanical designs—and killing them in order to restore life to your dead female companion. Easier said than done, as it happens, as what sounds like a series of bosses also turns out to involve some

sharp platforming sections as you literally clamber up your massive foes, dancing over arms and legs, clinging to fur and armor and bone, before delivering the killing blow.

As is the way with the team's first PlayStation 2 game, interpreting what your actions might mean is all part of the mysterious appeal, but, as time goes on and more of the monsters are felled, it's likely that you'll start to feel somewhat conflicted about your selfish slaughter. As such, *Shadow of the Colossus* is affecting as well as spectacular, thoughtful as well as violent, and a workout session for the conscience as well as the thumbs.

Regularly name checked and rarely criticized, the game isn't perfect—at the very least, it's pushing the aging PS2 somewhat—but it's so fascinating and troubling to play, most gamers are willing to overlook chugging frame rates and occasionally wobbly controls. The forthcoming third game, *The Last Guardian*, looks to merge the monsters of *Shadow of the Colossus* with the camaraderie of *Ico*, and the results promise to be intriguing. **CD**

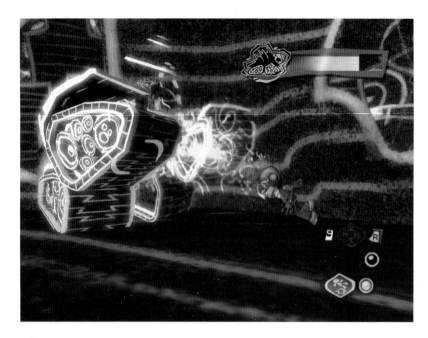

Psychonauts

Original release date : 2005
Platform : Various
Developer : Double Fine Productions
Genre : Platform

A colorful and largely rather undisciplined riot of smart japes and cutting one liners, *Psychonauts* has way, way too many ideas from which to make a single coherent game, but it's somehow found just about the perfect structure to tie all its loose ends together.

Raz, the stumpy child hero of a psychic summer camp, must travel inside the minds of the game's cast of lovable—and not so lovable—nutcases, working out what makes them tick by exploring the astonishing three-dimensional worlds sculpted out of their innermost psyches. Okay, so it's a platformer at heart, but it doesn't always feel like it. From the tangled conspiratorial brilliance of the Milkman's adventure—a paranoid fetch quest

extravaganza set in a Möbius strip Americana suburb that loops back on itself seemingly without end—to being thrust into the turn-based warfare of a nasty Napoleonic board game, every move in *Psychonauts* is a left turn. Each one taking you somewhere new, somewhere dazzlingly unexpected, and—seeing as the game was designed by veteran adventure game guru Tim Schafer and his team at Double Fine—somewhere entirely hilarious.

While *Psychonauts* never quite settles into a groove and its rampantly excessive collectible items merely serve to make everything even more of a muddle, it's a glorious exploration, and by-product, of the imagination. This title is a genre bending near masterpiece with far too many highlights to list in one go.

It's such a shame, then, that so few bought *Psychonauts* when the game first came out. Perhaps you should pick it up now on Steam, or Xbox Live's Xbox Originals download service, in order to make amends. It will entertain, enthrall, amuse, and delight you at every wicked turn. **CD**

The Movies

Original release date : 2005
Platform : PC
Developer : Lionhead Studios
Genre : Management Simulation

The Movies is Lionhead's attempt to turn machinima, the art of telling stories using repurposed game engines, into more than just an accident of the three-dimensional era. A far cry from the full-motion video experiments like *Steven Spielberg's Director's Chair*, it's as much a game as a creative tool (Spielberg's 1996 project is arguably neither), casting you as much as producer as director.

Prima donnas have to be hired, fired, cosseted, and detoxed; studios have to be built, staffed, and maintained; scripts have to be bought or composed from scratch. And with the timeline running from the silent era to today's CGI, you can't be caught napping on the research front. This is where comparisons with *Hollywood Mogul*, an acclaimed 1997 simulation by Carey DeVuono, stop. Incorporating a vast range of sets, props, actors, and events, along with track-based post-production tools, the moviemaking component of *The Movies* is a milestone in user-generated content. With enough wizards and templates to get anyone's efforts in the can, it's also complex and flexible enough to let you establish a directorial style. Every stage of the process and frame of film can be customized and exported for playback on any PC.

One of the first triple-A games to be aware of Web 2.0, it gave *The Movies Online* website the same care and attention as anything on the disk. Users could publish and share their movies with the world, budding Roger Eberts giving the thumbs-up or down through user comments. The game had thus achieved one of the highest goals of UGC applications: to let people enjoy them without actually owning or playing them. Sadly *The Movies Online* was retired in December 2008 with more than 33 million seconds of uploaded running time. **DH**

The Warriors

Original release date : 2005
Platform : Various
Developer : Rockstar
Genre : Adventure / Fighting

Rockstar Games didn't have to strain too hard to adapt Walter Hill's 1979 film *The Warriors* for the PlayStation 2 and Xbox. The story was about a New York City street gang who were falsely accused of murdering the city's highest-ranking gangster and who spent the rest of the night battling against increasingly difficult foes, from the Orphans, a bunch of scruffy wimps, to the Baseball Furies, painted freaks wielding baseball bats.

Comprising nonstop action, only the lightest hints of character and plot, and a storyline that followed the broad outlines of the epic journey, the movie was essentially a video game in its own right. Given that, it's surprising how much the video game version of *The Warriors* brings to the table. It is primarily a beat 'em up, in the proud tradition of *Double Dragon* and *Final Fight*, but with deeper fighting than those arcade games allowed. Rather than button mashing or sticking and moving, combat in *The Warriors* is a matter of messy brawling.

As befits the gang's "one for all, all for one" ethos, in most battles you'll be giving commands to your fellow Warriors. The strategy element is light, mostly encouraging them to attack or defend. And the grappling is brutal. Gang members can pick up lots of objects in the environment and bash their foes with them. Even basic strikes are swift and painful, though not as much as driving opponents to the ground and pounding them into submission

The Warriors is a more linear game than Rockstar is known for, but it still has plenty of optional objectives to distract you, such as looting storefronts, stealing cars, and tagging walls with your gang sign. With a storyline that actually expands upon that of the film, you don't have to be a fan of the movie to like it. **MK**

TimeSplitters: Future Perfect

Original release date : 2005
Platform : Various
Developer : Free Radical Design
Genre : First-Person Shooter

More of a refinement of the evergreen *TimeSplitters* formula than an enormously original addition to the series, *Future Perfect*, under the stewardship of Electronic Arts, is a slightly more polished affair than the previous two games.

Rather predictably, there are few changes to the multiplayer mode seen in *TimeSplitters 2*—it would take a brave developer to begin tinkering with what remains one of the fastest and finest death match models found on consoles. The provided playlist of classic arenas and beautifully designed new maps are more than enough to please hardened fans and newcomers alike. The single-player mode, by contrast, takes a fresh approach, and marks the series' first attempt at a more coherent storyline.

There are still levels culled from various points in history, but this time you spend the entire campaign in the boots of Cortez, the series' time-hopping hero, and at the points where the story doubles back on itself, you'll even find yourself cooperating with a version of Cortez from earlier or later in the game.

The entire challenge can be played with a friend in tow, and there are few games that offer as much variety from level to level. One minute you're preventing a nuclear missile launch on a speeding train and the next you're pumping ordnance into an enormous zombie deer in a transparent homage to *Resident Evil*.

Much of the rest is in the trimmings, including a more flexible map creator and a now unfortunately shuttered online mode, which included a directory of downloadable user made levels. The loss of the online service isn't perhaps as big a blow as it might initially appear, *Future Perfect* is still best enjoyed in classic four-way split screen mode alongside friends within elbowing distance. **MCh**

SC-20K FOREGRIP
29 / 179

Tom Clancy's Splinter Cell: Chaos Theory

Original release date : 2005

Platform : Various

Developer : Ubisoft

Genre : Stealth

Superspy Sam Fisher's third outing marks a high watermark for a particular kind of stealth-action game play. The evolution of dynamic lighting took *Splinter Cell's* shadowy tactics to a new level, but *Chaos Theory's* technical accomplishments would little have mattered if not married to the game's taut action and innervating soundtrack.

The tense stillness as Sam watches guards from darkened corners, the frantic rush as he surges forward to break a neck, the panic from being spotted—all these things are heightened by Amon Tobin's soundtrack, itself a masterpiece informed by cinematic scores of detective and spy fiction, exuding a sense of noire melancholy and industrial desolation. Every environment offers many

potential expressions of Sam's abilities. He is one of the most capable of all heroes, able to turn even the most innocuous setting into a weapon, such as a railing on a high gantry becoming a springboard for an unlucky goon's flight into the night sky.

Throughout, actor Michael Ironside growls bleak witticisms, often into the ears of Sam's frightened, captured prey who usually give up their secrets or, in at least one instance, bladder control.

Chaos Theory's single-player triumph is matched by a brilliant asymmetrical team multiplayer mode, and an uncommonly generous cooperative campaign, with a potential for smart collaborative tactics almost no other game has since recaptured. Although predictably one player is needed to boost another to a high ledge every now and again, it's when you split up and coordinate that the game's possibilities blossom. This freedom best expresses *Splinter Cell's* predatory charms. A dark night, a dozen necks, so many different ways to snap them. **MD**

Oddworld: Stranger's Wrath

Original release date : 2005
Platform : Xbox
Developer : Oddworld Inhabitants
Genre : Action / Adventure

The chaotic whimsy of Oddworld Inhabitants has made something almost unheard of in video games: a series in which anything can happen and very often does. In its PlayStation days, Oddworld was known for bringing gorgeous art design to a neglected format (the two-dimensional platform adventure) and finding hope and mirth where none had a right to exist. The game's story tells of the Mudokons, a pitiful race of workers who pack food at the factories of RuptureFarms, blissfully unaware that they're also the main ingredient.

Its universe, which expands and surprises with every game, is worthy of Tolkien or Lucas and yet borrows from neither. *Oddworld: Stranger's Wrath* was a masterpiece no one saw coming. In a corner of Oddworld better suited to spaghetti Westerns than fantasies, a bounty hunter called Stranger rounds up outlaws to save for a mysterious life-saving operation. In the plight of the Grubbs, nearby townsfolk enslaved by a genocidal demon, he finally senses the pay dirt he's been looking for. Stocking up on "live ammo" (actual living creatures fired from his crossbow, each with unique powers), he wanders into an epic battle of action and stealth, never suspecting that his stake amounts to more than just money.

To glance at this lyrical, sun-baked first-person shooter, you'd think it worlds apart from the *Oddworld*s of old. But the signature is there, masterfully hidden in textures, weapons, and attitudes, waiting to prove that cruelty comes in countless disguises. And when it finally emerges, joined by a twist that turns the game on its head, it does so with élan, shaming those that boast of maturity. This title does much to blow off the heads of those clichés and stereotypes specific to this genre. **DH**

Command
RESTRAIN

SWAT 4

Original release date : 2005
Platform : PC
Developer : Irrational Games
Genre : First-Person Shooter

Before going underwater for the critically acclaimed *BioShock*, Irrational Games settled for the underground world of latter-day urban crime. With a title that tells you everything and yet nothing, *SWAT 4* comes closer to emulating real-life law enforcement than any game since *Police Quest*, at least when it comes to the rules of engagement. Each of its missions could be an extract from a movie, from the serial killer arranging sick forensic tableaux to the nightclub full of captive revellers.

Made before shows like *CSI* had turned viscera into a teatime snack, it's an exceptionally bleak episode for the squad-based tactical shooter. More important than the objectives for each mission are the rules for every encounter. Unless it's a matter of life and death, lethal force is prohibited. If a suspect won't comply but keeps their weapon down, shooting them with anything but a Taser or less-lethal weapon incurs a heavy points penalty. The same goes for downing civilians or allowing, by negligence or tactical error, a teammate to be incapacitated.

More than even the US Army–sanctioned *Full Spectrum Warrior*, this is a thinking person's shooter. Every line of the pre-mission 911 call, slot of the load-out screen, and in-game menu option is vitally important. Willing to trade immersion for an extensive series of drop-down contextual menus, *SWAT 4* is more intelligent than recent *Rainbow Six* or *Ghost Recon* games, making the most of the PC's mouse and keyboard control scheme. With right and center mouse clicks invoking the menus, the left is free for the usual first-person shooter gunplay, shots being all too easily fired in haste. Its multiplayer modes, furthermore, include four-man cooperative support for the single-player campaign—a rare feat even now. **DH**

Ninja Gaiden Black

Original release date : 2005
Platform : Xbox
Developer : Team Ninja
Genre : Action / Adventure

Barring a dodgy camera, *Ninja Gaiden* didn't have much wrong with it. That didn't stop Team Ninja from obsessively tinkering with their masterpiece, however, and in *Ninja Gaiden Black* they improved on what many fighting fans already regarded as the greatest fighting game of its generation. Every aspect of the original is tweaked, from enemy checkpoints to Ryu Hayabusu's costume.

There's even room for a scornful new difficulty mode named Ninja Dog, accessible only after many deaths, which sends your warrior into battle with a pink ribbon tied around his arm. For those who reveled in the first game's difficulty, however, here is an even greater challenge. And though *Ninja Gaiden Black* is often criticized for what seems

like an insurmountable learning curve, it's the necessary prelude to one of the most rewarding fighting experiences around. Ryu is simply a joy to control, as responsive and fast as your own thinking, and capable of feats that leave you breathless. The enemies, meanwhile, are relentless warriors in their own right, a single one of whom is quite capable of decimating a player that loses concentration.

It's often said that the *Ninja Gaiden* series is all about the block button, but that is to totally undersell the depth of its combat. *Ninja Gaiden Black* is about blocking, but it's also about positioning, dashing, counterattacking, and refusing to be bullied by superior numbers. It's about waiting for that one lull in a fight when you can burst into a group of enemies and decimate them in a hundred-hit combo. The system rewards time spent with new layers of tactics, new types of enemies that alter your entire approach, and stunning scenes from the best ninja movie never made. *Ninja Gaiden Black* is the video game embodiment of a very basic truth: Sometimes you have to be cruel to be kind. **RS**

Resident Evil 4

Original release date : 2005
Platform : Various
Developer : Capcom
Genre : Survival Horror / Shoot 'Em Up

The codified world of the action game was rocked to its foundations by *Resident Evil 4*. One of the most heavily prototyped modern games, its early variations were so radical that while one stayed true to the fixed cameras of early *Resident Evil*s, another went on to become *Devil May Cry*. Eventually, out of the cauldron would come a game of such marvelous cunning that it swept away any sense of franchise ennui, restoring the series' status as the master of the survival horror genre.

The president's daughter has been kidnapped by a mysterious cult, and US government agent Leon S Kennedy is sent to rural Europe on a rescue mission. Little does he realize that in this neck of the woods, the locals are anything but cooperative. Los Ganados (which in Spanish can mean either "the mob" or "cattle") are an insular bunch who, when they're not driving their pitchforks into piles of hay, drive them through the faces of heretics they then burn in the town square. In the hills behind them, the castle of Ramon Salazar infects its subjects with Las Plagas, a mind-controlling parasite, while harboring the scientists and priests of the sinister Los Illuminados.

With a forced aspect ratio and over-the-shoulder camera, *Resident Evil 4* marks a true turning point in widescreen gaming. But its emphasis on crowd control and unpredictable artifical intelligence takes the survival horror into uncharted territory. Attacking from all sides with sporadic dodges and bursts of speed, eyes burning with parochial hate, Los Ganados and their neighbors are terrifying. Nowhere is safe from their ladders and medieval weapons, and nothing grips the heart like the nearby sound of a chainsaw. *Resident Evil 4* sees Capcom at the height of its powers. **DH**

X³: Reunion

Original release date : 2005
Platform : Various
Developer : Egosoft
Genre : Space Simulation

Before the *X* series, the three Elite games were the only choice for serious space traders. The combination of open-ended economics, combat, and genuine exploration originated by David Braben and Ian Bell had not been built on for a decade, but here, at last, intrepid pilots could venture out into new star systems. *X³: Reunion*, the penultimate game of the series, was perhaps the most revolutionary, ushering in an astonishing universe.

X³: Reunion is very much the *2001: Space Odyssey* to *Wing Commander's Star Wars* though—a somber, often lonely experience that capitalizes on vast scale and the unknown rather than more human struggles. While a mission plot can be followed, it's possible to dip in and out

of it, or even ignore it completely. It's all too easy to spend hours simply exploring the potential of other endeavors, such as space trading, piracy, or becoming hired help to the various galactic civilizations that populate the game. Trading is augmented by the ability to build factories and space stations, even as far as setting up trade routes with your own fleet of automated vessels.

Weighing the hefty manual in one hand should alert anyone to the game's depth, but even the hardiest of space veterans may be put off by the complete lack of tutorial and little direction. However, by plunging the player into a universal sandbox, accompanied only by their wits, Egosoft successfully reinforces the sense that there is real adventure to be had out there beyond the well-policed systems. Some bugs on release (later patched) initially marred the game's critical reception, but it is testament to the unique experience offered that none of the atmosphere was lost—and atmosphere is something you don't want to be short of in the vacuum of space. **BM**

Armadillo Run

Original release date : 2006
Platform : PC
Developer : Peter Stock
Genre : Puzzle

The subgenre of physics puzzle games doesn't boast too many titles that stand up as all time classics, but *Armadillo Run* could be said to be one. Like plenty of other games based around Rube Goldberg–type mechanical sequences, the win conditions are extremely simple: you have to get the rolled-up armadillo ball to the blue portal.

How you do that depends on the meticulous construction of an apparatus, the building of which is constrained by a budget defined by the level you are trying to complete. Working with a tool kit of physics objects, the player must propel the armadillo via a network of ropes, metal bars and sheets, cloth, rubber, elastic, and rockets, each of which has a specific cost within the main campaign game. Unlike previous instances of such games, *Armadillo Run* has a sophisticated three-dimensional physics engine, which makes the movement of the armadillo itself both realistic and predictable.

While the basic game contains some dynamic and beautiful solutions, it's the general level-editing suite that has produced the most spectacular results. Anyone can make their own run using the simple tools, and consequently there are thousands of user-created levels available. Many of these are highly ingenious and are more than enough to keep *Armadillo Run* veterans going once they've completed the core game.

Creative types, keen to show off both their own design skills and the *Armadillo Run* engine, have produced some spectacular contraptions. These can generally be downloaded as additional player levels via the *Armadillo Run* website, but there are plenty of player-created roller-coasters, windmills, and even giant clockwork cog systems to be seen on YouTube, too. Evidence, if any were required, that gamers are highly imaginative creatures. **JR**

Line Rider

Original release date : 2006
Platform : Internet
Developer : Boštjan Cadež
Genre : Action

Is *Line Rider* a game or a toy? Perhaps it doesn't really matter all that much. Whatever niche this particular game slots into, the results are charming and rather excellent fun. Here is a physics playground where the rules, like the scenery, all depend upon your own imagination.

Created by Slovenian university student Boštjan Čadež, *Line Rider* tasks you with drawing a ski slope on a blank page, and then watching carefully as a tiny little tobogganist flings himself energetically down it. The physics are absolutely brilliant. Even before the first ten minutes are up, you'll have put this tiny nobody through some truly vicious collisions.

The real pleasure lies in simply sitting back and watching your assault course come to life, bumping and jarring, and flinging the poor chap off course as he careens unpredictably downhill in a cloud of comic violence.

What happens next in *Line Rider* is entirely up to you. If you want to refine the longest possible run, you're absolutely free to do it. If you'd rather create daredevil spins and loops and twirls, that's perfectly acceptable too. Or possibly, as so many YouTube contributors have done, you want to simply sketch a picture, creating a fantasy landscape of your own or painstakingly copying an old master, before seeing what it does to this poor little man on his battered sledge.

Line Rider gambles that the future of games is all about freedom rather than rules, fun rather than easily defined achievements. Whether it's right or wrong remains to be seen, but with more complex DS and Wii versions failing to hit quite the same sweet spot, the best way to experience this odd little game is still for free on the Internet. And experience this game you must, for its simplicity and elegance hit a sweet spot few can match. **CD**

Mother 3

Original release date : 2006
Platform : Game Boy Advance
Developer : Brownie Brown / HAL Laboratory / Nintendo
Genre : Role-Playing

Mother 3 is perhaps better known for the story surrounding the game and its creator than the game itself. Released only in Japan, it encountered a slew of development problems and was originally slated to be released more than a decade earlier for the Super Nintendo console. A loose sequel to the previous two outings, *Mother* and *Mother 2* (*EarthBound*), it follows a team of characters led by Lucas and Flint in their battles against the Pigmask Army. Much like *Duke Nukem Forever*, the game *Mother 3* floated on in the ether, appearing in advertisements and discussed excitedly online.

Part of the mystique is due in part to the game's writer, Shigesato Itoi. Itoi has worn many hats during his lifetime, his work including voicing a role in Hayao Miyazaki's *My Neighbor Totoro* and co-writing a collection of stories with Postmodern author Haruki Murakami. It was Itoi who gave *Mother 3* its sometimes twisted narrative and flair. For example, one of the settings, Tanehineri Islands, is in fact an evil mirror image of the home of the two main protagonists, Lucas and Flint.

When Nintendo decided to keep the game as a Japan only release, a team of fans embarked on the process of translating it on their own. It was no small task. Like most good role-playing games, *Mother 3* is text heavy, featuring tens of thousands of lines of dialogue. After more than two years of work, a patch containing the final translation was released, a testament to the hard work of translators and their rabid appreciation of the series.

Mother 3 was downloaded more than 100,000 times and, although such a number wouldn't have made it a hit in commercial form, it did bring a great adventure to the attention of players worldwide. This is a delightful return to an old classic and well worth playing. **JBW**

Uno

Original release date : 2006
Platform : Various
Developer : Carbonated Games
Genre : Adaptation

To many gamers around the world, *Uno* was an obscure American card game until one day it turned up on Xbox Live Arcade, and its frantic multiplayer fun quickly saw it become a worldwide classic. Still one of the service's top sellers, there's something timeless about the vibrant delivery and astute control scheme that Carbonated Games brought to the family standard. The rules were so brilliantly poised in the first place that the developer could spend all of its time thinking about implementation.

A color- and number-matching card game that tasks you with getting rid of the hand you're dealt as soon as possible, *Uno*'s already an enjoyably devious time waster. Working within the established framework, Carbonated Games does a number of clever things to further enhance the fun, from ensuring you get a good look at the statistics of the players you're up against, to auto selecting the card it thinks you're most likely to play at the start of each turn. Shifting between your possibilities is slickly done and best of all, unlike the physical version of the game, *Uno* auto organizes all of your pick-ups, which should please the neat freak lurking within you.

And, as with the card game, *Uno*'s capacity for lavish viciousness is undimmed on Xbox Live Arcade, with the ability to skip, reverse, and land almighty pick-ups on whomever seems to be inching toward victory the quickest.

With a real potential for group victimization and all the fiddly things, like sorting decks and totting up high scores, handled by the computer, Carbonated Games's winner really does feel like the future of a nice game of cards. Since it is always lurking right there on your Xbox 360's dashboard, it's never more than a few clicks away from your TV screen. *Uno* is a light and entertaining game that's compulsive, addictive and, most of all, fun. **CD**

Gears of War

Original release date : 2006
Platform : Xbox 360
Developer : Epic Games
Genre : Shoot 'Em Up

The tight-knit family at North Carolina's Epic Games delivers blockbuster games while powering dozens more with its Unreal technology. But it wasn't until *Gears of War* that its design credentials and its ability to steer a genre rather than pander to it really started to shine. After just two games, this testosterone-driven alien-invasion saga has sold more than 10 million copies.

The invaders of *Gears of War* come not from above but below. The Locust Horde, a subterranean colony of bloodthirsty reptiles, decides to breach the surface of planet Sera and take it for its own. This Emergence Day sees the near annihilation of humankind, the last remnants of government and resistance forming COG, an army that resembles a bunch of American footballers playing *Laser Quest*. Led by Marcus Fenix, a battle-hardened ex-convict, a squad of COG soldiers has to infiltrate the Locust home world, the Hollows, and use an experimental bomb to remove the threat once and for all. That's the plan, anyway.

Gears of War is heavily inspired by *Resident Evil 4*, adopting its over-the-shoulder camera view, Baroque set design, and fascination with gory chainsaw kills. Being a fast and furious action game, though, it adds a point-to-point cover system that makes siege resistance and flanking its primary modes of combat. The most prominent face button on the Xbox 360 controller is devoted to it, snapping players to cover if it's close, triggering a Hollywood style "roadie run" if it's not, and mantling over if it's in the way.

Fashionable as it is to credit older games like *Kill Switch* and *Operation Winback* for the blueprints, this game's implementation, along with its dedication to cooperative multiplayer, set the standard for this particular brand of third-person action gaming. **DH**

Black

Original release date : 2006
Platform : Various
Developer : Criterion Games
Genre : First-Person Shooter

Black's curt title seems to speak of careful restraint, an assumption that would be entirely misleading. *Black* has focus, yes, but there's not much holding it back, and once the game kicks off, it's nonstop chaos until the very last clip has been emptied.

Criterion Games had already turned racing titles into exaggerated high-speed explosion carnivals with the deliriously enjoyable *Burnout* series, and *Black* is clearly an attempt to do the same for the first-person shooter. And you know what? It's a successful attempt. Set in Chechnya and viewed through the eyes of a slightly nutty Black Operations specialist, Criterion's blaster does have some semblance of a plot, but its real story—and the

narrative that drives its tight handful of missions to their crazy combustible conclusions—is the story of a man's love for his guns. These are the kind of guns that rip the environment apart, that send enemies ragdolling into the distance; guns that are lovingly detailed and take up a great deal of the player's vision; guns that, quite simply, are a joy to fire again and again.

Stealing the two-weapon-slot maximum from the *Halo* series, you'll have to think carefully about which of your beloved guns to take with you into battle, but in all honesty, there's not really a bad one in the bunch.

If you like shooting things—or if you just find yourself in a bad mood—*Black* is the only game you can depend upon 100 percent of the time. It's guaranteed to ease your mood after several hours of hardcore fighting, or cheer you up as you blast your way across the various levels. Play it through to completion to unlock the infinite grenade mode while you're at it. This game is yet another combustible delight you won't regret discovering. **CD**

Prey

Original release date : 2006
Platform : Various
Developer : Human Head Studios
Genre : Shoot 'Em Up

Eleven years in the making, *Prey* is one of the most notorious residents of game development hell, eclipsed only by its fellow 3D Realms project, *Duke Nukem Forever*. Finally released in 2006, it was originally pitched as an *Unreal* style showcase for its developer's in-house technology. *Prey* fell into a vicious cycle of announcing a release date, wowing audiences at industry events, collapsing under its own ambition, and resurfacing months later with new unobtainable goals. Finally the game was muscled onto shelves by the combined force of a new developer, Human Head Studios, publisher 2K Games, and direct supervision from 3D Realms.

All things considered, the finished *Prey* is surprisingly close to the original vision. Its hero is Tommy Tawodi (introduced in 1997 as Talon Brave), a Native American plucked from his reservation by a visiting alien spaceship, the Sphere. Like a giant gristmill, this organic leviathan is chewing up everything from flesh and bone to cars and houses, and isn't leaving until it's polished off the Earth. With girlfriend Jen and grandpa Enisi next on the menu, Tommy must side with a group of rebels to destroy it from within. Helping him on his way are the ghost of his pet hawk, Talon; his spiritual ancestors; and the bizarre portals scattered about the ship.

Much the game's backbone through the years, these holes in time and space are what sets it apart today. Embedded into more traditional levels than those of Valve's *Portal*, the portals conspire with a series of gravity switches to throw the whole game off its axis. As you hunt down exotic weapons and hideous foes, you never quite know if you're up, down, inside, or out. One of the few games built using *Doom 3* technology, it's the corridor shooter given a massive twist—literally. **DH**

ArmA: Armed Assault

Original release date : 2006

Platform : PC

Developer : Bohemia Interactive Studios

Genre : Strategy / Shoot 'Em Up

The journey of the Czech studio behind *ArmA*, Bohemia Interactive, has been fascinating to watch. Following initial commercial success in its partnership with Codemasters, for *Operation Flashpoint*, the studio subsequently decided to go it alone and went on to produce a controversial modern combat simulator, *ArmA: Armed Assault*.

Here, Bohemia had created a game that was as close to a genuine military simulator as a commercial game could be (and it was adapted as a military simulation, *Virtual Battlespace 2*, for the Australian Defence Force), while still containing a full-blown single-player campaign and support for online play. The game is both inaccessible and complex, yet it nevertheless maintains an intense popularity.

Ludicrously ambitious on both technical and game design fronts, *ArmA: Armed Assault* is one of the most forbidding combat experiences in gaming. Like *Operation Flashpoint* before it, the game relies on the community that surrounds it for much of its appeal. The modifying and content creation of the gaming community are largely what completes this game, and it is best approached with a view to spending some time experimenting on the latest version.

There are modifications for changing almost every variable that isn't dealt with directly within the game, and players have created thousands of scenarios using its powerful editing suite. Few people truly find what they're looking for in the vanilla single-player aspect of the game, and it's generally the multiplayer, user-created content—including highly complex multiplayer missions and campaigns, both competitive and cooperative—that bring life to the proceedings. Outmoded in some ways by its sequel, *ArmA 2*, this is nevertheless a design classic from a highly focused studio. **JR**

Company of Heroes

Original release date : 2006
Platform : PC
Developer : Relic Entertainment
Genre : Strategy

Prior to *Company of Heroes*, the role of the real-time strategy general was basically guilt free. You dug up some rocks, refined them into little squads of action men with macho catchphrases, and scoffed as they lost a hand-to-hand fight with a flamethrower tank. Then you tweaked your tactics and sent in the next round of volunteers. This game, with its brutal accounts of key battles in World War II Europe, is rather different.

Its trick is quite straightforward: It tries really, really hard to be HBO's *Band of Brothers*. So does *Medal of Honor: Airborne*, a first-person shooter you'd expect to bring you closer to life on the frontlines, but doesn't. Because as much as *Band of Brothers* is about people taking potshots at the

Nazis, it's more about the agony of choice. One foxhole over another during a mortar attack; the value of an objective next to the price of a dozen men; the need to press on versus a chance to save a stranded soldier. This is the action in HBO's series, and it is reflected here in *Company of Heroes* by Relic Entertainment.

The consequences are brought vividly to life by the Essence Engine, built from scratch by Relic to deliver top-down action with all the detail and special effects of a triple-A action game. Equally important is the use of Havok's physics engine to depict flying limbs, walls crushed by advancing tanks, billowing smoke, and the rushing debris of obliterated buildings.

It's thanks to these that you're captivated by the sight of a unit under fire, soldiers pinned by bullets and the pieces of their friends, begging for rescue. There are said to be almost 2,000 animations for a basic infantry unit alone in this impressive title, making it a definitive choice for anyone with a penchant for real-time strategy gaming. **DH**

Takase

Bully

Original release date : 2006
Platform : PS2
Developer : Rockstar
Genre : Action / Adventure

Inspired by the likes of ZX Spectrum game *Skool Daze*, *Bully* took its name from the fictional Bullsworth Academy where the action takes place, though it was given the less-controversial title *Canis Canem Edit* outside of the US—which actually gave a more accurate hint of the game's content. For all Rockstar's moral majority baiting attitude, this is a game that is, in many ways, a principled tale. Sure, there's more beating to a pulp than sermonizing from the pulpit, but this is a game that encourages players to stand up to the bullies, whoever they are.

You can mess about in lessons thanks to a raft of mini-games which encapsulate everything from art class to darts, while outside of lessons the action is similar to *Bully*'s bigger brothers. This is all the freeform mayhem that we have come to expect from Rockstar, except set in the playground. Would-be playground daddies have to negotiate the tricky challenges of romance and the social bear pit of the school corridors, and forge alliances with the different factions in the game, such as the Nerds, the Greasers, and the Jocks. *Bully* is far from child's play. **DM**

Yakuza 2

Original release date : 2006
Platform : PS2
Developer : Amusement Vision
Genre : Action / Adventure

A law unto itself, *Yakuza 2* sees producer Toshiro Nagoshi's crime saga at its finest. You'll have to endure a truckload of cut scenes, but the fighting system and deep diversions make *Yakuza 2* more than worth the investment.

A mix of hard-boiled posturing, daft twists, and some memorable characters, *Yakuza 2*'s story is helped immeasurably by its subtitles. It takes our man Kiryuu from convenience stores to the top of skyscrapers, and is always moved along by a scrap. Kiryuu's a responsive and brutal fighter, capable of taking out multiple foes in smooth combinations and getting down and dirty with the business end of a road sign, but it takes a while for your opponents to prove worthy of a flexible approach.

Alongside this are countless distractions, ranging from amusement arcades to a simple game of mahjong. It's that type of game, where even the tiniest details play off against something else, where exploring will always reward you, and where becoming immersed is a condition of play, rather than an option. Organized crime has rarely been imagined, or realized, so beautifully. **RS**

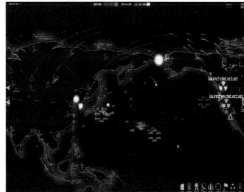

Dead Rising

DEFCON

Original release date : 2006
Platform : Xbox 360
Developer : Capcom
Genre : Survival Horror / Action

Original release date : 2006
Platform : PC
Developer : Introversion Software
Genre : Strategy

In February 2008, a complaint was filed in the US District Court by Richard Rubinstein, rights owner and producer of George A. Romero's *Dawn of the Dead*. The latest salvo in a long-running copyright spat, it drew several comparisons with the accused, Capcom zombie game *Dead Rising*.

Shortly before the case was thrown out by a magistrate, it was also noted that in both works, "many of the zombies wear plaid shirts." As well as being a howling rip-off, *Dead Rising* is a fusion of ruthless fights, a restrictive save system, and meticulous attention to character and detail. Its hero, photojournalist Frank West, stumbles when he jumps, says the wrong things at the wrong times, and isn't quite as good as advertised when it comes to saving others.

The atrocious artifical intelligence of the people he escorts is by far the game's biggest flaw, and with just a single save slot, underestimating the distance to a waypoint can irreparably harm your progress. However, with a zombie population that ranks among the greatest technical achievements ever in games, it is absolutely *Dawn of the Dead*, and then some. **DH**

Inspired by both the nuclear nightmares of the 1980s and the corny Matthew Broderick flick *WarGames*, this casual real-time strategy game treats the memory of the Cold War with both dread and kitsch.

The ambient soundtrack and the clinical war room–styled, wire-frame graphics instill a brooding atmosphere, and yet the game's simplifications duck any real world conflicts. The world is chopped up neatly into six simple regions that start on an equal footing. So China, Japan, and the rest of Asia work together as one block while the whole of Latin America stands just as well armed on the other side of the Pacific. As far as strategy goes, shooting down a nuke is easy, if your defenses are still up.

Other features of the game are all too believable. Private chats allow players to form alliances, but since only an individual can win the game, alliances break easily. And once a nation's defenses are wrecked, you'll want to keep pounding them for a higher number of megakills. Whether the experience is hilarious or horrifying depends on your attitude, and the people you consider your friends. **CDa**

Eets: Hunger. It's Emotional

Original release date : 2006
Platform : PSP
Publisher : Klei Entertainment
Genre : Puzzle

Like *The Incredible Machine* and *Lemmings* before it, *Eets: Hunger. It's Emotional* challenges players to lead a helpless creature to some goal using various tricks and gizmos to point him along the way. How do you motivate Eets, a cartoonish dog thing with a blank stare and a savage jaw?

Obviously, with food. Pelting him with chocolate chips makes him angry and more likely to jump from ledge to ledge, while tranquilizing him with a big marshmallow makes him timid and keeps him in place. He's also scared of the dark and prone to getting shot through the air by whales. He's riddled with other quirks that give you new ways to control him, but indirectly, and only through the most ingenious Rube Goldberg-esque setups. Relentlessly

cute, *Eets: Hunger. It's Emotional* puts a friendly face on a rigorous series of puzzles. Across a hundred levels—more if you count the user-made ones—the title steadily hands you new tools and new challenges, from glowing ginseng to a pig that shoots another flying pig from its backside.

In fact, skip to the editor, and you'll see a daunting set of options, each with a different purpose and a goofy illustration. But the levels introduce these options at a gradual pace, training you on how to get the most from each one, and then running you through easy and hard maps to test what you've learned.

Some of your best tricks have to be triggered in real time, and most of the puzzles have more than one solution to encourage creative thinking. The Xbox version, *Eets: Chowdown,* also adds new scoring opportunities and an action mode. Silly at first glance, *Eets: Hunger. It's Emotional* offers impressive depth for what looks like a lighthearted game. The brisk humor, the deranged action, and the silly food gags are just frosting. **CDa**

Elebits

Original release date : 2006
Platform : Wii
Developer : Konami
Genre : Action / Shoot 'Em Up

Motion controls? Check. Family friendly? Check. Easy to pick up, difficult to put down? Check. As one of the earliest third party Wii games, *Elebits* is also one of the first to lay out the blueprint for what makes a good Wii game. It doesn't try to compete with better-looking, faster-paced games on competing systems. In its own gentle way, *Elebits* stakes out territory all its own.

Picture a hide-and-seek game on steroids, and you've got *Elebits*. In the game world, alien creatures named Elebits are responsible for generating all the world's electricity, which is a fine arrangement until they revolt and the power goes out. Playing as a plucky young boy named Kai, your task is to recover the Elebits and restore power.

You won't travel far as levels only span from your house to your neighborhood, to a bland city center. All along the way, you'll need to find and retrieve Elebits, and you'll find them hiding in the darndest places.

The primary play mechanic is Kai's capture gun, a gravity beam that allows him to pick up and move objects, open doors, and ensnare Elebits. Some of the motion controls are gratuitous (is it really necessary to have to grab a doorknob, turn it, and open the door? Hitting one button used to work just fine for this), but the basic mechanic of digging through everyday environments to find hidden Elebits is a blast. They hide in boxes, in Dumpsters, in microwaves, and in other such delightful places.

Kai can pick up and fling objects with the capture gun, bouncing them off of each other in unpredictable ways. Each time Kai finds more creatures, nearby electrical appliances start to turn on, providing a real sense of progress. Add a multiplayer mode and a map editor, and you've got a first-generation gem of a Wii game. **MK**

Elite Beat Agents

Original release date : 2006
Platform : DS
Developer : iNiS
Genre : Music

Elite Beat Agents is one of the very few video games that simulates the experience of cheerleading. But don't get the wrong idea. In the West, cheerleaders are women who wear rah-rah skirts and wave pom-poms, performing impossibly elaborate dance routines to inspire overpaid sportsmen to play better. In Japan, cheerleaders, or *ouendan*, are men and women who provide motivational chants for every occasion, from year-end drinking parties to important sporting occasions. In this game's Japanese predecessor, *Osu! Tatakae! Ouendan!*, they are a sharp-suited team of spiky-haired men who turn up in times of trouble to inspire regular folk to overcome the everyday problems of ordinary life by means of one of the most inventive rhythm-action games of recent years. On their way to the West, however, they transmogrified into the *Elite Beat Agents*, a secretive government rhythm operations unit, out to save the world from despondency and upset.

The game's excellently absurd storylines incorporate everything from assisting babysitters to fighting giant robots. The climax sees the agents defending Earth against music-hating aliens, but the high point is rather more somber in tone, with the agents singing a cover of Chicago's soft rock love crooner, "You're the Inspiration," in order to reassure a grieving daughter. Other songs include "Sk8er Boi," "I Was Born To Love You," and "Canned Heat," each punctuated by cut scenes and accompanied by game mechanics evolved from iNiS's *Gitaroo Man*, requiring the player to tap the screen at the right time, spinning circles and tracing lines that follow the flow of the music.

In the unlikely event that music-hating aliens ever do invade Earth, just flash them a copy of *Elite Beat Agents*. If the best rhythm-action game in recent years isn't enough to fend them off, there's no hope for the human race. **DM**

Tomb Raider Legend

Original release date : 2006
Platform : Xbox 360
Developer : Crystal Dynamics
Genre : Action / Adventure

It's a feistier, more natural Lara Croft that swans into a Tokyo penthouse in *Tomb Raider Legend*, hobbling about in a dress until guns are drawn, at which point the bar gets jumped, the seams get ripped, and the holsters are revealed. The ensuing chase involves monkey swings between flagpoles high above the streets, a rooftop jump on a Ducati Superbike 999, falling scaffolding, laser fences, guard dogs, assault rifles, and a helicopter rescue.

If it sounds a lot like an American's idea of what *Tomb Raider* should be, that's because it is. What's more, that's exactly what it had to be. Britishness, a word best reserved for walnut dashboards in classic cars, was the last thing needed after the troubled James Bond-influenced installment, *The Angel of Darkness*. Clunky controls, sluggish combat, poor performance, and bugs aplenty, the series was left horribly out of step with games like *Prince of Persia: The Sands of Time*. So Eidos turned to San Francisco's Crystal Dynamics, famed for its progressive *Legacy of Kain* series, to start things over from scratch.

Opening with a flashback to the death of Lara's mother in a Himalayan temple, *Tomb Raider Legend* is an exhibitionist. It wants to show how much it's improved. When it isn't doing its action movie routine, it's parting a giant waterfall to reveal a Ghanaian temple, breaching a research facility run by the KGB, and having gunfights amid tumbleweed against Peruvian mercenaries.

Best of all is its Croft Manor standalone mission, a day-in-the-life treasure hunt that sees Lara raiding her own home, busting open walls to find secret passages before hitting the gym for some time trials. With moves you can finally do by instinct, rather than trial and error, it's an adventure that even Crystal's own sequel, *Tomb Raider Underworld*, would have a hard time keeping up with. **DH**

Exit 2

Original release date : 2006
Platform : PSP
Developer : Taito
Genre : Puzzle / Action

The definition of a hero is, for video games, relatively straightforward: someone who kills lots of things. Mr. ESC of *Exit 2* is a little different. He's a one-man emergency service, dashing through burning buildings, guiding children to exits, saving people from their own wanderings, and carrying the wounded out on his shoulders before disappearing with a flourish.

At once stylish and understated, *Exit 2*'s levels are two-dimensional environments with puzzles constructed from fires, blocks, and the victims themselves. The little people are scattered around. Some are brawny adults, some have broken legs, some are children trapped in corners and abandoned. They all follow you like lemmings, and they're

also a little like the creatures in *Lemmings*—each class of person has their own ability. The levels are thus split between Mr. ESC's own exertions and encouraging people to use their own abilities. All of this happens under severe time pressure that, when exceeded, causes Mr. ESC's flashy comic book adversary to rescue the situation.

The improvement over the original *Exit* is entirely in the new types of civilian, and in how their abilities allow the puzzle template to be varied. It's also a game that enjoys symmetry, many of its levels built to operate like clockwork, springing open with just the right sequence of moves. This is also one of the reasons that the game can also frustrate, as several restarts on the tougher stages are inevitable.

Exit 2's puzzles are often impenetrable to begin with, the sliding objects and order to solutions literally obscured by the surrounding disaster. This is why, when you've worked them out and whisked everyone to safety, dashing out through the door last with a doff of the hat, you don't just feel like a cog in the machine—you're a hero. **RS**

Earth Defense Force 2017

Original release date : 2006
Platform : Xbox 360
Developer : Sandlot
Genre : Shoot 'Em Up

Earth Defense Force 2017 disregards almost every expectation of how a contemporary video game should look and behave. Its plot could be mapped on a matchbox: giant insects are invading Earth, stop them with guns. Its visuals have a sort of proto-Godzilla charm, with Tokyo streets that crumple like flat-packed furniture at the mere suggestion of a missile, and hulking great ants and spiders that catapult around the game world like rubber balls when they are killed.

Add to this a grinding frame rate, no-frills mechanics, and meager extras, and you've a slender proposition. But while the rest of the world was trying to make their games as realistic as possible, developer Sandlot was happy to focus on what would make their game deliciously insane. The result is one of the medium's rough diamonds. You assume the role of one of the titular soldiers, sent to face off against an almost endless stream of huge insects, silver UFOs, and mirror-surfaced bipedal robots.

You take just two weapons into battle with you, and while they never run out of ammunition, once chosen they can't be changed. Enemies drop new, more powerful weapons, as well as small health packs that incrementally upgrade your soldier's health one hit point at a time. As such, the game's scenario is preposterous. Not in the sense of fantasizing about alien invasion, but in suggesting that the world's governments would send you to face it.

It's in this context of overwhelmingly stacked odds that the game flourishes, bringing to the fore all of the reasons why we love to play games. Liberally firing homing missiles toward 20-feet ants atop 250-feet skyscrapers in downtown Tokyo is a rare thrill and one that never grows old before the war of the worlds is won. **SP**

Fight Night Round 3

Original release date : 2006
Platform : Xbox 360
Developer : Electronic Arts
Genre : Fighting

Fight Night Round 3 seemed a distant prospect in 2005, until 8 p.m. on January 4, 2006, when Microsoft sparring partners Bill Gates and Steve Ballmer not only played the game live at the Consumer Electronics Show, but delivered it moments later to living rooms around the world.

This was high-definition gaming delivered with broadband efficiency, playable not from the desktop PC but the sofa. Textures for Electronic Arts's game had been snapped from pre- and post-fight dressing rooms, capturing everything from eyes swelling shut to open pores and wounds. Animation was motion captured, venues were intricately copied, and behavior was based on the realities of the sweet science—Ali's rope-a-dope,

Winky Wright's peek-a-boo, bobbing, weaving, orthodox, and southpaw. Movement was controlled by the same Total Punch Control system as in the excellent *Round Two*, thumbsticks used to make hooks and jabs as natural as throwing real-life fists. And then the sucker punch—advisors brought in from the *Matrix* movies to give every knockout a bone-crunching, toe-curling clout. To many, though, this last point is the game's undoing.

In a career mode dogged by product placement, the dominance of the flash knockout can make entire bouts feel like highlight reels, fighters hitting the canvas moments from the opening bell. And while an impression of health can be gained from puffed cheeks and dropping gloves, the promise of "HUDless" play isn't quite upheld. A flawed stamina system requires close scrutiny, and it isn't long before the optional health bars become essential. A more restrained sequel, *Fight Night Round 4*, remedies these problems by hanging back, calming down, and focusing on the essentials. **DH**

Rockstar Presents Table Tennis

Original release date : 2006
Platform : Various
Developer : Rockstar
Genre : Sports

Your eyes aren't deceiving you. *Rockstar Presents Table Tennis* is the game of Ping-Pong, from the guys who brought you *Grand Theft Auto* and *Manhunt*. Given that, what's most surprising about the game is how faithful it is to the sport. This isn't extreme table tennis. Competitors don't do backflips. At the end of a victorious match, you are not even given the option to execute your opponent. No, this is a rigorous and exacting sports simulation.

The inputs are simple. Your character will hit the ball automatically, presuming he can reach it in time. Your job is to aim the direction of your shot while putting spin on it to direct the angle of its bounce. You can also toggle a soft lob instead of the default smash. That's it. But from this

basic move set emerges a game of surprising complexity. The ball swiftly changes in its direction and speed, with endless variation. Whether against the computer or a live opponent, the key to victory is to change things up, which means adjusting your tactics with each shot.

The game's only theatricality comes when a rally starts to build. The ball glows with its increased speed, and underlying techno music pumps faster and louder. It all builds so gradually that you may not realize how tense you've become until the rally ends and you sink six inches into your chair.

The original Xbox 360 version of *Rockstar Presents Table Tennis* works suitably with the dual-analog control pad, and features online connectivity so an opponent is never far away. The Wii version is easier to pick up and play thanks to more intuitive motion controls, but actually provides less precise ball handling, and no online features. Still, whichever one you choose, you'll find it's fantastic. Just try not to forget to breathe. **MK**

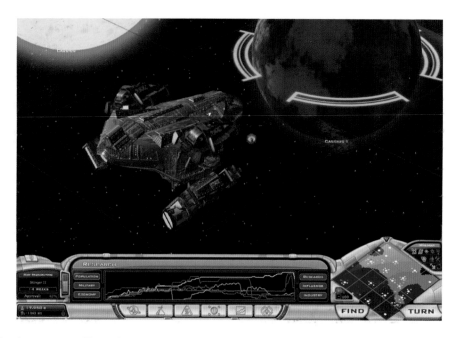

Galactic Civilizations II: Dread Lords

Original release date : 2006
Platform : PC
Developer : Stardock
Genre : Strategy

As the 2000s drew to a close, Stardock had positioned itself as the most outspoken developer/publisher in the PC gaming community, arguing that piracy is simply a nonissue, and that more restrictive controls by publishers only succeed in alienating customers. The best defense against piracy, Stardock suggested, lay in improving levels of service and simply making games that are of limited interest to pirates. Strategy games, for example.

It was Galactic Civilizations II: Dread Lords that laid out the company's intention, which was cemented with the publishing of 2009's Sins of a Solar Empire. Galactic Civilizations II: Dread Lords is a space empire game in the subgenre known as 4X—shorthand for "explore, expand,

exploit, and exterminate." Stardock considers game design as engineering, not art. As such, there's no shame in taking direct inspiration from genre classics like Ascendancy and Masters of Orion, and then developing these themes into something that is preferable to play today.

Putting aside the highly amusing ability to piece together your own ships using impractical designs, the standout feature in Galactic Civilizations II: Dread Lords is its artificial intelligence. This stands head and shoulders above that of most games, and in accordance with Stardock's philosophy was improved considerably after release.

How much the game improved following its excellent launch is best illustrated in the second expansion pack, Twilight of the Arnor. Here, each of the in-game species is given an individual techology tree that, at a stroke, turns the genre staple task of researching better equipment into an actual narrative device. This shows how each of the species differs fundamentally at an intellectual level. Such touches are marks of an inspired production. **KG**

Disgaea 2: Cursed Memories

Original release date : 2006

Platform : Various

Developer : Nippon Ichi

Genre : Role-Playing

Was creating a sequel to *Disgaea*, a tactical role-playing game (RPG) with a final level cap so high that you could just about slog away at it forever without reaching it, really necessary? While some of the game's later maps and battlefields were so ripe with strategic possibilities you could replay certain fights indefinitely, the game didn't scream out for a sequel.

Disgaea 2: Cursed Memories certainly belongs to the "more of the same" school of sequel design, but when the result is so polished, chirpy, and likable, it's hard to be too upset about it. It's hard to do anything, in fact, except prepare yourself for getting sucked back into the heady brew, and commence plugging away at the leveling all

over again. Having gotten to know the whims and foibles of a handful of Netherworld inhabitants over the course of the first game, an epic adventure quickly kicks off as a gaggle of adorable heroes race to break a powerful spell that is turning the population into demons.

What this translates into is another series of isometric fights crisscrossing a rich fantasy world, where the character design and insane battle effects conspire to create one of the most characterful experiences available on any platform. The item world has been expanded significantly, and the maps are even more devious than before, but, essentially, there's very little here at all to put off fans of the original game.

Like the first game, *Disgaea 2: Cursed Memories* has been ported to handheld platforms, turning up on Sony's PSP with the new title *Disgaea 2: Dark Hero*. It's a very playable incarnation of the original, but hardcore fans might want to track down the original PlayStation 2 release, which comes with a soundtrack CD. **CD**

Art Style: Orbient

Original release date : 2006
Platform : Various
Developer : Skip Ltd
Genre : Puzzle

Nintendo has always been a master of misdirection, and one of its greatest strokes is the *Art Style* series, developed almost entirely by Skip Ltd. In an industry overanxious about cultural legitimacy, from any other developer those two little words would signify excess with painterly visuals, complex systems, and purple passages pregnant with meaning. For Nintendo, they mean simplicity of concept and execution, with no baggage.

Art Style: Orbient is the exemplar of this: a sparse solar system, the visual style lifted straight from children's astronomy textbooks, and one planetoid moving through it. You don't control your planet directly, but can either attract it toward or repel it from other planets, the aim being to absorb smaller chunks and increase your size.

When you're small, you can enter orbit around bigger planets, and when you're big, you can pull smaller planets into your own orbit. When in an orbit, your planet's movement is locked, and you can choose when to slingshot it outward in another direction. The levels are built around the simple principle of moving backward and forward within the same setup, hoovering up different sizes of object at different times to make the final layout.

Two buttons and a basic understanding of physics are your only contributions to this system. But it's a core around which ever more elaborate structures of planets and asteroids are created, with the delicate synths and piano layering as more bodies begin to orbit you. Soon, your influence is sending that little circle pinwheeling from orbit to orbit with nary a pause, a Galactus on a relentless course in a universe changed beyond recognition. A shifting planetarium under your control, and a simple system that depends on little more than nudging in the right place, *Art Style: Orbient* is a bewitching creation. **RS**

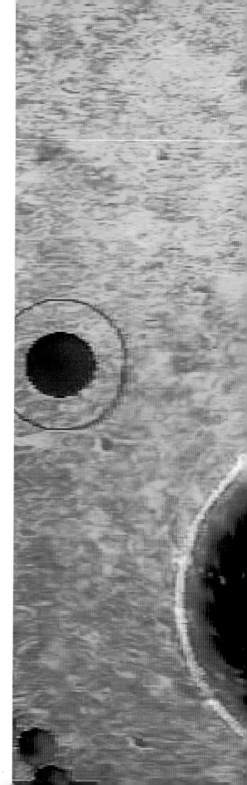

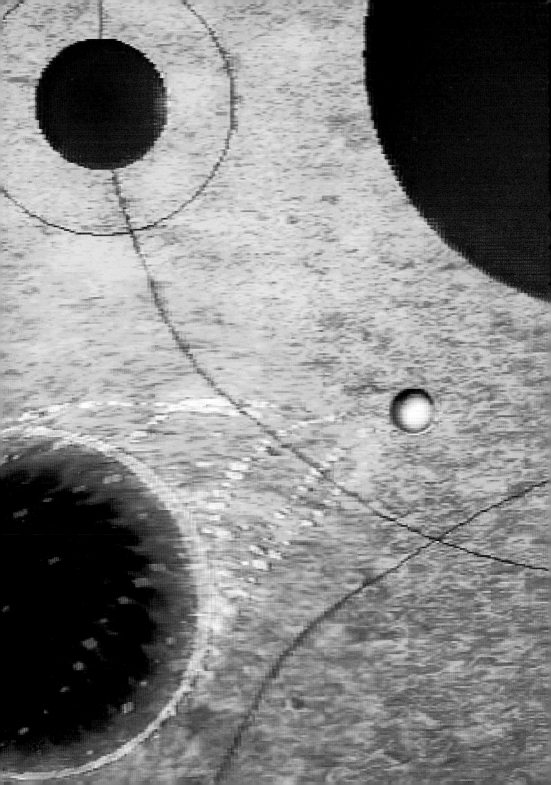

Final Fantasy XII

Original release date : 2006
Platform : PS2
Developer : Square Enix
Genre : Role-Playing

In *Final Fantasy XII*, Square Enix decided to update and redefine almost every central tenet of the template its designers helped established twenty years earlier. This game is still a sprawling epic, complete with a cast of hundreds—a huge game world to explore and thousands of monsters to defeat—but here turn-based random battles are discarded for free-flowing fights. You act more like a team manager than an active combatant during battles, thanks to the Gambit system, which allows hundreds of artificial intelligence directions to automatically set the behavior of your team.

Rather than following the series' familiar narrative trajectory, *Final Fantasy XII*'s plot focuses on grand political machinations. The game world is infused with European influence, every city given its own character and theme.

Fans were left a little disillusioned by its change of personality, while the series' critics just weren't interested enough. It's a shame that the relative commercial failure of such a large experiment seems likely to discourage such interesting innovation in the series' future. **SP**

Okami

Original release date : 2006
Platform : Various
Developer : Clover Studios
Genre : Action / Adventure

Okami is a more elaborate adventure than any Capcom had made before. The story of sun god Amaterasu, who assumes the form of a white wolf, *Okami*, developed by Capcom's off-shoot Clover Studios, sends the player on a magical quest to purify a cursed land. Playing out in a linear progression of quests, rife with regular opportunities for leveling up, *Okami* has an obvious debt to Nintendo's classic action role-playing game, *The Legend of Zelda*.

At the heart of the game is the Celestial Brush, a mechanic that allows players to pause proceedings and draw directly onto the game world, attacking enemies or altering the environment by drawing bridges or blowing obstacles about. It's a magical technique that gives *Okami* a welcome sense of its own identity.

Released just prior to Nintendo's *Zelda* follow-up, *The Legend of Zelda: Twilight Princess*, there are many who would argue *Okami* is actually the better title. It's certainly prettier, with its washed-out landscapes and parchment worlds. *Okami* was eventually ported to the Wii, where it's probably easiest to track down today. **CD**

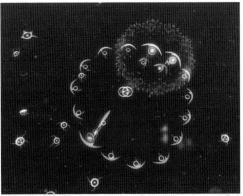

God Hand

Original release date : 2006
Platform : PS2
Developer : Clover Studios
Genre : Fighting

God Hand aims to be the best game ever made about kicking someone so hard that they fly into space. Gene, the hero of the piece, had his arm chopped off, but luckily it was replaced with the titular limb. It glows yellow and is capable of beating up everything in the cosmos.

God Hand certainly gets the humor right, from its midget Power Rangers to a fat hombre named Elvis who fights to remixes of the King. It's the intricate and evolving abilities of Gene that elevate this to the ranks of the great. Combinations are assigned to a single button, which you press multiple times to use, and any attack can be mapped to two farther buttons. This makes the fighting system easy to access while still allowing huge flexibility, but tallies with Gene's swift dodging abilities to make him untouchable.

This is a difficult game, but it's jammed with different ways to fight, many playful distractions, and a soundtrack that has yet to be bettered in terms of capturing the sweet thrill of comic violence. *God Hand*'s an offbeat ode to the joy of hitting things hard and repeatedly, and it's a brilliantly crafted one. **RS**

Flow

Original release date : 2006
Platform : Various
Developer : J. Chen, N. Clark, A. Wintory
Genre : Life Simulation

Flow is exceeding sensual. Part of this is due to the way the game plays with the tilt and sway of the motion sensitive PlayStation 3 controller. The remaining traits have been with the experience since it was born as a free Flash game.

Playing *Flow* is like returning to the amniotic fluid of pre-birth. Your surroundings swim with motes, single-celled creatures, and blue and red coded organisms which act as gateways from one plane of the liquid world to the next. Players take the shape of a microscopic organism, a living work in progress. The rest is all swerve and swim. Eat or be eaten. Every cell and flagellating life-form munched adds another tendril or feeler to the player's creature, new segments sprouting forth as it lengthens and grows.

Once everything's eaten, you dive deeper to find creatures like yourself that must be dueled first, weakened, then consumed. These encounters aren't the fights familiar to everyday gaming. They're micro boss battles, hiccups in a steady downward swim. And at the black bottom of *Flow* there's no princess or prize, just the chance to be reborn and take the dive again. **GM**

GTR 2

Original release date : 2006

Platform : PC

Developer : Simbin

Genre : Racing

Subtitled "FIA GT Racing Game," *GTR 2* proves definitively that simulation doesn't necessarily have to equal sterility. Not only is *GTR 2* still one of the most realistic recreations of the interaction between car and asphalt, it's also a glorious, noisy, petrol-soaked spectacle.

At least some of the credit has to go to the astonishing soundtrack. From the rich distant thunder of an idling TVR to the distinctive wail of a redlining V12 Ferrari, never has a squeeze of the throttle felt more potent, or more of an invitation. On track, SimBin's undisputed mastery of four-wheeled physics results in one of the most layered and detailed handling models ever produced. Even beyond what can be felt through the controller, there is an astonishing array of variables being considered behind the scenes, calculating things as seemingly trivial as the liquid fuel shifting inside the tank. *GTR 2* also sees the refinement of Live Track technology (now a standard concept in heavyweight simulations), the surface and grip level changing, depending on where player and opposition cars lay down rubber. The technology is most noticeable during the stunning wet weather events, as a drying line visibly materializes as the race wears on.

It might seem like overkill, but for players who genuinely want to test their abilities in a race-prepared GT car, this pedantry is both a reason to persevere and a reassuring validation of the results they achieve. Combine that with desirable models, such as Ferraris and Porsches, and some of the most popular circuits from around the globe, and this becomes something approaching racing game nirvana. As a result, while it might not be as well known as *Gran Turismo* or *Forza*, it's an essential addition to any racing fan's collection. **MCh**

Guitar Hero II

Original release date : 2006
Platform : Various
Developer : Harmonix
Genre : Music

Guitar Hero is ubiquitous now, but the delight that developer Harmonix showed in the creation of this sequel suggests that its success wasn't foretold by its makers. Guitar Hero did many things for the medium, but by far the most important was that it slapped the music industry out of its stupor and demanded that it began to pay serious attention to music games.

Guitar Hero II still included songs introduced by those little words "inspired by," indicating a track was being mimicked by a session group, but there were far more original recordings. Its wild success enabled a future where the Beatles would have their own game. This is the best of the Guitar Hero games, because it's the last one you felt was made by people who cared about good music. Harmonix is a developer composed of musicians, many of whom play in bands, and so Guitar Hero II finds room alongside the hits to push unknown gems onto the player.

It's a quality lost in subsequent entries. This game is about rocking out to songs you know, yes, but it's also about finding awesome new ones. Few players had heard of Drist, Megasus, or the wonderfully named Honest Bob and the Factory-to-Dealer Incentives, but everyone was glad they were in there. Little changes to the basic game made a difference. Practice mode, for one, is essential for when you begin that long journey through the difficulties.

The career feels like a more balanced progression, and there are songs to be unlocked while in career mode that may subsequently be played in other modes. One final note: As you finish that solo in "Freebird," and are playing the song out with an internal glow, remember that this turned out to be the series swansong for Harmonix, who were free as a bird to go and create Rock Band. **RS**

Hitman: Blood Money

Original release date : 2006
Platform : Various
Developer : IO Interactive
Genre : Stealth

The fourth game in the *Hitman* series saw the creative team at IO moving up a gear. The game is easily the most accomplished of the stealth assassination titles, with a series of highly sophisticated levels making the most of the bald protagonist's broad range of equipment and abilities.

Each level presents 47, the nameless hitman, with a complex situation and usually several targets to deal with. These scenarios range from a party in a seafront villa, through a mountaintop detox clinic, to an entire street carnival complete with hundreds of people. What is most rewarding about *Hitman: Blood Money* is the sheer range of ways any given hit can be performed.

Wealthy southerners getting married, for example, can simply be shot as they prepare for their wedding. Or they can be murdered at the altar with a grenade or, best of all, killed by a bomb in their own wedding cake. Meanwhile a mark in an opera can be killed onstage by timing your sniper shot to occur at the very moment when he is "killed" by a gun at the climax of the performance—this is, of course, assuming you're smart enough. You'll probably end up simply garotting him in his dressing room. Sometimes it's just best to do it the easy way.

Also, unlike previous games, it's often possible to botch a hit but shoot your way out, rushing to escape the scene of the crime. Other titles in the series were so strict that gung-ho attitudes always led to failure. In *Hitman: Blood Money*, however, there is scope for things to go hilariously wrong, while still allowing you to get out of the assignment alive. The game is framed with beautiful touches, such as the church on the menu screen that is populated with the people you've killed, and the newspaper between levels filled with stories that relate directly to the events that took place in the last mission. **JR**

Jeanne d'Arc

Original release date : 2006
Platform : PSP
Developer : Level-5
Genre : Strategy / Role-Playing

If a young peasant girl stood before you and demanded you help her save France, would you listen to her? Would you take her prophecies seriously and would you give her an army to lead? The life and martyrdom of Joan of Arc, and her miraculous fight against the English, is dashingly retold in Level-5's *Jeanne d'Arc*. Never mind that she's armed with an enchanted bracelet, some of her troops have animal heads, and a demon has possessed Henry VI. The story is fantastical anime fare, but this superb, tactical role-playing game (RPG) does justice to the real saint.

Take the opening scene, where a young Jeanne and her even more helpless friend, Liane, have to take up arms against the English who are burning their village. Jeanne will eventually become your strongest character, but until then she has to master her powers and persuade everyone she meets to follow her. Even then, some of her strongest comrades may be taken away or turned against her.

Jeanne d'Arc was Level-5's first tactical RPG and the studio's debut on the PSP, and it's a must-play, even for strategy newcomers. A rabble of secondary characters can join Jeanne in battle, and each map is unique, with upper levels or constrictive doors and bridges complicating each field. Though easy to learn, the strategies open up as players earn new powers, or take advantage of conflicting affinities to the sun, moon, and stars. And if you feel yourself falling behind, a few free maps offer easy grinding.

Even if you've read your history, Jeanne's story takes a few surprise turns. No matter how powerful Jeanne becomes, her character remains sympathetic. She's still the young heroine who came out of nowhere to fight and maybe die for her cause. *Jeanne d'Arc* is a brilliant take on an ancient and compelling tale. **CDa**

Shin Megami Tensei: Persona 3

Original release date : 2006
Platform : Various
Developer : Atlus
Genre : Role-Playing

As part of the larger *Megami Tensei* (translation: *Goddess Reincarnation*) series, *Shin Megami Tensei: Persona 3* flirts with demonic imagery and suicide themes—characters fire guns known as "evokers" at their heads in order to summon Personas that cast spells—and would doubtlessly raise tabloid panic if the series were better known.

But there's so much more to the game than that, as it cleverly contrasts these dark motifs with the pleasantly bright day-to-day experiences of a high school student in a modern-day Japanese town. Each day your character goes to school, experiences events, and then spends time doing whatever they wish; hanging out with friends, taking part in a school club, or singing karaoke. Breezy artwork, lively

music, and a true representation of the natural ebb and flow of a Japanese student's life would be a reward in itself, but players are also awarded new Personas for creating social links; this develops a unique symbiosis between your character's daytime life and his time in the "dark hour."

It's at the latter point that the player is able to explore Tartarus, an enormous tower of secrets that is randomly generated each night. It's a dungeon-crawling experience that brings to mind *Rogue* and requires that the player finely balance exploration and leveling up before having to retire for the day.

When discussing essential Japanese role-playing games (RPGs), it becomes all too easy to fall into the trap of reciting Square Enix's oeuvre, titles that, in setting and style, tend to maintain an otherworldly status. Games can offer a reflection and understanding of the culture that spawned them, and while this potential often remains unfulfilled, it's something that *Persona 3* offers for those willing to immerse themselves in its world. **MKu**

Just Cause

Original release date : 2006
Platform : Various
Developer : Avalanche
Genre : Action / Shoot 'Em Up

Parachuting into a lustrous island paradise backed up by a grappling hook, plenty of big guns, and an entirely questionable haircut, Rico Rodriguez is a strange kind of video game hero. He's friendly, foppish, and charming, even if he's reassuringly handy with a rocket launcher.

Just Cause is all about destabilizing a questionable political regime by taking on numerous open-world missions and blowing everything you lay eyes on into a billion pieces. Rather fittingly, given the overarching theme, the game itself is the first thing to start showing any signs of subsequent strain. *Just Cause*'s vast playground seems to be always teetering, entertainingly, on the edge of a devastating nervous breakdown. Garage doors needed

to end missions get stuck half open, and minor road traffic accidents are punished with attack helicopters trying to blast you into the next life with vicious homing missiles. Perhaps the latter is merely a sign of how repressive the island's dictatorship has become over the years, but it's harder to explain air drops that, when called in, land on the player and kill them, or the fact that a uniquely memorable bug early on transforms Rodriguez into a disembodied pair of trousers for large chunks of the game. At least it makes him invulnerable at the same time.

Despite such a distinct lack of polish, it's very hard not to fall in love with *Just Cause*. The island, with its sprightly foliage and craggy ravines, is often lovely, and Rico's barnstorming combination of parachute and grappling hook—taken to, frankly, insane levels in the forthcoming sequel—provide plenty of options for getting about. If you like open-world games because of their opportunities for chaos and impromptu hilarity, then this should probably be next on your list after *Crackdown*. **CD**

Metal Gear Solid: Portable Ops

Original release date : 2006
Platform : PSP
Developer : Kojima
Genre : Stealth / Action

Metal Gear Solid games have always been event releases, elaborate titles that push hardware, shift consoles, and set new records in terms of story complexity. Sony's PSP already had a few *Metal Gear* entries by 2007, but they were either esoteric oddities, like *Metal Gear Solid: Digital Graphic Novel*, or thoughtful asides, like the addictive card battler *Metal Gear Acid*. *Metal Gear Solid: Portable Ops* was an action title that looked and played like one of its genuine console brethren—and changed it all.

That's a staggering achievement in its own right. Fitting the game's cinematic stealth onto a platform with limited power and only one thumbstick is no easy task, but *Portable Ops* cuts barely any corners. Its story, picking up with Naked Snake in 1970 after the events of *Metal Gear Solid 3: Snake Eater*, is suitably convoluted, and its control scheme, although a little more cumbersome than normal, still finds room for shooting, moving bodies, and creeping your way through the game's militarized environments. It even has time to throw in a new squad-based element, with Snake recruiting various comrades throughout the story who can then be sent out to do his dirty work for him.

Where there are differences, they tend to make sense. Objectives have been tailored for the length of the average train journey, while the game's selling point uses the fact that you're on the move with a clever system that turns Wi-Fi hotspots and GPS data into additional comrades.

Portable Ops is all the Snake you could hope for—stylish, complex, and filled with clever trickery. It's a template for how things should be done when moving a series to the PSP and a reminder that, although *Metal Gear Solid* may always have a smirk on its face, it continues to approach the desires of its fans with the utmost seriousness. **CD**

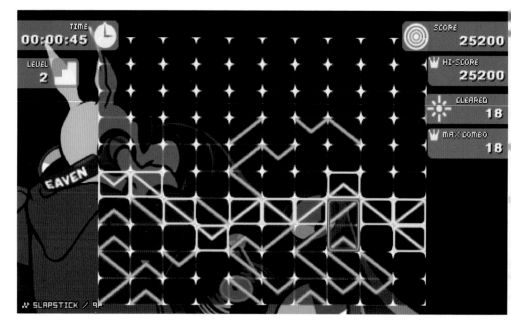

Gunpey

Original release date : 2006
Platform : Various
Developer : Q Entertainment
Genre : Puzzle

The story of *Gunpey* is the story of two gaming visionaries. The first is Nintendo's Gunpei Yokoi, the brilliant mind behind the Game Boy whose long and illustrious career with Nintendo came to an ignominious end after the failure of the pioneering, if considerably flawed, Virtual Boy console, and whose life came to an even more tragic end as the result of a car accident. The second: Tetsuya Mizuguchi is not only one of the nicest men in video game development, but also one of the most talented and the most open minded.

One of Yokoi's legacies is probably the entire video game industry as we know it today. Where would Nintendo's much talked about Blue Ocean Strategy approach to gaming be today were it not for the Game Boy? Another of his legacies is *Gunpey*. Starting life as a standard puzzle game for Bandai's Wonderswan handheld console (also designed by Yokoi), the game was eventually picked up by Mizuguchi's Q Entertainment and given a more modern makeover for the DS and PSP. Like *Tetris*, the object of the game is to construct lines out of fragments that descend from the top of the screen, clearing the screen before it fills up with disconnected fragments.

Like Mizuguchi's other portable puzzlers, *Lumines* and *Every Extend Extra*, the compelling conundrum mechanics at the heart of the game are re-housed in a structure devised from the colored lights and sounds of Mizuguchi's much-loved club culture. Indeed, having started out on titles like *Sega Rally*, Mizuguchi's subsequent career seems to be an attempt to distill peace, love, neon lights, and club grooves into video game form. How fitting that one of those attempts should be *Gunpey*, a memorial for one of video gaming's most cruelly overlooked visionaries. **DM**

Mercury Meltdown

Original release date : 2006
Platform : Various
Developer : Ignition Banbury
Genre : Puzzle

Great puzzle games are always rather fluid in play, but *Mercury Meltdown* was the first to exploit the possibilities of a liquid for its core mechanic. Having established that rolling a blob of poisonous mercury within the safety of a PSP could lead to satisfactorily puzzling possibilities in the original, developer Ignition went wild with the sequel.

The game remains a gloopier *Marble Madness*, in which you tilt a maze to encourage one or more blobs of mercury to go where you want, mixing them up to make new colors as required to open gates and release doors. But *Mercury Meltdown*'s levels are complicated affairs, there are more ways to mix and split your mercury, more hazards to overcome, multiway paintshops, and actively hostile

enemies, and times when you'll find your blob as hard and free rolling as a pinball. There are more than 160 levels to work through, many of which seem baffling when you first encounter them, even without a vicious mandatory time limit or the need to preserve a certain amount of metal to the end. They're divided into ten themed labs, all of whose levels are unlocked when you're granted access, sidestepping the blocks of the first game that left the disks of many unfinished games gathering dust—if they weren't hurled through the nearest available window.

Ignition also added party modes, as well as extensive multiplayer support. The first game's geeky chic—to put it generously—is made over too, with a much slicker look and feel reminiscent of Saturday morning kids' cartoons

Mercury Meltdown doesn't quite have the character to stick in the mind like a true classic, but to return to it after a long absence is to find you didn't quite finish all the levels and to happily lose another few hours to it anew. You can't ask for greater payback from a puzzle game than that. **OB**

Naked War

Original release date : 2006
Platform : PC
Developer : Zee-3
Genre : Strategy

Naked War presumably takes its name from the way your little soldiers lose their clothes instead of their lives when they're defeated in battle. But it's an appropriate name because of the way its creators laid themselves bare by choosing to make it. Created by the brains behind puzzle games *Wetrix* and *Aquaqua*, it resembles a cross between *Advance Wars* and *Worms*. Indeed, there's something of that do-it-yourself, bedroom coding ethic behind *Naked War* itself. It was devised, in part, as a response to the rising costs and market polarization of the blockbuster-obsessed, mainstream video game industry.

Eschewing the elaborately detailed thick necked space marines and graphics of those blockbusters, it keeps things simple—turn-based strategy between cartoon soldiers on two teams, red and blue. Those cartoon soldiers compete for resources housed in crates that contain various sorts of power-ups, like shields and med kits, and they can also jump in tanks, helicopters, and gun turrets.

Most important, they each carry a "doofer." The aim of the game is to capture all of them, but since they can be recaptured, each game contains an epic ebb and flow. With demobbed soldiers always able to reclothe themselves and continue fighting, the possibility of a comeback remains right until the end, which means fortunes twist and turn for the full duration of the game.

Naked War's main innovation, though, is that it's played over e-mail, allowing its creators to free themselves from the traditional publisher/developer model and players play for free, only paying a small fee to start games. But it's not the business model that makes *Naked War* such excellent fun, but the immersive and devilishly complicated tactical challenges that play out across the topographically fiendish, brightly colored maps. **DM**

Slitherlink

Original release date : 2006
Platform : DS
Developer : Hudson Soft
Genre : Puzzle

Ever played one of those games that refuses to let you sleep? That just snakes its tendrils into your brain and won't let you switch off? *Slitherlink* is one of those games.

Japanese publisher Hudson Soft was one of the first companies to capitalize on the unexpected success of the DS, unveiling a series of no-frills puzzle games as soon as it became apparent that Nintendo's new handheld had tapped into new audiences. The first game in the series, *Puzzle Series Vol. 1: Jigsaw Puzzle*, was released a little over a year after the launch of the DS and does exactly what it says on the box; it's a series of jigsaw puzzles, nothing more and nothing less.

Released about half a year after that, *Slitherlink* is similarly unadorned—but gaming drugs of such undiluted purity as this need no adornment. Originally devised by Japanese puzzle powerhouse Nikoli (the same company behind the extraordinary success of *Sudoku*), *Slitherlink* is a very simple, very complex logic puzzle. It's join the dots. Those dots form a lattice on a grid and the aim is to connect them with a line to make a single continuous loop. The challenge is that the grid is also scattered with numbers. Each number represents the number of lines that surround it, and so the gamer must use logic to work out which lattices can be joined by lines.

Like every great puzzle game it sounds boring, but it plays brilliantly, progressing from simple, small grids to huge sprawling fields of numbers. Just completing every puzzle in the game can take anything between seventy and a hundred hours, but even then you won't be able to stop yourself from revisiting those simpler puzzles to blitz them with the *Rain Man*–style number skills you will have acquired by the end. This is one of the sweetest puzzle games, and one of the most addictive. **DM**

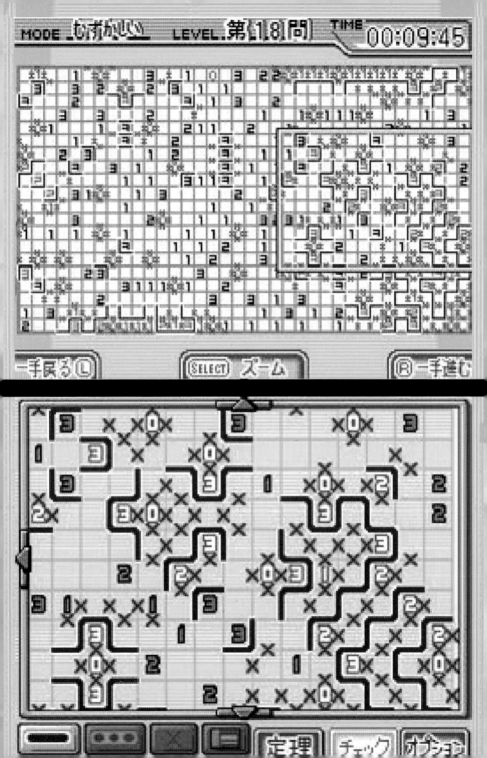

Gottlieb Pinball Classics

Original release date : 2006
Platform : Various
Developer : FarSight Studios
Genre : Pinball

Pinball afficionados are suspicious of video games. Their rise, after all, corresponds closely with the decline of pinball machines. So creating a video game from real world pinball machines—by the storied Gottlieb, no less—might seem like adding insult to injury. But the creators of *Gottlieb Pinball Classics* are clearly fans themselves, as this game is a meticulous tribute with a strong sense of pinball history.

Getting computerized three-dimensional pinballs to behave like real 1¹/₁₆-inch ball bearings is the most daunting challenge for the developer of a pinball game, and FarSight Studios does it better than anyone else. *Gottlieb Pinball Classics*'s digitized replicas are spot-on. You can even jostle the machine, which is critical—any pinball

player who doesn't apply a little physical emphasis is missing half the game. A few of the machines in the game's virtual arcade are playable for free from the start. To unlock the others, you must complete certain table goals, which function as a nice way to deepen play beyond the traditional pursuit of a high score.

The eleven-game collection spans seven decades, going as far back as *Play-Boy*, a poker-themed tabletop machine from 1932 that had no flippers, or electricity for that matter. That historic curiosity bears little resemblance to *Black Hole*, the glorious table that features a second mini-playfield (complete with its own flippers) under a window in the main playing area. Another highlight is *Central Park*, an ornate pre-electronic game from the 1960s, when Gottlieb produced its most beautiful cabinet art. *Gottlieb Pinball Classics* functions as a museum, preserving the memory of important machines that most people would never encounter otherwise. Far from an insult to pinball lovers, it's a gift that reignites enthusiasm for the game. **JT**

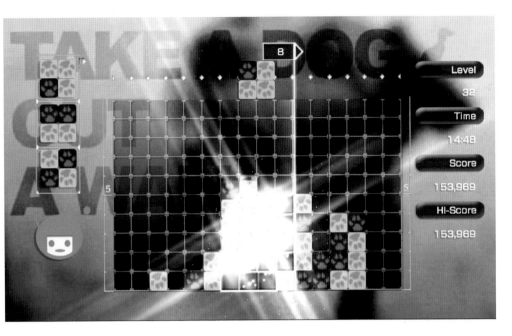

Lumines Live

Original release date : 2006
Platform : Various
Developer : Q Entertainment
Genre : Puzzle

Lumines Live showed there was room in the competitive world of falling block puzzle games if you had class and if you had style. The game offered beautiful multicolor backdrops pulsating to the rhythms of niche Japanese trance with a tight game mechanic embellishing its classic formula with a few neat twists.

On the PSP, it was the game that helped define the system in its early days, as perfectly built for the slick device's glorious screen as *Tetris* had been chunkily appropriate for the flickering green face of the Game Boy. Arriving late to the party on Xbox Live Arcade, however, the argument was mostly about price. *Lumines Live* came out on Microsoft's console, cut into a series of fairly expensive installments, and players were quick to suggest that they were being nickel-and-dimed by Q Entertainment, or the Xbox 360's famously rich platform holder, or, most probably, both at the same time.

Resistance was useless, however. *Lumines Live* is as bluntly addictive on a high-definition television as it is in the palm of your hand. While it may look like *Tetris* with its collapsing chains and passing timeline, the realization that it actually plays nothing like *Tetris* hits just as hard a second time. The unlockable skins that power your journey through the game may have suffered slightly under Xbox Live's download file cap at the time, but not even the odd blurry surface can take away from such a gloriously implemented port, with everything except the slightly disheveled multiplayer turning up trumps.

Meanwhile nothing, absolutely nothing at all, can diminish the undying pleasures of playing a brilliant title on a controller that no longer makes you feel like somebody stood on your knuckles. **CD**

Rise of Nations: Rise of Legends

Original release date : 2006
Platform : PC
Developer : Big Huge Games
Genre : Strategy

If you want to take the science of a real-time strategy (RTS) game in a bold artistic direction, who better to lead the way than Leonardo da Vinci? *Rise of Legends*, a spiritual successor to the historical *Rise of Nations* series, is a lesson in the true, broader meaning of fantasy. Instead of orcs and elves, axes versus swords, it features the oldest, greatest battle of human civilization: technology versus magic.

Into that it drops a theological bombshell, a third race of beings that unites the two, wielding the kind of divine power that might once have created man. That, game makers, is how you stage a war. The Vinci, with its clockwork soldiers, flying machines, and steampunk skyscrapers, is the game's driving force. Beset by war

between the provinces of Miana and Venucci, its ingenuity is focused largely on destruction, its leaders obsessed with vengeance and power. Atrocities litter the early story, starting with a single murder and eventually threatening mutual destruction.

Joining the fray are the mystical Alin, children of the desert with their own internal conflicts and beliefs. Both species are soon entangled in one another's affairs, just in time for the rise of the Cuotl, a sinister tribe that worships false alien gods and wields incomprehensible powers.

The forces at work in *Rise of Nations: Rise of Legends*, not least *Alpha Centauri* mastermind Brian Reynolds, are too great to simply fall in line with RTS tradition. Some of the game's units are city-sized, while its cities become megalopolises, thanks to a district-by-district expansion system. A whole district might then be a giant steam-powered hammer that fires a building-sized slug across the map. At the other end of the scale, the politics of the many neutral factions boast the same level of detail. **DH**

Medieval II: Total War

Original release date : 2006
Platform : PC
Developer : The Creative Assembly
Genre : Strategy

It's a testament to the brilliance of the *Total War* series' design that the weakest game in the series can still be such a strong outing. *Medieval II* was a remake of the second game in the series, *Medieval: Total War*, which came after the original *Shogun: Total War*, using the fancy, new three-dimensional engine that the company had created for the third game, *Rome: Total War*. The combination is thrilling.

Once again the formula is to mix real-time strategy with turn-based campaigning. The turn-based campaign sees you take control of one of the major medieval forces and ascend to power between the years of 1080 and 1530. The campaign sets a number of conditions for victory, including control of specific provinces for certain factions.

While the real-time battles are optional, the medieval battlefield themes mean that they are hugely engaging to play. This is the era of the famed cavalry charge and the mighty archer. Tremendous battles from history, such as Agincourt, are set up for play in the historical battles section, and they make for fascinating, historically concise experiences. They're also closer to the size of historical armies, too, with the engine able to support up to 4,800 individual troops in your army.

Unlike the original *Medieval: Total War* game, *Medieval II* stretches to the discovery of the Americas, and their conquest. For certain powers, control of North America is among the win conditions for the grand campaign. Despite all its strengths, and the success of the previous game, *Rome: Total War*, *Medieval II* is sullied somewhat by its poor artifical intelligence and path finding, which remained imperfect even after patching. This makes both campaign and battle-map experiences frustrating. Ultimately this is a flawed epic, but nevertheless a classic. **JR**

Test Drive Unlimited

Original release date : 2006
Platform : Various
Developer : Eden Games
Genre : Racing

"Enjoy the best of town and country," begins the tourist spiel for Oahu, Hawaii. "Discover striking contrasts from a tropical playground to an urban island fantasy. Enjoy Waikiki's trendy cosmopolitan vibe, surfing, and waterfall hikes . . . . Less than an hour away, the Windward coast is home to some of America's best beaches."

If ever there was a place that deserved the fast cars, expensive clothes, and beautiful people (the adjectives are interchangeable) of *Test Drive Unlimited*, it's this one. Dubbed a massively open-world online racer, Eden's reinvention of the *Accolade* series models this island from coast to coast, welcoming you to more than 1,000 miles of roads—an achievement recognized by *Guinness World Records*. You pick your character, help yourself to a pile of cash, and then hit the showroom to spend it.

Finding yourself an apartment, you then pull out onto the drive and check the game's map, causing the camera to shoot up into the clouds to try and take it all in. Pull it back farther, and you may as well be looking at a page from an atlas. Time trials, races, delivery missions, and police cars await, but the temptation throughout is to wind down the windows, crank up the stereo, and go wherever the next road takes you. The game offers not only the pleasure of getting behind the wheel and racing but also that of having in-game money to spend—on clothes for your character, houses, new cars, and vehicle upgrades.

The switch from micro to macro scales is the power of *Test Drive Unlimited*. Look at the car and you'll see furnished dashboards and polished grills; look away and the roads seem to stretch into infinity. Then it's on to the biggest world of all, the Internet, with multiplayer races you can start by simply drawing them on the map. **DH**

OutRun 2006: Coast 2 Coast

Original release date : 2006
Platform : Various
Developer : Sumo Digital
Genre : Racing

There are few things in life as exhilarating as sliding around Sega's sweeping, swooping highways as they arc along mountainsides, race under leafy green canopies, and hurtle through neon-lit cities in the remake of its classic arcade racer, *OutRun*. Go back to the original 1986 coin-operated game, and you'll find that nostalgia papers over a number of flaws, but its 2003 remake, *OutRun 2,* seems unlikely ever to be diminished by the passage of time.

OutRun 2 remains the most exhilarating driving experience in the history of video games, paying only the barest heed to real world physics in its bid to deliver nothing but the sweetest bursts of automotive pleasure. *OutRun 2006: Coast 2 Coast* takes that remade coin-operated racing game

and faithfully recreates it, proving that there is nothing sweeter than a perfectly timed power slide. Then it adds extra tracks to those brilliant originals, and throws in fifteen more Ferraris before going on to create a comprehensive single-player campaign around it.

More than just the extra few mini-game modes in *OutRun 2*, *OutRun 2006: Coast 2 Coast* makes the driving just the starting point before embarking on a most improbable vehicle-based voyage through logic tests, memory quizzes, driving tests, and more. None of which is necessary, really.

It's all perfectly well engineered, but ultimately there is nothing you can do to make the core driving experience at the heart of *OutRun* any more perfect than it already is. The truly interesting journey here is just the one on the roads. Whether those highways are steering you through a number puzzle or taking you down memory lane as Magical Sound Shower plays and you make the journey through modern versions of Cloudy Mountain or Desolation Hill. **DM**

Tom Clancy's Splinter Cell: Double Agent

Original release date : 2006

Platform : Various

Developer : Ubisoft

Genre : Stealth

The fourth of the *Splinter Cell* games, *Tom Clancy's Splinter Cell: Double Agent* casts shadows on a part of hero Sam Fisher that's always been brightly lit: his patriotism. It starts with a one-two punch of destabilizing events, the death of a rookie under his command and a more immediate tragedy: the loss of his only daughter in a drunk driving accident. Overcome with grief and unfit for his usual duties, he's transferred to the blackest of all operations— undercover work within a domestic terror cell in a bid to test and ultimately rebuild his identity.

After the universally acclaimed *Chaos Theory*, seen by many as the definitive *Splinter Cell* episode, Ubisoft was left with little choice but to break a few rules. The Sam Fisher of *Double Agent* often appears with neither stealth suit nor trifocal goggles. Most of his missions come with two conflicting objectives, some from the terrorist JBA and others from the NSA, who tug his loyalties back and forth while jeopardizing his cover. And because gamers place such implicit trust in their mission merchants, his allegiance feels divided from the start.

Double Agent also marks the series' first experiments with social stealth, its superb JBA safe-house missions letting you brush shoulders with the very people you're betraying, sneaking off one mission to satisfy another. Its closing act is also a first—a stealth mission set in an open battlefield in the cold light of day, where the rules of engagement are more disposable than ever. Some time before *Metal Gear Solid 4* made it a bulletpoint feature, this game did it with style. An entirely separate multiplayer mode deserves far more credit than space will allow, providing all kinds of courageous spy games. **DH**

The Elder Scrolls IV: Oblivion

Original release date : 2006

Platform : Various

Developer : Bethesda Game Studios

Genre : Action / Role-Playing

Every new generation of gaming hardware needs a title to prove it was worth the fuss. For the Xbox 360, *The Elder Scrolls IV: Oblivion* did the honors. From the first moment you take your customized character out of the sewers and into the open world of Tamreil, you'll be tempted to explore every corner just to enjoy the sheer beauty of it.

From the ruined temples and long vistas across hills and valleys (where the plant life changes realistically with altitude) to the game's cities and dungeons, *Oblivion* has a cinematic quality that's only enhanced by voiceovers from the likes of Patrick Stewart, Terence Stamp, and Sean Bean. Tamreil is absolutely gigantic, and it's yours to romp across as you will (or better yet ride across, once you get a horse).

Of course, there's a plot spanning the continent and most key locations but, as with the previous *Elder Scrolls* episode, *Morrowind*, it's up to you how and when you tackle it.

What's really impressive is how deep this sandbox style of play can take you. Do a lot of stealing or scrapping, and you'll attract the notice of the Thieves' Guild or the Fighters' Guild, respectively. Soon you're off on side quests, improving your bank balance as well as your skills through practice, and too engrossed to remember the main plot. Yet it's still there waiting until you're ready.

Combat is a free-form dance, a million miles from the rigid role-playing game encounters of old. Magic is dazzling. Nonplayer characters are numerous, and talking to them often is very useful. The skills progression system is elegant, and there's really very little micromanagement required anywhere. Instead, Bethesda's game is about the adventure, both in each moment and on a grand scale. If you're looking to lose yourself, you must seek out *The Elder Scrolls IV: Oblivion*. **OB**

The Legend of Zelda: Twilight Princess

Original release date : 2006
Platform : GameCube, Wii
Developer : Nintendo
Genre : Action / Adventure

While many enjoyed the *Legend of Zelda* episode *The Wind Waker,* fans of *Ocarina of Time* longed for a proper sequel—a game that kept the more traditional fantasy art style of the original three-dimensional game, and sent players back to the fields and meadows of Hyrule to explore the land as a grown-up Link once more. With *The Legend of Zelda: Twilight Princess,* they got their wish, but at a price.

This is certainly everything fans requested, but perhaps that's part of the problem. While *The Legend of Zelda: Twilight Princess* is still a magnificent adventure, compared to the rest of this astonishing series it can often feel a little hemmed in and by rote. So it's perhaps both a blessing and a curse that the return to Hyrule manages to work in so many traditional sequences and cameos. Races like the Gorons and the Zora return, as does at least one of the original game's temples—harder and more elaborate than it was before. There are new ideas, too. Link can transform into a wolf at the press of a button and search out scent trails, while the intrusion of the frightening twilight realm leads to a neon- tinged aesthetic that is a total departure for the series in general. Taken as a whole, the game itself can feel like something of a homage to the successes of the past with little to add for itself.

If any series can get away with inventively riffing on its own, rather restrictive, traditions, it's this one. While the last-minute conversion to motion control with a platform shift from GameCube to Wii can feel a little tacked on, *The Legend of Zelda: Twilight Princess* is still a lavish, memorable, and warm hearted adventure. This is a game that, in any other series, would stand out as a towering triumph, and only here, nestled in among such auspicious siblings, seems tainted with a tinge of disappointment. **CD**

Viva Piñata

Original release date : 2006
Platform : Various
Developer : Rare
Genre : Life Simulation

Released in tandem with a children's animated series, *Viva Piñata's* child-friendly marketing belies the richest strategy game on the Xbox 360. Saddled with a lonely, overgrown plot of land, the player's task is to attract a gorgeous menagerie of shimmering piñata animals to take up residence in your garden, breed, and eat one another until that shabby little plot of land becomes a self-contained ecosystem. The universally adorable looks make *Viva Piñata* stand out, but it is the gently addictive, well-paced strategy game at the core that makes it truly memorable.

If anything, the game is too complicated. There are layers of radial menus between thought and execution, which can make the pace feel hugely demanding in the early stages before the natural rhythm of plant watering and piñata animal care becomes second nature. This is a significant departure for Rare, which made its name with colorful platformers that presaged *Viva Piñata's* cuteness but little of its demanding complexity, and the developer struggles to make the interface accessible.

It's the character design and escalating pace of the game play that ultimately knocks down that pain barrier. The animals themselves are colorful and full of character, their paper feathers or fur ruffling and swaying in the wind. Breeding smaller piñatas attracts larger ones, and prospective new residents might prowl teasingly for weeks before finally setting foot inside. It's often the mark of a great game when it has you thinking in complete nonsense. "Why aren't my Buzzlegums attracting the Fizzlybear?," "Must protect the Bunnycombs," "GET AWAY, sour Shellybean." *Viva Piñata* infests the mind, and showcases a developer of enduring talent. **KM**

Trauma Center: Second Opinion

Original release date : 2006
Platform : Wii
Developer : Atlus
Genre : Medical Simulation

Atlus was not the first company to see the potential in steady-handed surgery, but its realization of the idea far exceeds the organ yanking of *Operation*. Steering clear of grim simulation, *Trauma Center* finds the arcade in the operating room. Stitching tiny tests of accuracy into one large, chaotic chest cavity, a balance must be struck between surgical finesse and damage limitation. Incisions are ranked with grades befitting *Devil May Cry* combinations, but it means nothing if the patient doesn't pull through.

Second Opinion is a remake of the DS original, *Trauma Center: Under the Knife*, but you couldn't tell, such is the natural fit of the Wii Remote. Stitches once sketched with the DS stylus are happily zigzagged with the Remote pointer. In fact, Atlus was able to expand on the original, transforming the Wii Remote and Nunchuk into defibrillator pads and using the Remote's rotating ability to enable a fanciful bit of bone restructuring. Particularly good use is made of the A and the B button pairing, pinching together with a satisfying tactility to tweeze slivers of glass from tendons.

Upscaling from the DS to the television screen also saw *Trauma Center: Second Opinion* take its place alongside the TV medical dramas Atlus liberally borrow from. Charting the rise of a man-made biological virus, GUILT (Gangliated Utrophin Immuno Latency Toxin, of course), as much time is spent manhandling lungs as observing flamboyantly coiffed doctors yell melodramatic ultimatums at one another. Patient names are even amalgamations of famous on-screen doctors and the actors who portray them. Later games add cooperative play, online leaderboards, and even bigger hair, but these grueling years in medical school are an essential precursor. **MC**

Slaves to Armok II: Dwarf Fortress

Original release date : 2006
Platform : PC
Developer : Bay 12 Games
Genre : Management Simulation

Dwarf Fortress is so phenomenally geeky that it merits every one of the colons in its full title, *Slaves to Armok: God of Blood Chapter 2: Dwarf Fortress*. It's also the most obsessional, singular achievement in 2000's game development. Nothing is bigger or madder or more glorious—or more alienating. At its core, *Slaves to Armok: Dwarf Fortress* is what's often termed a "Roguelike." That is, it's in the line of games in which you control a tiny (usually ASCII) letter, exploring randomly generated dungeons. It's a fair description, but it doesn't cover a fraction of what *Slaves to Armok: Dwarf Fortress* offers.

Placed in charge of a small expedition of the eponymous humanoids, you're forced to eke an existence from the rock and soil. The key note is simulation, because this is an attempt to make a true living environment. You start with generating the world, a process that realistically creates the terrain and then runs several thousand years of history. Masses of types of rocks, along with everything from plants to elephants, are modeled. Dwarf psychology is modeled too, so that they can mourn, crave, and go absolutely crazy. When you've bricked up a dwarf to prevent him from turning others into functional dwarf-skin boots, you know you've been playing *Dwarf Fortress*.

The heroes have an existence of almost unremitting woe. Indeed, the much quoted motto of the game is "Failing is fun." The catch is the interface, which is baroque to the point of lunacy. It will eventually be improved, but its creators see little point until the game's features are complete. Unfortunately it's unlikely that such a day will ever arrive. For developer and players both, this is an obsessional, singular, and glorious game. **KG**

Pokémon Diamond and Pearl

Original release date : 2006
Platform : DS
Developer : Game Freak
Genre : Role-Playing

There are many permutations of monsters in the *Pokémon* universe, with additions coming into play as the series has progressed, but the game sinks its hooks into players through an interlocking simplicity that is the cornerstone of the series' design. Electricity types (Pokémon with electric attacks, such as series mascot Pikachu) are "super effective" against water types, but "not very effective" against ground types, because the former conduct electricity while the latter are grounded.

From these basics grew a business empire (there's a rather amusing style sheet occasionally handed to writers that specifies, among other things, that "Pokémon are not creatures, they are Pokémon"), and a menagerie that, by the time of the *Diamond/Pearl* iterations, boasted more than 500 Pokémon and thirteen different types, as well as hybrids. What stays the same is the ease of those first few steps, the nurturing arm it throws around you for the first few challenges until you get a handle on things and the game lets you loose to discover things for yourself.

It helps that *Pokémon* is always a grand adventure. You begin as a young child with nothing but a single Pokémon and an ambition to be a great trainer, and end hundreds of hours later as a Pokémon master with an army in the hundreds at your beck and call. *Diamond/Pearl*'s online applications, such as worldwide trading and battling, mean that for some players it never ends.

In some ways this is one of the most complex role-playing games ever made, but at its core it is the most simple for its millions of players. *Pokémon Diamond/Pearl* plays out as nothing less than the game they want it to be, and the fun they want to have. **RS**

Tony Hawk's Project 8

Original release date : 2006
Platform : PS3, Xbox 360
Developer : Neversoft
Genre : Sports

Don't be fooled. *Tony Hawk's Project 8* may be full of chatter about ollies, grinds, and spine transfers. It may also feature motion-captured professional skaters, like Rodney Mullen and the Birdman himself. And, yes, it will let you heel-flip a Hosoi deck through 360 degrees while flying ten yards in the air. But it is not a skating simulator (see Electronic Arts's *Skate* for that), it's really a lifestyle simulation.

Load up *Tony Hawk's Project 8* and you're transported to a surreal American suburbia, part David Lynch, part *Lords of Dogtown*, where men in mascot costumes roam the streets and Nokia and Jason Lee's Stereo have product placement deals. You don't just skate; you dress up your avatar in obscure fashions and send them hurtling up

graffiti covered half-pipes to the sounds of Kasabian and Eagles of Death Metal. This isn't just a skating game, dude. It's a subculture in a plastic case.

What makes *Tony Hawk's Project 8* the pinnacle of the series' decade-plus run, though, isn't its lifestyle sell but its instant playability. Kick off through the game's sprawling suburban jungle (no load times but occasional frame-rate judders) and feel immediately empowered. Want to grind that rooftop to impress Tony and join his elite Project 8 team? Go for it. Want to do a One Foot Tailgrab over that pizza shack and then manual past the fat real estate lady? It's all yours. Even failure is fun as *Jackass*-style bails aim for the highest hospital bills possible.

It all comes to a head in Nail the Trick, a slow motion bullet-time mode that lets you do board flips in drawn out ecstasy. It's the *Matrix* of the skateboarder's art, allowing you to pull off feats real skaters could only achieve in their most extreme dreams. It's time to limber up, let loose, and join Tony Hawk in some styling moves. **JRu**

Virtua Fighter 5

Original release date : 2006
Platform : Various
Developer : Sega-AM2
Genre : Fighting

The fighting game of fighting games. No matter how good the latest *Street Fighter* or *Tekken* is, they'll still be undisciplined teenagers compared to *Virtua Fighter*'s cool, mature mastery of fighting. The reason's simple: Combatants don't just throw punches and kicks in *Virtua Fighter*, they connect with each other.

Initially the game can seem slower paced than its manic competitors, but underneath the surface *Virtua Fighter 5* is even more intense and reaction based. Watching professional players fight, you'll occasionally see moments of stillness where everything stops for seconds as they weigh up the last exchange, thinking about the next move before pressing anything, poised to react in the blink of an eye. In the hands of less skilled players, *Virtua Fighter 5* works just as well, though it does require a basic investment, demanding a knowledge of your character's style rather than simple mashing. What's going on under the hood is so impressive that you almost forget about its beauty in motion.

The smooth animation and modeling of martial arts styles and the simply stunning environments are superb. Atop an isolated rock, trapped in a cage surrounded by neon and noise, ankle deep in azure waters, or in the intense bronze surroundings of a temple, your fighting remains the centerpiece of every setting.

New characters such as El Blaze bring radically new styles to the game but slot effortlessly into a roster balanced and rebalanced to perfection over more than a decade of play. So to say that *Virtua Fighter 5* is the finest *Virtua Fighter* is to state the obvious. This is a series that refines rather than reinvents, and one that respects its players too much to risk ruining everything. **RS**

Virtua Tennis 3

Original release date : 2006
Platform : Various
Developer : Sega-AM3
Genre : Sports

Since the launch of the original arcade version in 1999, the *Virtua Tennis* series has thoroughly enlivened the staid world of the tennis simulation with its unique, and not altogether realistic, take on the sport. *Virtua Tennis 3* was released into arcades in 2006 and followed by a typically enhanced console version the following year. It is the pinnacle of the series, with beautiful animation, detailed arenas, and an exciting roster of world famous players.

At the game's core is a marvelously intuitive control system, with a range of context sensitive shots accessible from just three buttons—lob, slice, and top spin. While beginners are able to fumble their way through early matches, increasing confidence opens up a wealth of sly,

lightning fast shots, mostly accessed by holding down buttons as early as possible to increase power. Coupled with the utterly fluid player movement, it's an engaging experience. Indeed, authenticity for hardcore sports fans isn't really the key aim here. It's about fun and drama, hence the fact that almost every just-out-of-reach shot can be saved with a flailing dive across the baseline.

Another essential component of the home console versions is the World Tour mode. Here, players create their own rookie tennis stars and guide them through full careers, taking part in tournaments and trying out a huge range of practice mini-challenges. Designed to develop key areas of your game, from serving and volleying to footwork and precision ground strokes, these daft tasks have you smashing balls into advancing robots, serving at giant bowling pins, and attempting to pick up humongous fruits. That's the beauty of *Virtua Tennis*. 2K Sports's *Top Spin* series may have the gritty realism, but it doesn't have a tennis-powered bingo test. **KS**

Wii Sports

Original release date : 2006
Platform : Wii
Developer : Nintendo
Genre : Sports

Bundled with every Wii console sold, *Wii Sports* is an effortless introduction to the quirks, delights, and very occasional frustrations of Nintendo's unlikely world-beating console. However, the game itself is far more than a mere technical demonstration or a slick tutorial. Beneath the carefully anonymous interface, with its progress charts and bland menu screens, lies an addictive, brilliantly designed, and often elegant, collection of mini-games.

With bowling, boxing, tennis, baseball, and golf on offer, *Wii Sports* ensures you'll never be strapped for something to do. While some of the distractions are surprisingly good for a five minute workout (boxing, in particular, with its ducking, weaving, and fierce flurries

of jabs, can be uniquely winding for players inching past thirty years of age), some, like bowling or baseball, are the perfect accompaniment to an evening with friends. These are surprisingly deep and intense team sports that unfold in flurries of chattering recrimination as the sofa gets pushed out of the way and grandstanding takes over.

The ability to import your own Miis to play with in the game only raises the stakes—a perfect flyball caught at the last minute by your own granny is particularly galling. While no one likes to be aced out of the court by their younger brother, Jack Black, V from *V for Vendetta*, or the family dog, the game inspires sportsmanship and laughter.

Wii Sports is a modern classic and its swings and lobs have been calibrated to hide the inherent fuzziness of the Wii itself in a way that few other games have successfully copied since. If you have the console and you bought it through legitimate channels, there's no chance that you won't have the game in your possession already. In fact, it's likely you're nodding in agreement right now. **CD**

Dreamfall: The Longest Journey

Original release date : 2006
Platform : Xbox
Developer : Funcom
Genre : Adventure

To an adventurer, there can't be a much more appealing title for a game than *The Longest Journey*. The so-named 1999 point-and-click release more than lived up to expectations, revered today alongside *Grim Fandango* as an exemplar of the genre. The gestation period for its sequel was lengthy in itself (appearing seven years later), but *Dreamfall: The Longest Journey* was worth the wait.

Picking up ten years after the original, the player is cast as Zoe Castillo—street-smart, attractive, and studying bio-engineering. When she begins receiving strange electronic messages from a young girl imploring her to "save April Ryan," Zoe is thrust into an expansive adventure, which takes place between the science-fiction world of Stark

and the magical world of Arcadia. The imaginative art direction prevents dystopia fatigue from setting in and steadfastly refuses to capitulate to cliché, except when intended. Zoe's memorable description of an Arcadian city as looking like "something out of a role-playing game" is a great example of this game's playful self-awareness.

Like *Broken Sword: The Sleeping Dragon*, *Dreamfall: The Longest Journey* seeks to reinvigorate a genre declining in popularity by including fighting and stealth sections. The game is played from a close third-person perspective rather than from more traditional fixed viewpoints.

Players approaching the game as an action title will be disappointed. This is a title focused on narrative, and the pleasure to be derived here stems from the gripping script, exceptional voice acting, and passionate storytelling. While ardent point-and-click apologists may bemoan concessions to commerciality, Funcom should be applauded for its desire to innovate and for setting a high bar for game narratives that has rarely been met since. **BM**

Rayman Raving Rabbids

Original release date : 2006
Platform : Wii
Developer : Ubisoft
Genre : Party

Rayman Raving Rabbids is a bit like *Mork & Mindy*. The television show was a bizarre spin-off of the popular series *Happy Days*, and rested its hopes on the talents of newcomer Robin Williams. The Rabbids, buck-toothed, quizzical antagonists of Ubisoft's long-time hero Rayman, are slightly better known, but spin-offs are no more of a guarantee in video games than they are in television.

Moreover, *Rayman Raving Rabbids* was launched on the Nintendo Wii, which, until its launch, was something of an unknown quantity. *Rayman Raving Rabbids* would be the first among many for which the console would define its existence. A collection of mini-games, it was created to embarrass you in front of a room full of family members by

inviting you to swing your Remote as wildly as possible. One favorite involves having the Rabbids attempt a hammer throw with a cow. It's the same off-key humor that animated *Earthworm Jim* more than a decade earlier.

In fact, *Rayman Raving Rabbids* was something of an anomaly for its development studio, which, having adapted Peter Jackson's *King Kong* into video game form, seemed to have its sights focused on Hollywood blockbusters rather than competing with Nintendo for the family fun space. Indeed, publisher Ubisoft was behind the game of James Cameron's *Avatar*, and in *Prince of Persia* its own intellectual property has traveled in the other direction.

But perhaps *Rayman Raving Rabbids* isn't so far removed from the company's appreciation of the silver screen. Mischievous rabbits already have an established place in film, and the Rabbids are clearly crazy enough to sit comfortably within daytime children's programming. Their hilarious screams should be enough to grab some director's ear at the very least. **JBW**

Microsoft Flight Simulator X

Original release date : 2006
Platform : PC
Developer : ACES
Genre : Flight Simulator

For more than twenty-five years, Microsoft has been publishing the *Flight Simulator* series. That's long before the software giant had even dreamed of creating something like its Xbox console. Much like sports games, the incremental differences from year to year often mean little to the casual consumer, but for fans of this particular series, allowing the wings to bend to adjust the rate of descent or ascent and adding camera shake when a plane moves through turbulence are the little joys that make the series wonderfully complete.

In fact, as in any good simulation, overall perfectionism has been the series hallmark and *Microsoft Flight Simulator X* (or *FSX* as it's often termed) is the benchmark for those wishing to take an aerial jaunt. In terms of core game play, it performs as expected, but serious simulations are judged by their verisimilitude to the real thing, and *FSX* goes to extreme lengths in terms of attention to detail.

Baggage carts and fuel trucks jockey for position as your plane prepares to take off, and real road data now features across the game's terrain. Moreover, because the *Flight Simulator* series has such an active community, the inclusion of features such as Shared Skies, which allows multiple players to control the same cockpit, is a smart touch. One of the stranger additions, meanwhile, is the bump in the maximum flight height of aircraft to more than 1,000,000 feet, or more than twice Earth's diameter. The game's release marked a sad note for the franchise. Citing budget cuts, Microsoft closed the ACES studio, effectively ending *Flight Simulator* for the foreseeable future. However, that hasn't stopped eager fan communities from making their own additions in a bid to keep the game alive. **JBW**

Ultimate Ghosts 'n Goblins

Original release date : 2006
Platform : PSP
Developer : Capcom
Genre : Platform / Fighting

When a game industry veteran returns to a series they created decades earlier—not that it happens very often—the outcome can be divine or catastrophic. The same could be said of bringing any sprite-based classic into three dimensions, or from stick and buttons to a modern controller. Just ask *Golden Axe*, *Mega Man*, *Metal Slug*, *Bomberman*, *Earthworm Jim*, or any of the other casualties. But when Tokuro "Professor F" Fujiwara—a "scary master" according to *Resident Evil* creator Shinji Mikami—returned to *Ghosts 'n Goblins* twenty-one years after the first game, the result was a platformer fit for a king.

Ultimate Ghosts 'n Goblins is aptly named: locking its 3-D models to a side-scrolling plane, it leverages the power of

Sony's handheld while staying faithful to series roots. It is also still a game of mathematical precision, every jump requiring a cool head and fresh approach. Flinch, and you lose; hesitate, and you're lost. And don't think that the PSP widescreen gives you more space to breathe: It simply crams in more of those wonderfully imagined creatures from the devils at Capcom.

Unlockable teleports, shield-assisted flight, versatile levels, and surprise bosses take the format to its extreme, the game reinventing itself as you hop back and forth. You survive the levels first and only later complete them, using new weapons and abilities to achieve the impossible and reach the unreachable. But if that's "ultimate," then what does that make *Goku Makai-Mura Kai*? Never released outside Asia, this remix of Fujiwara's game restores the charged magic attacks of 1998 sequel *Ghouls 'n Ghosts* while tweaking difficulties and giving you more abilities from the start, playing with the formula without ever threatening its chemistry. **DH**

Ace Combat 6: Fires of Liberation

Original release date : 2007
Platform : Xbox 360
Developer : Namco
Genre : Flight Simulator / Combat

Namco's *Ace Combat* is a famously formulaic series that gets by on two things: increasingly realistic looks and the geometric beauty of a midair dogfight. Drama befalls the characters, and the backdrops always change, but the games are still best described by their post-flight replays, the paths of the planes twisting and circling like decorative ribbons. *Ace Combat 6: Fires of Liberation* stays the course while boasting the strongest of the series' stories.

It's also, at times, indistinguishable from reality. If you want a random screenshot, just lean from a window and look up. Don't look down because the ground isn't nearly as photogenic. Streets, houses, soil, and waves don't come as easily as an unreachable skybox, but at least they don't

look like porridge in *Ace Combat 6: Fires of Liberation*, which is an improvement, thanks to the Xbox 360. The game even goes as far as to make treacherous urban canyons out of streets and skyscrapers.

All that rolling to and fro can, as ever, feel like being trapped inside a washing machine, but Namco, with experience in making story-laden fighting games like *Tekken*, knows how to spice it up. Its conflict, a fictional war between the Republic of Emmeria and the Federal Republic of Estovakia, may be viewed from four different perspectives. There's a washed-up fighter ace assigned to desk duty on the ground, a squadron leader on the opposing side, a mother left wandering after an air strike wipes out her home, and a tank chief looking to make some easy money behind enemy lines.

Ace Combat 6: Fires of Liberation also makes time for several fan favorite multiplayer modes, filling the online skies with up to sixteen fighters at once. Is anyone still playing, though? That's another matter. **DH**

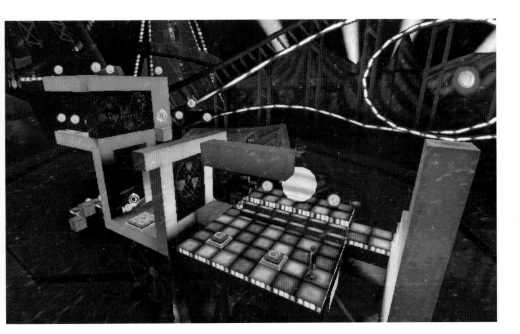

Crush

Original release date : 2007
Platform : PSP
Developer : Zoë Mode
Genre : Puzzle / Platform

If you're in the market for a forgotten gem, you may find that *Crush*—a cerebral PSP puzzler by British developer Zoë Mode—is just the kind of thing you've been looking for. *Crush* blends genres and styles in a way that few other titles would think to, and emerges, in the end, with something distinctive and brilliant, even if almost everybody subsequently ignored it. When you delve into its curious mix of spatial reasoning, twitchy platforming, and psychobabble narrative, you discover it is really no surprise that the game remains so unknown.

Playing as gawky insomniac Danny, *Crush* sees you navigating your way to the exits of a suite of intricate floating platform mazes designed around the main character's most persistent nightmare scenarios. Getting to the goal is impossible, however, if you stay within the strict confines and rules of the game's 3-D environment. Instead, you must regularly rotate the perspective left or right, up or down, and then "crush" it: flattening the 3-D levels into a 2-D space, joining platforms together that would normally exist on different planes, and creating paths where none previously existed. Be very careful, though—position yourself in the wrong spot, and you'll squash yourself to death; uncrush at the wrong time, and you'll materialize in thin air and promptly fall into the ether.

With nasty enemies to avoid and a clever arrangement of different rewards and trophies for speed-running levels, *Crush* was most likely held back from success by its eccentric, gap-toothed art style. A cult classic in all the right circles, however, Zoë Mode's oddity has aged remarkably well, and, due perhaps to its obscurity, has yet to see too many of its smart ideas stolen and repurposed by prettier competitors. **CD**

BioShock

Original release date : 2007
Platform : Various
Developer : 2K
Genre : First-Person Shooter

BioShock brought stylish brain-horror to a genre more familiar with cheap thrills, and bookish smarts to one that was happy to trade in paper-thin plots. Clever, intricate, and darkly funny, it's all the things games aren't meant to be, as well as all of the things they are.

BioShock kicks off with a plane crash that dumps its nameless hero, rather roughly, into the middle of the ocean. Waking to find the dark waters aflame with fuel, he makes his way to a nearby promontory of rock, where a staircase leads down to a diving bell that takes him even deeper, into a city built at the bottom of the waves. This is Rapture, an ideology-driven colony where mankind is free of petty morality and able to live a life based around the

objectivist theories of Ayn Rand: a life of unfettered self-interest and uninhibited greatness.

That's the idea, anyway, but it's all fallen apart a bit, and a good chunk of Rapture's survivors are slowly killing one another, while mysterious forces fight for the hearts and minds of those who remain.

At its most basic, *BioShock* is a shooter with a genetic upgrade system that allows you to unite your machine guns, pistols, and wrenches with a kinetic range of elemental and telepathic abilities. In truth, however, it's a narrative roller coaster, sucking you through the game's intricate environments, subverting your expectations, and pushing you out at the end with something unpleasant to think about. The game's Big Daddies have become a classic of modern video games: hulking Verneian nightmares clad in drill-armed, brass diving suits as they escort the creepy Little Sisters about. But it's the story—hubris, ideology, and the terrible wild card that is human nature—that really defines the experience. **CD**

Call of Duty 4: Modern Warfare

Original release date : 2007
Platform : Various
Developer : Infinity Ward
Genre : First-Person Shooter

Ian Fleming said of James Bond: "Exotic things would happen to and around him, but he would be a neutral figure—an anonymous, blunt instrument wielded by a government department." Consider that a rebuke to the theory that *Call of Duty 4: Modern Warfare*, with its charmless heroes hidden behind layers of army field equipment, is somehow unfit for 00 status.

Let's run through what takes place in Infinity Ward's sequel: a globetrotting hunt for a Russian ultranationalist, a breathless escape from a sinking cargo ship, a sniper assassination, a race against the clock to diffuse terrorist nuclear missiles, a showdown with a helicopter gunship, and, just when you're thinking it's over, a three-minute

dash through a hijacked passenger plane that, naturally, you exit at 30,000 feet.

That's half the story. The rest is left to intense, stylish missions that blast their way through all the places, buzzwords, and money shots of televised combat. Chief among the latter is the AC-130 bombing mission, which imitates surreal government-sanctioned, network news-friendly clips of enemies being annihilated. In fuzzy black-and-white and with unsettling accuracy, shiny antlike people are vaporized by puffs of incandescent flame. *Modern Warfare* or modern warfare? On this rare occasion, it's hard to tell the difference.

A massively successful multiplayer shooter, *Call of Duty 4* set the Guinness World Record for Most Played Online Video Game in 2009. This is partly due to a smart, savvy, and responsive studio, and also to an ongoing dialogue between Infinity Ward and its fans. But it's more a testament to just taking multiplayer seriously and making something you'd just as soon play as sell. **DH**

Anno 1701: Dawn of Discovery

Original release date : 2007
Platform : DS
Developer : Keen Games
Genre : Strategy

Few games dare take on dark imperialist history as their theme. And still fewer cloak that theme in a bright, well-to-do aesthetic. Yet *Anno 1701: Dawn of Discovery*'s subject matter runs counter to its bright, cartoonish visuals. As a settler in the new world of America, your task is to set about leveling the land and building houses, churches, pubs, quarries, and profits. The game's easy-to-use mechanics ensure that you apply yourself to these engaging tasks without so much as a second thought.

When a Native American chief enters your burgeoning settlement to request politely that you leave, the game's wider purpose becomes clear: to play invader, stealing land and resources from the indigenous people who already occupy it. In a sense, *Anno 1701: Dawn of Discovery* takes you through the story of capitalist America, as fundamental survival needs give way to expanding territory, building a military empire, fending off rivals, and defeating those who would seek to threaten your way of life.

The game's potency beyond the sharp metaphor is in its execution, which is perfectly suited to the handheld. It's a rare joy to see your miniature settlements grow and industrialize, splinter into social tiers, and develop their own geography and architecture. As you can micromanage every aspect of your city, from the amount of taxes you charge each social class to the evolution of technology and industry, the game world soon becomes uniquely yours. In turn you are inspired to provide for and meet your people's needs and wants.

The game's simplistic, streamlined, and effective approach works well for its system and audience. Pocket-size imperialism never slipped down so comfortably. **SP**

Final Fantasy Tactics A2: Grimoire of the Rift

Original release date : 2007
Platform : DS
Developer : Square Enix
Genre : Tactics / Role-Playing

When it was released, *Final Fantasy Tactics Advance* was unfairly assumed by critics and fans to be inferior to the original *Final Fantasy Tactics* (and its PSP remake, *The War of the Lions*). Unfairly because although the two games were ostensibly similar, they excelled in very different ways, and, while *Final Fantasy Tactics Advance* was perhaps too easy, it contained an infinite variety of strategy. This variety is most evident off the battlefield, in the way you nurture and develop your characters to maximize their abilities.

Grimoire of the Rift returns to the world of Ivalice, modeling itself on *Final Fantasy Tactics Advance* rather than the original *Final Fantasy Tactics*. The battles are still too easy, but, as in the previous game, the real challenge is in how you develop your clan, steering them through the various character classes to pick up skills and combos that expand your tactical horizons. As in so many other games, the point is not so much beating the game, but beating it well, and with style.

And visual style is something that is clearly important to the creators of the game. The precise re-creation of Ivalice is one of many delightful touches: The towns and villages and their inhabitants are as breathtaking as the cut scenes in which they're recreated during *Final Fantasy XII*, for example, and the lush jungle battlefields seem to teem with life. The style of the game, though, is the strategic equivalent of a free-roaming sandbox, giving players the freedom to go anywhere and do anything, choosing to follow the main quest or ignore it in favor of the auction houses or hundreds of subquests. This is nothing less than one of the most interesting realms in Square Enix's long and illustrious history of world building. **DM**

Crackdown

Original release date : 2007
Platform : Xbox 360
Developer : Realtime Worlds
Genre : Adventure / Shoot 'Em Up

Every developer loves *Crackdown* because every developer wishes they'd made it. A work of delinquency to match any *Grand Theft Auto*, it casually breaks rules that have run the action game since the dawn of 3-D. It has no story, just three underworld kingpins and their loyal gangs. It has no problem with you jumping hundreds of feet from a rooftop to the ground, and does little to stop you climbing back up. It has no order: If you think you're hard enough, you can run right up to the toughest boss and throw him off a balcony after just half an hour. Or you can just leave him be and make fireworks out of passing cars. Your choice.

The hero, an interchangeable avatar known only as "Agent," has no identity. Charged with freeing Pacific City from the cancer of crime, his relationship with its people is entirely of the player's making. *Crackdown* was made by Dundee studio Realtime Worlds and its founder, *Grand Theft Auto* co-creator David Jones. And just like Rockstar's game, it leaves all judgments to its cops, your superiors seeing the slaughter of civilians as little more than bad PR, punishable by the minor inconvenience of arranging your death.

With none of the usual crutches to fall back on, *Crackdown* is 100 percent game. Your abilities as a fighter, climber, runner, and driver are their own reward, and there's little else to it but excuses to improve them. Scattered about the spires and alcoves of Pacific City are 500 Agility Orbs, while a "skills for kills" system spits out tokens for weapons and melee combat. Radical support for drop-in/drop-out co-op play lets Xbox Live users find their own joint objectives. The freedom, the inventiveness, the bonus downloadable content, the ominous score—it all comes together to create a must-have game. Some call this a playground; others, a chemistry set; both are justified. **DH**

Everybody's Golf 5: World Tour

Original release date : 2007
Platform : PS3
Developer : Clap Hanz
Genre : Sports

Released nearly ten years after the first game in the series, *Everybody's Golf 5: World Tour* contains everything that made all the previous games so special: superbly polished graphics, simple controls, precise physics, and personality. Lots and lots of personality, which is embodied in the colorful selection of courses, clubs, costumes, and characters. It replaces the photorealistic bland—sorry, brand—sponsorship of Tiger Woods and the rest, opting instead for big-headed cute characters that range from super-kawaii, pink-obsessed young girls to bumbling tweed-wearing oldsters.

But it doesn't sacrifice realism where it matters. The ball travels with a real-world fidelity through the air, buffeted by the wind, bouncing through the rough, and rolling down the fairways on courses that are every bit as interesting, and as challenging, as the real thing. *Everybody's Golf 5: World Tour* doesn't dispense with realism, it just embroiders it to heighten the fun. The realities of golf playing are supplemented with all sorts of wacky powered-up shots and delightful little touches, like the caddies that scarper off at superspeed in pursuit of your ball, or the online lobbies that allow you to dress up as a scuba diver or schoolgirl (whatever makes you happy).

The game overhauls the shot system from previous games in the series, doing away with the pie-chart style swingometer, but it retains the one-button simplicity (which is every bit as inclusive as the more fashionable motion-sensed golf swing ushered in by the age of the Wii). And with a lengthy main campaign to unlock all of the courses, clubs, and costumes, plus an online multiplayer option accessible from the warmth and safety of your sofa, you'll never have to spoil a good walk again. **DM**

Contra 4

Original release date : 2007
Platform : Various
Developer : WayForward Technologies
Genre : Shoot 'Em Up

A direct sequel to *Contra III* (that may sound like a fairly obvious fact, but this is a tangled and complex series), *Contra 4* is a brilliant piece of back-to-basics side-scrolling action design.

It was built by the intriguing American developer WayForward Technologies, whose mix of licensed games and intricate boutique titles marks it out as a possible contender for the role of a Western treasure. Its recent output includes stylish mini-game collection *Duck Amuck*, based on the Warner Bros. cartoon, and the moody, cerebral survival-horror puzzler *LIT*. With this in mind it's clear that the *Contra* series finds itself in the hands of genuine fans whose main concern is simply to make good games. The game progresses as a straight-ahead blaster, its no-nonsense design ignoring potential pitfalls like the temptation to cram in touch controls and other DS gimmickry. Most levels use both screens as playing areas, allowing you to scamper about, shoot anything that moves, and collect regular power-ups to unleash new weapons.

With a plot that pits you against an extraterrestrial menace known as Black Viper, and a range of different game modes, this is some of the most elegant 2-D design since the original games wowed audiences back in the days of 8- and 16-bit consoles. The inclusion of faux 3-D sections, calling to mind the original *Contra*, only drives home the sensation that you're in safe hands.

Contra 4 is, rather frustratingly, not available in Europe, but with WayForward Technologies' recent games, such as its Wii remake of *A Boy and His Blob*, meeting critical success in the UK and beyond, it's not entirely impossible that a late budget re-release might put this into your hands. Otherwise, there's always eBay. **CD**

Free Running

Original release date : 2007
Platform : Various
Developer : Core Design / Rebellion
Genre : Sports

The moment *Jump London*, a documentary about athletes treating the UK capital as their own private obstacle course, aired on television in 2003, game makers scrambled to make parkour their own. A generational leap for action games, it formed the bedrock of Ubisoft's recent catalog, inspiring the return of *Prince of Persia* and the groundbreaking technology of *Assassin's Creed*. Other notables walk the same tightrope of trendy nonconformity as the sport's real-life stars, but currently, though, *Free Running* remains the only authentic parkour game, its "traceurs" and "traceuses" fleeing nothing but the streets in pursuit of self-improvement.

Adding the acrobatic elements that tend to separate free running from parkour—and the debate over that topic continues—*Free Running* was made by Core Design's Derby studio, but released after its purchase by UK superdeveloper Rebellion. Leaping between publishers Eidos, Reef Entertainment, and Ubisoft in a very short space of time, it was terribly publicized and largely forgotten by the few who noticed it in the first place—which is an injustice. Though its fiddly camera steepens its learning curve, it knows what makes a rational, fragile human being want to conquer a city by simply standing on top of it.

Surprisingly, it's not about height, challenge, or danger, though all play a part in the Tony Hawk–style objectives. It's about appreciating a world we take for granted, full of monolithic apartment blocks, concrete bollards, and immobilized cars. Momentum is its science; the game awards points and bonuses for chaining jumps, vaults, and rolls. But at its heart is its aversion to fantasy, and its ability to turn deliberately nondescript docks, bus shelters, and terraced gardens into worlds as exciting as an Arabian fortress or a gleaming police state. **DM**

FlatOut: Ultimate Carnage

Original release date : 2007
Platform : Various
Developer : Bugbear Entertainment
Genre : Racing

It's not all about the violence with the *FlatOut* series. True, it fires drivers through windscreens with some degree of zest, but only as part of a broader selling point: physics. It's a rougher, weightier experience, more like *The Dukes of Hazzard* than Eutechnyx's *The Fast and the Furious*. And it's unapologetically frustrating, to the point where Xbox 360 debut *FlatOut: Ultimate Carnage* features the telling Achievement "Perseverence," awarded for restarting the same race over and over again.

Ostensibly just a remake of Xbox game *FlatOut 2*, *FlatOut: Ultimate Carnage* feels transformed by the jump in technology, proving that the HD era stands for more than just "high definition." While higher texture resolution and parallax mapping pick out every crack and fiber of the American Midwest, the real change is in the complexity and dynamism of the races themselves. Forcing bumper-to-bumper action from first to last place, its tracks merrily disintegrate over the course of several laps, making the last lap as unpredictable as the first. Its redneck drivers, meanwhile, seem determined to drive over any obstacle, especially one another.

FlatOut: Ultimate Carnage offers no guarantees of a clean or fair race. You can't go into a destruction derby and expect to be chaperoned to the finish, and some racers simply reject the myth of playtime equaling progress. You are compensated, however, by vibrant, seductive track design that almost demands a kiss of the bumper. Military vehicle graveyards, lumber yards full of lazily discarded machinery, barns reduced to flying timber, riverside rooftops, treacherous storm drains, and gridlocked streets are just some of the highlights. For *Blues Brothers* fans, there's even a damaging trip to the shopping mall. **DH**

Crysis

Original release date : 2007
Platform : PC
Developer : Crytek
Genre : First-Person Shooter

Gaming had yet to reach its goal of true photorealism when Crytek decided it wasn't enough. Coining the term "video realism," it vowed that its next game would mimic the eye more than a camera, aided by techniques like depth of field, motion blur, diffuse transmission (light and shadow visible through semi-translucent materials), soft particles, and ambient maps (indirect lighting). Instinctively embraced by the "enthusiast" market, Crysis would promote an entire generation of software and hardware, from dual-slot graphics cards and multicore processors to Windows Vista and DirectX 10.

You are dropped straight into the action of a militaristic campaign. A fictional island chain plays host to man and beast, a dormant alien artifact prompting a standoff between America and North Korea. Stepping ashore before penetrating the interior, the player's US operative can make a weapon out of almost anything, from hijacked Jeeps to abducted chickens. Areas spanning land and sea are accessible from the start, though most of the action confines itself to mission waypoints and twists in the story. The biggest difference is the game's most potent weapon: you. Drawing superhuman powers from your nano muscle suit, you're what Crytek calls an "adaptable warrior."

Crysis remains a divisive game. Some feel it gives you more power than it knows what to do with; others praise its AI's versatility in a destructible world. Almost all gamers, however, concede that it is a sci-fi spectacle of the highest order. One thing's for sure: It demands a lot from your PC. Underscoring the gap between pre-launch screenshots and day-one performance, it continues to madden graphics obsessives years after release, bugbears including aliased foliage and steep hardware requirements. **DH**

Flywrench

Original release date : 2007
Platform : PC
Developer : Mark Essen
Genre : Puzzle / Action

Better known within art circles than by game consumers, thanks to his decision to demonstrate his work as art installations and in galleries, Mark Essen is associated more with his genre-blending—and often intentionally unplayable—art works, such as *Randy Balma: Municipal Abortionist*. Such association makes *Flywrench* seem out of character. It is a graphically stark and tightly designed test of reflexes that could be mistaken for a game from Atari's early, vector-graphics-led history.

In *Flywrench*, the player controls a ship (little more than a line) that changes color for each maneuver. In order to pass barriers, the ship must be a particular color. Doing nothing means the ship is white, allowing it to pass through white barriers (via previous momentum), while movement makes the ship "flap," flashing it red, requiring deft timing to pass red barriers.

The game world is also a maze, in which touching the edges means instant death (unless the ship is spinning, and thus colored green), and in many ways the design brings to mind electric wire puzzles. However, in this case the intent is to create flow rather than exacting tension. Because there is almost no time between a failure and restarting a level, and the player's ship is manipulated by using a limited number of possible interactions, a well-played game of *Flywrench* becomes almost a rhythm-action title, one where you define the rhythm yourself.

Ultimately this aspect reveals *Flywrench* to be in the same vein as Essen's more apparently artistic video game projects. It is a game about movement, and additions such as rich graphical detail would be redundant, only detracting from its aim to make the player intimately and precisely aware of their relationship with their ship. Playing *Flywrench* isn't gaming—it's dancing. **MKu**

E4

Original release date : 2007
Platform : Xbox 360
Developer : Q Entertainment
Genre : Action / Shoot 'Em Up

There's no denying it: Blowing stuff up can be lots of fun—particularly if the idea is taken to ridiculous lengths and if the general effect is as stylish as this. The most alliterative video game ever made, *E4* (aka *Every Extend Extra Extreme*) takes a simple mechanic and turns it into an unforgettable collision of style and high-score multipliers, tailor-made for wasted winter evenings in front of a huge HD television while the bass rattles the frosty windows.

The rules are simple: create chains by blowing up your tiny pulsating craft within reach of enemies. Your blast radius will cause any nearby foes to explode, sending out their own shockwaves and, ideally, the whole thing creates a chain reaction, extending outward in a vast, unpredictable rolling wall of points and power-ups. The music and visuals combine in a stirring, stylish spectacle. It is truly a beautiful thing to behold.

An Xbox Live Arcade updating of Q Entertainment's sharp PSP game, *E4* earns the "extreme" in the title with upgraded visuals and nice design tweaks, including proper multiplayer options, a funny little traditional shooter mode—which isn't actually all that brilliant, but is better than nothing—and the option to import your own music from the Xbox 360's media center to build your own procedurally generated levels.

Endless suicide for fun and profit: It's a concept that shouldn't really work. Luckily, it does, and exceptionally well, too. A game that should feel too clever and abstract and arty, in fact, feels visceral and immediate. Even if you're annoyed at the clever-clever name and put off by the trippily strange, warping artwork, don't miss out on *E4*. Once you've got it in your hands, and your eyes are unblinkingly following the action, you find your rhythm and the whole thing clicks. It's literally a blast. **CD**

Final Fantasy IV

Original release date : 2007
Platform : Various
Developer : Square Enix
Genre : Role-Playing

The fourth *Final Fantasy* wasn't the first to let you save the world—but for the first time, it blamed you for putting it at risk. Players start the game as Cecil, loyal servant to a king who's bent on murdering his rivals and burning their towns to the ground. Shocked by the atrocities that he's ordered to commit, Cecil rebels and sets out to redeem himself—aided by a cast of strange, often ill-equipped, sidekicks. You'll frequently get the impression that Cecil is carrying all the weight while his new companions level up, but the hassle suits the story: It's the most immediate way he can atone for his sins.

The best version of the game today is the 2007 reissue by Square Enix, released in time for the twentieth anniversary of the series. Following its success with a 3-D overhaul of *Final Fantasy III*, the publisher followed the same process with *Final Fantasy IV*, tweaking a few rules, adding mini-games, changing the purpose of certain characters, and inserting previously missing script sections. The greatest change, though, is reinventing its 2-D world in sparkling 3-D. The environments have never looked lusher, and the character designs are weirdly cute. In his skinny black armor Cecil resembles an ant, while Tellah is decked out in so much color that he should be leading a carnival.

What Square Enix couldn't revamp is the steady grind of the dungeon crawls. The player works through one tunnel system or mountain setting after another, battling through random encounters and optionally flipping on the autobattle when the enemies get repetitive. The fluctuating party lineup and timer-based battle system try to keep things moving, but it's not a big improvement over *Final Fantasy III*. Still, the engaging and epic story is worth the slog. In its day, this was the state of the art in RPG storytelling, and the narrative still tugs hearts today. **CDa**

Desktop Tower Defense

Original release date : 2007
Platform : Internet
Developer : Casual Collective
Genre : Strategy

Tower defense games, like so much else that is good and just in this world, came from veteran PC developer Blizzard. They originated in the form of a handful of custom maps for its million-seller strategy game *Warcraft III*, in which players placed turrets to see off waves of increasingly powerful enemies. But the genre only really broke into the mainstream with *Desktop Tower Defense*, a non-budget Flash title created by UK-based coder and *Warcraft* fan Paul Preece.

Using a handful of clever tweaks from a friend's tower defense game, *Elemental Tower Defense*, and taking his favorite elements from *Warcraft III*, Preece built *Desktop Tower Defense* in the space of a few weekends, mainly as a smart means of teaching himself the intricacies of Flash programming. He used hand-drawn art to ensure that players could choose between towers that were instantly identifiable, employed only the barest of sound effects and visual flourishes, and set the game against a photograph of his own work desk, complete with piles of transatlantic currency acquired on his various trips to the US.

The result looked crude, but played in a very refined manner, with the tiny enemy Creeps finding their ways around all but the smartest arrangements of towers, and a handful of design firsts—such as the button that allowed you to send the next wave—that have become genre standards. And although the visuals are primitive, they exert a certain appeal, all of which combines to make Preece's little side project a vivid piece of gaming history, one of the original—and still one of the best—entries in an increasingly voguish genre. It spawned a legacy, becoming one of the top Web applications of 2007, as well as launching updates and a recent sequel. Free to play online, *Desktop Tower Defense* is, even now, just a quick Google search away. **CD**

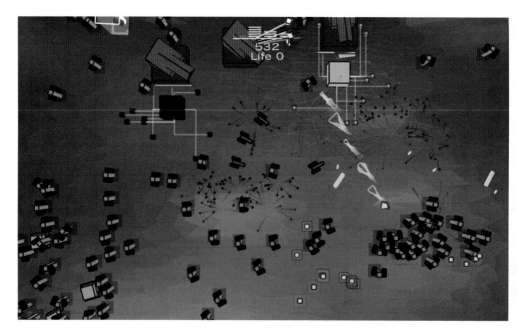

Everyday Shooter

Original release date : 2007
Platform : Various
Developer : Queasy Games
Genre : Shoot 'Em Up / Music

Everyday Shooter (*Riff: Everyday Shooter* in Europe) is a love poem to the shoot 'em up, a formal study of the chain combo, and a showcase for its designer's impressive guitar playing. It's a punishing action game with a tranquil presentation and the structure of a record album: Levels are "tracks," a shuffle mode lets you play them in any order, and each one lasts only as long as the song that forms its soundtrack. (Oh, and one of the bosses is Hayao Miyazaki's Porco Rosso. Did we mention it's also an art game?)

Designer Jonathan Mak has described the game as "an album of games exploring the expressive power of abstract shooters," which pretty much sums it up. The musical work that inspired Mak was Steve Reich's *Electric Counterpoint*, a minimalist piece featuring ten overdubbed guitar parts. Mak's score also sticks to guitars, and it casts the player as another instrumentalist. Your actions and mishaps trigger sound effects, and chain reactions play a cascade of sounds, which are different on each level, just like the moves that cause them. On some maps, you can push an object into a swarm of enemies and watch it detonate them all; in another, alien bodies connect like neurons, and killing one extinguishes the rest.

But Mak overstates the importance of the player. Not only are your musical contributions just accents to the score, your ship is shrunk to a tiny dot, which zips around the screen, firing in all directions. (In the style of *Robotron: 2084* and its descendants, one analog stick or D-pad moves the ship, the other points and shoots.) Your tiny stature matches your inability to control the pace of the enemies or the length of the levels. You don't beat the game so much as appreciate it; it presents a set of concepts that players study by way of their trigger finger. **CDa**

MotorStorm

Original release date : 2007
Platform : PS3
Developer : Evolution Studios
Genre : Racing

With more than a hint of *Mad Max*, *MotorStorm*'s vehicles jump, claw, maul, and stampede their way around the American West, roaring over tracks that end up in the mountains. One of the most compelling PS3 exclusives, it literally breaks new ground with its deformable terrain.

The game opens with a voiceover worthy of the late Orson Welles, just the kind of B-movie shtick that made the sci-fi racers of the 16-bit era so endearing. "In this ageless valley," it rumbles, "a new breed of warrior has been born." *MotorStorm* isn't sci-fi, but it isn't far from fantasy, either. Allowing a lethal mix of rally cars, big rigs, dirt bikes, mudpluggers, ATVs, trucks, and buggies to hare around at the same time, it rarely renders a frame without some

piece of wreckage—human or vehicle—chaotically flying across the screen.

With deliberately aggressive AI and almost terminally frenzied races, *MotorStorm* pops the cork on a very pent-up Evolution Studios. Having worked exclusively on *WRC Rally* games between 2001 and 2005, treating real-world tracks and cars with a legally enforced respect, it lets it all out with a passion. It also does it with brains—the giant, open tracks giving each of the vehicle types its own stomping ground, the monsters plowing through trenches of mud while the bikes stick to rocky elevations. The more laps you endure, the more the routes devolve into quagmires full of wreckage and dynamic shortcuts.

MotorStorm also makes an interesting early case for the updating of games via Internet-enabled consoles. Released in Japan with its entire multiplayer mode missing, then in Europe without rumble support or an efficient front-end, it took more than a year to emerge intact from PS3's rushed and mangled launch. **DH**

Forza Motorsport 2

Original release date : 2007
Platform : Xbox 360
Developer : Turn 10 Studios
Genre : Driving / Racing

The *Forza* series sits at the serious end of the racing game spectrum, but it's not staid. Indeed, though it shares *Gran Turismo*'s enduring fetish for car wax and torque ratings, its cars are far more tricksy and skittish to drive, demanding delicate braking and acceleration, their wheels riding the roads with stimulating fidelity.

Forza Motorsport 2's predecessor also added one of the friendliest additions to the racing game the casual driver has enjoyed for years: the braking line. This aid to road positioning and speed cuts out the need to exhaustively learn tracks before you have a chance of being competitive. It's even quite possible to win on entirely unfamiliar courses. And then there's *Forza Motorsport 2*'s customization feature: a supremely flexible paint shop that has you creating anything, from reproductions of official race cars to anime babes, with the only limit being your imagination. And knowing that showing off is the greatest reason for designing all this stuff, developer Turn 10 includes an auction house, in which players can spend in-game cash on other players' creations (and make some by selling their own), and a photo mode that allows screenshot uploads to the *Forza* website.

Of course, such abandon is tempered by attention to the stern delights of tuning and purchasing new parts—but even here, all players are catered for. Each car is given a rating that places it within each speed class. Tune it up, and your rating will rise, too. For dedicated players, then, the skill lies in raising a car's rating right up to the very limit of its class, so that it'll be the fastest on the track. For the rest of us, it tells us how good our car is without having to take it to the test track. With this in mind, you could say that *Forza Motorsport 2* was made for anyone. **AW**

Halo 3

Original release date : 2007
Platform : Xbox 360
Developer : Bungie
Genre : First-Person Shooter

Bungie's third—but not final—instalment in the *Halo* saga came with the bold agenda that it would "finish the fight." With the game hyped like few others and the focus of the most intense fan speculation in years, Bungie was inevitably not going to please everyone. It did a spectacular job all the same, providing a fittingly explosive—if rather familiar—end to the saga of Master Chief. In the process it managed to raise the bar for what people can expect from console multiplayer suites.

The single-player campaign is suitably epic, taking you from the jungles of Earth to the arid deserts of a distant world, and throwing in the requisite Warthog duels, Scarab attacks, and Flood eruptions as the war against the Covenant reaches its unlikely conclusion. Some bemoaned the disappearance of the Elites, but fighting the game's Brutes, with their AI significantly improved following a disappointing showing in *Halo 2*, more than makes up for that. The overall quality of combat is enhanced, especially with the addition of equipment to *Halo*'s arsenal, such as a button press allowing you to deploy portable bubble shields, antivehicle mines, and health zappers.

But multiplayer is where the game really excels, both in campaign co-op, with its support for up to four players, and in the peerless competitive options, with a brace of brilliant modes, a smart range of scaled maps, and Forge, an editor that allows you to create your own levels and variations. Save films, allowing you to plod through old matches from any camera angle, are simply another form of magic entirely, and, for a time, *Halo* owned multiplayer console shooting. Even now, with other teams learning to reverse engineer its tricks, *Halo 3* remains one of the classiest, and most generous, online console games around. **CD**

God of War II

Original release date : 2007
Platform : PS2
Developer : Sony
Genre : Action / Adventure

God of War II is thought by some to be the swan song of the PlayStation 2 era. It arrived amid huge expectations, controversial marketing, and went on to be critically acclaimed and seen by many to be the high point in the successful series. You pick up the story as Kratos, the newly appointed God of War, who's leading the Spartans in their conquest of Greece. The breathtaking opening pits you against a towering Colossus, and you battle it at the height of your powers—only to find those powers stripped away a minute later by Zeus, who's been thinking you're a little too dangerous. A one-way trip to Hades is interrupted when the Titans intercept Kratos' soul, help him regain his strength, and set the stage for a battle between the old gods and the older ones—with Kratos hacking and slashing in the middle.

But in the meantime you get another dozen hours of legendary characters and gigantic bosses borrowed from the best of Greek mythology, as well as an action-and-puzzle hybrid that's reminiscent of the *Legend of Zelda* games. Yes, unlike little Link, you solve puzzles by shoving giant boulders with your superstrength or by tripping a switch with a waterlogged corpse—but otherwise, the balance of thinking and smashing is similar.

Dodging, combos, and epic finishing moves elevate this above your usual button-smashing action-adventure. Weapons and magical abilities are acquired throughout the game, and Kratos's trademark dual blades-on-chains fling out and slice flesh with a satisfaction that's primal. It's not easy, and the game will even warn players to crank the difficulty down a notch if they're dying too often. If that happens to you, don't be stubborn; it's worth swallowing your pride to get through the story and see everything this exceptional game has to offer. **CDa**

GrimGrimoire

Original release date : 2007
Platform : PS2
Developer : Vanillaware
Genre : Strategy

The creatives at Vanillaware are torchbearers for traditional 2-D art. *GrimGrimoire* is their lesser-known offering, a turn-based strategy game launched during the twilight years of the PlayStation 2, neatly sandwiched between 2007's attention-grabbing *Odin Sphere* and the lovely Wii hack-and-slash actioner *Muramasa: The Demon Blade*. Like Vanillaware's other offerings, *GrimGrimoire* is rendered with an organic, hand-drawn feel—a striking reaction to the preponderance of games that attempt, and often fail, to recreate the real world with visual verisimilitude.

To dismiss *GrimGrimoire* as an exercise in style would be a mistake, since the game succeeds in nearly every way, achieving all its goals. It works as a real-time strategy game pared down for console players, and its art style works in its favor—units are iconic and easy to discern from the background. The controls are simple enough that the player rarely wishes to trade their dual-analog controller for a keyboard and mouse.

The plot riffs heavily on chords already struck by *Harry Potter*, but a heavy anime influence distances the story from Rowling's realm. Protagonist Lillet, a tow-haired sorceress in training, finds herself caught in a time hiccup. She relives the same five days over and over—the moments leading to the mass murder of the students and teachers at her alma mater, the Tower of the Silver Star.

In a rare move for PlayStation 2 games, *GrimGrimoire* was released in the West with the option to play the game with its original Japanese audio—another sign of gaming culture's turning tides. *GrimGrimoire* helped predict a movement toward retaining rather than whitewashing the cultural flavor of Japanese imports. As a keeper of the old-fashioned two-dimensional flame, Vanillaware proved forward looking. **GM**

TIME 00:16.10
LAP 1/1
POS 9/10

Colin McRae: Dirt

Original release date : 2007
Platform : Various
Developer : Codemasters
Genre : Racing

How much of Colin McRae was left in Codemasters's series upon his death in 2007? On the one hand, his name was still on the box (in Europe, at least) and his self-developed car, the R4, was in the game. But on the other you had Travis Pastrana, the real star of *Colin McRae: Dirt*, and everything he represents: America, the X Games, the freestyle sports scene, and the adrenaline-fueled reality TV show, *Nitro Circus*. The sixth game in the series still features those classic checkpoint races against nothing but the clock, but its loyalties are on the slide.

The title, *Dirt*, is pretty much all its races have in common. One-on-one crossover races, hill climbs in big rigs, ground-churning CORR events in superbuggies; had

the series started off like this, it would have been Ivan "Ironman" Stewart on the cover. Like stablemate *Race Driver: Grid*, *Colin McRae: Dirt* also tends to follow its markets as much as its globe-trotting instincts, sticking to races in Europe, Japan, Australia, and the US. No shakedowns in Jordan or Dakar here. The journey ends with rally's own version of the Nürburgring, the Race to the Clouds hill climb at Pike's Peak, Colorado.

"Dirt" doesn't have to signify anything, of course—it can just mean dirt. The spectacular depiction of filth—be it on the car, the ground, or someplace in between—was the selling point of several 2007 games. Codemasters's Neon engine gives *Colin McRae: Dirt* the upper hand, its real-time physics affecting trees, exhaust smoke, trackside flags, and the deformation of cars and track. The wind wraps around scenery, barriers wrap around errant hoods, and cars wrap around lampposts if you really lose the plot. Say what you like about the series' own direction, but there's no denying its progress. **DH**

Heavenly Sword

Original release date : 2007
Platform : PS3
Developer : Ninja Theory
Genre : Adventure / Fighting

Few games have shouldered the weight of expectation quite like *Heavenly Sword*. A flagship PlayStation 3 game at a time when there was little coherent vision of what Sony's console would bring, it arrived amid a haze of promises and hearsay. The foremost rumor, bizarrely, was that an entire PS3 processing unit had been devoted to its heroine's hair. It hadn't, just as developer Ninja Theory had not embarked on some grand career-ending folly. Its performance isn't rubbish. It isn't unplayable. And it isn't, as you may have heard, just another hack 'n slash.

Its title refers to a godly blade that, like Excalibur, waits for a divinely appointed heir to wield it in battle. Many believe in this prophecy while others, like the evil King

Bohan, simply believe in its power. Its latest custodian is Nariko, a fierce Amazonian clanswoman. Handed the sword by her father, she faces a dangerous choice: surrender it or use it. She chooses the latter, knowing its reputation for draining its owner's life, and the fates of warrior and weapon become entwined.

In a prophecy of its own, *Heavenly Sword* portended more than just the future of PS3. With its heavy use of performance capture and a scenery-swallowing turn from Andy Serkis (who famously brought to life Gollum in the *Lord of the Rings* movies) as Bohan, it fired the debate about movie-and-game-industry convergence. A close collaboration with effects company Weta Digital, it even piqued the interest of director Peter Jackson. A solid third-person fighter full of epic backdrops, parry-based combat, and stunning cinematics, it even puts the tilt controls of the PS3 joy pad to good use. Also of note is an original soundtrack by versatile composer Nitin Sawhney and sumptuous art by Alessandro "Talexi" Taini. **DH**

Hexic 2

Original release date : 2007
Platform : Xbox 360
Developer : Carbonated Games
Genre : Puzzle

After the universally acclaimed—and also universally addictive—delights of *Tetris*, Alexey Pajitnov was always going to have to work hard to top his first game. *Hexic*, included on the hard drive of every Xbox 360, is not as friendly and accessible as his early masterpiece nor as dazzlingly replayable, but it's a smart game in its own right. This sequel, released for Xbox Live Arcade in 2007, only builds on that formula.

Hexic's basic game play mechanic involves matching gems of the same color to clear them from the playing field, but this simple idea is thoroughly embellished over the course of a complex and challenging puzzle title. Rather than swapping individual gems as with many match-three titles, in *Hexic* players must rotate clusters of three hexagonal pieces, making a match with each turn. A dizzying number of variations and bonuses are quickly piled on top of this, and, while *Hexic* might look colorful and casual, it's actually an exacting and rather enjoyably strenuous game to experience. *Hexic 2* adds a handful of smart additions to the mix, including new pieces, a roomier board, and a two-player battle mode, the latter of which helps to make an austere game a little more warm-blooded and personal.

In many ways, *Hexic* is actually the antithesis of *Tetris*. It's a slow burner that's enduringly hard to master, whereas *Tetris* is easy for almost everyone to play, and its individual games can last for a half hour or more, while *Tetris* is limited to shorter bursts for all but the very best players. Comparisons can be made and argued over, but *Hexic 2* is a willful and independent game in its own right, and it's more than capable of adding a little more luster to Pajitnov's already world-beating reputation. **CD**

Hotel Dusk: Room 215

Original release date : 2007
Platform : DS
Developer : Cing
Genre : Adventure

Yes, *Hotel Dusk: Room 215* has a divisive rotoscoped art style reminiscent of a certain classic a-Ha video. Yes, it features an unusual selection of puzzles, almost all of which are drab, ranging from the tense delights of searching through a very small laundry basket to—cripes!—peeling a label from a bottle of wine without tearing it. But Cing's intriguing faux-noir follow-up to *Another Code: Two Memories* is worth your attention for the unique and bizarre story it crams onto its tiny DS cartridge.

Pretty boy Kyle Hyde used to be a New York cop until he shot his partner, who he suspected of corruption. Now he works as a salesman for the Red Crown Company, a job that has led him to the peculiar Hotel Dusk, home to a range of pensive eccentrics. Everybody has a secret, and everybody seems to be waiting for something or other. Before the night is out, Hyde finds himself knee-deep in a seemingly impossible mystery that involves art forgery, secret chambers, his dead partner, and a hotel room with the power to grant wishes.

It's not your average video game narrative: It's coy, involuted, and pleasantly ambiguous, and it casts a spell over the game. There is a strange, low-key tone to *Hotel Dusk: Room 215* that makes it a lot easier to forget the weaker elements as you explore the hotel, interrogating suspects in endless dialogue exchanges, and solving the strangely limp puzzles. It isn't a perfect game, then—at times, it isn't even that good—but it belongs to that rare breed of entertainment where you can genuinely say there's nothing else like it; not just in terms of presentation, but in terms of the stories it wants to tell and the characters it wants to explore—and, ultimately, the places it wants to take you while it does so. **CD**

Fai Dan: Looks like a dozen. Maybe more.
Can I help?
What's going on?
Only a dozen?

Mass Effect

Original release date : 2007
Platform : Various
Developer : BioWare
Genre : Action / Role-Playing

Apparently restless without a *Star Wars* game to work on—its previous was *Star Wars: Knights of the Old Republic*, its next would be MMO *The Old Republic*—RPG maker BioWare decided to make its own galactic saga, leaving no stone unturned when it came to sci-fi inspirations. Like *Star Trek*, it would feature a members-only club of humans and aliens it called the Human Systems Alliance. As in *Babylon 5*, the many species therein would meet in a city-sized space station, here named the Citadel, full of politicians, soldiers, thieves, and refugees.

And like some visually futurist piece from the 1970s, everyone would wear jumpsuits that looked like recycled Japanese cars. In place of the Force the game would have the titular Mass Effect, a universal phenomenon that beings in 2183 AD could sense and control. Instead of the starship USS *Enterprise*, there'd be the SSV *Normandy*, a prototype ship commanded by the player's own Captain Kirk—a customizable hero called Shepard. As in any geek fantasy, there'd be a ruthless separatist bent on messing things up and a wealth of back story about ancient warring races. And romance? If you played your cards right—as in, chose the right missions and dialogue options—maybe you'd get even more.

Wrap all that around the proven team play from *Knights of the Old Republic*, *Halo*-inspired vehicle sections, and a modern cover-based combat system, and you have *Mass Effect*. Using state-of-the-art lip-synch, film grain, and lens effects to really act like a blockbuster movie, it makes up for shortcomings in narrative and player choice. At times you're choosing less between good and evil than pious and petulant, but perhaps that's the influence of latter-day *Trek*, always straying from space opera to soap. **DH**

Odin Sphere

Original release date : 2007
Platform : PS2
Developer : Vanillaware
Genre : Action / Role-Playing

Odin Sphere was one of the first games in a high-definition 2-D renaissance that's now largely led by beautiful but bite-size downloadable titles. This, though, is a full-length action epic, framed in a series of lush storybooks being read by a little girl in her attic. Its characters are large, richly detailed 2-D sprites in almost Shakespearian costume, and they're set against a layered backdrop of scrolling 2-D environments that draw heavily from traditional Japanese art. *Odin Sphere* is a beautiful piece of visual artistry; its waves, snowflakes, and falling blossoms evoke a moving version of Hokusai-era ukiyo-e woodblock prints.

The game's five separate but interlocking stories play out independently, each with its own protagonist, a storytelling structure that gives *Odin Sphere* the atmosphere of an epic medieval myth. The storybook framework is a beautiful context for the art, lifted from a well-translated script that maintains the theatrical tone of the original Japanese instead of ruining it with second-rate voice acting.

Odin Sphere plays like a familiar scrolling 2-D fighter, with an uncomplicated, momentum-based combo system, meaning that, over the course of forty hours, the action can sometimes wear thin. Item synthesis and food play a secondary role; planting seeds grows plants that characters can either munch delicately or combine with other ingredients in a sumptuous-looking restaurant to create a more nutritious meal with greater hit- and experience-point bonuses. Very few games display such poise and delicacy in their presentation as *Odin Sphere*. There are better action games and better RPGs, but when it comes to sheer artistic vision, this stands among the medium's very greatest achievements. **KM**

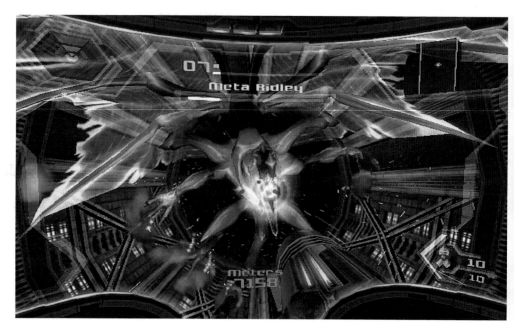

Metroid Prime 3: Corruption

Original release date : 2007
Platform : Wii
Developer : Nintendo
Genre : Action / First-Person Shooter

When Nintendo and Retro Studios brought the *Metroid Prime* series to the Wii, they kept intact the fundamental ideas that have guided the franchise for decades. Samus Aran, intergalactic bounty hunter, traipses across the galaxy to fight space pirates, gaining upgrades and abilities all the while. She fights massive bosses whose tricky attack patterns are counterbalanced by vulnerable spots that glow helpfully. And, of course, Samus can roll into a little ball for those hard-to-reach areas. But while Retro didn't aim to reinvent *Metroid*, it did reinvent *Metroid*'s aim.

Though other developers had attempted to use the pointer function of the Wii Remote for more lifelike first-person shooting, *Metroid Prime 3: Corruption* is the first to get it right. The Remote controls both Samus's aiming and turning functions on a continuum. In the middle of the screen is a large dead zone in which the aiming reticule will move freely without affecting movement, allowing Samus to aim at most enemies in her field of vision. Move the reticule toward the edge of the screen, and she will start to turn in that direction—slowly at first, but faster the farther out you go. This approach makes it easy to fight when enemies are near, and it's simple to navigate the twisted hallways and expansive vistas that make up the game's varied environments. Player intent is always respected.

Other motion controls include deploying Samus's grappling hook using the Wii's Nunchuk with a whip-like motion. Unlocking doors and using computers are accomplished by using the Wii Remote with one-on-one tracking. Even as other developers' experiments with motion control continue to feel clumsy and even gratuitous, *Metroid Prime 3: Corruption* shows how natural it can feel when done well. **MK**

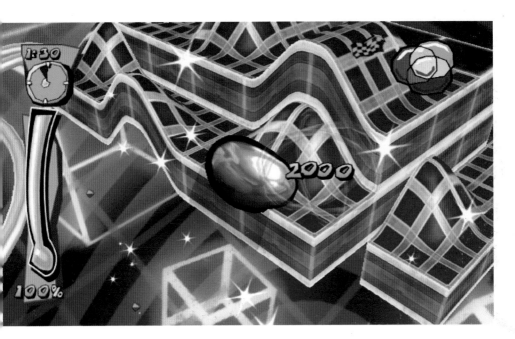

Mercury Meltdown Revolution

Original release date : 2007
Platform : Wii
Developer : Ignition Banbury
Genre : Puzzle

Mercury Meltdown Revolution spectacularly demonstrates what can be done with the Wii's accelerometers. Ironically, *Archer Maclean's Mercury* (the first game in the series) made its debut on Sony's PSP, and was intended to ship with a tilt-sensing plug-in. That particular gadget never made it beyond prototype form, but the game was a brilliant launch title nonetheless, yielding a sequel in the form of *Mercury Meltdown*. *Revolution* is essentially the same game with some additional levels, but it is also the definitive version thanks to the control afforded by the Wii's Remote.

The game combines elements of *Marble Madness* and *Super Monkey Ball*, but adds a complex puzzling element to the dexterity challenges. The titular element must be guided through abstract floating mazes (by manipulating the maze, not the quicksilver), but progression is impeded by varied obstacles, such as shifting blocks, disappearing platforms, and gates. The primary puzzle mechanics involve coloring or splitting the mercury. Multiple paths and edges without barriers need to be carefully navigated, while gates can only be passed through if your mercury is the same color; you may need to split your globule, color the segments differently, and then recombine them to achieve the required hue.

Ignition Banbury does a great job of imbuing the player's "character" with just that: the mercury is animated brilliantly, and if any drops away over the edges, it lets out a heartstring-tugging yelp of distress. Enough liquid metal must be deposited at the end of the level to progress to the next, so avoiding such calamity is essential. The lack of multiplayer is disappointing, but *Mercury Meltdown Revolution* is an all-too-rare example of a game interface that dissolves the barrier between player and play. **BM**

No More Heroes

Original release date : 2007
Platform : Various
Developer : Grasshopper
Genre : Adventure / Fighting

One of those games that is extremely hard to describe, and even harder to convey the appeal of, *No More Heroes* is a blisteringly stylized open-world game. You play as Travis Touchdown, wannabe assassin, big mouth, and full-on wrestling fan, scraping by in a deadbeat town filled with hicks and murderers. The crux of the game plays out in quirky white-trash dungeons as, tasked with working your way to the top of the local assassins leaderboard, you fight your way through to the insane, sexy parade of bosses, picking up loot, and earning money. In between that, you bomb around town on your Sinclair C5–alike and perform various menial tasks for incredibly low wages. How do you feel about collecting some coconuts?

A Japanese take on a Western game type, *No More Heroes*'s world itself is staggeringly empty, its sun-lasered California strip malls and apartment complexes devoid of almost anything to do except take on the incredibly repetitive jobs and kill time before your next dungeon. Luckily, the dungeons themselves are breathtaking: ultra-hip snaggles of corridors and arenas where you use your lightsaber-styled Beam Katana to dispatch wave after wave of oncoming baddies.

Combat is immensely satisfying: a muddle of swings, blocks, high/low attacks, and wrestling grabs that evolve over time and climax in discovering Travis's "Dark Side"—a secondary mode than can be accessed when three slot machine icons line up after delivering a successful death blow. With its distinct flat-color visuals and ragged, punky aesthetic, with its enemies exploding in splattery black showers of ink, and with its pick-ups built from blocky pixel art, there's no danger of mistaking the madness of *No More Heroes* for any other title. **CD**

Pain

Original release date : 2007

Platform : PS3

Developer : Idol Minds

Genre : Action

Pain didn't start off as anything particularly special: merely an entertaining but throwaway schoolboy-humor experiment with the Havok physics engine, featuring just one level and two characters. But when it unexpectedly became the best-selling game on PlayStation Network, Idol Minds began adding levels and characters until the game was big enough for a physical release, feeding a seemingly infinite appetite for launching a ragdoll character model from a massive catapult into a cityscape, just to see what happens. Now, there are multiple playable environments (including the Abusement Park) to explore, and it's the only game in the world that makes it possible to fire Flavor Flav into the mouth of a giant whale.

Pain proves a universal truth of video games: for a huge section of the game-playing public, ragdoll physics are inexhaustibly funny. A lot of *Pain*'s humor is a little too self-conscious to hit the mark, but when it isn't trying, the emergent humor can be brilliant. Once in a while in among the usual car pileups, explosions, and general chaos, one lucky launch sees some poor character end up bouncing off exploding barrels until they end up hanging improbably from a crane by their belt buckle, or headfirst through two windows and into a Dumpster.

It's a weirdly addictive high-scoring game, too, largely because it's so random that any launch could potentially land a 20-million score. It gives the illusion of control by letting you twitch a character's limbs post-launch to nudge them into the path of a car or an exploding crate, but *Pain* is mostly about watching and giggling, not playing. It's best regarded as a little case study of gamers' playful fascination with destructive chaos, and also our universal love for physics engines doing funny things. **KM**

Picross
DS

Original release date : 2007
Platform : DS
Developer : Jupiter
Genre : Puzzle

When it launched, the DS was touted as the first step in Nintendo's "Blue Ocean Strategy." Its unique combination of traditional gaming hardware with stylus and touch screen pointed to unparalleled gaming possibilities, and held the promise of exploiting those hitherto untapped audiences—the azure seas of Nintendo's analogy. But as any puzzle fan will tell you, the real killer use of the stylus and touch screen duo is the ability to emulate a pen and paper.

That has allowed it to house silicon versions of any and every notable pen-and-paper puzzle game, from tic-tac-toe played over PictoChat to conversions of games like *Sudoku* and *Slitherlink*. Of all of them, the greatest is undoubtedly *Picross DS*—a type of puzzle also known, in its pen and paper incarnation, as Nonograms, or Griddlers. It had actually appeared on other consoles with some success in Japan, but it was the addition of the stylus functionality that cemented its mainstream appeal in the West.

Picross DS takes a few simple logic rules and then layers them on top of one another until they create a tangled web of fiendish complexity. Your mission is to untangle that web—in this case, by working out which squares on a grid are shaded, and which are not. At the end of each row and column of the grid is a series of numbers. These numbers represent the number of contiguously shaded blocks, and by cross-referencing them until your brain hurts, it's possible to work out where they all go.

Like all of the best puzzle games, it boasts a learning curve that starts off deceptively shallow, but just gets deeper and deeper. You'll start off dangling a toe, and before long you'll find yourself bang in the middle of Nintendo's blue oceans. **DM**

Professor Layton and
the Curious Village

Original release date : 2007
Platform : DS
Developer : Level-5
Genre : Adventure / Puzzle

Level-5's plucky, uniquely European-flavored tale of polite derring-do and lateral thinking was a sleeper hit for the world-conquering Nintendo DS. It was an outcome neither developer nor publisher was remotely prepared for, and an early shortage of cartridges saw the game changing hands in the US and UK for some frankly ridiculous amounts.

Whatever you pay for it, the game's a charming—and often fairly challenging—adventure, as gentle genius Professor Layton and his cockney apprentice Luke (in the sequel, Luke has undergone a baffling change of class) arrive in the village of St. Mystere, to investigate the mystery of the fabled Golden Apple. The wider narrative will have to wait, however, as everyone the duo meets along the way has some kind of individual puzzle for them to solve—be it a conundrum with matchsticks, foxy questions about pitchers of water, or various more complex logic or math challenges. Some of the puzzles are trick questions—a card that was played far too much in the sequel, *Professor Layton and the Diabolical Box*—but all of them bring a warm thrill of achievement once they're completed. Beyond the specific challenges you've still got a sprawling series of murders to investigate, the solution to which will bring the fate of the entire populace into question.

The puzzles are sharp and entertaining, and the watery art is wonderfully distinctive. *Professor Layton and the Curious Village* is a game with a lot to recommend it. A huge hit with the DS's new nongaming audience, the game is one of those rare titles that pleases almost everybody, and with such a finely judged balance between modern game play and traditional puzzles, it's not particularly difficult to work out why. **CD**

"My village is on a road that leads to no other towns. I look forward to seeing you there."

Use your stylus to draw a circle around the right village, and then touch Submit.

Circle the village !

HINTS 1 2 3

QUIT

CLEAR

SUBMIT

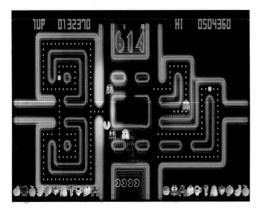

Pac-Man Champ Ed

Original release date : 2007
Platform : Xbox 360
Developer : Namco
Genre : Maze

Original *Pac-Man* developer Toru Iwatani appears to have taken the "remake" concept literally, crafting the game he might have made if the Xbox 360 were around in 1980. The result is engrossing, expanding the cat-and-mouse game play of *Pac-Man* without ever betraying its roots.

Most of the graphical enhancements in *Pac-Man Champ Ed* are lavished on the mazes. They pulsate with color and light; bonuses sparkle into existence; spotlights track the hero and his ghostly pursuers. These visual touches are always subtle, and the same goes for the soundtrack, which blends the classic game's sound effects (the siren, the "wakka-wakka") into a throbbing electronic mix. Iwatani's aesthetic restraint is a masterstroke that gives *Pac-Man* an immersive, moody sense of place—mazes seem like layers of a deep world rather than diagrams on a flat screen.

Pac-Man Champ Ed is more fragmentary than the original. There are no levels to speak of; the maze reconstructs itself as you go. And in the most striking departure, there's a time limit, shifting the focus from endurance to speed—yet the core thrill of the chase is still there. **JT**

Peggle

Original release date : 2007
Platform : Various
Developer : PopCap Games
Genre : Puzzle

Fire a ball bearing at an arrangement of colored pegs, clearing all the orange ones until you run out of ammunition. A bucket passing back and forth at the bottom will give you a ball bearing back if you manage to catch it, while everything you do in the game showers you with points—long shots, stylish bounces, prolonged hot streaks. Such is PopCap's brilliance with rewards that even missing all the pegs entirely leads to an entertaining bit of nonsense that may or may not reward you with another ball. Even when you crash and burn completely, the game manages to make you feel warm and fuzzy, without the slightest sense that you're being patronized.

It has a glorious air-brushed art style, a range of *Peggle* instructors, each of whom have their own secret skill to aid you, and the single best use of Beethoven's "Ode to Joy" in all of recorded history. Novices delight in the sounds and sights and constant chatter of point accumulation, while more seasoned players are thinking five bounces ahead, even racking up to 16 million points from a single shot. *Peggle* truly has something for almost everyone. **CD**

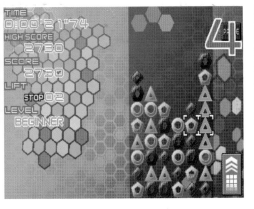

Planet Puzzle League

Original release date : 2007
Platform : DS
Developer : Intelligent Systems
Genre : Puzzle

Planet Puzzle League has a great understanding of interface, a masterful multiplayer, and refinements that seem slight but change games utterly. The interface is simple enough: You tilt the DS on its side and, using the stylus, drag your tiles by stroking the screen instead of pressing a D-pad repeatedly. This changes the way the game is played: Where once you had to jerk tiles across space by space, now smooth sweeps can pull colors together instantly. If you're quick enough with the stylus, you can line up other tiles to take advantage of the falling pattern. These combinations are where the magic of *Planet Puzzle League* is found, not only in the simple joy of their execution, but in the way you use them against other players and watch them used against you.

Online play is simple enough, but it makes one of the best puzzle games around even greater, and the DS's dual screens inspire hypnotic, frenetic competition by showing your opponent's playfield. The standard of play online can be ridiculously high, and foolish individuals that think themselves masters are quickly humbled. **RS**

Puzzle Quest

Original release date : 2007
Platform : Various
Developer : Infinite Interactive
Genre : Puzzle / Role-Playing

A match-three game built into a very basic RPG framework, Infinite Interactive's title was a sleeper hit, sucking people in before they'd realized they were even in danger. *Puzzle Quest's* great idea is to target the completer/finisher part of your brain, each victory suggesting that another is only five or ten minutes away.

The RPG elements couldn't be more basic: choose a character and explore a very limited game world, taking on quests, most of which will result in playing a tile-swapping game with some manner of monster, while leveling up and unlocking new skills and spells. The story is confusing and forgettable, the character design looks distinctly copyright-free, and the world is almost gloriously generic.

The puzzle game is a lot tighter, but the AI enjoys quite an unfair advantage, the monsters you battle possessing a freakish knowledge of the tiles that are about to fall into the screen, which allows them to set up the most elaborate chains while you fight through a few simple matches before failing out and having to do the whole thing all over again. **CD**

Ratchet & Clank: Size Matters

Original release date : 2007
Platform : Various
Developer : High Impact Games
Genre : Action / Shoot 'Em Up

The fifth *Ratchet & Clank* title released in five years (a release schedule normally reserved only for sports games), *Size Matters* represents the only entry for the main series on PSP, serving as a stop-gap in the transition between the series' last appearance on PS2 (*Ratchet & Clank: Deadlocked*) and its first on PS3 (*Ratchet & Clank Future: Tools of Destruction*).

Developed by High Impact Games (a breakaway from original developer Insomniac Games), *Size Matters* surprises by not feeling like a cut-down or neutered experience. While locations might be slightly smaller and there may be fewer enemies on-screen, the title offers the fizzing combination of shooting and platforming action the series has come to be known for.

Belonging to a series already four entries strong, *Ratchet & Clank: Size Matters* suffers for players unfamiliar with its setting and characterization, and even for devoted fans the PSP's lack of a second analog stick can make the gunplay somewhat awkward. However, as in its predecessors, *Ratchet & Clank: Size Matters* maintains players' attentions by the clever pacing of Ratchet's upgrades, with new weapons always only a few bolts (the game's collectible currency) away, and new armor placed across levels generally after bosses or other scripted events.

In addition, the game offers a well-paced storyline that keeps you guessing from one level to the next, as Ratchet and Clank find themselves on an adventure to understand the importance to their universe of the mysterious and ancient Technomite race.

Ratchet & Clank: Size Matters's title is gleefully ironic. It's really a perfect example of how handheld titles can now be just as comprehensive, epic, and fully featured as their home console relatives. **MKu**

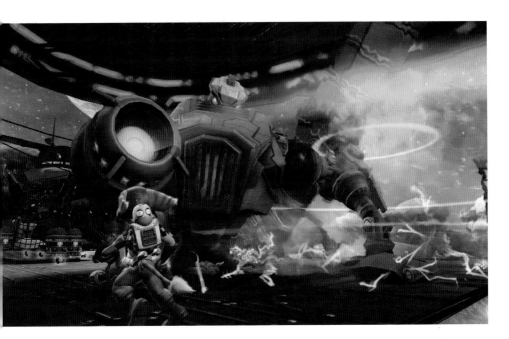

Ratchet & Clank Future: Tools of Destruction

Original release date : 2007
Platform : PS3
Developer : Insomniac Games
Genre : Platform / Shoot 'Em Up

The longest-running argument among gamers is whether graphics are a true measure of a game's worth. Most people would agree that flashy visuals don't amount to much without solid game play, but what if the point of a game is to show you new and thrilling sights? *Ratchet & Clank Future: Tools of Destruction* sends players across several stunning alien worlds, each with a distinct identity and appearance. It is at once a convincing case for high-definition gaming, and an argument that graphics and game play are impossible to separate.

Graphical horsepower is often best used in service of the fantastic, and that's the case here. Ratchet and Clank explore hot, muggy planets where dinosaurs still rule, and gleaming futuristic cityscapes where skyscrapers do just that. The environments look so good that you may not immediately realize how interactive they are; feel free to go ahead and climb the armor plates running along that apatosaurus's back. Equally as fun to ogle are the gonzo weapons that Ratchet employs in his battle against the evil Emperor Tachyon. His guns shoot metal blades, rockets, laser beams, even tiny swarms of creatures. Each one can be upgraded to an absurd degree. One weapon starts off emitting puffs of wind, useful against only the smallest of enemies, but as it powers up it eventually becomes a force-5 tornado, chewing up and spitting out everything on the screen.

Ratchet & Clank Future: Tools of Destruction is equally admirable for its storytelling and sense of humor. The earnest Ratchet and the acerbic Clank are the quintessential comic duo, the id and the superego constantly in tension. It can't be easy to make games that look this good and play this effortlessly, but Insomniac Games keeps pulling it off. **MK**

Portal

Original release date : 2007
Platform : Various
Developer : Valve Corporation
Genre : Puzzle / Action

Don't be put off by the overplayed in-jokes and Internet memes. There's so much more to Valve's clinical first-person puzzle game than non sequiturs about cakes and songs about science. A strange spin-off from the *Half-Life 2* universe, *Portal* is a non-Euclidean platformer that will warp players' minds into a Möbius strip. It looks like a shooter, and has its handful of twitchy moments, but it's more about forethought, lateral thinking, and experimentation than running and gunning.

Trapped inside a sinister and gleaming research facility, with only the unstable computer GLaDOS for company, the player's job is to use Aperture Science's delightful new portal gun to navigate through a series of challenges. The gun itself couldn't be simpler, especially if you're a fan of those old Hanna-Barbera cartoons where characters lug portable holes about: one trigger fires an entry doorway into a surface, the other fires an exit hole. Step through the first and emerge through the second. If there's a gap to cross, fire one hole into the walls on either side and simply walk through; if there's a platform up high, put a hole in the ground and another above the platform, and you're there in seconds. If you want to fall forever, put a hole in the ceiling and one in the floor, and just jump in.

Inertia, turrets, and the mysteriously lovable Companion Cube quickly intrude to make things a little more confusing, but *Portal*'s ultimate surprise is the astonishing story that's quietly unfolding throughout most of the game. The narrative unfolds in a teasing series of mysteries that culminates in a shocking and darkly hilarious revelation. *Portal*, then, is a frighteningly clever game: witty, head spinning, and a cold glittering joy to look at. Play it now—before someone spoils the ending for you, or the memes turn you off for good. **CD**

Quadradius

Original release date : 2007
Platform : Internet
Developer : Jimmi Heiserman, Brad Kayal
Genre : Adaptation

Few would argue that chess, a centuries-old battle of wits with the heritage and prestige of worldwide recognition and championship-level competition, is in need of refreshing. That didn't stop a high-school project, escalated after graduation by creator Jimmi Heiserman, from adding a little Macromedia Flash and Java networking color to a black-and-white board. Aesthetically catering to a generation brought up on industrial-themed strategy titles—deployable power-ups and a kitschy science-fiction interface are present and correct—*Quadradius* reins in the impatient user with classic turn-based rules that are indebted to the checkers family as much as *Command & Conquer*. The aim is to destroy enemy pieces one at a time by landing on top of them—or decimating them with a neatly timed carpet-bomb, if that's your prerogative.

Evolving to the changing state of individual matches is the cornerstone of the experience, and it's no surprise to find that same fluidity mirrored in the title's design and development in the years since inception. Power-ups are nothing without balance, and *Quadradius* embraces that rule and applies it as a stern lesson in the dynamics of satisfying, structured, turn-based strategy. Determining to pace the one-on-one battles by turns rather than reflexes allows the art design to breathe, and though functional rather than flamboyant, Brad Kayal's work manages to elicit a sense of static time and decision-making purpose with its subtle mood lighting and clunky, industrial audio.

Like the best of the genre, *Quadradius* is easy to play and hard to master. It's a contemporary and convincing display of how a modicum of gaming's inherent variable and core conceit—chance as a weapon—can be applied to an ancient system and enable an old dog to learn some new, bomb-dropping, multiplying tricks. **DV**

Retro Game Challenge

Original release date : 2007
Platform : DS
Developer : indies zero
Genre : Adaptation

As a form matures as a cultural artifact, there comes a need for works that consider the form while being part of it. Film has had it easy—documentaries have been used to investigate its history and meaning countless times—and even comic books have Scott McCloud's defining *Understanding Comics*. Games seem a harder prospect. How can there be time to reflect when you're busy interacting?

One answer comes in *Retro Game Challenge*, aka *Game Center CX*, a Japanese game based on a beloved television series (in which an affable comedian, Shinya Arino, attempts to complete famously difficult Famicom games within a set period of time). Outside of being set challenges by a virtual Arino, the cultural reference points are understandable to a wider audience.

Retro Game Challenge is as close as a modern game can get to representing the 1980s gamer experience. Each block of challenges is set around broad parodies of games of the time: Cosmic Gate is a *Galaxian*-esque shooter, Guardia Quest a *Dragon Quest*-aping RPG. But what sets the entire title apart is that these games are played from a virtual living room where your (child) avatar exists along with a junior version of Arino. During challenges you see them on the lower DS screen and hear Arino cheering you on, and as the game progresses, you can read magazines hyping up new titles you might play or find tips and cheats for the games you already have.

In an always-connected world, *Retro Game Challenge* is a context-rich reminder of a time when magazines each month were a window into a bigger world, each game was sucked dry before the next one could be afforded, and if you played video games with friends, it was in the same room. For that it deserves a place in the library of any student of the medium. **MKu**

Space Giraffe

Original release date : 2007
Platform : PC, Xbox 360
Developer : Llamasoft
Genre : Shoot 'Em Up

Although it shares some common DNA, *Space Giraffe* is not *Tempest*. Legendary designer Jeff Minter had already provided an eye-searing update of the Atari classic before with *Tempest 2000*, and here he used a similar framework—enemies advancing toward you along a forced-perspective playing field—but expanded the concept in hundreds of astonishing directions.

But be warned, it's not for everyone. Filled with meme-speak and in-jokes, sprinkled with the developer's fondness for ungulates, crowbarring in at least one photograph of former Xbox chief J Allard, and covered in a pulsing, warping light display, *Space Giraffe* is branded unplayable as often as it's embraced as a masterpiece. Certainly, Minter's flair for trippy visuals can make things hard to follow on occasion, but this is still a precise and exhilarating game in which you're constantly gambling on the odds in order to rack up the high scores. Let the enemies get to the edge of the grid where you can barge them with a bulling run or shoot them when they're still a safe distance away, knowing that you're missing out on points? Dodge incoming fire or try to ping it back, keeping it in play for Sneeze bonuses? Trim the deadly flowers as they come toward you or try to keep them alive until the end of the level?

It's a dazzling, complex world, filled with intricate beauty, and that only makes the game's relative failure to sell all the more disappointing. Despite adopting the lowest price point available for an Xbox Live Arcade title, *Space Giraffe* has struggled to sell more than 20,000 copies since its release on the console. That doesn't mean there's no reason to pick it up now, however (particularly since it's also available for the PC). Despite the spinning visuals and starbursts of color, Minter's game is a true evergreen, as enjoyable today as it was when it was first released. **CD**

Rock Band

Original release date : 2007
Platform : Various
Developer : Harmonix
Genre : Music

After its success with *Guitar Hero*, what was next for developer Harmonix? This is, after all, the studio that created the market for rhythm-action games in the West, both defining and popularizing a Japanese genre in which few industry types have previously showed any faith. The answer was obvious. *Rock Band* was apparently a part of the original *Guitar Hero* concept, and its basic elements owe almost everything to its predecessor. But the act of following the rhythm and hitting the right notes is changed utterly by the addition of one simple factor: friends.

Rock Band was the first music game to make multiplayer a fundamental part of the experience; previous titles, including Harmonix's own, had included support modes, but they were largely supplementary and not evolved enough to provide suitable entertainment for a roomful of gamers. In *Rock Band* there's little room for soloists. You and up to three friends—lead guitar, bass, drums, and vocals— play each track together, standing or falling as a group, and what seems like a simple change alters the experience beyond recognition. You play every note in a solo with crystal sweetness, backed by the pulse of your bassist in the middle of a groove, while the singer hits every note perfectly and the drummer pounds through like an artillery strike. When *Rock Band* peaks, there is nothing like it.

The comprehensive structure Harmonix builds around the game—tours, avatars, a great website, and a constant stream of new tracks via downloadable content—is wonderful, but simply irrelevant to the meat of the experience. It sounds nonsensical to make this claim for a jumble of plastic and a disk, but playing *Rock Band* feels likes performing in a band up onstage in front of a screaming audience. More important, it's the closest most of us will get to the experience of making great music in the company of our greatest friends. **RS**

Singstar

Original release date : 2007
Platform : PS3
Developer : Sony
Genre : Music

Sony's competitive karaoke started life as a research project prototype kicked about by the eggheads and engineers in Sony's London Studio. It would go on to become the ultimate party game and pop-culture compendium, a perennial part of any wannabe scenester's social whirl. Its genius was to assemble a track list in which pop classics such as Britney Spears's "Toxic" rubbed shoulders with the sounds of a more innocent era, embodied, for example, in Musical Youth's "Pass the Dutchie." Current hits like "Mr. Brightside" by the Killers sat alongside bits of musical history like Madchester anthem "She Bangs the Drums."

But for such a seemingly disposable piece of media, it is home to some staggeringly sophisticated bits of technology. It uses all sorts of math and physics to listen to the words sung by would-be crooners, and compares their pitch to the original to generate a point score. It also uses devoted handheld microphones and the PlayStation Eye to inject an almost scientific amount of fun.

Originally created for the PlayStation 2 platform, the PlayStation 3 version ushered *Singstar* into the modern era of downloadable content, with thousands of tracks available online to add to the thirty songs that appear as standard on the disk of the original game. High-definition music videos are also thrown in for good measure, and Sony supports a vibrant (and vocal) online community, including space for players to share and rate movies and pictures of *Singstar* parties. There is even a dedicated VIP room in PlayStation's virtual space, Home, that has been used for various promotional activities, including an appearance in 2009 by UK rapper Dizzee Rascal.

It is a twenty-first-century twist on the hairbrush and mirror, allowing anyone to experience the dizzying taste of fame in the safety and comfort of their own homes. **DM**

The Darkness

Original release date : 2007
Platform : Various
Developer : Starbreeze Studios
Genre : Action / First-Person Shooter

The Darkness is a comic-book series from Top Cow Productions that centers on Jackie Estacado, a hitman for the mob who, on his twenty-first birthday, becomes the latest host for a timeless evil power. As its name suggests, the Darkness can only manifest itself at night, creating all kinds of demonic weapons for Jackie to control. But who's wearing the trousers in this relationship? Is it the man, who quickly discovers he's been stabbed in the back by his gangster "uncle" Paulie? Or is it the monster that poisons his ear (in the voice of Mike Patton from Faith No More) and makes him watch as his enemies murder his girlfriend?

When the *Darkness* game was announced, Swedish developer Starbreeze had already made its name as a safe pair of hands for tricky adaptations. And, as with previous game the *Chronicles of Riddick: Escape from Butcher Bay*, it wasn't content just to wrap this material around a boilerplate FPS. Jackie's powers, which include spikes that impale enemies, tendrils that snake around walls to outfox them, and implike "Darklings" that even take the liberty of urinating on them, aren't just decorative kill animations; they're prominent characters, nuanced weapons, and the threads that bind the game's themes and environments.

Like the treacherous prison of Butcher Bay, the world of *The Darkness* isn't something you can ignore while shooting enemies in the head. Jackie's no more bulletproof than Riddick, and has to analyze his New York surroundings before every confrontation. Many of his bullets are spent knocking out lights rather than people, creating shadows from which to launch his most devastating attacks. And because so much love has gone into every frame of animation, his powers as enthralling when idle as when tossing cars and ripping out throats. You'll know just how it feels to be lured to the dark side. **DH**

S.T.A.L.K.E.R.: Shadow of Chernobyl

Original release date : 2007
Platform : PC
Developer : GSC Game World
Genre : First-Person Shooter

If the concrete sarcophagus around Reactor 4 of the Chernobyl nuclear power plant is a tomb, then the nineteen-mile Zone of Alienation is its graveyard. It's as real as the vehicles abandoned on April 26, 1986, the lava still trapped in the facility's basement, and the nearby ghost town of Pripyat, where the activities of that day remain frozen in time. It's a place in which nightmare, reality, history, and folklore seem effortlessly interchangeable, and where the image of a cold, forbidding Soviet Union full of lost souls and secrets can be indulged and embellished. The perfect place, in other words, for a survival-horror game and a limitless source of power for *S.T.A.L.K.E.R.: Shadow of Chernobyl.*

That it took Ukraine's GSC Game World more than five years to create the horrors only adds to this game's mystique. A buggy and tortuous first-person adventure, it features scavengers who survive amid warring factions, mutant predators, and shockwaves of unreality from the reactor itself. Powered by the enigmatic X-Ray Engine, it dares you to imagine a world in which this didn't happen, where the worst disaster in the history of nuclear power didn't spawn everything from poltergeists to burning winds.

Excellent combat AI and ballistics models make *S.T.A.L.K.E.R.* a top tactical shooter, but it owes its cult appeal to brutal RPG elements. Vicious creatures roam through long and impenetrable nights, inflicting lasting wounds that limit your inventory. Strange anomalies ravage the terrain, eating away at your weapons and armor. And by the time your Geiger counter sounds the alarm, you're well on the way to a lethal dose. It's just a shame GSC's grandest ambition, a truly seamless open world, was one of the earliest casualties of development. **DH**

The Witcher

Original release date : 2007
Platform : PC
Developer : CD Projekt
Genre : Action / Role-Playing

The player-character of *The Witcher*, an albino monster-slaying man-witch called Geralt of Rivia, wasn't too familiar to many fantasists before this game arrived. The books of Polish author Andrzej Sapkowski, which provide the character and subject matter, have nevertheless been doing big business for years. The witcher has been slaying monsters and wooing maidens since 1993, but it was in 2007 that he made a serious impression on the RPG scene.

A single-character RPG with a focus on mature content and real-time combat, *The Witcher* is enormously engaging, if rather dry at first. This is a huge game, rivaling even Japanese RPGs in the investment of time required for completion. The first five hours could probably have been jettisoned, however, as they constitute a grinding tutorial sequence through a castle and crumbling village. It's a long time before you get into the body of the game and begin moving between wider areas of the world.

The gritty, realist environment and various subtexts of racism and corruption in a fantasy world make this a fairly dark RPG. These themes are splendidly conveyed by the beautiful, textured visuals, which are enhanced by BioWare's Aurora engine. *The Witcher* remains one of the more visually impressive RPGs, especially in its delivery of swordplay and general combat.

It is crucial to point out that the game was revised just a year later, with the Enhanced Edition, which overhauled both voice acting and character animation in order to create a more pleasing experience. Nevertheless, many English-speaking players elected to keep Polish voice acting and English subtitles. This gives *The Witcher* a foreign-language film quality, and results in an experience that reduces much of the kitsch value of a vanilla game. **JR**

John Woo Presents Stranglehold

Original release date : 2007
Platform : Various
Developer : Midway Chicago
Genre : Shoot 'Em Up / Action

One of the few games considered an official sequel to an acclaimed motion picture, *John Woo Presents Stranglehold* marks the return of Inspector "Tequila" Yuen, star of seminal Hong Kong crime flick *Hard Boiled*. Made in close collaboration with director John Woo by Midway's Chicago studio, it features the voice and likeness of action superstar Chow Yun-Fat. Prior to its development, the actor and director hadn't worked together since the 1992 movie.

In latter-day Hong Kong, a police officer has gone missing. The local Triads issue a ransom demand and call a meeting in a quiet marketplace: one cop, no funny business. Knowing it's a trap, Tequila heads in regardless, that *Hard Boiled* adage still fresh in his mind: "Give a man a gun, he's Superman. Give him two, he's God." Rescue soon turns into revenge, of course—this is John Woo, after all—and the trail leads to Dragon's Claw, one of the country's oldest and most powerful crime families.

John Woo Presents Stranglehold is widely underrated. With its physics-based stunts, polished scoring system, and "Massive D" destruction technology, it only truly comes together on its hardest difficulty setting. That's when elaborate venues like the Mega-Restaurant and Casino, Tea House, and Chicago skyscraper reveal their strategic depth, the newly hardened enemies and bosses forcing you to slide, swing, and dive into every available alcove.

It's also when you realize that this isn't a game about being Chow Yun-Fat but rather Woo, the master choreographer. Style is as important as survival in this game, and you're given more than enough tools to create the ultimate action sequence. True, you'll probably get killed in the process, but that's the mark of a great action game: It's as fun to lose as it is to win. **DH**

Team Fortress 2

Original release date : 2007
Platform : Various
Developer : Valve
Genre : First-Person Shooter

Team Fortress 2 is a tremendous and hugely successful improvement on the original. You can use anything from machine guns to foldout shovels (that feature surprisingly sharp edges). There are plenty of maps and classes to choose from, and most of the laws of physics do not apply. It has an expertly realized cartoon-style look and feel, along with brilliantly evocative sound effects. And the voice acting is impeccable: hearing the heavy talk so lovingly about his "sandvich" feels spot-on.

The game is an incredibly accessible first-person shooter built with the very intention of being easy to pick up and play. The same thing never happens twice, and each class of character is imbued with an engaging sense of fun. If you feel like burning hundreds of cartoon characters in a game of capture the flag; or sneaking around unnoticed before viciously stabbing people in the back; or even building a large fortress of gun turrets, teleporters, and dispensers, then this is the game for you. The wildly entertaining possibilities and combinations in Team Fortress 2 are almost endless.

Despite being available for both the PS3 and Xbox 360, it is best suited to the PC, whose version comes complete with extra unlockable weapons and clothing options for its diverse range of characters. Thanks to its open-ended nature, it also enjoys the benefits of a huge modding community, making it easy to join a game online, download one of countless maps, and start playing.

The vast majority of first-person shooters conduct their affairs with a completely straight face, and Team Fortress 2 ranks above most of them not only with its extensive online features, but also with its unashamed and unbridled sense of fun. **SG**

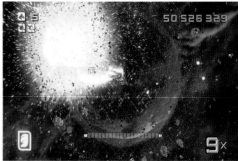

Super Mario Galaxy

Super Stardust HD

Original release date : 2007
Platform : Wii
Developer : Nintendo
Genre : Platform

Original release date : 2007
Platform : PS3
Developer : Housemarque
Genre : Shoot 'Em Up

Super Mario Galaxy has the distinct sense of imagination let loose, its colorful and inventive tendencies toward excess racing as far out into the ether as possible, and the results—a beautiful and precise platformer set in the colorful nebulae of space itself—are completely intoxicating. *Super Mario Galaxy* has more ideas in a single one of its tiny planets than many games can fit into their entire campaigns. Its dreamy brilliance is seemingly endless, as each new solar system brings new power-ups, new tasks, and new ways to have fun.

The biggest—and greatest—idea is to set much of the game on spherical worlds, where Mario can utilize every surface of the planet, even heading inside them for some equally mind-bending challenges. Star-shaped shooter pads propel the heroic plumber swiftly from one planetoid to the next, while phantom platforms lurk in asteroid belts ready to pull themselves into shape as necessary.

The game's simple structure—find stars, open up new levels—provides a satisfying hook to the experience, and *Super Mario Galaxy* even has room for a second player, allowing stragglers to collect fragments of stars while Mario himself heads off on the main adventure. **CD**

A high-def polishing of an Amiga classic, *Super Stardust HD* is one of the shiniest games ever made, emerging onto the PlayStation Network in a self-confident shimmer of space dust and lens flare, proving that simple shooters can be stylish, slick, and, frankly, rather expensive-looking.

Super Stardust HD is somewhat derivative, but a handful of clever tricks means it retains a strong identity of its own. First, there's a range of upgradeable weapons available to you as you blast hulks of space rock—and the odd alien—into dust. With flame, ice, and, erm, green options, all of which are particularly strong against a certain kind of target, they're a pleasure to use and a pleasure to upgrade—the whiplike trail of fire being a particular favorite. Then there's the playing field itself—each level is a planet, with your unending game space wrapped neatly around its orbit.

Power-ups are hidden inside the biggest chunks of space rock, and every direct hit generally breaks a boulder into a dangerous smaller piece. *Super Stardust HD* gets an additional shot in the arm every so often with a sudden onrush of creepy aliens, and even the odd boss fight. Smart and slick, this is a very memorable and effective addition to a crowded genre. **CD**

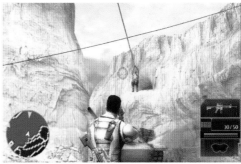

Supreme Commander

Logan's Shadow

Original release date : 2007
Platform : Various
Developer : THQ
Genre : Strategy

Original release date : 2007
Platform : Various
Developer : Sony Bend
Genre : Stealth / Shoot 'Em Up

Chris Taylor is a towering legend of real-time strategy design, a master of the massive computer game battlefield in which players capture resource points before building factories and military installations and then pump out units to take other armies down. But with *Supreme Commander*—shortened, colloquially, to the rather charming *SuppComm*—he outdid himself. A game built around the idea of scale, it allows players to zoom right from the overworld map, deep down into the action, and create a staggering amount of units before taking out the enemy mobile command center—vast, stylish mechs—in a thrilling climax. This comes very close to providing the ultimate RTS template.

It is an incredible game to experience. Building all those units might be something of a grind, but *Supreme Commander*'s big pay-offs, in which the battlefield is literally swamped with swarms of fighting units, are something no RTS fan should miss out on. Coated with a hard, sci-fi, utilitarian design and with mini-missions requiring real tactical brilliance, Taylor's hardly created the most friendly of games, but as a supercharged treat for the genre's elite, it's simply second to none. **CD**

Sony Bend proved it could summon incredible performance from PSP hardware with *Syphon Filter: Dark Mirror*, and the team proved there was still more to eke out with this sequel, which adds further game play mechanics to Gabe Logan's secret agent arsenal.

The story is surprisingly deep, twisting around world politics and the wild-card terrorist element, who've got their nefarious paws on world-threatening technology. The hero's team is called on to use all of its spying talents and gadgets to chase down answers.

This sixth entry in the *Syphon Filter* series boasts fluid game play by allowing health to regenerate and supplying more information on potential threats, such as where those pesky grenades are going to land. Supported by the context-sensitive ability to take cover and hide behind walls, the variety of combat situations is pretty significant. The slick design makes play mostly intuitive. You can enjoy a stylish solo adventure and then test out the options in ad hoc or infrastructure multiplayer, including new modes Retrieval and Sabotage. It's an impressive package squeezed into the PSP, and remains one of the most acclaimed games on the platform. **RSm**

The World Ends with You

Original release date : 2007
Platform : DS
Developer : Square Enix
Genre : Action / Role-Playing

Fresh and familiar by turn, Square Enix's brightly colored RPG is like few other games in the genre. Its big-haired manga kids suffering from overwrought existential doubts might be de rigueur for at least certain facets of the field, but while *The World Ends with You* has staples like item management, leveling, and instanced battles, it manages to put such a unique and fresh twist on them that they become almost unrecognizable.

Teenage misfits Neku and Shiki are dead, apparently, and find themselves trapped in Tokyo's Shibuya district and forced to mingle with the living while playing a deadly game created by the villainous Reapers. What this translates to is a series of brisk missions in which a revolving cast of characters must work to a strict countdown while buying items, engaging in fights, and reading the minds of the living—a particularly spooky addition to the game.

And the fights are like nothing else. Using the DS's peculiar capabilities in the most literal sense, players control two characters simultaneously—one on each screen—each of whom battles it out in a distinct manner. On the top screen, Shiki—or a handful of other teens as the game progresses—fights with presses of the D-pad, hopefully lining up certain arrangements of icons in order to trigger powerful specials; while below, Neku attacks enemies with taps and swipes of the stylus.

Badges offer different perks and attacks, and they also help add to the punky *otaku* aesthetic of the whole piece. Consistently fun is choosing which load-out to go into the next battle with. With a surprisingly gripping story and a combat system that, initially, is utterly overwhelming, the *World Ends with You* is a brilliant, shining curiosity. **CD**

The Legend of Zelda: Phantom Hourglass

Original release date : 2007
Platform : DS
Developer : Nintendo
Genre : Action / Adventure

Keeping the cel-shaded aesthetic of GameCube big brother *The Legend of Zelda: The Wind Waker*, *Phantom Hourglass* is yet another sign of the *Zelda* series' terrifying dexterity, washing up, in hardware terms, on the most inhospitable of shores, but learning to thrive very quickly.

The Legend of Zelda: Phantom Hourglass is, above all else, a masterpiece of control, as you lead hero Link about with the stylus, tap enemies to attack them, draw quick circles for a deadly spin move, and even plot courses for your little steamboat by sketching them onto the map. In a much-needed mechanic, given the series' inherent complexity, you can also scribble helpful notes to yourself directly onto the schematics of the game's dungeons.

But it's not just a brilliant piece of interface design: tasked with rescuing his friend Tetra, Link finds himself back on the seven seas in the company of the woozy, oddball coward, Captain Linebeck. He's a great character to hang out with, and the game throws up plenty of opportunities for Link to keep him out of trouble.

There are some smart changes to the game's overarching structure, too, with the regular suite of elemental dungeons joined by a single massive temple that runs through the spine of the experience and is accompanied by a nasty time limit.

Phantom Hourglass is not always *Zelda* at its very best. Despite the regular brilliance on display, it's lacking in the series' true sense of adventure at times, and repeatedly returning to a particular dungeon can wear a little thin. But it's a very skillful piece of work for a portable outing, and it more than deserves a place in that special handful of must-have titles for the DS. **CD**

Ghost Recon Advanced Warfighter 2

Original release date : 2007

Platform : Various

Developer : Ubisoft

Genre : Strategy / Shoot 'Em Up

This sequel was released just a year after the original *Ghost Recon Advanced Warfighter*. It maintains the near-future setup, and the concentration on a fictional South American crisis, but polishes every element of the brand's impressive battle armor.

The result is a squad-based tactical shooter that feels more like an action game than a dry strategic think piece. There's trouble brewing in Mexico again, and the elite Ghost squad is sent in to quell rebel forces and prevent a possible nuclear attack. In the single-player campaign, Captain Scott Mitchell returns as the key participant, but players also command a unit of AI-controlled soldiers through a series of combat missions, taking in stealthy ambushes, mass firefights, and the odd vehicle section. The key to the game is its intuitive squad controls. Troops can be directed with the D-pad, while a handy camera view lets players see through the troopers' eyes to allow the precise planning of reconnaissance and flanking missions. Furthermore, the presence of a controllable drone aircraft means enemy positions can be scoped out and ascertained without having to send in the AI guys like glorified bait. The design brilliantly combines well-planned military interventions against enemy encampments with moments of tense, chaotic drama.

Ghost Recon Advanced Warfighter 2 is a comprehensive multiplayer shooter, mixing a robust range of competitive options with a considerable co-op mode boasting a separate story and objectives. Together with the detailed urban environments and agenda-setting use of lighting effects (the explosions are awesome), this game is the barometer of contemporary military styling against which every subsequent example must have measured itself. **KS**

Uncharted: Drake's Fortune

Original release date : 2007
Platform : PS3
Developer : Naughty Dog
Genre : Adventure / Shoot 'Em Up

Uncharted: Drake's Fortune is a self-consciously cheesy adventure with a charming Saturday matinee style. It is a fun, colorful, and exhilarating blend of folklore, treasure hunting, globe trotting, and zombie Nazis that leaves film fans thinking of classic Indiana Jones moments, and gamers acknowledging debts to Tomb Raider.

But the game, the first PS3 title made by Jak and Daxter developer Naughty Dog, is far more than just a Lara Croft clone. Its chatty hero, Nathan Drake—a rogue, lover, and all-round straight-up guy—spends more time engaged in cover-heavy shoot-outs than clambering between rocks and prodding ancient machinery back into life (although there's plenty of that, too), while Uncharted: Drake's

Fortune's handful of genuine location-based puzzles are endearingly simple. In truth it's not all smooth running, with climbing sections occasionally grinding against too many shooting galleries. But, crucially, the game gets the guns right in ways that Lara Croft has consistently struggled to, with an over-the-shoulder aiming mode and a smart pop-and-stop cover system. Derivative, but Naughty Dog blends genres rather cleanly, and the development team makes its own contribution felt in terms of the good-natured character work: Drake is brought to life in a truly stellar performance by voice actor Nolan North, placing Uncharted: Drake's Fortune several notches above the best game audio out there at the time of release.

With amazing animation and some beautiful locations, it's a slick adventure, only really let down by a few irritating Jet-Ski sequences. The game brings a touch of class to a genre that is often about gems and statues and creepers and not much else. It isn't perfect, certainly, but it's yet another sign that games are growing up. **CD**

Wii Fit

Original release date : 2007
Platform : Wii
Developer : Nintendo
Genre : Fitness

Aiming to do for your body what *Brain Training* did for your mind, *Wii Fit* starts with a surprisingly traumatic event. You are asked to step onto the rugged plastic set of scales—or "balance board" in Nintendo's terminology—that the game comes bundled with. The board then calibrates the results and makes your Mii bloom or shrink depending on your BMI. Few exercise incentives are quite as powerful as seeing your Mii wobble around in a tubby fashion, so it's no real surprise that *Wii Fit* has gone on to sell millions of copies despite its rather hefty price tag, and become the second best-selling video game in history.

Beyond the bloated Miis, *Wii Fit* is a series of exercises designed to help you tone up a bit. These include everything from yoga and light stretching to a series of gamelike challenges. Just how much you'll tone up is up for discussion, of course. Like *Brain Training*, there's a lingering suspicion that Nintendo might be offering a push in the right direction rather than a genuine workout (for that, EA's *Sports Active* is a much more strenuous choice for the serious gym fan). Nevertheless, the challenges are handled with grace and style, and certain activities, particularly the on-the-spot jog around the delightful Wiifity Island, are guaranteed to leave you out of breath.

The mini-games are almost worth the price of admission alone, as you shift your weight on the balance board to guide a bubble through a stream, avoiding sharp rocks and bees; tight-rope walk between skyscrapers; even launch yourself down a ski jump and into the air.

A sign of just how far Nintendo has come with this hardware generation, *Wii Fit* might be a long way away from the hardcore pleasures of *Zelda*, but its design is filled with the same kind of clever tricks. **CD**

Wipeout Pulse

Original release date : 2007
Platform : Various
Developer : Sony
Genre : Racing

There was a suggestion that Sony was preaching to the converted with *Wipeout Pulse*. Another few years, another decal-spangled, trance-music-backed spin for its futuristic franchise, albeit only the second for PSP. Unlike an action-adventure brand, an FPS, or even a real-time strategy game, there's a limit to how much a racing game can evolve beyond what made it successful. Take away *Wipeout's* breathe-and-you'll-crash-it steering mechanics or its once-revolutionary club styling, and you take away *Wipeout*.

Yet within these confines, *Wipeout Pulse* does bring new material and motivations to the races. The most exciting are the mag strips that stick your craft to the track, enabling you to navigate white-knuckle rides through what would otherwise be impossible loops, bends, and vertical drops. There's also an admittedly confusing but novel grid-based progression system: Instead of the usual slog through lesser craft to earn your right to the best, you're given access to a matrix of different race meets. There are also varying setup conditions and racing modes, including the Eliminator, which does what it says on the box, and a Zone mode that's all about speed.

As is traditional, *Wipeout Pulse's* twelve courses are near-impossible on first encountering them, and here the pain is doubled by some events being conducted in reverse. The AI is, at times, a bit random, but does provide a worthy opponent. That *Wipeout Pulse* hails from 2007 rather than 1997 is demonstrated by the customization options—including vehicle skin editing and custom tracklists—various online capabilities, and how the game obsessively collates your stats. It's still surprising to find all this running without a glitch on the little PSP, but it'd be more surprising if you didn't find it a challenging play. **OB**

Professor Layton and the Diabolical Box

Original release date : 2007
Platform : DS
Developer : Level-5
Genre : Adventure / Puzzle

The second of Level-5's *Professor Layton* puzzle-adventure games for the Nintendo DS is another charming, well-mannered mystery, and though it took the best part of two years to reach audiences outside of its native Japan, it did at least arrive in sufficient numbers to circumvent shameless profiteering from secondhand merchants. *Professor Layton and the Diabolical Box* puts an Agatha Christie spin on the series by taking protagonists Luke and Layton on a train journey in search of a mysterious artifact known as the Elysian Box.

Every sight, sound, and encounter is an opportunity for a puzzle, naturally, and the game (called *Professor Layton and Pandora's Box* outside of the United States) has as varied and abstract a selection as its predecessor. As before, the individual puzzles and the overarching mysteries of the story have no meaningful relevance to each other, but each aspect of the game is compelling in its own right, and when the player is weary from one too many matchstick puzzles or trick questions, the story maintains just enough intrigue to encourage them to push onward. In keeping with series tradition, the characters and towns that Layton comes across are always *most* peculiar.

The game's greater scope makes for a less comfortingly provincial game than *Professor Layton and the Curious Village*, even if players of the predecessor might well feel that they've seen quite enough similar-looking block puzzles and mazes, thank you. Equally, there are plenty of humorous references that *only* those who have played the earlier game will understand. In all, this is a superb, original presentation, with a sharp script and a generally excellent cast of voice actors adding to its undoubted charm. **KM**

Unreal Tournament 3

Original release date : 2007
Platform : Various
Developer : Epic Games
Genre : First-Person Shooter

Unreal Tournament is the fastest-moving multiplayer shooter in more ways than one. As a game of blasting fellow humans into pieces, it has enough foot speed, firepower, and body count to make its competitors blush. As a project for Epic Games it's even more restless, adding a wealth of new features to each new installment, including characters, maps, vehicles, and game modes. And as a lifelong promoter of modding as both a hobby and career move, it comes with some of the most versatile home development tools around, giving free access to the prolific Unreal Engine. Just head to its online forums for some extraordinary user-created maps.

The problem with speed, though, is that it tends to leave people behind. Hence the reputation of most PC shooters for precipitous learning curves and hardcore communities: If you weren't there from the start, what business do you have playing now? Previous *Unreal Tournaments 2003* and *2004* did little to shake this attitude. But *Unreal Tournament 3* is different. With a single-player story mode full of tutorials and sparring sessions, it's as much a game for rookies as veterans.

This was vital for *Unreal Tournament 3* because it wasn't just the average PC game. It was a PS3 game, too, and one of the first to let console gamers see what they were missing. In a gesture that's unlikely to be repeated any time soon, it gave PC modders the tools they needed to "bake" content for both platforms, a map that works on one being just mouse clicks away from the other. Someone even added *Halo*'s Master Chief, much to the ire of Xbox 360 owners; their version offers no mod support thanks to Microsoft's content approval process. **DH**

Warhawk

Original release date : 2007
Platform : PS3
Developer : Incognito
Genre : Shoot 'Em Up

Warhawk had a troubled development, and as the game lurched toward release, its appeal could initially seem fairly hard to understand. A multiplayer-only shooter (the solo campaign had been stripped away following concerns over its quality), with an emphasis on quirky vehicles, didn't seem like a recipe for success. Then there was the fact that Sony's approach to online games was often rather muddled in general, with its PlayStation Network lacking the infrastructure—and users—of Microsoft's Xbox Live.

Over time, however, *Warhawk* has made a name for itself, with a rich core of devoted fans playing every evening on the game's expansive and varied maps, where factories loom out of the desert sands, and strange spikes

of rock hang in the air. Part of the reason for Incognito's success is that *Warhawk* gives players exactly what they want. Plenty of options are available, whether you're after a night of close-quarters ground-based warfare or spiffy dogfight runs through the skies.

And it's balanced almost perfectly, with planes causing devastation to ground troops only as long as they're moving, while even the big vehicles can be taken out by a common foot soldier if they play their cards right. Piloting the titular Warhawks themselves was initially divisive; for some players, the ability to switch between various flight modes will always seem a little weird, but most people find they only need a couple of hours' practice before they're up to speed and ready for combat.

More than anything else, however, the game has benefited from decent post-release support with a handful of weighty updates providing new maps and vehicles, and, finally, adding rocket packs. *Warhawk* is a smart, underappreciated game. **CD**

Zack & Wiki: Quest for Barbaros' Treasure

Original release date : 2007
Platform : Wii
Developer : Capcom
Genre : Adventure / Puzzle

It may have been the name that sealed it for Capcom's pirate-flavored adventure title. Perhaps the cute, sprightly pairing of "Zack & Wiki" makes one of the best third-party Wii games around sound a little too much like a children's cartoon series tie-in. Whatever the reason for its relatively poor sales, it wasn't because of the reviews: Magazine and website staff all over the world just loved this game. They lavished praise on its brilliant use of the Wii Remote and optimistically declared that this, finally, might be the way ahead for one of gaming's most beloved—and more venerable—genres: the adventure game.

Zack & Wiki: Quest for Barbaros' Treasure follows the struggles of its two heroes—a treasure hunter and his strange enchanted monkey. Zack yearns to be a great pirate, and, accompanied by the talking skull of a deceased pirate, he and Wiki seek their fortune on a quest for the legendary Treasure Island, at the same time fending off the rival Rose Rock pirates. This light narrative plays out for the most part as a traditional, if intricate, adventure in which the player navigates environments by pointing the Remote and sidestepping enemies, and interacting with various objects to solve puzzles.

Interaction switches the game from a third-person to first-person perspective, and often throws in some kind of motion-controlled twist when manipulating the fairly large inventory. Puzzles are smart but never too smart, and the only real irritation comes from a slight fiddliness when the environments get too complex for their own good.

For the most part, then, *Zack & Wiki: Quest for Barbaros' Treasure* is just the kind of game Wii owners often complain that there aren't enough of: It's thoughtful, carefully made, and completely unsuited to any other console. **CD**

World in Conflict

Original release date : 2007
Platform : PC
Developer : Massive Entertainment
Genre : Strategy

Recent attempts to reboot the real-time strategy genre have been met with limited success. *World in Conflict* represents one of the most significant advances, especially with its Soviet assault incarnation, which includes more missions from the invaders' perspective.

The game is set in a counterfactual history where the Soviet Union of the 1980s attempts a land invasion of North America to redress the balance of a war it is losing in central Europe. The campaign tells the story of a number of protagonists, with all the missions being undertaken by these key personnel. The game is really an excuse to pit the Cold War powers against one another in a straight fight and to see the battlefield technology from that era in action.

It's a bleak and beautiful spectacle, with tank battles across open fields, titanic artillery bombardments, and entire towns flattened in colossal exchanges of ordnance between groups of armor and infantry. *World in Conflict* is extraordinarily detailed, right down to the individual impact craters, and the real-time battles often evolve into thrillingly destructive firework displays. The resource mechanisms of reinforcement aren't ideally suited to single-player sessions, however, making some of the scripted events seem absurd, such as being told to retreat when you could clearly fight all day.

The multiplayer component is a strong one, making for a kind of tactical death match between players who opt for armor, infantry, air, or support units. Playing to support one another in capturing victory points across the map is remarkably engaging. The combined resource-pool options ultimately mean that players are able to deploy a single tactical nuclear weapon, which often turns the tide of any given game to spectacular effect. **JR**

Patapon

Original release date : 2007
Platform : PSP
Developer : Sony
Genre : Music / Management Simulation

A quirky delight from Sony's Japan Studio, *Patapon* sees you controlling an army of the titular eyeballs through rhythm—a control scheme based around memorizing simple beats that you match up to a background track.

It's a curious innovation: Your control over the army at first seems a little indistinct, even sluggish, thanks to having to keep religiously to a metronomic "pata-pata-pata-pon," with troops only responding after a full four beats have been played. But that steady beat soon hardwires itself into your fingers, helped immeasurably by a border that flashes in time, and you realize that the challenge here is not in a switching response to a new beastie, but in keeping your army moving and singing no matter what.

They're a tough little bunch, the Patapons, and especially so when in Fever mode—triggered when you've beaten out five regular instructions without missing a trick. So your obsession becomes keeping them there: "Pata-pata-pata-pon" moves them forward, "pon-pon-pata-pon" makes them attack, and as you progress, more beats and potential instructions are revealed. Fumble your instructions, and the beat collapses catastrophically, dumping your army out of Fever mode just as a horned monster pops up on the horizon.

Along with this fantastic game play mechanic, *Patapon*'s distinctive art style cements its place as a special game. Bloated, colorful dragons vie with big-eyed elephants and distended crabs for your army's attention, while the Patapons themselves are a beguiling creation: simply eyes with legs, the tribal touches added to their different types and their unquestioning worship of the player making them unquestionably yours. Just as you end up, despite your role as a god, being unquestionably theirs. **RS**

Carcassonne

Original release date : 2007
Platform : Xbox 360
Developer : Sierra On-Line
Genre : Adaptation / Strategy

In the early days of Xbox Live Arcade, the sheer novelty of a new game appearing every Wednesday was so incredible that players routinely subjected themselves to some genuinely bizarre wastes of time, in the manner of lab rats willingly lining up for chemo trials. While *Carcassonne* would superficially seem to fall into that category, this is, in fact, a polished and uncomfortably addictive title. Named after a medieval French town, the whole thing actually began life as a German board game. What was originally an enjoyable, award-winning tabletop game is enhanced and, arguably, perfected as a video game. The almost iconic cardboard and wooden "meeples" are made into a rich virtual experience.

Carcassone's a simple tile-placing game in whic[h] players lay out a series of cards, slowly generating [a] complex medieval terrain filled with roads, cities, ar[d] cloisters, and occasionally positioning "follower" piec[e] to claim ownership of a particular tract of the emergin[g] territory. The game ends when the last card has bee[n] placed and scored in a manner that initially seems rath[er] elaborate and baffling, but which quickly becomes secor[d] nature. It's a very nice way to spend an afternoon, and th[e] Xbox Live version makes things even easier, shuffling ar[d] collecting the cards, allowing for a slightly more fulsom[e] sense of place, and taking care of the irritating—and ofte[n] controversial—aspects of group games, like working ou[t] whose turn it is next, and deciding who has won.

With expansions available and both online and offlin[e] multiplayer catered for, *Carcassonne* was a surprise h[it] garnering very positive reviews. With a free demo availabl[e] it is a game nobody should miss out on playing, no matte[r] how unappealing it initially seems. **CD**

Banjo-Kazooie: Nuts & Bolts

Original release date : 2008
Platform : Xbox 360
Developer : Rare
Genre : Platform / Vehicle Construction

Rare might just have made the best LEGO game that never was, or perhaps even the game of 2008. Instead it made *Banjo-Kazooie: Nuts & Bolts*, which welded a vehicle construction kit onto a platforming franchise, creating a game of brilliant wit and ambition, locked away in a prison of incomprehensible make work and lengthy loading screens.

The redirection of the series as a sort of DIY *Wacky Races* is introduced with self-effacing charm. Banjo and his feathered sidekick have been put out to pasture, growing tubby and complacent on a diet of pizza and video games. When their old nemesis Grunthilda shows up, their bloated bellies scupper their chance to fight back. Luckily the Lord of Games sweeps in and calls time-out, declaring that the

platforming paradigms of yesteryear should stay there. Instead he introduces a series of automotive challenges across a number of colorful worlds, often mocking gaming convention, the *Banjo* series, and even the Xbox 360 itself.

Banjo's task is to build the vehicles to match the challenge—snapping on high-grip wheels or egg cannons to get that extra edge in a race, or constructing an elaborate spinning armature to thrash away concentric circles of dominoes. It's here that the game excels: The building tools are intuitive and powerful, and the vehicle physics rewards smartly weighted builds. But while still retaining a joyous, cartoon buoyancy, the game remains one of the great near-misses of the decade. Although there's a thrill in engineering the perfect solution, the process of iteration is weighed down by a fiddly back-and-forth between loading screens. It is also fueled by the kind of tiresome "collectathon" that the Lord of Games derides as old hat. A few twists of the spanner here and there, and *Banjo-Kazooie: Nuts & Bolts* could have gone off like a rocket. **MD**

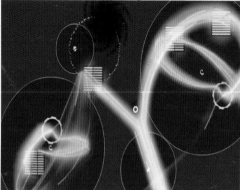

Audiosurf

Original release date : 2008
Platform : Various
Developer : Dylan Fitterer
Genre : Puzzle / Music

While the major music games tailor their game play to a limited set list, *Audiosurf* tackles the problem from the other side: It generates an abstracted response to any song on your hard drive, creating a new way to experience your favorite music. Point *Audiosurf* to an Mp3, and in a few seconds it creates a racetrack floating in space. Big beats make the track throb and bump beneath you, while sudden crescendos and fast, lurching stops spark starbursts and spirals in the sky. As you drive, different colored gems litter the track, and your job is to match, combine, or avoid them for the highest possible score.

The game can work at odds to the sheer pleasure of the visuals. Some may find it like playing *Tetris* on a mobile phone while cruising down the street. But maxing your high score will put you on the global leaderboards, which track every single song that's been played in the game.

Audiosurf's support for a live community and for the millions of songs on the Internet make the game a special social experience, as well as the coolest visualization tool since the lava lamp. **CDa**

Auditorium

Original release date : 2008
Platform : PC, Mac
Developer : Cipher Prime
Genre : Puzzle / Strategy

Like a scene from *Fantasia*, *Auditorium* visualizes music as threads of light and gives the player the power to manipulate them—redirecting them like water, coloring them with filters, or losing them into silent voids. Your goal is to assemble a musical score by directing the streams to volume bars fixed around the screen. The music pours in from one direction, and you'll use clear widgets to control its waves, steer its flow, and even splash it randomly at your targets. Hit all the targets, and the score swells to life before it fades and takes you to the next one.

Like many indie games of the 2000s, *Auditorium* combines a novel mechanic with a distinctive look and then exercises it through a series of puzzles. And while the music is a little self-serious, the synthesized tunes are captured in a top-notch recording that lives up to the visuals.

Above all, the game will relax you. The puzzles are rarely a challenge even at the final levels, and trial and error will crack almost any of them. But the real pleasure lies in just manipulating the controls and watching the streams of light do their thing. **CDa**

Bejeweled Twist

Original release date : 2008
Platform : Various
Developer : PopCap Games
Genre : Puzzle

If you thought casual games were easy to make, spare a thought for PopCap, which spent four years creating *Bejeweled Twist*. As the long-awaited sequel to its most important franchise, PopCap knew it had to get the game just right, settling on a mechanic that managed to change the central dynamic of the match-three game dramatically, while retaining a crucial sense of familiarity.

While in previous *Bejeweled* games players form chains of three or more gems by swapping them one at a time, in *Twist* you rotate two-by-two blocks of jewels in a clockwise direction. You don't have to make matches with each turn, either, which initially feels a little bit scandalous, but you're rewarded with chains for working as efficiently as possible. It all adds up to a game that is as superficial or as deep as you want it to be: A puzzler that rewards players who just wants to kill time between appointments, as well as those who look forward to a mammoth five-hour session.

Bejeweled Twist is a worthy installment in the franchise: densely constructed, simple to understand, and beautiful to look at. And, as ever, it's very, very hard to put down. **CD**

Afrika

Original release date : 2008
Platform : PS3
Developer : Rhino Studios
Genre : Safari Simulation

One of the more interesting PS3 exclusives, *Afrika* is a safari game that has you shooting the world's most precious and enigmatic creatures—not with a gun, thankfully. You are a freelance photojournalist making a name in the plateau continent, working your way up through cameras, lenses, and unknowing subjects. Early assignments include nearby zebras and giraffes, but the commissions are rarely simple, often asking for a specific pose or close-up. Persist, though, through some timid early stages, and you'll be treated to something wildly ambitious.

Afrika brings to mind PlayStation series like *Aquanaut's Holiday* and *Everblue*, but it places much greater emphasis on the realism of its world and virtual equipment. It's hard to decide which is more nuanced: the camera that blurs if you shake the Sixaxis controller or the wildlife that noses tentatively around your jeep, balking at your approach and dashing—or, indeed, charging—with any sudden moves.

All too often, whether by escaping it, exploiting it, or devaluing it with violence, gaming makes our world feel cheap; this one reminds us that it's not. **DH**

Critter Crunch

Original release date : 2008
Platform : Various
Developer : Capybara Games
Genre : Puzzle

Not many games spare precious pixels to lecture players on the importance of filial piety, but cute, fuzzy puzzle *Critter Crunch* routinely places tongue in cheek and scolds: "Remember to call your grandparents. They miss you!" This is a challenging, carefully designed game that nonetheless acts like a Saturday morning cartoon, reveling in the randomness of its wit. "Don't feel bad for the Critters you're popping," it chirps after your carnivorous hero, Biggs, clears the puzzle board of delicious creatures. "Believe it or not, they really like being exploded!"

Biggs is a rotund rodent with very specific tastes. He spends the game gobbling up the various creatures that slowly descend the grid of vines above his head, but he always ends up spitting them back out. But he's not consuming the critters; he's feeding them to one another until they burst from overeating. When they explode, they release enormous jewels from their innards. And in the bizarre world of *Critter Crunch*, these gems are Biggs's true dinner. If you line the grid up just right, putting together a series of food-chain explosions, Biggs's son—his name is Smalls, of course—shows up to eagerly lap up a stream of rainbowed gem vomit from his father's mouth. If that sounds like too much for you, not to worry: The makers thoughtfully include a tutorial on barfing.

Don't be misled by the game's deranged ecosystem, though, as *Critter Crunch* is a focused mental challenge. For most of his journey across the island of Krunchatoa, Biggs operates in the standard eat-everything-in-sight mode, but there are also challenge modes that place rather tight restrictions on how to clear the board—time limits, move limits, and so on—forcing you to choose your moves carefully. There's a serious logical structure underlying this game; it just refuses to act the part. **JT**

Galcon

Original release date : 2008
Platform : Various
Developer : Phil Hassey
Genre : Action / Strategy

Once an entry in a game development contest, then a successful browser game, *Galcon* is now best known as a simple and admirably intuitive real-time strategy game on the iPhone. Numbered planets of different colors populate the screen. By tapping their own planets, the player can send a squad of ships toward neutral or enemy planets in order to take it over. Planets with higher numbers take more ships to conquer, and larger conquered planets produce ships at a faster rate. It's more about quick thinking than careful planning, but nonetheless it feels intellectually satisfying, and its five different modes proffer sufficient variations on the theme to keep *Galcon* a home-screen staple for some time.

It's a numbers game, essentially, about sending ships out to conquer new territories without leaving key planets exposed and underdefended. If a fifty-ship squad is halfway across the map and your planets are suddenly attacked, it's game over. *Galcon* is unexpectedly additive; managing the percentages is far more frantic than it has any right to be, and seeing the screen buried under swarms of green ships moving in for a final takeover is exhilarating. Stealth mode adds extra tension by making the ships invisible, leaving nothing but small explosions and rapidly decreasing numbers to warn of an attack. There are a few dirty tactics that fox the AI on lower difficulty settings, but with ten different levels of computer-player fiendishness, *Galcon* isn't lacking for challenge.

Other iPhone games boast sharper visuals—ultimately the interface consists of a lot of circles with numbers on them against a generic space wallpaper—but on a platform whose games are often more famous for style than substance, it's refreshing to be left to concentrate wholly on the action. **KM**

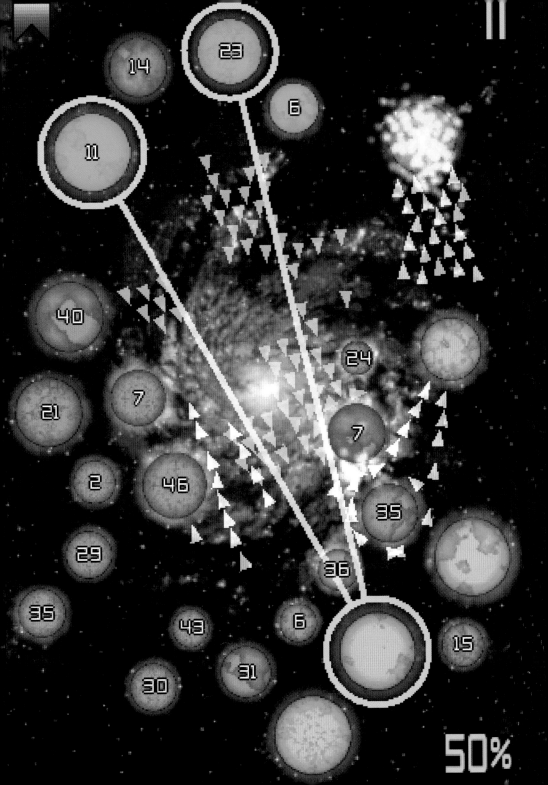

Battlefield: Bad Company

Original release date : 2008
Platform : PS3
Developer : Digital Illusions CE
Genre : First-Person Shooter

The release of the stylish, innovative but flawed *Mirror's Edge* in 2008 demonstrated that Swedish studio DICE is at its most effective with first-person shooters. Games like *Battlefield: Bad Company* consolidate its position as a world-leading developer within the genre, changing not only the weapons and style of its approach, but the way players can interact with their environments. The game focuses on enhanced destructibility, offering the ability to destroy walls, sandbags, fences, and other objects that remain impervious to damage in most other games. No longer is the inside of a house a safe haven for fleeing soldiers.

Battlefield: Bad Company, like many of its predecessors, promotes the use of squad play. Players are able to make up their own squads with a group of their friends, or fight in one giant squad made up of their entire team. Although the game lacks the ability to give out orders, there remains nonetheless a high level of cooperation possible with other squad members.

Players quickly realize that moving stealthily behind cover as they did in previous *Battlefield* games is not the best way to avoid death this time around, however. Staying in one place and waiting for the enemy to come to you is *definitely* not the way forward; you must be constantly on the move and aware of the position of the rest of the squad and your surroundings.

Though in its multiplayer mode *Battlefield: Bad Company* feels a little more intimate than its revered PC-based predecessors—such as *Battlefield 1942*—thanks primarily to the reduced number of players that can take part simultaneously, its core innovations and excellent all-round production values make it a first-person shooter worthy of serious attention. **SG**

Bionic Commando Rearmed

Original release date : 2008
Platform : Various
Developer : GRIN
Genre : Platform

Oh dear, Super Joe's been lost behind enemy lines, and now it's all down to Nathan "Rad" Spencer to head into the mouth of hell and get him back again. What's more, he's armed only with a couple of rubbishy guns and a grappling hook that shoots from his arm.

Besides coming up with sufficiently stupid names for its lead characters, Capcom's 8-bit classic *Bionic Commando* had to get just one thing absolutely right: the sensation of swinging from one grapple point to the next as you make your way across a network of platforming levels without the fallback of a traditional jump button to help you out. Luckily, GRIN delivered in spades in this perky updating of the original, which uses new 3-D models against a 2-D

plane, but keeps practically all of the game's previously used levels and structure intact.

Most famous at the time of its original Japanese release for its sensitive casting of Adolf Hitler in the role of villain—at least it didn't cast him as the hero—today, *Bionic Commando* is seen as a masterpiece of addictive, if brutally unforgiving, side-scrolling adventure. And *Bionic Commando Rearmed* is a perfect example of the pitch-perfect update, cleverly handled.

GRIN would go on to make a big-budget 3-D version of the series with expansive aerial arenas and a hero with murky dreadlocks. But mixed, generally rather unforgiving, reviews and poor sales helped put an end to the developer—and, perhaps, to Capcom's greater plans for the franchise. At least we got this before it all went wrong: a perfect blend of action and adventure, and an ideal introduction to a classic game for a generation that may not have been alive for the original. Plus, there's not an Adolf Hitler in sight. **CD**

Mario Kart Wii

Original release date : 2008
Platform : Wii
Developer : Nintendo
Genre : Racing

The original *Super Mario Kart* hit the world of video games like a bolt of lightning. Released for the SNES in 1992, it simply dwarfed the ambitions of every other racing title, its fan-friendly cartoon aesthetic disguising a staggeringly deep racing game. Shaving seconds off your personal best was a cerebral affair as much as a test of your fast-twitch muscle fibers, as you graduated from the entry-level all-rounders like Toad to the hard-to-master heavyweights like Donkey Kong. The game set a benchmark that other carting games just could not match.

It also established the template for all of the other games in the series, which spans four home consoles and two handhelds: Nintendo characters racing carts across

a series of Grand Prix that featured fiendishly engineered tracks, escalating engine sizes from 50cc to 150cc, and a bonkers array of weapons, from humble banana skins to all-powerful lightning bolts.

Mario Kart Wii takes that template and transforms it for the mass popularity of Nintendo's motion-controlled gaming machine, introducing a plastic peripheral that turns the Wii Remote into a steering wheel and unleashing an online mode that allows twelve racers to compete with one another over the Internet. Some more numbers: There are twenty-four characters, thirty-six vehicles, thirty-two tracks, including sixteen based on levels from previous titles in the series. Nearly 20 million copies were sold. If you count the moms, dads, grandmas, grandpas, little sisters, and older brothers Nintendo's console attracts, that's a lot of happy drivers enjoying Nintendo's potent mix of colorful characters, wicked weapons, hopping, sliding, and speed boosts—the latter achieved, this time around, by drifting at the right angle or performing stunts in the air. **DM**

Braid

Original release date : 2008
Platform : PC, Xbox 360
Developer : Jonathan Blow
Genre : Puzzle / Platform

A high watermark for cerebral puzzlers, or a platformer with ideas above its station? *Braid* provides fuel for both its fans and detractors, but the argument over its artistic pretensions must always take a backseat to its mechanical excellence as a game. A platformer that depends on Mario's tropes while simultaneously satirizing them, its key idea is time: If you can rewind your mistakes, you don't need to worry about making them.

Braid's variations and growth of this central mechanic should be a set text in every game-design course. At first it's as simple as rewinding. Then you play levels where your own movement left and right causes time to proceed or reverse. The ability to spawn doppelgangers, reversing time to solve a puzzle with your earlier self, is soon in play. Then there are pockets of time that can be dropped and picked up, placing one element in a bubble as the rest of the world moves on.

The puzzles created around these abilities are often miniature masterpieces of their own, depending on lateral thinking much more than the ability to gauge a jump. Each puzzle's completion wins you a jigsaw piece, which goes to make up each world's individual picture, part of an allegorical story draped over the game. At once an elegy for love lost, it's simultaneously a portrait of myopia and obsession, with a weighty and sometimes ponderous subtext about the creation of the atom bomb—a whole metagame, and one that mocks those players brave enough to undertake it, demanding hours of investment for little reward other than making this subtext obvious. Demanding of players in all the right ways, but also occasionally condescending toward the tropes on which it (and they) rely, *Braid* is a singular experience. **RS**

Burnout Paradise

Original release date : 2008
Platform : Various
Developer : Criterion Games
Genre : Driving

Even to its fans, *Burnout* was in danger of living up to its own name. Ever since developer Criterion joined the EA family—though not necessarily because of it—the celebrated battle racing series had been supercharged to breaking point. Rewards and ephemera would vie with oncoming traffic for screen space, the wants of an attention-deficit mainstream sitting awkwardly with the needs of a slick but philosophical racing game. Surely at this speed and with this many people tugging at the wheel, an accident lay just around the corner.

Yet at a rumored cost of $50 million, *Burnout Paradise*, the seventh game in the series, is a death-defying stunt of which Evel Knievel himself would be proud. An open-world

Burnout, it isn't just a sequence of tracks but a sprawling, unbroken junction. Covering five boroughs, twenty-six square miles, and multiple terrains, Paradise City provides the ultimate answer to the question: Which way now? It leaves it up to you. Wherever you point the car, a gauntlet of traffic awaits. If you want to race, just stop at the relevant traffic lights. Or a time trial? Ditto. A crash challenge? Hit the switch at any time to just flip into a point-scoring roll, earning Crashbreaker bombs to rack up the damage.

With a Freeburn mode that lets you switch just as easily into drop-in/drop-out multiplayer, *Burnout Paradise* offers freedom for its fans, but more important, for itself. An unprecedented run of downloadable content—dubbed "The Year of Paradise"—has added a sequel's worth of features that might never have left the whiteboard: bikes, an online community hub, a day/night cycle, handling fixes, a long-awaited restart option, and an entire island are just some of the additions to be found, many based on feedback from players. **DH**

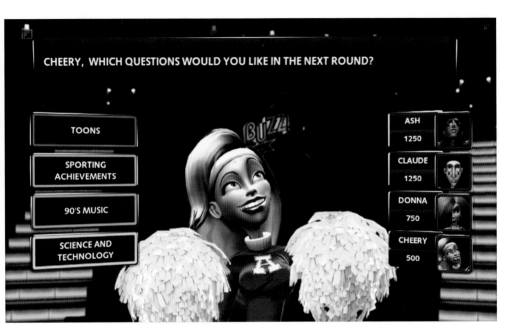

CHEERY, WHICH QUESTIONS WOULD YOU LIKE IN THE NEXT ROUND?

TOONS

SPORTING ACHIEVEMENTS

90'S MUSIC

SCIENCE AND TECHNOLOGY

ASH 1250

CLAUDE 1250

DONNA 750

CHEERY 500

Buzz Quiz TV

Original release date : 2008
Platform : PS3
Developer : Relentless Software
Genre : Quiz

A video game quiz show was always going to work, but that doesn't mean it had to work as well as *Buzz Quiz TV*. For some, it's all down to the chunky plastic buzzers that come packaged with the game, for others it's the Muppet-headed presence of cult favorite Jason Donovan as the snarky, shiny-suited question master. For most, the brilliant ticking heart of Relentless's PlayStation best-seller is simply the raucous in-fighting and bickering it can bring to your living-room sofa as you tussle over answers and use complex psychological tricks like sneering and snatching away the controllers to unsettle your familial opponents.

Buzz Quiz TV offers the wholly expected HD makeover as the aging series makes its debut on the PS3. However,

on this occasion the real star of the show is the ability for players to construct their very own quizzes and organize them into party-friendly playlists. The integration with the new *Buzz Quiz TV* website is smart and pretty much seamless—indeed, within a matter of minutes of unpacking the game, even the least technically savvy of contestants will be piecing together quick-fire buzzer rounds built around family pets, hereditary illnesses, or even the hereditary illnesses of family pets.

The pace is fast, the visuals are stylish, and, as the host, Donovan has just the right tone of mean-spirited smarm. *Buzz Quiz TV* may not be a recipe for the most complicated and challenging of evenings in, then, but it can probably be counted on to provide one of the loudest.

An elegant rebuttal to all who find the sleek, black PS3 a little too stylish and impersonal for its own good, Relentless's chart topper is also a clarion call to anybody who thinks video games lead only to lives of moody introspection and miserable isolation. **CD**

Castle Crashers

Original release date : 2008
Platform : Various
Developer : The Behemoth
Genre : Role-Playing / Action

You see a certain kind of cooperative competition when kids play beat 'em ups together. When scimitar-wielding soldiers or laser-waving aliens flood the screen, everyone on the sofa has to band together to fend them off. But the one who killed the most will start bragging about it, while someone else tries to grab the best loot. And if, at the end of the level, you tell the players that only one of them can have the biggest prize—the chance to smooch the princess you've spent all this time rescuing—in no time, all four of them are beating one another senseless.

Castle Crashers is a retro throwback best played by grown-up gamers who wish they were still thirteen years old. The humor may be crass, but in a way that anyone can appreciate: After all, the deer that poops when danger arrives is dead-on for this context. In any case, what else would you expect from the team of lead programmer Tom Fulp and lead artist Dan Paladin, who created the bully-bonding action of *Dad 'n Me* and the anatomical platformer *Sack Smash*?

Castle Crashers is a raucous beat 'em up, but the art is the clincher, with its brave color-coded knights and its wide array of collectible pets and weapons. While a single-player campaign lets you build up your character and explore the map in peace, the game is most fun with multiple players. It also comes with death match modes if you'd rather just skip ahead and beat one another up.

As an adventure, *Castle Crashers* is somewhat limited: Repetitive button-mashing wins the day, weapon choices vary more in their visual style than their abilities, and there's no real story to speak of. But if you can get the right mix of pals on your sofa, ply them with enough sugar, it'll be just like old times. **CDa**

Sid Meier's Civilization Revolution

Original release date : 2008
Platform : Various
Developer : Firaxis Games
Genre : Strategy

The idea of a simplified spin-off of Sid Meier's venerable *Civilization* series sounded like heresy at first. After all, this was the ne plus ultra of strategy games, made legendary by its limitless depth and complexity. And some whippersnapper developers wanted to dumb it down? Is nothing sacred? No, it isn't—and the armchair emperors who dip their toes in *Sid Meier's Civilization Revolution* will be grateful for that. Though the *Civilization* games have always been the thrall of micromanagers, here we have an addictive "one ... more . . . turn ..." game play in a package that will also be of interest to big-picture types.

The goal is still to grow your civilization from a pack of cavemen to a world-girdling juggernaut. You accomplish that by founding cities and enlisting citizens to build your military-industrial complex. That's the traditional route, at least. You can also win by cultural supremacy, economic domination, or by placing first in a space race to Alpha Centauri. The multitude of victory scenarios means that you have freedom in how you shape your civilization; it also means that rival nations have more ways to beat you. Players lulled by the calm isolation of prehistoric times will be snapped to attention in the industrial era, when they discover that foreign powers have been scheming all along. There may be fewer units, fewer rules, and less shuffling of resources here than in full-fledged *Civilization*, but it's still a layered experience.

In fact, the game's great achievement is not that it simplifies the series' formula, but that it can preserve so much of the PC classic in a console-friendly format. Even on an iPhone, the megalomaniacal thrill of the game comes through, as you spread your imperial fingers across the globe and wait for the right moment to squeeze. **JT**

Cursor*10

Original release date : 2008
Platform : Internet
Developer : Nekogames
Genre : Puzzle

*Cursor*10*'s challenges are silly and, at first, seemingly impossible. For example, you are instructed to click on a box exactly ninety-nine times to get it to open: but there's no way to do that before the timer runs out, so you need another player or two to help out. On another level, clicking on a plate reveals the next staircase—but if you're clicking the plate, you can't climb the stairs, so, again, you need the assistance of at least one other player. And in *Cursor*10*, a simple, ingenious free Flash game you play in a Web browser, the other player who helps you out is none other than…*yourself*. The job at hand is a tricky one: You steer ten cursors through the game, each cursor working alongside "recordings" you've already made of the others. So there are, in effect, ten versions of *you* that must plan cooperation with one another. This is the only way to solve the puzzles needed to get you to the sixteenth and final level.

With *Cursor*10*, Japanese game designer Yoshio Ishii puts his own spin on the idea of multiplayer at a time when online and cooperative play are commonplace. While shooters and sports games encourage real-time head-to-head play, Ishii and others are exploring the idea of letting players cooperate without actually playing at the same time (see also Jesse Venbrux's *Deaths*, where the bodies of past players litter your game, or *Demon's Souls*, where players can aid or invade one another's games to create a "massively single-player" adventure).

Short in length and visually sparse, *Cursor*10* can feel like a proof of concept rather than the finished work, but playing it for any longer would be a maddening experience. By the time you get to your last few cursors, you're racing against the timer, all the while your previous mistakes repeating before you again and again. And, of course, if you fail, you have only your past selves to blame. **CDa**

Fable II

Original release date : 2008
Platform : Xbox 360
Developer : Lionhead Studios
Genre : Action / Role-Playing

All of the games Peter Molyneux has produced for Lionhead Studios have tended to polarize audiences. None, however, did that quite so thoroughly as *Fable II*. A rich masterpiece of the imagination, or a broken childproofed abomination—depending on who you talk to about it—the pleasure ultimately comes in finding out for yourself which line you take. This, in other words, is a game that everyone should play at least once.

At the center of the controversy is a fairly laudable design objective: Lionhead wanted to make a game almost anyone could pick up and play, an exercise in audience pampering in which combat is reduced to the press of a single button, death is banished entirely, and a shining bread crumb trail is there to show you your next objective no matter how far you wander from the main path.

None of this is as comprehensively hobbling as it sounds. The combat is actually as complex—and thrilling—as you want it to be. Death is replaced with the shame of permanent scarring, and the bread crumb trail can be turned off or ignored, but is generally rather brilliant, anyway, encouraging neophytes to explore, safe in the knowledge they will never get lost.

Some love this approach. Others find it cloying and uniquely irritating in a game world where morality, for the most part, simply translates into a sartorial choice, as your character zips between lordly angel and thuggish blue demon, and where you can step outside of the main quest line at any point to raise children, murder prostitutes, or become a bigamist—the choice is yours.

Whatever your own feelings on the final game, however, it's harder to argue that the inclusion of a dog who will love you no matter how unlovable you become is anything other than a stroke of genius. **CD**

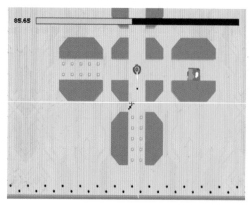

N+

De Blob

Original release date : 2008
Platform : Various
Developer : Metanet Software
Genre : Platform

Original release date : 2008
Platform : Various
Developer : THQ
Genre : Platform / Puzzle

Slick and compact, *N+* lives up to its minimalist title as a fiercely pared-down platformer, with sprites that look like clip art, levels that look like architecturally inclined doodles, and a color scheme composed of grays, blacks, yellows, and beiges. Oh, and don't forget the reds, too, because as *N+*'s lithe and skillful ninja leaps and hops and throws himself across perilous platforms to get to the exit of each level, he's likely to spend rather a lot of time being blown into wet crimson rags again and again.

Jumping and running may be the main tools at your disposal, but success relies upon understanding the game's peculiar physics, as you learn to rely on wall hopping, sliding into full stops, and then generally beginning to push gravity to its very limits.

While *N+* started as a free Web game, the smart visuals, pounding soundtrack, wealth of levels, and editor allowing you to create your own masterpieces—not to mention the explosive online multiplayer feature—earn the game its ambiguous Microsoft Points price tag with ease, bringing a genuine touch of indie chic to Xbox Live Arcade. **CD**

De Blob started life as a course project at the Utrecht School of Arts, its original aim to highlight possible approaches to urban planning improvements for their local city center. The simple trackball-driven software was designed to be a half hour of colorful fun for passing pedestrians in a local mall. Having bought the game concept, THQ spent months turning this vivid sketch into a fully featured console game, and the end result is one of the most exciting and creative titles on Nintendo's system.

De Blob puts you in control of a large lump of paint that is rolled around a series of urban levels, splashing the scenery with blasts of bright color. It's the perfect premise for a video game—messy, brilliantly silly, and rather unworldly—and the finished product benefits from endlessly cheerful art design and a great camera system, imported, wholesale, from the students' original code.

As for the students themselves, with the money they received from THQ, they set up their own studio, turning out *Swords & Soldiers*—a colorful RTS for WiiWare that is rather brilliant in its own right. **CD**

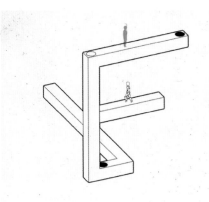

Echochrome

Original release date : 2008
Platform : Various
Developer : Sony
Genre : Puzzle

Look past the fact that *Echochrome* resembles your math homework. Sony's PSP title may have an austere and rather minimalist graphical presentation, but it's a smart and deeply entertaining puzzle game all the same, an Escher-influenced hop, skip, and jump through the monochrome world of magical geometry.

Like the best puzzles, *Echochrome* is very simple: Each level presents the player with a strange and complex piece of free-floating architecture and tasks them with rotating the perspective until all gaps in the course are covered up, enabling a little stick man to move around collecting tokens. Hide a gap behind a wall, and it will cease to exist, a piece of simple dream logic that initially seems rather quirky and difficult to understand but which quickly becomes second nature as the game scales in complexity.

Stylish and cold, this is a game that you'll inevitably warm to all the same, and yet another title to show doubters when they suggest that all video games are about shooting people, blowing things up, or driving around in flaming red sports cars. **CD**

Fantastic Contraption

Original release date : 2008
Platform : Internet
Developer : inXile Entertainment
Genre : Puzzle

Fantastic Contraption is about the thrill of creativity under tight constraints. The game provides a pitiful tool set—a few wheels and connecting rods—and asks you to create a vehicle. With a bit of ingenuity, those circles and sticks come alive as a rumbling, bumbling machine.

The aim is simple: to build a machine that will move a little red payload to a target area that is obstructed by gaps, stairs, tight corners, and other obstacles. It sounds simple enough, but the action can be surprisingly complex as you attach ever more wheels and rods to your machine. You tweak your design, press the start button, watch it go, and then head back to the drawing board if you fall short.

It is appealing that the physics engine smoothly animating your contraptions ensures that the failures can be just as entertaining as the wins. It's hard not to laugh as you watch your car-tank-bicycle-kazoo monstrosity amble its merry way right off a cliff. The masterstroke is that you can share your inventions—it's fun enough to experiment with your own ideas, but trying out everyone else's makes *Fantastic Contraption* a blissful time sink. **JT**

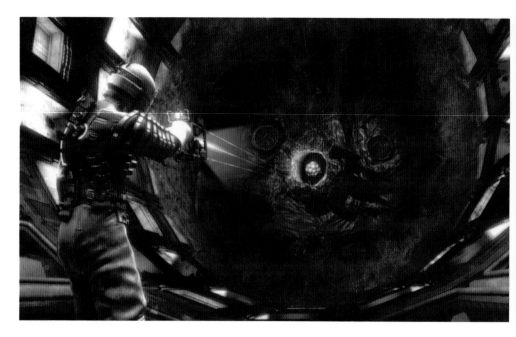

Dead Space

Original release date : 2008
Platform : Various
Developer : Electronic Arts
Genre : Survival Horror / Shoot 'Em Up

When a studio known for licensed action games, yearly sports updates, and franchise sequels announces a game called *Dead Space*, hopes aren't high of imaginative sci-fi horror. Indeed, when EA's workhouse in Redwood Shores, California, unveiled its game to public and press, it sounded as fresh as a shambling corpse. To wit: A team of workaday deep-space engineers (*Alien*) is sent to investigate the *USG Ishimura*, a vast mining ship turned haunted house (*Event Horizon*) by an evil relic, and its grotesque minions (*Hellraiser*). They crash on arrival, leaving a tool-wielding survivor (*System Shock 2*) to brave uncanny visions and scenes of bloody murder (*The Shining*) while keeping a very close eye on his inventory (*Resident Evil*).

But masters of horror care little for story: *Dead Space*'s power lies in design, execution, and that vital ingredient—misdirection. Taken individually, its production values are a cut above. In concert, though, the lighting, decor, music, and surround sound play such cruel and calculated games with players that many find them unbearable. The reactors, rec rooms, and vestibules of the *Ishimura* are never as you'd expect, though bumps in the night are assured. Sometimes it's just the random clatter of a nudged table, or the slow thump of a crew member's head against the wall, or the malignant drumming of limbs against a bulkhead. Then comes the rush—for which you're never quite prepared.

At its hardest, *Dead Space* is almost a strategy game. Its combat—full of upset rhythms, spasmodic dodges, and fierce ambushes—leeches ammunition you can't afford to waste. A weapon bought on one level becomes currency in the next, shops acting as pawnbrokers to players limping back from an impasse. "Strategic dismemberment" is the *correct* term—only a fool would take it lightly. **DH**

Fallout 3

Original release date : 2008
Platform : Various
Developer : Bethesda Game Studios
Genre : Action / Role-Playing

In September 2007, Bethesda Softworks paid $5.75 million for the acclaimed *Fallout* franchise, its goal being to wrap a post-apocalyptic skin around the lucrative bones of its previous game, *The Elder Scrolls IV: Oblivion*. The result is very much *Oblivion* with guns—which is to say it's a breathtaking artistic feat with strictly defined concepts of morality and free will. As your character flees the life-long safety of Vault 101, a crowded bomb shelter full of lies about the outside world, they discover an epic, hand-crafted vision of a decimated 1950s, reborn centuries later as a scene from *Mad Max*.

In the former Washington DC, Coppertone billboards peddle gizmos that now crunch beneath the feet of marauding street gangs. Towering mutants patrol what's left of the National Mall, mysterious armies claim government, and rebels compete over pirate airwaves. Others eke a living as scrapyard merchants, slave drivers, bounty hunters, and hermits. A few, including your missing scientist father, pursue dreams of a fertile future.

It's not easy to connect with all this, not least the idea that 200 years have failed to fix a toxic and monotone world. Then there's Bethesda's fondness for cataclysmic moral choices, which often involve being either Christ reborn or the devil incarnate. In one mission, the Automated Man, you face a disarmingly real dilemma over the fate of a fugitive android.

Much like *The Elder Scrolls IV: Oblivion*, *Fallout 3* has a thriving modding community on the PC, which continues to fashion weapons, clothes, armors, and rules by the hundred. All of this ensures that the game's world, which has expanded in several unlikely directions through downloadable content, continues to find new life. **DH**

Bangai-O Spirits

Original release date : 2008
Platform : DS
Developer : Treasure
Genre : Shoot 'Em Up

Bangai-O Spirits is a game that defies description. Even more than its brilliantly off-the-wall predecessors, it refuses to be pigeonholed, offering up a chaotic, confusing, bewildering, brilliant mix of bite-sized amusements, like an effervescent box of chocolates. Or fireworks. Or chocolate fireworks. It is a heady brew.

A mix of art house curio, puzzle-game compendium, and old-school shoot 'em up, it ransacks video gaming history for half of its jokes. Sniff the vapors, and you're liable to become just as confused as its creators evidently were. Some 160 levels contain everything that the original *Bangai-O* was and more—a tiny giant robot shooting and bombing its way through puzzles, bosses, shoot 'em ups, physics experiments, and pastiches of old games.

It even comes with a comprehensive editing suite, giving players the same set of tools with which Treasure's development team distilled this inspired concoction. The best thing about that, though, is that if players want to share their newly minted missions with others, they have to send them as sound files, using the DS microphone and speakers to work with the sort of whirrs, bleeps, and clicks that haven't been heard since games stopped being distributed on audio cassettes.

Everything about *Bangai-O Spirits* displays an utter love of video gaming. It is a joyful sashay through the history of the medium, with missions inspired by everything from *Gradius* to *Mr. Driller* and beyond. What's more, since players can now choose their own weapons, there is a seemingly infinite variety of ways to play. You can use baseball bats to swipe enemies out of the air, or even freeze the entire screen for a few seconds in your quest to unleash gloriously silly waves of destruction and collect every last piece of space fruit on the screen. **DM**

Devil May Cry 4

Original release date : 2008
Platform : Various
Developer : Capcom
Genre : Action / Fighting

Dante, the clown prince of hack 'n slash, isn't controllable until the second half of *Devil May Cry 4*—you can blame *God of War* for that. Sony's Olympian romp was a huge hit in Japan, especially for a "*yoge*" title (a game made in the West). It proved that there was a market for the press-button-to-win type of action game. But while every gamer likes to feel powerful, few want to work quite as hard for it as learning six different combat styles and dozens of moves. So while Dante takes a mythical backseat, much of *Devil May Cry 4* features Nero, a dead ringer boasting simpler moves and tactics.

Setting up a show-stealing battle shortly before the hand-over point, Nero is charged with capturing Dante after a massacre at an opera house. Little does he realize that the victims, not to mention his superiors, are part of a holy order in league with demons. From a laboratory hidden under a castle (a Capcom fetish) it hopes to harness demonic energy using fragments of Yamato, a sacred sword. Nero's girlfriend, Kyrie, is later abducted by the high priest, Sanctus, prompting alternate navel gazing and shouting at the sky.

Critics of *Devil May Cry 4* may resent how the game repeats itself almost entirely, the Dante levels tracing the same levels and bosses but in reverse order, and in decidedly irreverent fashion. In one cut scene, Dante chats up the lesbian antennae of an angry slobbering frog; in another, he turns closing a demonic portal into a vaudeville routine that ends with him gripping a rose between his teeth. Next to this, Nero's harpoon grappling and combo gauge feel like something of a warm-up act—or even an apology. But seeing as nothing has really been culled from the *Devil May Cry* format, it's hard to begrudge Capcom's overindulgence. **DH**

Far Cry 2

Original release date : 2008
Platform : Various
Developer : Ubisoft
Genre : First-Person Shooter

Crytek's original *Far Cry* dumped you into paradise and let you shoot the place up without much in the way of a care in the world. The plot took a last-minute lurch into science fiction, and the characters never rose above the level of pretty cannon fodder. It was a simple, free-form pleasure to play, and like a holiday in the tropics, it left you feeling pretty good about things.

Built by a different team, with some very different objectives, *Far Cry 2* throws you into hell instead: into the stinking jungles of an African state on the sweaty fringes of a brutal and horrific civil war. It's a world where death lurks and slithers in the damp trees; where bullets must be pulled out of your flesh with pliers; where both of the

potential governments waiting to leap into the power vacuum are hopelessly compromised, and the whole thing is about to descend into chaos once the Jackal, an international arms dealer with mysterious motives, starts pumping cheap guns and grenades into the area.

If *Far Cry* was *The Island of Doctor Moreau*, then, the sequel is *The Heart of Darkness*, an inquisition into the grim soul of man. A self-consciously literary game, Ubisoft's title still has time to work as a hilariously explosive free-form shooter, however, as you set fire to the jungle, announce yourself to the enemy by blowing up your own car, or stagger to a lofty vantage point only to be smacked about by a gazelle. In its scrabbling toward realism—vehicles that constantly need repairing, guns that rust and stop working in the middle of battles—*Far Cry 2* is arguably at its most gamelike, but in its adult handling of its narrative, and the glorious way it stitches a group of playable NPC characters around you as your adventure unfolds, it's taut, memorable, and as clever as it is well-read. **CD**

Gears of War 2

Original release date : 2008
Platform : Xbox 360
Developer : Epic Games
Genre : Shoot 'Em Up

Epic Games presided over a new landscape of action games after *Gears of War*, the game's cover-based combat becoming more than just the template for fast-paced tactical shooters. When TV and movies wanted to capture the zeitgeist of our screen-addled times—*Entourage, Live Free or Die Hard, The Hurt Locker* are examples—*Gears of War* made an appearance. And when the US Army hosted a controversial recruitment drive disguised as a game tournament, there it was again. So what next?

Reuniting the A-team of Marcus Fenix, Dominic Santiago, Augustus "Cole Train" Cole, and Damon Baird, *Gears of War 2* is a game built to command. Its confidence as a progressive co-op bloodbath surpasses any debts to older games, while the ever-evolving Unreal Engine gives it freedom to go wherever its creators choose—into the guts of a giant worm or the topsy-turvy innards of a city in midcollapse. Leaving proven features untouched, it piles its energy into art direction, enemy variety, AI versatility, and multiplayer dynamics, culminating in Horde, a rapturously received take on *Resident Evil*'s Mercenaries mode.

If only its story was so effective. Time has shown that if there's one thing this series understands, it's games and movies that blow stuff up. And no game knows them better. The way humans react to personal tragedy, though, is a more delicate matter. In a flabby midsection that sees a morbid twist, *Gears of War 2* scales the heights of melodrama and swan dives over the top, forgetting itself momentarily before reverting to casual slaughter. It's a moment of inadvertent comedy that made Epic proud, even optioning Clive Owen for a hypothetical movie version. (The alternative, presumably, being a fridge that's learned how to speak.) **DH**

Defense Grid: The Awakening

Original release date : 2008
Platform : Various
Developer : Hidden Path
Genre : Strategy

Tower defense games work like this: bad guys come at you, trying to steal your resources, while you build a network of gun towers to stop them. How this process unfolds varies from game to game, but in *Defense Grid: The Awakening* most of the towers do projectile damage and have an opportunity to shoot the enemies on their way in *and* their way out. Each tower has a different role: some are anti-air, some slow down opponents, some bombard from afar, others are short-ranged flamethrowers. The enemies, meanwhile, have their own powers. Some are fast, numerous, and storm your defenses in rapid succession; others are slow but practically invulnerable, and must be hammered with potent weaponry as they make their run

through your citadel. Getting the "grid" right will decide whether you win or lose a level. That's tower defense for you—and it is ludicrously compelling.

Defense Grid: The Awakening's strength is in its presentation. While there are lots of low-budget angles on the basic concept out there, this particular example is a beautiful 3-D production with exquisite little invading aliens, meticulously modeled weapon towers, and a vaguely humorous voiceover provided by the uploaded intelligence of an engineer who once ran the complex you are trying to defend. There's little innovation here, perhaps, but the improvements on the basic idea are implemented sensibly and efficiently. Towers can be upgraded, for example, and you soon learn the value of an upgraded tower over those that have simply been erected and left in their basic fire mode. Massive power-ups are also available to wipe out enemies en masse in tight situations. Half puzzle game, half action-strategy—and with a strange side plot about raspberries—this one is an offbeat classic. **JR**

Fatal Frame IV: Mask of the Lunar Eclipse

Original release date : 2008

Platform : Wii

Developer : Tecmo / Grasshopper

Genre : Survival Horror

While the Internet is littered with alleged ghost photographs, *Fatal Frame IV: Mask of the Lunar Eclipse* proves it takes more than an iPhone to catch an angry spirit. In Tecmo's spooky survival-horror game, the camera obscura—a creaky device capable of entombing vengeful spirits on film—is your only defense. The catch? Photographers must allow the phantoms perilously close to get the best snaps. Capture a ghost's bloodstained eyes close up and you'll achieve the high-scoring, "Fatal Frame."

Where *Silent Hill* and *Resident Evil* trade on the grotesque and intense, *Fatal Frame IV* peddles a more traditional brand of dread. Locating action in a hospital provides a suitably stark setting, but it's decorated with dolls, masks, lank-haired children, and other J-horror tropes. Anchored before incoming terrors, you succeed by holding your nerve and refusing to fumble. The arcade-style post-photo score tally deflates the tension somewhat, but then it's straight back to ratcheting up the fear.

Fatal Frame IV: Mask of the Lunar Eclipse ups the terror by opting for *Resident Evil*'s behind-the-protagonist visual style. And bringing the camera to waist level not only offers a better sense of location, but also removes scary signposts. Ghosts can, and do, emerge from anywhere, with fleeting glimpses weighing heavily on every step.

The most mischievous development belongs to one particular action command. Prompted to reach for objects, be they behind curtains or tucked in the gloom below a bed, your character's hand extends only for as long as the A button is held. Preset animations would leave your actions to play themselves out, but this demands personal bravery. The wavering sense of should-I-or-shouldn't-I has rarely been better captured. **MC**

God of War: Chains of Olympus

Original release date : 2008
Platform : PSP
Developer : Sony
Genre : Adventure / Fighting

Destiny brought *God of War: Chains of Olympus* to the PlayStation Portable format. And to honor its release, Sony shipped a red edition of the handheld, with a silkscreen of Kratos' constipated grimace beaming from the back. Even on the small screen, his deeds are big and bloody: the dual blades and other foe skinners spill just as much blood, and boss battles are just as epic, starting with a giant Cyclops who's immediately crushed by an even bigger Basilisk. And a handful of logic puzzles give you pause to think on your way to the next evisceration.

God of War: Chains of Olympus is a must-play for owners of Sony's beleaguered handheld; the graphics shine on the tiny screen, and the control scheme maps well to the handheld's single analog stick. But the portable version does have a number of shortcomings compared to the console editions. Maps are duller, made up of long, identical hallways with dull, breakable containers. The "press this button to trigger something awesome" mechanic barely engages the player—like when Kratos chains Atlas to the bottom of the world with a few well-timed clicks. At least the obligatory sex mini-game loses nothing in the translation.

But like the console versions, *God of War: Chains of Olympus* also has its melodrama. Kratos runs into Calliope, the daughter he accidentally slaughtered in a murderous rage. Calliope enters the game as an eerie wisp of a thing, flitting in the distance ahead of Kratos until he finally meets her in the Elysian Fields. Will they be reunited? Will his wrath be quenched? If you have to ask these questions, then you must be new to the series—but suffice to say that if the gods ever did right by Kratos, they wouldn't be anything like as much fun to kill. **CDa**

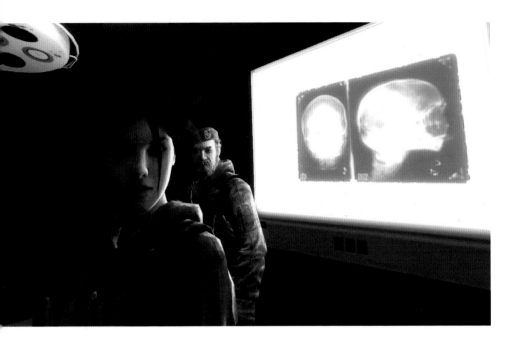

Left 4 Dead

Original release date : 2008
Platform : Various
Developer : Valve Corporation
Genre : Shoot 'Em Up / Survival Horror

Zombies, okay, along with pirates and ninjas, make up the aristocracy of Internet culture, so it's only fair that Valve, the most iconic and well-respected of modern video game developers, should turn the undead apocalypse into a full-blown sport. Left 4 Dead may carve its handful of campaigns into elaborately staged schlock films, complete with titles, posters, and direct-to-video taglines, but in truth it's something like the Super Bowl for a nerd-ruled twenty-first century: a four-player team equipped with guns and ammo, and a range of cleverly convoluted environments to work through as its playing fields.

Thrown into one of four characters, players collect supplies, choose weapons, and fight off zombies as they make their way from one safe house to the next, across an America crippled by the unexpected eruption of the end of the world. The guns are nice and varied, four "special" zombies add dangerous twists to the regular onslaught of the brainless, brain-hungry horde, and cooperation is absolutely essential as the alarms go off and dead-eyed murderers race to your positions, ready to club you to death and gnaw lustily on the remains.

At the heart of the game is the AI director—an ingenious chunk of code that constantly mixes up spawn points and attack waves, depending on how you play. It's a teasing, deadly presence as the campaigns heat up, pushing you into states of twitchy panic as it holds back on enemies for long stretches before swamping you with death just as you're in sight of victory.

In single-player mode, Left 4 Dead is slick enough fun, but played with three friends—or more in versus mode, with some filling in for "specials"—it's an absolute freewheeling riot. **CD**

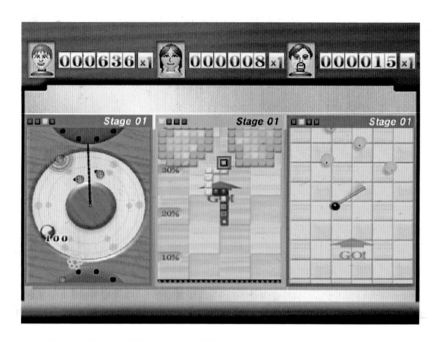

Maboshi: The Three Shape Arcade

Original release date : 2008
Platform : Wii
Developer : MindWare
Genre : Puzzle

If you're sick of incompetent friends messing up your multiplayer games, here's an idea: play with yourself. *Maboshi: The Three Shape Arcade* is composed of three simple games, all controlled with one button: Square, a snakelike battle against a rising wall of fire; Circle, a momentum-based arena where you have to bash encroaching beasties; and Stick, a bouncy race upward through an obstacle course.

Each game's basic visual style hides a great idea, and individually they'd easily qualify for Nintendo's Art Style series. But by combining the three and allowing them to influence one another, MindWare crafted a singular puzzler that's as much about panic as planning, last-

minute escapes as overconfident falls. It can be played as a multiplayer, each of the three games assigned its own portion of the screen, and if you're going solo, the computer will step in to play along on the other games.

But *Maboshi: The Three Shape Arcade* also allows you to save your best runs on each of the games, and then play in tandem with your ghostly self. It's a high-score chase bolstered by your old high-score chases, where you know what's going to happen with *Stick* and can plan accordingly, or where you know that *Square* is soon going to bottom out, so you'd better be prepared to push on alone. Single multiplayer *Maboshi* not only lets you help yourself, but exposes the frailties within your own play, pointing out just how badly you played last time around.

The only aim is simple: Mr. Maboshi keeps popping up and asks if you'll bag a million points for him. The game is all about racking up scores—but where in other games you do it for yourself, here it's for the sake of the game. The better you get at *Maboshi*, the better *Maboshi* gets for you. **RS**

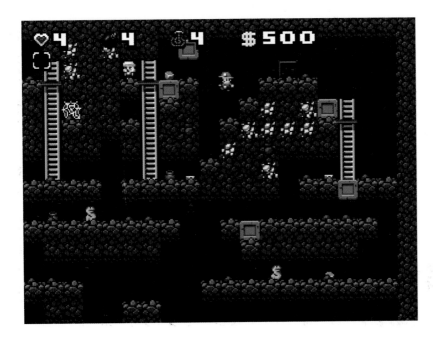

Spelunky

Original release date : 2008
Platform : PC
Developer : Derek Yu
Genre : Action / Adventure

Speaking at the 2009 Game Developers Conference in San Francisco, Derek Yu explained the importance of death in *Spelunky*, his freely distributed game that had drawn endless pleasure and hair-yanking frustration from thousands of admirers. *Spelunky* is a "Rogue-like"—a descendant of games like *Rogue* and *Nethack*—with which it shares two key characteristics: the map changes with every game, and once you die, it's gone. While most RPGs let you save and restore your progress, in a Rogue-like, each adventure is unique and every life—and death—has meaning. Yu boiled it down to a slogan: "Death is fun."

In the introduction, an Indiana Jones–style explorer sets out for gold and treasure. Through level after level, he climbs and dashes through procedurally generated maps, fends off animals with his whip, dodges spikes and traps, and sometimes even saves a damsel in distress. Those with experience of 1989's *Rick Dangerous* from original *Tomb Raider* studio Core Design will immediately feel a sense of familiarity with the character.

For a roguelike, *Spelunky* is accessible: The graphics are cute (and owe a debt to *La Mulana*, the 2005 PC game from independent Japanese developer GR3 Project), and while some of the moves are initially awkward, the game's difficulty makes you learn quickly. In no time you're weighing the ever-greater risk and ever-more-tempting rewards on each map, putting up with capricious instakills while plowing ahead to more loot.

Until *Spelunky*, Rogue-likes were a niche genre occupied by ASCII games or hardcore Japanese RPGs. While the game remains a cult hit, Yu has created new fans of the genre, and with an Xbox Live Arcade port in the works, its influence will just keep spreading. **CDa**

Age of Empires: Mythologies

Original release date : 2008
Platform : DS
Developer : Ensemble Studios / Griptonite Games
Genre : Strategy

In the beginning, there were *Age of Empires* and *Age of Empires II*, both superb real-time strategy games for the PC. Out of these evolved *Age of Mythology*, another outstanding PC game, and finally there came *Age of Empires: Mythologies*, a brilliant turn-based strategy title on the Nintendo DS. And the clue's in the title: while *Age of Empires* plundered history for inspiration, the *Mythology* games ransack myth and legend, drawing on the ancient cultures of Egypt, Greece, and Scandinavia to bestow armchair generals with a touch of the divine.

The relocation to the DS forces a transformation from real-time strategy to turn-based tactics, but the essentials remain true to the series: simple-but-deep resource gathering and base-building support the rise of armies that are put to work wiping out your enemies. Of greatest interest are the resources themselves: gold and food are normal enough, but it's divine favor that makes the difference. And although it dispenses with history, advancing through the epochs still plays as important a part of *Age of Empires: Mythologies* as it did in the earlier games, opening up new technologies and units and granting access to better godly powers. The Greeks start out with the support of Zeus, for example, but they also get to acquire the favor of other gods, like Athena and Heracles, as they pass through the game's different eras.

Those eras span twenty-four lengthy missions and a host of multiplayer options supporting online, hotseat, and wireless download play. It's a comprehensive package of perfectly balanced strategy gaming that demonstrates the timeless appeal of the *Age of Empires* series, able to endure its own journey through the ages. **DM**

Grand Theft Auto IV

Original release date : 2008
Platform : Various
Developer : Rockstar
Genre : Action /Adventure

After the PlayStation 2, *Grand Theft Auto* games—riots of black humor, violence, and cartoon slapstick—*Grand Theft Auto IV* can sometimes seem a little serious. Its magnificent reincarnation of the first game's Liberty City, an alternate New York, introduced a new tone to the series, a darkness that permeated the streets and crafted a cast of memorable and tragic characters. The American Dream has rarely been manhandled like this.

The ambition is huge: *Grand Theft Auto IV* aims to be the best crime movie you'll ever play. Its narrative pits the immigrant experience against the capitalist dream, the cheap and nasty crimes in back alleys and burger joints, leading to escapades such as an ambitiously staged bank heist. Its protagonist, Niko, is a reluctant antihero, although that doesn't stop him being a nasty piece of work when the time comes (and when you're mowing down civilians, his character is never an issue). And his story's end, however you play it out, is not a happy one. It never could be.

The world is soaked through with Rockstar North's sharp humor, which now crops up on the in-game Internet and television sets, as well as the outstanding radio stations, effortlessly skewering consumer culture and, in particular, right-wing America (you imagine this may be somewhat personal for developers previously investigated by the FBI). The jokes don't always succeed, the gunplay isn't perfect, and some players find the disconnect between your actions and the narrative jarring, but this is still one of the medium's great achievements. In terms of vision, nothing else gets close. If *Grand Theft Auto IV* isn't the greatest game in the world, it holds a distinction of equal value: It's the greatest game ever made about the world. **RS**

Guitar Hero World Tour

Original release date : 2008
Platform : Various
Developer : Neversoft
Genre : Music

There are all kinds of reasons why we may never get to see a *Guitar Hero: Pink Floyd*, the least being that the average human hand simply wouldn't survive the ordeal. But in the set list of the series' fourth game, it comes preciously close to its prog-rock masterstroke. The subject is Tool, the taboo-breaking art-rock band who last licensed a tune back in 1996. Its three-track suite—played in a hallucinatory limbo inspired by its album art—is an odyssey for both the senses and the fingers. An antidote to the series' less fortunate cameos, it does *not* feature any of the band's members.

It's moments like this, indifferent to the endless churn of hardware and features, for which the series will be remembered. Nevertheless, *Guitar Hero World Tour* is a pivotal game in all respects. Answering the call of *Rock Band* by adding drums and microphone to the ensemble, it holds its own thanks to superior hardware and two genuine innovations: a studio mode and the accompanying music exchange, *GHTunes*. Far from the expected gimmick, this feature-rich creation mode would at least give loyalists a champion, even if it couldn't heal the rift between fanboys.

As much as the *Guitar Hero* engine outperforms that of *Rock Band*, its characters more diverse and its visuals smoother, the artistic struggle continues. With a blemish here (the entire front-end interface) and faux pas there (the ongoing use of rock legends as mere puppets for performing any old song), the inheritors of *Guitar Hero*, be it publisher or developer, have still to put their integrity beyond doubt. Based on *Guitar Hero World Tour*, you have to wonder if it's that old rock star dilemma: The artists seem to get it, but sometimes the management just don't. **DH**

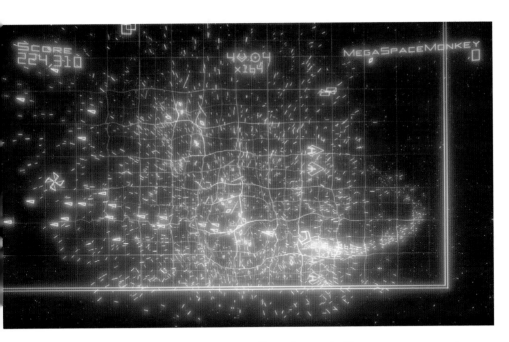

Geometry Wars: Retro Evolved 2

Original release date : 2008
Platform : Xbox 360
Developer : Bizarre Creations
Genre : Shoot 'Em Up

While Bizarre Creations's sadistically replayable neon light display would make it onto the Wii and DS, albeit in the hands of other developers—in the expanded form of the *Galaxies* titles—players hoping for a genuine sequel would have to wait for *Geometry Wars: Retro Evolved 2*, created by the original team, and released on Xbox Live Arcade alongside its older brother. The results did not disappoint.

The sequel provides all the expected tweaks: nattier visuals with a 3-D twist; deeper, richer colors; a handful of new enemies, all of which fit so nicely into the game's aesthetic that it can be tricky to tell which are actually new. But things evolved further, breaking the game down into discrete chunks by providing a range of different unlockable game modes of which the traditional endless play, rebranded as Evolved, was just one option.

It's a brilliantly inventive collection, from Deadline, which enforces a three-minute time limit, to King, which gives you flickering pockets of invulnerability in a sea of increased danger; Waves, a one-hit wonder imported from *Project Gotham Racing 4*, and Sequence, a rush of different missions that are so difficult that it's uncommon to reach the end of the series. Best of all is Pacifism, a mode born out of an achievement in the original game, in which players find themselves entirely unable to shoot, and must destroy ranks of enemies by racing through explosive gates.

The inclusion of Geoms, imported from *Galaxies*, gives you something to collect as well as something to shoot, and *Geometry Wars: Retro Evolved 2* allows you to retain your multiplier if you die. Otherwise the game is as brutal as the original. And while the game features multiplayer options, the real competition with other players is based around the game's leaderboards. **CD**

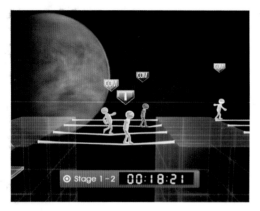

Let's Tap

Original release date : 2008
Platform : Various
Developer : Prope
Genre : Music

Tetris Party

Original release date : 2008
Platform : Wii
Developer : Hudson Soft
Genre : Puzzle

The problem with creating an icon is that you can labor under its shadow for the rest of your career. But Yuji Naka, cocreator of *Sonic the Hedgehog*, found a neat solution with the first game from his own start-up studio: He decided to work with the one thing about the blue blur that no one else had picked up on: the simple controls. Where most Wii games see its Remote as an opportunity for exaggerated gestures and simulated thrusts, *Let's Tap* doesn't even want you to hold it. Placing the controller inside the game's cardboard packaging, you drum your fingers, and control the game through delicate vibrations.

Let's Tap rejoices in the simple act of play. It comes with more than thirty brilliant J-pop jangles and just wants you to beat along to their infectious rhythms. The visualizer mode, meanwhile, gives you five artistic options, then lets you loose to see what tapping can produce; it's a mode full of little Easter eggs and quiet surprises.

Let's Tap wasn't just the name of the game, but a mission statement: Why do more when we haven't begun to explore what can be done with the bare minimum? **RS**

Such is the strength of *Tetris* as an endlessly replayable masterpiece that the development team at Hudson Soft could have almost been forgiven for resting on their laurels and letting the ancient gears of Alexey Pajitnov's title drive the sales for them. Happily, they didn't: *Tetris Party* may feature the classic game, as well as throwing in expected multiplayer options and quirky gimmicks involving Nintendo's balance board peripheral, but at the heart of the experience is a handful of new game modes, all of which should be enough to draw in fans of the series.

The new editions really aren't bad, from a two-player co-op that invariably results in total chaos, to variations like Field Climber, where your pieces help an on-screen character reach the top of the playing field, or Shadow, in which you match Tetris pieces to background images—rather like painting by numbers.

It seems, then, that the days of churning out lazy *Tetris* retreads is on the way out, buried under a fall of blocky new titles that test the boundaries of the classic even as they give in to its delirious capacity for brilliance. **CD**

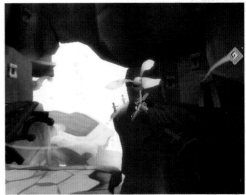

LocoRoco 2

Original release date : 2008
Platform : PSP
Developer : Sony
Genre : Platform / Puzzle

A plasticine playground that likes to break off from the player's control to go on roller coaster rides, LocoRoco 2 doesn't do anything revolutionary to the formula of the original: It just makes it better. It works because it understands its host. Where others try to graft existing platformers onto the PSP's slightly cramped controls, LocoRoco 2 uses just the two big shoulder buttons. Thus, you tilt the world on the pin-sharp PSP screen to the left or right, which makes the LocoRoco roll as gravity dictates, and occasionally press both buttons together for a little hop.

The flipside of this is that there's a greater degree of latitude in level design than in other platformers—with such slippery controls it couldn't be otherwise. But although you may struggle to bag a particularly out-of-the-way piece of fruit, it's not going to stop you completing a level.

This game bounces. It sings as you play and encourages luxuriating in a mad ecosystem where the guts of a huge animal can be used as a slide. There's an infectious joy about LocoRoco 2 that makes it one of the few games that will put a smile on anyone's face. **RS**

Lost Winds

Original release date : 2008
Platform : Wii
Developer : Frontier Developments
Genre : Platform / Adventure

The cold, mercilessly capitalist wastelands of deep space seem a very long way away in this whimsical WiiWare title from Frontier, headed up by David Braben, the cocreator of Elite. Instead, the brutal and uncaring universe of the future is replaced with green grass, a gentle fall of cherry blossom, and the tale of a young boy called Toku, and his explorative adventures with the wind spirit, Enril.

As the player, you get to control both: the Wii's Nunchuk allows you to steer Toku through the complex, 2-D environments. The Remote gives you access to Enril and his capricious wind powers, as you unlock the abilities to gust Toku across gaps, tug flames about in blustery strands, create swirling vortices, and let your tiny boyish charge soar across the sky on his billowing cape. It's a tightly conceived adventure, each new level bringing a handful of clever new platforming ideas to the game.

Although Lost Winds was one of the first games to appear via Nintendo's WiiWare service and has since been followed by a sequel, it remains one of the most accomplished downloadable Wii games. **CD**

Ninja Gaiden II

Original release date : 2008
Platform : Xbox 360
Developer : Team Ninja
Genre : Adventure / Fighting

If you were making the sequel to a game with a near-perfect fighting system, what would you do? Team Ninja decided to build a better one around a new feature that, the first time you hear of it, sounds suspiciously like a gimmick: the de-limbing of your enemies.

In fact, this mechanic is an invention of genius, as well as the answer to a question no one else had thought to ask: what is an enemy who doesn't react to being hit until its arbitrary health bar is depleted, and then suddenly keels over when it is? It is a missed opportunity for complexity and a missed opportunity for feedback.

By making your individual blows capable of lopping off an opponent's arm or leg, *Ninja Gaiden II*'s fighting system added a new layer to the brilliant brutality of the original. Enemies can become much more vulnerable, yet at the same time dangerous; be open to one-hit kills, yet willing to sacrifice themselves to get you back.

This is only one part of *Ninja Gaiden II*'s system, but it's the change that lifts it above the original, adding a visceral edge and a palpable danger to Ryu's skills. The rest is as good as ever: enemies that never quit and can fillet you in a moment, bosses the size of buses, crazy locations that mix *Blade Runner* with *Bushido*, and a selection of weapons that are somehow all as brilliant as one another.

That's not the half of it, of course. There is still the difficulty curve that, once again, welcomes new players by killing them over and over in the first battle; the set-piece battles that take the breath away (battling against a werewolf king in a colosseum full of lycanthropes is a particular highlight). And, of course, the reward for mastery—although when you learn to survive in *Ninja Gaiden II*, that's all the reward you'll ever need. **RS**

Metal Gear Solid 4: Guns of the Patriots

Original release date : 2008
Platform : PS3
Developer : Kojima
Genre : Stealth / Action

With plot strands everywhere and two distinct identities, *Metal Gear Solid* would need one hell of a finale. How would creator Hideo Kojima do it? What would he sacrifice, and who would he try to serve: his fans or himself? In the end, he went for nothing and everyone. Across battlefields designed to reflect a century of wars, generations of characters would have their fates decided.

Opening in the Middle East, the game introduces Old Snake. Formerly Solid Snake, this legendary soldier is losing the fight against two deadly enemies: decrepitude and a man-made virus called FOXDIE. Five years after the Big Shell incident of *Metal Gear Solid 2*, the world has entered a new age of warfare, where armies owned by

private military companies feed the world economy with neverending conflict. Chief stakeholder is Liquid Ocelot, a mutant mix of Snake's two fiercest rivals. Controlling the system, however, are the Patriots, a secret government who have managed to implant every soldier and weapon on Earth with controllable nanomachines. Unbeknown to Snake and his allies, that power is about to change hands.

Confused? Guess what? So is this game. *Metal Gear Solid 4* is a spectacle like no other, taking the series' production values to new heights, thanks to the power of the PlayStation 3. Previously limited to mountains of text and mannered voiceovers, emotion is now visible on the faces of its characters, seldom more so than with Hal "Otacon" Emmerich—a series regular with a tragic past. But its attempts to reconcile everyone and everything add an element of madness, not to mention an incredible range of control options. It confirms the suspicion that the ultimate *Metal Gear Solid* might never have been the *best*, but is as fascinating a creature as gaming has provided. **DH**

Midnight Club: Los Angeles

Original release date : 2008
Platform : PS3, Xbox 360
Developer : Rockstar
Genre : Racing

On the face of it, setting a motor racing game in Los Angeles seems like a bit of a joke. Clearly, for anyone who's been caught in the sludge of I-5 or US-101, the City of Angels is the last place to use as a racetrack—unless, that is, you're looking to test whose blood pressure can rise the fastest. Nonetheless, Rockstar San Diego chose to adopt the glitz, if not the grind, of Los Angeles for its 2008 iteration of the long-running *Midnight Club* series.

It's not always the case that a publisher instills consistency across its myriad titles, but *Midnight Club: Los Angeles* really *feels* like a Rockstar game. Of course, the RAGE engine now used in all of the company's titles adds its particular visual patina, but the open-world approach to

game play is fundamental in that *you* get to chose exactly how you'd like to proceed. Finally, of course, there's an appropriately ridiculous plot, which involves a character known only as the Player, making you wonder why Rockstar San Diego bothered naming him at all.

For all its bombast, though, nothing can prevent *Midnight Club: Los Angeles* from hiding what it is: a racing game—albeit a particularly accomplished one. And despite the open environment, there's only so much to do if you don't carry a deep personal interest in car culture, even if there is entertainment to be found in unlocking new cars and edging out rivals, or using special features, such as EMPs, for disabling other cars.

To give the game an additional layer of interest, the makers wisely launched the Rockstar Social Club, allowing players to compete with one another online, thus ensuring that *Midnight Club: Los Angeles* retains appeal once the novelty of seeing Mann's Chinese Theatre recreated in virtual form has passed. **JBW**

MotorStorm: Pacific Rift

Original release date : 2008
Platform : PS3
Developer : Evolution Studios
Genre : Racing

Evolution Studios's sequel to the early PlayStation 3 classic retains the frantic, battle-racing of the original, but improves on proceedings in some crucial ways. Polish and variation are the keys, as the developers rethink the environments and broaden the roster to up the ante on a series that could no longer rely on next-generation freshness alone to see it through.

The biggest change is in the location. No matter how much you loved the mud and grime of the original MotorStorm's dusty canyons, the sheer amount of orange rock on display in every course inevitably wore out its welcome with time. For the sequel, Evolution packs you off to an island paradise, where a range of distinct ecologies offer a real range of tracks, as you plow through thick green stretches of jungle, race around gloomy caverns, and sandy beaches and—of course—make detours necessary to negotiate the lava flows and deadly debris from a disturbingly active volcano.

If the original MotorStorm ever had any *real* connection with reality, this is the game that severs it, plunging you into the kind of maps that are only a toadstool away from the tracks encountered in *Mario Kart*. The whole thing dazzles, of course, and it's as smart as it is pretty, with neat little touches—like the way that driving through water instantly cools your engine down—that add a new layer of tactics to the racing.

Best of all, though, are the monster trucks, a new class of vehicle capable of crushing both foliage and much of the competition under their hulking tires. Brash and pleasantly trashy, they fit in perfectly, slotting into the jarring, bone-jangling core of the game, as if they'd been there from the start. **CD**

Race Driver: Grid

Original release date : 2008
Platform : Various
Developer : Codemasters
Genre : Racing

Race Driver: Grid was one of the first games to recognize the fallacy of chasing photorealism. While titles like *Project Gotham Racing 3* took pride in capturing real-world cities, some believed they barely succeeded at all, the attention to roads and buildings failing to snag the most important aspect: the air in between. Similarly, cars won't shine by merely importing them as accurately as possible. Like a stage performer, a video game needs to project and exaggerate. So *Race Driver: Grid*, taking its cues from movies like *Bullitt* and *The Fast and the Furious*, moved up a gear.

To begin with, its forty-three cars were chosen not according to speed or variety, but by status. Only the most iconic would get in, including the Aston Martin DBR9, the Ford Mustang Boss 302 (the most commonly reproduc "muscle car" in video gaming), the McLaren F1 GTR, a the Pontiac Firebird Trans Am (yes, that's the one fro *Smokey and the Bandit*). Its racing styles are those ma famous by its three regions, Europe favoring open whe and touring cars, Japan hosting nighttime street races a drift contests, and America pitting its larger-than-life citi against growling muscle cars. The cities include a *Di Harry*–flavored San Francisco and a neon-dressed Tokyo.

Race Driver: Grid is a spectacular racing game, its roarir cars eclipsed only by another engine: Ego—a successor the Neon engine that powered *Colin McRae: Dirt* and th crowds its races with god rays, smoke particles, spectato and fluttering physics objects. Its most important mov however, is the "flashback" feature that lets you rewir and replay a section if you mess it up, rescuing races fro otherwise ruinous slipups. Kudos, also, to its front-er menus, which, like those of the *Colin McRae* games, a works of art. **DH**

S.T.A.L.K.E.R.: Clear Sky

Original release date : 2008
Platform : PC
Developer : GSC Game World
Genre : First-Person Shooter

After the torrid development of *S.T.A.L.K.E.R.: Shadow of Chernobyl*, the Zone of Alienation was left a place where the unknown and the unfinished sat awkwardly side by side. Uncharted regions pepper its idea of an open world, its X-ray engine full of unused features, its nomadic characters leading unrealized lives. Attempting to fill in the blanks are two "expandalones" set before and after the first game's events. The prequel, *S.T.A.L.K.E.R.: Clear Sky*, rises to the task while succumbing to its creator's worst habits: overambition and a tendency to meddle.

One of the first games to support DirectX 10, it's also one of few to actually leverage the technology, adding more of those all-important details to its environment.

Rainstorms visibly drench the buildings of newly accessible Limansk so that morning sunbeams can dry them out, smashing the game's frame rate in one of several technical anomalies. Deadly emissions from the Chernobyl NPP, meanwhile, frazzle the screen, sending everyone running for cover, fearing for their deteriorated nervous systems.

Less successful is the "faction wars" feature, an arguably misguided attempt to bring order to the Zone's territorial scuffles. Turning the map into a place of conquest rather than mystery, it creates a dynamic into a schism, the gun combat at odds with its role-playing and survival horror. Furthermore, the AI's newfound grenade-tossing ability makes even the lower difficulties mercilessly hard, while the nights are overpopulated to the point of being truly impenetrable. But as you beat a new path to Chernobyl, enjoying a 50/50 split of new and old locations, it's hard to suggest that the Zone is worse off. A place of insufferable hardships and exquisite doom, it turns the best and worst of PC gaming into something extraordinary. **DH**

Resistance 2

Original release date : 2008
Platform : PS3
Developer : Insomniac Games
Genre : First-Person Shooter

The battle to create the biggest and craziest weapons and modes continues in *Resistance 2*, sequel to PS3 launch title *Resistance: Fall of Man*. By its own admission, developer Insomniac Games only knows how to make giants—games with the scope and generosity to match its other hit series, *Ratchet & Clank*. It's certainly evident here, with the game's multiplayer mode, supporting up to sixty players in a single match. It's not the highest in a PS3 game (that would be *MAG*, a tactical combat game that supports 256) but *Resistance 2* has a few other numbers up its sleeve.

Nineteen, for one—the number of weapons shared by the game's warring armies. Having vandalized places like Grimsby and Manchester Cathedral last time—in the process having a real-world fight with the Church Of England—*Resistance 2* lands on US soil, continuing the story of resistance fighter Nathan Hale. The Chimera, an alien race determined to invade somewhere glamorous, have launched a full-scale attack on San Francisco and turned Chicago into a lake. Hale, among the last of a squad of superhumans infected with a Chimeran virus, only has days left to live but vows to make them count.

Here's another big number: 300. That's how many feet there are to the game's biggest boss, the Leviathan. Opinions differ as to what it all adds up to, battles like this one confined to theme park–style routes around a largely immobile enemy. Others go to the opposite extreme, spawning more fodder than your cannons can cope with. The game's most convincing numbers are its most variable: the persistent experience points that make every multiplayer game count, rewarding you with weapons and power-ups. Teams of up to eight can play the cooperative modes, which divide from the story campaign to offer random roaming objectives. **DH**

Yukiko

Let's go on ahead... I think they're going to be a while.

Shin Megami Tensei: Persona 4

Original release date : 2008
Platform : PS2
Developer : Atlus
Genre : Role-Playing / Life Simulation

As the "what if?" offshoot for Atlus's underground classic *Shin Megami Tensei* series, *Shin Megami Tensei: Persona 3* saw the side attraction overtake the main event in terms of popularity. *Shin Megami Tensei: Persona 4* merely cements that state of affairs, offering an effortlessly fascinating slice of high-school life and demon fighting, with a crazy jazz soundtrack and extraordinarily attractive visuals.

Previously set in inner cities, *Persona 4* takes the action out to a spooky rural town, where the local populace is being menaced by a vicious serial killer. Moving in with the local cop, you play a prim and unusually elegant exchange student who is tasked with making friends at school, attending to your studies, and taking the occasional trip

through the television set when night falls in order to fight through massive dungeons, leveling up and giving a bizarre variety of enemies a righteous shoeing.

The combat is as satisfying as ever, and the replacement of *Persona 3*'s single tower with a range of themed dungeons is very welcome, but the real strength, once again, lies with the bizarre social sim ticking away at the heart of the whole experience. With each demonic mission given a firm deadline by which it has to be completed, a lot of the fun of *Persona 4* comes with planning your time and fitting in school, social clubs, and hanging out with friends in order to level up your vital social links.

Shin Megami Tensei: Persona 4 is absolutely vast and terrifyingly intricate, but its friendly atmosphere and quirky mechanics also make it a pleasure to play. And, polished and witty as *Persona 3* may have been, this fourth installment is slightly more refined. It also stands on its own, which means it's a fine entry point for anyone wanting to sample the series' unorthodox delights. **CD**

Pure

Original release date : 2008

Platform : Various

Developer : Black Rock Studios

Genre : Racing

Let's be honest: Quad bikes—those stunted, rather malformed motors that seem more at home in a garden center than roaring up and down the racetrack—are hardly the sexiest of vehicles. Synonymous with famous people braining themselves, they're squat and unlovable and hard to get a feel for. And even if they *are* fast, they just don't particularly look like they are.

What attracted Disney's racing specialist Black Rock Studios to the vehicle, however, was very simple: They're zippy and surprisingly light—the perfect choice for a game that handles and corners like an off-road racer, but allows you to get the kind of airtime you might expect from a snowboarding game like *SSX Tricky*.

SSX Tricky isn't a bad analogy, as it happens: Black Rock's ruggedly beautiful game plays out on a series of frantic, looping roller coaster tracks that wouldn't be out of place on one of EA's mountains. At the core of the experience is a trade-off between pulling off elaborate—and often entirely ridiculous—midair tricks or boosting yourself into oblivion, making every corner a gamble, every jump an opportunity to get ahead of the crowd. When you add to that a handful of chirpy characters from which to choose, excellent animation, and some world-class audio—all of which helps to convey a real sense of speed—and customizing options that allow you to build your ideal ride from the frame up, it makes for an entertaining and challenging all-round package.

As fast and hilarious as *Burnout*, as race-tuned as *Ridge Racer*, *Pure* is the grade-A racer that helped to put its venerable UK-based developer firmly on the map. (And it seems more than likely that 2010's explosive car battler *Split/Second* will ensure the team stays there.) **CD**

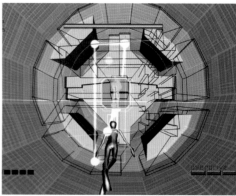

World of Goo

Original release date : 2008
Platform : Various
Developer : 2D Boy
Genre : Puzzle

The story is as irresistible as the game itself: two ex-EA employees go solo in San Francisco and capture worldwide acclaim and success from their bedrooms. *World of Goo* shows how far a great original idea can stretch, and, perhaps just as crucially, the standards of polish and production independently made games can reach—as well as their potential for reaping financial reward.

This is a game about building things. Its bricks are gooballs and its goals are reaching pipes that suck them all up. From these elements come more ideas than you'd ever think possible, from the simple act of building a skyscraper to guiding a thin line of gooballs through a corridor of spikes by adding balloons as you build. And both those examples are from the first world.

Later stages add different types of gooball, enabling ever more daring flights of imagination in the challenges the player is set. And, as for the universe, a cartoon dystopia where a mysterious corporation controls all . . . Well, let's not ruin it. *World of Goo* isn't a game that's worth reading about, it's a game that has to be experienced. **RS**

Rez HD

Original release date : 2008
Platform : Xbox 360
Developer : Q Entertainment
Genre : Shoot 'Em Up / Music

For all that it owes to the *Panzer Dragoon* series (its on-rails control system and much of its talent), the hypnotic and emotional *Rez HD* is a game without equal. Inseparable from one of the great video game soundtracks, it put the power and meaning of "synaesthesia"—the seamless fusion of sight and sound—beyond doubt.

Trapped in a sentient computer network called the K-Project—inspired by the artist Kandinsky—you are a hacker guiding an avatar through the system, breaching its defenses in an effort to reboot Eden, an AI overwhelmed by its universe of knowledge. Moving along a fixed path but able to look and shoot in all directions, you build combos by locking on to multiple targets or weak spots, then releasing the button to fire volleys of pent-up energy.

A deceptively deep and rigorous score-attack game, *Rez HD* is defined more by the progressive techno that courses through every object on-screen, from avatar and enemies to virtual landscape. The game eventually reaches a truly awesome final level—a dreamlike account of Earth's history told by a computer. It's all quite remarkable. **DH**

PixelJunk Monsters

Original release date : 2008
Platform : PS3
Developer : Q-Games
Genre : Strategy

PixelJunk Monsters was one of the first big-console attempts to take on the tower defense genre. Eschewing the fancy 3-D graphical effects that marked many big-budget attempts to cash in on the craze, it instead went for an artful visual style made gently surreal by Japanese music duo Otograph's burbling soundtrack.

The game riffs on the genre's basic premise, embodying the traditional mouse control in the form of the strange, masked, turtlelike player character. It's not just an aesthetic trick, it also adds time management and physical risk to the traditional tenets of tower placement and resource management. Since your turtle man walks slowly, you need to strictly prioritize his movements.

The game comes into its own when played with a friend, but the advantage of having two turtles on the job is quickly lost if actions are not choreographed—fervent strategizing turns to fuming admonishment as the wrong tree is chosen for a tower. An appealing fusion of mellow atmosphere and grinding tension, *PixelJunk Monsters* charms as much as it challenges. **AW**

Top Spin 3

Original release date : 2008
Platform : Various
Developer : PAM Development
Genre : Sports

With simplicity and hidden depths, much like those of the great *Mario Tennis*, *Virtua Tennis* seemed indomitable. But after a rally that's lasted six games between them, the *Top Spin* series has gone from underdog to favorite. Indeed, PAM takes its reputation so seriously that its third incarnation, despite the precipitous learning curve of its predecessor, creates an entirely new game from scratch. It's a game that newcomers simply cannot play—and neither, for that matter, can anyone else. Not at first, anyway.

As in real tennis, power, position, and angle are all vital ingredients of a *Top Spin* shot. This isn't to say they're the difference between a stunning cross-court winner and a simple return; here they're the difference between the ball going over the net or into the stalls—or into orbit. One of four face buttons has to be held and then released as you approach the ball, a tweak of the analog stick fixing the direction. But there's no gauge to indicate too much or too little—and no margin for error of any kind. Make no mistake, this is a career sport, and you can't expect any success at all without *a lot* of practice and effort. **DH**

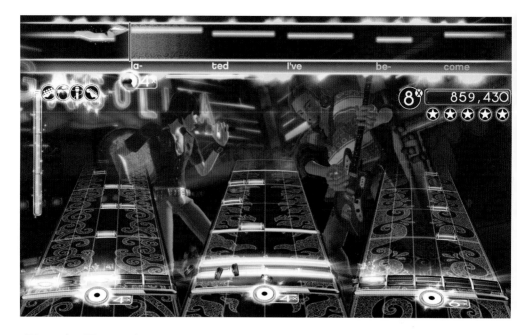

Rock Band 2

Original release date : 2008
Platform : Various
Developer : Harmonix
Genre : Music

With its second edition, *Rock Band* grew from a novelty to a platform. *Rock Band 2* shipped with a new set of songs, a few slicker features, and the instruments were improved. But essentially it delivered more of the same experience—and the point of that experience had become clear.

Coming just a year after the first *Rock Band*, the sequel cemented the drums/guitar/mic platform. After this release, Harmonix would focus on shipping weekly song downloads, and for 2010 it announced the Rock Band Network, which flung open the doors to band- and label-submitted content: Anyone who took the time to author a track could try to sell it through the service, and maybe score a hit. Meanwhile, the instruments supported the

2009 spin-off game, *The Beatles: Rock Band*. (Although the Fab Four's music *obviously* wasn't allowed to mingle with hoi polloi in *Rock Band*'s set lists.)

If anything, the sequel proved that it wasn't just a stripped-down simulation of how a rock band works. For many, it was a first step to learning to play music firsthand. The drum kit is no toy—as a legion of modders proved—but a real electronic instrument, and the lesson that ships with the disk teaches you the basic beats. Similarly, the microphone and pitch-scoring coaxed would-be singers to try something more rigorous than drunken karaoke. And even that plastic five-buttoned guitar had the effect of enticing people to try the real thing.

Doubters still asked the same question. Why would anyone spend time woodshedding on this game when they could play the guitar for real? But Harmonix reminded us that teaching amateurs to make music was part of the vision of the company and that its products could be the first step in that journey. **CDa**

Saints Row 2

Original release date : 2008
Platform : Various
Developer : Volition, Inc
Genre : Adventure / Shoot 'Em Up

When looking at the progression of the *Grand Theft Auto* series, something became notably less visible in the transition from the early 2-D titles to 3-D: sheer, irreverent fun. That's not to say there's no joy in *Grand Theft Auto's* sardonic parodies of American culture or the wholesale destruction that takes place in Liberty City, but if you long for a return to a series that delights in running over a line of chanting religious types, *Saints Row 2* is for you.

For this is a game in which cruising in a stolen police car might see you asked to break up a fight between ninjas and pirates—especially troublesome if your gang is already staffed with ninjas. And a full character creation system means that playing a Rastafarian clown with a cockney accent for the length of the game is arguably one of the most sensible choices.

Played straight, *Saints Row 2* is clearly a reprehensible product, since it undoubtedly glorifies cold-blooded murder, drug use, and misogyny. However, the tabloid-bating storyline (which feels more like an attempt to appeal to antisocial teenagers than *Grand Theft Auto's* satirical celebration of the criminal underworld) is only one symptom of a title that tries to be over-the-top in every way. Within a scant few missions you'll be firing rocket launchers at helicopters and—if you choose to take part in one of the game's many side jobs—doing everything from spraying neighborhoods with liquid feces from a truck to throwing yourself in front of cars to perform insurance fraud.

Saints Row 2 is not perfect—its glitchy combat is frequently clumsy, and it's rather ugly all round—but a decent checkpoint system means it's never frustrating. And even if it was, violent, crazy, and fun relief would only ever be another mission away. **MKu**

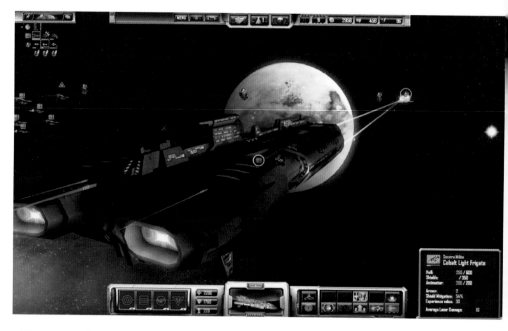

Sins of a Solar Empire

Original release date : 2008

Platform : PC

Developer: Ironclad Games

Genre : Strategy / Space Simulation

Both massive and ambitious, *Sins of a Solar Empire* belongs to the 4X genre of strategy games, a term that stands for "explore, expand, exploit, and exterminate"—which, after all, surely sums up all the functions of a large-scale space empire. By no means the first 4X game (the term dates back to 1993's *Masters of Orion*), *Sins of a Solar Empire* is nonetheless one of the few that handle their empire-building tasks in a real-time, rather than using a turn-based format. Developed by Canadian new boys Ironclad—formed by ex-employees of video gaming giants Barking Dog and EA—on a relatively lean budget of just under seven figures, *Sins of a Solar Empire* balances impressive complexity with a manageable pace and smooth controls.

The game's premise pits three warring factions—two human, one alien—against one another. The overall aim is for you to grow from a single planet to a series of conquered systems, expanding your fleet and developing your technology along the way. Massive capital ships can gain experience and new abilities with time, and you can pay off pirates to harass your enemies—provided your enemies haven't already paid them more.

With both single- and multiplayer capabilities, the game covers the bases of a modern real-time strategy title, but its true attraction lies in its scale. Fighting across a dozen to a hundred planets with a massive fleet at your command, you'll explore new systems on one side of the map while you curry favor for an alliance on the other, and your competitors never have to wait for your turn to end in order to plot and scheme against you.

Sins of a Solar Empire is a deep game and a slow one, where the simplest match can last hours. But it set a new benchmark for galactic conquest. **CDa**

Siren: Blood Curse

Original release date : 2008
Platform : PS3
Developer : Sony
Genre : Stealth / Survival Horror

The survival-horror genre has largely been defined by the *Resident Evil* and *Silent Hill* franchises—and imitated by so many other wannabes. Sony's Japan Studio took a bold, modern approach in updating its *Siren* franchise by integrating a TV serial format in the episodic distribution that would propel the narrative in concise segments. Rather than waiting a week for the next hourly installment, however, players can download the entire game at once.

The protagonists in this chiller are members of an American TV crew who descend on the mythical Japanese lost village of Hanuda, to document practices thought to include human sacrifice. Yes, that's just asking for trouble. The team quickly becomes embroiled in the devilish shenanigans, and they have to sneak and skulk to avoid the attention of the deadly zombielike *shibito*.

The game design, constructed around tightly focused encounters dripping with the kind of terror that makes gamers anticipate death with every opened door, uses a system that lets players see scenes through the eyes of the enemies. Displayed in a split-screen format, it's used to solve puzzles and locate potential danger. After viewing the enemy's movement patterns, you can then use that information to sneak past undetected—this is crucial in many instances since there are few weapons, and some characters who can't use any. Combat, in general, is to be avoided as these *shibito* are absolutely deadly.

Throughout the twelve episodes the story intersects across the multiple characters, each providing fresh perspective and skill sets. What emerges is a horror game that doesn't create its shock through blood and gore, but instead crafts a well-paced build-up of tension that makes the "BOO!" moments so much more terrifying. **RSm**

LittleBigPlanet

Original release date : 2008
Platform : PS3
Developer : Media Molecule
Genre : Puzzle / Platform

Okay, it's a platform game, but it's *also* a platform for making games. But, depending on your ingenuity and patience, the games you make don't have to be platformers themselves. Indeed, they don't even have to be *games*. Bedroom geniuses have turned *LittleBigPlanet*'s quirky tools toward puzzle titles, racers, side-scrolling shooters, mechanical calculators, roller coasters, animatronic photo albums, jukeboxes, and absolutely everything in between.

The tools are unavoidably quirky, with the tool-shed hobbyist's love of complexity. Torque setting, emission ratios, rigidity, and all manner of other calibrations a certain type of person will love to mess around with feature heavily—the same pleasures that may make other players

want to run a mile. Stephen Fry takes a rare break from Twittering about what he had for breakfast to provide a rumpled, avuncular guide to the game's complexities, yet, mesmerizing as it all is, *LittleBigPlanet* inevitably loses a certain proportion of its audience from the moment they realize that there's more than one variety of bolt on offer.

But the genius of the game is that you don't have to create. You can merely consume, logging in daily to see what the community has built for you to enjoy, play through the developer's own (frequently brilliant) levels, and marvel at the handicraft art style that revels in buttons, felt, sponge, cork, and anything else you might find at the bottom of the world's greatest desk drawer. There are even downloadable add-ons, such as an inspired paint gun–focused *Metal Gear Solid*–themed pack.

LittleBigPlanet isn't a game everybody will want to stick with, but it's a game everybody should have a chance to play. Muddled, ingenious, and staggeringly imaginative, like Fry himself, it is a very British eccentricity. **CD**

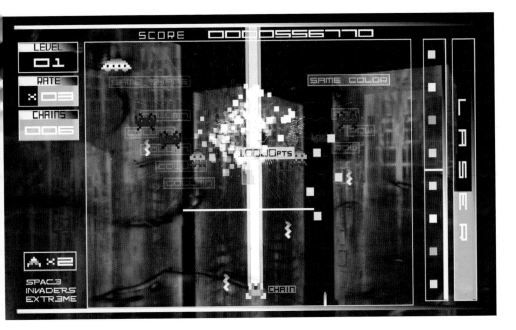

Space Invaders Extreme

Original release date : 2008
Platform : Various
Developer : Taito
Genre : Shoot 'Em Up / Action

Space Invaders was a landmark arcade phenomenon that has picked up more than a little dust over the decades. A title for the history books rather than a game to be played regularly, it took this bold, colorful DS and PSP reinvention to shake most of the cobwebs away.

Space Invaders Extreme retains the vital core of the original series—Aliens! Shoot them!—while wrapping the whole thing up in a colorful and contemporary mess of sound and vision. Lights flicker, backgrounds warp, scores spill into the air, and the soundtrack shakes your handheld console right down to its tiny internal organs. And yet at the core of such an excessive vision the original principle remains as sharp as ever.

The art of taking on Space Invaders Extreme is in chaining different colored enemies together in order to get an array of beefy power-ups: spread shots, explosive charges, and searing laser beams you can roll across the screen, destroying all in your wake. Naturally, of course, the enemies have been similarly upgraded, and now enter battles with shields and new moves: They can even come together to form pulsating bosses that can only really be taken down in stages or via the Russian roulette option of that single lucky shot.

Elsewhere in the game, bonus rounds and high-score challenges drop in to mix things up. At times, snatches of the original design can even be seen through the crazy clouds of color, as UFOs warp past, and old familiar formations rise from the ashes of the new. You couldn't really ask for a more fitting update. Space Invaders Extreme is a bold and relevant reinvention of a classic that retains the spirit of the old, while throwing in the colorful rags of the fresh and voguish. **CD**

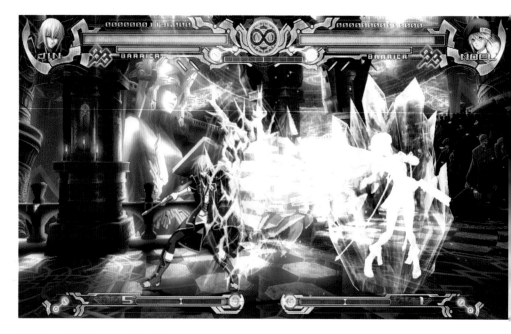

BlazBlue: Calamity Trigger

Original release date : 2008
Platform : Various
Developer : Arc System Works
Genre : Fighting

Most developers of fighting games left the prohibitively expensive 2-D aesthetic of the genre's formative years for dead with the medium's switch to high definition. Not so with Arc System Works, whose loud and brash heavy-metal fighting series, *Guilty Gear*, continued to eschew a more affordable 3-D approach in favor of hand-drawn, pin-sharp sprites. When it lost the rights to the *Guilty Gear* name, the Yokohama-based developer continued pursuing the sort of cartoon spectacle that had established its reputation. The result—*BlazBlue: Calamity Trigger*—treads a careful line between innovation and tradition.

In terms of the character design, hard-rock soundtrack, and screen-filling effects that punctuate every special move, the game has more than a little in common with its forebear. Indeed, the two main characters, sword expert Ragna and blonde-haired Jin Kisaragi, are clear substitutes for *Guilty Gear*'s Sol Badguy and Ky Kiske, both visually and in play. But the more muted color palette—all blues and purples to *Guilty Gear*'s fierce reds—bespeaks the slightly slower pacing of the experience, as well as its more distinguished balance.

A four-button fighter in the SNK tradition, attacks are divided into weak, medium, strong, and "drive"—and can be chained together in a variety of ways. Special moves are based on the *Street Fighter* style, while the drive feature gives characters their own unique effects when triggered, from temporarily freezing an opponent in a block of ice to sweeping a gust of wind across the battlefield in order to knock any projectile off course. A considered and fully featured online mode underpins the spectacular visuals, making *BlazBlue: Calamity Trigger* a dazzling debut for a new fighting game series. **SP**

Soul Calibur IV

Original release date : 2008
Platform : Various
Developer : Namco
Genre : Fighting

Let's get this out of the way: Yes, *Soul Calibur IV* is the one with the *Star Wars* characters. In an infamous and unlikely crossover, this edition of the venerable fighting series lets you pit Darth Vader and Yoda against *Soul Calibur* mainstays, such as Cervantes and Voldo. The creeping tendrils of George Lucas, though, shouldn't distract from the substantial innovations at work in *Soul Calibur IV*, most notably the online play capabilities—a first for the series. And although graphical improvements are obligatory in any sequel, it's nonetheless worth mentioning that this is the most beautiful *Soul Calibur* yet.

All the HD body detailing and swoosh effects would be wasted, though, if Namco had strayed from the accessible game design that gives *Soul Calibur* its ... well, soul. When developers make a fighting game, they generally have two choices: option A is a button-mashing beat 'em up that anyone can play; option B is a combo-heavy test for the diehards. But *Soul Calibur IV* refuses to choose. Its design is layered, so a ham-fisted punter can land some killer blows while a more advanced player still has a rich system of moves and countermoves to explore.

Critics may gripe about the weak narrative in fighting games, and the threadbare tale woven by *Soul Calibur IV's* story mode won't win any awards. But there's more than one way to tell a tale, and the true narratives come out of heated competition with friends. The amazing comebacks, the hot streaks, the oh-so-satisfying acts of revenge— these are the legends you'll recall years from now, after the game's back story is long forgotten. By allowing players with a wide range of skills to craft their own sagas, *Soul Calibur IV* established itself as one of the essential games in the fighting genre. **JT**

Wipeout HD

Original release date : 2008
Platform : PS3
Developer : Sony
Genre : Racing

When Sony's futuristic racing game *Wipeout* found its way onto the PSP format, many felt its days as an audiovisual trendsetter were over. The new controls were not as fine, the smaller screen seemed anathema to its eye-scorching looks, and its licensed tunes owed a shred of novelty to the handheld format. And then came the announcement of a PS3 follow-up, apparently little more than a download-only bundle of old tracks and modes boosted to high resolution and sold at a knockdown price. Even collaborator, the Designers Republic, was on its last legs, its influence trapped in the 1990s, its own demise coming in early 2009.

All of this seems rather silly and irrelevant now that *Wipeout HD* is here. Sticking to its founding principles of speed and fluidity, not to mention a heady mix of danger and glamour, the new *Wipeout HD* has leapfrogged a generation that can still appear flummoxed by today's technology. It's sixty frames-per-second performance, seen by many as a hallmark of precision, remains as rare in the video game world as ever: speed is often a trick created by motion blur and special effects, especially in racing games; and even HD, the watchword for this entire generation, has to be faked from time to time. That's *Wipeout HD*'s one trick: a dynamic frame buffer that trades resolution for speed to keep things moving smoothly. But that's it, and it's genuinely imperceptible.

As for the game itself, tracks like Vineta K (which flies over and under a sparkling coast) and Sol 2 (a minty-fresh ride above a mountain range) never feel like the PSP imports they are, while the *Tron*-like dreamscapes of Zone mode finally find their time and place. Perfect material, then, for a photo mode that lets you freeze the action, pan and zoom until you've found the right shot, then add a finishing touch like tilt-shift effects and sepia tones. **DH**

Monster Hunter Freedom Unite

Original release date : 2008

Platform : PSP

Developer : Capcom

Genre : Action / Role-Playing

Capcom's Herculean efforts to market the multimillion-selling *Monster Hunter* series to gamers outside of Japan might seem like a suicide mission, because this is as Japanese as games get: forbidding, hard as nails, and quietly self-effacing in contrast to the brash self-promotion and accessibility of many Western supersuccesses. But once you're past the five-hour pain barrier, *Monster Hunter Freedom Unite* develops into one of the most rewarding and nuanced games in Capcom's repertoire. It's not for everyone, but then neither is mountain climbing or *Street Fighter*, and they can be life affirming too.

Hunting monsters is a matter of picking one of eleven weapon types (everything from improbably large swords to light crossbows to enormous lances that shoot shells from their tips), mastering it, and heading out into the wilds in search of a forty-foot dragon to fell. *Monster Hunter Freedom Unite*'s large, organic world is full of dinosaur-like monsters, big and small, that are killed and carved to gain the materials to craft an ever-extending selection of different weapons and armor.

Monster Hunter Freedom Unite is at its best in a group, where different players' strengths can come together to overcome odds that would be near-insurmountable alone. It's about that sense of terrified awe on the first sighting of a new, intimidating foe, and the pure elation of finally taking it down. It makes players work hard for their rewards, but they are rewards worth having. There's also an endearingly whimsical sense of humor—dancing cat chefs and BabyGro-clad piglets adding a dash of silliness.

Monster Hunter Freedom Unite isn't just one of its decade's most popular games, it's one of the most interesting—and, if it gets under the skin, one of the best. **KM**

Spore

Original release date : 2008
Platform : Various
Developer : Maxis
Genre : Life Simulation / Strategy

Developed by Maxis and designed by the *Sims* mastermind Will Wright, *Spore* promises the universe. Conceived in 2000 as *SimEverything*, it was duly described as everything from a "toy galaxy" to a "life simulator"—favoring comparisons with the SETI Project over anything seen in gaming. Unveiled in 2005, *Spore*'s thirty-plus prototypes simulated, among other things, gravity wells in cloud formations, forest fires, cell cultures on varying planets, and SSPSF (the process by which interstellar gas gives rise to stars). Evolution versus intelligent design? This game seemed like both.

The catch? There is no game. As Chris Hacker of Maxis would explain: "There never was some other version of *Spore* that got changed at some point, only a growing number of technologies that solved problems." Yet such was the difference between the promise of *Spore* and the reality, the game emerging years later as a kid-friendly pastiche of other games, that few knew what to make of it.

Split into five sections—Cell, Creature, Tribal, Civilization, and Space—*Spore* follows life from its earliest days in a rock pool to its conquests of tribes, nations, and the stars. Each stage lets you customize your species in different ways, the results launched into an online "data cloud" so they can rain back down into other players' games. So as you fight for survival in Creature and seek power in Civilization, everyone you meet is a product of this global "Sporepedia." The challenges might be simple—often too simple for adult tastes—but this take on asynchronous multiplayer is *Spore*'s great breakthrough.

Nevertheless, it's hard not to wonder what the game could have been in a parallel universe, one where *The Sims* had exerted a little less gravity. **DH**

Super Street Fighter II Turbo HD Remix

Original release date : 2008

Platform : PS3, Xbox 360

Developer : Backbone Entertainment

Genre : Fighting

It's not like there isn't precedent: This is the seventh iteration of *Street Fighter II*, Capcom's genre-defining and enduring one-on-one fighter. But *Super Street Fighter II Turbo HD Remix* is the most stark example of what modern download services and the chugging hype-train of the Internet can do for old games—and what they can't.

Undoubtedly inspired by the re-release of *Street Fighter II Hyper Fighting* on XBLA, which racked up sales far in excess of anything Capcom anticipated, the game's development process was an open one. Character models and development updates were drip-fed to an eager audience by Seth Killian, an expert player employed by Capcom to help in the rebalancing of the game, and from

this came a series of wonderful articles on the principles underlying many of the characters.

All of the sprites were redrawn, and almost all of the characters were tweaked in some way to further balance the game. Cannily released mere months before *Street Fighter IV*, the sales were good. But many players were left wondering if they'd been sold the definitive version of a classic, or a rather shiny piece of old rope.

This was no fault of the designers: You can't question the workmanship on offer here. Nevertheless, it exposes the old game's skeleton: There's no opportunity to add new animations, for example, thanks to the havoc it would wreak on the underlying systems, so it means the game looks jerky in a way that your trusty nostalgia specs would never let you view the originals. So this is what download services can do: You can take advantage of nostalgia for sales, and you can starkly expose the mechanics underlying old games. But, with just a coat of HD paint and a few tweaks, you can't make something old new again. **RS**

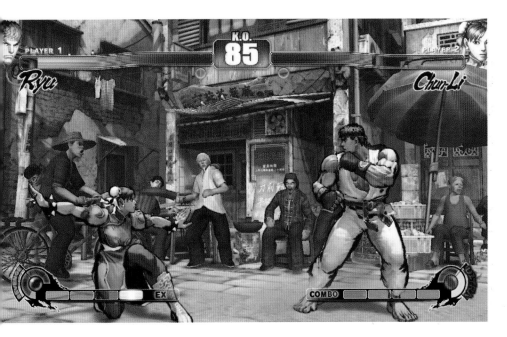

Street Fighter IV

Original release date : 2008
Platform : Various
Developer : Capcom
Genre : Fighting

Street Fighter IV is, without doubt, a masterful reimagining of one of gaming's great formative institutions. By reassembling many of the team who worked on the seminal *Street Fighter II*, Capcom managed to rediscover the alchemy that made its 1991 arcade hit the definitive 2-D fighting game for twenty-odd years. But more than that, *Street Fighter IV* is a powerful rebuild of the genre, effortlessly translating the excitement and spectacle of sprite-based fighting games into 3-D (in a visual sense, at least; combat still plays out on a 2-D plane) in a way no other title has managed.

Simplifying move lists, lengthening the windows of opportunity for combos, and making inputs more forgiving in terms of the speed required to execute them, the game lowers the entry bar to newcomers. But in introducing a flexible focus attack, allowing grandiose ultra specials to be inserted into combo strings and balancing the character roster with rare grace, *Street Fighter IV* also delivers one of the longest and deepest learning curves for those willing to set out on the warrior's journey.

Street Fighter IV has also managed to reinvigorate the tournament scene by attracting a huge online community, inspiring scores of competitors to try their hands at more serious competitive play—something that bespeaks the game's depth and balance.

With Capcom's inevitable and incremental updates, iterations adding new characters to the mix, tweaking move lists and rebalancing the cast, none will have quite the impact that *Street Fighter IV* initially managed. It is, in no uncertain terms, a sucker punch to propel an aging genre into the future, one that has rekindled long-dormant passions in a generation of retired Kens and Ryus. **SP**

Super Smash Bros. Brawl

Original release date : 2008
Platform : Wii
Developer : Nintendo
Genre : Fighting / Action

There's fan-service, and then there's *Super Smash Bros. Brawl*, the latest installment of the ludicrously popular mascot fighting game. This time it's for the Wii, and goes further than any previous versions in its quest to be the ultimate pugilistic museum of all things Nintendo, while also finding time to include a few more famous faces from the wider world of video games.

Any truly in-depth overview of *Super Smash Bros. Brawl* would simply devolve into a trawl through the star-studded cast list, but while there are plenty of obscure Nintendo favorites to unlock, the most high-profile newcomers include Pit, the dainty cherub from old-school classic *Kid Icarus*, and outsiders like Konami's supersoldier

Solid Snake, and—gasp!—Sega's Sonic the Hedgehog. While it's always good to have grizzled old Snake aboard—though sadly it's not in his geriatric *Metal Gear Solid 4* incarnation—the speedy blue mammal is perhaps the most timely inclusion here. After all, the great "Who would win in a fight: Mario or Sonic?" question has been a staple of schoolyard debate for as long as there have been control pads and lunch breaks.

It's not all about the characters, though. There are additions to the fighting mechanic itself, and for a while there was even a level-creation uploading service in operation. But the main impulse, of course, for any *Smash Brothers* game is initially who you can fight as, where you can fight (the addition of a level set in the Earthbound universe is a particularly thoughtful inclusion this time), and the title. Yet while *Super Smash Bros. Brawl* is a serious fighting game in its own right, it is really most useful as a glorious interactive Nintendo compendium—a role it performs with brilliance. **CD**

Valkyria Chronicles

Original release date : 2008
Platform : PS3
Developer : Sega
Genre : Strategy

Tiny, pastoral Gallia has come under attack from an overwhelming empire, and its people have assembled a peasant army to defend it. Underdogs all, the troops in this army are also the most important thing about it. The major characters tell their stories in a series of engrossing cut scenes, but the minor characters that make up your squad also have a story to tell. For your sniper, do you choose Oscar, who's shaky but eager, or Marina, a lone wolf with a cold glare? Who do you risk on the frontlines of your desert assault? Always reliable Rosie or dumb but dependable Hannes, who grunts "YOU DIE NOW" as he puts down foe after foe? Browsing their profiles and weighing up their kills and flaws, their personality types, and even their sexual preferences, you can spend hours deciding who you want by your side.

Valkyria Chronicles is a bittersweet tactical RPG that has attracted a cult following. The game tells the story of the Gallians' war through major turn-based battles, in which players strategize from a top-down view and then execute each move from an over-the-shoulder perspective. The technique lets you experience both the general's-eye view of the battlefield and the troop's view from the trenches as your orders bring them under fire.

Learning the tricks of each encounter and the traits of each soldier makes the battles complex and rewarding, although thanks to quirks in the AI, your enemies are erratic and not a little stupid. In addition, many of the battles can be won by mastering a simple trick or just by knowing in advance where to hide. But the story is strong enough to distract you from the rough edges. *Valkyria Chronicles* is both epic and intimate, and it makes you responsible for every single life you command. **CDa**

THROWING GRENADE INFILTRATE

0 2

144563 172000

1
27 x 6

TEAM COMMAND - THROW SMOKE GRENADE

Tom Clancy's Rainbow Six: Vegas 2

Original release date : 2008
Platform : Various
Developer : Ubisoft
Genre : First-Person Shooter

What were the terrorists thinking? Take over Sin City, and you're really going to feel the wrath of the military, the highly trained members of Team Rainbow only too happy to liberate the extravagant hotels on the Strip. This sequel provides some of the background to the original terrorist takeover in *Tom Clancy's Rainbow Six: Vegas 1* and then picks up the story—since it's clear that the terrorists didn't get the message the first time around.

Things have changed, though. Team Rainbow now comes armed with more aggressive tactics as well as a few new tricks, even if the heart of this tactical FPS beats a familiar rhythm. You also get a new character to control, and customizing his skills and equipment is part of the freshened grab bag of features. Moving your squad into position and out of danger requires the familiar level of micromanagement, though they will use cover effectively and watch your back when you need support. A better option, however, is to have a friend come along for cooperative ride through the story, with the ability to drop in and out at any point.

But *Vegas 2*'s heart beats still stronger online, where the format has been finely tuned into an absorbing tactical challenge. Three new modes make the cut this time, adding a fresh take on the attack and defend challenge and introducing a Team Leader format that puts an even greater focus on teamwork and communication. A new system also tracks your playing style and sets up match types that suit you and your friends, while the persistent experience-points system lets you chase higher ranks and cosmetic upgrades. Each piece has been expertly finessed by a studio that clearly has this game play style down pat and understands what its audience demands. **RSm**

Tomb Raider Underworld

Original release date : 2008
Platform : Various
Developer : Crystal Dynamics
Genre : Action / Adventure

After the slick, modern-day reboot of *Legend*, with its Tokyo skyscrapers and Cold War military bases, and after the lavish fan service of *Anniversary*, which remade the original *Tomb Raider* using Crystal Dynamics's dazzling new engine, *Tomb Raider Underworld* feels like a timely reinvention of some of the series' oldest ideas. Staying, for the most part, far out of the way of modern civilization, Lara Croft—still wonderfully voiced by Keeley Hawes—explores a range of complex tumbledown temples, spanning everywhere from the coast of Thailand to Central America, on the trail of a Norse supermyth that may tie many of the ancient world's greatest secrets together, while bringing *Legend*'s increasingly complex plot to a conclusion.

After the quick-snack speed-run levels of Crystal Dynamics's first game, *Tomb Raider Underworld* can initially hit players with the shock of the old: Its levels are massive, often featuring multipart puzzles to keep you busy for hours, and there's an intricacy to the smallest environments that makes you feel like you're genuinely exploring the unknown again. Lara's motorbike makes a return, in a much more fully featured manner than in the on-rails shooting sections that broke up *Legend*. A few old enemies are back, too, as the epic storyline involving the mysterious disappearance of Lara's own mother tidies itself away for good.

With highlights including an item that allows Lara to move huge objects, and an exhilarating escape from a flooding tanker ship, *Tomb Raider Underworld* has more than enough spectacle to match its forebears, and while some players felt that the end of the game seemed rather rushed, two short but excellent downloadable episodes round out the experience perfectly. **CD**

Reset Generation

Original release date : 2008
Platform : N-Gage, PC
Developer : RedLynx
Genre : Puzzle / Strategy

With its bright colors, wacky sound effects, and chirpy cartoon cast, *Reset Generation*—created for Nokia N-Gage–equipped mobile phones—appears to be a casual game, but it isn't. And with its pixel-emphasized graphics, vibrant sprites, and familiar muddle of castles and heroes, it has the appearance of a retro game, but it isn't that either. Instead, RedLynx's bright mobile app is a complex and irreverent puzzle game, and a real curate's egg; a witty and self-referential offering that casts many glances back at gaming's greater history, while taking players somewhere they've rarely been before.

After choosing your character from a range of stereotypes that gamers of any age will find amusingly familiar—a hedgehog, a plumber, a monster trainer, an elf—your job, naturally enough, is to rescue your princess from a rival's castle. This is significantly harder than it sounds, however, as players must piece together a road to get themselves to the princess by dropping various puzzle blocks onto the game's grid, while at the same time guarding their own castle from enemy attack.

A frantic multiplayer muddle, the game makes far too many quick-wink references to other titles—*Sonic the Hedgehog*, *Super Mario Bros.*, *Tetris*, etc.—for any quick overview to catalog in their entirety. But in spite of such frippery, the important thing is that once the flurry of homages fade away, what you're left with is a distinctive and memorable puzzle game in its own right.

Created to bring people flocking to Nokia's ill-fated N-Gage platform and fend off the ubiquity of the Apple iPhone, *Reset Generation* happily managed to migrate as a free, Windows-only browser game, thus enabling its vibrant community to weather the final closure of Nokia's mobile gaming service in 2010. **CD**

Drop7

Original release date : 2008
Platform : PC, iPhone
Developer : Area/Code
Genre : Puzzle

Crossing the addictiveness of *Tetris* with the basic math of *Sudoku*, *Drop7* was a big viral hit on the Web before it moved to the iPhone. The setup is simple. Numbered circles appear at the top of the screen, and you have to drop them into columns. Line them up in the quantity written on the circle—for example, two twos in a row, or three threes, and so on—and the circle explode, sometimes setting off chain reactions as new combinations slide together. Chain reactions boost your score exponentially, but you'll also deal with circles whose numbers are hidden in shells that must be steadily broken apart, mixing dumb luck into your best-laid plans.

Unlike *Tetris*, your session can't go on forever; the concealed numbers will eventually pile up beyond your ability to crack them open, and when the numbers exceed the columns that hold them, you're done for. But the game's abacus-like aesthetic compels you to keep giving it one more try. Superior players can line up astounding chain reaction scores, but a casual player can have just as much fun watching the numbers vanish row by row.

But the most surprising thing about *Drop7* is its background story. The game was created by the developer Area/Code as a front for an alternate-reality game named *Chain Factor*, built to support the television crime show *Numb3rs*. Serious players explored an intricate storyline through fake Web sites and clues on public billboards. Meanwhile, casual fans could just swing by to play *Drop7*—and their number crunching would still aid the experience by unlocking more content for the hardcore crowd. This gave players a sense of mystery, as they helped a cause they didn't understand and aided a community that was larger than themselves—all by simply sliding numbers down a screen. **CDa**

163,109

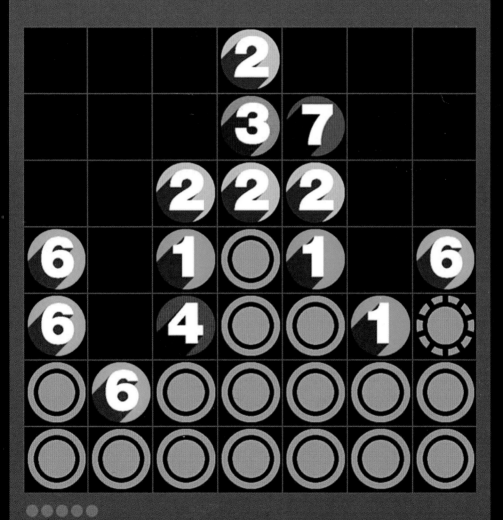

●●●●●

LEVEL 10

DOUBLE-TAP FOR MENU

TrackMania: United Forever

Original release date : 2008
Platform : Various
Developer : Nadeo
Genre : Racing / Puzzle

The trickiest thing about *TrackMania* is working out which incarnation of the game you are playing. That's not so much a criticism of the naming conventions Nadeo has chosen for its many expanded/alternative versions since the 2003 original as it is an admiring recognition of how remarkably accessible this physics-free racing series is. There is simply *nothing* to get confused or frustrated about ... except the name.

In spite of the game's instantly cheering simplicity—it feels comfortably familiar from the first second of play—it's oddly tricky to pinpoint this French title's influences. There's a touch of *Micro Machines*, perhaps, a dash of *Stunt Car Racer*, for sure, but ultimately it has a toonish-

but-believable form all its own: outlandish tracks that couldn't exist but look as if they do, cars that look like serious business but handle like unbreakable toys, and all the respawns and restarts players could possibly desire. It hoists the flag of fun above all concerns in such a way that any and every player feels they're doing well and can do better yet—and without any all-too-obvious trickery such as, say, *Super Mario Kart*'s cheating opponents.

The sublimely joyous action would be more than enough to earn *TrackMania: United Forever* a place on any PC—but we get a bizarre car-based platform/puzzle mode too, a test of absurdist logic rather than braking distance.

Better still is the construction set that enables the creation of any kind of course. Track design is outrageously simple—just a matter of placing blocks into the shapes you want. As a result, the global *TrackMania* community is huge: as of 2013, a twelve-million-strong-and-counting hub of design, sharing, and commentary. And there's no reason not to join it. **AM**

TrackMania DS

Original release date : 2008
Platform : DS
Developer : Firebrand Games
Genre : Racing / Puzzle

Nintendo's consoles have always boasted something of a toylike quality, in the best possible sense. Discovery and play seem to go hand in hand, which makes TrackMania DS a good fit. Its dedicated fan base is attracted to the sheer wealth of possibilities the game offers, but underneath it all, TrackMania DS is LEGO meets Scalextric. It's about building things, and racing cars really fast.

The core of Trackmania DS is an editor that lets you quickly build big tracks full of loops and chicanes and immediately try them out with cars. This is all handled via the DS's touch screen, which makes for the odd fiddly moment, but is otherwise straightforward. TrackMania DS is largely the PC original, although there are small

omissions (it has fewer environments, for instance) and one big one in the form of no online connectivity. While this instantly negates a large part of the TrackMania experience, which is all about swapping tracks online, it means TrackMania DS is about the odd fifteen-minute grand prix with friends rather than anything broader.

Online aside, TrackMania DS is a near-perfect translation of the original on limited hardware, and a near-perfect fit for Nintendo's handheld. The sensation of speed is brilliantly achieved, leaving other DS racers on the starting line, and the vertigo-inducing twists and turns are liberally scattered over a substantial career mode. There's no touch-screen fiddling to spoil the racing itself, the frame rate is smooth throughout, and the pruning undertaken to fit the game on smaller hardware is judicious. It's not quite the everlasting behemoth that is the PC version, which has an endless supply of new content, but TrackMania DS is quite distinct from that world, anyway. It's a great toy, and magnificent fun. **RS**

Art Style: Intersect

Original release date : 2009
Platform : DS
Developer : Q-Games
Genre : Puzzle

Art Style: Intersect was originally developed by Q-Games (better known for the *PixelJunk* series of PlayStation 3 downloadable titles) as *Digidrive*, the final installment of Nintendo's Japan-only *Bit Generations* experiment. Despite not being as well known and not quite as accessible, *Art Style: Intersect* is perhaps the most distinctive puzzle experience seen since the watershed of *Tetris*.

The game begins somewhat awkwardly. The screen features a crossroads upon which arrows of three different colors can move, and it is initially difficult not to interpret it as a road system with cars traveling along it. You want to apply preconceived attributes to it, but *Intersect*'s play is in no way intended as an abstract representation of any real-world analog. It is something entirely of its own.

Game play does not involve traffic management, as arrows do not collide and do not leave the screen once they appear on it. What it does require is treating each of the four "roads" as a stack and guiding enough arrows of a certain color down each until you begin to collect that color in a reservoir. You can then use that reservoir to project the "core" (represented on the DS's screen) away from an encroaching spike and hopefully toward a high score. Sending the wrong color down a road can destroy, combine, or double your reservoir, depending on the situation at the other roads.

It is willfully complex, and impossibly abstract, but that's okay. Once the game's internal logic begins to click, it leads to an inbuilt understanding that goes beyond conscious thought. Within a few games you begin to feel like an idiot savant playing *Tetris* with the down key depressed. Each move you make to flow the arrows to the correct reservoir, carefully managing and unleashing them at just the right moment, proves bountifully rewarding. **MKu**

Borderlands

Original release date : 2009
Platform : Various
Developer : Gearbox Software
Genre : First-Person Shooter

Even if you didn't know that *Borderlands*'s developer Gearbox Software hailed from the depths of Texas, ten minutes playing this brilliant mash-up of a first-person shooter and a role-playing game would probably lead you to that conclusion. *Borderlands* has a wonderful sense of place, from the roadkill-heavy opening to the jarring white-trash soundtrack, all contained within the game's insane alien world—a scrubby patchwork of trailer parks, hicks, and mutated hillbillies. The snarky sense of humor makes the simple mechanics seem fresh, all the way until the last headshot.

Choose one of four character classes and step off the bus into the Arid Wastelands, and *Borderlands* tasks you with finding a mysterious alien vault buried somewhere in the wilds of Pandora, a truly hellish and inhospitable planet. You don't have to be the most advanced of classics scholars to realize that this probably isn't going to end well. But the plot is pure misdirection, a lure to draw you into Gearbox's loot-heavy world, where you use crazy guns to shoot crazy enemies who in return drop more crazy guns for you to cause mayhem with. Repeat until satisfied.

Procedurally generating upward of 150,000 different weapons, *Borderlands* boasts some insane artillery: shotguns that fire lightning, sniper guns that unleash rockets, SMGs with long-distance scopes, and much more besides. Brimming with humor and ideas, and absolutely chaotic in four-player co-op, games don't get much simpler than this. But they also don't get much better. If you're itching for a little more of Gearbox's crazy creation, you might want to check out the first downloadable add-on, *The Zombie Island of Dr. Ned*—a hilarious, nutty expansion featuring zombies and WereSkags—and 2012's equally entertaining *Borderlands 2*. **CD**

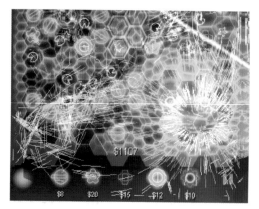

[T: 00:00:34]   [NAV: +000x +001y +031a +001dx +002dy +000da]   [LAW:]

/---------------------------------------\
Attention: Survivor
You have experienced a sector-wide explosion
of unknown origin. Beware that other pilots
in this region may resort to piracy.
Drag emergency relief modules onto your
ship to begin reconstruction.
\---------------------------------------/

[COM: (Info Buoy) Message Delivered   ] [HLP: Press (P) for command reference.]

GeoDefense Swarm

Captain Forever

Original release date : 2009
Platform : iPhone
Developer : Critical Thought Games
Genre : Strategy

Original release date : 2009
Platform : Internet
Developer : Farbs
Genre : Shoot 'Em Up

Pastiche can be a wonderful thing. As a game designer you can take another developer's mechanic, give it a new sheen, and release it as your own. At least Critical Thought Games had the manners to incorporate its influences into *GeoDefense Swarm*'s title—no false advertising here.

GeoDefense was one of legions of clones that emerged in the wake of *Desktop Tower Defense*. It's well suited to the iPhone: the touch screen makes placing defending units a breeze, and its bite-sized nature is perfect for trips on public transport. *GeoDefense* is also emblematic of the shortened path to success that developers can travel nowadays. Without a publisher's backing, a studio of Critical Thought's diminutive size still can be a critical and commercial hit.

GeoDefense Swarm has the added bonus of adopting the look of another popular small game: *Geometry Wars*. Enemies explode into neon fireworks, evocative of *Tron*, the screen pulsing with color. But Critical Thought makes its own contribution: enemy paths are clearly delineated in the honeycomb interface, making it easier to prepare your units. This positions the game as superior in its genre. **JBW**

Captain Forever succeeds in innovating on multiple levels, while resting on Australian creator Jarrad "Farbs" Woods's love of retro aesthetics.

You start as a spaceship, complete with an arcade-neon glow appropriated from *Captain Forever*'s main inspiration, Hikware's *Warning Forever* (2003). You fly around, blowing apart opponents. Remaining pieces can be picked up and attached to your ship. The action alternates seamlessly between being an inertia-heavy shooter and a construction game. How large will you make your ship? When should you upgrade? What do you do when half your vessel has been blown asunder and you're desperately trying to rebuild while being bombarded by horrors seemingly birthed from a 1980s arcade game?

Even in its business model, *Captain Forever* innovated. It was solely available as a Web browser game, with a fee granting access to an improved version—minimizing piracy, creating a community, and funding Farbs's future plans, which included the sequels *Captain Successor*, *Captain Imposter* and *Captain Jameson*. **KG**

Boom Blox Bash Party

Original release date : 2009
Platform : Wii
Developer : Electronic Arts
Genre : Puzzle

When Electronic Arts announced that Steven Spielberg was collaborating with one of its studios on a video game, *Boom Blox* was not what anyone expected.

Its sequel, *Boom Blox Bash Party*, is a cross between interactive Jenga and those fairground attractions where you attempt to knock glued-down cans from a platform with baseballs. Broadly, the aim is to knock down as many blocks as possible with each throw for points, or remove blocks without tumbling the entire structure. Special challenges and explosive or special indestructible blocks turn it into a precise puzzler or a chaotic party game.

Aiming and throwing with the Remote is intuitive, and the physics respond perfectly, sending blocks spinning and flying and wobbling precariously just like they ought to. It's brilliantly, childishly satisfying.

Boom Blox Bash Party is more varied than the original *Boom Blox*, adding toys like paintballs and a slingshot, as well as environmental factors like zero gravity and underwater levels. Their core principle is the same, though: Making things fall over is really good fun. **KM**

Canabalt

Original release date : 2009
Platform : Various
Developer : Semi Secret
Genre : Adventure

Originally a hit as a free Flash game, *Canabalt* casts the player as a lone man outrunning the apocalypse. You never learn what you're running from, although the giant tripodlike monsters on the horizon give one clue. As for safety, you'll never reach it. From rooftop to girder to office corridor, with rockets falling from the sky and flocks of pigeons erupting at your feet, your only goal is to keep running—while jumping over the gaps and debris that could slow your momentum or stop you dead. Crisp grayscale graphics feed the impression of speed and, when the end comes, your epitaph is brief: It's simply a report of the distance you covered before you died.

Designer Adam Saltsman built the game in just under a week for the Experimental Gameplay Project, entering it in a competition with the theme "Bare Minimum." True to the theme, *Canabalt*'s simplicity is its greatest strength. The sessions are short and relentless, and the sequence of obstacles changes every time—there's nothing to do at the end but try again. Quick, addictive, and most of all, thrilling, *Canabalt* hits the spot for casual gaming. **CDa**

Assassin's Creed II

Original release date : 2009
Platform : PS3, Xbox 360
Developer : Ubisoft
Genre : Action / Adventure

It's hard to figure out which is the real star of *Assassin's Creed II*. Is it the cities—the thronged alleys, grand squares, and fine facades of Florence and Venice—or the graceful Ezio, the game's lethally capable assassin? Set amid the lethal machinations of shadowy organizations and family power struggles of the Renaissance, it's a fascinating re-imagining of history that immediately charms. Though the cities are pastiches of the real things, tuned for play rather than facsimile, they're studded with period buildings—the background of each (along with leading personalities, from Lorenzo de' Medici to Caterina Sforza) documented in a database. Indeed, a quick dig through historical records reveals that though the game's winding plot of murder and intrigue seems far-fetched, it plays surprisingly faithfully to reality—under the overarching Dan Brown–style conspiracy story, at least. Ezio, meanwhile, is a delight—scrambling up stucco, leaping between terracotta roofs, and diving from towers, slashing, pouncing, and stabbing as he goes.

The first *Assassin's Creed* (2007) was criticized for failing to provide much of a game, so its sequel responded with a tumult of content. There are special dungeon-like locations in which to exercise Ezio's acrobatic talents; there's his Tuscan town, Monteriggioni, to develop into bustling prosperity. Glyphs found on certain buildings unlock various abstract puzzles. There are letters to deliver, retribution on adulterers to dole out, and races to be won. There's so much to do that you're still being introduced to new features and mechanics hours into the game. But it never feels too much, and each collectible and challenge nets you a specific reward, from a special set of armor to the revelation of a grand secret behind the game. **AW**

Batman: Arkham Asylum

Original release date : 2009
Platform : Various
Developer : Rocksteady Studios
Genre : Adventure / Fighting

What makes Batman so much fun to play? He's stealthy, lurking in the shadows to catch his prey, yet he's also brawny and built to slug his way through any mob of goons. He's the world's greatest detective, using a belt full of gadgets to sniff out a trail, but his suspects tend to be larger-than-life sociopaths with outlandish costumes. He's a troubled hero and probably crazy, but in a stoic way; nobody wants a Batman who doesn't keep it cool.

The Batman experience includes many contradictions, and Rocksteady's *Batman: Arkham Asylum* threads its way through all of them. The third-person action adventure throws him into a wide-open setting—Gotham City— but constrains all the action to the buildings and caves of Arkham Island. Batman gets to throw down with the goons, but also hangs from the rafters and squeezes his buff physique through narrow ventilation shafts. We might not get the opportunity to dive too deeply into his psyche, but the darkest parts of his past are drawn out and mirrored in the skewed surroundings of Arkham Asylum, the dungeon-like equipment that litters this institution and, most of all, a few nightmarish doses of a hallucinogen.

The main antagonist is the Joker, and the cat-and-mouse game he plays with Batman mirrors the structure of the game itself. He runs "the Bat" through a maze of traps and challenges, all built to distract Gotham's biggest hero while a more sinister plan plays out in the city. The final battle with the Joker—and, really, most of the boss fights—are the weakest elements of the game, but don't miss the hidden tapes of interviews with Poison Ivy, the Riddler, and the rest of Batman's rogues gallery. The villains are almost as fascinating as Batman himself—acting, arguably, as two sides of the same coin. **CDa**

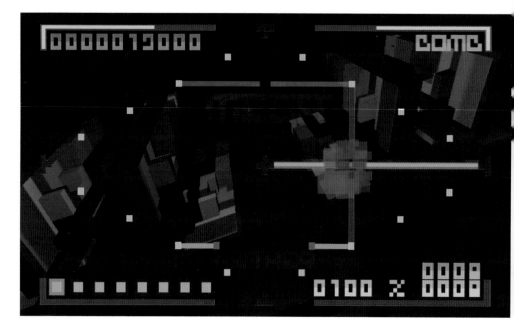

Bit. Trip Core

Original release date : 2009
Platform : Wii
Developer : Gaijin Games
Genre : Action / Music

Looking to gaming's deepest roots for its inspiration, *Bit.Trip Core* is a neatly self-reflexive rhythm game built around the 8-bit sound, simplicity, and geometry of the '80s arcade. Its visual vocabulary comprises moving dots, blocks, and flashing primary colors, backed by cascading, ever more complex music. Though it boasts all the visual hooks and brutal difficulty of its decades-old aesthetic influences, *Bit.Trip Core* is a modern, higher-definition reinvention—the backdrop music visualizer depicts sweeping landscapes of 3-D pixels, clumped together as strange, light-emitting towers or undulating hills and valleys. If we could see and hear what an 8-bit computer were thinking, this is what it might be like.

Unlike the first game in the series, *Bit.Trip Beat*, which is literally a twitch game, you don't twist the Wii Remote to play. Instead, a stationary D-pad at the center of the screen shoots a four-directional beam to intercept floating pixel dots, which blip and beep as they cross paths. Before long these patterns form crisscrossing lattices across the screen, building from rhythmic beeping into an intensely complicated torrent of beats.

If you do well, the music gets better, gradually adding more and more to the track. The visuals, too, step up gradually, becoming intensely hypnotic as the beat starts to syncopate and layers of synth begin to fold in on themselves. Making it to the end of the fourteen-minute sensory assault that comprises each of its three modes is an enormous feat of pattern recognition, patience, and dexterity. *Bit.Trip Core* uses lethally complicated geometry to fashion a fiercely hardcore challenge of pattern interpretation for modern players accustomed to nothing but scrolling note charts in their music games. **KM**

Grand Slam Tennis

Original release date : 2009
Platform : Various
Developer : Electronic Arts
Genre : Sports

There are seemingly insignificant moments that quietly change the way you feel about controlling video games: the first time you push an analog stick, for instance, or tap a DS screen, or tilt an iPhone. *Grand Slam Tennis* is the first third-party game to use the Wii's MotionPlus add-on for accurate, three-dimensional motion control and, after the first few imaginary racquet swings, it's difficult to imagine ever wanting to play *Wii Sports Tennis* again. It is an effortlessly instinctual system, meaning ball placement, velocity, and follow-through suddenly matter.

An entertaining side effect of this newfound technical accuracy is that hardened gamers can suddenly find themselves defeated by their own lack of real-life physical coordination. *Grand Slam Tennis*'s learning curve is brutal for players without an instinctive feel for a racquet, and the absence of a training mode beyond a simple ball machine is inexplicable—it's odd to pioneer a radical control system without providing a little guidance on how to use it. Instead of imbuing the business of virtual tennis playing with any meaningful sense of investment or improvement, the career mode is mainly a sequence of frustrating tournaments against AI players who don't have to struggle with motion control that actually works.

With two or more real people, however, *Grand Slam Tennis* is far more accessible. It swaps sports games' typical attempts at realism for a cartoonish visual style, caricaturing vintage players like John McEnroe and Pat Cash alongside Roger Federer, Rafa Nadal, and Andy Murray. Its lovable looks don't excuse the lack of depth and breadth in the game modes—but, by virtue of its control system alone, *Grand Slam Tennis* still earns a place near the top of the tennis game pile. **KM**

Battlefield 1943: Pacific

Original release date : 2009
Platform : Various
Developer : Digital Illusions CE
Genre : First-Person Shooter

The modestly sized, download-only experiment *Battlefield 1943: Pacific* is, for some, where the team shooter series hits its stride. Revisiting both the idyllic tropical locations and giddy, explosive lunacy that made famous the very first game, it offers a smartly balanced and pared down version of *Battlefield*'s multiplayer staples. Instead of the muddle of customizable classes, nuanced abilities, and weapon load-outs, *Battlefield 1943: Pacific* asks players to choose between long-, short-, and mid-range specializations. And even then it tempers each bias with a secondary weapon to help you out of scrapes. Both health and ammunition automatically replenish, and the HUD is a master class of readability. Even the island settings themselves guide players with their geography, raising objectives up on visible landmarks or funneling players to the frontline, down sandy spits dotted with palm trees.

While other *Battlefield* games' weapon upgrades, complex game variants, and sprawling levels have given themselves over to a longer commitment, *Battlefield 1943: Pacific* aims to crown itself as the king of instant action. With no need to fuss about what you are doing, where you are going, and what to pick up along the way, the game invites the kind of throwaway experimentation that sees players piling detonation packs onto vehicles and plowing through enemy lines with macabre jollity. It revels in its pyromania, and while *Battlefield: Bad Company* chased the series toward gritty soldiering, here blue skies, swaying palms, and glittering lagoons encourage a peculiarly light-hearted approach that is mirrored in the absurdity of the action itself. Accessible in a way that few shooters are, and delighted by its sense of mayhem, *Battlefield 1943: Pacific* tells us it's a charming day to have a war. **MD**

Bayonetta

Original release date : 2009
Platform : Various
Developer : Platinum Games
Genre : Action

Formed from the ashes of Clover Studio, Platinum Games arguably represented the cream of a particularly talented crop of Capcom developers. *Bayonetta*, Platinum's second release, is their crowning achievement.

Playing as the eponymous witch, you have to batter your way through all of heaven's minions in a series of set pieces that simply get more ridiculous and more brilliant as you progress. One moment you'll be surfing the ocean on a piece of airplane wreckage as you battle a giant mechanical shark, the next balancing on a rocket as it flies toward the enemy base.

The endless replayability of *Bayonetta* doesn't come from these magnificent moments, however. It comes from

the control of *Bayonetta* herself, the most capable and responsive fighter ever to be placed in a player's hands. In the midst of chaos, she moves when and where you want her to: dodging the instant you demand it, crashing down when you want her to, and generally doing everything spectacularly. As the challenge ramps up, so does your understanding of her capabilities. In other games you might get tossed around like a rag doll by enemies. Here, you are the one in control.

Ally this to original and polished art direction, a magnificent score, and visual effects that look good and synchronize beautifully with the mechanical elements of the game, and you have *Bayonetta*. It falls short of perfection on occasion: Certain quick-time events can be a pain, cut scenes can drag, and you'll see the odd location reused as the adventure unfolds (rather a Capcom tradition). But none of that stuff really matters because, in terms of wish-fulfilling fantasy action, *Bayonetta* is up there with the very best. **RS**

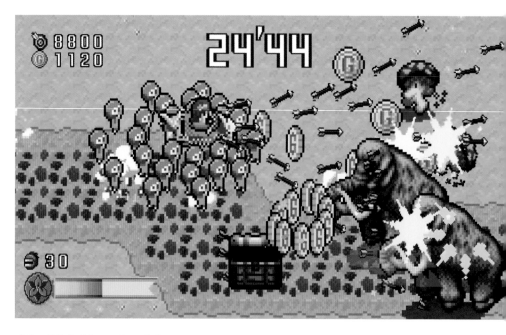

Half-Minute Hero

Original release date : 2009
Platform : PSP
Developer : Marvelous Entertainment
Genre : Strategy / Action

Games have always looked backward as well as forward for their inspiration, but it's only recently that they have developed the self-confidence to make fun of—as well as pay homage to—their forebears. Witty and inventive, *Half-Minute Hero* condenses all the pomp and self-consciously epic grandeur of the archetypal Japanese RPG into a thirty-second race to save the world. The spiky-haired boy hero, evil world-ending overlord, and 8-bit–inspired aesthetic are all familiar, but the game reinvents the J-RPG as a fast-paced strategy game—the first credit screen rolls about forty-five seconds into the game.

Every mission is a tiny micromanagement puzzle. Reaching the overlord's castle turns into a complicated sequence of small tasks, sending you off to retrieve sacred artifacts or persuade villagers to build a bridge, all within the same thirty seconds. You can buy the right to reset the clock at villages, an ability that quickly develops from last resort into a tactical imperative. High scores are the result of a delicate balance between leveling up enough in the overworld to defeat the evil lord in his castle and leaving just enough time to get there. Striking the final blow with less than a second left on the clock is exhilarating.

Half-Minute Hero—relaunched in 2011 as *Half-Minute Hero: Super Mega Neo Climax*—displays self-assured humor in its super-speed, 8-bit–style soundtrack, the late '80s art style of its anime characters, and the brilliantly random battles, in which hero and enemies simply ricochet crazily off one another in a shower of numbers until one or the other topples over.

Far from a naked, derivative appeal to nostalgia, *Half-Minute Hero* is a bold and modern concept with appeal that actually goes far deeper than its satirical premise. **KM**

Fat Princess

Original release date : 2009
Platform : PS3
Developer : Titan Studios
Genre : Action

You would think that a world in which slices of delicious birthday cake spontaneously appear in a meadow would be a great place to live. Not so in the land of *Fat Princess*, which would be a magical, Disney-esque realm were it not for an endless war between two groups of elves, each vying to kidnap the other team's princess and imprison her in their castle. Following the standard rules of multiplayer capture-the-flag, *Fat Princess* carves out a niche with the silliness of its setting and the gentleness of its play.

At the game's start, players spawn as elves on their side of the map. Elves can wear many hats—literally. Throughout each castle are machines that belch out different caps, each of which grants its wearer a different ability. Picking up and donning an engineer hat will allow an elf to repair damaged castle walls and upgrade other hat machines; the ranger hat makes an elf a long-range threat; the priest can heal allies; and so on. Choosing one hat doesn't lock a player into a class for the rest of the game—the hats can easily be changed at will.

Unlike most competitive online games, *Fat Princess* doesn't play like bloodsport. Elves do battle, and can be killed, but combat is so simple—with the control consisting of two buttons—that winning a fight feels like a coin flip more than anything. The emphasis is on trying to perform well at whatever job you are currently doing, despite the various distractions. Navigating world maps in particular can be highly hazardous, especially when shifting between lava pools and occasional trampolines.

Oh, and that cake? You feed it to your own princess so that she gains weight and is harder for your opponents to carry away. There's no designated job class for cake feeding—it's just the right thing to do. **MK**

Forza Motorsport 3

Original release date : 2009

Platform : Xbox 360

Developer : Turn 10 Studios

Genre : Racing

If the *Forza* racing series was built to satisfy pretty much anyone, it took the principle even further in its 2009 incarnation. The first two games featured rather orthodox fictional tracks, Maple Valley Raceway's autumnal trees being one of their few strays toward fantasy. But the new tracks in *Forza Motorsport 3* even have a taste for the theatrical: The roar of the crowd on entering the oval section of Sedona Raceway Park brings to mind a coliseum, while you will be arrested by the rocky vistas of Camino Viejo de Montserrat and thrown by the narrow village passages and switchbacks of the Amalfi Coast.

Though the game's simulation is as keen and playable as ever, it caters to a casual audience even more carefully

than its forebears, entirely stripping away the need to tinker with your cars with an automatic tuning system that upgrades cars according to the race ahead. Once you get on the grid, you will start at the back of the pack and almost inevitably surge a few places ahead before the first corner is even in sight. And if you don't, there's a rewind system that you can use as many times as you like, in order to dissect where it all went tragically wrong.

These features amount to a strange mix of realism and arcade, but most serious players will be racing for a good lap time on the online leaderboards and taking care not to incur penalties for going off-road or hitting competitors. Not to forget the suitably deep multiplayer option, which supports many kinds of events, from endurance races to games of tag. And for those who don't like driving, there are always the virtual occupations of making decal and paint jobs. Put it this way: *Forza Motorsport 3* is crafted to entertain such a broad audience that you don't even have to race to play it. **AW**

Colin McRae: Dirt 2

Original release date : 2009
Platform : Various
Developer : Codemasters
Genre : Racing

Even the death in 2007 of Colin McRae himself didn't stop *Dirt 2* from shipping in 2009, and this game about the niche sport of off-road racing proved one of the year's most entertaining driving games. It is an improvement on its predecessor, featuring a new sound engine, expanded multiplayer, and downloadable content. *Colin McRae: Dirt 2* straddles the extremes of racing games, borrowing the rough and tumble of *Burnout* and marrying it to the polish and realism of a refined simulation. It's a well-rounded game that's perfect for amateurs, because perfection isn't the point. From the first track, you're skidding through puddles or being bumped from behind by other wannabes aiming for a shot at the X-Games.

Your fleet ranges from performance saloons to buggies and Hummers. A simple set of statistics—acceleration, top speed, and drivability—helps you choose which vehicle you can handle. Once you pick your ride, you can enjoy the rich, vivid sights: skidding through a Moroccan village; flipping your truck beneath the baking sun of Baja, California; or barging into ancient stone walls along the road in Croatia. Even the spectators who jump back when you slam into their barrier don't seem scared: This is challenging and enjoyable racing, but never dangerous, and a mysterious sponsor will gladly repair your bruised and broken car after every brutal match.

More than a hundred events give the game depth and variety, and the real-world drivers you race against befriend you and help your career. The relationships you build are shallow, but they may give you a twinge of guilt when you muscle your buddy out of the way and hear him chide, "Did you *mean* to do that?" If they have to ask, perhaps they're in the wrong sport. **CDa**

Dead Space Extraction

Original release date : 2009
Platform : Wii
Developer : Visceral Games
Genre : Survival Horror / Shoot 'Em Up

Cementing the series' reputation as a shock tactician extraordinaire, *Dead Space Extraction* leaped from the murkiest of all shadows: the on-rails gun game genre. More moribund than even survival horror, this most basic arcade hand-me-down enjoyed a revival on Wii thanks to the crosshair-friendly Remote controller. Few saw an opportunity, though, for anything more than coin-op remakes and mildly adventurous, mildly gory parodies. True to form, *Dead Space Extraction* had other ideas.

If the first *Dead Space* was a homage to *Alien* and *System Shock 2*, *Dead Space Extraction* is more like *The Poseidon Adventure*. A roller coaster, its rails twist and turn through a series of interleaved stories, the player assuming various roles from the previous game's back story. There's the colonial security chief Nathan McNeill; his counterpart on the ill-fated *USG Ishimura*, Gabe Weller; a winsome and plucky surveyor, Lexine Murdoch; and a thoroughly devious mining executive, Warren Eckhart. They're worth mentioning by name because—thanks to a macabre early twist—you have no idea who will live and who will die. You care about all of them, even though you never fully control any of them.

Combat in *Dead Space Extraction* again involves the relationship between brutal industrial tools and the limbs of the Necromorphs, humans reborn as bloodythirsty mutants. It's arguably better on Wii, the Remote putting a new twist on many of the secondary fire modes while introducing a host of intuitive puzzles. It takes a steady hand to solder the *Ishimura*'s elevator and door controls back online, and a steady nerve to do it while stemming the tide of thrashing mandibles. This wasn't a game that just happened to work on Wii—it could *only* have worked on Wii. A shame, then, that it bombed on release. **DH**

Eliss

Original release date : 2009
Platform : iPhone
Developer : Steph Thirion
Genre : Puzzle

If you'll forgive the slight hyperbole, the App Store can be divided into pre- and post-*Eliss* eras. In the months prior to its release, with few exceptions, the iPhone's offerings were a sea of generic, pastel, over-easy, overaccessible, casual-focused, bottom-shelf titles; quickly knocked-out franchise cash-ins by major console publishers and amateur would-be gold rushers, hoping for a slice of the millions they had heard were there to be made.

And then along came *Eliss*, chirping a song from its toy-box electronic kit and simply in love with the idea of color, shape, and movement, of interaction and design in its most basic forms. Willfully and deliberately obscure, neither its screenshots nor its name give you any indication of what you're in for (until, perhaps, you find out that the latter is a play on Russian constructivist designer El Lissitzky). Solo creator Steph Thirion relents only to providing you with iconographic instructions: circles of like colors, you guess, can be joined or separated by pushing or pulling them apart, placed inside larger wire frame receptacles to be cleared off the board, and must never touch other colors. There's also some mad space babble about "squeesars" and galactic vortices.

It's not until you actually lay your fingertips on the screen itself that you realize that there's never been a game like this before. The reason is that there hasn't been the hardware to support it. Although its color-sorting and combining interactions are quite basic, at any given time *Eliss* is two handfuls (or ten fingerfuls) of responsibility: a compelling and compulsive blend of organizing and tidying the interstellar chaos that continually bubbles up to its surface. *Eliss* was one of the first signs of intelligent life that showed us how the iPhone could end up being, in every sense, a game changer. **BB**

DJ Hero

Original release date : 2009
Platform : Various
Developer : FreeStyleGames
Genre : Music

With a luxurious controller, tentative audience, and greater relevance in Europe than the US, what did Activision want from *DJ Hero*? Simple: It wanted the initiative. In a costly tit-for-tat battle between *Guitar Hero* and *Rock Band*, the developers at Neversoft were seen—somewhat unfairly, given the marvelous *Guitar Hero: Metallica*—as mere groupies to the rock gods at Harmonix. Something fresh was needed, something unrivaled.

Virtual turntablism has been the thrust of the *Beatmania* series for more than a decade, while Harmonix was dabbling with electronica years before it struck its first chord. But just as *Guitar Hero* made its Japanese antecedent *Guitar Freaks* a saleable prospect in the West,

DJ Hero's refined mechanics, desirable controller, star turns, and irresistible tunes are a defining package. So while FreeStyleGames, a UK studio split between veteran game makers and London DJs, deserves much of the credit, the rest belongs to Activision and peripheral maestro RedOctane.

DJ Hero isn't easy. It takes an almost scientific interest in cut chemistry to master the arcane symbols on-screen prompting directional scratches, timed button-taps, freestyle effects, and precise use of the cross-fader to chop and change the tracks. Player control of the mixes—a ninety-three-strong lineup splicing the Beastie Boys, DJ Shadow, Tears for Fears, Daft Punk, and a great many more—is largely illusory, the worst mistake just distorting or muting the sound. But creation isn't the object of these games—they're more about performance and appreciation, taking you deep inside the music, shining a light on the process, and, in this case, providing a channel between the artist and the audience. **DH**

Death Tank

Original release date : 2009
Platform : Xbox 360
Developer : Snowblind Studios
Genre : Strategy / Shoot 'Em Up

Death Tank began life as one of the most famously obscure games in existence. Lobotomy Software, an American first-person shooter specialist, tucked it away in its first game, Exhumed (a.k.a. PowerSlave), as a reward for collecting twenty-three hidden dolls representing members of the development team—but only on the US Sega Saturn version. The practically identical sequel, Death Tank Zwei, was hardly more accessible: It could only be reached by destroying every single toilet in Lobotomy's Saturn port of Duke Nukem 3-D or by having a save file from one of the developer's other games on the system memory. Barely anyone knew that Death Tank even existed. Why hide such an excellent multiplayer game?

Death Tank appears to be the product of sheer inventive boredom on Lobotomy Software's part. More than a decade later, the game's creator Ezra Dreisbach made Death Tank less impossible to play by working with Snowblind Studios to port it to Xbox Live Arcade. Significant graphical updates aside, it's much the same. Up to eight tanks battle on a destructible 2-D landscape, adjusting their gun turrets' trajectories to score hits. Death Tank turns a traditionally turn-based game type into real-time chaos; where Worms or Scorched Earth subject players to slow, menacingly inevitable defeats, in Death Tank you can rarely predict which shot is going to kill you.

The Xbox Live Arcade version attempts to offer some single-player value for its price tag, but Death Tank is only fun when played against other people. Sadly, it only supports four players locally; for the full complement of eight, you'll have to go online. It's also tragically missing the classic thrash-metal Death Tank theme song, which was at least eight percent of the original's appeal. **KM**

Demon's Souls

Original release date : 2009
Platform : PS3
Developer : From Software
Genre : Role-Playing

Its devotees describe *Demon's Souls* as a masochistic pleasure. This action role-playing epic takes control of your life and makes you slowly claw it back. In the tutorial, you are just getting the hang of the controls and learning how to block and when to parry, when suddenly you meet a demon ten times your size, who kills you with a single blow. You spend the next few hours as a ghost, weak and helpless, crawling through the same castle again and again. Unlike your usual role-playing game, you can't even gain a level until you beat your first boss. Your only choice is to get faster and craftier until you finally make your way back to life and start the game for real.

The isolated kingdom of Boletaria is thoroughly damned. Demons and dreglings prowl the ruins, and the few humans left are crazy and abandoned—and sound like they are speaking from their graves. But the more you get the hang of the place, the better you understand how to beat it. The game never wastes your time with bashing open crates or collecting random clutter. Where other role-playing games send you through dungeon after dungeon, each map of *Demon's Souls* is compact and hard-won, and you'll memorize every meter as you slowly overpower your enemies.

Demon's Souls is without a doubt a hardcore role-playing game but, with time, it doesn't seem difficult so much as absorbing. Every decision and act has a purpose, and you'll be startled by how much control you gain over your fate. The smoke-stained walls and echoey asylums that originally felt like a punishment start to feel pleasantly familiar as you persevere against them. And in a novel twist on cooperative play, other players will leave crucial hints or even jump into your journey, staving off the loneliness that the game tries so hard to instill. **CDa**

Dissidia Final Fantasy

Original release date : 2009
Platform : PSP
Developer : Square Enix
Genre : Role-Playing / Fighting

In the *Final Fantasy* RPGs, characters step forward and attack fresh air, while a number over the opponent's head indicates damage. In the *Final Fantasy* CGI movies, spiky-haired warriors clash at blistering speed, channeling some artful, manic hybrid of *The Matrix* and *Crouching Tiger, Hidden Dragon*. In *Dissidia Final Fantasy*, Square Enix tried to find common ground.

Blending the fighting and RPG genres is next to impossible, so *Dissidia* simply separates them and places itself in a category described as "dramatic progressive action." The face-offs are frenzied battles in which two fighters cover every square inch and surface of the arena. Outside of this, there's a leveling and equipment system

straight from an RPG. The 3-D battles are spectacular and full of counter-attacks, midair dashes, counter-counters, flourishes, and ridiculously excessive finishing moves. Thanks to its innovative health system, which sees players seesawing between attack points and health points that impact each other, fights can turn in seconds and a bad beating doesn't necessarily mean a lost match.

Outside of this, the RPG element seems a little bit of a pain at first, particularly the banal board game that has to be played while progressing through each location. As missions are cleared and the characters begin leveling up, however, it acquires a new importance. Perhaps the key to beating a new opponent lies in a bracelet that absorbs their main attack, rather than just relying on your reflexes, for example. *Dissidia Final Fantasy*'s stitching together of the genres rarely threatens to unravel, and even if you ignore the RPG aspect altogether (entirely possible), its innovative take on one-on-one 3-D fighting is more than enough to recommend it. **RS**

The House of the Dead: Overkill

Original release date : 2009
Platform : Wii
Developer : Headstrong Games
Genre : First-Person Shooter

The *House of the Dead* games have long been known for their ability to make players laugh as well as scream. However, the humor generated by the original arcade light-gun favorites was often of the fiercely unintentional variety, brought on by hammy scripts, ridiculous plot contrivances, and stiff animation that made most characters look like they had neglected to remove the coat hangers from their clothes before stepping into them.

The House of the Dead: Overkill is different. It plays out like a grindhouse drive-in movie (particularly influenced by 2007's *Planet Terror*), with scratches, pops, bursts of overexposed film, and genuinely memorable continuity errors. The game embraces its schlocky scripting with brilliantly contrived cardboard characters and wondrously inane dialogue. It's a joy to watch—so much so, in fact, that you would be forgiven for giving it space on your shelves even if the core game itself were terrible.

Luckily, it's not. *Overkill* may be a fairly basic on-rails shooting gallery, but its environments are atmospheric, the controls are excellent, and the crazy plastic six-shooter with which the game is packaged turns your Wii Remote into a curlicued hand cannon, perfect for sending zombies back to the grave with a few extra holes in them.

It's also elaborately disgusting, the final boss going to unexpectedly amusing lengths to coat the game in a gynacological membrane that is hard to escape. The perfect update to a guilty pleasure, the British-made *The House of the Dead: Overkill* has a great sense of humor and style, and doles out its sexy violence with a smirk and a winning wink. It is certainly a *House of the Dead* game, but it is not one gamers had seen before, presenting the most confident and imaginative entry for many years. **CD**

Dragon Age: Origins

Original release date : 2009
Platform : Various
Developer : BioWare
Genre : Role-Playing

Dragon Age: Origins represents BioWare's attempt to reimagine the fantasy adventure by making it darker, bloodier, and sexier. The modern fantasy role-playing game template had been largely defined by the company's earlier efforts, and BioWare intended to repeat what had worked about those games, while at the same time modernizing the approach, both technologically and thematically. The result is a visually impressive 3-D fantasy with grim themes, harrowingly bleak quests, and a dynamic cast of entertaining characters.

The fumbling love scenes and occasionally plummy voice acting might have come in for a bit of stick, but BioWare's intentions are well-founded. *Dragon Age: Origins*

is a fantasy for more mature audiences, and the writing, world-building, sexy bits, and blood-spattered heroes are all a testament to this focused vision.

Set against the backdrop of a collapsing, corrupt, and racist kingdom, you struggle to raise an army against the invading Darkspawn, a kind of orc-undead hybrid overseen by the "Arch-Demon." The decisions you characters face are more grave than in previous BioWare games, and the battles you engage in are tough enough to satisfy even the most experienced gamers.

The primary accomplishment of *Dragon Age: Origins* however, is the construction of a world with believable tensions. The downtrodden elves live as a slave race and the dwarves strive against a corrupt society blighted by toxic class struggle, overseen by a fierce religious order.

Epic in all senses, the game is best played on a PC—the interface of its console-based counterparts doesn't stand up to mouse and keyboard. Its legacy is upheld by *Dragon Age II* (2011) and *Dragon Age III: Inquisition* (2013). **JR**

Empire: Total War

Original release date : 2009
Platform : PC
Developer : The Creative Assembly
Genre : Strategy

Empire: Total War is a game focused on large, nineteenth-century armies doing battle, immersing players in the vast scale of war and the varieties of tactics required to overcome adversaries. This is a real-time strategy game that is by no means easy to master, constantly challenging the player, demanding that they be aware of what's going on in the battlefield and always be ready with a backup plan. Using one unit alone will not bring victory, and the player soon realizes that a combination of approaches is needed to defeat the enemy.

Upon release, Empire: Total War represented a real step forward (at the time) in the five-games-old Total War series, giving the player even more armies to choose from, even more countries to play as, and even more units to control and maps to manipulate them on. The game also gives the player the ability to fight in naval battles, adding an entirely new dimension to this already large offering. The attention to real-time detail in the design of the naval battles is fantastic: Your ships will only move as fast as the wind will take them, and sailing into the wind will slow you down. You can choose from a variety of battleships, and you will soon discover that it's unwise simply to pick the biggest variety since you'll be a sitting duck if you're attacked by five small, nimble craft. Ultimately the naval game play isn't the most polished part of the package, however, and the artificial intelligence used throughout the game as a whole feels far from robust.

Nevertheless, its other achievements ensure that Empire: Total War remains an accomplishment in the real-time strategy genre, and it's certainly as impressive, ambitious, and spectacular to behold as the best entries in the classic series. **SG**

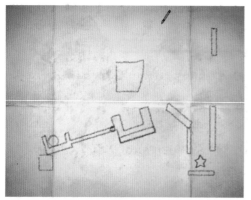
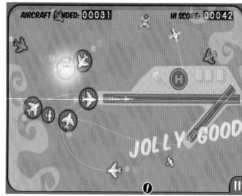

Crayon Physics Deluxe Flight Control

Original release date : 2009

Platform : Various

Developer : Petri Purho

Genre : Puzzle

Original release date : 2009

Platform : Various

Developer : Firemint

Genre : Management Simulation

Crayon Physics Deluxe espouses a new movement in game design of player empowerment and creativity.

The object of Crayon Physics Deluxe is to move a ball from one part of a 2-D level, cutely presented as if on a creased piece of paper, to touch a star by drawing objects with a virtual crayon, using your mouse. As the title suggests, everything in a level is subject to physics—balls roll and fall, blocks slide, ropes coil and pull taut. Pin one object to another, and it will swing from that point. The levels therefore require a series of intuitively deduced solutions to solve, from carrying the ball in baskets to flinging it with counter-weighted catapults.

It's open to many cheap tactics, but the intention is for you to be creative. As a note at the game's start says, "It's not about finding just any solution. It's about finding the awesomest one." As such, each level releases another star, but only if you can think up another three solutions.

The secret of Crayon Physics Deluxe is simple and liberating: With a crayon in your hand and a canvas before you, it's all down to your own imagination. **AW**

Flight Control was developed into a functional app with little fanfare. Yet, upon release, it rocketed to the top of the App Store sales charts.

The game play consists of simply drawing flight paths for incoming aircraft to follow. That may sound almost tediously simplistic, but with multiple landing strips corresponding to separate types of aircraft (which can also vary individually in size and speed), it becomes a tense management task, with lines needing to be redrawn quickly and skillfully to stop planes from colliding.

The game initially offered just one airfield to play on—and an interminably slow ramp-up of difficulty—but one of the great benefits of the App Store is its ability to quickly modify titles to better suit the audience. Accordingly, Flight Control was quickly updated to offer three airfields, online leaderboards, and a "fast-forward" button for when confidence (perhaps unwisely) overflows.

Thanks to a clean visual design, it's an attractive experience, looking every inch the kind of app that belongs on the system. **MKu**

Noby Noby Boy

Original release date : 2009
Platform : PS3
Developer : Namco
Genre : Action

A session with *Noby Noby Boy* goes like this: You independently control the bulbous head and tail of your snakelike boy, moving him around a randomly generated slab of world, populated by abstract structures, statuettes, and an assortment of animal and human life. Swallow any object, and it lumps its way through his body, from which it can be spat out the tail end. Then you discover the boy can stretch to a biologically impossible, rainbow-striped, physically unmanageable degree, until he's draped limply over—and intertwined with—every object in the world.

That, it turns out, is his true purpose. The yards he stretches are continually tallied and then broadcast, as a unit measurement of love, to the universe's only girl. She is an infinitely larger copy of Boy, and is growing linearly through a scale model of our solar system at a rate determined by the yards sent from all collective Boy players in the world. With each successive planet she reaches in real time (Mars took a matter of months), new levels are unlocked for every player. A true original, and a surprisingly affecting, innocent, and naive pleasure. **BB**

Flower

Original release date : 2009
Platform : PS3
Developer : thatgamecompany
Genre : Adventure

Flower is all pretty fields of grass, blowing in the wind, beneath blue skies that suddenly burst into color to a musical accompaniment of twinkly, jingly-jangly wind chime tunes. It comes dangerously close to being a little cutesy—until you actually start playing the thing and realize it is one of the most exhilarating games of recent times. It takes you on an emotional voyage, from the sun-filled simplicity of early levels to the darker later sections—all moody and storm-filled, with lightning arcing across the screen. You swirl and swoop through the skies to retrieve flower petals, transforming the landscape—and soundscape—as you go.

That soundscape is one of the key reasons for the elemental sense of freedom. The other is the superb motion control, which truly seems to capture the gleeful sense of floating on the wind.

There are no armies or worlds to conquer here; no buildings to leap from. And it is all the better for it, highlighting the artistic and dramatic possibilities of the video game medium. **DM**

F.E.A.R. 2:
Project Origin

Original release date : 2009
Platform : Various
Developer : Monolith Productions
Genre : First-Person Shooter

Creating a sequel to the original *F.E.A.R.* meant answering some questions. What happened after the cataclysmic explosion at the end of the first game? What will monstrous psychic girl Alma do now that she is free? *F.E.A.R. 2: Project Origin* addresses these issues in style, delivering a shattered city, frantic combat, and more hair-raising supernatural experiences.

F.E.A.R. 2: Project Origin is a potent mixture of combat and spookiness. The visions and weirdness keep you on your toes, even though you're a superpowered death machine who can slow down time to outpace his enemies. This slow-motion mode was at the heart of the original, because it allowed the game to show off its physics-drenched environments and sophisticated AI. This remains in the sequel, with the AI diving for cover and even knocking things over to block your fire. This time, however, you're also able to do that, and can take shelter behind makeshift barricades.

In terms of action, *F.E.A.R. 2: Project Origin* is a step up, too, not least because it allows you to pilot the machines against which you fought so fiercely in the original. These stompy little battle-suits stumble through walls and disgorge firepower into their environment in an enormously satisfying manner—a splendid power-fantasy in a game that delivers combat brilliantly.

If there's a problem with this sequel, it's that it is never ambitious enough. We could have done with even more horror, and more of that dread feeling of helplessness evoked by the original. Also, the game throws so many supernatural enemies at you that the experiences of the uncanny become devalued and are less terrifying. **JR**

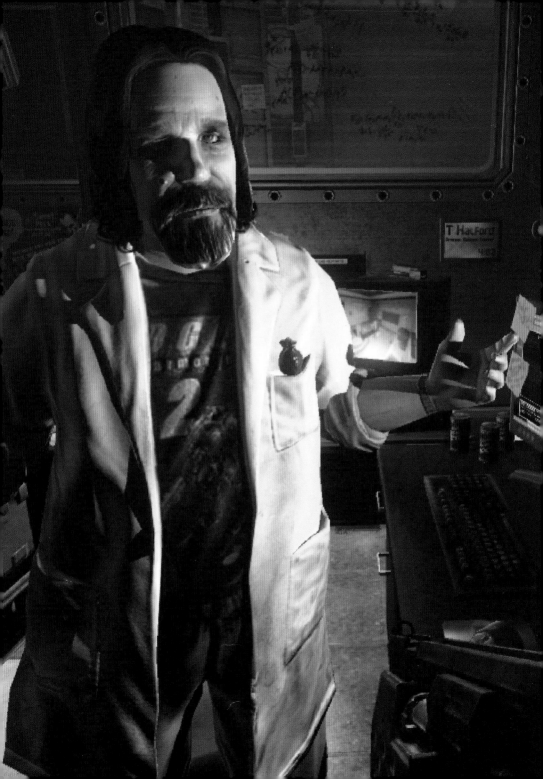

Fuel

Original release date : 2009
Platform : Various
Developer : Asobo Studio
Genre : Racing

Post-apocalyptic environments have long proven popular among game designers in the past decade, but it's unusual to see them in racing games. *Fuel* is an open-world racing game set in a climate-ravaged North America, where the continent has largely been abandoned to extreme-sports racing on quadbikes, buggies, jeeps, and even hovercraft—ideal for getting across the various stretches of water.

Unlike previous open-world racers in which events took place within a relatively small area, such as a city, *Fuel*'s backdrop is a zone of 5,560 square miles—about the whole area of Connecticut or half the size of Wales. Visually, this vast terrain is a kind of ruined and

miniaturized United States, its landscape varying from temperate forests to salt flats, through deserts and swamps, drowned cities, and abandoned farms. The weather is a particularly startling feature of the world, with huge lightning storms and twisters adding unpredictable and elemental spice to the races. The game events take place via a number of nodes across the landscape, all of which can be activated to start races. As regions are opened up by racing, players are able to move about quickly via a transport helicopter. The entire world is open to explore, and a round-trip of the map takes around eight hours, even without visiting all of the major locations.

Fuel is not a stunning racing game in mechanical terms, but a significant and awe-inspiring act of creativity in the wider scheme of video games. The sheer enormity of the seamless terrain makes a fine example of what other games should be doing with their world creation. If one small French studio can create something so broad and rich, what is the rest of the gaming world doing wrong? **JR**

Call of Duty: Modern Warfare 2

Original release date : 2009
Platform : Various
Developer : Infinity Ward
Genre : First-Person Shooter

The best-selling sequel to the best-selling original, *Call of Duty: Modern Warfare 2* is the gaming equivalent of a Bond movie. At times, it's an actual Bond movie. Developer Infinity Ward has worked on the series since its founding in 2002 and, with *Call of Duty: Modern Warfare*, brought its pyrotechnics bang up-to-date while simultaneously crafting the most popular, and some would say greatest, FPS multiplayer experience on this generation of consoles. *Modern Warfare 2*'s mission is simple: bigger and better.

Admittedly, its single-player campaign is influenced by its predecessor rather too much. Indisputably it is blemished by the controversial and clumsy airport level (in which you gun down civilians), though even this provides thrilling ideas and spectacular moments. More inspired is the Spec Ops mode, which lets you and a chum shoot, sneak, and explode your way through twenty-three of the best moments from both *Modern Warfare* games. Here you confront a hair-raising litany of explosions and panicked communications as you try to protect your friend from an orbiting AC-130 gunship, or during a silent and tense creep through snow and past dog patrols.

But it's when playing against other people that *Call of Duty: Modern Warfare 2* really finds its feet, and can't be faulted. It's one of the deepest multiplayer shooter experiences, with a rewarding leveling system that responds to every style of play, and constantly unlocks new goodies and accessories. The ability to create any type of soldier you wish leads to infinite tinkering between rounds, and a game that not only suits but positively encourages individual styles of play. *Modern Warfare 2* is a behemoth of the FPS landscape, and a shooter that tangibly rewards investment like few others. **DH**

Grand Theft Auto IV: The Lost and Damned

Original release date : 2009

Platform : PS3, Xbox 360

Developer : Rockstar

Genre : Action / Adventure

After the brilliantly miserable conclusion of Niko Bellic's tragic tale came this tense and edgy story of biker gangs and madmen—of friendship, rivalry, and creeping suspicion. In terms of the kind of errands it gets you to run, the adventures of Johnny Klebitz, pockmarked Jewish biker turned narcotics dealer, proved to be not dissimilar to *Grand Theft Auto IV* itself. The endless backtracking, escort runs, and shoot-outs could simply be more of the same, but the grim tone and frightening characters make it a very different beast. While it slots in rather cleverly with the narrative of the original game, *The Lost and Damned* serves to deepen our sense of Liberty City as a real place, with its own histories and subcultures.

Johnny Klebitz has been looking after a biker gang, the Lost, while Billy Grey, the boss, is enjoying a prolonged period of rest and relaxation in a mental institute. Klebitz is a thinker, and a tortured soul: He wants to set aside the casual violence, forge bonds with rival outfits, and make a fortune selling drugs. Once Billy's out, though, Johnny's plans are abandoned as the game turns into a test of wills as the two former friends battle over their shared future.

There are plenty of new toys for players to enjoy: the rather unwieldy bikes have been refined, weapons have been expanded, and there's a new mini-game revolving around riding in formation. But the real appeal for this first downloadable episode is undoubtedly to see Rockstar's storytellers at work again.

Grand Theft Auto IV: The Lost and Damned doesn't reinvent the wheel in any way, but it's a supremely polished offering with genuinely exciting moments, that serves to remind players why Rockstar all so often seems to belong in a class all its own. **CD**

GetaLife

Grand Theft Auto IV: The Ballad of Gay Tony

Original release date : 2009
Platform : Various
Developer : Rockstar
Genre : Action / Adventure

The second and final episodic expansion to the superb Grand Theft Auto IV, The Ballad of Gay Tony reintroduces some of the pyrotechnic bombast and gleeful carnage that had been sidelined in the grit and grime of the revamped Liberty City. While the original's immigrant story went for a somber approach, chastising America, this is an ebullient affair, reveling in the extremes that its cast of superwealthy eccentrics can afford.

It follows the travails of Luis, bodyguard and business partner to nightclub owner "Gay" Tony Prince. Once Tony was a leading light of Liberty City's glitterati, but his clubs are flagging, and a string of dodgy investments are coming back to haunt him. Strung out and drugged up,

he looks to his friend and partner, Luis, to help set things straight. However, setting things straight seems to involve a huge amount of explosive violence: High-rise buildings detonate while you BASE jump from their shattering windows, pleasure cruisers are sent to Davy Jones's Locker in a hail of rocket fire from a stolen attack chopper, and subway trains are stolen at the behest of playboy billionaires while they're still clattering along the tracks. The addition of a riot shotgun with exploding rounds indicates the overcaffeinated thrills offered by the episode.

But despite the preoccupation with fireworks, the surprisingly warm-hearted tale of Luis and Tony's see-sawing friendship is told with just as much skill and energy as Niko Bellic's grimmer story in Grand Theft Auto IV. One difference is that players can opt out of much of the socialization mini-games and distractions—a generous move from Rockstar, which, until Gay Tony, had even largely ignored concessions such as save points. But that's Gay Tony to a tee: generous and happy to please. **MD**

NEAR MISS

Mon 15:04

Grand Theft Auto: Chinatown Wars

Original release date : 2009
Platform : Various
Developer : Rockstar
Genre : Action / Adventure

If the DS thought that modest hardware, touch-screen controls, and a wholesome reputation were going to save it from *Grand Theft Auto*, it thought wrong. *Chinatown Wars* is an incredibly provocative episode, its lo-fi veneer hiding enough "hot coffee" to keep the tabloids busy for months. Though it reverts to a top-down look that's closer to the earliest *Grand Theft Autos*, it also recaptures their surreal levels of violence and destruction. Flamethrowers, chainsaws, bombs, and hoods are its weapons of choice.

The hero is Huang Lee—who, like most arrivals to Liberty City, has his hopes and ambitions dashed by those of family and friends. No sooner has he stepped off the plane than he's locked in a car and dumped in the

canal. Then a treasured family sword, Yu Jian, is stole by anonymous assassins. Punching his way throug the windscreen (with sharp jabs of the stylus), Lee find himself even worse off: Dishonored along with h conceited uncle Kenny, and caught among rival Triad crooked cops, the Korean mob, and the Italian mafia. All, c course, think that he's the solution to their problems.

Unlike the *Grand Theft Auto Stories* games on PS *Chinatown Wars* isn't a port. It doesn't make a mocker of the DS either: its mini-games are as enjoyable as the are subversive. You can imagine the stylus squirming a it negotiates backstreet dope deals, hot wires cars, an roots through bins for guns and ammo. But this isn't jus wanton crime. Much of Lee's income depends on buyin and selling needles, pills, and powders, then taxiing ther across Liberty City in the vain hope of a clear run. With you earnings now contraband, this sets up the most thrillin police chases since *GTA* began, a dink on a passing sid mirror being enough to sound sirens across the city. **DH**

Guitar Hero: Metallica

Original release date : 2009
Platform : Various
Developer : Neversoft
Genre : Music

Neversoft's best *Guitar Hero* game to date—an indispensable artifact for followers of the multi-million-selling band—oozes authenticity at every turn. Many of the usual platitudes are made, but for once they actually apply. The twenty-eight Metallica tracks are original recordings, based on original master tracks for everything, right back to their 1983 debut *Kill 'Em All* (those tapes found, it's said, in the basement of a former manager).

The twenty-one songs from "their personal favorites and influences" are just that—drummer Lars Ulrich fought Microsoft personally for the inclusion of thrash legends Slayer. The support for dual kick pedals exists purely to ensure accurate versions of Ulrich's drum tracks. Even

the cartoon story of adoring fans becoming the band's opening act is genuine—artistic license notwithstanding.

What's most startling is that this is the band vilified as regressive, technophobic fan haters during a high-profile fight with file-sharing service Napster. Say what you like about its handling of that affair—and you have to admit Ulrich had a point—but that couldn't be less true of its work with Neversoft, the band making repeat visits to provide additional motion capture and feedback. If there's a niggle with the result, it's the relegation of ex-bassists Cliff Burton and Jason Newsted to mere bonus ephemera. Newsted's struggle with the band is well documented, but a more poignant memorial to his predecessor wouldn't, surely, have put too many noses out of joint.

Crucially, the most formidable thing about *Guitar Hero: Metallica*—the thing that guarantees a miserable time for games trying to follow it—is the music itself. In the band that brought metal from the clubs to the stadiums, the series found its muse. **DH**

Halo 3: ODST

Original release date : 2009
Platform : Xbox 360
Developer : Bungie
Genre : First-Person Shooter

Two words lingered over *Halo 3: ODST* at it headed toward release: contractual obligation. Did Bungie, freshly free from Microsoft ownership and on record as wanting to leave the series behind, really have its heart in even another six hours of fighting the Covenant? The answer, happily, is yes: *Halo 3: ODST* may be short, and may be light on a certain hero in green armor, but it is thoughtful, exciting, and easily the most experimental game the brilliant development team has made in quite a while.

With Master Chief out of the way, *Halo 3: ODST* travels back to events from *Halo 2*, returning to the streets of New Mombassa inside the thinner cladding of an Orbital Drop Shock Trooper, or "hell jumper"—an extreme sports commando who rockets out of the sky and into the thick of the action. For the bulk of the game you play the Rookie, exploring the ruined metropolis on foot under cover of darkness, occasionally reliving daylight flashbacks from the rest of your team as you struggle to piece together what happened to your comrades.

With its moonlit streets, sultry soundtrack, and regular blasts from the recent past, *Halo 3: ODST* is Bungie's entirely laudable attempt at a film-noir mystery. That said, fans are more likely to enjoy the fact that each flashback sequence centers on a single core aspect of *Halo*'s game play. So, even though your superhuman jump, rechargeable shield, and dual-wielding habits are gone, the game still manages to feel like a greatest hits, with Warthog runs and plentiful frantic skirmishes. Rounding out the likable package is Firefight, a cooperative multiplayer addition in which teamwork allows you to fight off waves of advancing enemies—or at least die trying. **CD**

Might & Magic: Clash of Heroes

Original release date : 2009
Platform : Various
Developer : Capybara Games
Genre : Puzzle / Adventure

Might & Magic: Clash of Heroes might at first glance appear to fit into the same milieu as the Nintendo DS's defining puzzle/RPG hybrid *Puzzle Quest*, but it has far more in common with its PC-based namesake franchise, thanks to a surprisingly deep strategy system at its core. While *Might & Magic: Clash of Heroes* requires that you "stack" like-colored units in order to activate them in the game's battles, play is less about pattern matching than it is about finding and exploiting weaknesses in your opponent's formations. Through clever use of artifacts (equippable unique items that offer tactical nuance) and troop selection, players can switch between offense and defense on the fly. You can choose to position troops horizontally to create walls (literally) or to stack and link troops into all-out attacks, with bonuses for carefully timed offensives.

Might & Magic: Clash of Heroes has a steep learning curve for those expecting a simple match-three puzzler (sometimes the best tactics can be stymied by the random draw of new units). However, the play is streamlined to ensure the challenges never feel insurmountable.

The game makes especially good use of the dual-screen nature of the DS—opponents' formations on the top screen facing off against the player's on the bottom, and with both touch and D-pad controls equally usable. And special note must be made of *Might & Magic: Clash of Heroes*'s visual design, with the craft of bold pixel art made relevant through gorgeous portrait and background work. The art lends heart and gravitas to a story that not only fits within the franchise's continuity but is also accessible to newcomers, completing a title that is a uniquely polished fusion of puzzling and strategy. **MKu**

Machinarium

Original release date : 2009
Platform : Various
Developer : Amanita Design
Genre : Adventure

In 2006, Czech visionary Jakub Dvorsky invited friends to collaborate on a new video game project. Dvorsky had been building games throughout his life and, after graduating from art school, launched a company called Amanita Design. The assembled team toiled away with no pay and only vague prospects of success.

However, with new channels of digital distribution available and an award from the Independent Games Festival, *Machinarium* became an international sensation, and has since allowed Dvorsky and his partners to work on their projects full-time. It is a bold illustration of the changing landscape of independent games. The game's artwork is perhaps its most distinguishing feature.

Vaclav Blin's distinctive style is heavily evident in the paintbrushed aesthetic. The color palette is dominated by browns and grays, but not in any oppressive, overwhelming sense. The world feels positively ancient under Blin's care, and the set design takes on Tim Burton–esque tones in both its surreality and morose disposition.

Machinarium's dedication to simplicity makes the title sing. As a lonely robot, you're searching for your one true love. Yet there isn't a lick of dialogue. The little automatons communicate via speech bubbles, expressing their joy, frustration, and disappointment.

The game play, meanwhile, is quaint. Point-and-click adventures are a vestige of a bygone era, and Dvorsky's choice to follow that route arises both from financial necessity and a commercial reality. In fact, *Machinarium* is part of a newer generation of games that use point-and-click to new creative and narrative ends. The world is much bigger now for independent designers—a niche of ever increasing proportions. **JBW**

Halo Wars

Original release date : 2009
Platform : Xbox 360
Developer : Ensemble Studios
Genre : Strategy

With the advent of the Xbox 360, Microsoft was ready to begin "diversifying" the *Halo* universe. The choice of game to do this, however, was an odd one. Ensemble Studios had been acquired by Microsoft Game Studios in 2001, and veterans of the *Age of Empire* series were working on the problem of translating the RTS genre to console. Microsoft saw brand synergy, and *Halo Wars* was born.

The secret to *Halo Wars*'s success is that it's not a real-time strategy game: It's an action game with strategic elements and an RTS viewpoint. The missions rely on smaller armies and micromanagement of troops rather than resources. Spartans hijack enemy vehicles while you direct a Warthog through a barrage of grenades, before switching to your foot troops and beginning a skirmish with Covenant forces, directing their flanking maneuvers just like you did the Warthog—all with little more than the use of a single button.

It's an interface of great simplicity, and it means *Halo Wars* is a simplistic game in terms of strategy—this is no *Age of Empires: Master Chief* edition. You could even call it shallow at times, but the fact remains that it does work, and boded well for the genre on console. Unfortunately, Ensemble Studios was shuttered by Microsoft just as work was completed, an undeserved end for the developer's big ambitions (it certainly makes the reward unlocked for completing the game, "Ready for the Sequel," a little bittersweet). *Halo Wars* didn't do for the console RTS what the original *Halo* did for the console FPS, but how could it? Playing the game reminds you how close Ensemble got: a strategy game not only built to be played with a joy pad but positively responding to it, thrillingly careening from objective to firefight with scarcely a pause. **RS**

IL-2 Sturmovik: Birds of Prey

Original release date : 2009
Platform : Various
Developer : Gaijin Entertainment
Genre : Flight Simulation / Combat

As the sequel to one of the most popular and demanding World War II simulators on the PC, *IL-2 Sturmovik: Birds of Prey* faced a problem in the form of the relative restrictions presented by console joy pads. But developer Gaijin Entertainment's masterstroke is in pitching the game's various difficulty levels perfectly. Those after Battle of Britain-style action thrills and those who require the threat of blacking out during a loop-de-loop high above the white cliffs of Dover are equally catered for.

At the lower difficulty level the game fools you into thinking that the outcome of the war hinges on your skills, with Jeremy Soule's *Band of Brothers*–style soundtrack adding pomp and circumstance to the proceedings. But

with an anachronistically futuristic HUD lighting up enemy birds as bright-red diamonds on-screen, the game hardly presents a realistic challenge. Conversely, up the challenge to "realistic" and every joystick adjustment must be finely balanced with throttle and rudder to avoid barrel-rolling into the cornfields below.

From the green and yellow patchwork fields of Dover to the sun-soaked coastal holiday spots of Italy, and on to the gray, burning skies of Berlin, *IL-2 Sturmovik: Birds of Prey*'s vistas are both grand and beautiful. Missions are divided evenly between ground and air targets, some requiring you to shoot down a squadron of airborne fighters, others asking you to sink a fleet of battleships.

A story told through a combination of archive footage and contemporary voiceovers delivered in character adds a sort of sentimental authenticity to the package, but it's via its virtual skies that the game soars into the canon. It even stands up transferred from console to PC under the title *Wings of Prey*. **SP**

Infamous

Original release date : 2009
Platform : PS3
Developer : Sucker Punch Productions
Genre : Action

Infamous is a sparking, spitting video game equivalent of a superhero origins movie, with all the delights and frustrations that such a concept suggests.

Taciturn Cole MacGrath—who gurns like a pirate when left to idle and moves in a sinewy crouched run when busy, accompanied by the constant jingle-jangle of his rucksack—is a bike courier who's just accidentally blown an entire metropolis to pieces. Cut off from the mainland, forgotten by the rest of the world, the citizens of Empire City go quietly mad together, giving in to a frenzy of looting and murder that further destabilizes the already ravaged environment. Mostly, they're angry at Cole, it seems, who they blame for causing the destruction.

Not that he really cares: He's woken up at the epicenter of the blast, entirely unharmed, and filled with gradually evolving electrical powers, which mean he can blast cars through the air, fry the bodies of the nefarious Reaper gangs, and—eventually—soar through the sky in a scientific, albeit rather ambiguous, manner.

There's a limp karma system in place as Cole breezes through the plot, a range of upgradeable powers that react to whether you're killing people or saving them, and three derelict islands to explore along the way. But *Infamous*'s real charm is its no-fuss traversal, which sees you sticking to walls in an entirely fuss-free manner, scampering up drainpipes, surfing over power lines, and gadding about on the rooftops with glee. *Infamous* doesn't have the mindless joy to match *Crackdown*, with its formidable draw distances, but as a more narratively inclined strain of up-market chimney jumper, it's certainly an entertaining and inventive accompaniment to Realtime Worlds's dazzlingly simple classic. **CD**

Left 4 Dead 2

Original release date : 2009
Platform : Various
Developer : Valve Corporation
Genre : Shoot 'Em Up / Survival Horror

Despite Valve's well-earned reputation as one of the most careful and community-minded game studios, their announcement of a speedy follow-up to *Left 4 Dead* saw a vocal minority of the gaming population turn against the Washington-based developer with a real viciousness. A sequel within a year of the original game might be *de rigueur* for a sports title or a cuddly platformer, but Valve's productions were meant to take eons to build, pieced together in dark secrecy before emerging, blinking, into the light with all their brilliant secrets still untapped.

The truth is, however, that as the original *Left 4 Dead* team performed a postmortem on their first title, they realized there was so much more that they wanted to do:

daylight levels, hideous new specials, and melee weapons like frying pans, cricket bats, and *katanas*. Along with elaborate behind-the-scenes changes to the AI director itself, a new product was surely inevitable. With all this in mind, why not do it straightaway?

And it's hard to feel too angry once you've played the result. *Left 4 Dead 2* moves the zombie apocalypse to the Deep South, throwing in new enemies—the best being the Jockey, a horrible mutant who leaps on to your back and tries to draw you away from safety—plucky new heroes, and dazzling new scenarios, including creepy fairs and swamps. Melee weapons add a dash of queasy comedy to proceedings, and the AI director's influence has increased to include control of the weather and the ability to screw around with the game's geometry.

Plenty who signed angry petitions have been won over by the quality of the final product—and, as ever with Valve, the end result is simply something that gives you more options to enjoy, and more ways to play. **CD**

Killzone 2

Original release date : 2009
Platform : PS3
Developer : Guerrilla Games
Genre : First-Person Shooter

Announced by a trailer made by Glasgow CG expert Axis Animation, *Killzone 2* is a testament to presentation. Perhaps the most remarkable thing about that clip—a stunning portrait of a futuristic battlefield but not, infamously, the game as it then existed—is that it isn't actually that misleading.

Upping the ante from 2004's *Killzone*—a game that wasn't quite the "*Halo* killer" many had hoped for—the sequel depicts an endgame scenario between the forces of Earth (the ISA) and a race of mutated human colonists, the Helghast. Having weathered the storm in the first game, the ISA mounts a full-scale invasion of the enemy homeworld, Helghan, unaware of its formidable defenses.

With a complete absence of telltale flaws, and pioneering uses of deferred rendering (a technique that allows greater control of dynamic light) and motion capture, *Killzone 2* simply doesn't resemble any other game. Battlefield debris is spun into vortices by passing drop ships, weapons look as real down the barrel as they do from afar, and soldiers squirm against cover when suppressed by enemy fire. Lens effects, like horizontal light streaking, meanwhile, heighten the visual drama.

Dour though it might be, with a palette of browns, greens, and grays in a world of shantytowns and ruins, it's a unified style. Frustratingly conventional at times, the action still captures the burden of soldiers at the limit of their endurance, sluggish but yet frosty enough to handle some crafty enemy AI. Pitting a contentious (but intuitive) cover system against nonstop incoming bullets and grenades, it keeps you constantly on your toes. A separately developed multiplayer component takes this dynamic online, spicing it up with persistent stats and rolling objectives. **DH**

Madden NFL 10

Original release date : 2009
Platform : Various
Developer : Electronic Arts
Genre : Sports

In 2008, the perennial chart-topping *Madden* franchise celebrated its twentieth anniversary. That version was marked by numerous feature upgrades to support visuals aimed at producing a style tightly in tune with the broadcast TV images devoured by US audiences every Sunday. So maybe incremental features and minor enhancements would be expected—and even accepted—for *Madden NFL 10*. But the surprisingly impressive range of updates to the on-field action takes the experience strides farther down the realism path.

A system called Pro-Tak has the most immediate impact on both the look and flow of each play. The new animations allow more players to pile into tackles and create realistic plays as the quarterback drops into the pocket before throwing downfield. Other tweaks fine-tune the game play with more realistic momentum as players run with the ball and attempt dekes and stiff-arms. Similarly, the contact and coverage between wide receivers and defensive backs generate realistic timing patterns that can take many, many tries on the practice ground to perfect.

Half-time and post-game highlights, plus numerous camera angles, allow you to dissect every move from multiple perspectives. Cuts to the coaches patrolling the sideline, or the quarterback talking on the phone to the offensive coordinator, all add flavor without getting in the way of the on-field action or slowing down the pace. The wealth of options to build a franchise, draft players (now the AI specifically addresses its team needs), and play online guarantee football fans a full year of action after the sixteen-game regular season is done. **RSm**

Henry Hatsworth in the Puzzling Adventure

Original release date : 2009
Platform : DS
Developer : Electronic Arts
Genre : Adventure / Puzzle

It's no great surprise that one of gaming's greatest experiments should come from designer Kyle Gray. He was a cofounder of the Experimental Gameplay Project at Carnegie Mellon, a student-led organization that challenged its participants to constantly prototype and iterate on as many ideas as they could jot down. What's more surprising, perhaps, is the studio Gray would eventually produce the game through: EA's Tiburon studio, known then almost exclusively for its sports series.

How Gray managed to sneak *Henry Hatsworth in the Puzzling Adventure* through the greenlight process isn't as important as the fact that he did. Without it we wouldn't have received the first simultaneous platformer and block-matching puzzle game. It's a balancing act as precarious as it sounds. Defeating enemies in the platforming sections above converts them to enemy blocks that are dropped to the DS screen below, where you'll have to pause the action above to play a light version of SNES-era classic *Tetris Attack* to clear them off the board. Doing so, though, refills health and charges up the attacks you perform in the platformer above, creating a constant feedback loop throughout the entirety of the adventure.

Which isn't to say the stop-start required doesn't occasionally frustrate, or that it doesn't indulge in uneven difficulty (a charge mitigated by reminding yourself of the latter half of the loop above). But the game is so alive with vibrant characters (including the tea-sipping titular gentleman himself and his rival members of the Pompous Adventurers' Club) and gorgeously realized worlds that there should never be any doubt that this is a puzzling adventure well worth undertaking. **BB**

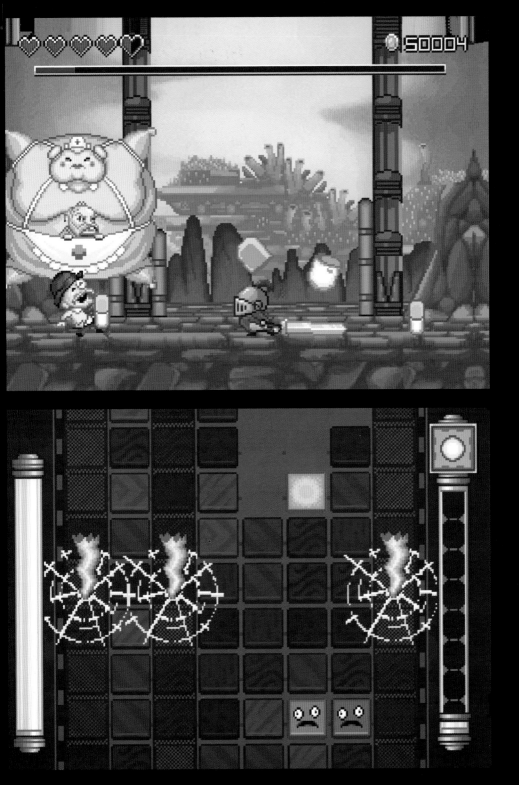

Lost Winds: Winter of the Melodias

Original release date : 2009
Platform : Wii
Developer : Frontier Developments
Genre : Platform / Adventure

Developed, like the original *Lost Winds*, by a small team on a tight schedule, *Lost Winds: Winter of the Melodias* proves that there is always room for a little extra invention, even within the constraints of a downloadable game's limited file size. Its art style is at once sumptuous and beautifully understated. Its world is simple and two-dimensional, but the generous incidental detail in the characters and environments suffuses it with character.

The player controls the winds with intuitive gesture controls, suspending boulders in a vortex, gusting protagonists across gaps, or gathering up water or fire in a slipstream. The whole world reacts to the winds, tempting you to dally playfully with branches, grass, and blossoms, or sweep up leaves in eddies. For the early part of the game, little hero Toku is stuck in an eternal winter, forced to stay close to sources of heat until he finds a warm coat. From then on, the power to change the seasons at will not only showcases the flair and diversity of the game's art style, but adds an extra level of strategic depth to its elegant puzzles.

Lost Winds: Winter of the Melodias is often about playing with the dynamics of water, snow, and ice, sweeping up snowballs with the winds or draining pools to create icy pathways. Its internal logic is beguilingly clever—each time you solve a puzzle, you're not just smiling at your own sense of accomplishment, but at the slick inventiveness of the game design itself.

Helpful maps and hints reduce time spent wandering, searching for puzzles. It plays smoothly, but it's over quickly. Successful downloadable games marry a simple and involving concept with a distinctive visual style; given how effectively this game commands these key strengths, it's difficult to begrudge its length. **KM**

Little King's Story

Original release date : 2009
Platform : Wii
Developer : Cing / Town Factory
Genre : Role-Playing / Strategy

When he isn't making *Harvest Moon*, Yasuhiro Wada has varied interests. He worked on *No More Heroes* with Goichi Suda, and he oversaw this delightful Wii strategy game from its inception, pulling in artistic and design talents with experience of everything from *Super Mario* RPG to super-obscure Japanese cult titles, such as *Moon* and *Chulip*. *Little King's Story* is quirkier than it first appears. The gently bizarre character design and dialogue lend personality to what might be dismissively branded a *Pikmin* clone.

Pikmin is an influence, obviously, but the game also channels the insidiously addictive nature of *Harvest Moon*. The player is merely the brains—it's a steadily growing army of little followers with different hats who do all the

game's dirty work. Little King launches his subjects at enemies and obstacles to get them out the way and collect resources to build up the area around his castle with more and more houses, barracks, and carpenters' shops, improving the quality of life for his little citizens.

The game is characterized by a dreamlike childishness, with cut scenes drawn in moving crayon, tutorial screens written on chalkboard, and a fuzzy, friendly supporting cast of bumbling knights and sentient cows. There's a gentle inference that the whole game is going on inside the head of a bored but imaginative five-year-old.

But it's deeper than it looks; one of the first challenges comes when a threatening religious zealot demands that you build a church or face God's punishment, and it leaves the options open. Its simple simulation of feudalism isn't quite as adorable as it might appear, either, necessitating the systematic eradication of quite harmless-looking little monsters in order to expand the kingdom. *Little King's Story* might be cute, but it's in no way immature. **KM**

Race Pro

Original release date : 2009
Platform : Xbox 360
Developer : Simbin
Genre : Racing

There was a time when everything knew its place. Simulations were firmly the realm of the PC, while arcade thrills were best handled by consoles. Game consoles grew more powerful, however, and with power came the ambition to tackle genres that had previously been beyond the hardware's processing capabilities. (Or was it PC developers sensing better economic opportunities within the broader and bigger console audience?)

Whatever the reason, *Race Pro* is one such example of that crossover. Previously a PC-hosted sim-racing series, the path to console proved rocky (including a change of publisher after the ignition cables of the initial project were cut), but well worth the effort. Based on a fine assortment of vehicle types—everything from Mini Cooper to F3000—raced on thirteen real-world tracks that eschew the traditional circuit menu, the *Race Pro* experience is further refreshing, thanks to a handling model that isn't afraid to stick to its roots. Keep all of the driving aids switched on and the accessibility is impressive. Not as notable, though, as being able to achieve such user-friendliness via a joypad input, *without* it compromising the underlying feel of a serious sim racer. But if you remain unconvinced (and have the skill), simply switch off the aids.

Perhaps a little too true to its nature, aesthetically, things can be rather functional, and off the track the menu-driven system can be disappointingly awkward and player progression insufficiently rewarded. Yet for every mile you travel on the tarmac, battling for apex space against credible AI opponents on some uncommonly demanding racetracks, and at the wheel of one of the most rewarding handling models on a console, those concerns somehow fade into the distance. **JDS**

Need for Speed: Shift

Original release date : 2009
Platform : Various
Developer : Slightly Mad Studios / Electronic Arts
Genre : Racing

For many years, Electronic Arts has been doing the video gaming equivalent of trying to sell us a used car without a full service history. For a while, the well-rehearsed salesman routine worked a treat, too. The publisher would simply point to the big, shiny 18-inch alloys, detail the extensive pearlescent bodywork, and finish the tour with the enormous carbon spoiler; gamers would then be reaching for their wallets, having forgotten to use their heads and have a good look around the engine and check out the paperwork.

Over time, however, players have gotten wise to EA's shiny trick. The Need for Speed games may enjoy a long pedigree (dating back to the 1994 original), but some of the more recent outings detach themselves from the original titles in the series, not only by including countless Nordschleife-length laps but by losing drive and direction, too. While they're delivered in an undoubtedly beautifully presented shell, it's one lacking the necessary internal components to properly power the series against the arrival of games like Project Gotham Racing, Forza Motorsport, and Race Driver: Grid—all experiences that are heavily focused on the realism end of the scale.

Hence, Need for Speed: Shift. A change in name as well as approach, it discards the glass fiber and the chrome rims and instead welds an intense motorsport experience to EA's renowned production values. It's a more serious proposition than before, the detail evident throughout, its in-cockpit viewpoint an illustration of the game's positioning. Though its handling dynamic falls short of the systems employed by the big boys at the front of the grid, it's a refocus and a brave new road for a franchise that was in danger of succumbing to corrosion. **JDS**

Space Invaders Infinity Gene

Original release date : 2009
Platform : Various
Developer : Taito
Genre : Shoot 'Em Up

Space Invaders arrived early on the iPhone in a somewhat traditional cash-in incarnation. It wasn't, however, worth getting back into that lone turret until it received the bespoke treatment. That appeared in the form of Space Invaders Infinity Gene, a pacy mash-up of Space Invaders Extreme and the wire-frame aesthetic of Rez, which combine to create a luminous free-wheeling shooter, wrapped up in a gloriously pretentious coating of deep-space bobbins about evolution and mutation.

It starts simply enough, loading up with the original game's iconic alien grid, before dissolving into a frantic static roar, flinging hundreds of new invaders against you as you plow through elaborately reimagined levels. Along the way, each victory levels you toward infinity, new power-ups, different shot types, and even unlockable extras as you race to the end. The tiny chittering aliens of the first game are joined by spectral cruisers and suicide bombers, then by vast armadas and flotillas of craft that march across the screen, all with their own unique attack to explore and exploit. Finally, given that the whole thing unfolds on an MP3 player, you can use your iPhone's music catalog to generate one-off levels—an experiment that quickly becomes ridiculously addictive.

Crucially, Space Invaders Infinity Gene controls like a charm, too, with firing handled automatically, while you steer your ship around with your finger. Your iPhone will end up smeary and in need of a good wipe down, but as you rocket through the leaderboard in what turns out to be an engagingly easy and satisfyingly spectacular game, even Apple's most hardcore product fetishists probably won't stop to notice too much. **CD**

Mario & Luigi: Bowser's Inside Story

Original release date : 2009
Platform : DS
Developer : AlphaDream Corporation
Genre : Action / Role-Playing

Having touched the extremities of the universe in Super Mario Galaxy, where else could there be left for the intrepid brothers to travel but inner space through the internal organs of Bowser himself? But this is a cartoonish sort of introspection, far from the gory literalism of Marcus Fenix's exploits inside a giant worm in Gears of War 2. Here, Bowser's arteries, cavities, and intestinal tract, through which you guide Mario and Luigi, have primary-color appeal. AlphaDream's aim is not to disgust players, but enthrall them by turning biological cogs and wheels into a playground, one ripe with puzzles and unusual purpose.

As with Nintendo's best games, the premise not only sets up the story, but also the mechanical conceits. So play switches between Mario and Luigi on the inside, and Bowser on the outside, the former pair fixing Bowser's various ailments in a bid for freedom, while Bowser himself works to uncover the mystery behind his swallowing the contents of Princess Peach's kingdom.

Action in one space affects the other. Guide Bowser to a fountain for a deep draught of water, for example, and his insides will fill with liquid, changing the terrain of the other side of the game. From this spatial relationship the developer builds out a plethora of interesting puzzles, with the Mario & Luigi RPG mechanics providing an engaging chaser to these macro puzzles.

Full of variety and ingenuity, Mario & Luigi: Bowser's Inside Story turns its back on Japanese RPG convention, even taking time to parody the habits of its closest genre. Bristling with exemplary dialogue and riotous humor, it represents the pinnacle of its series; a game that, like its antagonist, is greater than the sum of its parts. **SP**

Operation Flashpoint: Dragon Rising

Original release date : 2009
Platform : Various
Developer : Codemasters
Genre : Shoot 'Em Up / Strategy

The first installment of *Operation Flashpoint* was the result of a group of ex-servicemen being unhappy with the way war was portrayed in games. Consequently, it's something of an acquired taste. Being felled by a bullet you didn't hear, fired from half a mile away by the ever-alert AI, is peculiarly engaging, but requires a sadomasochistic surrender to which many weren't prepared to commit. At the very least, however, it created a climate in which *Operation Flashpoint: Dragon Rising*, Codemasters's sequel, could exist, offering a clear alternative to the arcade-style bombast of series such as *Call of Duty* and *Ghost Recon*.

Operation Flashpoint: Dragon Rising distills the severe complexity of its inspiration into an experience that not only works well on the PC *and* consoles, but succeeds in avoiding compromise. A huge sandbox island, believable plot, and great attention to detail ensure an incredibly immersive experience. While the AI can occasionally cause frustration (thanks to a lack of self-preservation and sparse save points), played cooperatively with three friends the game is capable of bringing you within what feels like an uncomfortably close proximity to war.

Requiring the use of real-world tactics and cover, firefights can be drawn-out, tense affairs. Taking only a few hits, even on the lowest difficulty setting, will result in death, and even a small injury will need attention to avoid bleeding out. The fear of coming under fire is powerfully communicated through the game's audio, even though sometimes it won't be clear to you where the shots are coming from. In offering an antidote to the sanitized take on war available elsewhere, *Operation Flashpoint: Dragon Rising* takes a brave gamble. It's one that pays off, but it takes a brave individual to enlist. **BM**

Chronicles of Riddick: Assault on Dark Athena

Original release date : 2009

Platform : Various

Developer : Starbreeze Studios

Genre : First-Person Shooter

Originally intended as an expansion to *Chronicles of Riddick: Escape from Butcher Bay*—a sweetener to justify its re-release on today's consoles—*Chronicles of Riddick: Assault on Dark Athena* blossomed into a full-blown sequel during a prolonged, uncertain development. The merger of publisher Vivendi with Activision Blizzard saw the project dropped for several months before it drifted into the path of its savior—a reinvigorated Atari. None of that time went to waste, the result being a bumper pack of the full-length sequel and original, both titles given a significant HD upgrade.

The new game picks things up where the first one left off, Riddick's *Butcher Bay* escape craft floating into view of the *Dark Athena*, a pirate ship that sells brainwashed captives on the black market. Headed by the dreadlocked Captain Revas (voiced with relish by Michelle Forbes), its crew of mercenaries has no idea that its latest quarry might well be its last. Sneaking into the ship's shadows, Riddick sees this as a prison like any other: breakable.

Beyond the introduction of the Ulaks, the twin blades seen in the *Chronicles of Riddick* movie, little has changed on the combat front. Thugs in the *Dark Athena*'s cabins get pulverized and stabbed, snaring the attention of gun-toting guards. But the addition of the Ghost Drones—remote-controlled cyborgs made from hapless prisoners—gives Riddick something new to play with. Finding occasion to take over their command consoles, he can guide them into battle or, when a puzzle demands it, a gory demise. Just when you half-expect the game to draw to a conclusion, it goes planetside for another act, adding enemies, weapons, and hours of play. Congratulations, Riddick. You're a bona-fide serial killer. **DH**

Shatter

Original release date : 2009
Platform : Various
Developer : Sidhe Interactive
Genre : Sports

The digital download model of PlayStation Network and Xbox Live Arcade has created a new space for small, tightly focused high-quality games. It's a space full of surprises— there was certainly nothing in Sidhe Interactive's back catalog to prepare us for the stylish, *Arkanoid*-echoing success of its PSN hit, *Shatter*.

The hook is very much *Wipeout* meets *Breakout*, matching the industrial futurism of Sony's racer with traditional ricochet-and-reaction game play. *Shatter* pulls us through pulsing 3-D spacescapes, housing the individual blockbusting levels, to the rhythm of a pumping trance soundtrack. Rather than a ball, *Shatter* features a pointed disk carving through zero gravity. And rather than a flat paddle, *Shatter*'s disk deflector is the polished, curved shield of a small sideways-shuffling ship, with each successful save met with a ringing metallic schwing.

For all the sci-fi bluster, the game play seems too neat a fit for preexisting genre slots. You bust blocks by juggling the destructive disk until each level is cleared, but there are surprises: *Shatter* toys with the traditional bat-and-ball playing area, testing reflexes with horizontal and spherical reconfigurations. And, more significantly, it introduces a game-changing risk-and-reward system in the form of your craft's ability to repel and attract floating screen objects. On a basic level this gives players control over their projectile post-collision, dragging or lifting the disk to curve its path into objects with labor-saving precision. But the attraction/repulsion also affects bonus-multiplying fragments of destroyed blocks—the key to building a high score. Later levels show a twitching sea of items to collect and avoid, behaving more like a hardcore shooter than an *Arkanoid* clone—a label that does little justice to this interesting and innovative gem. **ND**

Swords & Soldiers

Original release date : 2009
Platform : Wii
Developer : Ronimo Games
Genre : Strategy

Real-time strategy games were born on the PC and tend not to travel well to other platforms, depending on the kind of swift, yet complex, controls only a mouse and a handful of hot keys can really deliver. While it *is* possible to find excellent console-based strategy games, it's usually a job for a huge team armed with a big budget and plenty of development time. Not, then, the kind of feat that a dozen or so ex-students from Utrecht School of the Arts in the Netherlands should be expected to take on. And yet that's exactly what happened with *Swords & Soldiers*.

With cash made from selling their coursework project *De Blob* to publisher THQ, the plucky graduates quickly formed Ronimo Games. With their eyes set on Nintendo's downloadable WiiWare service, *Swords & Soldiers* is the team's first release—even if the polish and imagination on display can make that hard to believe.

Ditching the traditional top-down perspective for a side-on view, *Swords & Soldiers* allows you to create a range of units and set them moving across the game's rolling battlefields. Once units have begun walking, they largely take care of themselves, which leaves you free to get involved more directly, providing what is essentially sniper support with a series of godly powers you unleash by aiming the Wii Remote.

It's all extremely satisfying, and the three separate campaigns are built around distinct factions—the Vikings, the Aztecs, and the Chinese—each with their own strengths and weaknesses to learn about and their own zany storylines to follow. Local multiplayer rounds out the package, the whole thing proving that although Ronimo may not be particularly gifted at naming games, it's already frighteningly skilled at making them. **CD**

Plants vs. Zombies

riginal release date : 2009
latform : Various
eveloper : PopCap Games
enre : Strategy

starts with the gentlest of introductory tutorials and ends
ith the joyous tinkling of Laura Shigihara's lovely "There's
Zombie on Your Lawn"—and in between lies one of the
harpest, most constantly entertaining strategy games
f recent years. As is PopCap's way, almost every single
spect of *Plants vs. Zombies* seems designed to make you
huckle with delight, from the rhythmic bopping of your
wn units to the slack-jawed moaning of the zombies, to
1e terrifying chug of the approaching Zomboni.

PopCap calls the game a "lawn defense" title: The
ndead are coming for you in your house, so your
arden—and backyard, and eventually even rooftop—
epresent your last lines of security. You're left, in other

words, with no alternative but to fight off the shambling
apocalypse using horticulture. Luckily, the game's arsenal
is a constant delight, from the explosive Cherry Bombs
and Potato Mines, to the old reliables like Peashooters and
Wall-Nuts. Day and night cycles alter your attack options,
while each victory leaves you with a new seed packet to
experiment with on your next outing.

The zombies scale just as inventively, from the
standard tweedy varieties, to shock troopers reinforced
with road cones or buckets, and on to zombie dolphins,
linebackers, and monstrous overgrown types who loft
hideous rotting midgets past your defenses. It all makes
for a masterful game: witty, charming, and endlessly
replayable, and its enormous success with hardcore
gamers apparently took PopCap itself a little by surprise.

Three years in the making, *Plants vs. Zombies* was
always going to be a treat. If there's one disappointment,
it's that legal wrangling dictated that the developers
couldn't call the final product *Lawn of the Dead*. **CD**

Prototype

Original release date : 2009
Platform : Various
Developer : Radical Entertainment
Genre : Action / Adventure

Prototype is what happens when a developer famed for making *Incredible Hulk* games loses the right to make them, but makes one nonetheless. Radical's lead is a lot like Bruce Banner: infected by something he can't control, vilified by state and society, and dangerously detached from his fellow man. "My name is Alex Mercer," he begins. "They call me a killer, a monster, a terrorist. I'm all of these things." Worse, he's a video game player with dozens of special moves, freed to test them out on a terrified New York City. If you were the military, you'd be after him too.

Mercer has no memory of his past, and wakes on a mortuary slab to find himself hounded by Blackwatch, a special-forces unit dedicated to fighting biological warfare. It has its hands full: A man-made infection h turned hundreds of New Yorkers into feral canniba wrapping entire buildings in protoplasmic gunk. Soc there'll be thousands, and within days there'll be nothir left to save of the quarantined Manhattan Island. A he feasts upon his first victim, absorbing their valuab memories, Mercer discovers he's the alpha mutant, able t sprint up buildings, slice apart tanks, and shape-shift int civilian disguises. Whose side does he take? His own.

The problem with vast open-world action game is that the action has to *fill* all of that space. Happil *Prototype* succeeds brilliantly, for fights in this game don just involve dozens of soldiers, vehicles, and monsters, bu actually travel beyond their flashpoints to places you don expect. What starts on the ground could end on a rooftop in the air between two skyscrapers, or in a helicopter battl that crosses the entire city.

Prototype has been described as *Grand Theft Aut* meets *Devil May Cry*—and it's not hard to see why. **DH**

Punch-Out!!

Original release date : 2009
Platform : Wii
Developer : Nintendo
Genre : Fighting

Punch-Out!! was surely the least likely Nintendo franchise to ever make a return to our television screens. Ignoring the unfortunate matter of the original game's Mike Tyson branding, and the fact that it had been more than a decade since Super Punch-Out!! skipped and shimmied onto the SNES, there's the simple reality that boxing games had come a very long way. The likes of EA's dazzling Fight Night series had brought realistic physics and freakishly good animation to a field Nintendo had approached as if the sweet science was a form of puzzle game, dumping you into a lineup of caricatured boxers, where each rumble was all about memorizing your foe's attack patterns and working out the specific timings for your own openings.

Inevitably, Nintendo changed very little, and—perhaps even more inevitably—the result is an unqualified success. Essentially an enhanced reimagining of the original NES title, Punch-Out!! for the Wii brings back a world of familiar faces and moves, but mixes it up with optional motion controls, satisfying multiplayer, and a brilliant recreation of the 2-D past in chunky, cartoonish 3-D animation.

From King Hippo through to Von Kaiser and Glass Joe, almost all of Little Mac's original opponents return for a nostalgic thumping, and a handful of careful new additions pad out the lineup while maintaining the series' now rather worrying penchant for cultural stereotypes.

Putting aside such modern-day concerns, the results are a burst of even-handed nostalgia the likes of which only Nintendo seems to have the skill and heritage to pull off. Of course, Punch-Out!! was never going to take Fight Night's crown, but this is a smart adaptation of a genuine classic, a welcome piece of fan service in a Wii lineup filled with far less inspiring fare. **CD**

The Path

Original release date : 2009
Platform : Various
Developer : Tale Of Tales
Genre : Adventure

The warning is clear: "Don't go off the path!" But as you steer each of six Little Red Riding Hoods to Grandma's house, you can't help but wander into the woods. And the deeper you go, the more trouble you find. While good girls make their way to safety, the ones who misbehave have to confront their own "wolves."

As a work of interactive storytelling, *The Path* is gripping and disturbing. The misty woods lead to a horror show of surreal imagery, and while the player witnesses what happens to each girl, it's impossible not to feel complicit. Are you expected to stop Carmen from enjoying a beer with the lonely woodsman? Or Ruby for getting in that car with the older boy from school? The elliptical stories and symbols invite the player's interpretation, and the best questions are left open. (Are the girls sisters, or are they the same girl at different ages? Do their wolves kill them, or force them to grow up?) *The Path* is effective because it's interactive: By involving you in each girl's fate, it never lets you sit back and judge what you're watching. After all, you're the one who made it happen. **CDa**

EyePet

Original release date : 2009
Platform : PS3
Developer : Sony
Genre : Pet Care Simulation

EyePet is a curious entrant from the London-based developer best known for creating the *SingStar* karaoke games. In fact, it's more like the kind of product you'd expect from a Japanese studio.

Virtual pets have been around since Bandai Tamagotchi arrived in 1996, and later in video game manifestations such as the *Nintendogs* franchise. *EyePet* takes the pet-and-care approach of previous generations of digital cats and dogs and merges it with the PS3 PlayStation Eye technology to produce something that wouldn't be out of place at a science museum.

A cross between a monkey and puppy, *EyePet* does all of the little adorable things you would expect such a creature to do. It frolics and smiles and sticks out its tongue. You can change its outfits. And it interacts with you on-screen. You can tickle it or startle it with a clap of the hands. If it gets sick, you have to scan the forlorn little creature to identify its ailment. *EyePet* blurs the line between game and amusement—but there's no winning or losing here, only blissful playing around. **JBW**

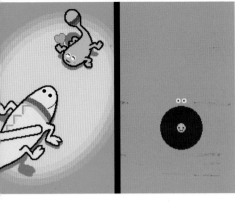

Rhythm Heaven

Original release date : 2009
Platform : DS
Developer : Nintendo
Genre : Music

Rolando 2

Original release date : 2009
Platform : iPhone
Developer : HandCircus
Genre : Adventure / Puzzle

Rhythm Heaven is a quirky slice of Nintendo's old-school sensibility. A rhythm-action game, its controls are so ludicrously pared down that the action largely consists of tapping a dot on the touch screen. It's simple enough to be played by just about anybody, yet endearing enough that few who pick it up will fail to fall under its spell.

Whether you're punching bolts into nuts, filling cartoon robots with bright pink gasoline, or helping to teach a chorus of chubby doughboys how to sing in harmony, Rhythm Heaven is constantly reinventing itself for your visual and aural pleasure. Designed by the same hare-brained team who pieced together the crazy ludic scrapbook of the WarioWare games, this has the same bemusing mix of graphical styles and animation types, while the soundtrack is a glorious collection of oddities encompassing weird-out techno to cutesy J-pop.

The single stages are tough enough, but it's the regular medleys, flinging random games and rhythms together with a delightful trickery, that really remind you that Nintendo knows how to challenge as well as charm. **CD**

Casual-game newcomer ngmoco was the first publisher to take the Apple iPhone and iPod Touch seriously as a gaming platform. A company formed by ex-EA design legend Neil Young, with a remit to develop and publish the best games on the platform, it quickly made a name for itself as one of the App Store's most reliable brands.

The first Rolando, published in 2008, was an inventive 2-D platformer, but it was the sequel that really defined the game as something special. Rolando 2, with its stylish shift to a 2.5-D perspective and cheery tropical holiday atmosphere, is a miniature masterpiece. Each new level throws in a new toy—from vehicles that roll over enemies, to bows and arrows to shoot down baddies—while reveling in the consistently cheeky art design.

Rolando 2 isn't just a wonderful platformer, it's a testament to the way that the iPhone has opened up game design to a new kind of developer, and a reminder of what can get lost—and may now have been regained, at least in some small way—whenever games grow too big, too serious, and too unwieldy. **CD**

Resident Evil 5

Original release date : 2009
Platform : Various
Developer : Capcom
Genre : Shoot 'Em Up / Horror Survival

As beautiful as it is dumb, *Resident Evil 5* raises as many questions as it answers. Its defining characteristic is a slavish aping of *Resident Evil 4*, by some yardsticks the greatest third-person adventure in gaming, and yet it never threatens to approach its predecessor in atmosphere while holding on to mechanics that, arguably, were already dated when you were using them the last time.

But let's be clear: *Resident Evil 5* is a very good game, and if it were a player's first engagement with the series, they'd be forgiven for thinking it a magnificent one. The setting is inspired: a sun-baked Africa with the kind of brightness that reveals every wrinkle, infested with the latest victims of Umbrella's nefarious biological research.

It's a parched, weird, unsettling environment in which to be battling biological disasters, and shot through with the craziness only a crescendo of Capcom bosses can bring.

It's also cooperative. And although from time to time the campaign sags, tackling it alongside a friend strengthens its weaker moments while making its high points nothing less than magnificent. The game moves at a rip-roaring pace, and at its best—when it simply abandons you in an environment and pours in the enemies, mixing them up to confuse tactics and surprise you with their deadeningly efficient approach—it sets up some memorable encounters.

Resident Evil 5 has other great moments, such as the superb mercenaries mode, which places you and a friend in an arena with a time limit and infinite enemies for a score attack. But in the end, you *have* seen its shocks and scares before, and no amount of visual polish can hide that. So it remains a tribute to its masterful predecessor, albeit a very good one, rather than breaking new ground. **RS**

Sin & Punishment: Successor to the Sky

Original release date : 2009
Platform : Wii
Developer : Treasure
Genre : Shoot 'Em Up

When you're faced with a game that features chickens next to cruise missiles, it's hard to know where to start. It's said that the bosses in Treasure games are based around the personal interests of the team, a rather prosaic fact that comes to life when you find yourself hoverboarding in front of a stereo system belching out bullets. Judging by *Sin & Punishment: Successor to the Sky* (or *Star Successor* as it's known in Europe), the team's other fascinations include stealth bombers, parrots, visiting aquariums, and hamsters.

An unexpected sequel to the ill-fated (although excellent) N64 *Sin & Punishment*, *Successor to the Sky* throws several years' worth of brainstorming sessions at you in every level. Moving on a 2-D axis and shooting at enemies flying in and out of the 3-D space around it, batting them away when they get too close and hurtling forward relentlessly, this is a lesson in not only how to build a shooter, but how to balance risk and reward within it.

One example involves that breathtaking pace, the clouds of bullets that are constantly flying toward your character, and the question of how to increase your score multiplier. You could do it by remaining stationary with feet planted on the ground. Or you could knock enemy projectiles back at them, sacrificing the more regular onslaught of your weapon for a bigger chunk of points.

Mostly you'll be too busy just trying to stay alive to concentrate on such questions, dodging out of one frying pan into another, and always in the line of fire. As a shooter, *Successor to the Sky* is a showcase for the player's skills and offers tantalizing multipliers for self-imposed limits—the reward of nothing more than a higher number for working out the order of its apparent chaos. But most of all, it's an invitation to make the developer's interests your own. **RS**

The Sims 3

Original release date : 2009
Platform : Various
Developer : Electronic Arts
Genre : Life Simulation

What do you wish for? For many fans of *The Sims*, the answer might be simply "more Sims, please!" However, to publisher EA's benefit, following a glut of add-on packs, it chose *not* to reward the franchise's long-term fans with little more than another optional expansion when it produced the first genuine sequel to *The Sims 2*.

The big difference is that the Sims are no longer governed by their wants and fears, but by long-term "wishes" that form lifetime goals, and they've also developed the confidence to look after themselves. Even the most die-hard Sim fanatic will admit that the majority of time spent playing previous iterations of the series lay in tending to their most basic needs—to be clean, fed, not sleepy, and never bursting for the loo—but in *The Sims* this kind of dull stuff can be fully automated. It's necessar[y] too, because the emphasis has now shifted away fro[m] domesticity and is placed on how they interact with the community. So while previously you would have bee[n] expected to concentrate on a single household—an[d] were required to load "community lots" laboriously, [or] invite friends over to keep your Sims happy—the who[le] town is now accessible at all times, with Sims living, lovin[g] and growing old all on their own.

This fundamental change in approach turns *Th[e] Sims 3* into what the franchise had always been imagine[d] to be: a life simulator with a touch of soap opera. N[o] longer is play about maximizing comfort for your Sim[s] but in enjoying the situations you can engineer. Tempt [a] neighbor into an affair, deny a Sim his wishes, make Sim parents treat one child well and the other badly—all thes[e] possibilities and others are available, and that's more than you or your Sims would ever have known to wish for. **MK**

Spider: The Secret of Bryce Manor

Original release date : 2009
Platform : iPhone
Developer : Tiger Style
Genre : Action

Randy Smith, designer at Tiger Style, wrote in his column in video game magazine *Edge* about his team's struggle with telling a "human" story in the context of a game about a spider. While the focus in *Spider: The Secret of Bryce Manor* rests on its titular hero and the arachnid's quest for more and more bugs, the person in control becomes increasingly aware of the surroundings. We're exploring an old house, with newspapers piled up at the door; hints of a sibling rivalry or a lost love are littered around the place, hidden behind the furniture and even down the drains. It's down to the player to connect the dots and try to figure out what all these "clues" actually mean, but the spider doesn't care. He's just in it for the bugs.

The game itself is relatively simple: The player uses the iPhone's touch screen to create a series of webs. This is achieved by swiping the finger over the screen, which causes the spider to jump from surface to surface. As he moves he leaves behind strands of silk; a web appears where they intersect, catching any bugs that attempt a crossing. Nothing in the game can kill your spider, but hunger can drain your silk, so the challenge lies in catching the most insects with the fewest webs. This forces the player to invent creative solutions, as well as to explore the different rooms for secret hideaways—useful for both clues to the story as well as extra snacks.

As Smith wrote, his team *could* have let the spider affect the human story that surrounds it in some way—to change the course of events, instead of digging them up after they had happened. But in the end, this isn't a story about the Bryce family; it's a story about a spider. And all that spiders can do after a tragedy is clutter the place up with a lot of cobwebs. **CDa**

Skate 2

Original release date : 2009
Platform : Various
Developer : Electronic Arts
Genre : Sports

If you've ever seen skateboarders in the flesh, you've probably noticed that they don't seem to be having a whole lot of fun. Over and over they attempt the same trick, either bailing after the first ollie or failing to stick the landing. And when they do nail it, there's that brief moment of self-congratulation before they move on to the next challenge. It seems more like work than play. Yet when you play *Skate 2* for any length of time, you will understand exactly why they do it.

The real work of the game is trying to identify a good line, that stretch of obstacles that will allow you to ollie, grind, and maneuver your way across the city, racking up style points all the while. But don't think for a second this is simple to achieve. *Skate 2* uses an innovative control system in which almost all maneuvers are accomplished with the analog sticks. To jump, you pull back on the right stick, and watch your skater dip low. Then you flick it upward, and he leaps along with it. Mastering the timing of even the simplest ollie takes some doing. After that, however, things get more complex. Flicking the stick in different directions results in more advanced maneuvers, such as kickflips and heelflips.

Despite the steep learning curve required to master the controls, after a while it becomes clear that no other approach could feel as natural or precise. You really do have full control over your skater's every action, right down to the last millimeter, so there can be nobody else to blame but yourself when you fail, over and over, to land that perfect trick. Of course, when you do finally succeed, you can edit a video of your skater in action and upload it to EA's servers for all the world to scrutinize. And nobody will ever know that it took you six hours of practice to make that fifteen-second clip. **MK**

Uncharted 2: Among Thieves

Original release date : 2009
Platform : PS3
Developer : Naughty Dog
Genre : Adventure / Shoot 'Em Up

Games that aspire to cinema have to go a long way to beat *Uncharted 2: Among Thieves*, the sequel to 2007's *Drake's Fortune* and one of the most polished titles yet created.

It's all about pace and character. Throwing you into the game with an astonishing platforming tutorial set on a train dangling over a precipice, Naughty Dog's adventure then slips into a skillful series of flashbacks, breaking game mechanics like shooting and platforming down into handy chunks, while teasing you through a potentially confusing story of backstabbing high adventure and last-minute stabs of conscience. On the trail of Marco Polo's fabled lost fleet, Drake finds himself in a world where no one can be trusted, and while there are old friends and new love interests—the latter in the form of Chloe, a seductive Australian. This is a darker, more isolated tale than the original game, playing out in frosty temples, war-torn Nepalese cities, and mountain-top villages where poverty and spectacle rub shoulders. Drake even spends a little bit of time in a Turkish prison—something that certainly never happened to Lara Croft.

Forget open worlds and sandboxes, this is the most tightly controlled of roller coasters—enabling astonishingly cinematic set pieces, such as a race down through a crumbling building or a fight across the roof of a speeding train. Nolan North's winningly natural voice work (brilliantly, the actor recorded his lines, and was then recorded again, ad-libbing as he actually played through the game) is as charming as it was in the original, and while the staccato rhythm that swings you from gunfight to platforming and then back to gunfighting is only a marginally improved, *Among Thieves* toughs it out, for the most part, through sheer force of personality. **CD**

The Beatles: Rock Band

Original release date : 2009
Platform : Various
Developer : Harmonix
Genre : Music

Peter Jackson and *Lord of the Rings*, Sebastian Faulks and 007, Harmonix and The Beatles . . . surprisingly often, the job of handling a national treasure has fallen into the right hands. For the creator of *Guitar Hero*, however, that didn't make things easier for *The Beatles: Rock Band*. Close collaboration with surviving Beatles Ringo Starr and Paul McCartney (reportedly now a development guru, having watched a few Pixar movies) meant numerous demands and revisions. Then there was Yoko Ono, who felt that the flutter of John Lennon's hair during the game's closing set didn't reflect the winds above Saville Row on January 30, 1969—scene of the band's final performance. As if *that* gig wasn't trouble enough the first time around.

But Harmonix persevered. Charting the band's escape from Liverpool to America, then the globe, and the inner worlds of personal ambition and psychedelic fantasy, *The Beatles: Rock Band* is an adorable companion. Bold enough to tackle this eclectic body of work in chronological order, even when later songs like the "Yellow Submarine" offer no difficulty whatsoever, it waits until you've reached the end—actually "The End," the closer from *Abbey Road*— before shuffling the complete setlist into order of difficulty.

The breezy pop and marionette-like performances of the early days get things off to a slow start, but the game is transcendent during its *Abbey Road* sessions. Locked in the studio, recording classics like "Something" and "While My Guitar Gently Weeps," the band daydreams into its own music, visiting lush landscapes littered with in-jokes and artifacts. It's a plateau from which the game never falls, the action bookended by inspirational cinematics from Pete Candeland, a long-time collaborator with another virtual rock band, Gorillaz. **DH**

Starship Patrol

Original release date : 2009
Platform : DSi
Developer : Q-Games
Genre : Strategy

The stylus makes all the difference here, as *Starship Patrol* brilliantly introduces touch-screen controls to the tower defense game. The genre is built on micromanagement, calculating increments of damage in relation to gradual motion—killing enemies by a thousand cuts—and in *Starship Patrol* the most basic skills and most complex tactics are built around micromanagement through touch.

Each of the thirty levels has a unique structure to defend, with holes for plugging in your defenses of choice, and a unique combination of enemies. The game is achingly lo-fi, from the pixelly design of the batlike invaders from space to the background of cosmic graph paper, and a great flourish is a dotted line telling you exactly where each wave of enemies will travel before they arrive. Games of this type often suffer from enemy paths being either too predictable or too random; by giving you advance warning, *Starship Patrol*'s able to lull you into a false sense of security and execute vicious back-door attacks without ever seeming too unfair.

When preparing for attack, you dot your hulls with weapons, fine-tuning their aiming zone to where it's most effective. As the action starts to kick off, your stylus has to be swept over the energy spat out by defeated foes, quickly using it to fund more weapons or banking it for the surprises of the next wave. In later stages you'll have to adjust aiming zones as a matter of course during attacks to squeeze the maximum from your tool set—which is also upgradeable during every level to the point that devastating combinations can be discovered. *Starship Patrol* doesn't waste a single one of its stages, each layout a new challenge, each new combination of enemies having surprising consequences for your offensive choices—and vice versa. It's a work of rare craft. **RS**

Scribblenauts

Original release date : 2009
Platform : DS
Developer : 5th Cell
Genre : Puzzle / Action

With the ever-increasing scope of *SimCity* creator Will Wright's output, it seemed all but assured that he'd be the first to offer us a game about *everything*: As it happens, the kudos is awarded to indie developer 5th Cell—previously best known for the kid-friendly *Drawn to Life*. *Scribblenauts* has its player-created sights set significantly higher. For here, rather than simply color inside the lines to create your own protagonist, the designers ask that you think outside the box to solve problems—getting a cat out of a tree, knocking through a piñata, cleaning a mechanic's garage—using . . . well . . . *anything*.

Throughout the game's development, artists pored through dictionaries and encyclopedias, creating a database of more than 20,000 everyday and historic objects. *Scribblenauts* swiftly went viral—YouTube videos began to appear showing players successfully putting the game through a series of ever more arcane tests. What happens if you conjure "god" plus "death"? (Death kills god.) Surely you can't summon one-time ubiquitous Internet meme Keyboard Cat? (Actually, you can.)

In the end, an oversensitive control interface means that solving puzzles relies more often on simple pragmatism than flights of imaginative fancy. And all too often a gun works as well as anything—some video game tropes die hard, it seems, even though you do receive an extra reward for clearing levels *without* relying on firearms.

The killer punch, however, is the addition of an extra mode for each level, where you are asked to solve a puzzle three times in succession without using any of the objects used previously. This ends up being the game's strongest draw—apart from that, is, being the ultimate portable tool for settling those "jackalope versus stegosaurus versus kraken versus Einstein" debates. **BB**

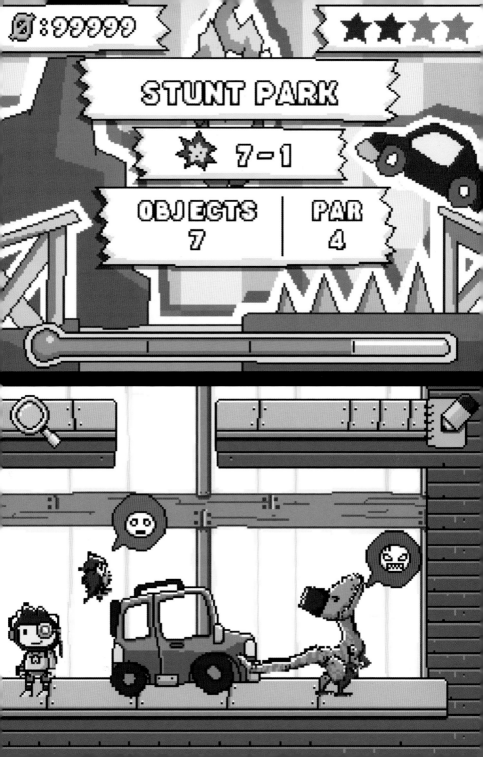

Trine

Original release date : 2009
Platform : Various
Developer : Frozenbyte
Genre : Platform / Puzzle

Side-scrolling adventures with ultra-high production values were a relative rarity in 2009. *Trine* bucks the trend with a storybook world and some intricate physics puzzles. As a single-player game it's pretty absorbing, but the action becomes far more dynamic when it's played cooperatively by two or three people at the same time.

In the single-player game you're able to transform into any of the three characters: a rogue, a wizard, or a knight. The rogue is able to fire arrows and use a grappling hook on wooden surfaces to scale and swing. The knight is armored, and can use either a sword, shield (which offers some protection), or a powerful hammer (which does lots of damage to enemies, but offers no protection).

The wizard is able to conjure up platforms, blocks, and planks, and can telekinetically interact with special objects throughout the world. *Trine* is filled with environmental puzzles that this combination of characters and their assorted abilities can, through collaboration, overcome.

As a solo player the solutions are fairly straightforward, or they can be bypassed entirely by clever use of the rogue and wizard. The real fun comes in the cooperative game, however, as players take on these roles individually, radically altering the dynamics of the puzzles and the combat. To give an example, getting past a spike pit as a single player might just require you to swing across as the grapple hook–using rogue; with two players it might mean finding another route, such as using the wizard's ability to create objects including floating platforms.

As puzzle games go, *Trine* is both accessible and rewarding, especially in multiplayer mode. The package is tarnished only by a hectic final level that's frustratingly out of sync with the rest of the experience. **JR**

Torchlight

Original release date : 2009
Platform : Various
Developer : Runic Games
Genre : Action / Role-Playing

A dungeon-crawling game with one town (Torchlight); one deep, randomly-generated dungeon to explore; and a regular stream of esoterically named equipment and loot, *Torchlight* feels a lot like 1996's *Diablo*. There's a good reason for this. Designed by Travis Baldtree (the man behind *Diablo* clone, *Fate*) and Max and Erich Schaefer (co-designers of *Diablo*), the game transcends the status of clone and is more like a spiritual sequel to *Diablo II*.

Players can choose from one of three character classes—the hulking Destroyer, magical Alchemist, and feminine Vanquisher—but rather than be tied down to a particular style of play, varied class-specific skill trees allow a twin pistol-wielding Alchemist to function as well as a

axe-equipped Destroyer, particularly when paired with the right equipment. For gamers who find the need to return to the surface to sell unwanted items an interminable bore, an artificially intelligent pet (either a dog or a lynx) that fights alongside your hero can be sent back to town to unload loot, making the addiction to finishing "just one more floor" harder to beat than ever.

Torchlight features bright art that, despite its near nonexistent storyline, makes the world a much more pleasant place to explore than the dark realms of *Diablo*. And, with equipment changes accurately reflected on player characters, it becomes an obsession not only to have the most powerful gear but the best-looking.

Though it can be a little lonely at times, *Torchlight* is a compelling reminder that collecting loot and leveling up is almost always obscenely pleasurable—even when stripped of the MMO conventions with which such activities have come to be associated. Just make sure that you avoid playing one more floor. **MKu**

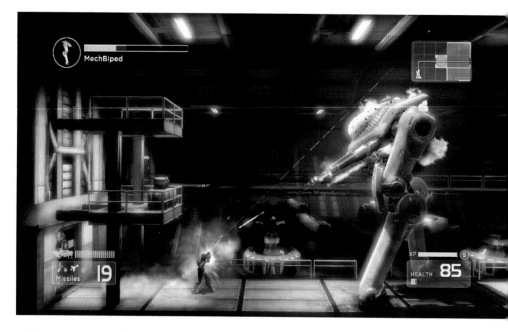

MechBiped

Missiles **19**

HEALTH **85**

Shadow Complex

Original release date : 2009
Platform : Xbox 360
Developer : Chair Entertainment
Genre : Action / Adventure

Xbox Live Arcade has a dual role as a clearinghouse for new indie productions with commercial potential and a marketplace for retro games with updated graphics and, if we're lucky, new game play. *Shadow Complex* may be a new property, but older gamers will immediately recognize its inspirations: the side-scrolling action of *Castlevania*, mixed with the exploration of *Metroid*—all run through *Epic*'s modern Unreal Engine.

Players control a hapless guy who stumbles across a supersecret military complex in the woods, where a legion of bad guys plot against the government. The player occupies a two-dimensional plane within a three-dimensional world. The limitation leads to satisfying

platforming exercises, and it narrows your search for the hidden passageways and stashed treasures that fill the game world. But as a design decision, it's also frustrating and almost cubist: Enemies can lurk in the background where you're not allowed to go, and aiming at them takes a lot of practice. You'll even find yourself jet packing from landing to landing of a stairwell because you can't just sidle over and walk up the steps.

There's also the so-called ludonarrative dissonance (or the "game/story conflict," if you favor a less florid form of English) that comes when the story beats tell you that time's running out—they're taking your girlfriend to the chopper. They're about to bomb the country—and yet you're still lured to collect all ten passcards, so you can go back to the basement and pick up a fusion helmet. But don't worry: The nuclear attack won't start without you, and you can take your time before the final set piece that caps off the adventure. After all, you never asked questions the first time you played this kind of game, did you? **CDa**

Red Faction Guerrilla

Original release date : 2009
Platform : Various
Developer : Volition, Inc
Genre : Shoot 'Em Up

As technology has advanced and video games have become more lifelike, one question has always nagged at players: Why, given the firepower we've grown accustomed to packing, can we never destroy most of what we see? Fire a rocket launcher at a building in *Grand Theft Auto IV*'s painstakingly realistic rendering of New York City, and when the smoke clears, it will still be standing. Developer Volition has given this matter some thought, and delivered *Red Faction Guerrilla*, a game in which everything you see can be tipped, toppled, and trashed. From a small shipping container to a sprawling industrial building, there's nothing in this game you can't reduce to rubble with a little elbow grease or some big explosives.

A perfunctory storyline casts you as a resistance fighter named Alec Mason on a colonized planet Mars, trying to throw off the yoke of the oppressive Earth Defense Force. There was a chance here for a topical, thought-provoking narrative about the perils of an empire and the limits of imposing government through force; instead it's a flimsy excuse to send players on one mission after another, the objective of which is invariably to smash as much stuff as possible. Not that there's anything wrong with that.

Alec's most trusty weapon is a sledgehammer that he swings with the power of Thor. It's good for dispatching enemies and for chipping away at building supports. The structures in the game are constructed logically. They'll keep standing if you punch holes in the walls, but if you weaken the frames, they'll groan and crumble. There is also a side game entitled *Wrecking Crew*, which removes the enemies and lets players compete to see who can cause the most damage to a small section of map. This is *Red Faction Guerrilla* in its purest and most irresistible form. **MK**

The Legend of Zelda: Spirit Tracks

Original release date : 2009
Platform : DS
Developer : Nintendo
Genre : Action / Adventure

Nintendo had been making *Legend of Zelda* games for twenty-two years by the time of *Spirit Tracks*'s release. Although this series has pioneered many of the standout technical, stylistic, and artistic innovations in video game history, it has definitely found its rhythm. But familiarity needn't breed contempt. *The Legend of Zelda: Spirit Tracks* taps into the childish glee at the core of *Zelda*'s appeal, and adds generous daubs of innovative, playful color to a rather strictly delineated template.

It's all about the train, really—set in the *Zelda* episodes *Phantom Hourglass* and *Wind Waker*'s living cartoon of a world, *Spirit Tracks* replaces the previous games' head-in-the-clouds seafaring with a toy train that's as fun to play with as any real-life equivalent. It's impossible to resist the chunky levers and dangling whistle cord on the DS's touch screen. As the game's map slowly opens out and more track sprawls across the landscape, characters start asking for more and more favors—deliveries; lifts to far-off lands; or to be brought a flock of chickens, some lumber, or a potential husband—and the train really comes into its own, becoming the focal point of *Spirit Tracks*'s world.

The touch screen feels a more natural interface than any controller before it. Nintendo's mastery of its own platform is evident in every one of *Spirit Tracks*'s clever items and puzzles. It's a superb example of tight, assured design—a technically perfect video game—but it's got a sense of humor and soul, too, in the central relationship between young Link and Zelda. Their banter, shared glances, and unselfconscious high-fiving add an aspect of childish romance and camaraderie that previous games in the series have always left implied. **KM**

Zen Bound

Original release date : 2009
Platform : iPhone
Developer : Secret Exit
Genre : Puzzle

Here's proof positive of the magical properties of video games: Hand an average person a rabbit-shaped piece of whittled wood with a rusty nail attached to a length of twine rudely jutting off its tail, and you'd be hard pressed to either call it a game or convince your lucky recipient that they were in for a fun time. Hand that same player Secret Exit's iPhone debut, *Zen Bound*, though, and suddenly everything's changed.

Because even though *Zen Bound* is little more than an exact digital representation of the object above, running layers of complex surface area calculations can turn *nothing* into *something great*. In it, your goal is simply to bind each increasingly complex wooden sculpture in paint-soaked rope, hoping to spread a coat evenly over its surface—even between its finely carved ears or woven through spindly legs—and it's no exaggeration to say that the result is one of the iPhone's most mesmerizing experiences . . . or, as its title would suggest, its most zen.

Secret Exit is keen to play up that Eastern mystique at every turn, through a gorgeous interface of paper-lantern-lit bonsai trees and a soothing glitch/click score by Finnish electronic outfit Ghost Monkey, and both those menu screens and the game itself are marvelously tactile achievements of 3-D code. Aided by the hardware's multi-touch capabilities and startlingly accurate string physics that sees your rope wind, tangle, and catch on every corner—just as the genuine article would, twisting the sculptures with gentle glass-smooth swipes—is a sensory delight, and one unlikely to be reproduced soon. After all, who would've thought a hunk of wood and some twine could be this much fun? **BB**

Zeno Clash

Original release date : 2009
Platform : Various
Developer : Ace Team
Genre : Shoot 'Em Up / Fighting

The first-person-viewed beat 'em up is a rare species. After all, the mechanics of punching and dodging when tied to this perspective are tricky to pull off convincingly. *Zeno Clash*'s central accomplishment is in creating a credible simulation of fisticuffs using *Half-Life 2*'s Source engine, so that punching people to the floor and then kicking them into submission makes sense . . . if of a brutal kind.

While the game features a significant amount of traditional gunplay, weapons can generally be knocked from the player's grasp, resulting in melee action. But this is far from being as frustrating as it sounds because the man-on-man combat is enormously responsive. Indeed, getting up close and personal in *Zeno Clash* is deeply satisfying, especially when it's with an enemy who looks like he's been plucked from He-Man's nightmares.

Nightmares are a common ongoing theme for *Zeno Clash*. The background story makes a *certain* kind of sense: You find yourself on the run from a city where a giant bird-like creature called Father-Mother presides over a cult of assorted humanoids—said to be her children. Your character is an outcast son, apparently human, who has attempted to slay Father-Mother and who must eventually return to the nest for a final confrontation.

The journey that he undertakes is strange, indeed. Accompanied by a beautiful horned woman, he travels through haunted lands, via a forest full of people too mad to live, takes a trip on a skeletal boat, and fights a masked assassin on the body of vast, beached whale. Few other first-person combat games manage to include pigs, insanity, squirrel bombs, and cryptic dialogue as key themes and get away with it. **JR**

Mighty Flip Champs

Original release date : 2009
Platform : DSi
Developer : WayForward Technologies
Genre : Puzzle / Platform

You can tell that WayForward Technologies spends much of its time toiling away on licensed games. That's because whenever the team stretches out with its own ideas—even when it's a snug little title for the DSi's downloadable service—you can always expect a riot of color and imagination, backed up with some ingenious level design.

Mighty Flip Champs is, at heart, a very simple game. You're presented with a series of single-screen platforming challenges, and all you have to do is reach the exit point of each level. There's a problem, though: You can't jump. This means that while you can still climb ladders and scale wire fences, when you need to get to a higher ledge with no obvious access points, you're kind of stuck.

That's where things start to get clever. A quick press of a button switches the screen for another similar—but not quite identical—screen, moving the level furniture around while keeping you exactly where you were. It's like trading one dimension for another: using a ladder that's only available in the first to get to a switch that's only available in the second. But what starts with some fairly simplistic spatial puzzlers quickly ramps up in complexity, until you find yourself flicking between four or five different versions of the same map, superimposing the differences in your head, and trying to exploit the tiny nuances of each.

It's a brain bender, in other words, but a delightfully smart one, shot through with some sweet music and lovely anime-influenced art design. Speed-running is on hand to provide this smallish game with some deep replayability, and while you may get stuck—and you may even get angry—you'll never stop being dazzled by such a simple concept, so brilliantly executed. **CD**

Muramasa: The Demon Blade

Original release date : 2009

Platform : Wii

Developer : Vanillaware

Genre : Action / Role-Playing

Vanillaware has created some of the most attractive and artistically accomplished titles ever seen. *Muramasa: The Demon Blade* is endowed with all the beguiling beauty of predecessor *Odin Sphere*'s, but condensed into a shorter span. It's a decision that actually does the game a lot of favors, the mesmerizing combat more enjoyable in small doses rather than stretched over a forty-hour epic.

At heart, *Muramasa: The Demon Blade* is a traditional side-scrolling 2-D fighter, streamlining its predecessor's sprawling, multipronged story into just two different plot threads. Combat is uncomplicated—one button controls practically everything, with one more for screen-emptying special moves—but stunning to look at, with an almost choreographed feel. Switching between the three differently equipped blades makes it possible to maintain an almost infinite combo, the rhythm altering subtly as you switch between powerful two-handed longswords that sweep across the screen and *katana*s that unleash a fast flurry of slashes.

It's these weapons, which branch out in elegant and complex upgrade trees, that provide the variety. The two-player characters also assert their individuality with different animation and fighting styles. Compensating for a relative lack of diversity in the action are hugely detailed backdrops: *Muramasa: The Demon Blade*'s layered, parallax-scrolling settings even outdo *Odin Sphere*'s on occasion.

Every minute of the game feels enriching—it's worth playing for the lovingly drawn food and eating animations in the village *izakaya*s alone. The game is suffused with Japan's artistic, mythological, and culinary tradition, and beautifully communicates that aesthetic to its players. **KM**

UPDATE **Parker McLachlin scored a BIRDIE on hole 13**

Tiger Woods PGA Tour 10

Original release date : 2009
Platform : Various
Developer : Electronic Arts
Genre : Sports

As predictable as the seasons, sports franchises are updated iteratively and annually, like downloadable content but without the download. While other games based on sports compete for market share, *Tiger Woods PGA Tour* is the only serious choice for golf fans, but that monopoly might be the result of evolution measured in putts rather than drives. The 2010 edition, however, introduces the concept of live tournaments, and in doing so breaks not only the mold but the fourth wall. 'Play the Pros' mode allows players to pit themselves against professional players, in real-time, while real-life events take place. Statistics are updated as they happen, and the player is stripped of aids, such as after-touch spin and

predicted ball paths. Serious fans are also treated to the official introduction US Open and USGA Championships, as well as the USGA Rules of Golf. Add dynamic weather (drawn from data made available online) and extensive character customization options, and the gap between simulation and the real thing diminishes farther.

The successful analog swing and three-click control schemes return, along with sixteen of the world's best courses, improved graphics, and various difficulty levels. While the Xbox 360 and PS3 versions are the most visually appealing, the Wii version's MotionPlus compatibility—interpreting your movements with detailed fidelity as you stand in front of your television and thrash around with a virtual golf club—give it a different kind of edge.

Of course, all of this is to be expected, and while *Tiger Woods PGA Tour 10* predominantly conforms to the iterative sports sequel model, it is the game's blending of reality with fantasy that really sets this apart as the definitive virtual golf experience. **BM**

NBA 2K10

Original release date : 2009
Platform : Various
Developer : Visual Concepts
Genre : Sports

Think sports, and you think EA. It's hard not to, but in its NBA franchise, 2K Sports owns the gold standard and critical darling. The overall package is crammed with top-quality features, with enhancements for this version adding more depth to the excellent franchise mode. Managing your team through season upon season is surprisingly accessible, potentially costing you hours in trade assessments, on-court practice, opponent research, and finally the games themselves. As with the best Vegas buffets, dip into every available option, and you can fill yourself until you're stuffed.

The on-court action apes real TV broadcasts with perfect camera panning of the play, and highly detailed player likenesses (even down to individual skill moves) means that even a brief glance seems uncannily like what you expect to see on ESPN.

Basketball at its highest level is a showcase of gravity-defying athletic endeavor: Using its complex, tough-to-master—but ultimately rewarding—control system, *NBA 2K10* captures this excitement as accurately as a game can. Dunking from under the basket, for example, is harder to execute than it should be, and the amount of analog stick manipulation can leave the inexperienced player with serious cramp issues, but patience and practice pay off.

Practice is certainly required with the new My Player mode, in which you take a kid from the Summer League, through to the NBA. It's tough, and you'll feel that you've earned that multimillion dollar contract if you make it as a pro. *NBA 2K10* is capped by excellent sports commentary, perfectly cast and delivered with context-aware remarks. In fact, the game's theme—Kanye West's "Amazing"—couldn't be a more appropriate choice. **RSm**

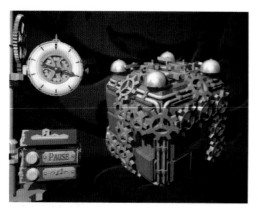

Cogs

Original release date : 2009
Platform : Various
Developer : Lazy 8 Studios
Genre : Puzzle

The term "mechanical advantage" is used to describe the multiplication of force afforded by gears placed in a series, so you get out more than you put in. The same is true of *Cogs*, a game built from simple components that delivers a challenge of rich complexity. Ostensibly a sliding-block puzzler, play consists of reorganizing a field of tiles in order to complete a mechanism of cogs.

Levels are hugely imaginative and consist of anything from a rocket that requires an unbroken path of pipes in order to light all four boosters, to an abstracted musical instrument in which cogs must be orientated to strike a series of bells in the correct order.

The steampunk visuals fit perfectly with the game's themes, making *Cogs* one of the most handsome puzzles available. The variety of modes ensure that it scales well to the player's ability, and solving each puzzle opens up "time" and "move" challenges that ask either that the puzzle is completed in no more than thirty seconds or no more than ten moves. By turns panicked and flustered, or thoughtfully frugal, budding da Vincis will be well catered for. **BM**

Wii Sports Resort

Original release date : 2009
Platform : Wii
Developer : Nintendo
Genre : Sports

While the success of *Wii Sports* made a sequel inevitable, Nintendo took its time. The results were worth the wait: *Wii Sports Resort* takes the delightfully simple premise of the original game and gives it a jolt of genuine character, moving its expanding roster of events to a tropical island setting where players can go fencing in the hills, pull off simple tricks on Jet Skis, and even buzz over the mountain ranges in a dinky little plane.

If the games can't quite match the spectacular sky-diving intro for exuberance, they more than make up for it with variety, as you dash between sword slicing challenges, engage in Ping Pong, and play Frisbee with the accompaniment of a delightful, if worryingly shiny, dog.

The biggest development, though, is the way in which *Wii Sports Resort* capitalizes on the increased movement fidelity of the Wii MotionPlus add-on bundled with the game. This extra precision opens the door for a range of activities that simply wouldn't have been possible before, and the results are generous, colorful, and, if played with friends, an absolute riot. **CD**

A Boy and His Blob

Original release date : 2009
Platform : Wii
Developer : WayForward Technologies
Genre : Platform / Puzzle

Based on the similarly named 1989 NES title, *A Boy and His Blob* is a love letter to a past generation of platform games. The plot is the innocent stuff of Disney cartoons: a planet in peril under an evil emperor births a sole refugee, the titular "blob"; said blob encounters young boy; they battle on Earth, and head for the stars to free the blob planet. To battle the evil minions, the blob can transform into a wide variety of apparatus, from ladder to parachute to trampoline. Each ability is created as the boy feeds the blob jellybeans, naturally. Art director Marc Gomez pulls the aesthetic sensibility from the world of Japanese filmmaker Hiyao Miyasaki, softening the edges and using loose brushstrokes to animate the imaginary environment.

But what emerges is a lovely connection between the boy and the blob, much in the tradition of *Fable II*—the blob is indispensable to your mission, yet completely reliant on you for its care and direction. But nothing makes more sense than the developer's choice to include a "hug" button, which does nothing but allow the boy to embrace his companion. We should all hope to be so lucky. **JBW**

PixelJunk Shooter

Original release date : 2009
Platform : PS3
Developer : Q-Games
Genre : Shoot 'Em Up

Fluid Dynamics: The Game. Not an enticing pitch, but that's the joy of being an indie developer like Dylan Cuthbert—it's his house; he gets to make what he wants. *PixelJunk Shooter*, the fourth title in the series, is set in an underground world where you maneuver your tiny ship around gushing rivers and oozing pockets of magma. Rendered in gorgeous 2-D animations, those liquid delights are the focus of a game that flows in every sense of the word.

The gist of the game is simple: A bunch of your fellow explorers are trapped inside a volatile planet; it's your job to zoom down from the mothership and rescue them. This means carefully making your way through subterranean landscapes and shooting the hideous aliens that pop out of the ground. But your main nemesis is the shifting terrain, which poses a constant puzzle-solving challenge.

PixelJunk Shooter is a pleasure to play, thanks to the tight, effortless controls. The movement of the ships is so smooth that after a few levels, the PS3's analog sticks feel like an extension of your thumbs—making it a joy to go with the flow. **JT**

Warhammer 40,000: Dawn of War II

Original release date : 2009
Platform : PC
Developer : Relic Entertainment
Genre : Strategy / Role-Playing

As sequels go, Canadian developer Relic took a bold approach when updating *Warhammer*, their most popular franchise. Ejecting much that was popular in the original—traditional *Command & Conquer*–like base building—they replaced it with a resource-free combat campaign that focuses on a small band of heroes in the form of squad leaders of space marine units.

Spend just a few minutes with *Warhammer 40,000: Dawn of War II* and Relic's intentions become clear—to make it more like *Diablo* or *World of Warcraft*, a game of loot, linear combat, and character development. Your heroes can be upgraded between missions, and there's scope for acquiring items that enhance their abilities.

The new race, the biomechanical Tyranids, also offer a pleasingly fresh angle, even if they never really swarm enough to sell the fiction of their insect-hive nature.

The base building returns in the multiplayer option although the game is still more about the hero and point capturing than its predecessor. Patches have boosted up the accessibility and playability of the game online, but it is still dominated by an ultra-hardcore community, making for some daunting matches if you're an outsider.

Fortunately for both single- and multiplayer aspects, the visceral, kinetic impact of the original game has been surpassed. *Warhammer 40,000: Dawn of War II* is preposterously violent, with dreadnoughts now able to crash straight through scenery as they valiantly pronounce their faith in the emperor, while assault marines jump-jet and sky-stomp around them. The battles with boss characters exemplify this violence, with ruins collapsing around gargantuan ork war bosses as they slam energy-swathed battle-bludgeons into the terrain. **JR**

This dino appears to be dead.

Time Gentlemen, Please!

Original release date : 2009
Platform : PC
Developer : Zombie Cow Studios
Genre : Adventure

While some claim *Grim Fandango* to be the last of the point-and-click adventures, the genre itself didn't die—just its ability to scale the upper reaches of charts. The underlying mechanics have informed many experimental contemporary games, from *Dreamfall* to *Heavy Rain*, but the fervent adventurer has also been spoiled for choice when it comes to traditional mouse-driven interactive tales. Of course, not all live up to the Sierra On-line and LucasArts classics, but the occasional gem still surfaces. *Time Gentlemen, Please!* is certainly one of them, and no less than a love letter to the adventure game's heyday.

The sequel to *Ben There, Dan That*, the game begins where its predecessor left off, tasking the player with cleaning up the huge mess left by the eponymous heroes' previous interdimensional (mis)adventure. Cue time travel, Nazi dinosaurs, and the attempted abolition of the coat hanger. Although the scatological humor may paint a picture of juvenility, there is a rich, polished and genuinely amusing experience behind the facade. Self-referential and certainly reverential—the time-traveling puzzles and access to a lab via a grandfather clock pay tribute to *Day of the Tentacle*, for instance—it always manages to elicit nostalgia with its in-jokes.

Players gorged on big-budget audio may be disappointed by the lack of voice acting, but its absence seems fitting in a game so enamored of its inspirations. Compensation comes in the form of great music and atmospheric sounds that match the striking hand-drawn visuals. An intuitive interface and genuinely logical puzzles make this a pleasure to play, while the volume of dialogue encourages a try-it-and-see approach—if only to see how many offensive jokes it's possible to cram into a game. **BM**

FONTAINE'S
CENTER
FOR THE POOR

- Kinect, developed by Microsoft, enables gamers to interact with the **Xbox 360** without ever touching a game controller

- Nintendo works on consoles producing 3-D images that can be viewed without the aid of 3-D spectacles

- Developers focus increasingly on games for social communities of all ages rather than individuals playing at home

- Gaming communities are increasingly linked via mobile technology, such as the iPhone, and by websites, such as Facebook

- Physically interactive games, popularized by the **WII**, challenge couch-based players

2010s

Max and the Magic Marker

Original release date : 2010
Platform : Various
Developer : Press Play
Genre : Puzzle

The notion of drawing pictures that come to life, and the potential adventures to be had therein, has been a popular one in children's cartoons over the years, and it seems plenty of game developers share the daydream too. As a result, we've seen many titles featuring drawing mechanics, from *Yoshi: Touch & Go* to *Scribblenauts*.

Max and the Magic Marker, however, is more like a combination of *Crayon Physics Deluxe* and *Lost Winds*, effortlessly combining physics-enabled puzzling with whimsical platforming. Anything you draw becomes part of the game world. Perhaps a ledge lies tantalizingly out of reach—do you draw a staircase, or do you create a seesaw, stand on one end, and scribble a counterweight over the other? When faced with an enemy, do you trap them or draw a boulder and let it roll right over them? Of course, pens run out of ink, so grabbing the globes that refill Max's pens provides a brilliant contextualization for some classically satisfying platform token collection.

But even collecting won't provide you with unlimited ink, meaning that thrifty deployment of your resources is essential, as well as ingenious solutions. This freedom to improvise means that every player will approach puzzles slightly differently, and you'll need flexibility to stop the vandalizing monster you accidentally released when first experimenting with your magical pen.

As is befitting for a game about drawing, *Max and the Magic Marker* sports a charming aesthetic that switches from childlike scribbles (when using the pen) to colorful caricature. Simultaneously balancing tradition with freedom of expression is no mean feat, but one the game takes in its stride. However you approach it, it's one title that's sure to draw out the artist in everyone. **BM**

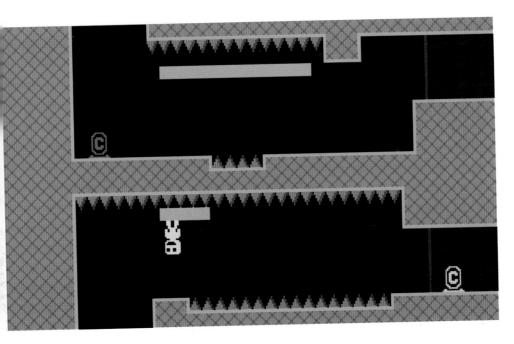

VVVVVV

Original release date : 2010
Platform : Various
Developer : Terry Cavanagh
Genre : Platform / Puzzle

Independent developer Terry Cavanagh has made a name for himself for the last few years with a number of free downloadable games that revel in 8-bit style visuals and unlikely puzzle mechanics. While they all suggested he was a smart designer with a keen eye for getting the most out of limited budgets, it took *VVVVVV*, a fiendishly tricky platformer, to really put him on the map.

Cavanagh's first genuinely meaty game is a devious romp through an abandoned space station, as a heroic captain tries to gather together the scattered members of his crew. The retro graphics and cheeky room names found at the bottom of each screen inevitably bring 1980s computer classics like *Jet Set Willy* to mind, but *VVVVVV*

actually has more in common with complex exploration titles like *Metroid*. As players progress through Cavanagh's spooky world, they steadily fill in the game's generous map, unlocking secret areas and collecting trinkets as they go. Platforming is still crucial, of course, but so is a willingness to fearlessly set off into the unknown, and a good memory for the way that the play area fits together.

At the very center of it all is a single ingenious idea. *VVVVVV* is a platform game in which you can't jump. Instead, progress is made by flipping yourself between walking on the floor and walking on the ceiling, with a press of the *V* key. It's a simple concept, but one for which Cavanagh never runs out of ideas. As the game progresses he puts in some genuinely devilish twists, as you navigate crumbling platforms, evade spikes, and abstract enemies, and bust through seemingly insurmountable roadblocks. It's mean-spirited, extremely difficult, and occasionally frustrating, but *VVVVVV* is so consistently ingenious that it remains a joy to play regardless. **CD**

Mass Effect 2

Original release date : 2010
Platform : PC, Xbox 360
Developer : BioWare
Genre : Action / Role-Playing

Mass Effect 2, the aggressively streamlined sequel to the 2008 original, *Mass Effect*, feels like the product of judicious editing. If a bit of *Mass Effect* didn't work, developer BioWare jettisoned it into the vacuum of space. With *Mass Effect 2*, story and choice move to the fore; the rest (especially item management) is tangential.

But BioWare tells one hell of a tale here. The plot picks up after the death of Commander Shepard, a spacefaring agent tasked with defending the galaxy from extra-dimensional invaders called Reapers. Reincarnated via expensive science, Shepard owes a favor to Cerberus, the megacorp that footed the bill. And since Cerberus is the only entity that has Shepard's back in the fight

against the impending invasion, there's an undercurrent of compromise to the affair. *Mass Effect 2* is, like the *Dirty Dozen* and *Seven Samurai*, as much about preparing for a confrontation as it is about the final face-off. From the moment of Shepard's rebirth, the game continually challenges the player to question whether they truly believe that the ends justify the means.

Most of these tests occur during conversations. As in the original *Mass Effect*, players steer the chatter in real time, making spur-of-the-moment decisions that push the discussion in one direction or the other.

Stellar writing and a particularly strong performance by Jennifer Hale (as the female Shepard) add a sense of ownership to the character and the sensation that the player isn't just watching a story unfold, but participating in its telling. As futuristic and evolved as *Mass Effect 2* seems, the game is really a throwback to the days when role-playing was about a bunch of friends sitting around a table, telling a story. **GM**

BioShock 2

Original release date : 2010
Platform : Various
Developer : 2K / Digital Extremes / Arkane Studios
Genre : First-Person Shooter

BioShock isn't subtle. Laden with direct references to objectivist philosophy, it stands out not only because using a philosophy to construct a game space is a unique decision, but because the philosophical concepts are so definitively hammered home by the intertwining of design and plot. If there is a flaw to *BioShock*, it is that it doesn't make the exploration of freedom of choice to its logical conclusion in its design, instead keeping the player locked to its scripted narrative.

Taken on these terms, a *BioShock 2* that offers more of the same would be a disappointment. While it doesn't mess with the original's formula, it succeeds in using the underwater city of Rapture to tell a much more subtle story, one that doesn't need to force understanding upon the player. Set nearly eight years after the conclusion of the original, *BioShock 2* casts the player as a Big Daddy trying to reunite with his Little Sister, and while the rantings of a new overlord, Sophia Lamb, swirl in the ether as Andrew Ryan's once did, they are merely color.

Indeed, *BioShock 2*'s story is so slight it could almost be overlooked completely in favor of the game's take on freedom of choice, which comes in the form of the combination of weapons and plasmids (genetic tonics that allow offensive powers such as electricity and fire) you choose to take into each battle. With a dizzying selection—weapons even have different kinds of ammo—it is a unique experience. It's particularly joyful when players find themselves defending a Little Sister and are given the opportunity to set up plasmid traps and decoys while also engaging in brutally direct combat. The one area of *BioShock 2* that outstrips its predecessor is conversely its least subtle, but who could object? **MKu**

Heavy Rain

Original release date : 2010
Platform : PS3
Developer : Quantic Dream
Genre : Interactive Drama

Writer and director David Cage isn't averse to narrative, or dialogue-heavy productions with aspirations. *Omikron: The Nomad Soul* and *Fahrenheit* were each burdened with the ambitions of a director out to make an innovative mark on the video game medium, whether by challenging notions of interactivity and existentialist themes (in the former) or a penchant for the cinematic (in the latter).

Heavy Rain walks a tightrope somewhere between the two, toppling generic preconceptions of users' authorial input by positioning them as an active participant in, and detached voyeur of, a traditional thriller narrative. The story follows the multiple characters linked to a series of murders by the so-called Origami Killer. More *Gone*

Baby Gone, perhaps, than the grandiose Hitchcockian pretensions the production values suggest, the unfolding of the unremittingly bleak plot is, in a market saturated by action blockbusters, something of a rarity.

Blending the environmental interactions of point-and-click adventure and the dynamic action systems of traditional combat titles, input is conducted in response to subtle symbolic cues, with functions ranging from the perfunctory to the crucial. The juxtaposition of the domestic and the extraordinary is the crux of Cage's creative oeuvre, encapsulated by the origami motif and prevalent in the admittedly tall tale's many twists and turns. It's a shame, however, to find a lack of tangible humanity and emotional resonance beneath the orchestral posturing and cinematic framing.

Crucially, though, *Heavy Rain* pioneers a synergy between video game and film that is admirable for its determination to take one avenue of this convergence to its natural, imperfect conclusion. **DV**

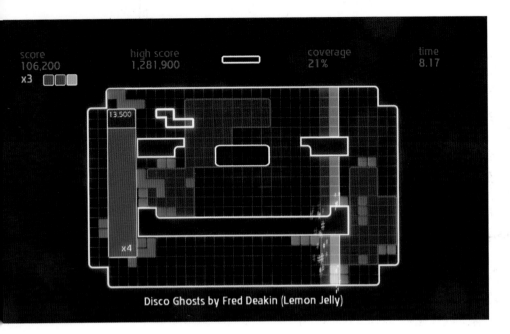

Disco Ghosts by Fred Deakin (Lemon Jelly)

score	high score		coverage	time
106,200	1,281,900		21%	8.17

x3

13,500

x4

Chime

Original release date : 2010
Platform : XBox 360
Developer : Zoë Mode
Genre : Puzzle

The inaugural release for philanthropic game publisher OneBigGame, *Chime* is anything but a throwaway charity case. Drawing inspiration from *Tetris* and *Lumines*, it is a music-themed puzzle game that turns convention on its head by asking you to fill the screen with objects rather than empty it of them.

You place blocks of various shapes and sizes onto the playing field, which resembles the stave of a music sequencer. The pieces can be rotated and moved around the area before being placed, and then clustered to form larger squares or rectangles. When a "quad" of sufficient size has been constructed, it disappears, painting the grid beneath with color. The object of the game is to fill in the entire playing field within the time limit, adding seconds to the clock as you pass certain thresholds of coverage. Intertwined with the game's puzzle systems is a layer of thoughtful, musical feedback. Blocks act like lyrical flourishes, read by a bar that moves at a constant pace, from left to right and then looping back to the start.

When the bar strikes a block, it triggers a stab of audio that complements the music playing in the background. While essentially irrelevant to the game mechanics, the layered audio adds greatly to the experience, injecting color and character to what might otherwise have been a fairly dry stacking exercise.

The musical aspect of the game is diverse and appealing, with Philip Glass joining Moby and Orbital in creating a prestigious, ambient soundtrack that suits the game's mesmerizing interactions. Best approached as a score attack game by competing against friends over Xbox Live, *Chime* is a deep and enthralling experience that would stand tall even without its philanthropic bent. **SP**

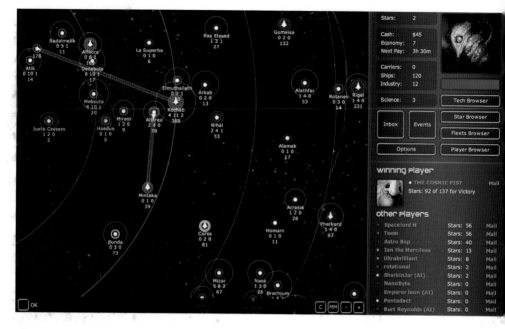

Neptune's Pride

Original release date : 2010

Platform : Internet

Developer : Iron Helmet Games

Genre : Strategy

Before the Internet became pervasive, online gaming was fragmented and halting, limited by trickles of data and the paucity of players capable of remaining connected. One effective solution was play by e-mail—turn-based games that required players to e-mail their moves to a host, who would compile all of the moves and distribute the results. *Stars*, by Jeff Johnson and Jeff McBride, exemplified the form, a complex strategy game set in a galaxy filled with opposing player factions that would explore, expand, exploit, and exterminate, one e-mail at a time.

Fast-forward to today, and we have its direct successor, *Neptune's Pride*. Played in real-time through a browser window, it might be stripped down from

Stars's overwhelming mechanical intricacies, but it's no less absorbing. Players again spread their civilization throughout the game's randomly generated galaxies building infrastructure to generate money, research new technology, and build spaceships through basic systems that are dizzying in their tactical depth

That's because *Neptune's Pride* is all about diplomacy and communication. Your most important tool is the in-game messaging system, or the instant messaging client, the phone, or, in a case of ironic continuity with its forebear, e-mail. Knowing your enemy, making lasting friends, and choosing the right time to stab them in the back is *Neptune's Pride*'s real heart.

With fleets taking hours to travel between stars, the ritual of logging in to spend your daily salary, and the slow reveals of the people you play against, *Neptune's Pride* is a long-term commitment. Even with its fifteen-year-old mechanics and functional graphics, it's one of the most nuanced and gripping of all online strategy games. **AW**

Super Mario Galaxy 2

Original release date : 2010
Platform : Wii
Developer : Nintendo
Genre : Platformer

Back on the good old N64, Super Mario's first adventure in 3-D space would define how an entire generation of games coped with traversing complex landscapes. Fourteen years later, *Super Mario Galaxy 2* proves the crowning achievement of that approach: a platformer of such depth and ambition and poise that it often seemed to be dismantling the entire genre as it went.

Whether upside down, floating around in mid-air, or transitioning from 2-D to 3-D sequences, *Super Mario Galaxy 2* copes with each and every challenge it sets itself without breaking a sweat. The best levels construct themselves around you as you move, and frequently pack themselves away again while you depart. Meanwhile, the deep-space theme gives the most playful designers in the entire video game business a chance to toy with gravity and material physics as effortlessly as the 2-D games had meddled with inertia. Vivid colours and elaborate, shifting landscapes collide creatively in every stage: if ever there was a developer whose collective imagination was perfectly suited for the Hubble generation, it's this one.

All of this had been accomplished before, of course, in the form of the first *Super Mario Galaxy* game. What marks the sequel out is a generous, gimmicky nature that throws a new toy your way every few minutes, and the kind of sharpened focus that only a second pass over the terrain can provide. *Super Mario Galaxy 2* is gorgeous, clever, inventive, and endlessly elegant—qualities that prompted glowing reviews and sales in the multi-millions.

Most of all, though, it's playful: a knockabout adventure that elevates the mysterious business of fun to dazzling new heights, and an exploration of outer space that leaves our own world so much the richer. **CD**

Red Dead Redemption

Original release date : 2010
Platform : PS3, Xbox 360
Developer : Rockstar
Genre : Action / Adventure

The scrubland stretches away towards a red rock mesa, a silhouette against the raw red light of the setting sun. Wind rustles, somewhere a coyote calls, and a few sparse twangs of a score recall an Ennio Morricone soundtrack, before falling back into silence. *Red Dead Redemption* homes in with precision on the Western's predilection for the lonesome landscape; the fraught relationship of a single man against the enormity of nature.

But this is an illusion, albeit a deft one. Rockstar's recreation of the Old West is a bustling place, crammed with all the distractions you expect from a game roughly cast from a *Grand Theft Auto* mold. Even a parched stretch desert offers diversions: a hijacked stagecoach here, a

damsel in distress there, a bounty to capture or a beast to skin. And your interactions with this world announce a powerful physicality: from the pounding of horses' hooves, the swish and tug of a well-thrown lasso, or, most commonly, the thudding of a bullet finding its target.

Like *Grand Theft Auto*, again, it is an attentive pastiche of cinema. Here we get all the principle facets of the Western: the redemption story, the pastoral and finally a furious revenge. John Marston is as complex a rough-cut hero as any in Rockstar's catalog—and his arc is one of the most potently tragic.

If the plot feels like three tales in one, that's nothing in comparison to its seamless blend of Old West geography. From prarie to bayou, wintry hills to sunscorched planes, *Red Dead Redemption* is a picture postcard flipbook—every turn in the road offering up a vista of natural beauty, perfectly framed and lit. It's testament to Rockstar's skill that, even amid a fine cast, it can make the world itself the game's most enduring character. **MD**

Limbo

Original release date : 2010
Platform : Various
Developer : Playdead
Genre : Platform / Puzzle

Tales of the deep dark wood have held children rapt with trepidation and wonder in fables from *Little Red Riding Hood* to *The Gruffalo*. While *Limbo* definitely lays claim to this tradition, it finds its niche in the darkest, most gruesome part. Though described as a 2-D puzzle platformer, the eerie atmosphere elevates it to something like folklore: shot in the grainy, flickering, black and white of a cinematograph reel, and painted in stark silhouette, *Limbo* is like a shadow play of the grimmest of Grimm tales.

You control a young boy, alone in a forest. The mood is intensely melancholic, then foreboding, but often gruesomely funny, as your prepubescent protagonist falls foul of the lurking horrors. A giant spider stalks you among the woodland furrows, a pack of feral children persecute you with arrows and spears, and no small number of bear-traps invite sticky, abrupt ends.

Gloomy as it may appear, *Limbo* possesses a searing slapstick wit—never failing to introduce a puzzle by killing you with it first. The boy's silhouetted head pops from his shoulders as a man-trap snaps shut around his body, or he'll end up hanging limply off an improvised skewer. Then, when you take pains to avoid the first pitfall, *Limbo* punctures your pride by tossing you straight into a buzz saw. The old one-two.

Its puzzles don't orbit a central gimmick, as *Braid*'s or *Portal*'s do. Instead, *Limbo* moves skittishly between disparate ideas, unified only by their reliance on your character's weight and momentum. But this constant dislocation adds to the feverish, fabular aesthetic—and it's this that remains, long after the memory of its mechanics have faded: a ghostly realm, as undwindling and woebegone as the title suggests. **MD**

Deus Ex: Human Revolution

Original release date : 2011
Platform : Various
Developer : Eidos Montreal
Genre : First-Person Shooter

A young studio makes its first game a prequel to one of the best loved and most ambitious PC games. Good luck with that, you might think—and yet *Deus Ex: Human Revolution* stays true to the themes, tone, and action of the pioneering RPG-FPS hybrid, while adapting beloved mechanics to modern tastes. It's also astute in making its darkly satirical cyberpunk future seem more relevant than ever. While *Deus Ex* offered an hysterical pastiche of conspiracy theory—blending secret genetics projects, human-created plagues, the Illuminati, aliens and more— *Human Revolution*'s preoccupations reflect the issues of our time, presenting uncertain steps into transhumanism against a backdrop of overweening corporate control and a fast growing divide between the wealthy and poor.

The game isn't, however, a grim bit of sermonizing: it's a brutishly brilliant shooter, or devious sneak-'em-up, depending on how you wish to play it. In the role of growly-voiced cyborg, Adam Jensen, you unravel a world-spanning conspiracy, primarily by sniffing out secrets in places you are not meant to be. As long as the ferociously dynamic AI doesn't scupper your plans, whether you choose to do this by leaving a trail of crumpled bodies or not is up to you: the game's intricate environments and Jensen's upgradeable skills are crafted to support discretion or aggression as you please, and larger narrative choices shunt the story in different directions too.

Few games invite such audacious heists, or allow you the freedom to devise them, but the real steal in *Human Revolution* is the way that it lives up to PC gaming's most august and intimidating legacy—and casts a long shadow all of its own. **MD**

Uncharted 3: Drake's Deception

Original release date : 2011
Platform : PS3
Developer : Naughty Dog
Genre : Action / Adventure

Uncharted 1 and *2* were jungle and ice. The third is fire and sand, with a little sky and sea on the side. So many scene changes might muddle a lesser game, but Naughty Dog' blockbuster treasure hunter romp infuses its world with detail and beauty. Its triumph is witnessed in the grandiose architecture of lost civilisations: vast crumbling edifice strewn with towering statues and murals.

But it's the more humble details that create acute vérité: the way light falls on parched rock, scorching a wall with glaring white, and blushing the surrounding stone with a vivid red glow; the way sand collapses and sinks beneath Drake's stumbling feet; the way seawater flushes through a ruptured cargo hold. These mark the very cusp of technical prowess for this generation of hardware, and the skill with which they are deployed establishes a high water mark in video game aesthetics as a whole.

The player's action blurs seamlessly with directorial control, maintaining the series' tradition of cinematic action and binding it into a story of unusual character and depth. Though always a likable rogue, Nathan Drake was thus far an enigma. While *Deception*'s story is guilty of repetition (a megalomaniac villain exploits Drake's savvy to capture a cursed treasure), *Uncharted 3* finally unfolds our hero's backstory and his relationship with mentor Sully. The paternal bond between Sully and Drake—a rare subject for video games—is told with surprising sensitivity and warmth, while the ongoing will-they-won't-they romance with Elena tightens its grip on the heartstrings.

In these ways, *Uncharted* demonstrates its command of gaming's emotional palette: exciting, wowing and wooing all at the same time. **MD**

Minecraft

Original release date : 2011
Platform : Various
Developer : Mojang
Genre : Sandbox

The most significant game of the past ten years isn't a big-budget spectacular filled with bullets and bombs, or even an addictive puzzler with smart visuals and bright colours. It's a defiantly primitive building game that comes with no real aim, a near-total absence of story and tutorials, and a server user interface best described as 'inadequate'.

It's hard to know if it's even finished. Issued after a short period of development, *Minecraft* has continued to take shape. Its blend of exploration, survival, and Lego-like construction initially rendered it a curio; four years and millions of downloads later, it's a phenomenon. Children can't stop playing it, industry veterans debate what made it a hit, and Lego itself got in on the action, releasing its

own *Minecraft*-themed kits—an appropriate gesture given that the game is pure toy and pure creativity, and comes with almost no barriers to entry. Stump up the pittance needed to download it and you'll find yourself cast as a modern Robinson Crusoe, stranded on a huge, evocative world where a couple of clicks build anything you want: a cave, an axe, a castle, a scale model of the Earth.

The *Minecraft* parade shows no signs of abating. Nor do the groups of imitators, hoping to ape the model and win a slice of the riches that Minecraft's Swedish creator Markus 'Notch' Persson has accrued. Notch himself, meanwhile, conducts himself admirably, releasing free content updates with alarming regularity, appearing faintly amused by his good fortune, inspiring others, and acknowledging his own inspirations.

Can *Minecraft*'s astonishing trajectory be replicated? That's a question a lot of people would like to know the answer to. Even if the answer is 'No,' having just one game like *Minecraft* is something of a treat. **CD**

Portal 2

Original release date : 2011

Platform : Various

Developer : Valve Corporation

Genre : Platform / Puzzle

Wedged amid the colorful antics of Valve's *Orange Box* compilation, the original *Portal* is perhaps video games' greatest shaggy dog story: a short narrative filled with vivid moments of comedy and capped with a perfect twist. So *Portal 2* had a hard act to follow: You can't tell the same joke twice and expect the same result.

Inevitably, then, the sequel is very different. It's a full-length release, complete with a separate co-op campaign. Its environments are more expansive and its mechanics more varied. At heart, though, it uses the same ingenious hook: you're a human lab rat in an ancient science establishment, armed with a 'portal gun' that allows you to connect and travel between disparate points in the world by blasting the entry and exit sides of a hole—and the puzzles are delivered with the same knowing humor.

It's an intoxicating mixture: warm comedy as you team up with the monstrous super-computer GLaDOS, and cold-hearted challenges along the way. New gels— one that allows you to pick up speed, another that lets you bounce—keep traversal fresh, while the abandoned factories and test chambers through which you move give the whole thing the scope and the scale of myth.

For all its brilliance, *Portal 2* can't quite compete with the tart delights of its predecessor. Towards the very end of the journey, the mechanics begin to feel slightly overstretched, and Valve's legendary focus on gathering player feedback throughout the design process has yielded a game in which perhaps too much of the friction has been removed. In the end, though, that could be another layer of this ingenious meta-narrative: an adventure set inside a series of fantastical laboratories is, in the final analysis, a product of one as well. **CD**

Dark Souls

Original release date : 2011
Platform : Various
Developer : From Software
Genre : Action

A hazy myth, an elegant contraption, an eccentric vision, an unforgiving mistress: *Dark Souls* has many sides, all of which reflect the character of its creator Hidetaka Miyazaki. An uncompromising visionary and long-time fan of dark fantasy fiction, Miyazaki has once again created a haunting and haunted netherworld of cobblestones, crumbling clock towers and knights in tarnished armor to explore in this pseudo-sequel to 2009's cult classic *Demon's Souls*.

As far from the churning mainstream of gung-ho action games as one can trek, in *Dark Souls* you skitter through narrow sewers and dense forests while cowering behind a shield, questing in hope of finding one of the bonfires that punctuate the unforgiving world: a rare point of safety, a place to trade currency for statistical upgrades, and, a little farther into the mystery, a respawn point.

It's a game with a reputation for difficulty but, in truth, its character is one of unrelenting fairness. The feeling as you set out time and again to penetrate a little deeper into the medieval world of Lodran—with its clifftops patrolled by skeletons and dragons and valleys guarded by ice giants and hydra—is one of banging a weak fist against overwhelming odds. But this is simply a game that asks you to improve your own skills in order to progress – and the rewards for those who persevere are as lasting as the muscle memory you gain along the way.

Then, once the story is complete and the most terrible monsters lurking in its belly are defeated, *Dark Souls* allows players to turn on one another, pledging allegiance to one of a variety of covenants before invading each others' worlds in combat. Rarely has a game that values the mysterious and unspoken been so urgently talked of—not least the buzz for the inevitable *Dark Souls II*. **SP**

The Elder Scrolls V: Skyrim

Original release date : 2011
Platform : Various
Developer : Bethesda Game Studios
Genre : RPG

With two intervening *Fallout* games maintaining Bethesda's RPG model, fans had plenty to demand of a fifth *Elder Scrolls*. They wanted an escape from the dungeon-craft and loveliness of *Elder Scrolls IV: Oblivion*, even if that meant a spiritual return to the feral shores of *Elder Scrolls III: Morrowind*. They wanted an end to those metastasizing bugs that break quests, corrupt saves, and make non-playable characters do the Riverdance when they should be sipping mead. And—though they didn't know it yet—they wanted dragons.

Two hundred years after the 'Oblivion crisis,' a new threat is rising in the land of fire and ice that is Skyrim, home to the resilient Nords. Amid the hostile canyons of The Reach, the exclusive College of Winterhold, and the war rooms of Whiterun and Solitude, its myriad human squabbles are about to be wreathed in dragons' breath, as prophesied by the Elder Scrolls. Only you, the mythical (and unsuspecting) 'Dragonborn,' have the power to master the dragons' ancient tongue and take down Alduin, destroyer of worlds. Being an *Elder Scrolls* game, all this is made unobtrusively melancholy by characters locked into fragile routines that all too often break.

Despite a new name and partial dynamic shadowing system, the game's Creation Engine is a mere upgrade of creaky old Gamebryo. But these and other side effects of Bethesda's cost-efficient world-building are suffered gladly by players who prize adventure over linear story-telling. (PS3 players who suffered the worst effects may, admittedly, be less indulgent.) The dragons bring majesty to Skyrim's wonderfully embedded regions and cities, but it's the players' own stories, enriched once again by modding on PC, that keep the series unbeatable. **DH**

Ni No Kuni

Original release date : 2011
Platform : Various
Developer : Level 5
Genre : RPG

Drawing together the considerable talents of Studio Ghibli, the animation house behind some of Japan's most enduring and critically acclaimed modern cinematic fairy tales, and Level 5, creator of some of the most inventive and vivid video game fables, *Ni No Kuni* has a rich and enviable lineage.

The premise—a parentless child at the precipice of puberty who will save a world but, to quote the script, "must first save himself"—may be well-worn. But the execution has all of the flair and generous detail one might expect of such a heavyweight creative collaboration.

Oliver, the game's thoroughly likeable thirteen-year-old protagonist, is called to save the fantasy world of Ni No Kuni in a bid to save the life of his mother in his own reality after she is fatally wounded in a tragic accident in the game's opening moments.

Accompanied by his favourite toy—a tubby, saucer-eyed fairy called Mr Drippy (brought to life by Oliver's tears) who sports a small red lantern dangling from a ring through his elongated snout—he tours the colorful world, righting its wrongs and watching how kindness performed in one realm affects the other.

Of course, various enemies stand in Oliver's way. Over the course of the adventure, he takes familiars (Pokémon-esque creatures that fight on his behalf) into battle. What first appears to be a simple system soon reveals satisfying depths, and the combat-driven heart of the game is sound. But its more attractive soul is to be found in the town and villages, where Oliver uses spells he has learned to spring locks, rejuvenate tired objects, and share emotions with people in the world. It's an endeavor that's unusually philanthropic and warmly instructive. **SP**

Far Cry 3

Original release date : 2012
Platform : Various
Developer : Ubisoft Montreal
Genre : FPS

Far Cry has always been a wayward series. The first game struck out for the sands of tropical islands while other shooters skulked in grey corridors and grim sewers. The second dropped you into a ravaged African state on the brink of civil war. Despite no overlapping characters or plot points, both looked beyond the normal bounds of video games, and let environment dictate action.

Far Cry 3 is probably the series's biggest surprise so far —not because the island setting's a departure, but because a franchise that often felt packed with smart ideas that never came together suddenly feels complete.

You play an American vacationing in the tropics whose holiday is interrupted when his friends are kidnapped by a group of maniacs. From there, the narrative doesn't unfold the way you might expect. Rather than offering a linear revenge mission, *Far Cry 3* quickly blossoms into a bizarre carnival of distractions, offering animals to hunt, flowers to pick, and—best of all—a series of communication towers to scale and capture. Systems pile up on one another in a pleasantly confusing tangle, while your map fills with icons tempting you off the main track.

Your favorite moment is likely to lie with a millisecond of hilarity rather than a rigorously scripted set-piece, as *Far Cry 3*'s main campaign is laden with postmodern trickery and symbolism that reduces storytelling to a series of codes to be broken. "This game is about entertainment, and about how far will you go in these loops . . ." said writer Jeffrey Yohalem, "Are you willing to kill these characters in the game in order to finish your entertainment?"

In the end, this self-conscious, almost self-defeating approach serves *Far Cry 3* rather well. The island's crazy, the game's demented, so why not go nuts yourself? **CD**

Journey

Original release date : 2012
Platform : PS3
Developer : Thatgamecompany
Genre : Action

Rumor has it that *Journey* was inspired by a retired astronaut and his insight into the strange blend of intense distance and intense connectedness his adventures had left him with. Eschewing sci-fi clichés, Thatgamecompany expanded on the idea with a game set in a nameless but semi-familiar fantasyland, thrusting players onto an endlessly shifting desert and tasking them with making their way towards a glowing mountain in the distance.

As objectives go, that one's as old as the *Bible*, yet it adds mythic power. It also orients players throughout this short but striking adventure, whether they're traversing the open sands of the early levels, or leaping and singing as they march up the frigid steppes of later environments.

Journey, in fact, goes out of its way to evoke a feeling of spiritual transcendence: church architecture, empty spaces, and nameless forces swirling in the skies abound.

A brilliant multiplayer component randomly connects you with others around the world, with whom you cannot chat or communicate in any traditional sense. Instead, you dance, sing, and urge each other onwards. So while *Journey*'s outer layers are beautiful but rather chilly, its center pulses with warm humanity. **CD**

XCOM Enemy Unknown

Original release date : 2012
Platform : Various
Developer : Firaxis Games
Genre : Strategy

This reboot's close quarters warfare boasts a neat turn-based system that gives you room to sneak up, fire on an enemy, and hopefully make it back to cover before you take a laser bolt through the head. It also renders said warfare personal, as you provide names for troops, pets, and friends, making it all the more painful when they die.

And they *will* die. It's part of the fun: so much so, in fact, that it would feel shameful to resort to a save game when it happens. *XCOM* makes defeats—even squad-shattering washouts—entertaining. They offer a chance to work out what went wrong, but are also an opportunity to watch game mechanics turn into full-fledged storytelling devices as you think back over a calamitous mission and ponder all the improbable things that went hilariously awry.

It does all this with dazzling economy: a handful of units within the human XCOM initiative, alien enemies, a simple selection of environments, and a spin on *Unreal Engine 3* that gives everything you encounter just the right gloss of direct-to-video cheapness. It's ugly, but beautiful too, as you watch the internal clockwork that powers each turn-based firefight, and refine your base-building to ensure that not one inch of your HQ is wasted. **CD**

Hotline Miami

Original release date : 2012
Platform : PC
Developer : Dennaton Games
Genre : Action

Thirty Flights of Loving

Original release date : 2012
Platform : PC, Mac
Developer : Blendo Games
Genre : Interactive Fiction

Scrappy and luridly detailed, *Hotline Miami* will go down in history as the game that gave doors their moment in the limelight. Dennaton's debut is stocked with weapons, both machine tooled and horribly improvised, but none is quite as satisfying to deploy as a door. Lurk in the hallway, wait for the right moment, then kick the thing in, scattering wood and human flesh as you go. Bam!

Set in the shimmering sweatpool of 1980s Florida, this action game has a quick pulse and a taste for inventive slaughter. Your slobbish hitman is despatched to a series of locations to turn them all into the kind of crime scenes that see police busting out carpet cleaners as well as body bags. Each level unfolds in a few blistering minutes as you clear one room, then the next, killing everyone you find.

You're deadly but vulnerable, and the mission swiftly becomes a cerebral challenge in which you build a route between weapon, victim, and safe haven, then refine that route over the course of many failures. Atop is a narrative that unsettles at every turn. Without this final element, *Hotline Miami* would just be another clever game with a knack for violence. With it, however, it becomes a queasy exploration of the strange *attraction* of violence. **CD**

Brendon Chung's colorful chunk of interactive fiction sends you racing pell-mell through a crime caper filled with ambiguity and a palpable sense of impending doom. But while you can collect all the weaponry and all the ammo you want, you'll never get to use any of it.

Thirty Flights of Loving skirts elegantly, maddeningly, and thrillingly around the kind of set pieces other games wallow in. The story depicts the build-up to—and aftermath of—some manner of heist, but neglects to show the main event itself. The whole thing's geared to leave you off-kilter, unnerved, and forever on the back foot.

Mesmerizing jump cuts make a case for Chung as the first *great* game editor. The world he creates is slyly suggestive, throwing in nods to the likes of *The Great Gatsby* and the films of Wong Kar-wai, with a romantic subplot that conjures moments of real tenderness.

Chung's the cleverest of designers, but also the most human. His block-headed characters might not look much like the people you see on the street, but are animated with wonderful economy and powered by what feels like a genuine eagerness to understand the mysteries of our personalities a little better. **CD**

Mark of the Ninja

Original release date : 2012
Platform : PC, Xbox 360
Developer : Klei Entertainment
Genre : Stealth

Vancouver's Klei Entertainment made its name with the beautifully animated brawlers of the *Shank* series: a lavish collection of two-fisted beat-'em-ups. Characterized by a deceptively elegant combat design that lurked behind simple heroics and a gorgeous, off-the-cuff cartoon aesthetic, they were stylish but surprisingly substantial.

Mark of the Ninja retains the art, but turns its attention to stealth and indirect combat. The sun is swapped for the moon, skyscraper shrines replace wrestling rings and dingy bars, and a developer that once reveled in violent excess is now more concerned with steely minimalism.

It's a beautiful transition, and *Mark of the Ninja* emerges as a modern masterpiece of sneaking and backstabbing.

Set across a string of gloriously murky 2-D levels, your mission of vengeance is told in a series of broken lamps, distracted guards, and whispering footfalls. Play well, and the enemy will never see your blade darting from the shadows. Play even better, and you won't actually have to take anyone down in the first place.

This is, in other words, rather noble sneaking: a game that values both forethought as you read a complex, ever-changing landscape, and quick-witted improvisation, as you react to that landscape even as you dash across it. "We really wanted to make a game where you actually felt like a ninja," declared Klei founder Jamie Cheng, "as opposed to one that just bombs in and kills everybody."

If you thought stealth games were all about patience, rote memorization, and banging around in a closet while guards flutter past, this is the one to prove you wrong. And if you thought Klei could handle only straightforward button-mashing and heroes equipped with buzzing chainsaws, *Mark of the Ninja* may leave you breathless. **CD**

The Walking Dead

Original release date : 2012
Platform : Various
Developer : Telltale Games
Genre : Adventure

Set within the unflinching vision of a zombie apocalypse outlined by writer Robert Kirkman and artists Tony Moore and Charlie Adlard in their comic book series, this five-part episodic adventure spins its own yarn. The premise may be shared across the graphic novel and TV series—how can humans survive the dangers of a world ruined by degenerative disease?—but the characters with which we share the adventure are new and their story untold.

That story flows in the vein of the best post-apocalyptic fiction, presenting only glimmers of hope in a world fraught with peril. The decisions that players are called upon to make—split-second, devastating choices involving which of two people to save, for example—

almost extinguish what little optimism exists. In contrast to the ever-increasing body of zombie games, *The Walking Dead* is less about staving in the heads of flesh-eaters (although you are frequently prompted to do so via a series of on-screen buttons) but more about human relationships, involving the taut conversations of survivors close to the edge of physical and mental collapse.

Your character, a teacher convicted of murder, stands at the center of these conversations as he negotiates new friendships with other survivors while protecting a young girl he meets in the game's opening stages. Conversational choices, a rudimentary inventory and scripted action sequences form the bulk of interactions.

While the dramatic choices presented in each episode are distressing in the moment, a second playthrough reveals that their implications are usually fleeting. Still, few games communicate such measured characterization and plotting, and *The Walking Dead* stands as a high point in a medium longing for narrative sensitivity and power. **SP**

Dishonored

Original release date : 2012
Platform : Various
Developer : Arkane Studios
Genre : Stealth

Dishonored should have been a disaster: a stealth game set in a complex, rather cerebral fantasy universe, created by a studio known for wayward over-ambitiousness. In the end, then, what is startling about this dark-hearted action adventure is not that it's so creative, but that it's so complete, and so vividly uncompromised.

Set in the neo-Victorian city of Dunwall during an outbreak of plague, you're cast as Corvo Attano, once protector of an empress, and now—after an early cutscene—her willing avenger. How you go about that vengeance is almost entirely up to you, with possibility-riddled levels that are as comfortable supporting approaches that focus on mindless blood shedding as they are handling devious, almost invisible sneaking.

To aid you in your quest, you learn a variety of skills —the best of which is undoubtedly Blink, a short-form teleport that utterly transforms the game's traversal options. You also meet a series of grisly, rather depraved characters, all of whom hint at a society that's rotten to its leaking core. Your allies are drunkards, your headquarters is an abandoned pub, and the city you're trying to save is in thrall to dainty entertainments like dog-fighting. Rarely has a game let so little light through its greasy windows.

Will you redeem Dunwall or ultimately damn it? That's your choice to decide, too. The only thing that's set in stone—literally—is the landscape itself: a mesmerizing blend of Edinburgh and Victorian London in which every street corner promises grim adventure and each alleyway hides nasty secrets. Dunwall's the centerpiece of *Dishonored*'s shrine to artful disrepair—and, if the place feels strangely familiar, that's probably because it was designed in part by Victor Antonov, the architect of *Half-Life 2*'s gloriously threadbare City 17. **CD**

Year Walk

Original release date : 2013
Platform : iOS
Developer : Simogo
Genre : Adventure, Puzzle

Year Walk is a game about discovery—which makes it a tough one to write about, for fear of diluting the new player's experience. You're cast into its Swedish folkloric world with no guide other than the knowledge that you are to take part in the mysterious, age-old 'year walking' ritual. Those who undertake the year walk will, it is said, know the future—whether they will be wealthy, contented, and loved.

It's up to you to discover how to go about that as you set out from a wooden shack in the forest, snow crunching underfoot. Simogo's lack of hand-holding is a major part of the game's charm, as is its impressive audio work. This is, after all, the studio that brought us *Beat Sneak*

Bandit (2012), and its affecting music and creepy sound effects beg to be experienced through good-quality headphones. But it is no spoiler to tell you that the studio's iOS adventure is both groundbreaking and terrifying—a journey that should not be missed.

That journey is a relatively short one—depending on how skilled you are at solving puzzles—but it spills out into the real world in interesting ways. Simogo makes clever use of the iPhone and iPad's touchscreens and accelerometers, playfully disrupting your expectations.

More interesting still is the option to download a companion app (at no extra cost) that functions as an encyclopedia of the game's richly realized lore. But it's that app's role in a fraught, unexpected endgame that makes this freshly-minted gem stand out. Combined with the fact that Simogo is not afraid to ask you take notes as you break *Year Walk*'s more complex codes, the result makes you feel like you have just discovered a doorway from your home into another world. **BM**

BioShock Infinite

Original release date : 2013
Platform : Various
Developer : Irrational
Genre : First-Person Shooter

Rapture, the underwater city in which the first *BioShock* plays out, is one of the finest, and most memorable, game worlds ever created. It's no small compliment, then, to say that *BioShock Infinite*'s Columbia—a floating city that both inverts and echoes Rapture's essence—matches it brick for brick in majesty, meticulous detail, and menace.

Infinite also marks a return to original developer Irrational (after 2K Marin took up the reins for *BioShock 2*), who take the series to new heights—literally. That's not to say there aren't echoes of the past—the game's combat is only slightly more developed—but the core gameplay is augmented spectacularly by the tools and populace that exist within its new environment.

Most notable among these are Elizabeth and your Sky-Hook. Elizabeth—the reason you find yourself in Columbia, and your companion for most of the game—is one of the most human, and most likeable, sidekicks since *Half-Life 2*'s Alyx Vance. But her story is more moving, and delivered with greater subtlety, despite her ability to give as good as she gets when the bullets and brimstone begin flying. Part of her repertoire is the ability to opens tears in the fabric of space and time, pulling aid and allies through. This also provides Irrational with a dizzying opportunity to play with your perception of the world in quieter moments, too.

The Sky-Hook, meanwhile, serves as both a disturbingly gory melee weapon and a key to the city's Sky-Line, a series of tracks that sweep and bank around Columbia, linking its various districts. If you manage to stave off vertiginous feelings near the edge of Columbia's cloud-borne islands, dangling on magnetized rails as you hurtle *over* that edge will hammer them home. **BM**

Contributors

Chris Baker (CB) writes and edits stories about video games and other topics for *Wired* magazine. He contributed a chapter to *The Splendid Magic of Penny Arcade: The 11 ½ Anniversary Edition* and has written for publications like *Slate*, *Entertainment Weekly*, *Giant Robot*, and the *1-Up* zine.

Tom Benjamin (TB) began playing video games in the late 1970s and nowadays collects vintage hardware and software. He is currently collaborating on a book dedicated to the history of arcade games.

Owain Bennallack (OB) has held editorial roles on *Edge*, *MCV* and *Develop*, as well as the PocketGamer website, which he co-founded. He chairs the Develop in Brighton advisory board, and his work has appeared everywhere from *The Times* to the BBC.

Brandon Boyer (BB) is founder of game culture outlet Offworld and chairman of the Independent Games Festival, and has variously contributed to and edited publications including *Edge*, *Gamasutra*, *Giant Robot*, and *Boing Boing*.

Jason Brookes (JB) is a former editor of *Edge*. Since then he has worked for the Asian gaming press, primarily as a foreign correspondent for Japanese media company Enterbrain, Inc (publisher of *Famitsu Weekly*).

Jamin Brophy-Warren (JBW), formerly a *Wall Street Journal* reporter, is the founder of video game magazine *Kill Screen* and also a writer covering arts and entertainment. His work has appeared in the *LA Times*, *Fast Company*, *Vanity Fair* and *Slate*.

Matthew Castle (MC) writes for and is the games editor of *NGamer* magazine. His work has appeared in many magazines and websites including *Edge*, *GamesMaster*, *Xbox World 360* and *Official Nintendo Magazine*.

Mike Channell (MCh) is reviews editor of *Xbox 360: The Official Xbox Magazine*, a regular presenter of the OXM Report on Inside Xbox and has been published in most of the major UK video game magazines including *PC Gamer*, *Official PlayStation Magazine UK* and *Edge*.

Chris Dahlen (CDa) is the editorial director of *Kill Screen Magazine* and a columnist at Edge Online. He has written for *Pitchfork*, *Paste*, *Slate*, and *The Onion*'s *The A.V. Club*.

Christian Donlan (CD) writes about video games for magazines and websites. A regular contributor to *Edge* and Eurogamer, his work has appeared in numerous other publications including *Design Week*. He has also written for children's television in Europe and the US.

Martin Davies (MD) is a writer and illustrator. His work on video games has appeared in *Edge*, *GamesMaster*, *The Guardian*, *NGamer*, *Official PlayStation Magazine UK*, *Official Xbox Magazine*, *PC Gamer* and *PSM3*. He's currently making games for Channel 4 and writing a novel.

Joao Diniz Sanches (JDS) is a freelance writer who has written extensively about video games since 1997. He is a former editor of *Edge* and the author of *The Video Gaming Manual* and *The Driving Games Manual*.

Nathan Ditum (ND) is associate editor of interactive PS3 show FirstPlay, and has been writing for *Official PlayStation* magazines for over five years. He's also a regular contributor to *Edge* and *Total Film*, and is writing a PhD on authorship in contemporary Hollywood.

Kieron Gillen (KG) has written professionally about video games for 15 years. In 2007 he co-founded Rock, Paper, Shotgun, Britain's most popular PC gaming website. He also wrote the script for Channel 4 game The Curfew, and writes comics for Marvel, Image and Avatar.

Sam Grant (SG) writes about video games for numerous websites and magazines. He is also a games developer, working across a wide variety of platforms.

Duncan Harris (DH) is a features writer, critic and design consultant whose work appears in *Edge*, *PC Gamer* and *Official Xbox Magazine*. His other projects include the open source media interface Aeon and the videogame photography site Dead End Thrills.

Mitch Krpata (MK) is a freelance writer based in Boston, Massachusetts. His work has appeared in magazines such as *Paste*, *Slate*, and *Kill Screen*, as well as at his blog, Insult Swordfighting.

Mathew Kumar (MKu) is a Scottish, Toronto-based freelance journalist who has written extensively about games for magazines including *Edge* and websites such as Gamasutra. He also publishes *exp.*, his own independent games magazine, available from expdot.com.

Keza MacDonald (KM) has spent more than five years reporting on video game culture in Europe, the US and Japan, where she lived while studying for a Masters in modern languages. Her work can currently be found in numerous publications including *Edge*, *Eurogamer* and *The Observer*.

Gus Mastrapa (GM) is a freelance video game critic from Apple Valley, California, who has contributed to *Wired.com*, *Edge*, *The Onion*, G4TV's *X-Play*, *Paste* and *Hustler*.

Ben Maxwell (BM) is a freelance journalist who also writes a blog under the pseudonym I Am The Manta. He has been gaming for 24 years, and is a contributor to Pocket Gamer and Edge Online.

David McCarthy (DM) is a former writer for *Edge* magazine and co-author of several books about video games, including *Game On! From Pong to Oblivion: The 50 Greatest Video Games of All Time*. He has also contributed to *Guinness World Records Gamer's Edition*, and his work has appeared in magazines including *GamesMaster*, *Official PlayStation 2 Magazine*, *Sight & Sound* and *Zoo*.

Jim McCauley (JM) is online editor for Computer Arts and .net magazines, and has been writing about games for 15 years for a variety of titles including *Edge*, *PC Gamer*, *Official Playstation Magazine UK*, *Arcade* and *GamesMaster*. He was launch editor of *PC Gamer*'s first website.

Alec Meer (AM) is a founder and editor of the gaming site Rock, Paper, Shotgun. Over the last ten years, his video game writing has appeared in titles and sites including *PC Gamer*, *Official Xbox Magazine*, IGN, Eurogamer and *Edge*.

Simon Parkin (SP) is a long-time contributor to *Edge* magazine. His work has also appeared on Eurogamer, Yahoo and Gamasutra and is often collected on his own site, Chewing Pixels. He also curates the Box Art blog, a collection of the very best video game box art from across the years.

Jim Rossignol (JR) is an author and an editor at the PC gaming blog Rock, Paper, Shotgun. His book *This Gaming Life* was published by University of Michigan Press in 2008. He has also written for the BBC, *The Times* and *Wired* magazine.

Jamie Russell (JRu) is a contributing editor on *Total Film* magazine and writes about video games and movies for *Edge*, *Radio Times* and *Sight & Sound*. He has published several non-fiction books and is currently writing a history of Hollywood and video games.

Ben Schroder (BS) is a video game writer and developer. He has contributed to *Edge*, *PC Gamer* and Next Generation Online, and has worked on titles across a variety of platforms from mobile phone applications to massively multiplayer online games.

Rob Smith (RSm) is the former editor-in-chief of *PC Gamer*, *Official Xbox Magazine*, and *PlayStation: The Official Magazine* in the US. He is also the author of *Rogue Leaders: The Story of LucasArts*, and his work has appeared in numerous video game publications.

Richard Stanton (RS) writes for and is the features editor of *Edge* magazine. His work has appeared in many magazines and websites including *PC Gamer*, *GamesMaster* and *PSM3*.

Tim Stone (TS) is one of *PC Gamer UK*'s longest-serving freelancers. His writing on simulation and strategy games has also appeared in *Edge* and *PC Pilot* magazine and at the websites Eurogamer and Rock, Paper, Shotgun.

Keith Stuart (KS) is a technology correspondent for the *Guardian* (London), and a veteran video game journalist. His work has appeared in a wide range of magazines, including *Edge*, *Official PlayStation Magazine UK*, *FHM*, *Esquire*, *FourFourTwo* and *Frieze*.

John Teti (JT) oversees gaming coverage for *The A.V. Club*, the entertainment section of *The Onion*. His writing and video work have appeared in Crispy Gamer, UGO, *Paste* and Eurogamer. He was formerly an associate producer at *The Daily Show with Jon Stewart*.

David Valjalo (DV) is a video game journalist with experience in various sectors of the industry. He has worked for Sony Computer Entertainment, Jazz Publishing and in video game retail. He is currently a staff writer for *Edge* magazine.

Ben Wilson (BW) is editor of *Official PlayStation Magazine UK*. He has previously worked for *Zoo*, *More*, *Bliss* and *Nickelodeon*. He has also written for *Loaded*, *New Woman*, *Empire*, *Edge*, *PSM3* and *GamesMaster*.

Alex Wiltshire (AW) is editor of Edge Online, having previously worked on design and architecture magazine *Icon*. His work has also appeared in *PC Gamer*, *Official Xbox Magazine*, *New Statesman*, *The Architects' Journal* and *Design Week*.

Index of Developers

Every effort has been made to credit the copyright holders of the images used in this book. We apologize for any unintentional omissions or errors and will insert the appropriate acknowledgment to any companies or individuals in subsequent editions of the work.

Acknowledgments

Tony Mott would like to give special thanks to:

Thanks to the team at Quintessence Publishing, including Helena Baser, Tristan de Lancey and Jane Laing, for their work and support throughout the production of this book. For providing valuable resources and assistance, thanks also to Arcade History (www.arcade-history.com), Taneli Armanto, Carousel Leisure, Giant Bomb

(www.giantbomb.com), Andrew Hind, Brian Hirt, Christophe Kagotani, the Killer List Of Videogames (www.klov.com), Moby Games (www.mobygames.com), The Fighters Generation (www.fightersgeneration.com), Pocket Gamer (www.pocketgamer.co.uk) and Super Mario Wiki (www.mariowiki.com).